Parking Lot Picker's Songbook

By Dix Bruce

GUITAR EDITION

I0901142

Online Audio www.melbay.com/96864BCDEB

A collection of over 200 great Bluegrass, Old Time, Country, and Gospel standards. Melodies are presented with standard notation and tablature along with lyrics and chords. The audio recording includes EVERY song in the book with Dix Bruce on guitar, mandolin, and vocals and Bill Evans on banjo and vocals.

Learn to play songs written and recorded by the giants of traditional American music: Bill Monroe, The Stanley Brothers, Flatt & Scruggs, Ralph Stanley, The Osborne Brothers, Jimmy Martin, Doc Watson, and many more.

Also included: Step-by-step instruction on how to transpose any song to any key!

Special thanks to Sherry Shachter, Bob Bergman, and Lorna Swain for their help in preparing this book. Their kind suggestions improved it greatly.

Cover photos by, clockwise from top, center: Dix Bruce, Tom Tworek, Gene Tortora, Bill Evans, Bill Evans.

MEL BAY

WWW.MELBAY.COM

Table of Contents

Introduction

The Parking Lot Picker's Songbook is an all-in-one sourcebook for musicians to help build their bluegrass repertoire and more effectively play with others in jam sessions and in bands.

Bluegrass and old time music is unlike most other types of music. Aside from the obvious differences in sound, bluegrass fans are usually players in addition to being listeners. Bluegrass fans typically bring their instruments to concerts and festivals and spend as much time swapping songs and jamming as they do watching the headline acts. Everybody picks: young and old, male and female, beginners to professionals. It's a wonderfully communal, world-wide group that welcomes like-minded strangers who pack a guitar, banjo, mandolin, fiddle, or a voice to sing with.

The shared repertoire is what brings them all together and it's a powerful phenomenon. You can go to a bluegrass get together in Tokyo, Buenos Aires, Paris, Reykjavik, or anywhere else in the world, and the local players will know the same Bill Monroe and Stanley Brothers songs and fiddle tunes that you know. You'll be able to break musical bread and communicate with strangers no matter what the local language is. *The Parking Lot Picker's Songbook* is my attempt to collect a large number of these songs in one place and present them to you with melody, lyrics, chords, tablature, and a recording of each individual song. *The Parking Lot Picker's Songbook* provides easy access to much of this core repertoire and is a great resource for both the newcomer and the more experienced player who is looking to expand his or her song repertoire.

So, what's a "parking lot picker"?

The term "parking lot picker" grew out of the early bluegrass festivals where fans would stand around in parking lots adjacent to festival or concert sites and jam or "pick." These days you're likely to find assorted groups of parking lot pickers jamming, swapping tunes and licks, and sharing their love of the music at any bluegrass event you attend. Parking lot pickers play music together at every opportunity. If you have an interest in playing and singing bluegrass music with others — no matter what your experience or ability level — then you are a "parking lot picker" and this book is for you!

What songs are included in this book?

Many of the most loved and important songs in traditional American music are collected in *The Parking Lot Picker's Songbook*, including many traditional favorites from gospel music. I love every one of them! I've heard many of them all my life, around home, at school and in church. Every one is special to me. Each represents a favorite theme, artist, or period in the history of American bluegrass, country, gospel, and old time music. It is my hope that you too will love these songs and use this book at jam sessions and performances sharing great music with friends and family.

In compiling this anthology I combed though my LPs and CDs, song books, and set lists. I paid special attention to the works of the pioneers of bluegrass and American old time music: Bill Monroe, the Stanley Brothers, Flatt & Scruggs, Ralph Stanley, the Osborne Brothers, Jimmy Martin, Doc Watson, along with many other important artists. You'll find them strongly represented, both with traditional pieces that were part of their repertoires and with songs they composed themselves. Over 100 years of American music is contained in these pages. From Stephen Foster's tragic "Hard Times" to Dean Webb and Mitch Jayne's "Old Home Place," to the traditional-turned-jam band favorite "I Know You Rider." You're bound to encounter many of your favorites as well as discover new songs that you'll want to add to your repertoire. Of course I had to leave out hundreds more. Maybe someday there'll be a *Parking Lot Picker's Songbook Volume Two!*

Most of these songs have been recorded again and again by bluegrass, country, gospel, and old time artists. I've listed the names of some of them on each song. If I left out your favorite artist, I apologize. My aim was to give you a representative group for each song rather than a comprehensive or all-inclusive list. I did lean toward the pioneers of the styles mentioned above. I also included some personal favorites that I wanted you to know about. I mentioned a few of my own recordings, both solo and with Jim Nunally.

It's important that you seek out and listen to these seminal recordings. I didn't name specific CDs the songs can be found on since collections, titles, and availability are constantly changing. Anything I might have included would likely be out of date within a month or two. Since the advent of box sets, compilations by the great artists are widely available. These days you can also search for instantly downloadable versions of your favorite songs on the internet. iTunes and other downloading services are convenient and reasonably priced and seem to be the wave of the future.

Some of the songs are more obscure and may not have been recorded by a great number of artists. Still they are special favorites of mine that I hope you will enjoy both in the book and on the accompanying CDs. And I couldn't resist putting in a few of my original compositions.

How do I use the Parking Lot Picker's Songbook?

The songs are listed alphabetically and I've designed this book to minimize page turns. Song titles are shown centered at the top of each page. Composer information, if known, is shown on the upper right. CD and track locations are shown on the upper left under key designation. For example, the recording of "Are You From Dixie?" is on CD number one, track six. Complete track listings for both CDs are on pages 303 and 304. Most song titles are shown in the "Notes on Selected Songs" section on page 283 where alternate titles are listed. This section includes any additional information or comments I might have on individual songs. Following this, you'll find a listing by artist.

Most of these songs are based on traditional sources and as such can be heard with a variety of versions, melodies and lyrics. I went with the versions I was most familiar with. Feel free to do the same and substitute your favorite chords, lyrics, and melodies as the mood strikes you.

Typical performance keys for both male and female voices are shown in the upper left corner of each song. I used my own voice as a starting point. My voice is a fairly typical male voice, not too low, not too high. I have found that if I sing a song in the key of G, a typical female voice will sing the same song in the key of C or D, a fourth or fifth higher than where I sing it. This is reflected in the notation:

M: G
F: C or D, capo 5 or 7.

"M" stands for "male voice," which will sing the song in the key of "G," *"F"* stands for "female voice," which will sing the song in the key of "C" or "D," when the chords shown in the music are capoed and played as suggested at fret 5 or 7. Of course there will be cases when these suggested keys might not fit your voice, whether you are a male or a female. Never fear, we'll learn to transpose the songs to any key.

Most of the songs are pitched in the keys of G and C. There are several reasons for this. G and C are probably the most popular keys for bluegrass, gospel, and old time music, and many of the "original" recordings of these songs are in G or C. G and C are also relatively easy keys to play in and capo around. However, most of the songs fit well into other keys too. Don't be afraid to move songs to other uncapoed keys. You'll discover all sorts of tonal characteristics unique to different keys. See the information on transposing on the following page.

What's the best way to learn a song?

It's a good idea to listen to the recorded version of the song first to get an idea of how it goes. CD and track numbers are listed under the key designations on each page. Short representative excerpts of **all** the songs have been recorded with guitar, mandolin, banjo, and vocals on the CDs accompanying this book. My friend, banjo player and singer Bill Evans, recorded them with me. I sing and play guitar and mandolin. Bill wrote the banjo version of this book. It's identical to this one and includes chords, lyrics, melodies in standard notation, plus banjo tablature. I also wrote a mandolin version of *The Parking Lot Picker's Songbook*. It's just like this guitar edition except that it includes mandolin tablature instead of guitar tab. Special thanks to Bill for letting us use his great photos in all three books!

As you listen to a song, follow along with the lyrics, music and tablature. Then play along. Try singing with the recording to determine if the song is pitched in your key. Since Bill and I have fairly typical male ranges, we pitched the songs for our voices. If your voice is pitched higher than ours, you'll want to sing in a higher key. All you have to do is place the capo on various frets and sing along until you find the perfect key.

As I mentioned above, I've found that a typical female range is usually a fourth or fifth musical interval above the male key. Key designations on each song reflect this. Of course everybody's voice is a little different and we're looking at this rule only as a starting point. So, if a song is written here in the key of D, to back up a female voice, you'd start by capoing at the fifth fret and playing the chords as written. Adjust up or down from there and you're in business.

What if your voice is lower than the written key or capoing is not an option? Read on!

How can I change the key of a song to better fit my voice or instrument?

Let's say the suggested keys or capo positions just don't work for your voice or for how you want to play your instrument. It's a simple process to transpose the chord progression to other keys. It's a bit more involved to change the melodies and write them out, but the same principles apply. Most of you will probably just need to transpose the chords so you can accompany yourself in a new key.

Let's look at "Amazing Grace" on page 9. It's presented here in the key of G, noted in the upper left hand corner of the page. Again, *"M: G"* means that a typical male voice would sing "Amazing Grace" in the key of G. If the key of G is too low for your voice, you can simply capo up until you find a key and capo position that works. What if the key of G is too high? If that's the case, you'll have to substitute a whole different set of chords. The ***Scale and Transposition Chart*** will make the process of transposing easier.

Scale and Transposition Chart

	Key signature	***Major scale***	***1***	***2***	***3***	***4***	***5***	***6***	***7***	***8 (1)***
Key	**♯/♭**		**I**	**ii**	**iii**	**IV**	**V**	**vi**	**vii°**	**I**
C	none	C	C	Dm	Em	F	G	Am	B°	C
F	1 - ♭	F	F	Gm	Am	B♭	C	Dm	E°	F
B♭	2 - ♭	B♭	B♭	Cm	Dm	E♭	F	Gm	A°	B♭
E♭	3 - ♭	E♭	E♭	Fm	Gm	A♭	B♭	Cm	D°	E♭
A♭	4 - ♭	A♭	A♭	B♭m	Cm	D♭	E♭	Fm	G°	A♭
D♭	5 - ♭	D♭	D♭	E♭m	Fm	G♭	A♭	B♭m	C°	D♭
G♭	6 - ♭	G♭	G♭	A♭m	B♭m	C♭	D♭	E♭m	F°	G♭
C♭	7 - ♭	C♭	C♭	D♭m	E♭m	F♭	G♭	A♭m	B♭°	C♭
C♯	7 - ♯	C♯	C♯	D♯m	E♯m	F♯	G♯	A♯m	B♯°	C♯
F♯	6 - ♯	F♯	F♯	G♯m	A♯m	B	C♯	D♯m	E♯°	F♯
B	5 - ♯	B	B	C♯m	D♯m	E	F♯	G♯m	A♯°	B
E	4 - ♯	E	E	F♯m	G♯m	A	B	C♯m	D♯°	E
A	3 - ♯	A	A	Bm	C♯m	D	E	F♯m	G♯°	A
D	2 - ♯	D	D	Em	F♯m	G	A	Bm	C♯°	D
G	1 - ♯	G	G	Am	Bm	C	D	Em	F♯°	G

The chart shows the scales, chords, and key signature (number of sharps or flats) that identify each key. If you look in the key of G line at the bottom of the chart, you'll see in the second column ("key signature") that the key of G has one sharp in its key signature. If you read across to the right you'll see "G Am Bm C D Em F♯°." These are the chords of the key of G and all are made up using only the notes of the G major scale. Songs in the key of G can have other chords as well, like E or A7, but to make these chords we need to use notes from outside of the G major scale.

If you remove all the "m" (or minor) and "°" (or diminished) chord designations, you'll come up with the G scale, which is "G A B C D E F♯." Be sure to leave the sharps and flats shown or the scale changes. So, how do we use this to transpose?

Going back to "Amazing Grace," we see that the chord progression to the first line of the song is G—C—G. Since "Amazing Grace" is written here in the key of G (noted in the upper left hand corner of the page, "M: G") let's see where these chords occur in the "key of G" line in the chart. The G chord is in the "I" (upper case Roman numeral one) column. The G chord in the key of G is a "one" chord. The C chord is in the "IV" column and is a "four" chord. We need to know where these chords fit numerically in order to transpose them. All chords are identified by Roman numerals, upper case for majors (I, IV, V) lower case for minors (ii, iii, vi) and the lone diminished chord which has a little circle as part of the chord name (vii°).

As I mentioned, we're assuming that "Amazing Grace" is pitched too high to sing in the key of G. We need to transpose it to a lower key, which will be to a key "earlier" in the musical alphabet (A, B, C, D, E, F, G) like F, E, etc. Let's transpose "Amazing Grace" to the key of E. Start with the first chord of the original key, the G chord, in the "I" column. Follow up in the "I" column to the key of E row. The I chord in the key of E is an E chord. Write an "E" in everywhere you see a G chord on the music to "Amazing Grace." (I suggest that you write in pencil in case your voice changes!)

The next chord in the key of G version of "Amazing Grace" is a C. The C chord is in the IV column of the key of G row. Follow that column up to the key of E row and you'll find the new chord is an A. Write an "A" in everywhere you see a C chord in the music to "Amazing Grace."

There's one more chord in the key of G version of "Amazing Grace" and that's the D. Once again, find the D in the key of G row. It's in the "V" column and is a "five" chord. Follow up in the V column to the key of E row and you'll find a B chord. Write a "B" in everywhere you see a D chord in the music to "Amazing Grace." Now you've changed every G chord to an E, every C to an A, and every D to a B, transposing the chord progression from the key of G to the key of E.

Transposing other songs

Some songs are in kind of nebulous keys like "I Know You Rider," "Shady Grove," and "Wayfaring Stranger." The first two are sometimes described as "modal," the last as "minor." In cases like this, it may not be clear to you which key row to use. If you match the number of sharps or flats in the key signature of the song to the second column ("key signature") of the chart, you can't go wrong. Just make sure that you follow up or down in the correct column.

There will be times when the exact chord you're transposing can't be found on the chart. In "Wayfaring Stranger" there's an "A7" chord but there's no "A7" in the key of F row, only an "Am" in the "iii" column. **You can still use this column as long as you maintain the original "quality" of the chord as you transpose**. For example, if the original is a seventh, the transposed chord needs to be a seventh. If the original chord is a minor, the transposed chord needs to be a minor also. Let's transpose "Wayfaring Stranger" from the given key of F/Dm up to G/Em. The first chord is a Dm. Find the Dm in the key of F row. It's in the "vi" column. Follow the "vi" column down to the key of G row and you'll find an Em. Pencil in an Em everywhere you see Dm in "Wayfaring Stranger." Find the next chord, the Gm, in the key of F row, in the "ii" column. Follow the "ii" column down to the key of G row where you'll see Am. Write Am in the music where you see Gm. The next chord in the original key of F is B♭. Find the B♭ in the "IV" column of the key of F row. Follow this down to the key of G row, where you'll find a C. Pencil it in. Do the same with the original F chord changing it to G. Finally, find the A in the iii column, where it's listed as Am. The original chord is an A7. Follow down in the iii column until you get to the key of G row. There you'll find a Bm, which you'll change to a B7 to preserve the dominant seven quality of the original. That's all there is to it, you've transposed the chords of "Wayfaring Stranger" from the key of F to the key of G.

A similar thing happens in "Little Maggie." It's printed in the key of G and the second chord is an F. However, there's no F chord in the key of G row, only an F♯ in the "vii" column. F♯ is one half step higher in pitch than F natural. All you have to do is take that into account in the transposed key. Let's transpose "Little Maggie" to the key of D. The first chord of the original key is a G. The G chord is in the I column of the key of G row. Follow this up in the I column to the key of D row and our first chord is transposed to a D chord. Now go back to the key of G row and the "vii" column, which is still an F♯. Lower it one half step to get the F chord from the song in the original key of G. Follow up in the vii column to the key of D row. You'll find a C♯. Since we lowered our original F♯ one half step to F natural, we'll need to do the same here and lower the C♯ one half step to C natural. So, the first two chords in the key of D version of "Little Maggie" are D and C. If you're interested in reading more about music theory, transposing, and how a capo works, check out my *Guide to Capo, Transposing, & the Nashville Numbering System* from Mel Bay. The "Transposer Wheel" on page 301 and the Capo Chart on page 302 will also be helpful in transposing.

Here's hoping you enjoy this collection of great songs! Visit me online at www.musixnow.com. Lots of music, tablature and MP3s to download and learn. My e-mail address is dix@musixnow.com.

— Dix Bruce

Dix Bruce is a musician and writer from the San Francisco Bay Area. He has authored over forty books, recordings, and videos for Mel Bay Publications. Dix performs and does studio work on guitar, mandolin, and banjo and has recorded two LPs with mandolin legend Frank Wakefield, eight big band CDs with the Royal Society Jazz Orchestra, his own collection of American folk songs entitled "My Folk Heart" on which he plays guitar, mandolin, autoharp and sings, and a CD of string swing and jazz entitled "Tuxedo Blues." He contributed two original compositions to the soundtrack of Harrod Blank's acclaimed documentary film "Wild Wheels." He has released four CDs of traditional American songs and originals with guitarist Jim Nunally, most recently a collection of "brother duet" style recordings entitled "Brothers at Heart." Dix arranged, composed, and played mandolin on the soundtracks to four different editions of the best selling computer game "The Sims."

Books and instructional DVDs: (For song lists and full details, as well as info on new books, CDs and DVDs, contact Musix, e-mail: info@musixnow.com)

The Parking Lot Picker's Songbook for Guitar, Mandolin & Banjo (with Bill Evans).
You Can Teach Yourself Country Guitar book & CD, DVD or video set.
You Can Teach Yourself Mandolin book & CD, DVD or video set.
Getting into Bluegrass Mandolin book & CD.
First Lessons Mandolin book, CD, & DVD set.
Bluegrass Mandolin Solos book & CD.
Bluegrass Guitar Solos book & CD.
BackUp Trax: Old Time Fiddle Tunes Vol. I book & CD set. Jam all night long with the band on old time and fiddle tunes.
Doc Watson & Clarence Ashley 1960-62 book & CDs set. Transcriptions with chords, melodies, lyrics, Doc's solos & rhythm playing. Incredible collection of songs that have become standards of bluegrass, folk and country music.
BackUp Trax: Swing & Jazz Vol. I book & CD set. Jam all night long with a great band. You play all the leads and the band never gets tired!
BackUp Trax: Traditional Jazz & Dixieland book & CD set. Jam all night long with the band on the basic Dixieland repertoire.
BackUp Trax: Early Jazz & Hot Tunes book & CD set. Jam all night long with the band on more traditional jazz standards.
Basic Swing Guitar (DVD). Learn swing chord comping on the classics of the genre.
Basic Country Flatpicking Guitar (DVD). Explores easy Carter-style solos.

Recordings:
Brothers at Heart by Dix Bruce & Jim Nunally. Brother duet-style songs, & hot guitar picking (FGM CD 111).
From Fathers to Sons by Dix Bruce & Jim Nunally. Folk, bluegrass, & hot guitar picking (Musix CD/C 104).
In My Beautiful Dream by Dix Bruce & Jim Nunally. Great new songs & old classics by the duo. (Musix CD 106).
The Way Things Are by Dix Bruce & Jim Nunally. More hot picking & great new songs by the duo. (Musix CD 105).
My Folk Heart by Dix Bruce, solo & small group, traditional American folk music (Musix CD/C101). With Jim Nunally, Tom Rozum, and John Reischman.
Tuxedo Blues by Dix Bruce, string swing & jazz (Musix CD/C102). With Bob Alekno on mandolin, David Balakrishnan on violin, Mike Wollenberg on bass.

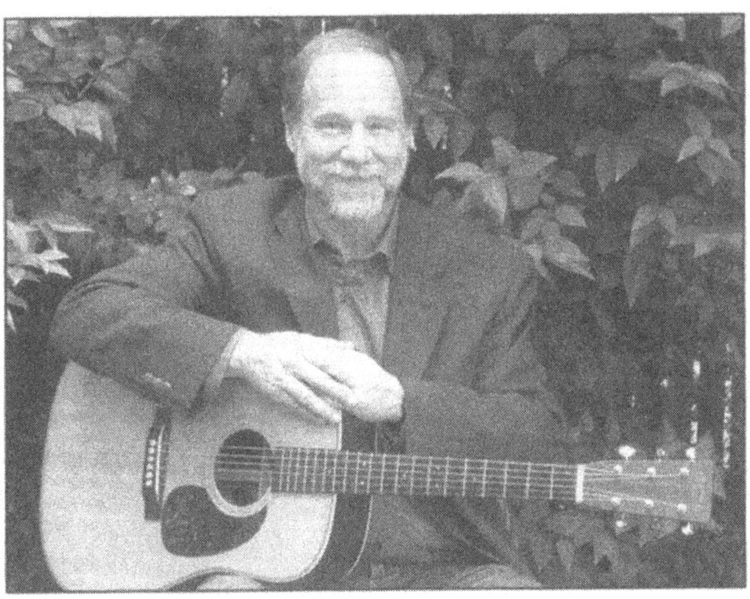

photo by Gene Tortora

Dix Bruce

All the Good Times

M: G; F: C or D, capo 5 or 7
CD 1-Track 1

Traditional

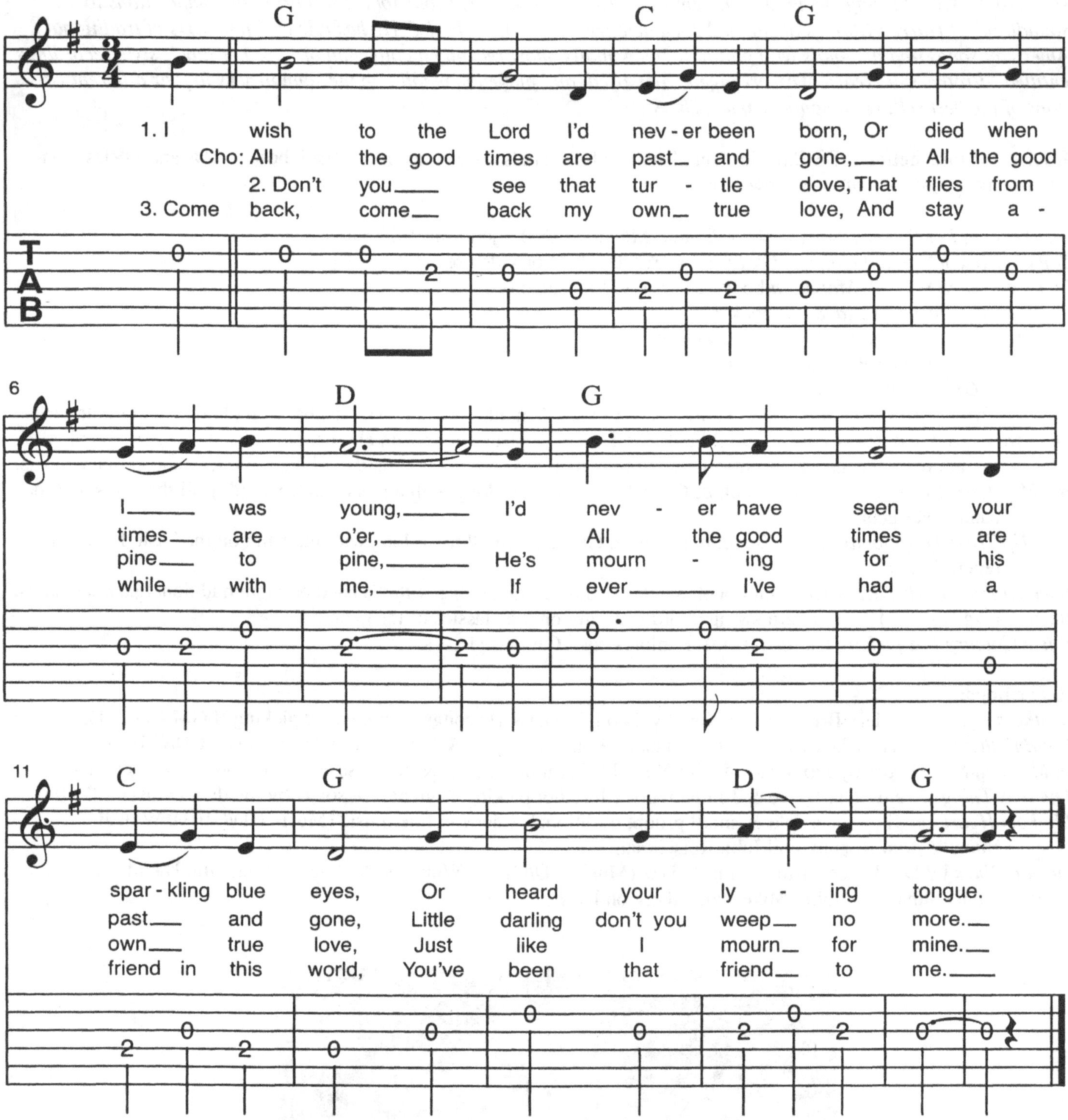

 B. Monroe, Monroe Bros., Flatt & Scruggs, R. Allen & F. Wakefield, Ken. Colonels, J. Martin

Amazing Grace

M: G; F: C or D, capo 5 or 7
CD 1-Track 2

John Newton, ca. 1779

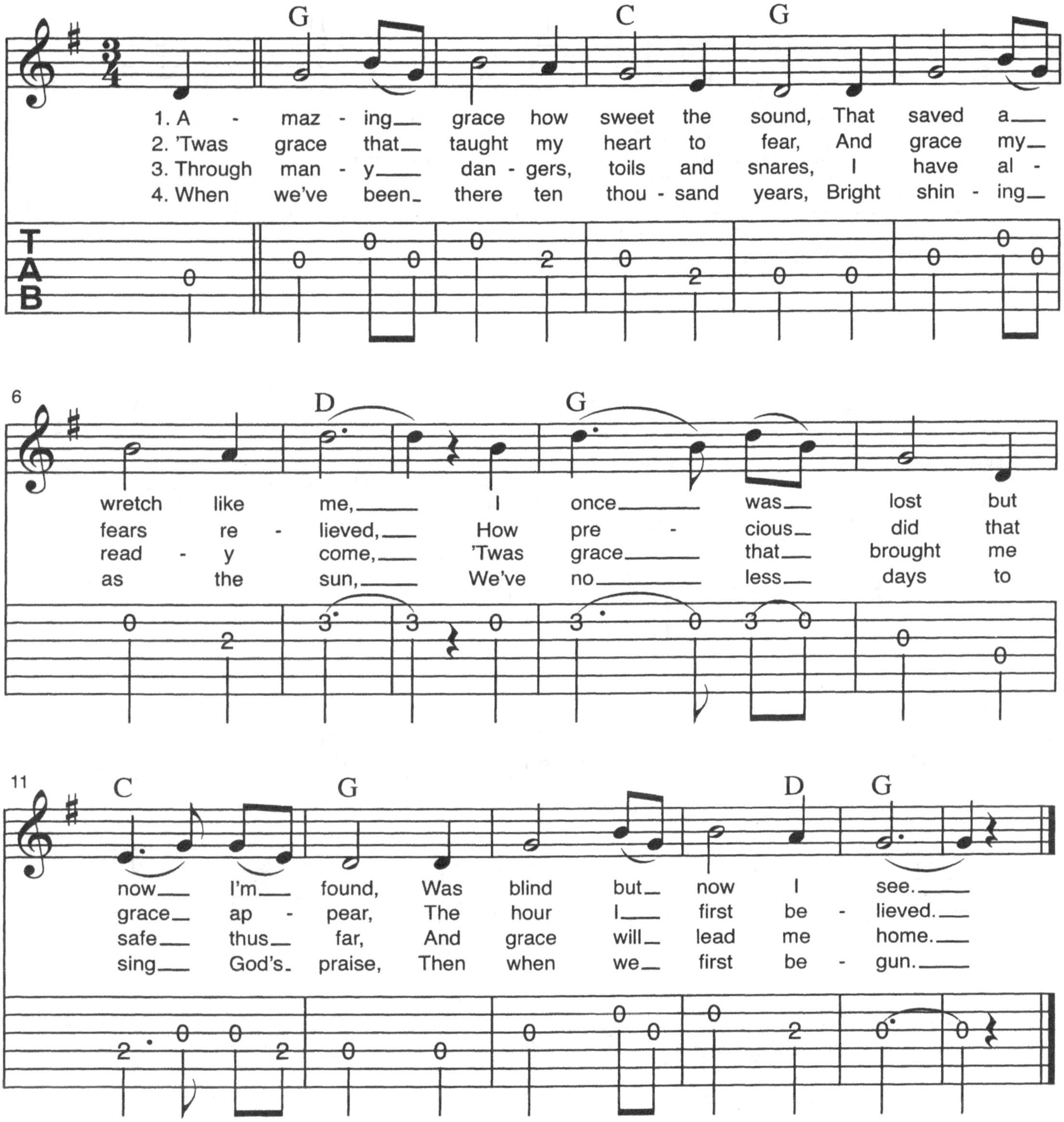

Angel Band

M: G; F: C or D, capo 5 or 7
CD 1-Track 3

Hascall & Bradbury, ca. 1860

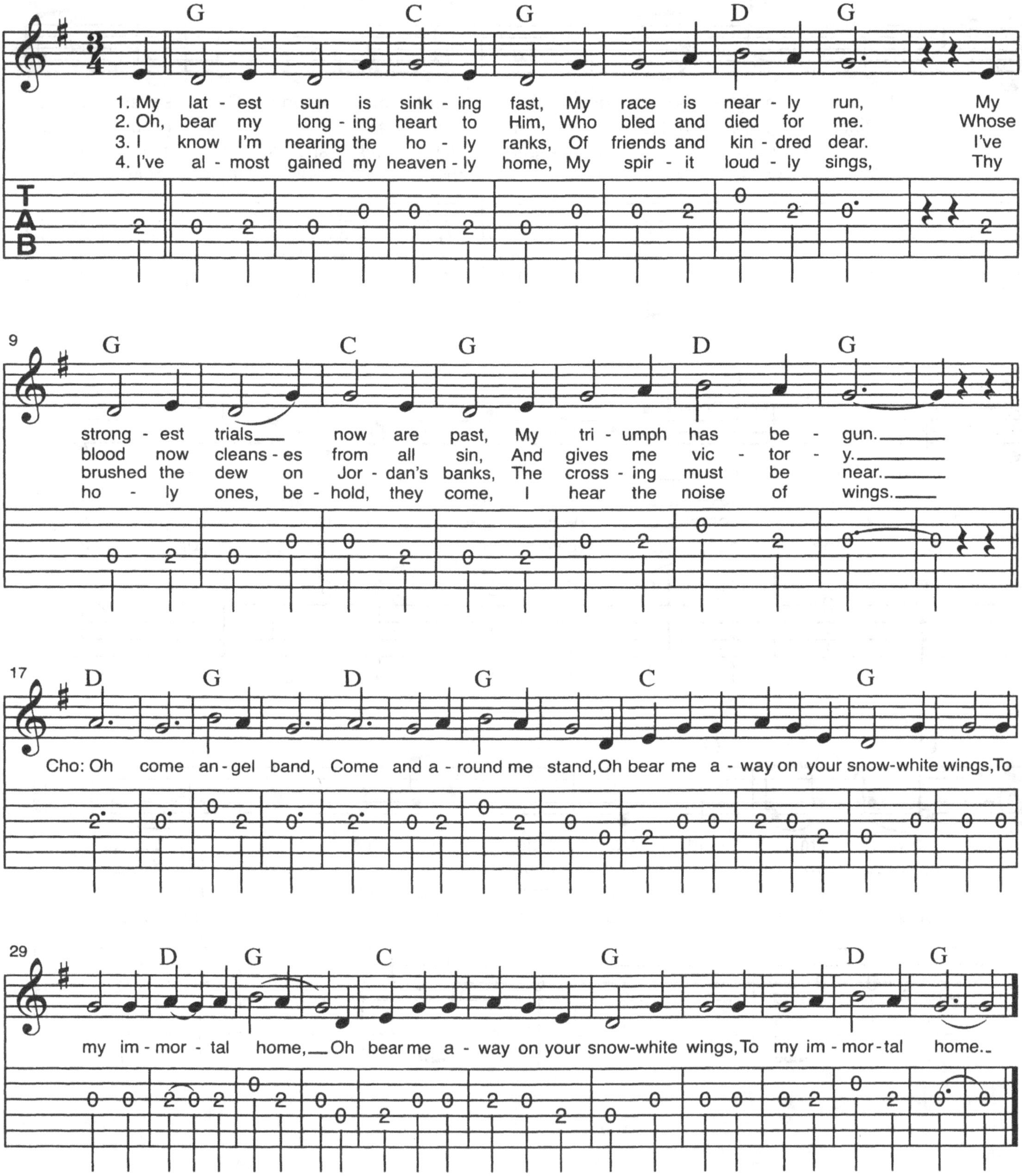

 Stanley Bros., R. Stanley, Flatt & Scruggs, Old & in the Way

Angelina Baker

***M**: C; **F**: F or G, capo 5 or 7*
CD 1-Track 4

Stephen Foster, 1850

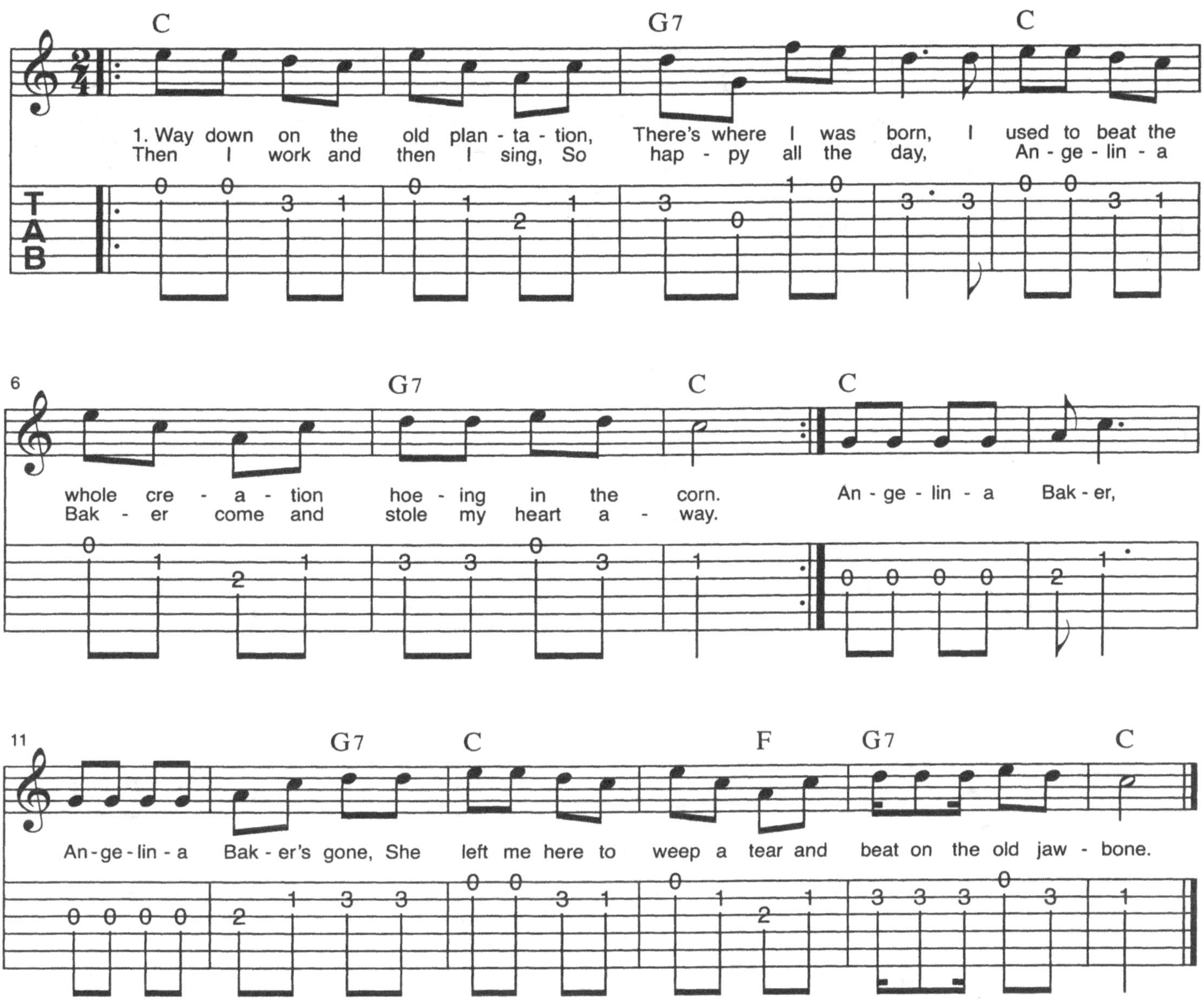


```
        C                                    G7
2. I've seen my Angelina in the Springtime and the Fall,
     C                                    G7          C
I've seen her in the cornfield and I've seen her at the ball,
        C                            G7
And every time I met her she was smiling like the sun,
     C                                      G7      C
But now I'm left to weep a tear cause Angelina's gone.
```

3. Angelina is so tall, she never sees the ground,
She has to take a wellumscope to look down on the town.
Angelina likes the boys, as far as she can see 'em,
She used to run old master 'round, to ask him for to free 'em.

4. Early in the morning of a lovely summer day,
I asked for Angelina, and they say "she's gone away."
I don't know where to find her, 'cause I don't know where she's gone,
She left me here to weep a tear, and beat on the old jawbone.

Angels Rock Me To Sleep

M: G; F: C or D, capo 5 or 7
CD 1-Track 5

Traditional

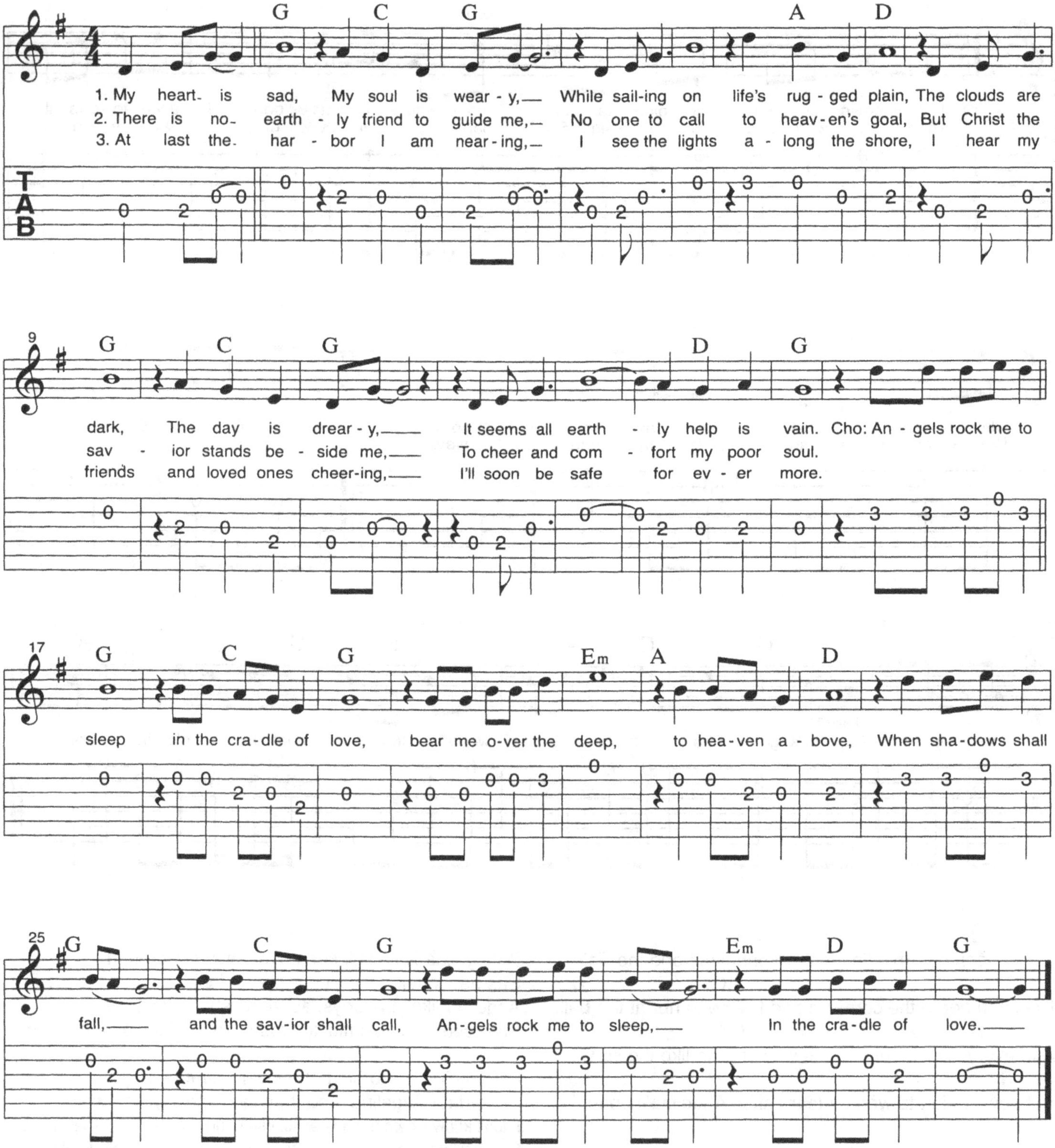

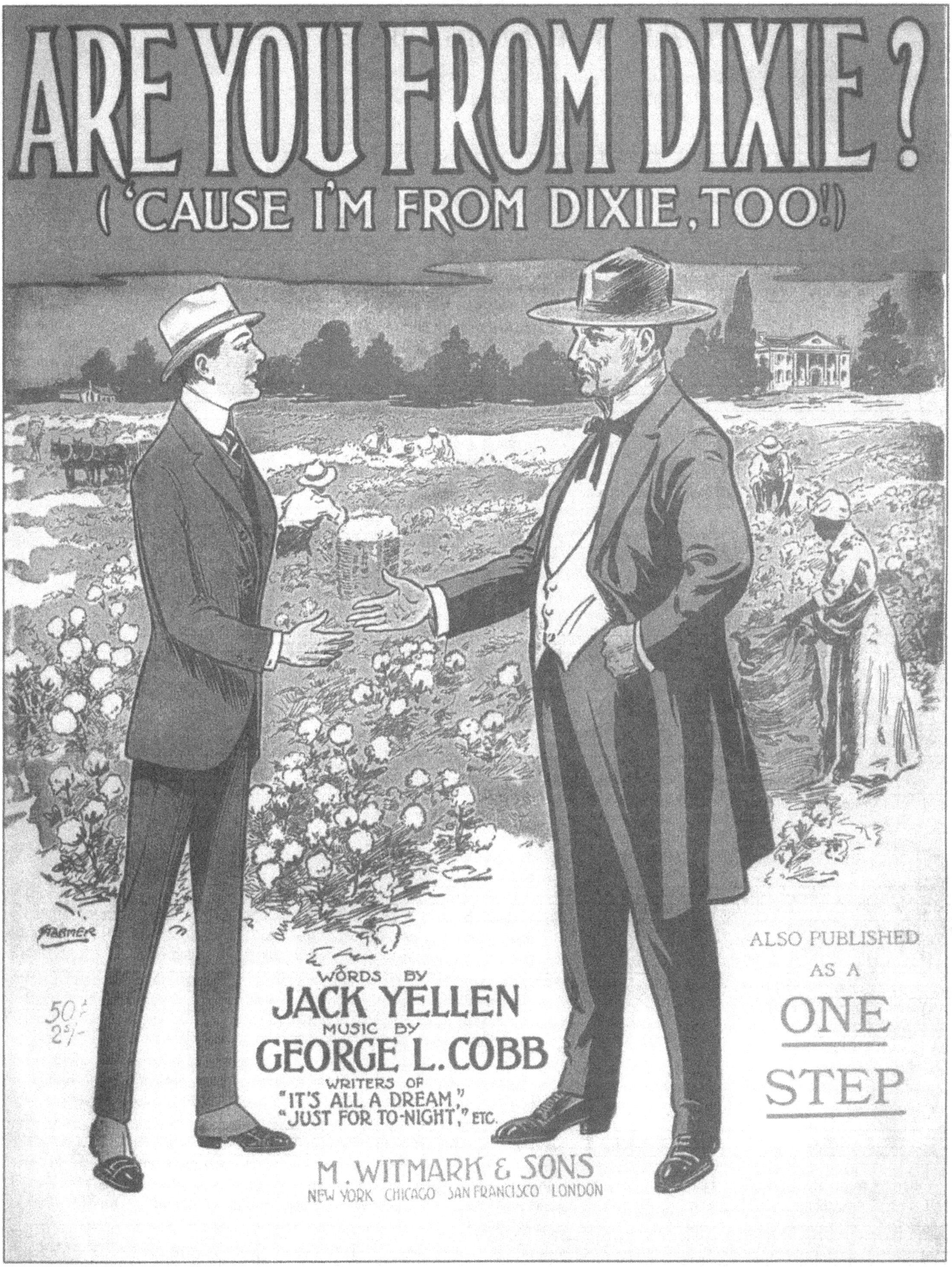

Original 1915 sheet music cover from the collection of Dix Bruce.

Are You From Dixie?

M: C; F: F or G, capo 5 or 7
CD 1-Track 6

Cobb & Yellin, 1915

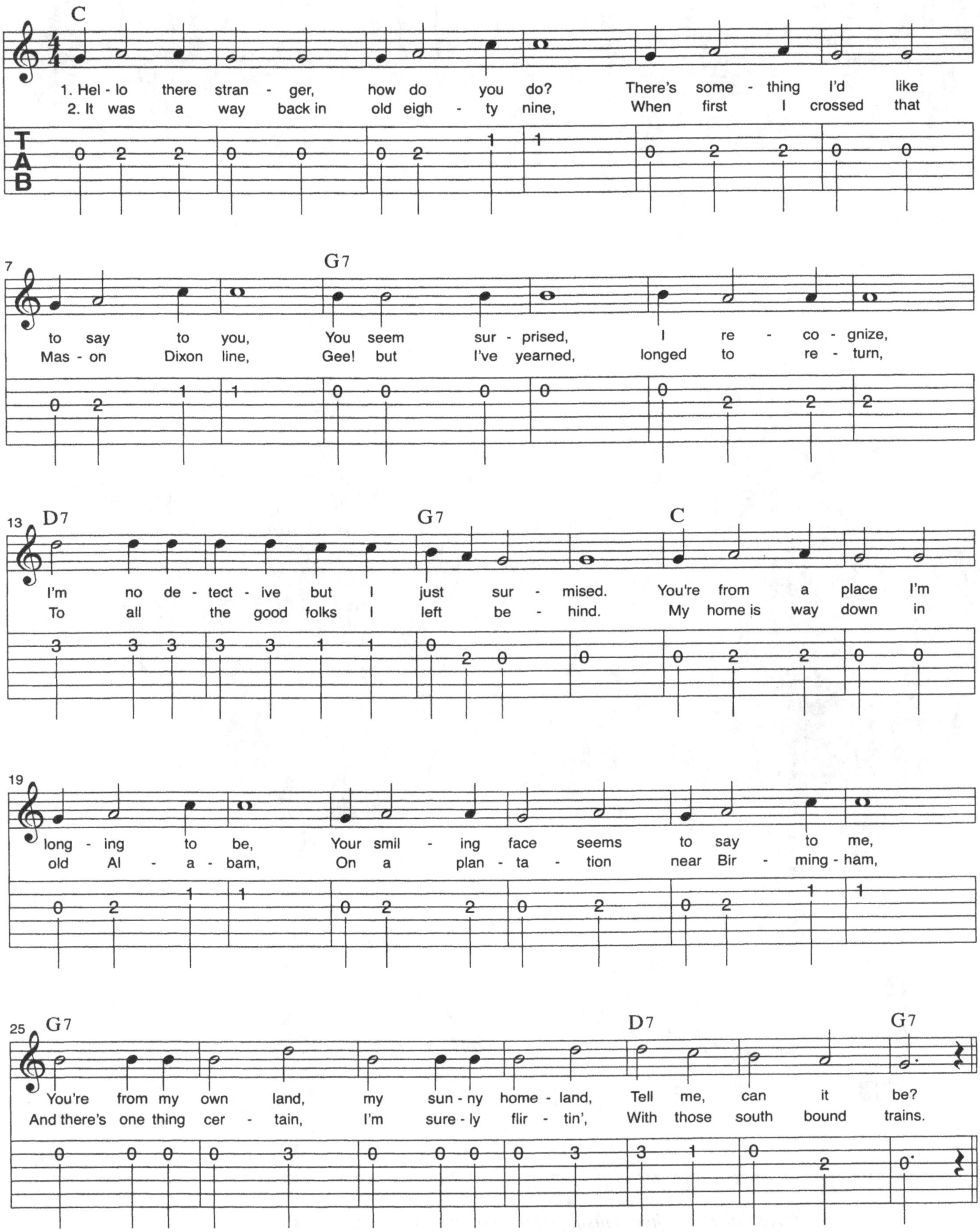

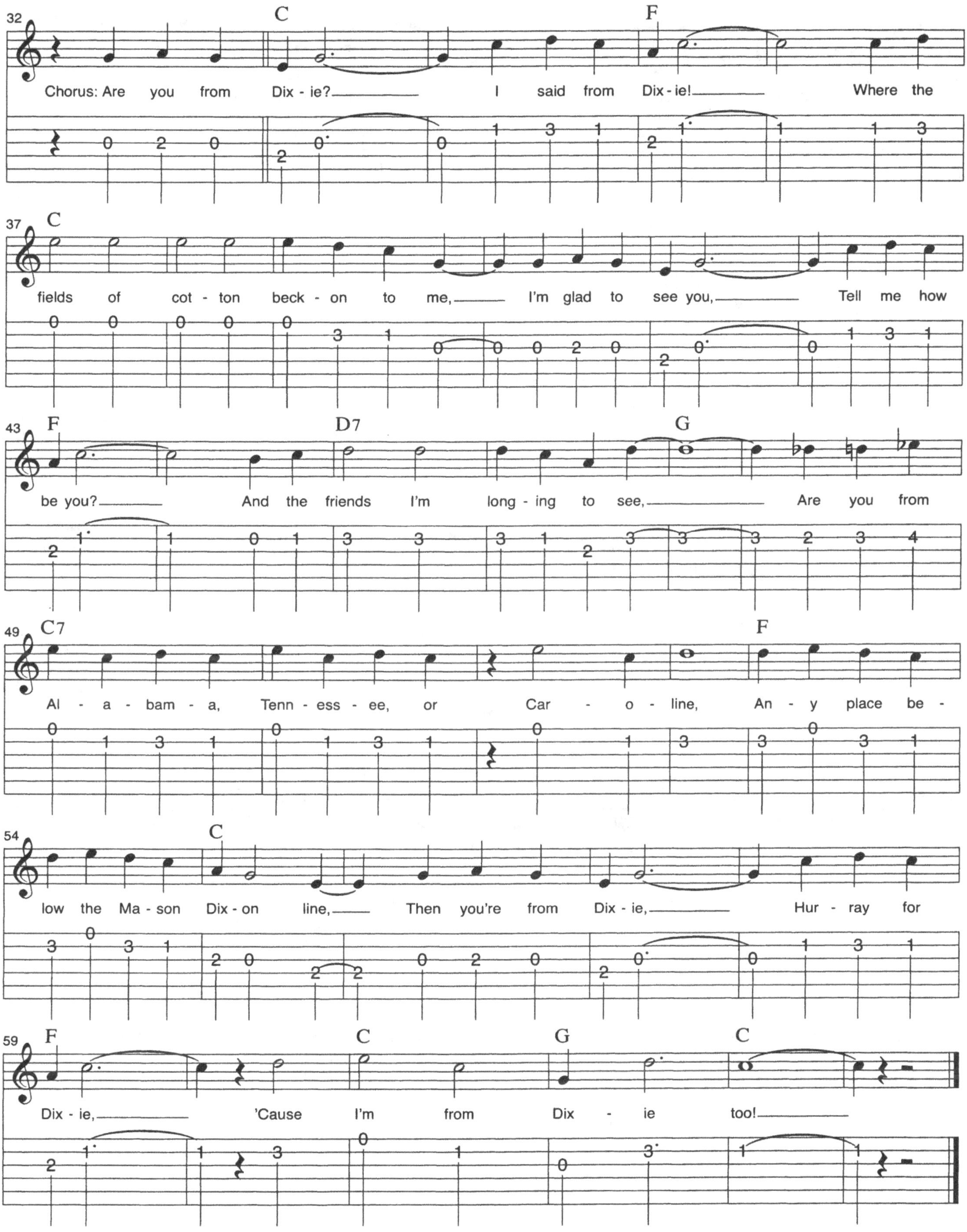
32 C F
Chorus: Are you from Dix - ie? I said from Dix - ie! Where the
37 C
fields of cot - ton beck - on to me, I'm glad to see you, Tell me how
43 F D7 G
be you? And the friends I'm long - ing to see, Are you from
49 C7 F
Al - a - bam - a, Tenn - ess - ee, or Car - o - line, An - y place be -
54 C
low the Ma - son Dix - on line, Then you're from Dix - ie, Hur - ray for
59 F C G C
Dix - ie, 'Cause I'm from Dix - ie too!

Are You Washed in the Blood of the Lamb?

M: G; F: C or D, capo 5 or 7
CD 1-Track 7

Elisha A. Hoffman, 1878

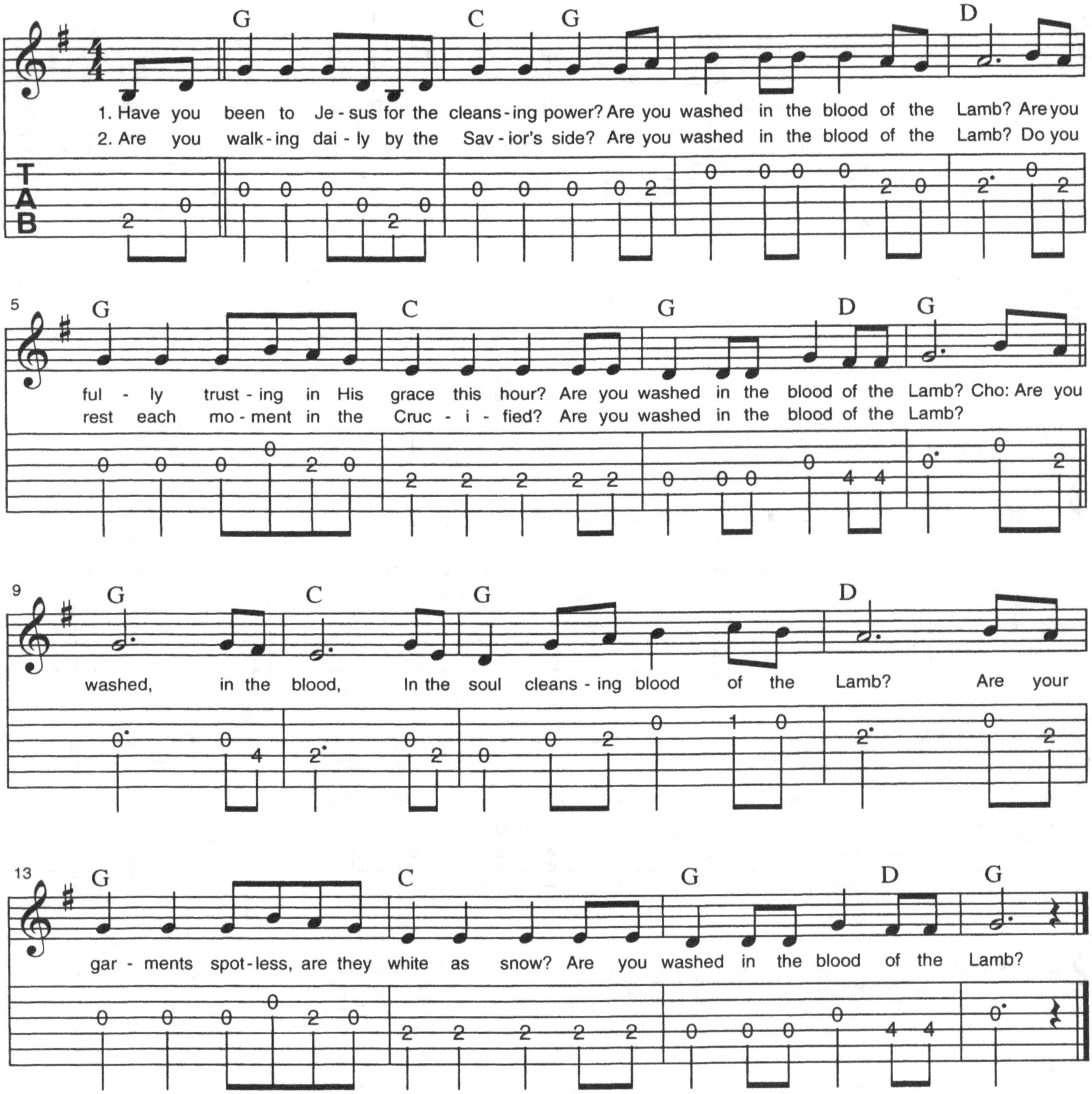

3. When the bridegroom cometh will your robes be white? (G C G)
Are you washed in the blood of the Lamb? (D)
Will your soul be ready for the mansions bright, (G C)
And be washed in the blood of the Lamb? (G D G)

4. Lay aside the garments that are stained with sin,
And be washed in the blood of the Lamb;
There's a fountain flowing for the soul unclean,
O be washed in the blood of the Lamb!

Arkansas Traveller

M: G; F: C or D, capo 5 or 7
CD 1-Track 8

Traditional

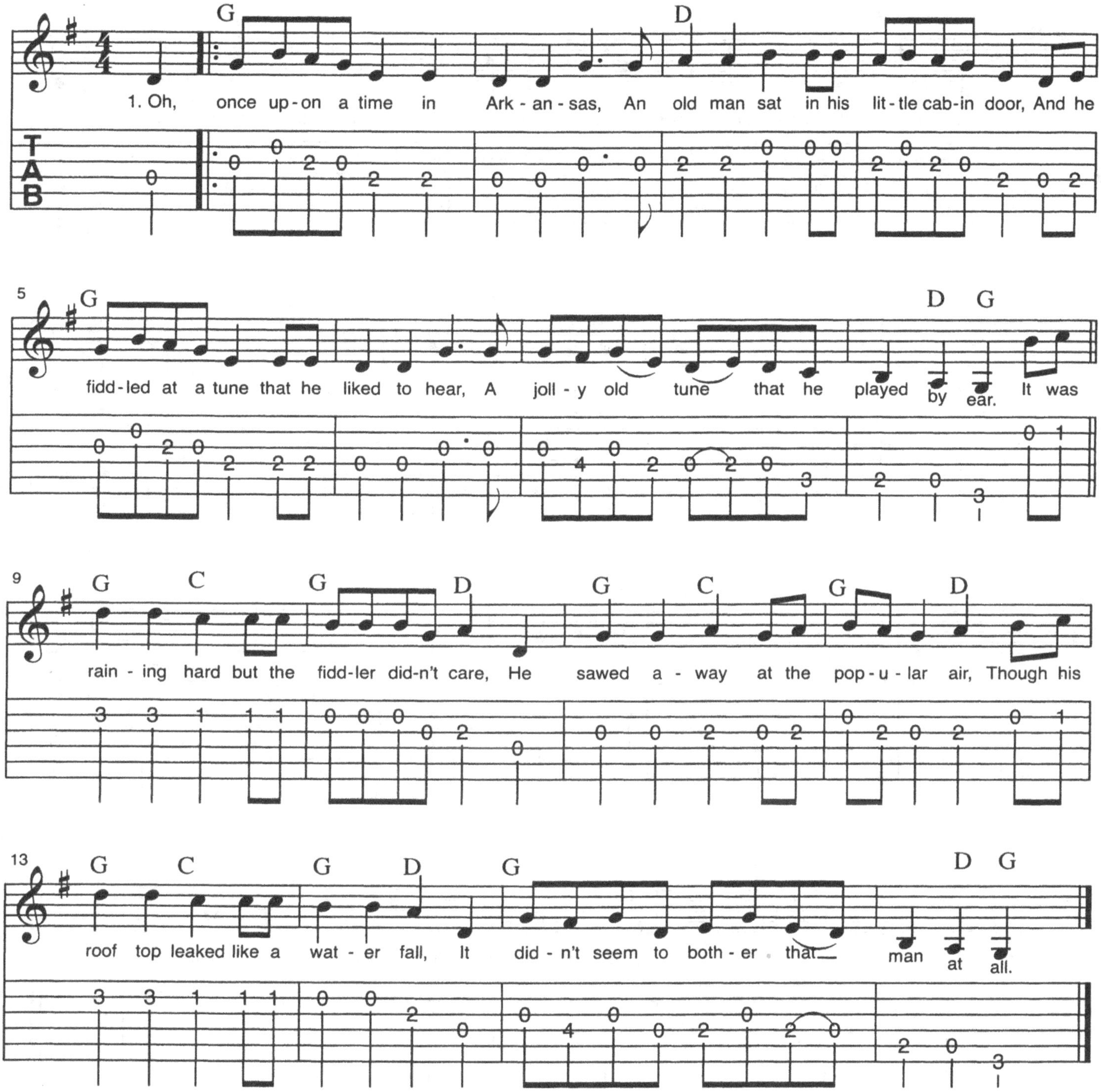

G
2. A traveller was riding by that day,
D
And stopped to hear him a-practicing away.
G
The cabin was afloat and his feet were wet,
D G
But still the old man didn't seem to fret.
G C G D
So the stranger said: "Now the way it seems to me,
G C G D
You'd better mend your roof," said he.
G C G D
But the old man said, as he played away:
G D G
"I couldn't mend it now, it's a rainy day."

3. The traveller replied: "That's all quite true,
But this, I think, is the thing for you to do;
Get busy on a day that is fair and bright,
Then pitch the old roof till it's good and tight."
But the old man kept on a-playing at his reel,
And tapped the ground with his leathery heel:
"Get along," said he, "for you give me a pain;
My cabin never leaks when it doesn't rain."

Aunt Dinah's Quilting Party

M: A; F: D or E, capo 5 or 7
CD 1-Track 9

Kyle & Fletcher, 1856

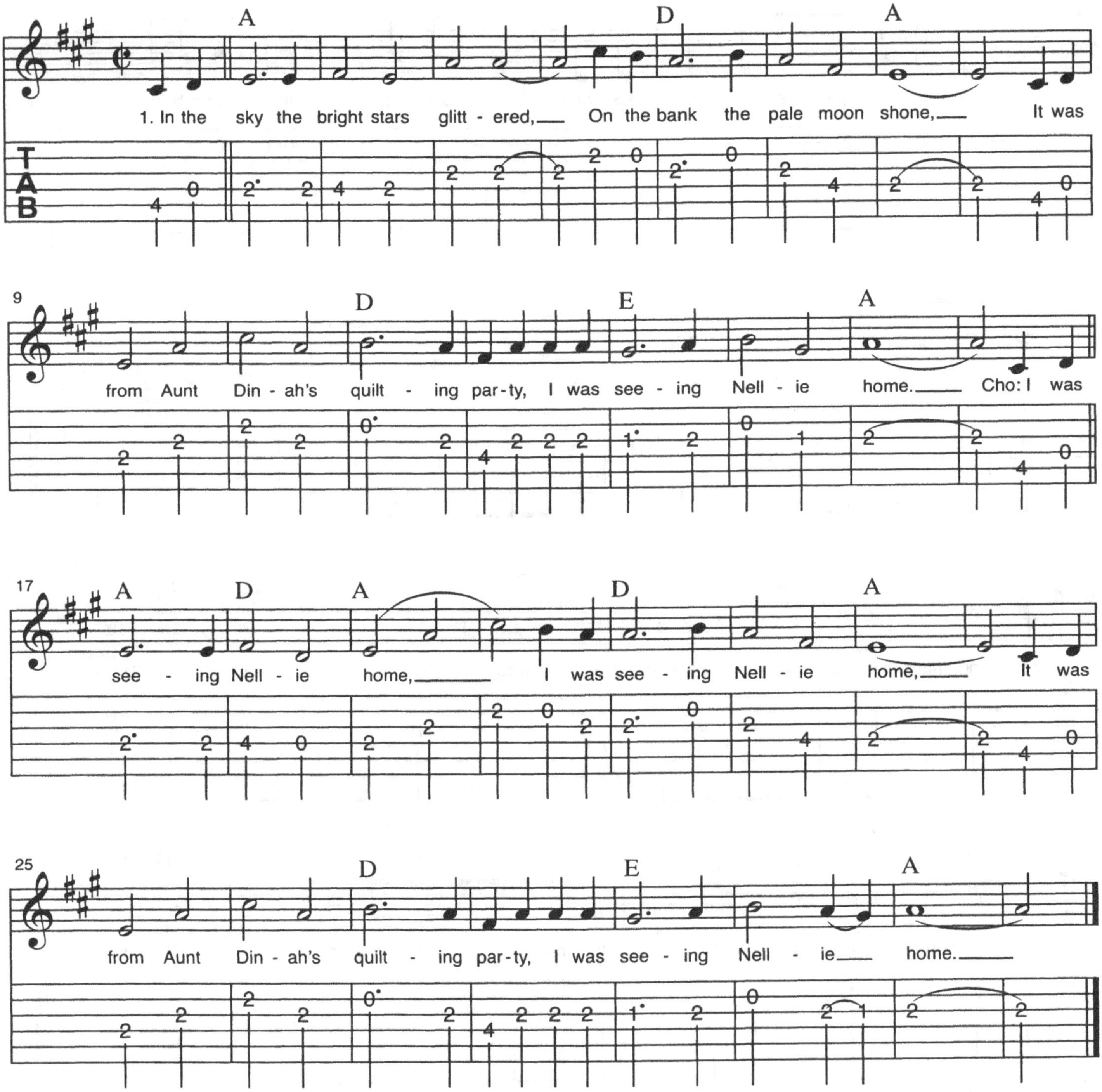

A
2. On my arm a soft hand rested,
D A
Rested light as ocean foam,
D
And 'twas from Aunt Dinah's quilting party,
E A
I was seeing Nellie home. (*Chorus*)

3. On my lips a whisper trembled,
Trembled 'til it dared to come,
And 'twas from Aunt Dinah's *(etc., chorus)*

4. On my life new hopes were dawning,
And those hopes have lived and grown,
And 'twas from Aunt Dinah's *(etc., chorus)*

Away in a Manger

M: G; F: C or D, capo 5 or 7
CD 1-Track 10

Luther & Muller

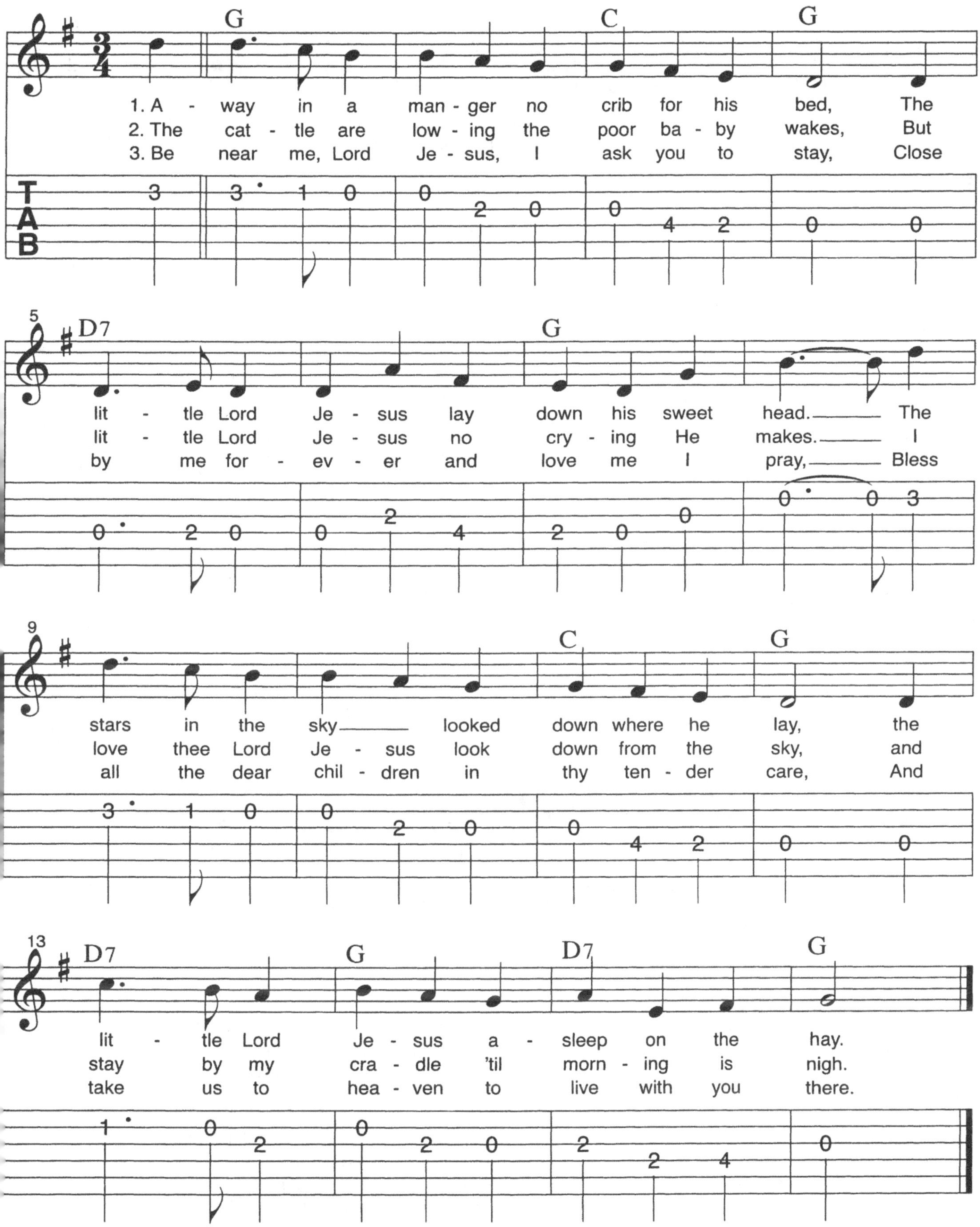

Banks of the Ohio

M: D; F: G or A, capo 5 or 7
CD 1-Track 11

Traditional

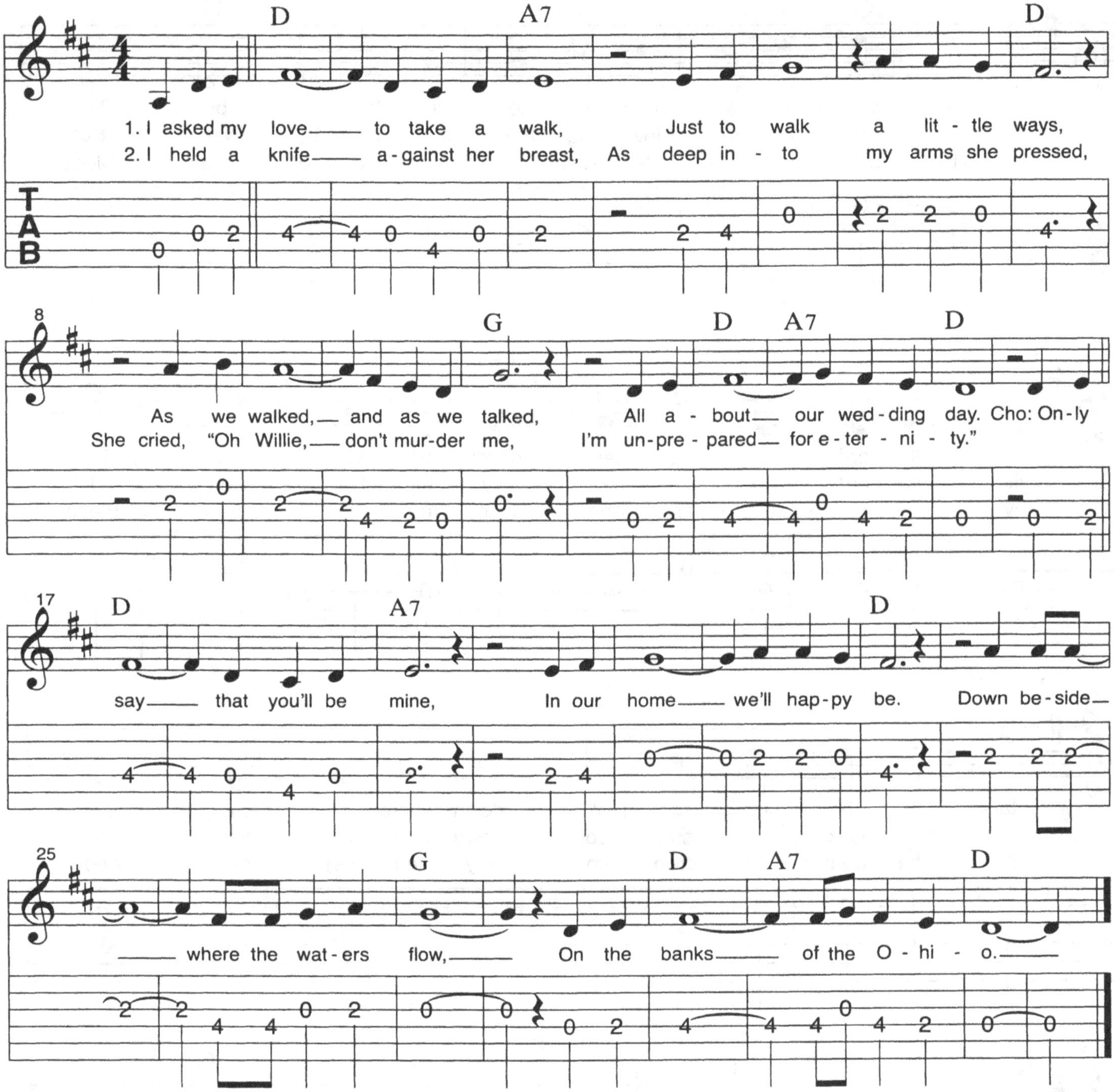

D A7
3. I took her by her lily white hand,
D
Led her down that bank of sand,
G
There I pushed her in to drown,
D A7 D
And watched her as she floated down.

4. I started home 'tween twelve and one,
Crying "God, what have I done?
I've killed the girl I love you see,
Because she would not marry me."

5. Next morning was about half past four,
The sheriff knocked upon my door,
Says "Young man, come go with me,
Down beside the deep blue sea."

 B. Monroe, Monroe Bros., T. Rice, D. Watson, D. Grisman, C. White, J.D. Crowe, Country Gentlemen, Stanley Bros., Blue Sky Boys

A Beautiful Life

M: G; F: C or D, capo 5 or 7
CD 1-Track 12

Wm. Golden, 1918

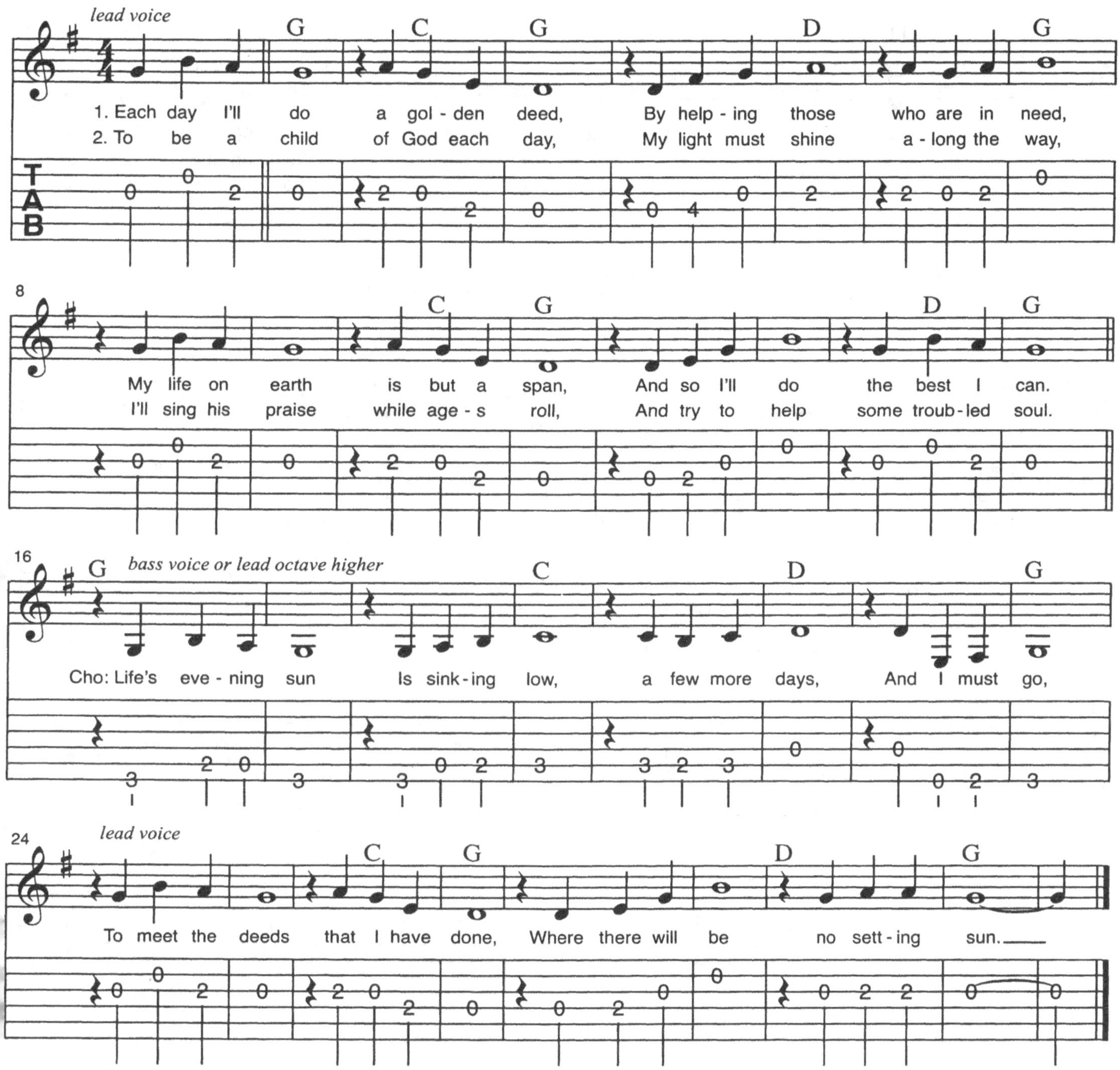

3. The only life that will endure,
Is one that's kind and good and pure,
And so for God I'll take my stand,
Each day I'll lend a helping hand.

4. While going down life's weary road,
I'll try to lift some traveler's load,
I'll try to turn the night to day,
Make flowers bloom along the way.

B. Monroe, J. Martin, Stanley Bros., Ken. Colonels, Country Gentlemen, Doyle Lawson

Beautiful Star of Bethlehem

M: D; F: G or A, capo 5 or 7
CD 1-Track 13

Boyce & Pace

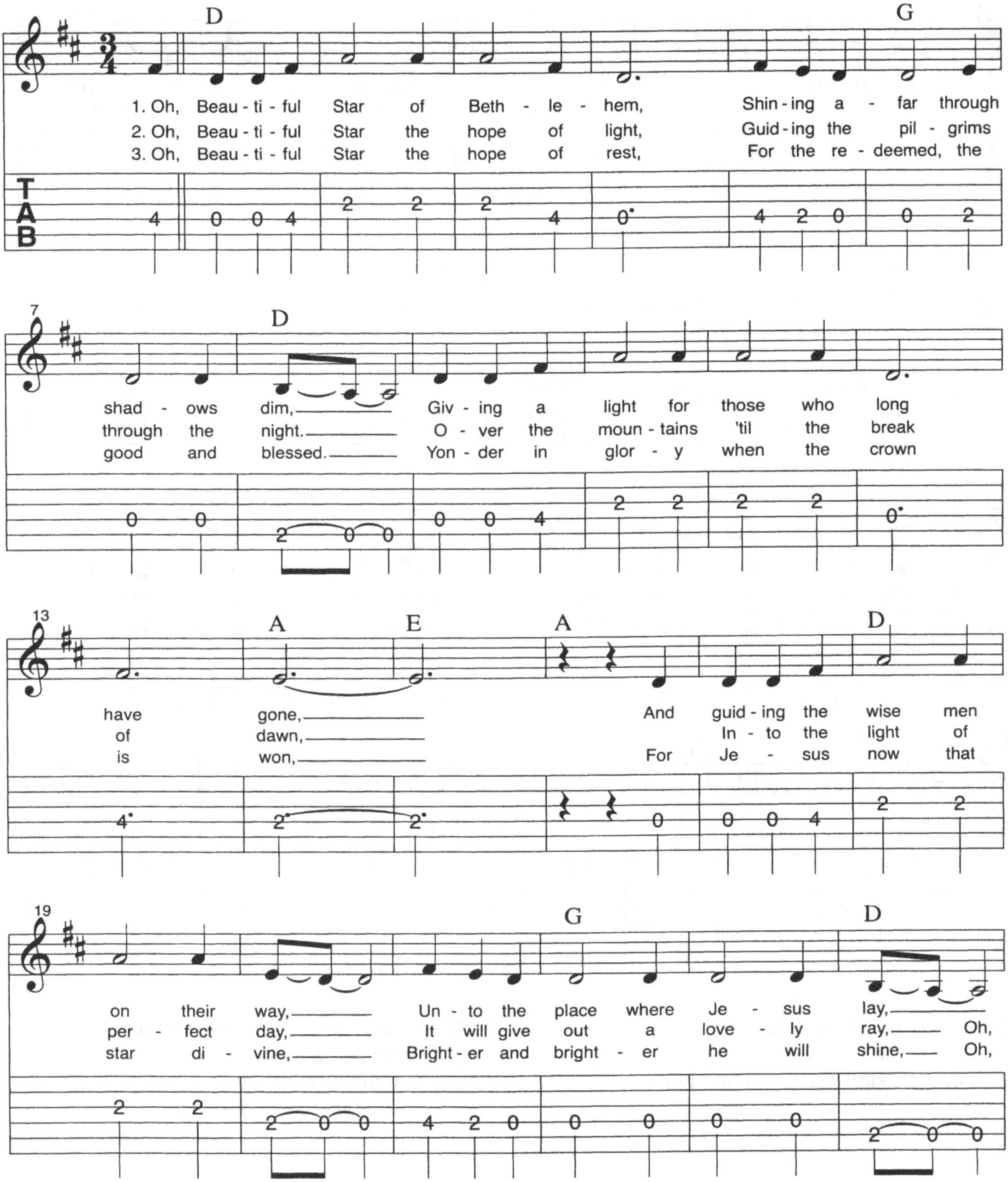

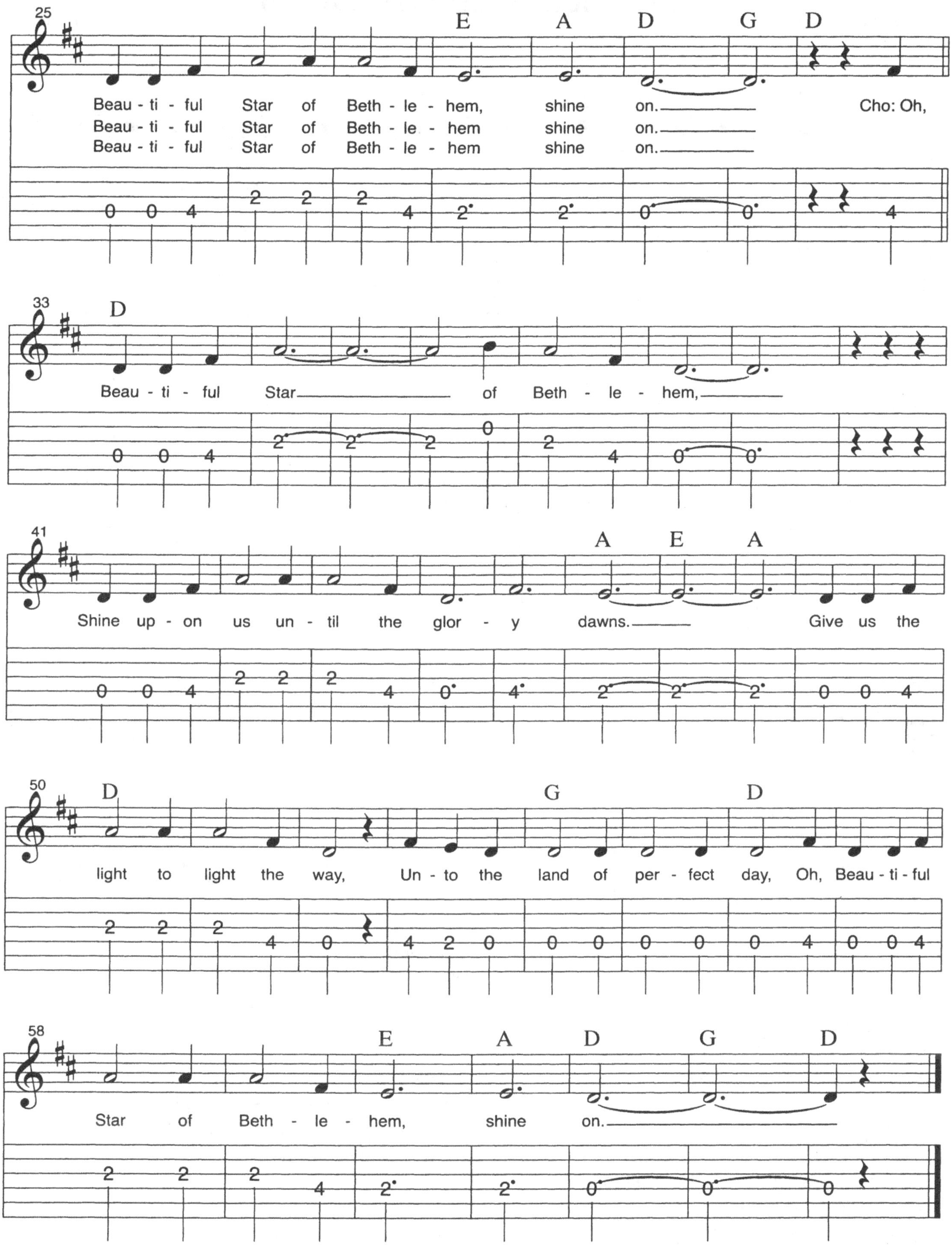
25
E A D G D
Beau - ti - ful Star of Beth - le - hem, shine on.
Cho: Oh,
Beau - ti - ful Star of Beth - le - hem shine on.
Beau - ti - ful Star of Beth - le - hem shine on.
33
D
Beau - ti - ful Star of Beth - le - hem,
41
A E A
Shine up - on us un - til the glor - y dawns.
Give us the
50
D G D
light to light the way, Un - to the land of per - fect day, Oh, Beau - ti - ful
58
E A D G D
Star of Beth - le - hem, shine on.

Bile Them Cabbage Down

M: G; F: C or D, capo 5 or 7
CD 1-Track 14, medley pt. 1

Traditional

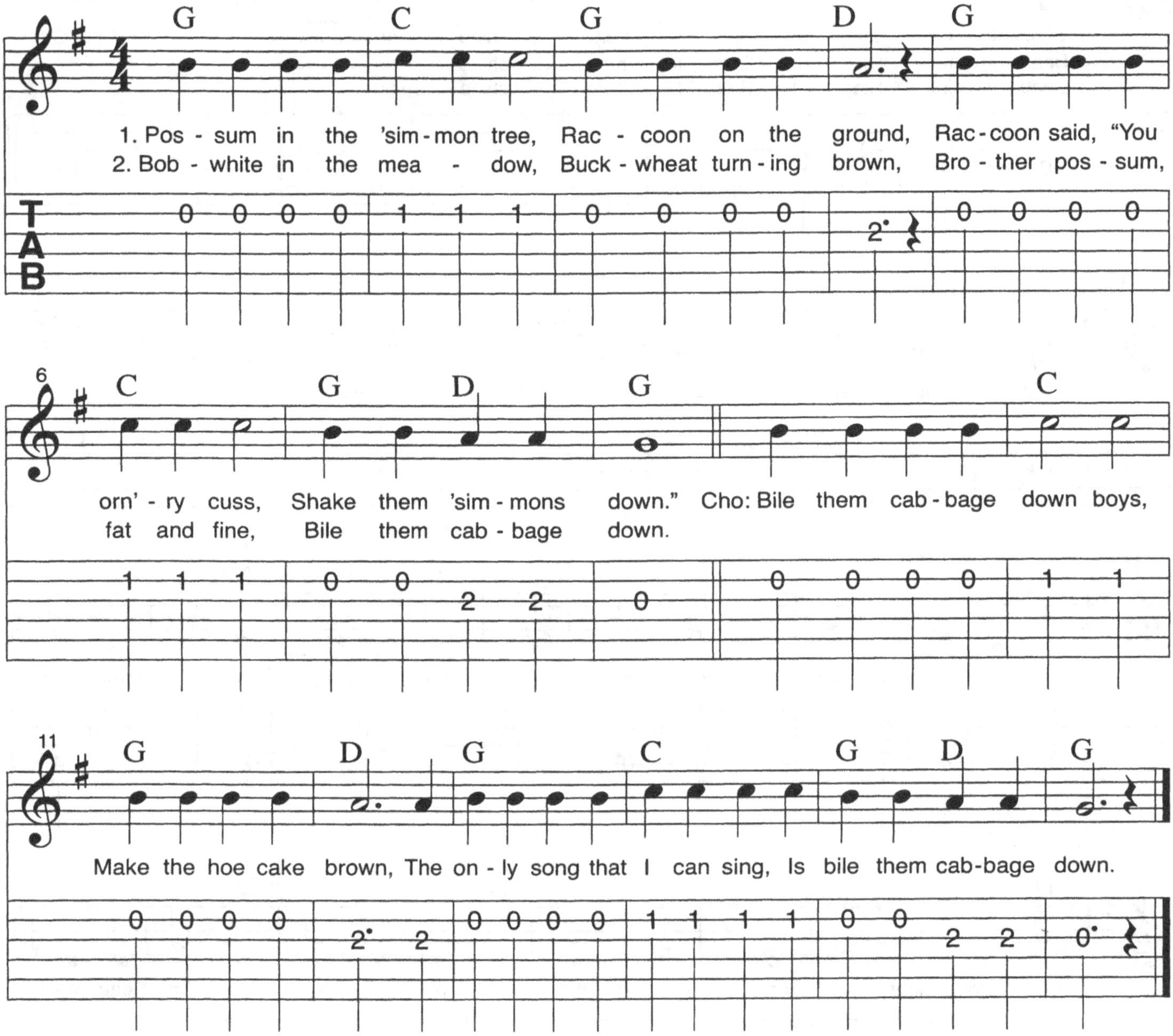


```
G                C
3.  Pork roast in the oven
G                  D
Taters turning brown,
G                    C
Buttermilk and cornbread too,
G             D     G
Bile them cabbage down.
```

4. Corn blades rustling in the breeze,
Pumpkins on the ground,
Squirrels chirping in the trees,
Bile them cabbage down.

5. I bought my gal a bicycle,
She learned to ride it well,
She ran into a telephone pole,
And broke it all to pieces.

6. Grandpa had a muley cow,
She was muley when she was born,
It took the jaybird forty years,
To fly from horn to horn.

7. Grandpa had a setting hen,
He set her as you know,
Set her on three buzzard eggs,
Hatched out one old crow.

Black Eyed Susie

M: G; F: C or D, capo 5 or 7
CD 1-Track 14, medley pt. 2

Traditional

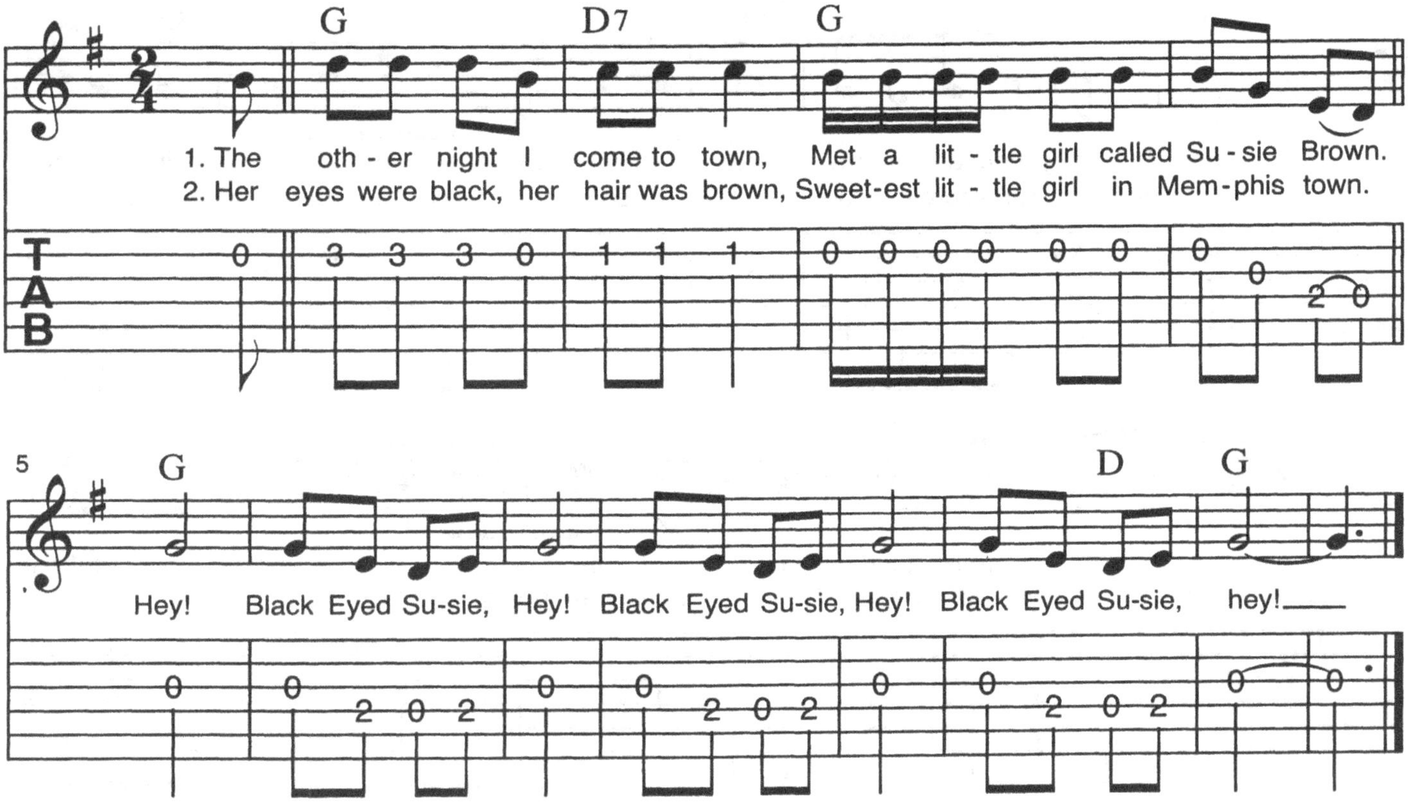

G D
3. All I need to make me happy
G
Two little boys to call me pappy,
G
Hey! Black Eyed Susie,
Hey! Black Eyed Susie,
D7 G
Hey! Black Eyed Susie, hey!

4. One named Paul and the other one Davey,
One loves ham and the other one gravy. (Chorus)

5. Some got drunk and some got woozy,
I went home with Black Eyed Susie.

6. I fell in love with her that night,
Sent for the preacher and the preacher was tight.

7. We said "I do" by the lantern light,
Promised that preacher we'd never fight.

Blue Ridge Mountain Blues

M: G; F: C or D, capo 5 or 7
CD 1-Track 15

Cliff Hess

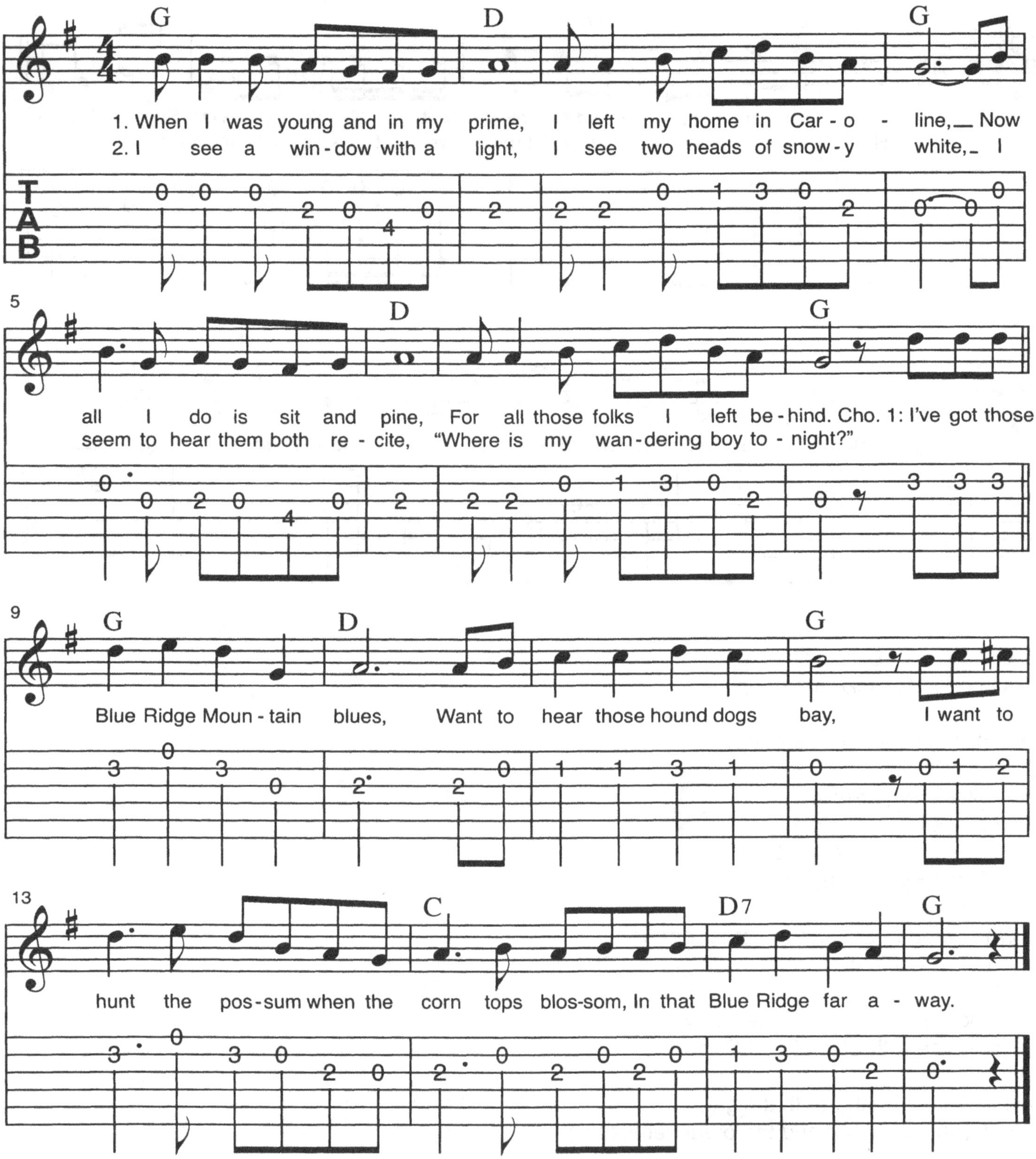

G D
3. I'll always do right by my Ma,
G
I'll always do right by my Pa,
D
I'll hang around that cabin door,
G
No work, no worry anymore.

G D
Cho. 2: I've got those Blue Ridge Mountain blues,
G
I want to stand right here and say,
C
My grip is packed to travel and I'm scratching gravel,
D7 G
To the Blue Ridge far away.

 B. Monroe, Jim & Jesse, Flatt & Scruggs, D. Watson, Bill Clifton

The Bluebirds are Singing for Me

M: C; F: F or G, capo 5 or 7
CD 1-Track 16

Mac Wiseman

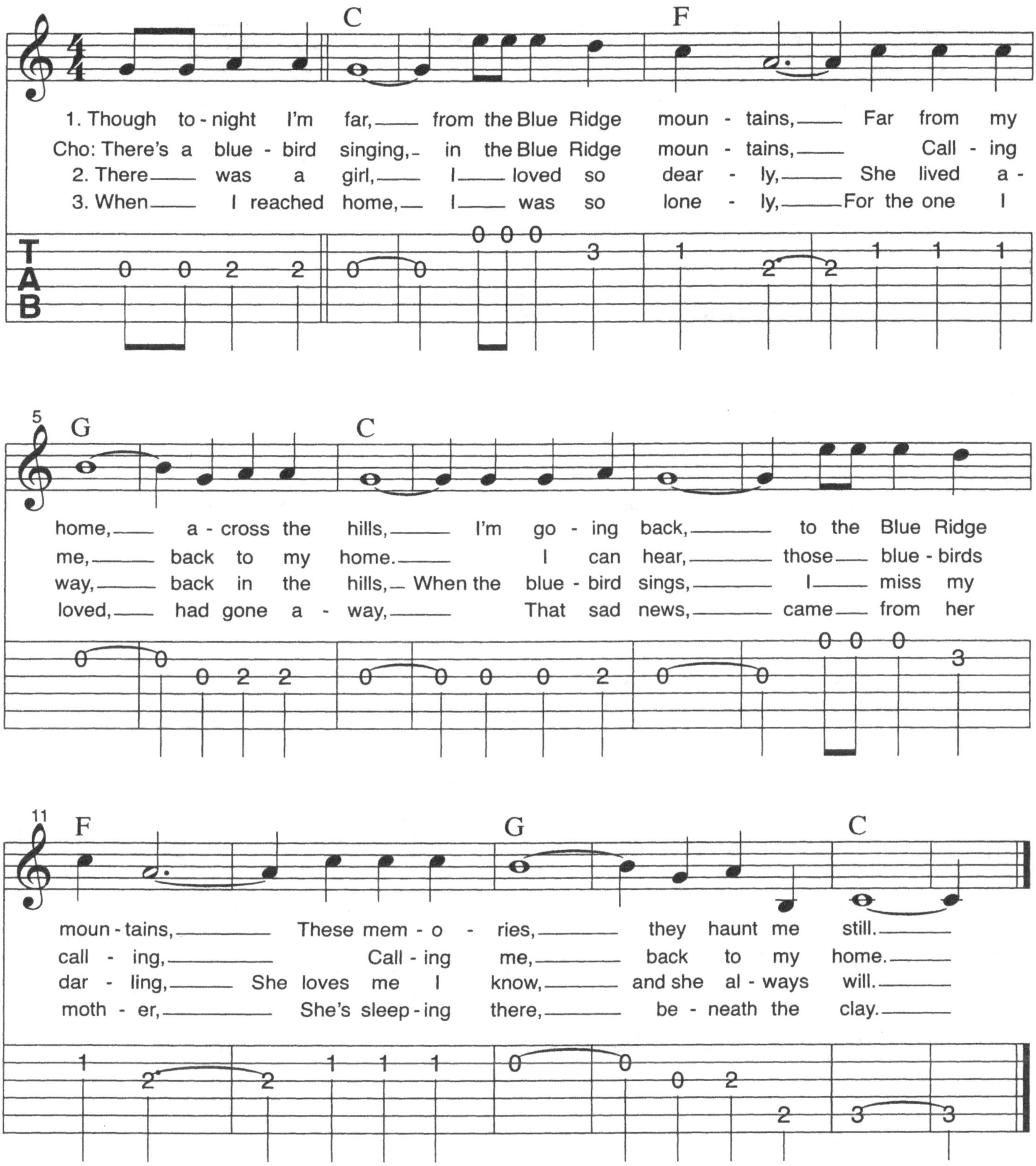

Bound to Ride

M: G; F: C or D, capo 5 or 7
CD 1-Track 17

Traditional

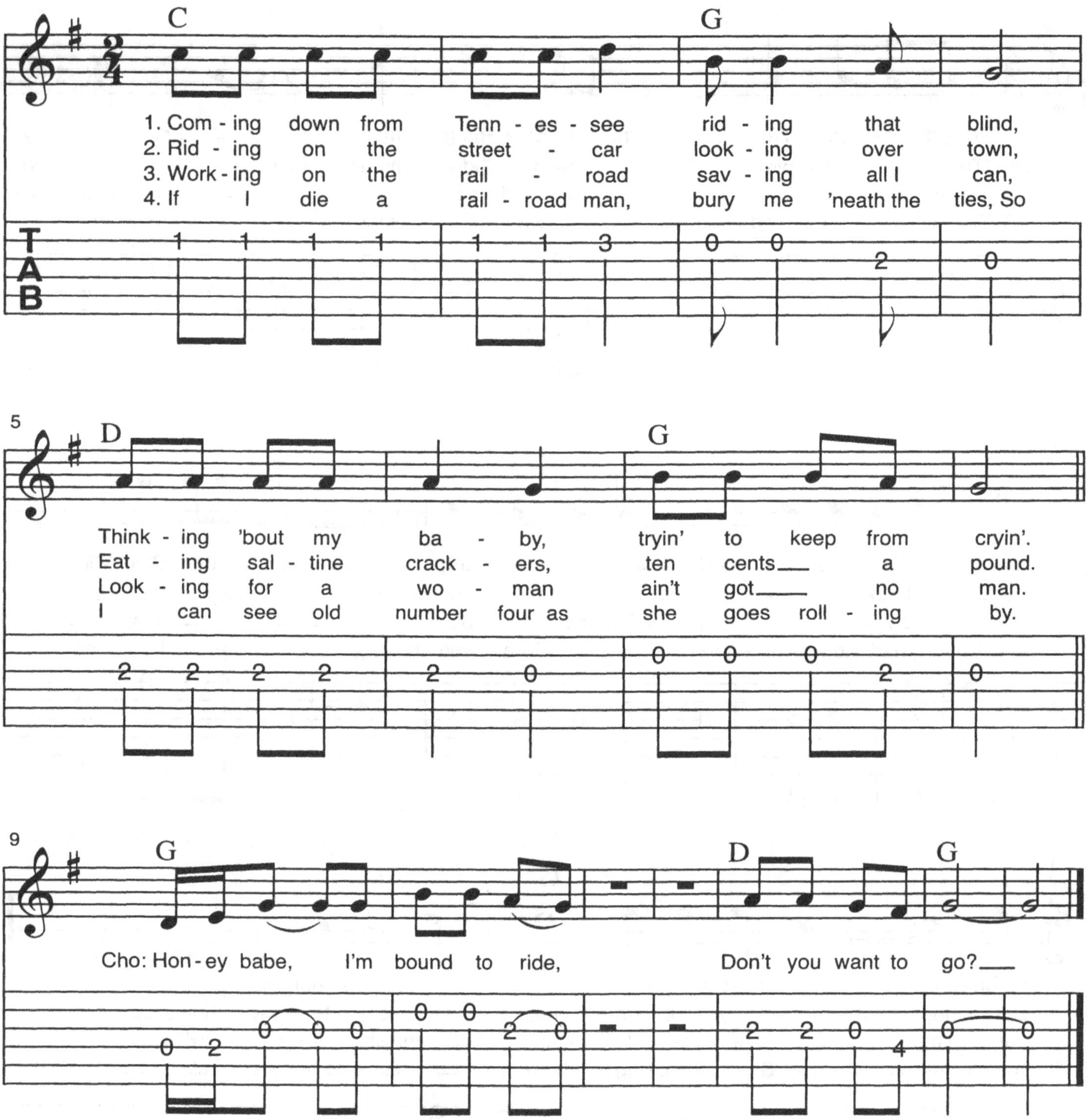

 Stanley Bros., Flatt & Scruggs, R. Stanley

Bright Morning Stars

M: C; F: F or G, capo 5 or 7
CD 1-Track 18

Traditional

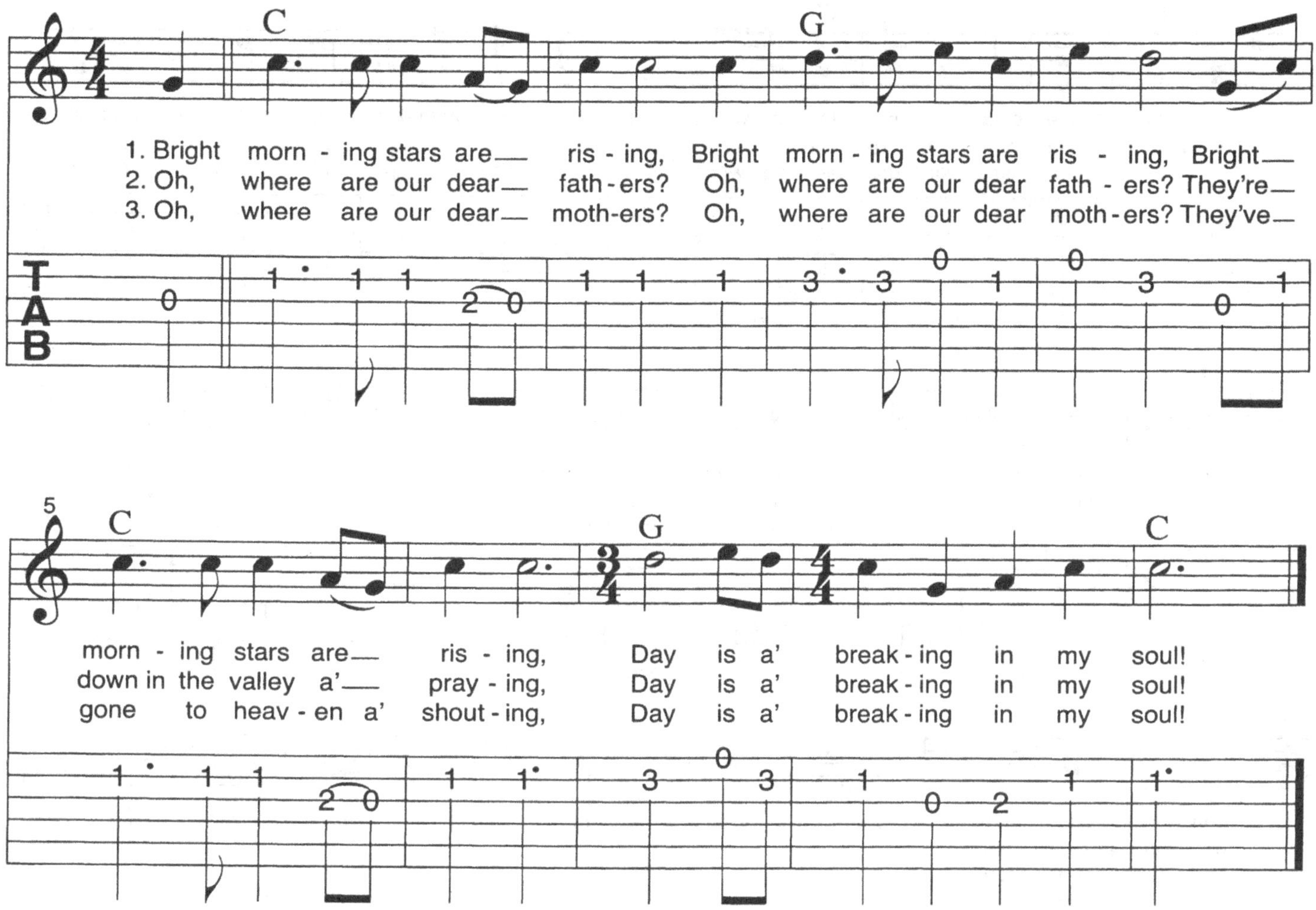

Bring Back to Me My Wandering Boy

M: G; F: C or D, capo 5 or 7
CD 1-Track 19

Traditional

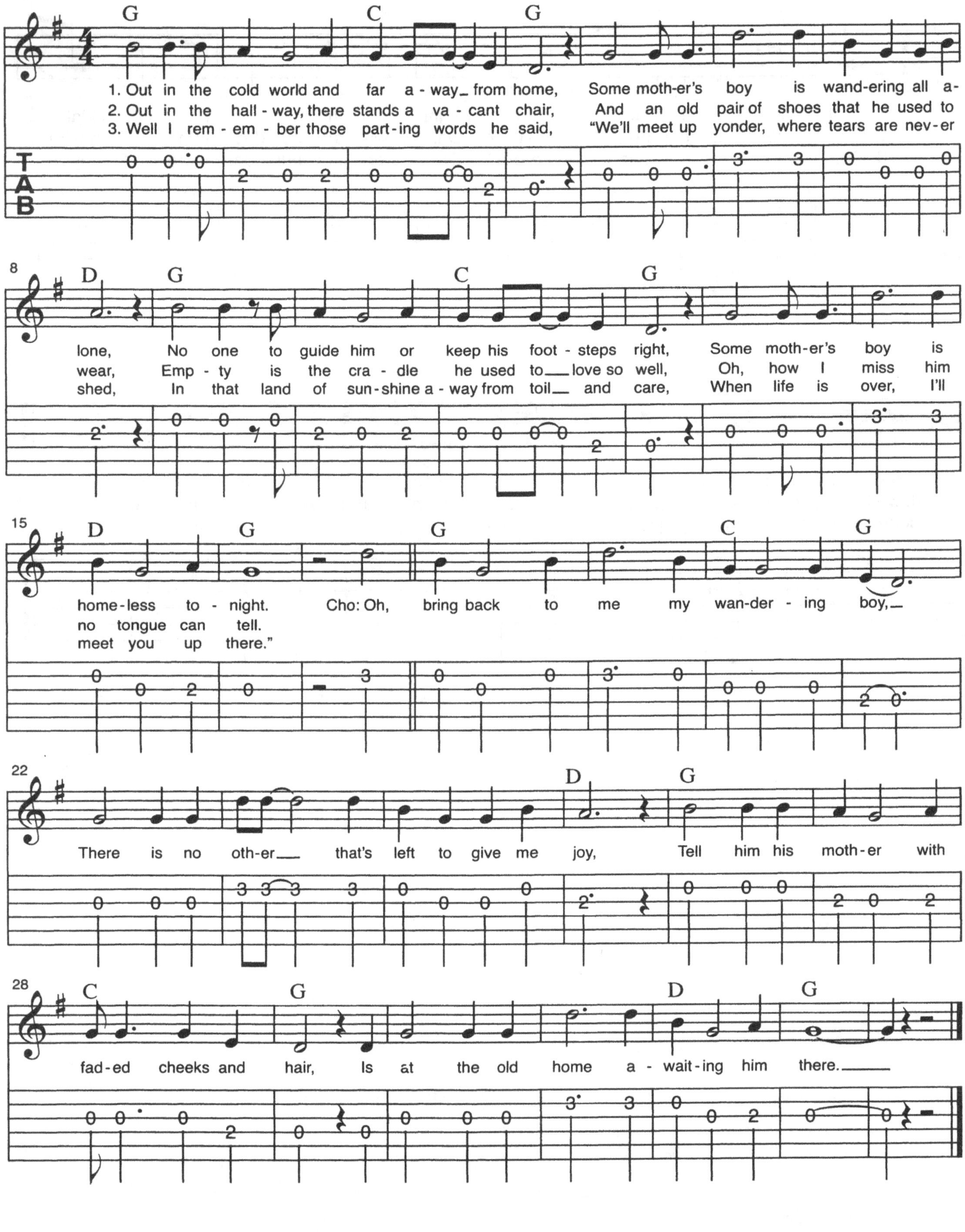

 B. Monroe, Flatt & Scruggs, Blue Sky Boys, Carter Fam., J. Val

Buffalo Gals

M: C; F: F or G, capo 5 or 7
CD 1-Track 20

Traditional

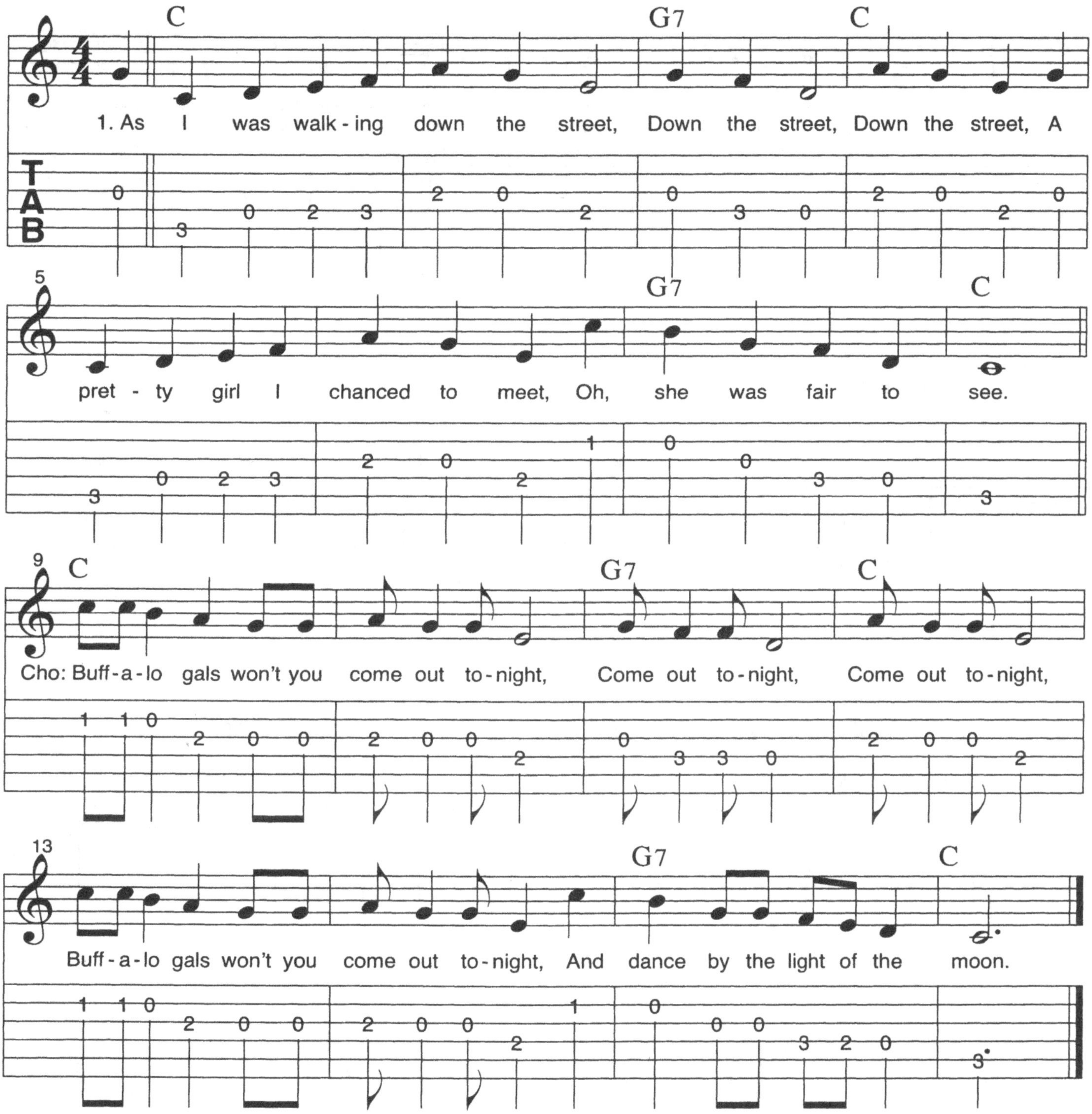

2. I danced with a gal with a hole in her stockin', (C)
Her heel kept a-rockin', her knees kept a-knockin', (G7 … C)
I danced with a gal with a hole in her stockin',
We danced by the light of the moon. (G7 … C)

3. I asked her if she'd like to talk, (like to talk 2X)
Her feet took up the whole sidewalk,
Oh, she was fair to see.

4. I asked her if she'd have a dance, (have a dance 2X)
I thought that I might have a chance,
To shake a foot with her.

5. I asked her if she'd be my wife, (be my wife 2X)
Then I'd be happy all my life,
If she'd marry me.

The Bully of the Town

M: G; F: C or D, capo 5 or 7
CD 1-Track 21

Unknown, 1895

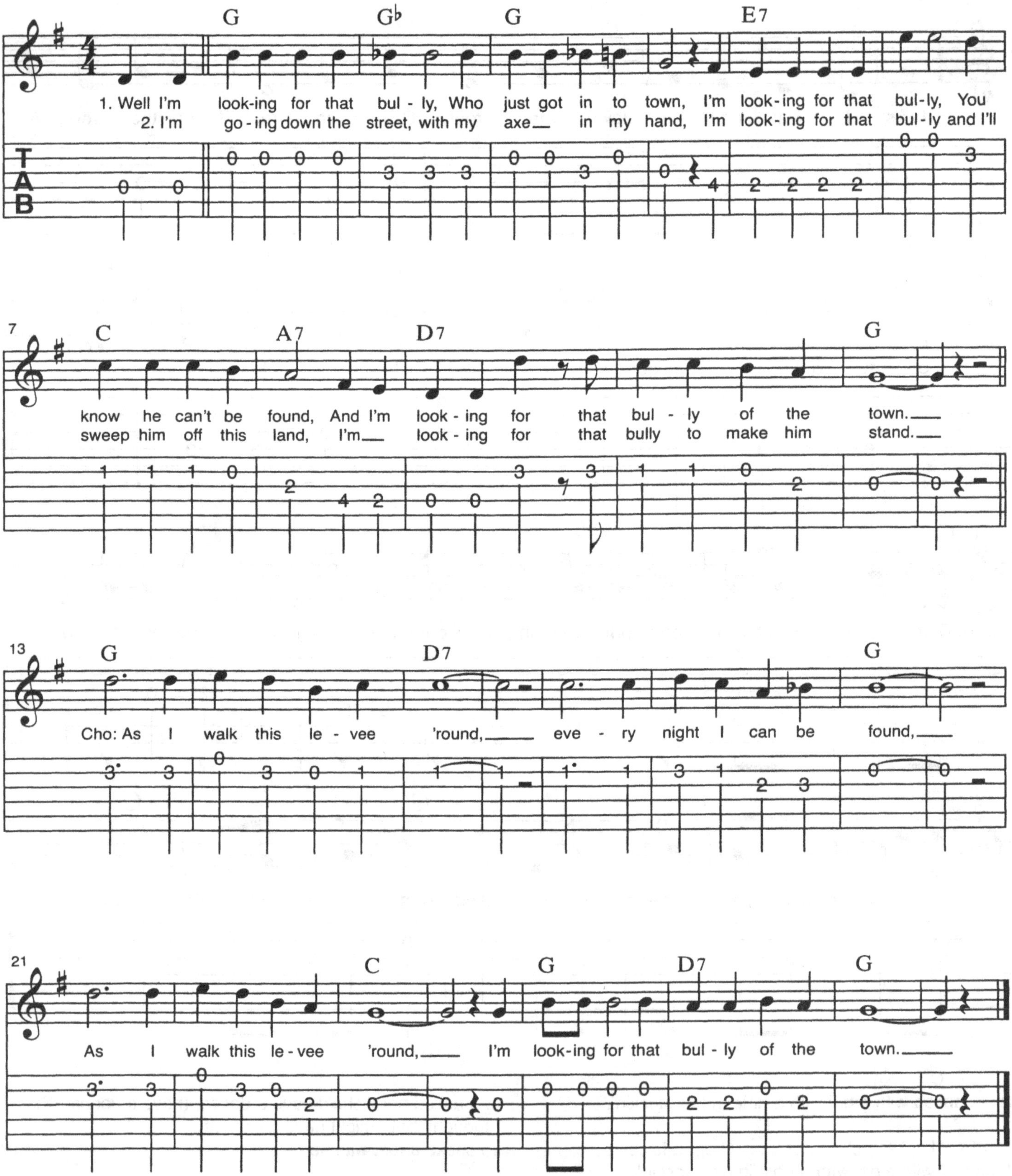

```
         G                  G♭        G
3.  I'll take my long razor, I'm going to carve him deep,
      E7                          C                A7
And when I see that bully, I'll lay him down to sleep,
     D7                                   G
I'm looking for that bully to make him weep.
```

4. I went a winging, down at Parson Jones',
Took along my trusty blade to carve that fellow's bones,
Just a'looking for that bully to hear his groans.

5. I walked in the front door, the men were prancing high,
For that levee fella, I skinned my foxy eye,
Just a'looking for that bully and he wasn't nigh.

6. I asked Miss Pansy Blossom, if she would wing a reel,
She says, "Laws, Mr. Johnson, how high you make me feel,"
Then you ought to see me shake my sugar heel.

7. I rose up like a black cloud and took a look around,
There was that new bully, standing on the ground,
I've been looking for you fella and I've got you found.

8. When I got through with bully, a doctor and a nurse,
Were no good to that man, so they put him in a hearse,
A cyclone couldn't have torn him up much worse.

9. You don't hear about that fella, that treated folks so free,
Go down upon the levee and his face you'll never see,
There's only one boss bully and that is me.

10. When you see me coming, hoist your windows high,
When you see me going, hang your heads and cry,
I'm looking for that bully and he must die.

11. My madness is a rising, and I'm not going to get left,
I'm getting so bad that I'm scared of myself,
I was looking for that bully now he's on the shelf.

H. M. Rounders, B. Keith, Fiddlin' John Carson, Skillet Lickers, Stanley Bros, Alan Munde, Allen Shelton, Doug Dillard

Bury Me Beneath the Willow

M: D; F: G or A, capo 5 or 7
CD 1-Track 22

Traditional

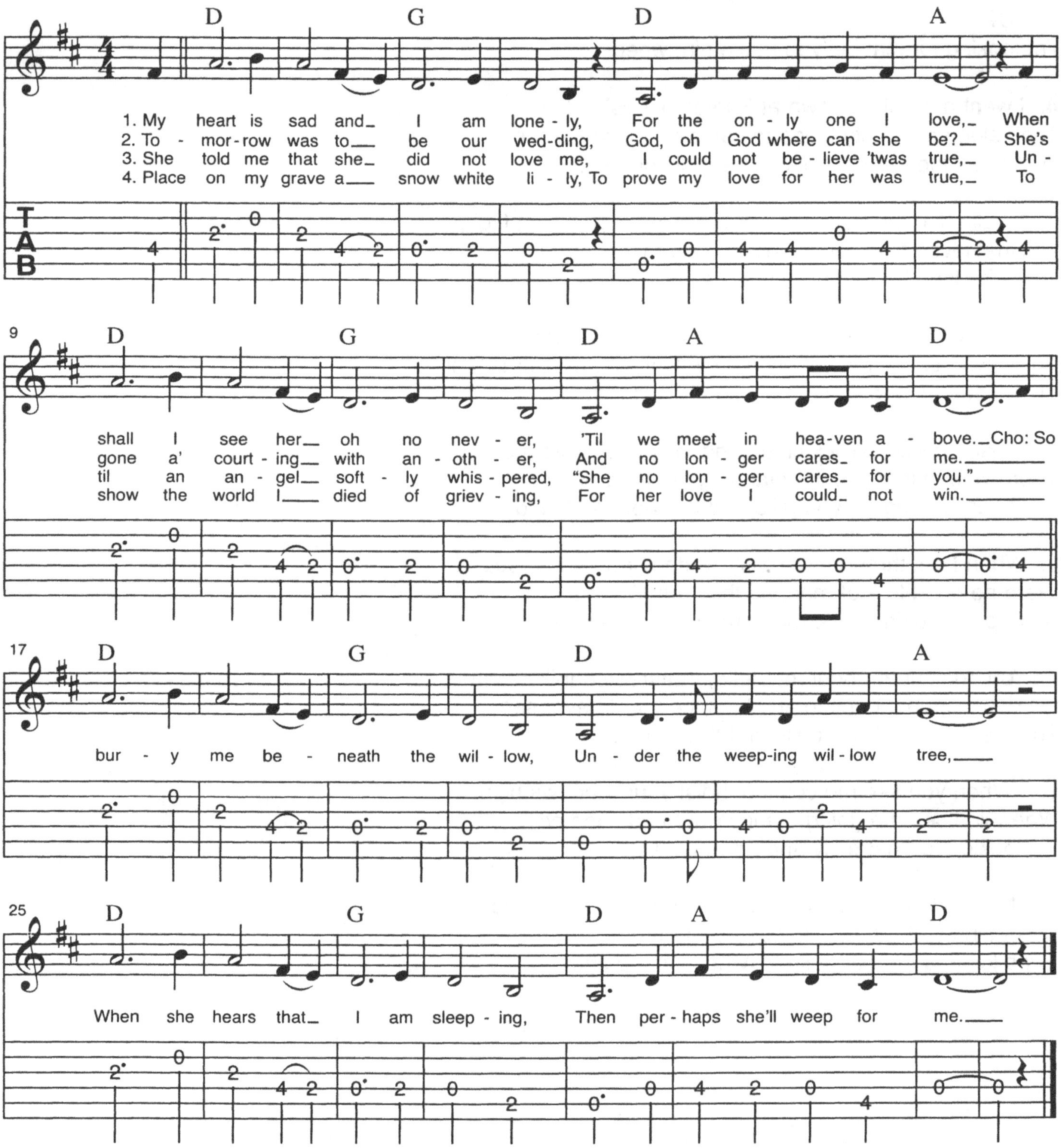

 Carter Fam., Rice and Skaggs, C. White, W. Guthrie, Ken. Colonels

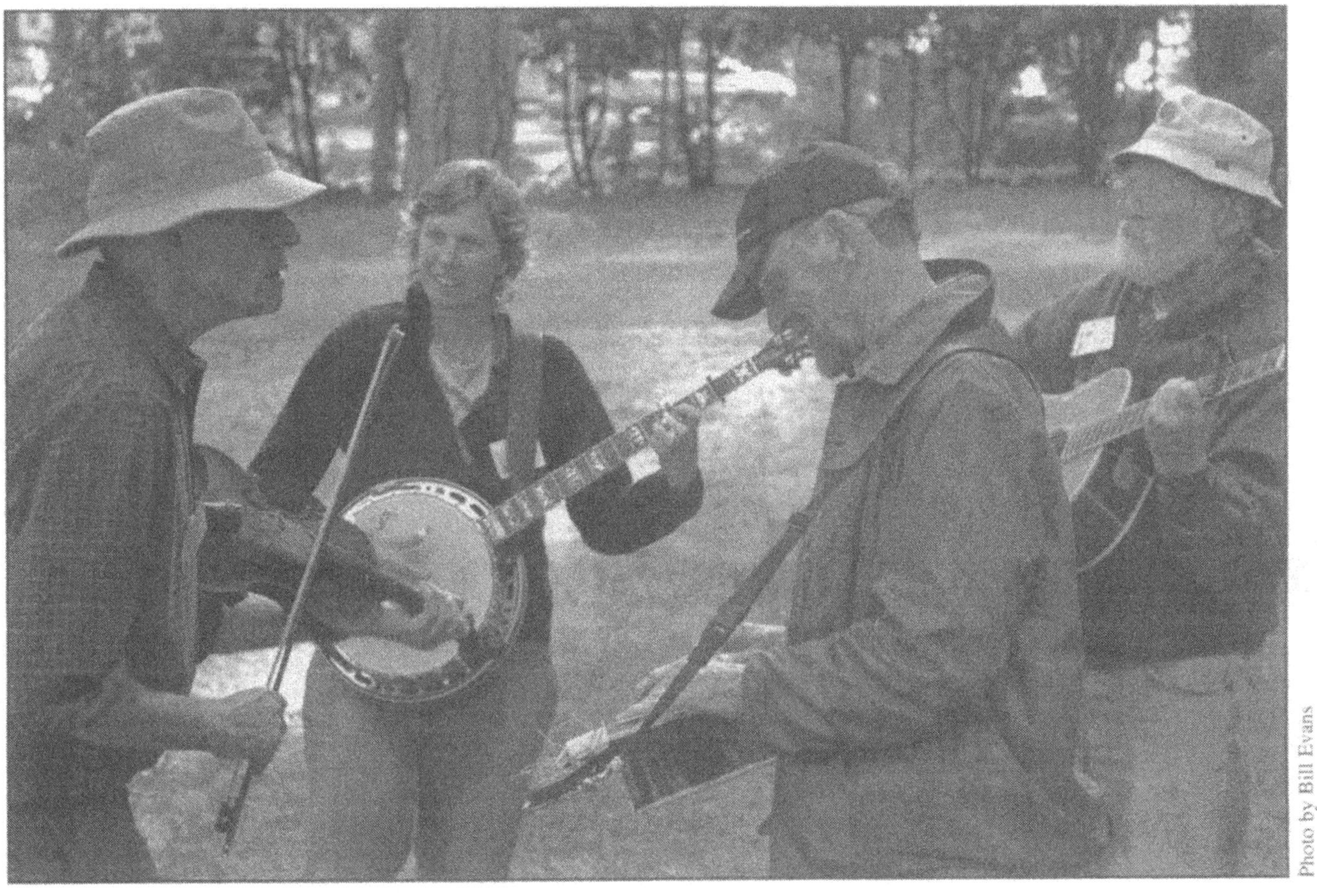

Photo by Bill Evans

Don't these folks look like they're having a good time?
It's tough not to smile when you're playing music with friends old or new.

C-H-I-C-K-E-N

M: C; F: F or G, capo 5 or 7
CD 1-Track 23

Perrin & Slater, 1902

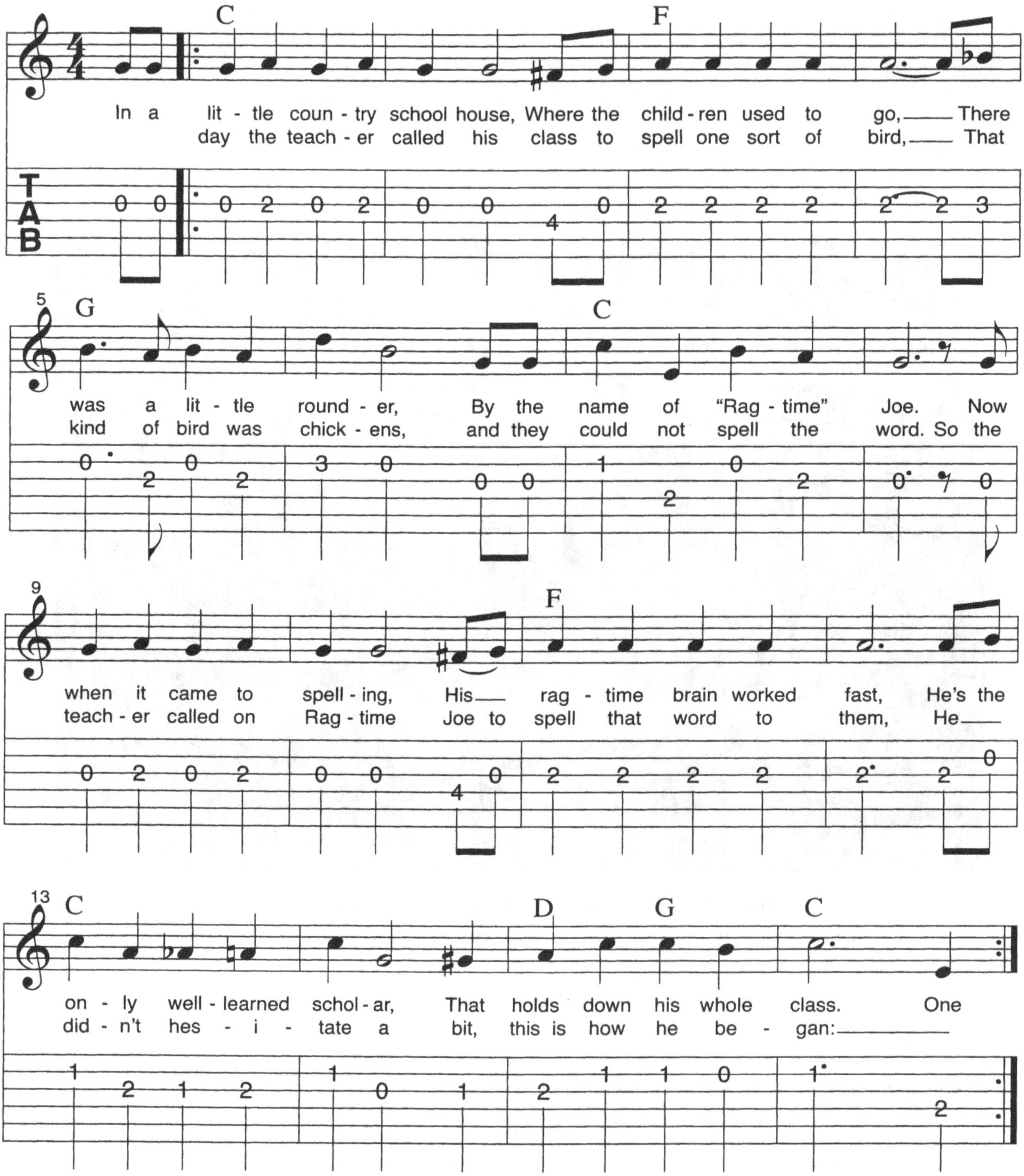

 Greenbriar Boys, Sam McGee, Kathy Kallick

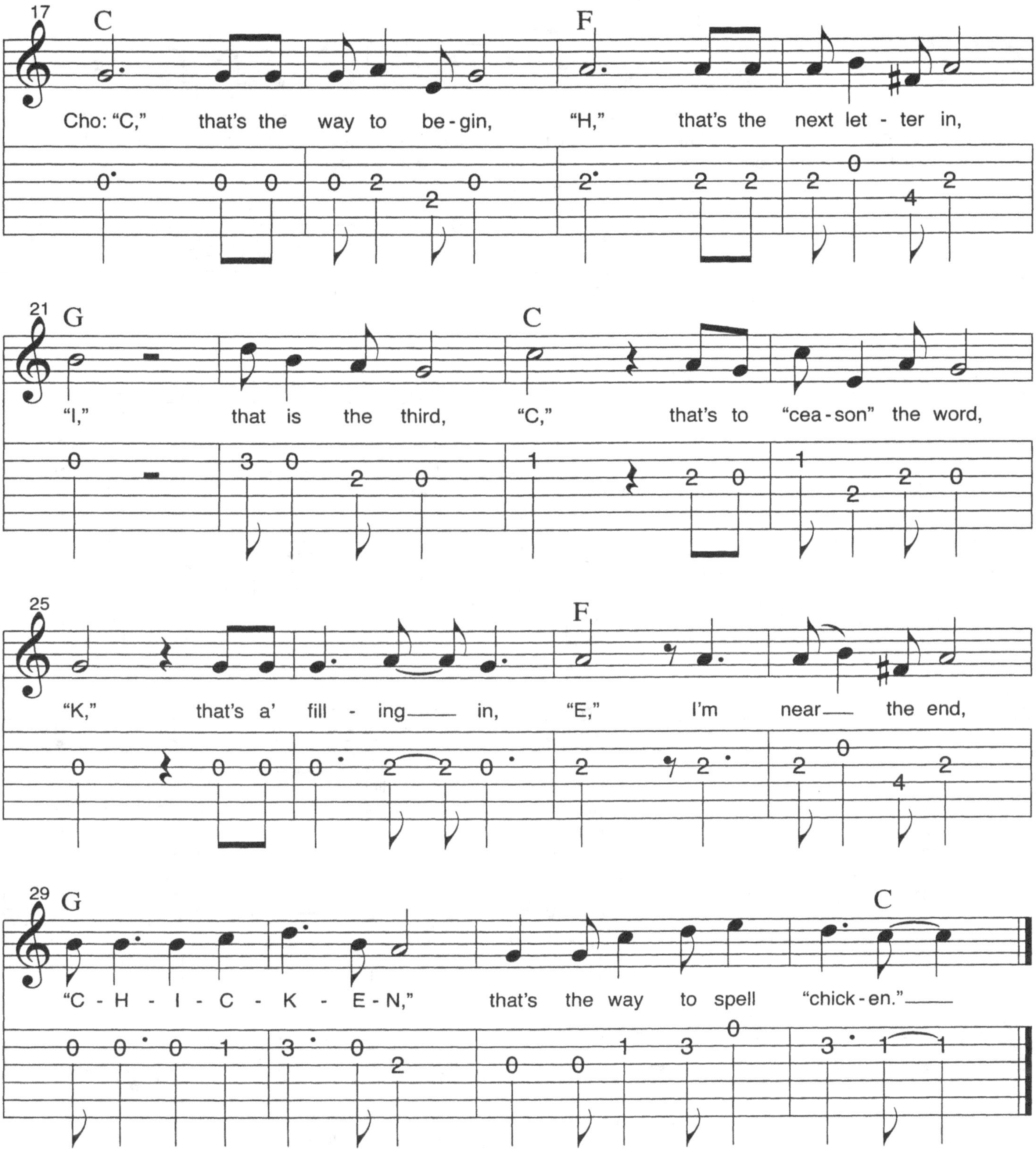
C F
Cho: "C," that's the way to be-gin, "H," that's the next let - ter in,
G C
"I," that is the third, "C," that's to "cea-son" the word,
F
"K," that's a' fill - ing in, "E," I'm near the end,
G C
"C - H - I - C - K - E - N," that's the way to spell "chick-en."

Can't You Hear Me Callin'?

M: D; F: G or A, capo 5 or 7
CD 1-Track 24

Bill Monroe

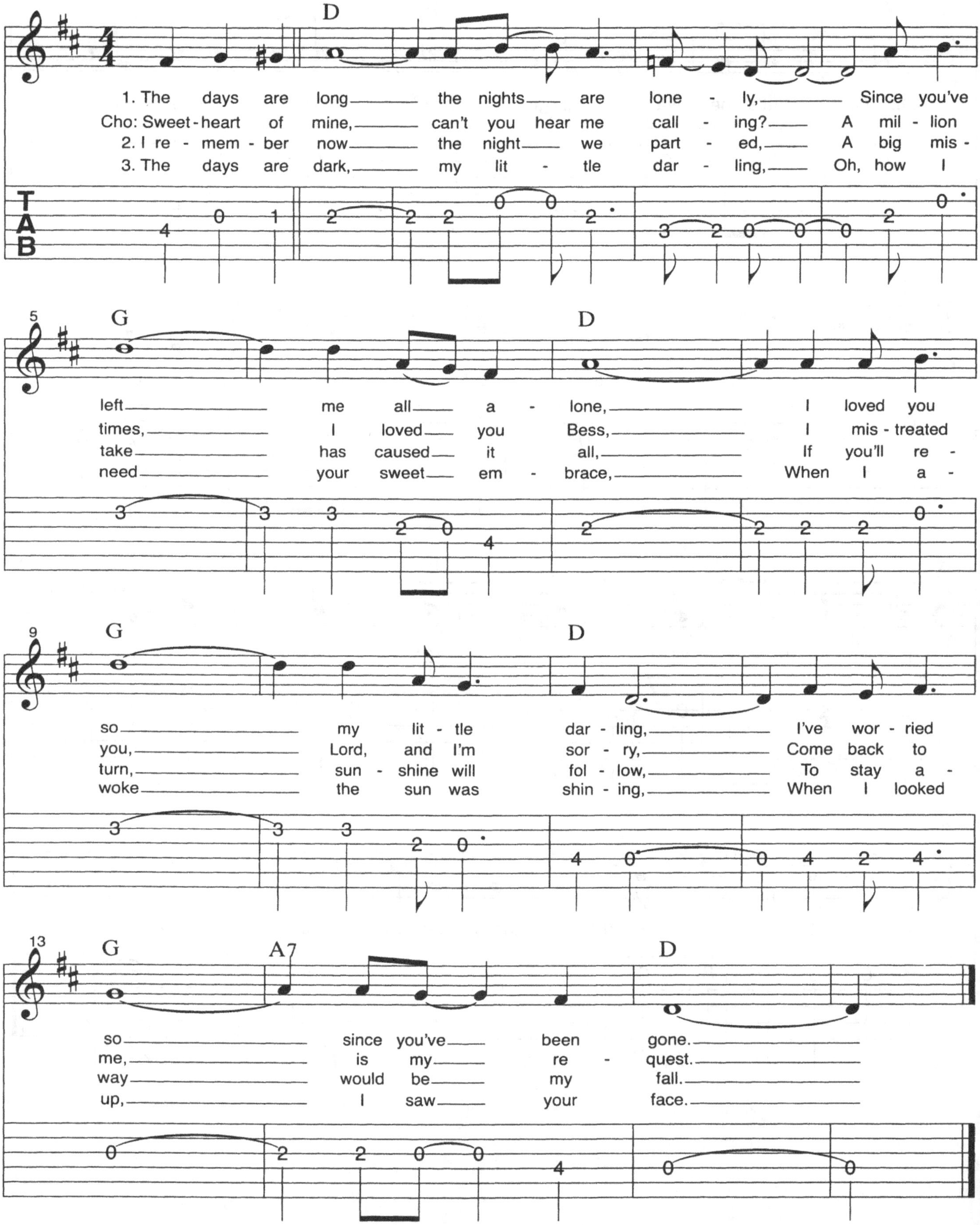

Careless Love

M: F; F: B♭ or C, capo 5 or 7
CD 1-Track 25

Traditional

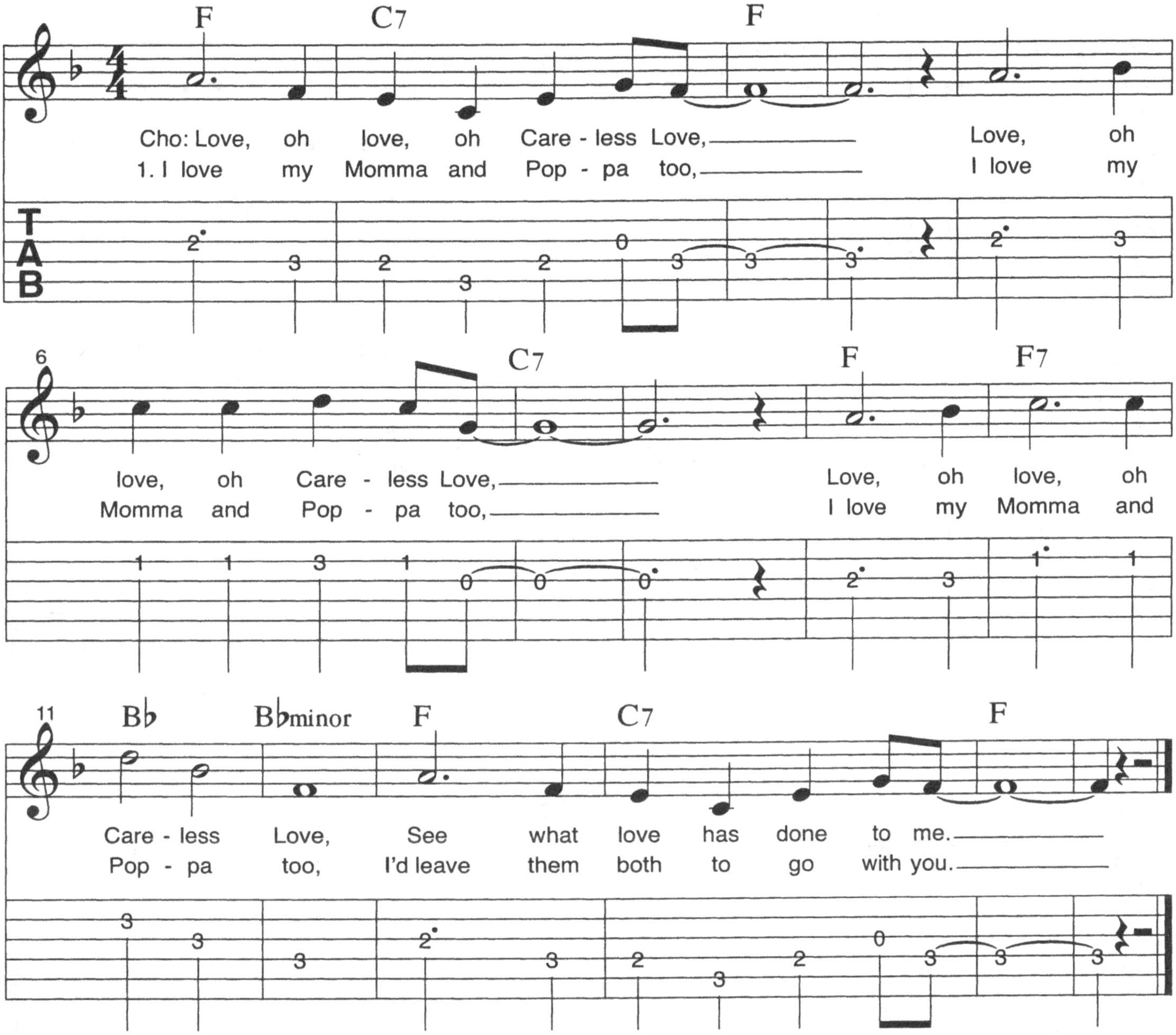

F C7 F
2. Sorrow, sorrow to my heart,
C7
Sorrow, sorrow to my heart,
F F7 B♭ B♭m
Sorrow, sorrow to my heart,
F C7 F
Since we two have been apart.

3. What, oh what will Momma say? (3X)
When she learns I've gone astray?

4. Once I wore my apron low, (3X)
Scarcely keep you from my door.

5. Now my apron strings don't pin, (3X)
You pass my door and you don't come in.

Children Go Where I Send Thee

M: D; F: G or A, capo 5 or 7
CD 1-Track 26

Traditional

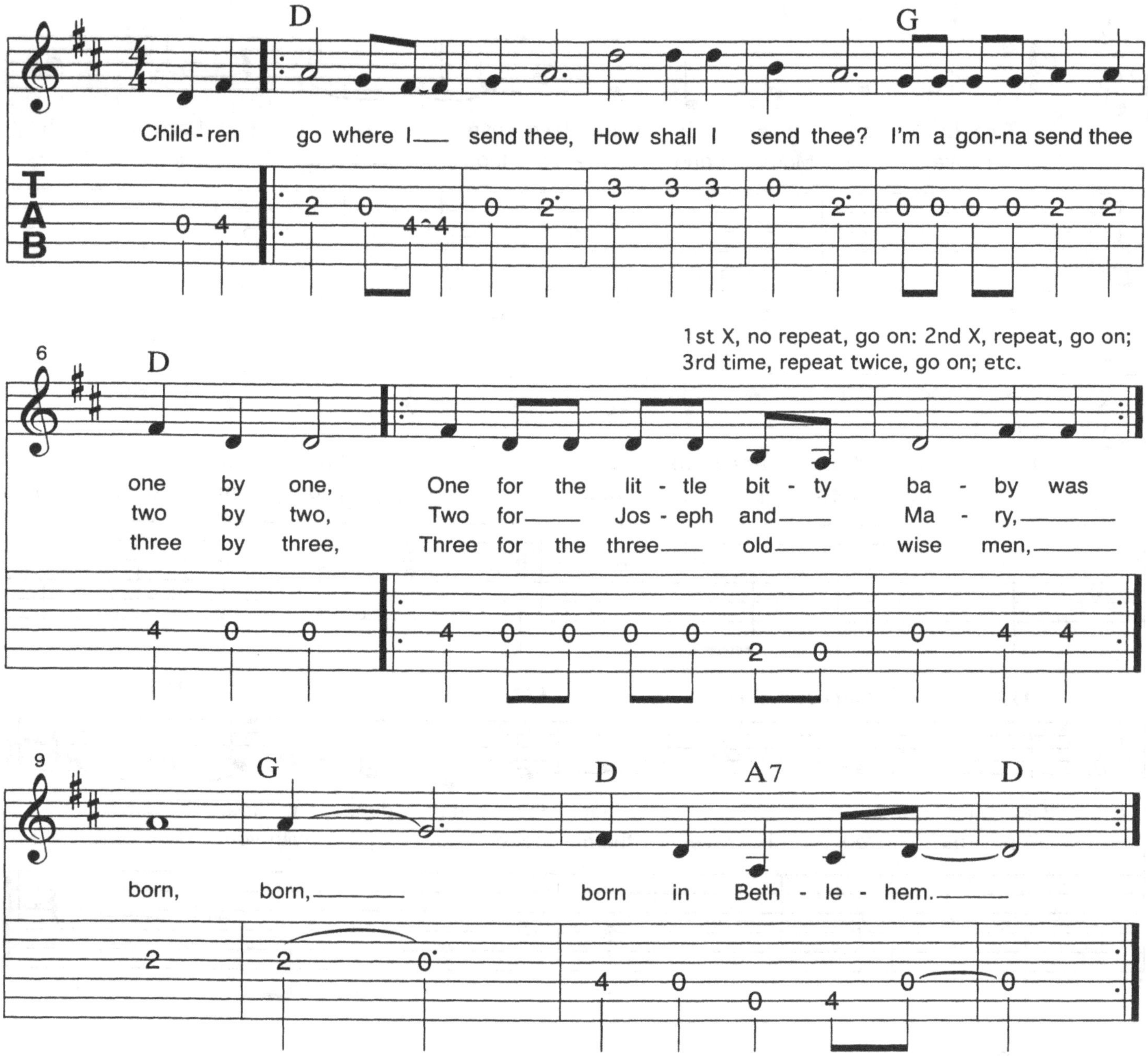

Four for the four who stood at the door,
Five for the Hebrew children,
Six for the six who didn't get fixed,
Seven for the seven who couldn't get to heaven,
Eight for the eight who didn't get straight,
Nine was the nine that stood in the line,
Ten for the ten commandments.

 Stanley Bros., R. Stanley, R. Skaggs

The Church in the Wildwood

M: A; F: D or E, capo 5 or 7
CD 1-Track 27

Wm. Pitts, ca 1850s

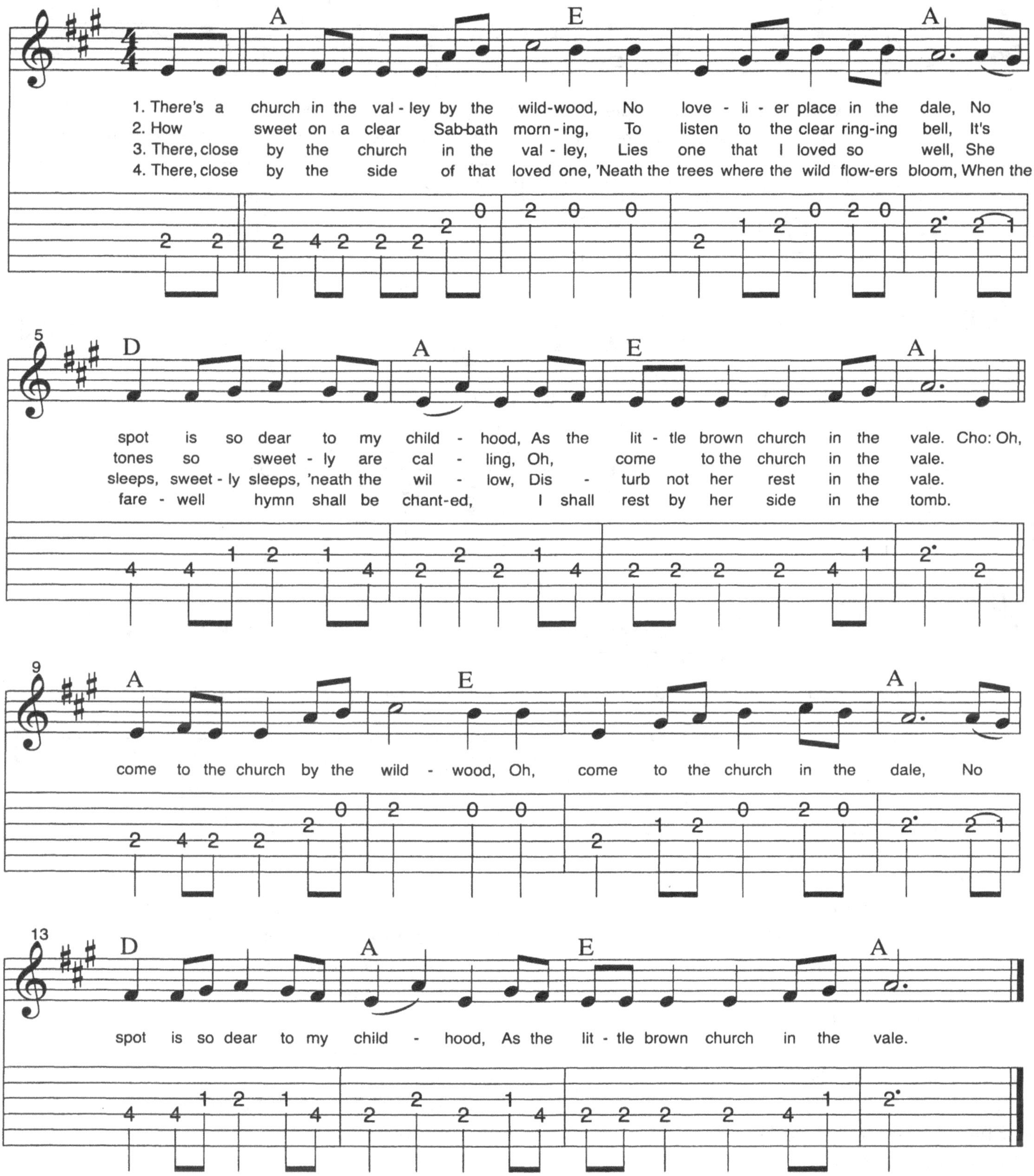

Cindy

M: G; F: C or D, capo 5 or 7
CD 1-Track 28

Traditional

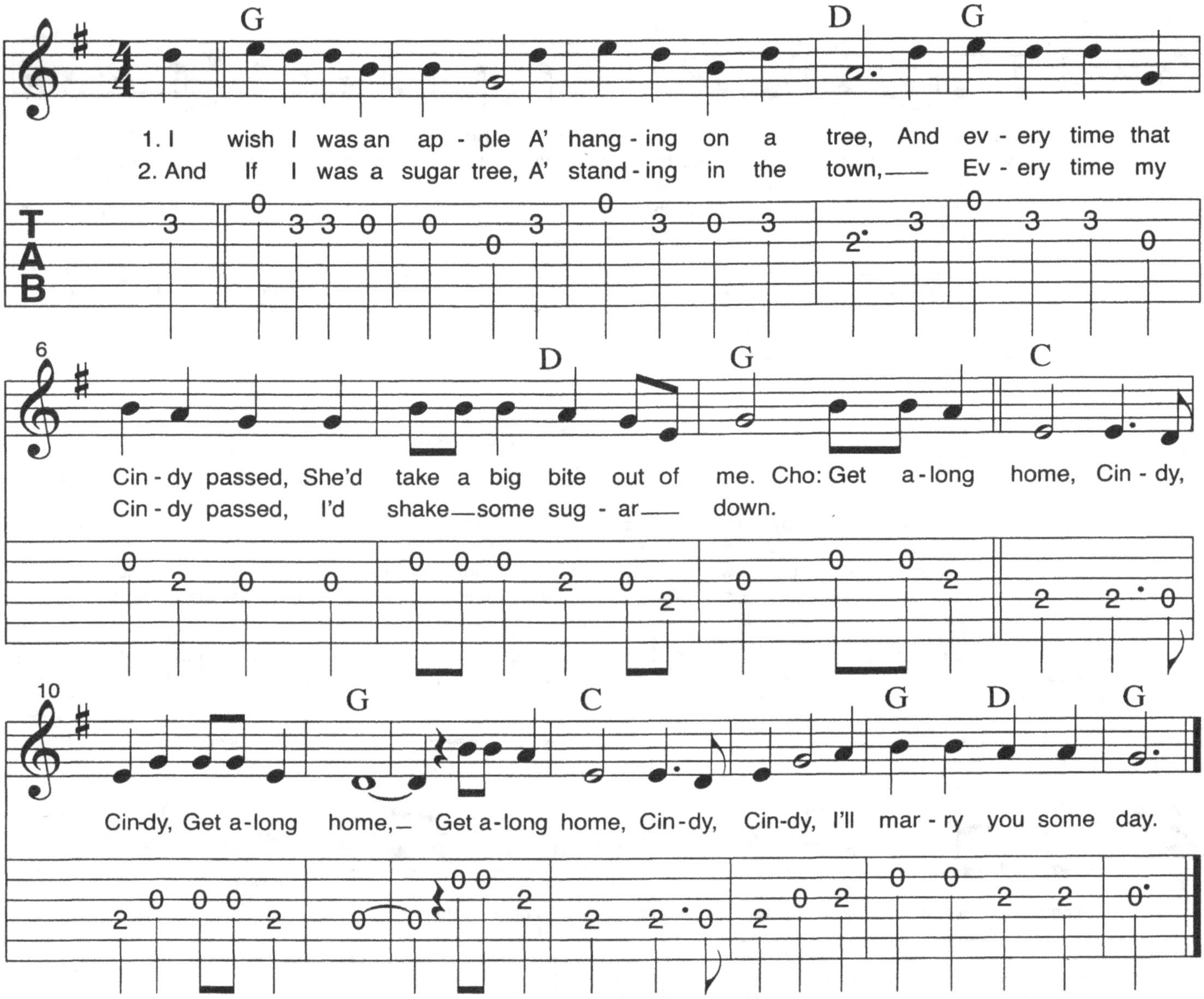


```
         G
3. The first time I saw Cindy,
                          D
She was standing in the door,
        G
Her shoes and stockings in her hand,
                 D       G
Her feet all over the floor.
```

4. She took me to her parlor,
She cooled me with her fan,
She said I was the prettiest thing,
In the shape of mortal man.

5. She kissed me and she hugged me,
She called me "Sugar Plum,"
She throwed her arms around me,
I thought my time had come.

6. Oh, Cindy is a pretty girl,
Cindy is a peach,
She threw her arms around my neck,
And hung on like a leech.

7. If I had a thread and needle,
Fine as I could sew,
I'd sew that gal to my coat tails,
And down the road I'd go.

Columbus Stockade Blues

***M**: G; **F**: C or D, capo 5 or 7*
CD 1-Track 29

Traditional

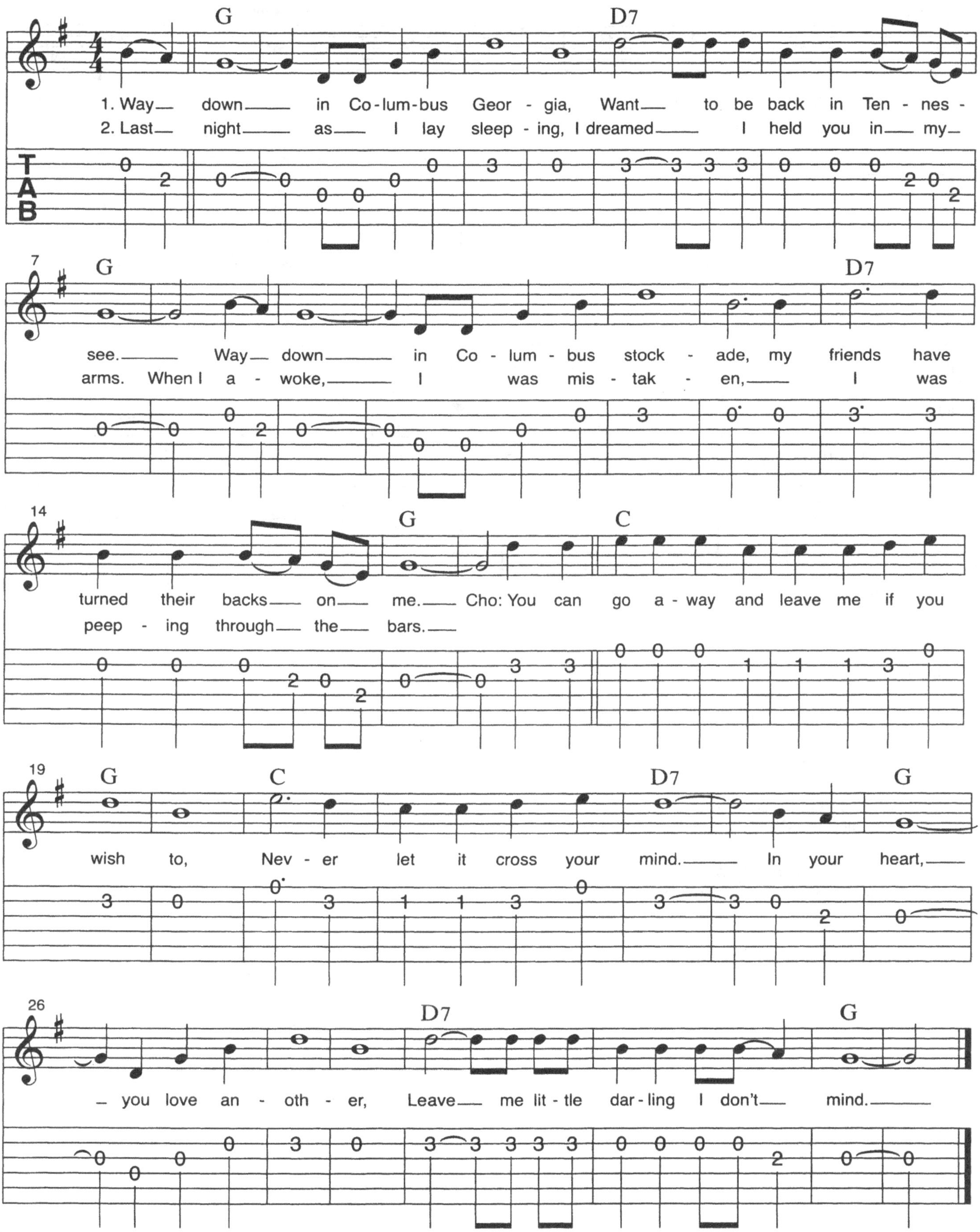

Cotton-Eyed Joe

M: G; F: C or D, capo 5 or 7
CD 1-Track 30

Traditional

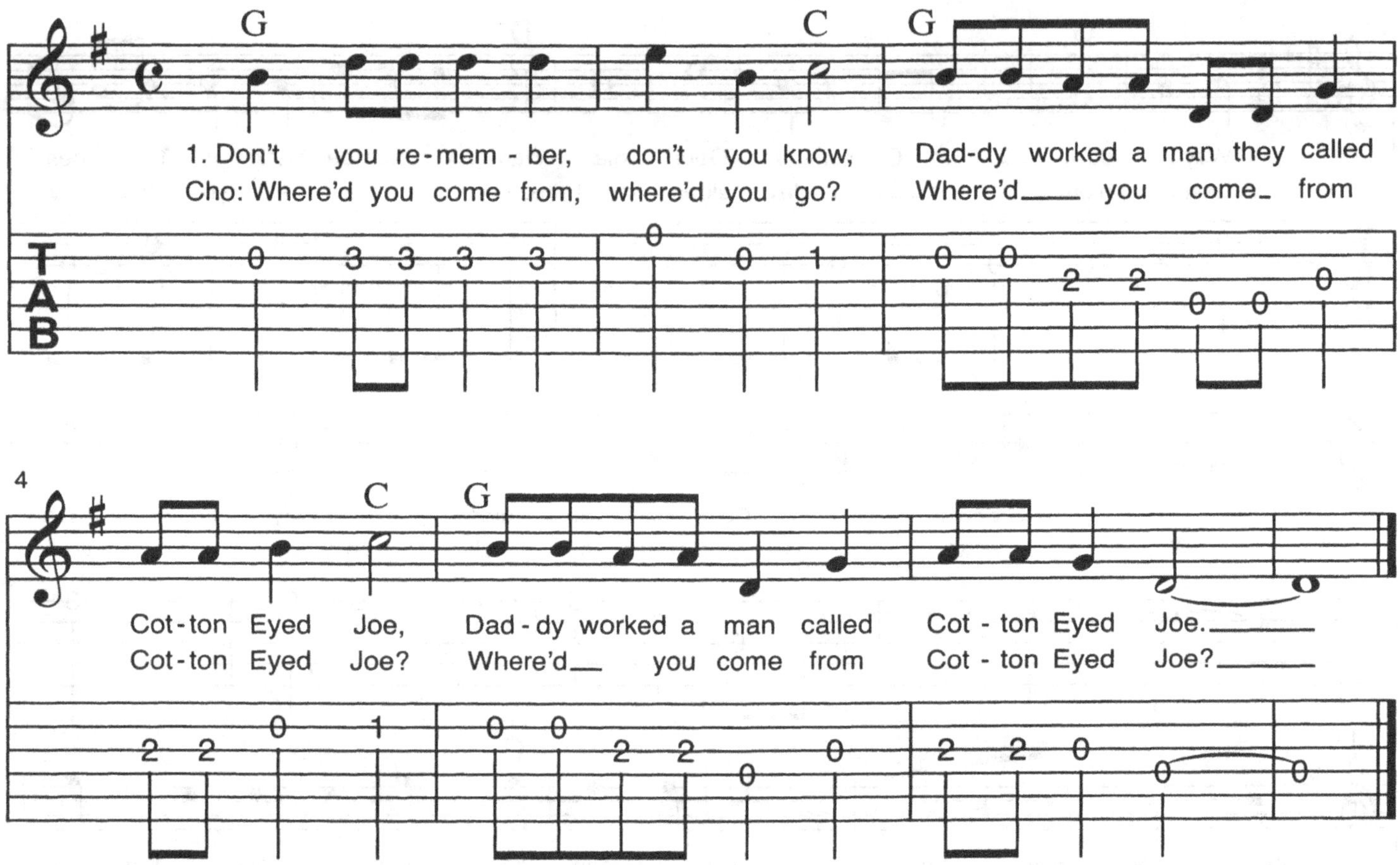

G C
2. Had not been for Cotton-Eyed Joe,
G C
I'd a'been married a long time ago,
G
I'd a'been married a long time ago.

3. Down in the cotton patch, way down low,
Everybody singing the Cotton-Eyed Joe. (2X)

4. I know a gal lives down below,
I used to go to see her but I don't no more. (2X)

5. I fell down and stubbed my toe,
Call for the doctor, Cotton Eyed Joe. (2X)

C. White, D. Watson, Fiddlin' John Carson, M. Seeger, Ken. Colonels, NLCR, E. Taylor, Skillet Lickers, K. Hall, D. Reno & R. Smiley, Kathy Kallick

Cowboy Jack

M: C; F: F or G, capo 5 or 7
CD 1-Track 31

Traditional

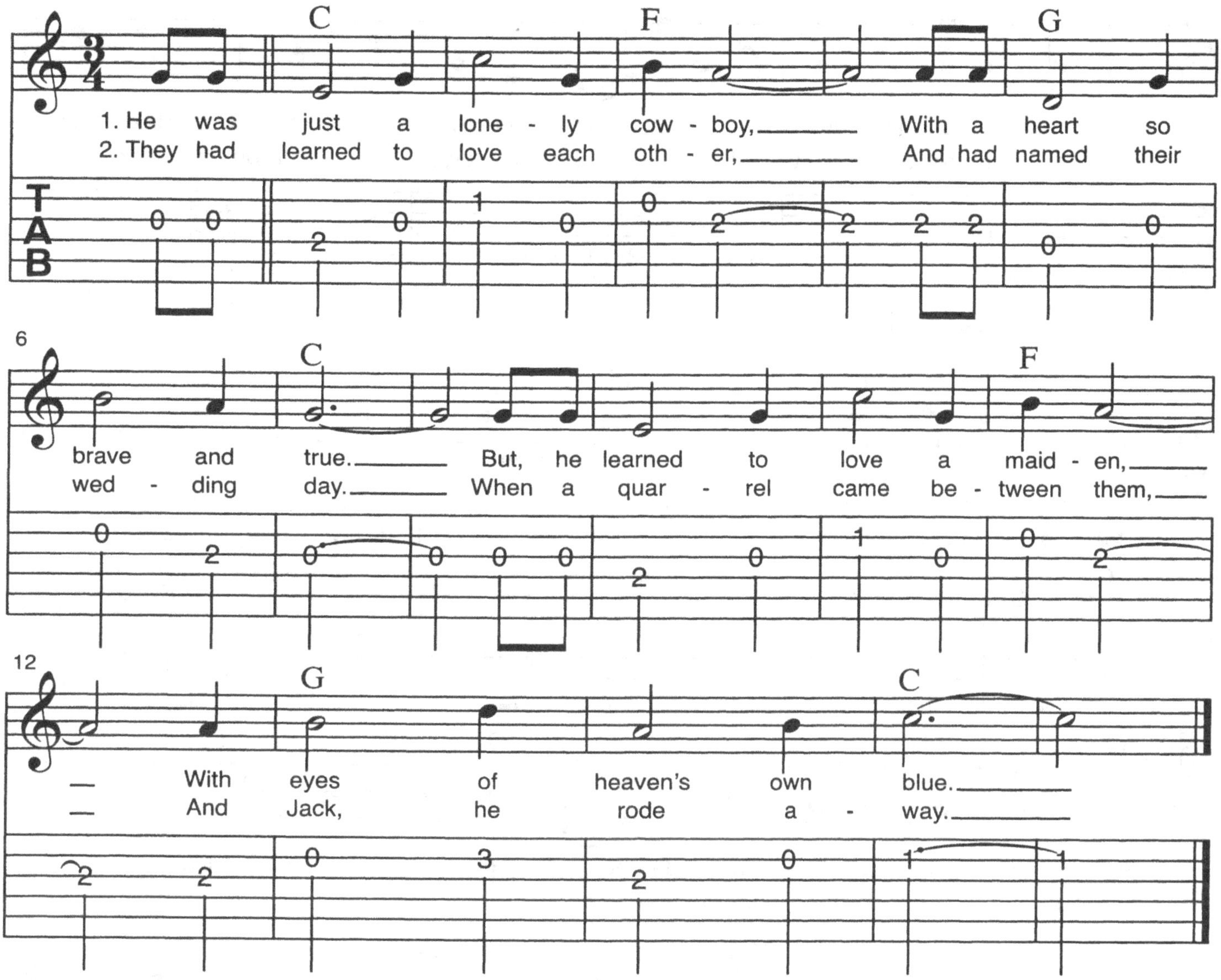


```
C                         F
3. He joined a band of cowboys,
      G                         C
And tried to forget her name.
                                    F
But, out on the lonely prairie,
      G                      C
She waits for him the same.
```

4. Your sweetheart waits for you, Jack,
Your sweetheart waits for you.
Out on the lonely prairie,
Where the skies are always blue.

5. One night as the work was finished,
Just at the close of day.
Someone said, "To sing a song, Jack,
T'will drive dull care away."

6. When he began his singing,
His mind it wandered back.
For he sang of a maiden,
Who waited for her Jack.

7. Jack left the camp next morning,
He was breathing his sweetheart's name.
He says, "I'll ask forgiveness,
For I know that I'm to blame."

8. But, when he reached the prairie,
He found a new made mound.
And his friends they sadly told him,
They had laid his loved one down.

9. They said as she was dying,
She breathed her sweetheart's name.
And asked them with her last breath,
To tell him when he came.

10. "Your sweetheart waits for you, Jack,
Your sweetheart waits for you.
Out on the lonely prairie,
Where the skies are always blue."

Carter Fam., Country Gentlemen, V. Williams

The Crawdad Song

M: G; F: C or D, capo 5 or 7
CD 1-Track 32

Traditional

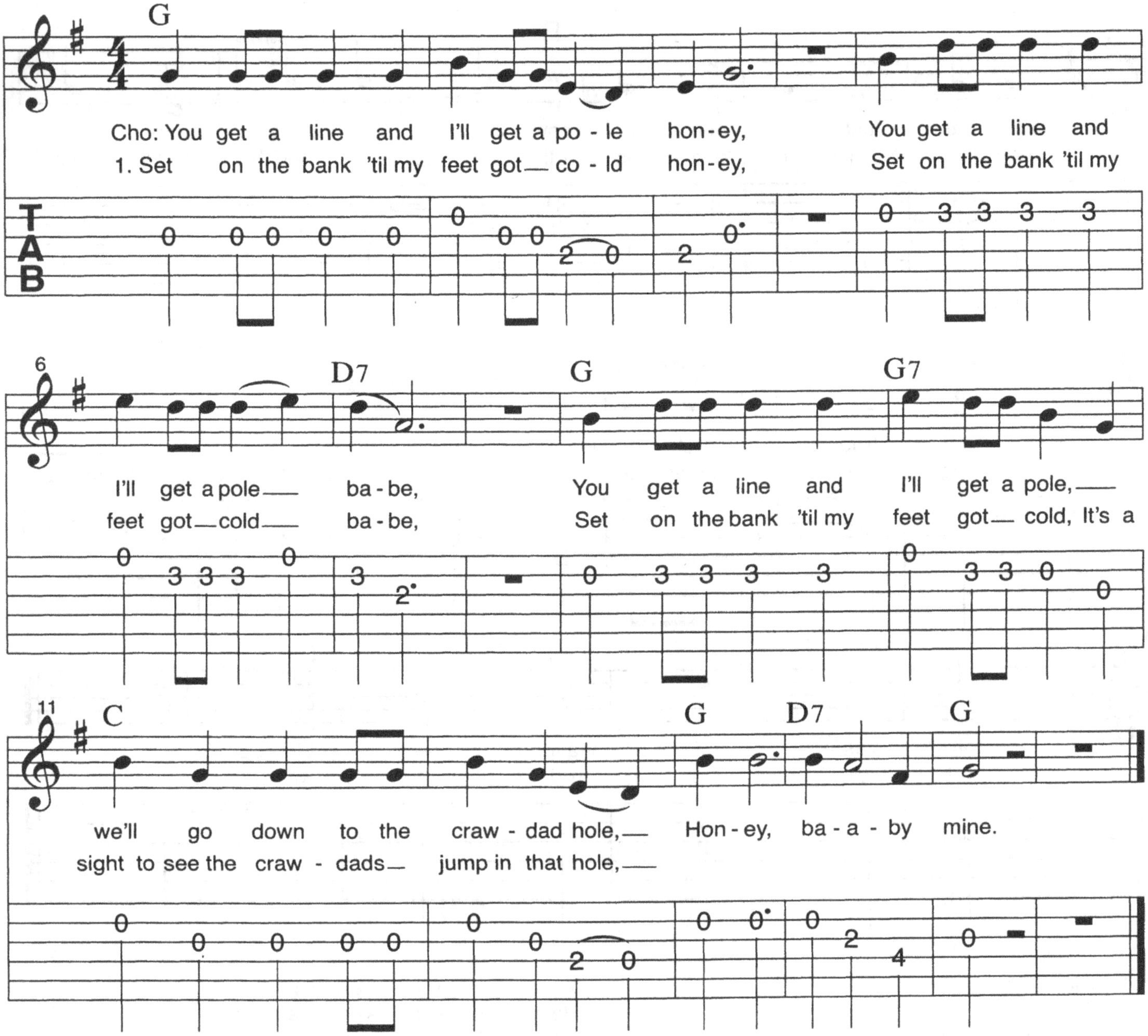

G D7
2. Yonder come a man with a sack on his back honey, Yonder come a man with a sack on his back babe,
G G7 C G D7 G
Yonder come a man with a sack on his back, He's got more crawdads than he can pack, Honey, baby mine.

3. He fell down and he broke that sack honey, He fell down and he broke that sack babe,
He fell down and he broke that sack, Was a sight to see the crawdads backing back, Honey, baby mine.

4. What did the hen duck say to the drake honey? What did the hen duck say to the drake babe?
What did the hen duck say to the drake, "There ain't no crawdads in that lake," Honey, baby mine.

Cripple Creek

M: A; F: D or E, capo 5 or 7
CD 1-Track 29

Traditional

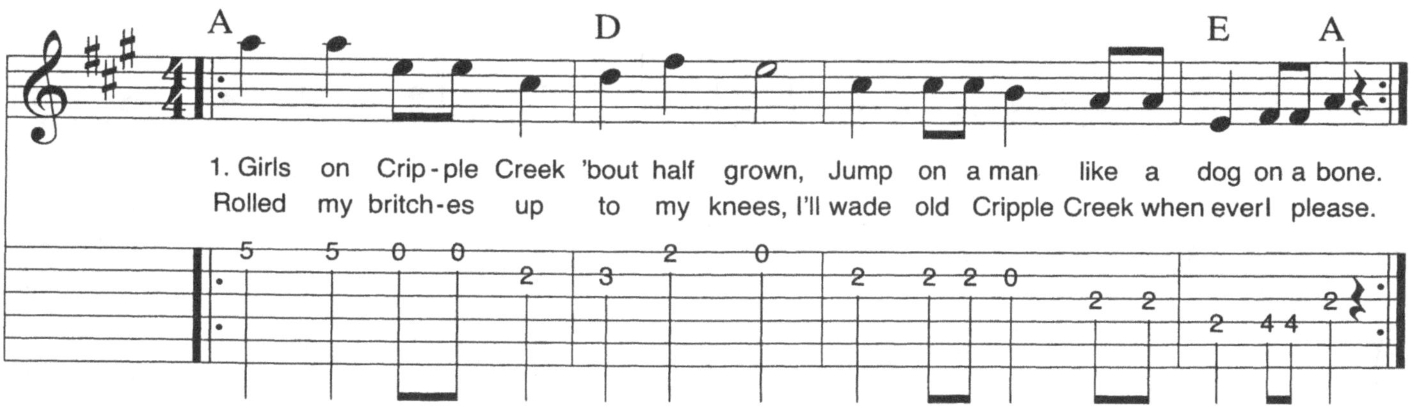

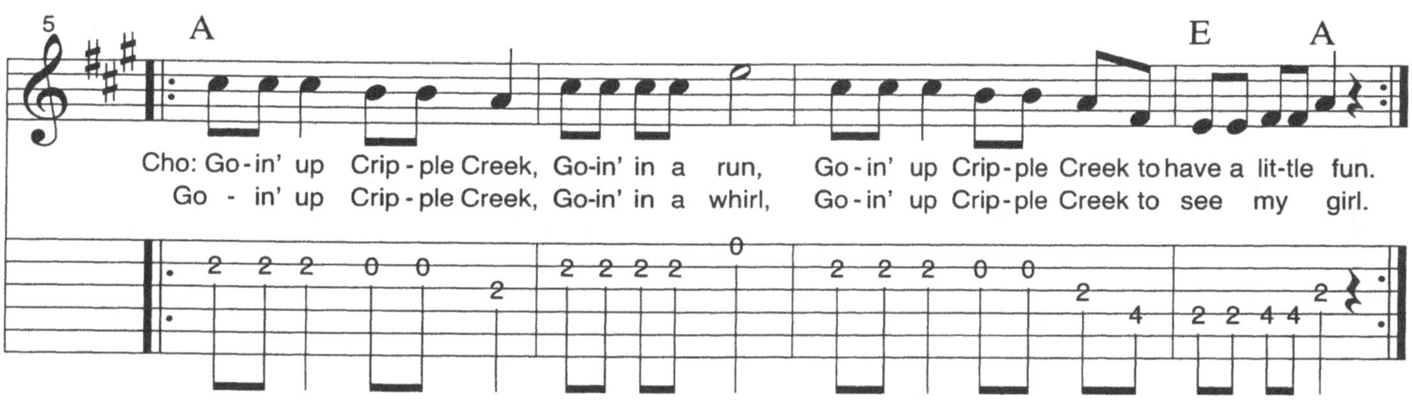

A D A
2. Cripple Creek's wide and Cripple Creek's deep,
E A
I'll wade old Cripple Creek before I sleep.
A D A
I got a girl and she loves me,
E A
She's as sweet as sweet can be.

3. I went down to Cripple Creek,
To see what them girls had to eat.
I got drunk and fell against the wall,
Old corn likker was the cause of it all.

4. I got a girl and she loves me,
She's as sweet as she can be.
She got eyes of baby blue,
Makes my gun shoot straight and true.

Monroe Bros., Flatt & Scruggs, R. Stanley, Jimmy Martin, C. White, D. Watson, Fiddlin' Doc Roberts, K. Hall, A. Munde, Country Gentlemen, John McEuen

Crying Holy

M: G; F: C or D, capo 5 or 7
CD 1-Track 34

Traditional

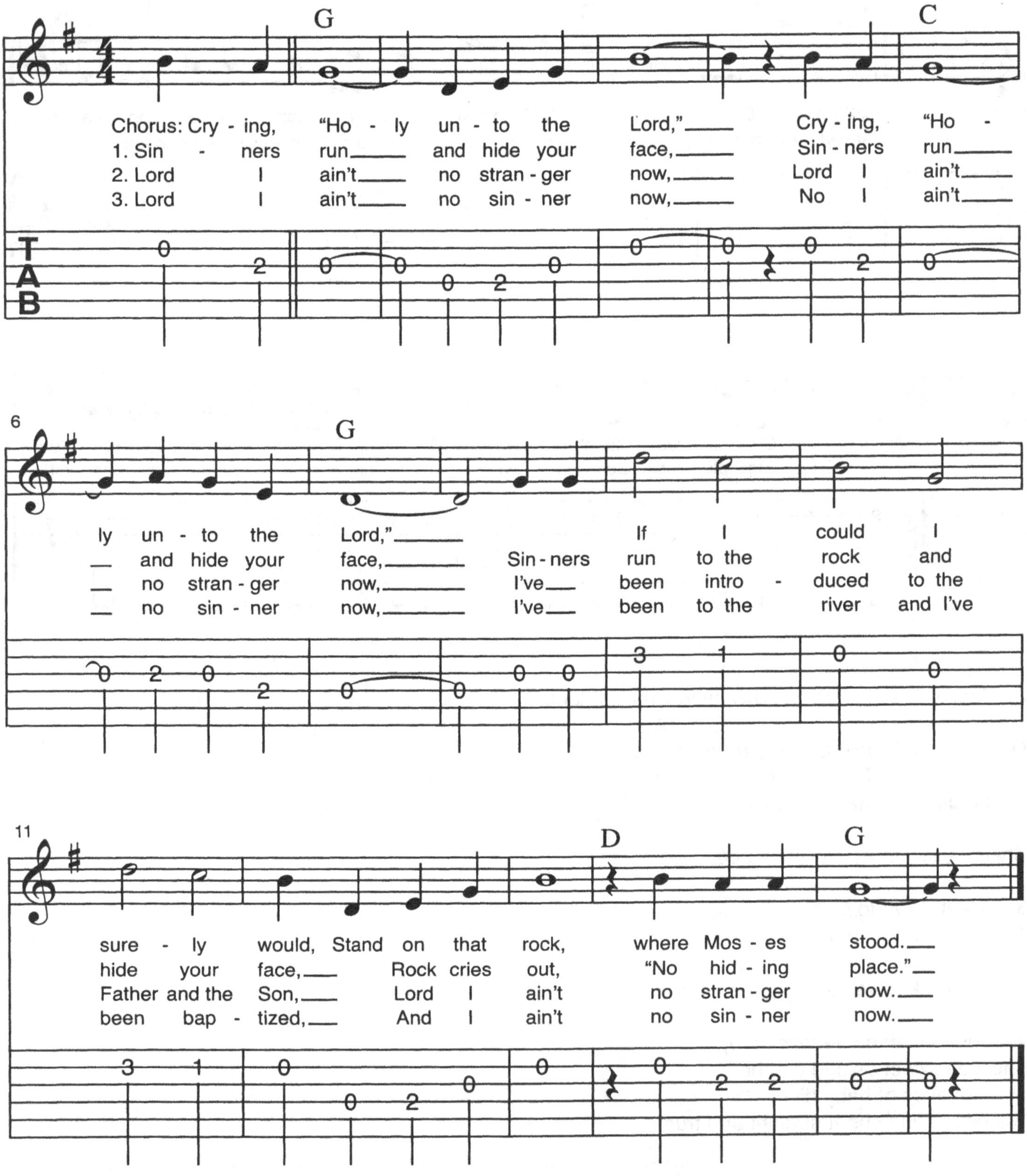

 B. Monroe, Flatt & Scruggs, Carter Fam., J.D. Crowe, Country Gentlemen, J.E. Mainer

The Cuckoo

M: Dm; F: Gm or Am, capo 5 or 7
CD 1-Track 35

Traditional

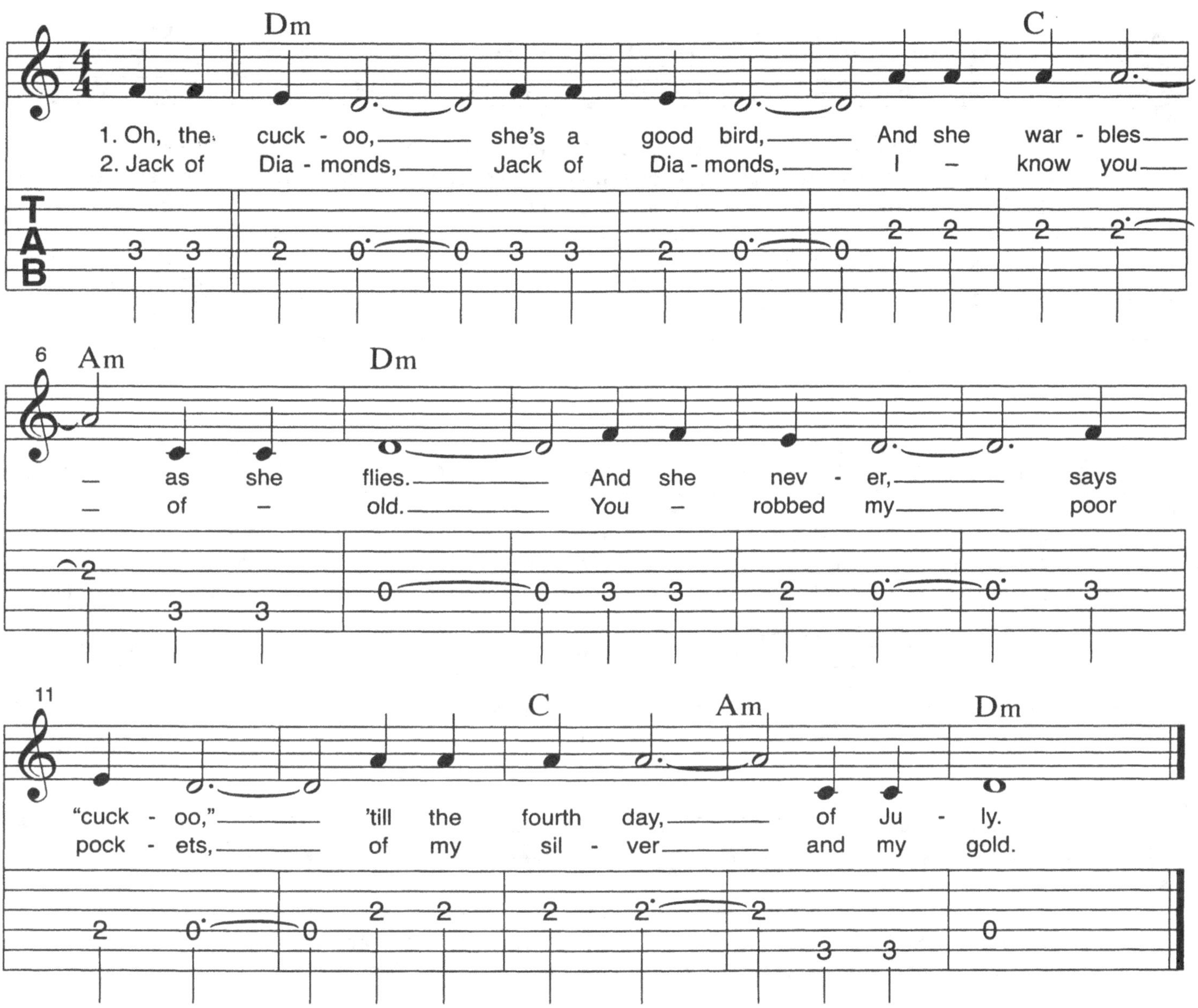


```
      Dm
3.  I've played cards in England,
     C           Am   Dm
I've played cards in Spain,
I'll bet you ten dollars,
     C      Am       Dm
I'll beat you next game.
```

4. My horses ain't hungry,
They won't eat your hay,
I'll drive on a little further,
I'll feed 'em on the way.

5. Gonna build me log cabin,
On a mountain so high,
So I can see Willie,
When he goes on by.

6. Oh the cuckoo, she's a pretty bird,
I wish that she was mine.
She never drinks water,
She always drinks wine.

Osborne Bros., C. Ashley, D. Watson, M. Seeger, D. Bruce, Dry Branch Fire Squad

Daniel Prayed

M: G; F: C or D, capo 5 or 7
CD 1-Track 36

Traditional

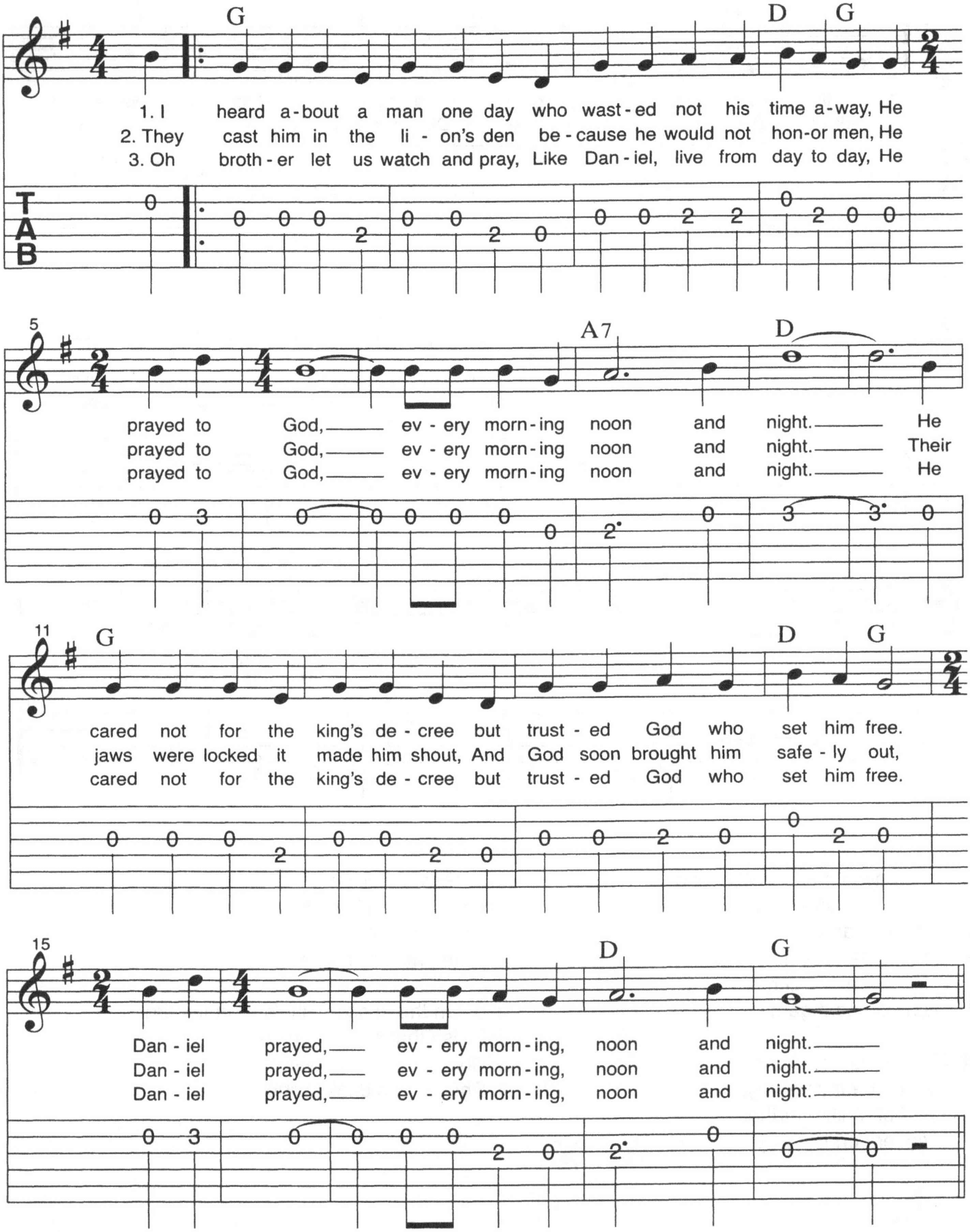

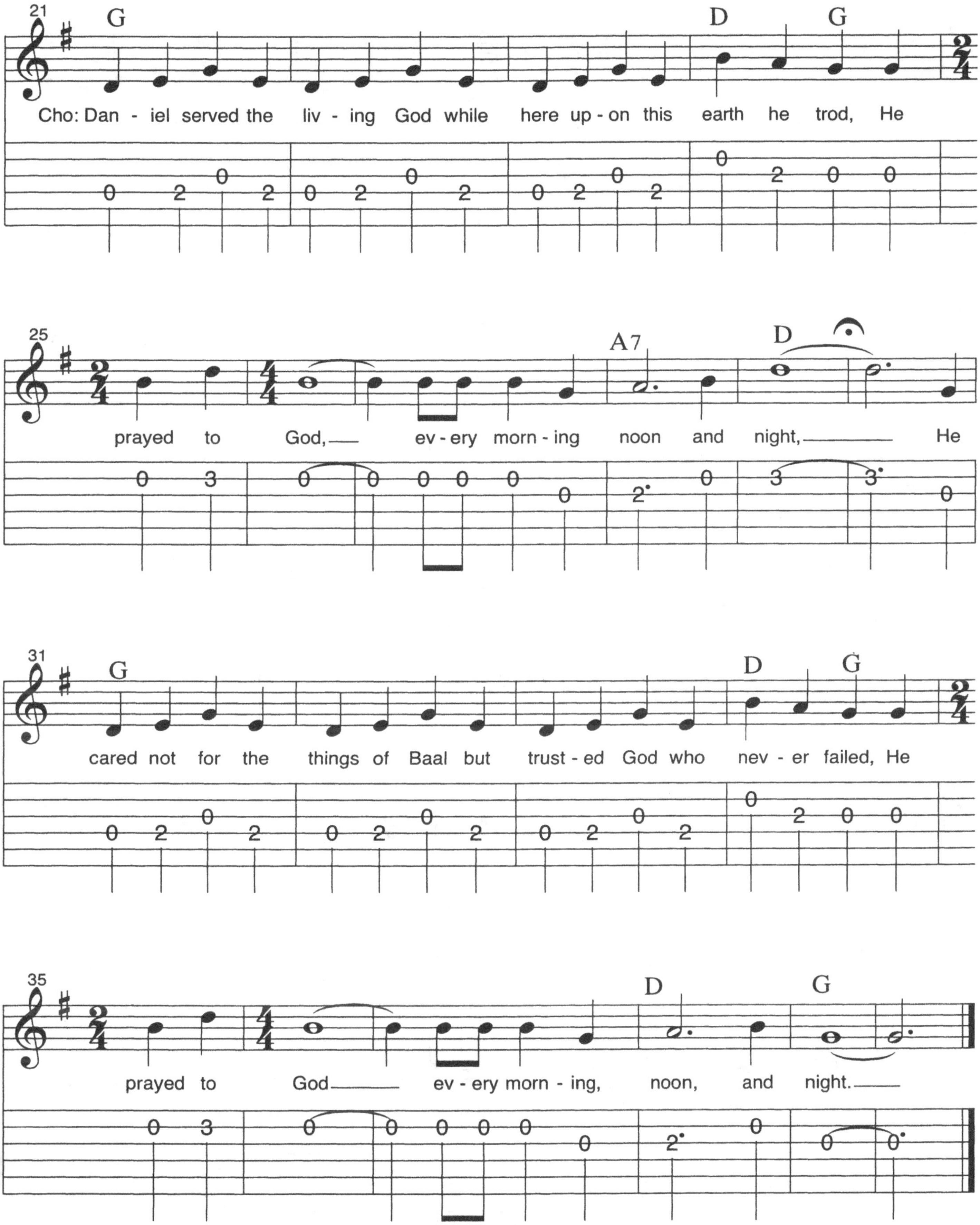
21
G D G
Cho: Dan - iel served the liv - ing God while here up - on this earth he trod, He
25
A7 D
prayed to God, ev - ery morn - ing noon and night, He
31
G D G
cared not for the things of Baal but trust - ed God who nev - er failed, He
35
D G
prayed to God ev - ery morn - ing, noon, and night.

Danny Boy

M: C; F: F or G, capo 5 or 7
CD 1-Track 37

Traditional

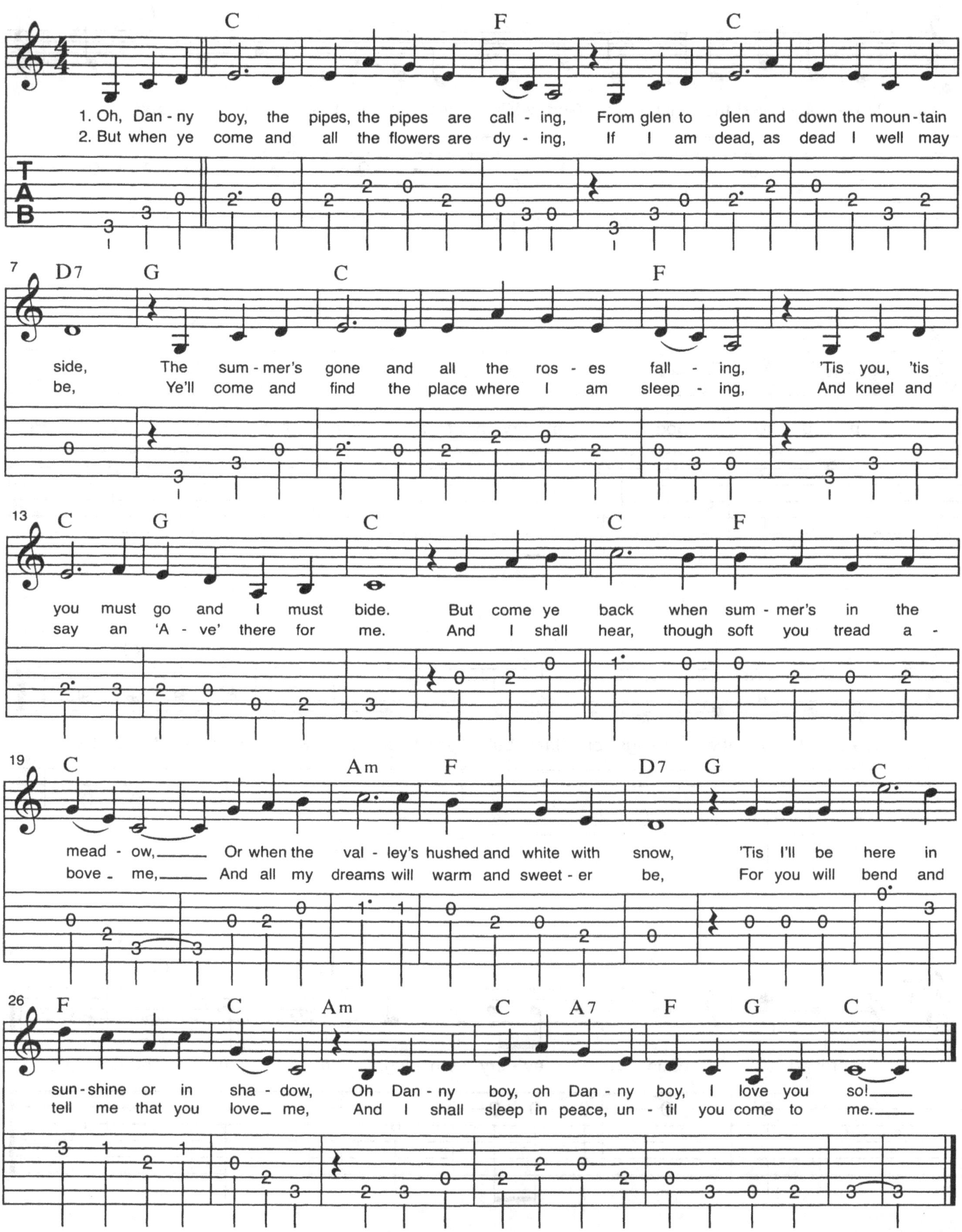

Darling Corey

M: C; F: F or G, capo 5 or 7
CD 1-Track 38, medley pt. 1

Traditional

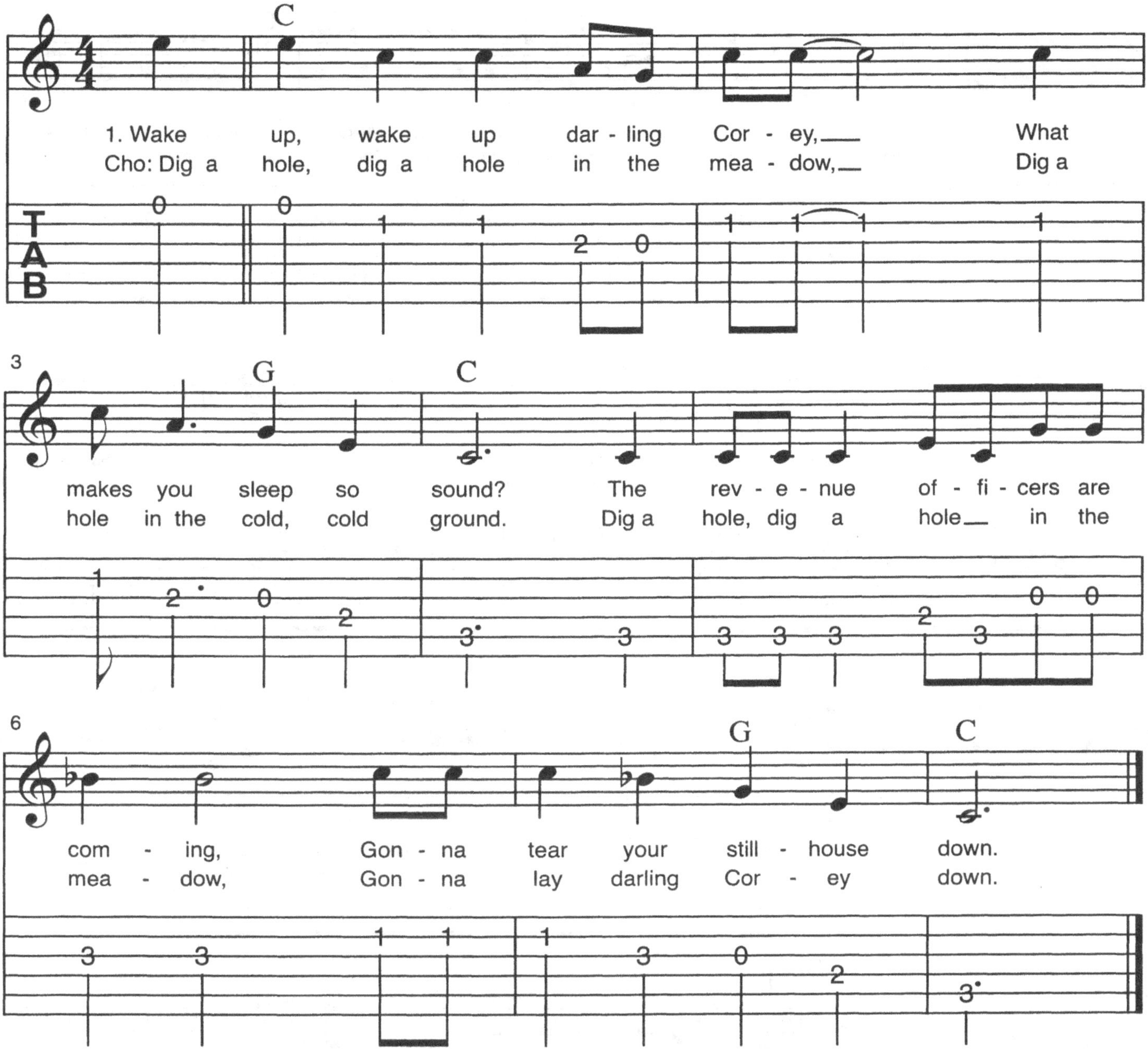

C
3. Well, the first time I saw darling Corey,
G C
She was sittin' on the banks of the sea,
Had a forty-four around her body,
G C
And a banjo on her knee.

4. Go away, go away darling Corey,
Quit hanging around my bed.
Bad liquor has ruined my body,
Pretty women gone to my head.

5. Can't you hear those bluebirds a'singing?
Don't you hear that mournful sound?
They're preaching darling Corey's funeral,
In some lonesome graveyard ground.

6. Wake up, wake up darling Corey,
Go and get my gun,
I ain't no man for trouble,
But I'll die before I'll run.

Monroe Bros., B. Monroe, Flatt & Scruggs, D. Watson, Country Gazette, NLCR, Seldom Scene, Gibson Bros.

Darling Nellie Gray

M: C; F: F or G, capo 5 or 7
CD 1-Track 38, medley pt. 2

B.R. Hanby, 1856

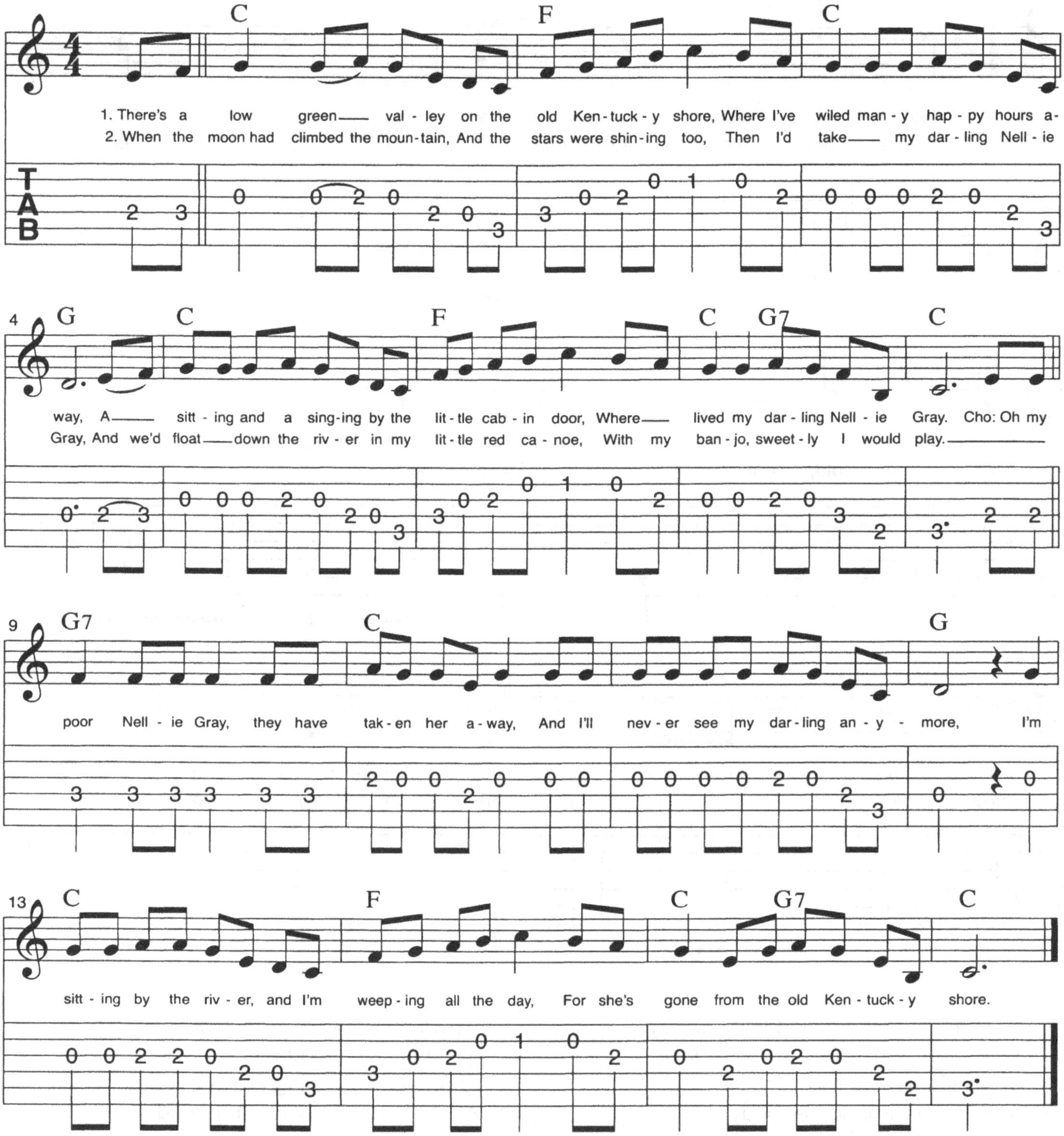

 Stanley Bros., Goose Island Ramblers, B. Clifton, M. Wiseman, D. Bruce & J. Nunally

        C   F
3. My canoe is under water and my banjo is unstrung,
            C   G
Lord, I'm tired of living anymore,
     C   F
My eyes shall look downward, my songs shall be unsung,
          C   G7   C
While I stay on the old Kentucky shore.

4. One night I went to see her, "She's gone," the neighbors say,
The white man bound her with his chain,
They have taken her to Georgia, for to wear her life away,
As she toils in the cotton and the cane.

5. My eyes are growing blinded and I can not see my way,
Hark, there's someone knocking at the door.
I hear the angels calling, and I see my Nellie Gray,
Farewell, to the old Kentucky shore.

Last chous: Oh, my darling Nellie Gray, up in heaven, there they say,
That they'll never take you from me anymore.
I'm a'coming, coming, coming, as the angels clear my way,
Farewell, to the old Kentucky shore.

Darling Will You Ever Think of Me?

M: D; F: G or A, capo 5 or 7
CD 1-Track 39

Dix Bruce

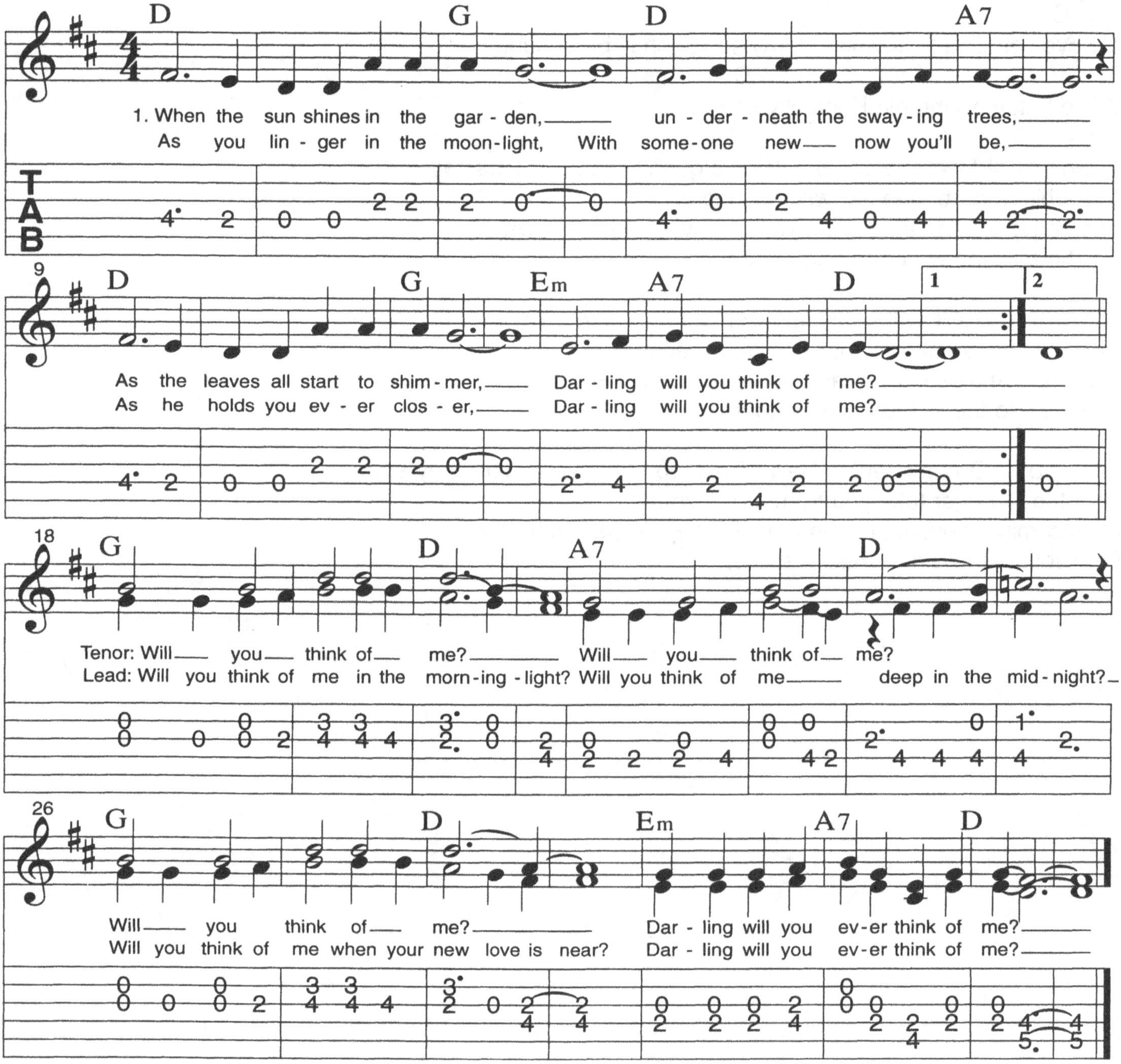


```
D                                  G
2. With the scent of summer fading,
D                              A7
From the gentle autumn breeze,
D                  G
As you pause in reflection,
Em     A7                D
Darling will you think of me?
I will love you in September,
As in summer I will be,
Ever loving through December,
Darling will you think of me? (Chorus)
```

3. Worlds away my heart is beating,
Always lost in revery,
Pleading though the night won't answer,
Darling will you think of me?
Can I ever find escape love,
From your tender memory?
Need I ask and be heartbroken,
Darling will you think of me?

Deep Elem Blues

M: C; F: F or G, capo 5 or 7
CD 1-Track 40

Traditional

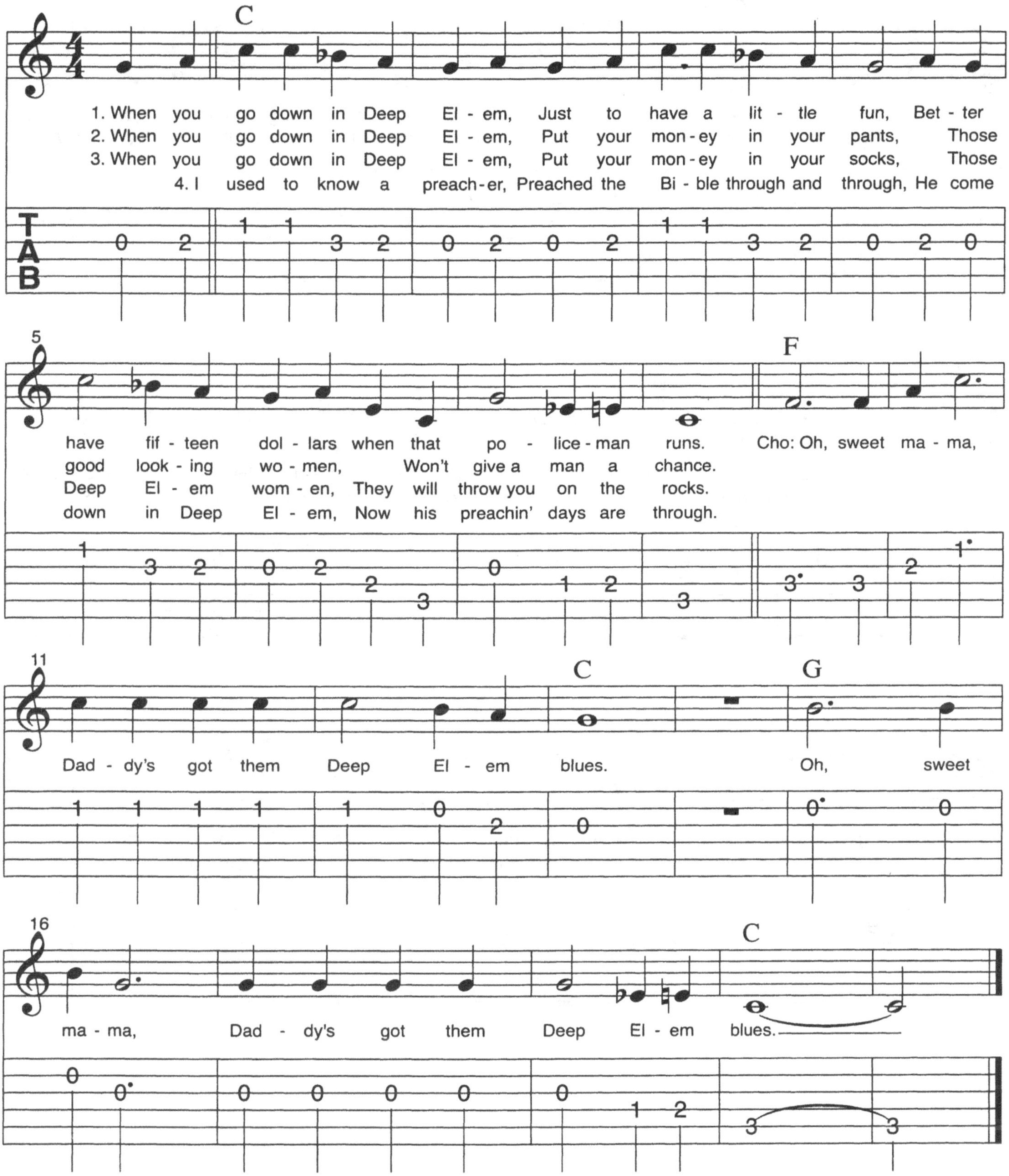

Diamonds in the Rough

M: G; F: C or D, capo 5 or 7
CD 1-Track 41

C.W. Bryson

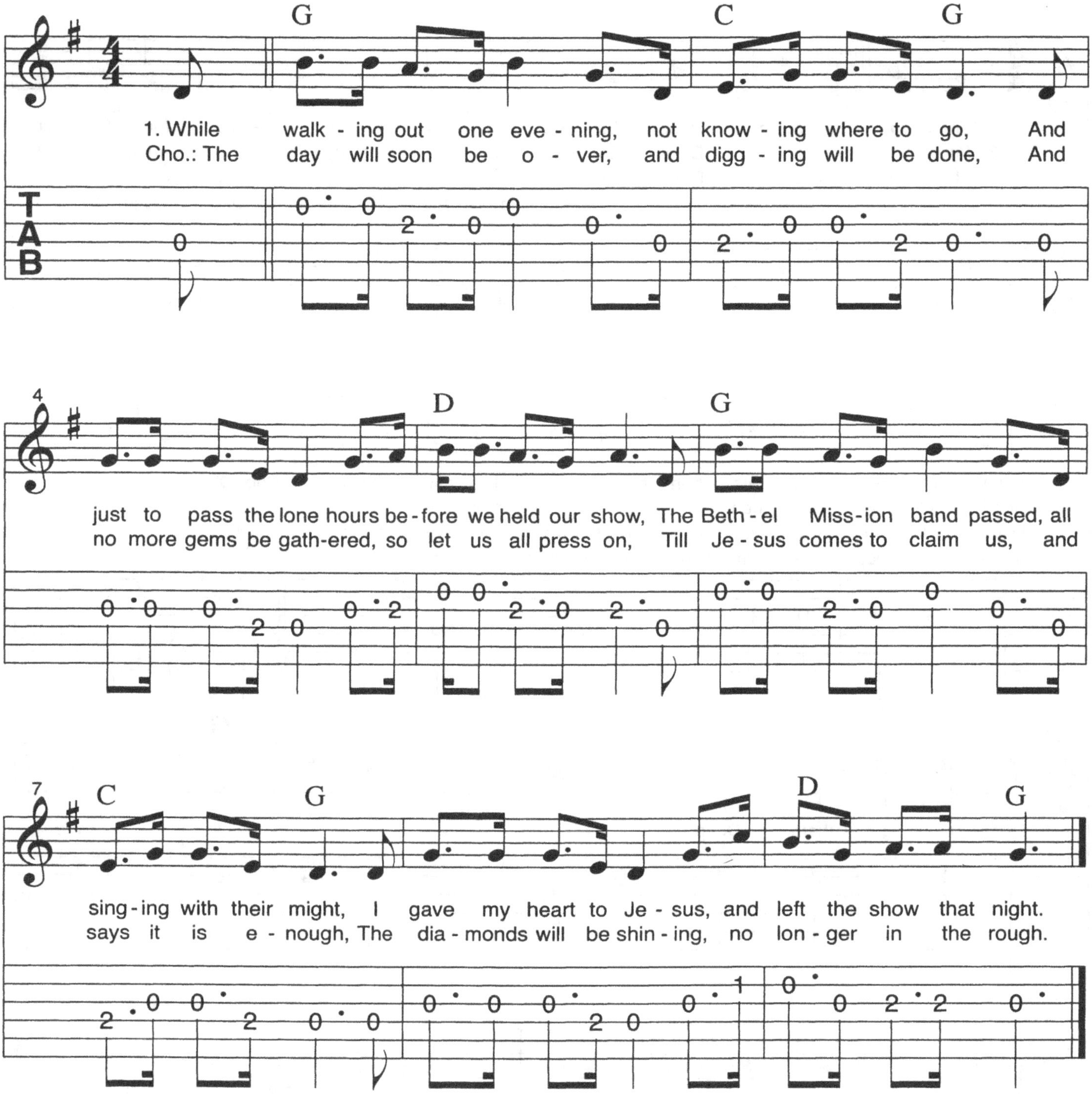

```
          G                                             C                          G
2. I used to dance the polka, the schottische and the waltz,
                                               D
I also loved the theater, its glitter vain and false,
          G                                              C                    G
And Jesus, when He found me, He found me very tough,
                                                                          D          G
But praise the Lord, He saved me, a diamond in the rough.
```

3. One day, my precious comrades, you, too, were lost in sin,
When some one sought your rescue, and Jesus took you in,
When you are tried and tempted, by sinners' stern rebuff,
Don't turn away in anger, they're diamonds in the rough.

4.While reading through the Bible, some wondrous sights I see,
I read of Peter, James, and John, by the sea of Gallilee,
And when the Savior called them, their work was rude enough,
Yet they were precious diamonds, He gathered in the rough.

5. Now keep your lamps all burning, the lamps of holy love,
And unto every sinner point out the way above,
The dying love of Jesus, will help you love the tough,
He'll polish into beauty, the diamond from the rough.

Do Lord

M: A; F: D or E, capo 5 or 7
CD 1-Track 42

Traditional

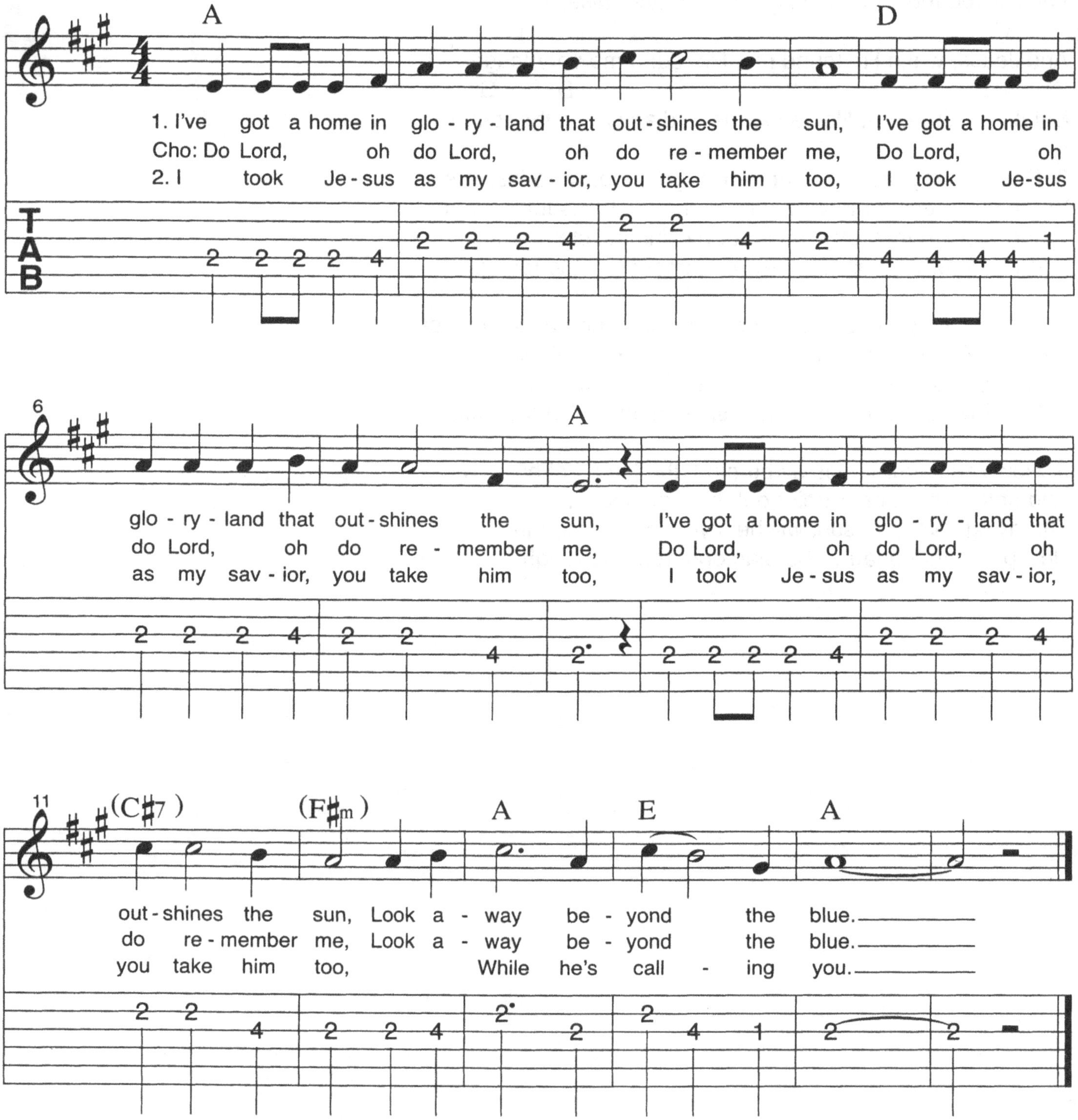

Don't Let Your Deal Go Down

M: G; F: C or D, capo 5 or 7
CD 1-Track 43

Traditional

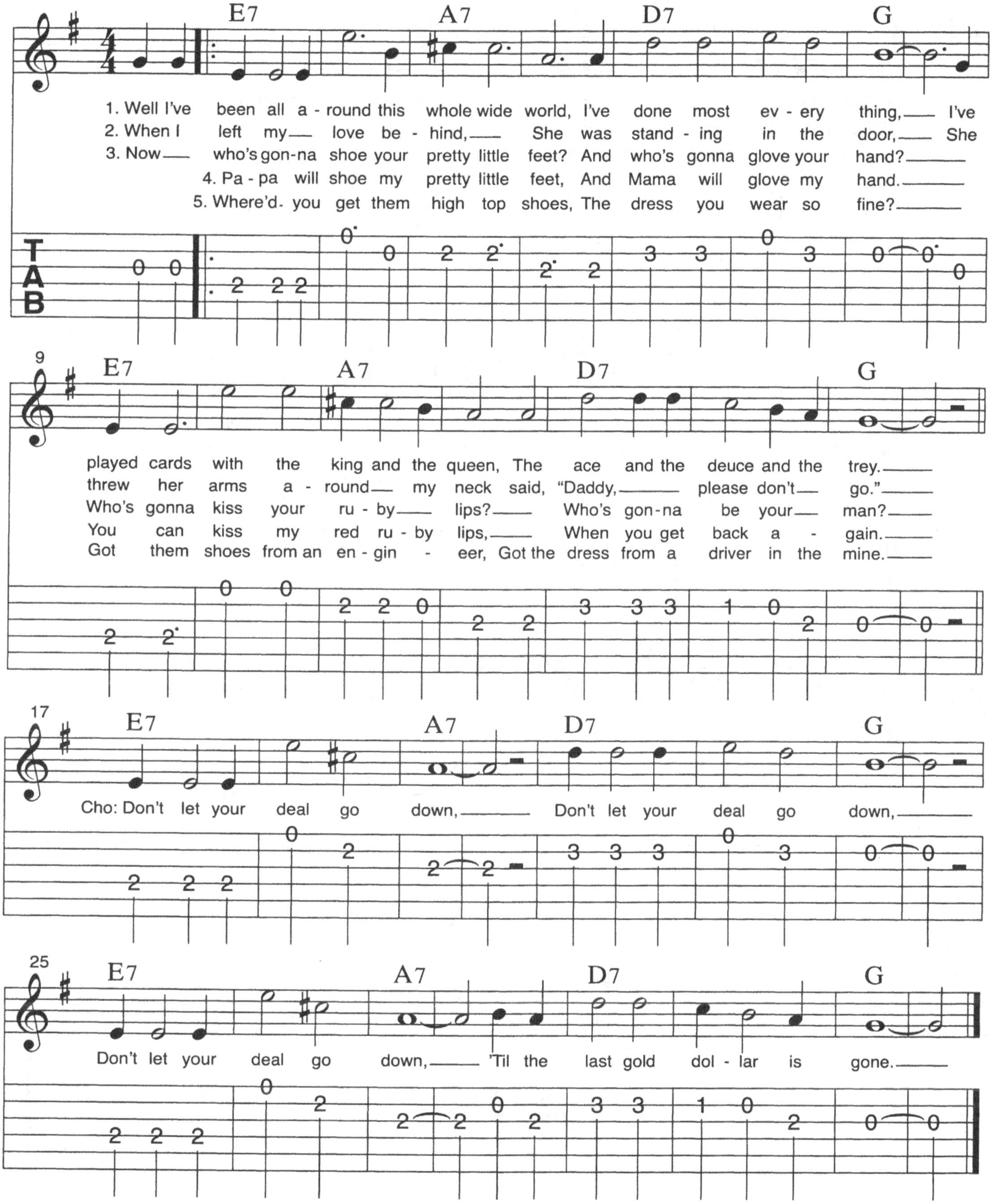

Don't This Road Look Rough and Rocky?

M: D; F: G or A, capo 5 or 7
CD 1-Track 44

Traditional

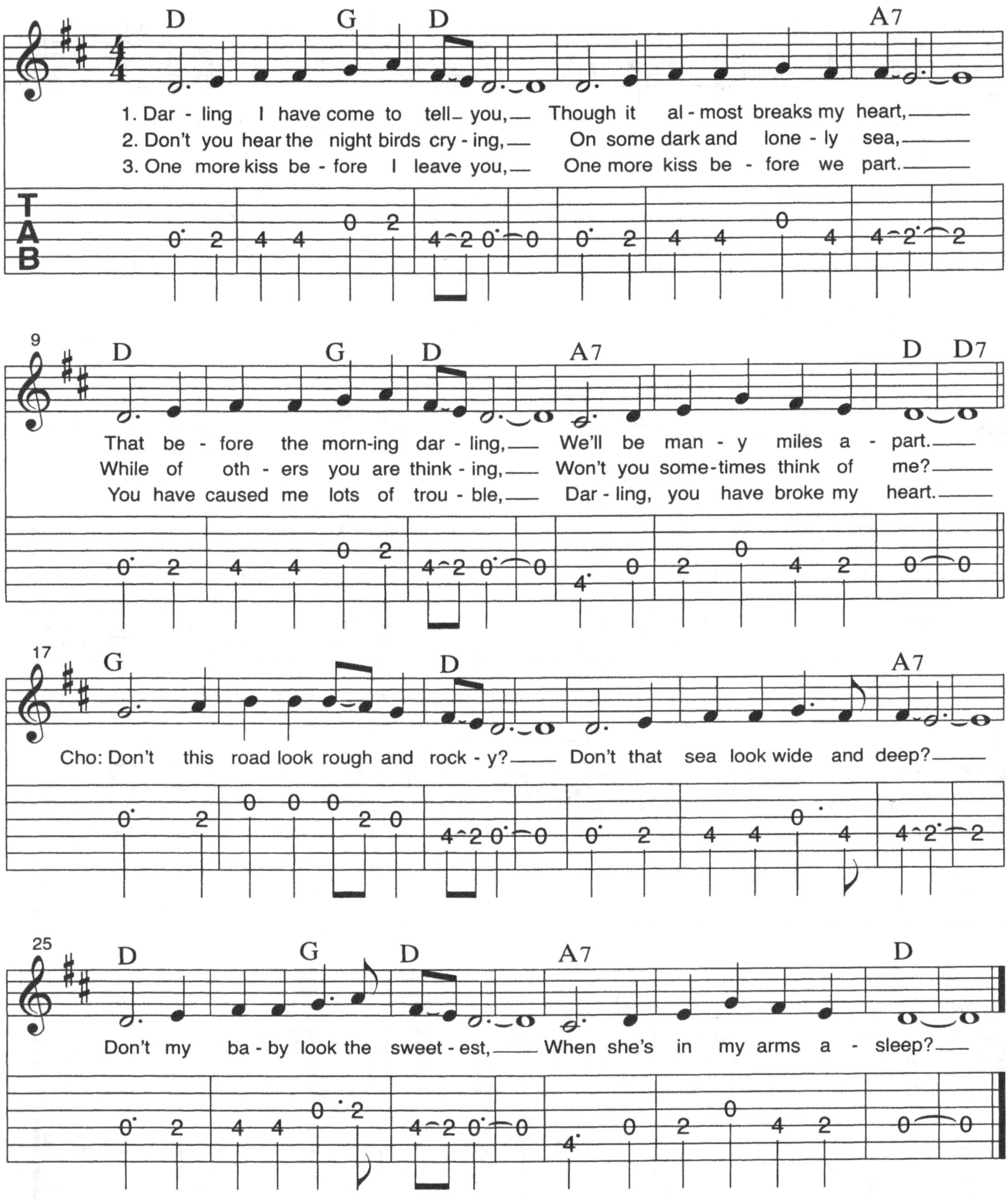

 Flatt & Scruggs, Blue Sky Boys, Bluegrass Album Band, Johnson Mtn. Boys

Don't You Hear Jerusalem Moan?

M: G; F: C or D, capo 5 or 7
CD 1-Track 45

Traditional

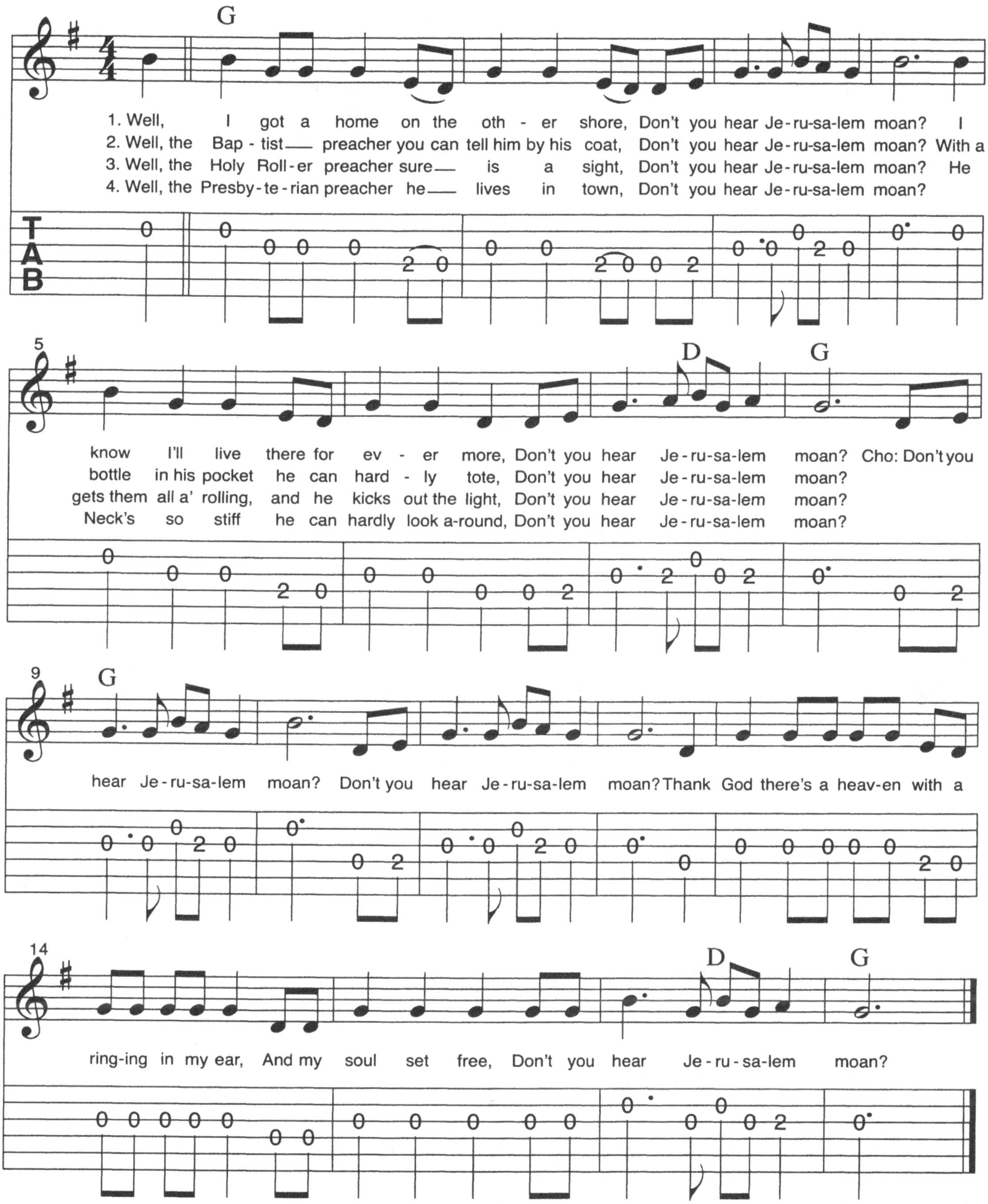

Down Among the Budded Roses

M: C; F: F or G, capo 5 or 7
CD 1-Track 46

Traditional

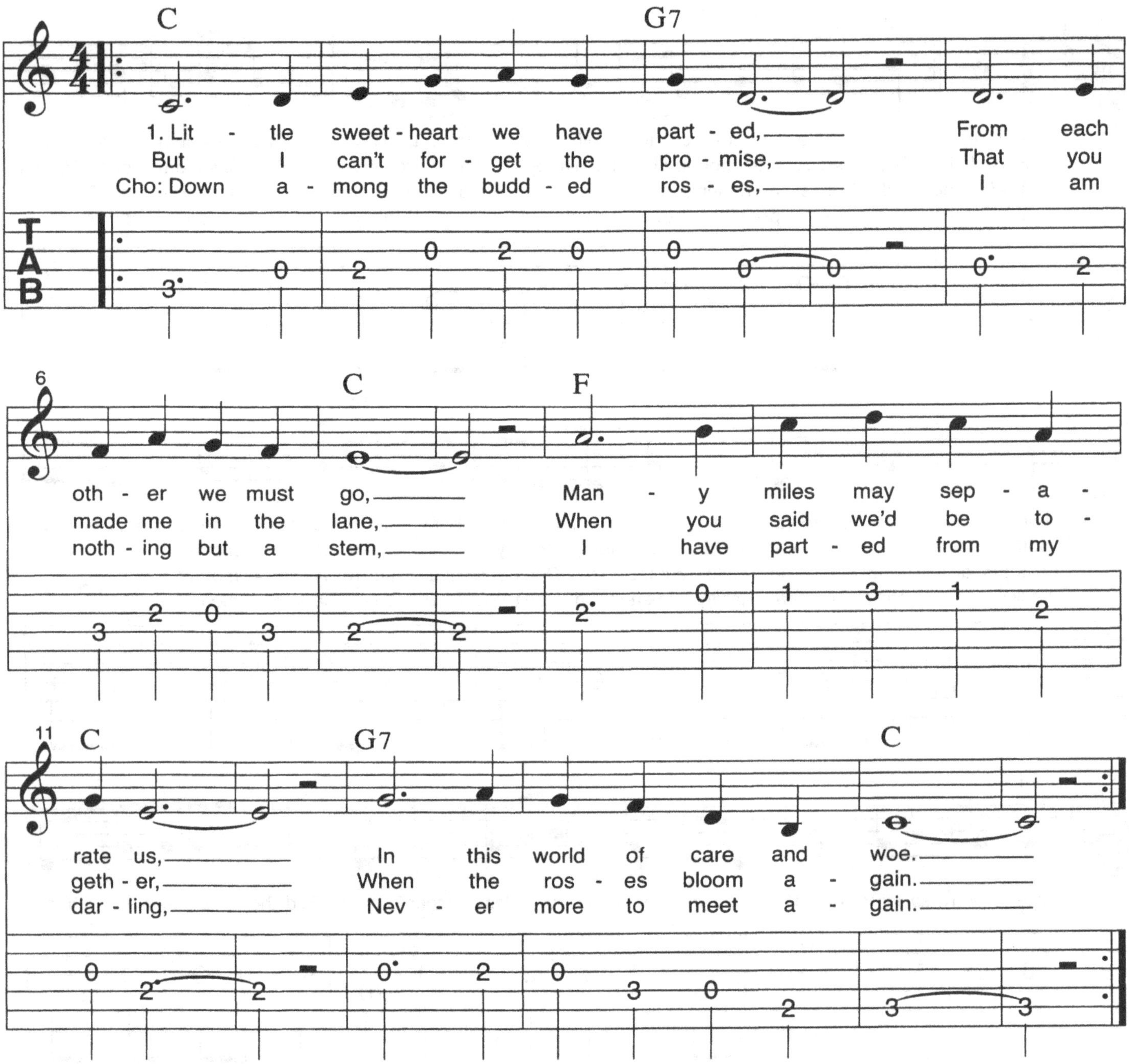


```
C                          G7                           C
2. Now this parting gives me sorrow, And it almost breaks my heart,
F                       C        G7                    C
Tell me darling will you love me, When we meet, no more to part.
Or will this parting be forever, Will there be no coming day,
When our hearts will be united, And all sorrows pass away?
```

3. Darling, meet me up in heaven, That's my true and earnest prayer,
If you love me here on earth dear, Then I'm sure you'll love me there.
There our hearts will be united, Free from every pain and care,
In the land of life eternal, In that city bright and fair.

 Goose Island Ramblers, V. Williams, Keith Little, Bob Paisley

Down in the Valley to Pray

M: G; F: C or D, capo 5 or 7
CD 1-Track 47

Traditional

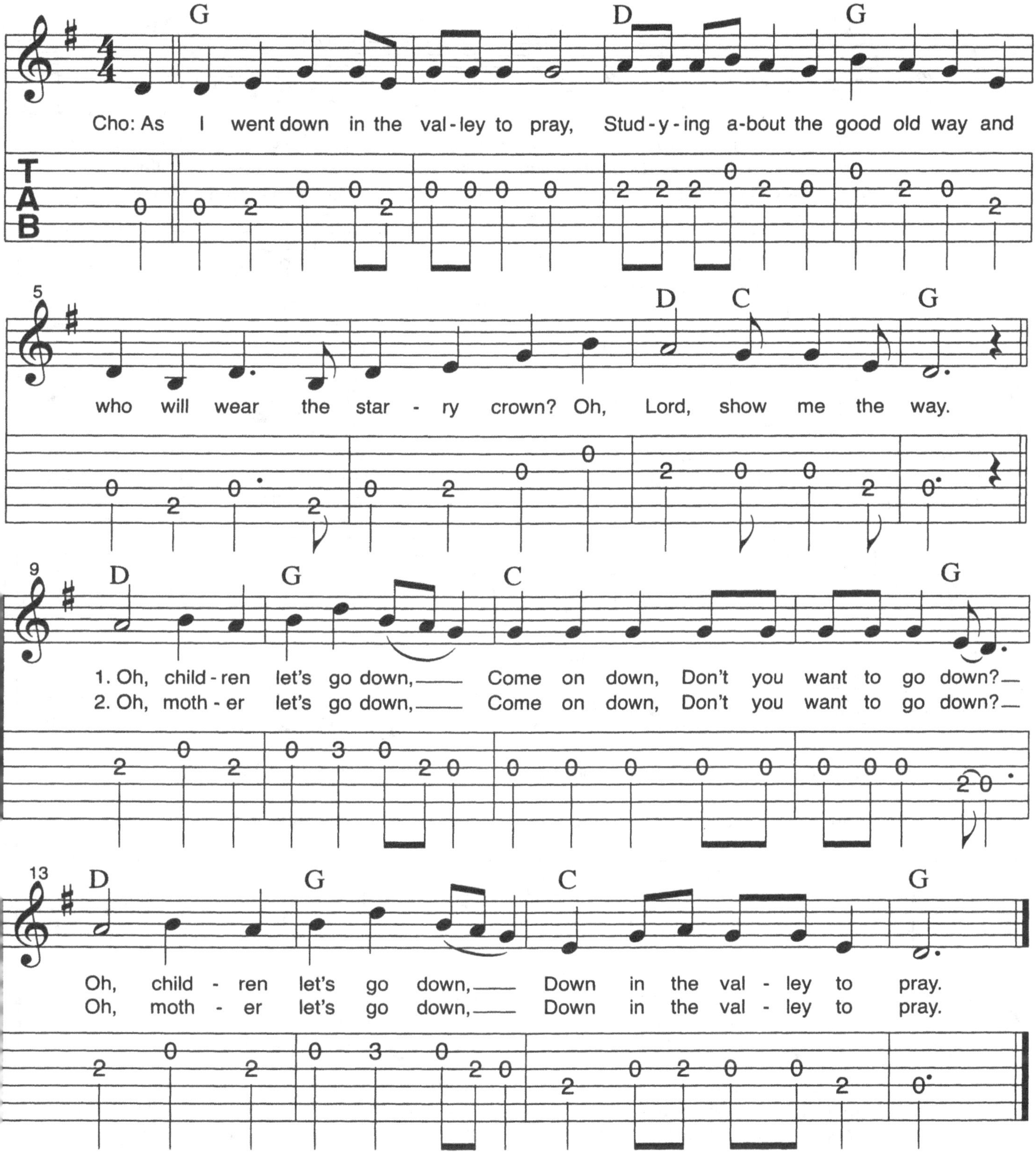

Additional verses:
Oh, brother, father, etc.

Down in the Willow Garden

M: Capo 4 to play in E; F: transpose to A or B (see page 5)
CD 1-Track 48

Traditional

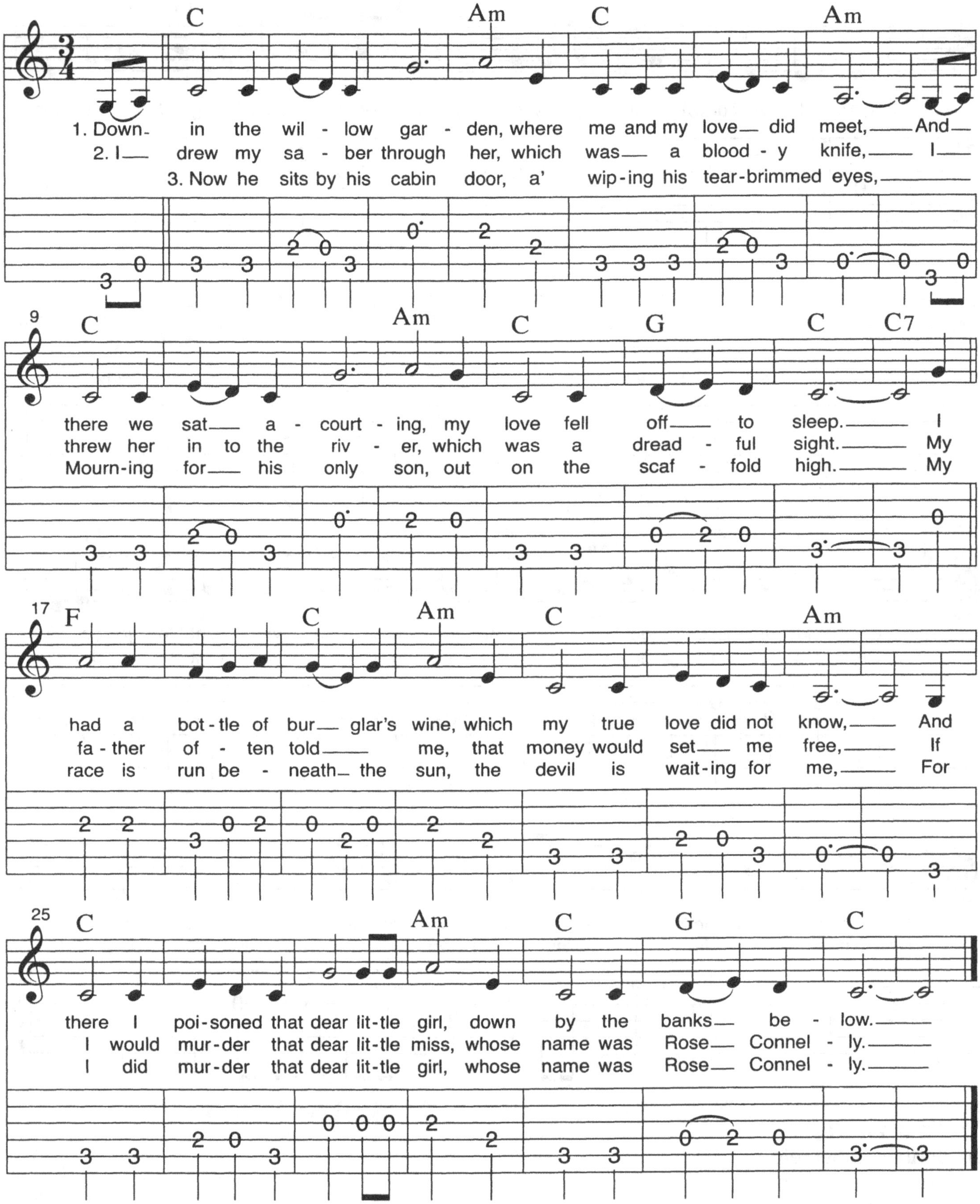

 C. Monroe, R. Allen & F. Wakefield, D. Grisman, NLCR, K. Hall, Everly Brothers, Osborne Bros., Lonesome River Band

Down the Road

M: G; F: C or D, capo 5 or 7
CD 1-Track 49

Traditional

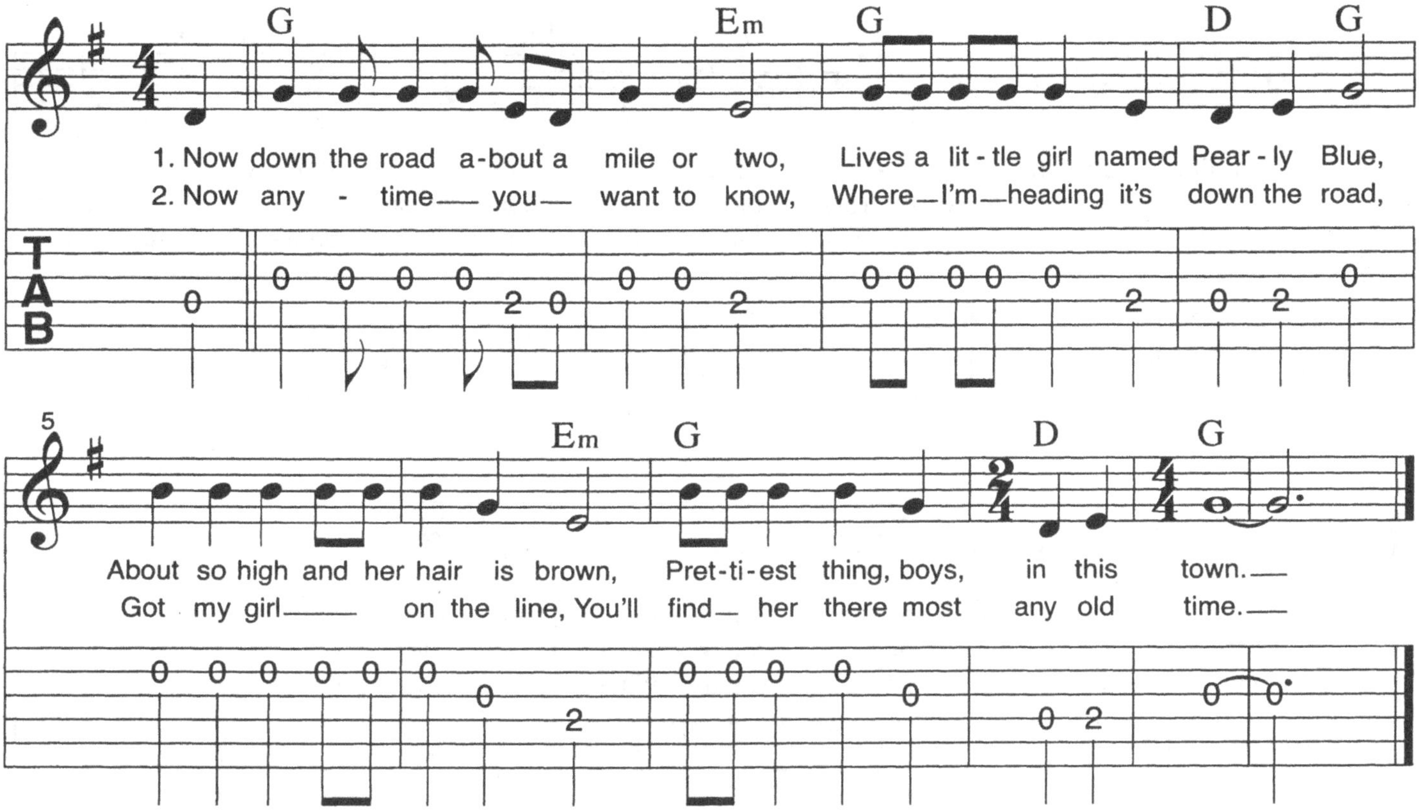

3. Now every time I get the blues,
I walk the soles right off my shoes,
I don't know why I love her so,
That gal of mine lives down the road.

4. Now everyday and Sunday too.
I go to see my Pearly Blue,
Before you hear that rooster crow,
You'll see me headed down the road.

5. Now old man ___* he owned a farm,
From the hog lot to the barn,
From the barn to the rail,
He made his living by carrying the mail.

** your name here*

Drifting Too Far From the Shore

M: G; F: C or D, capo 5 or 7
CD 1-Track 50

Chas. Moody

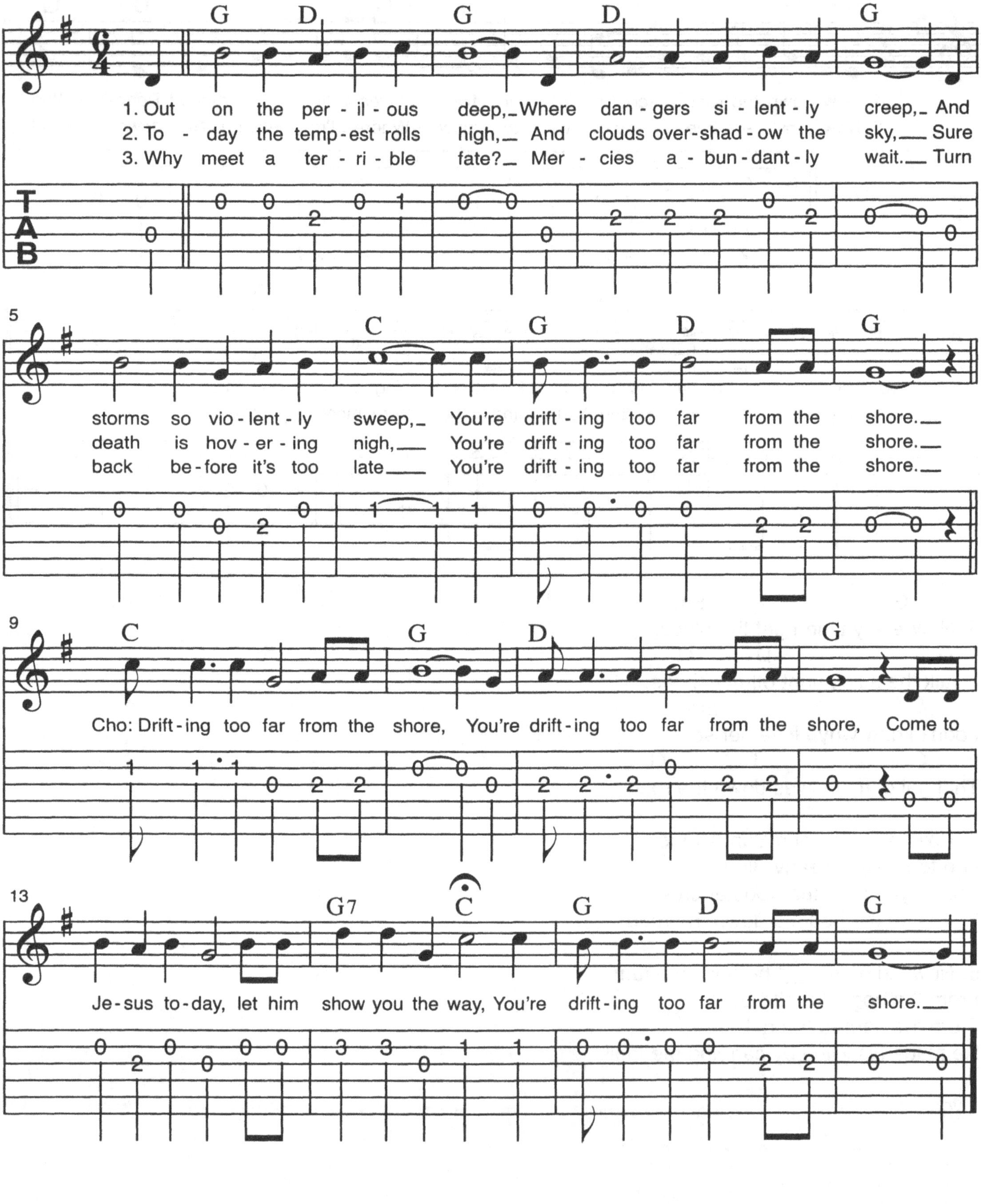

Monroe Bros., B. Monroe, Blue Sky Boys, Country Gentlemen, Boone Creek, Grisman-Garcia-Rice, Stanley Bros., Seldom Scene, Old & in the Way, IIIrd Tyme Out

East Virginia Blues

M: E; F: A or B, capo 5 or 7
CD 1-Track 51

Traditional

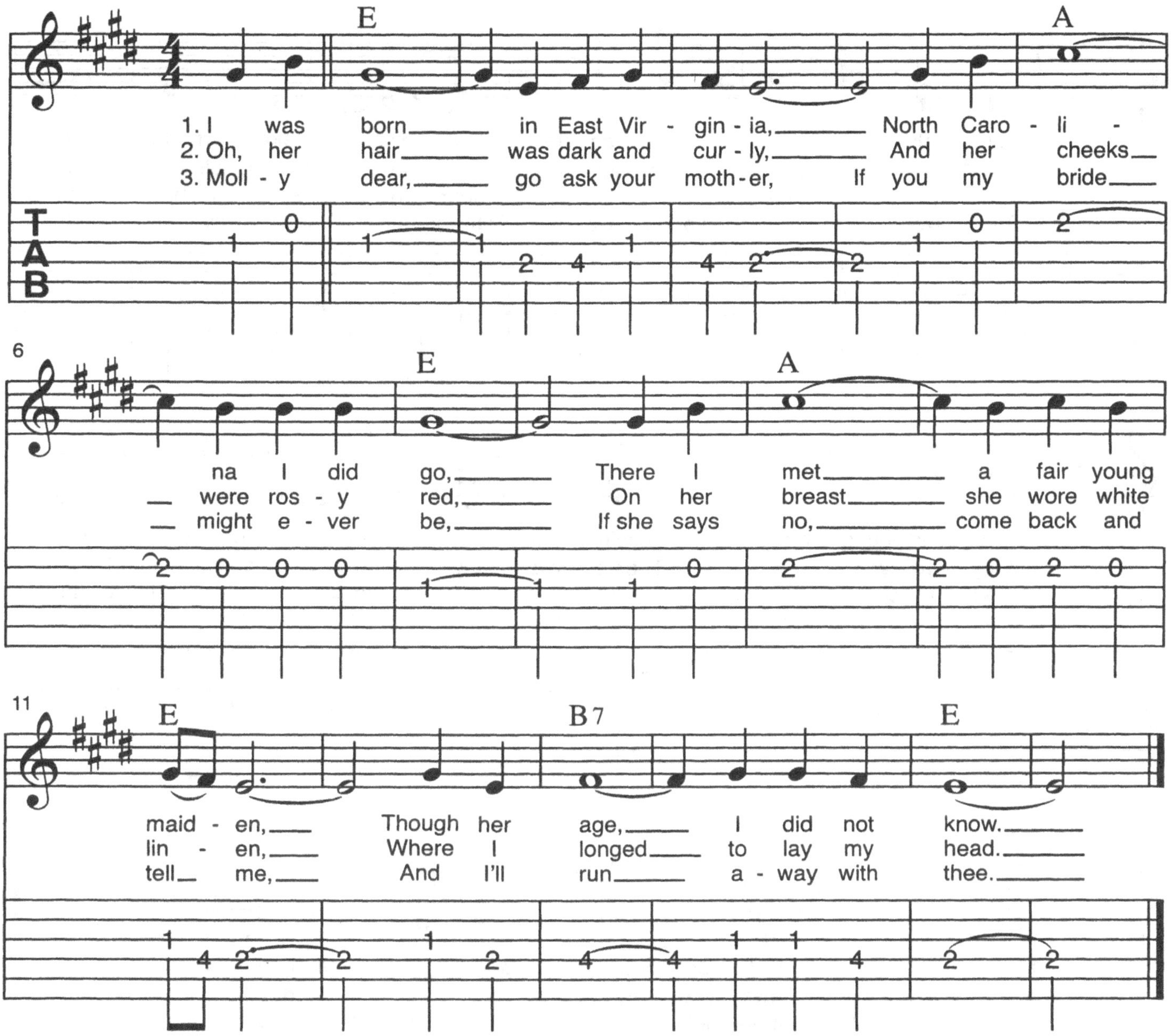

E
4. No I'll not go ask my mother,
A E
Where she lies on her bed of rest,
A E
For at her side she holds a dagger,
B7 E
To kill the one that I love best.

5. I don't want your green back dollar,
I don't want your watch and chain,
All I want is your heart darling,
Say you'll take me back again.

6. The ocean's deep and I can't wade it,
And I have no wings to fly,
I'll just get some blue-eyed boatman,
For to row me over the tide.

7. I'll go back to East Virginia,
North Carolina ain't my home,
I'll go back to East Virginia,
Leave old North Carolina alone.

8. Oh, you know I'd like to see you,
At my door you're welcome in,
At my gate I'll always greet you,
For you're the girl I tried to win.

Carter Fam., Flatt and Scruggs, Stanley Bros., R. Stanley, J.D. Crowe, Country Gentlemen, Kathy Kallick, NLCR

Fair and Tender Ladies

M: D; F: G or A, capo 5 or 7
CD 1-Track 52

Traditional

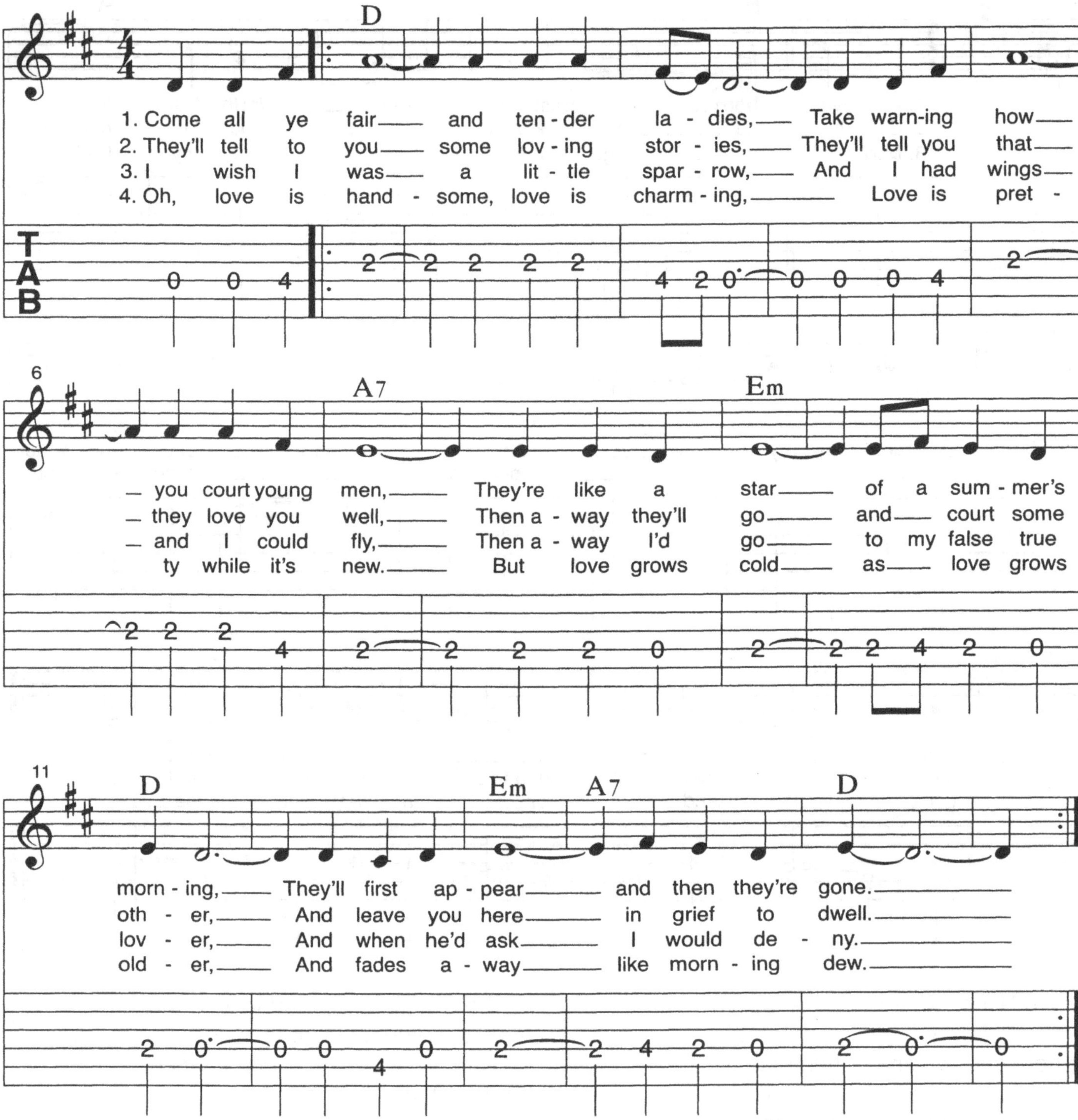

 Country Gentlemen, Ken. Colonels, J.Val, Osborne Bros., P. Rowan

Fathers Have a Home Sweet Home

Traditional

***M**: G; **F**: C or D, capo 5 or 7*
CD 1-Track 53

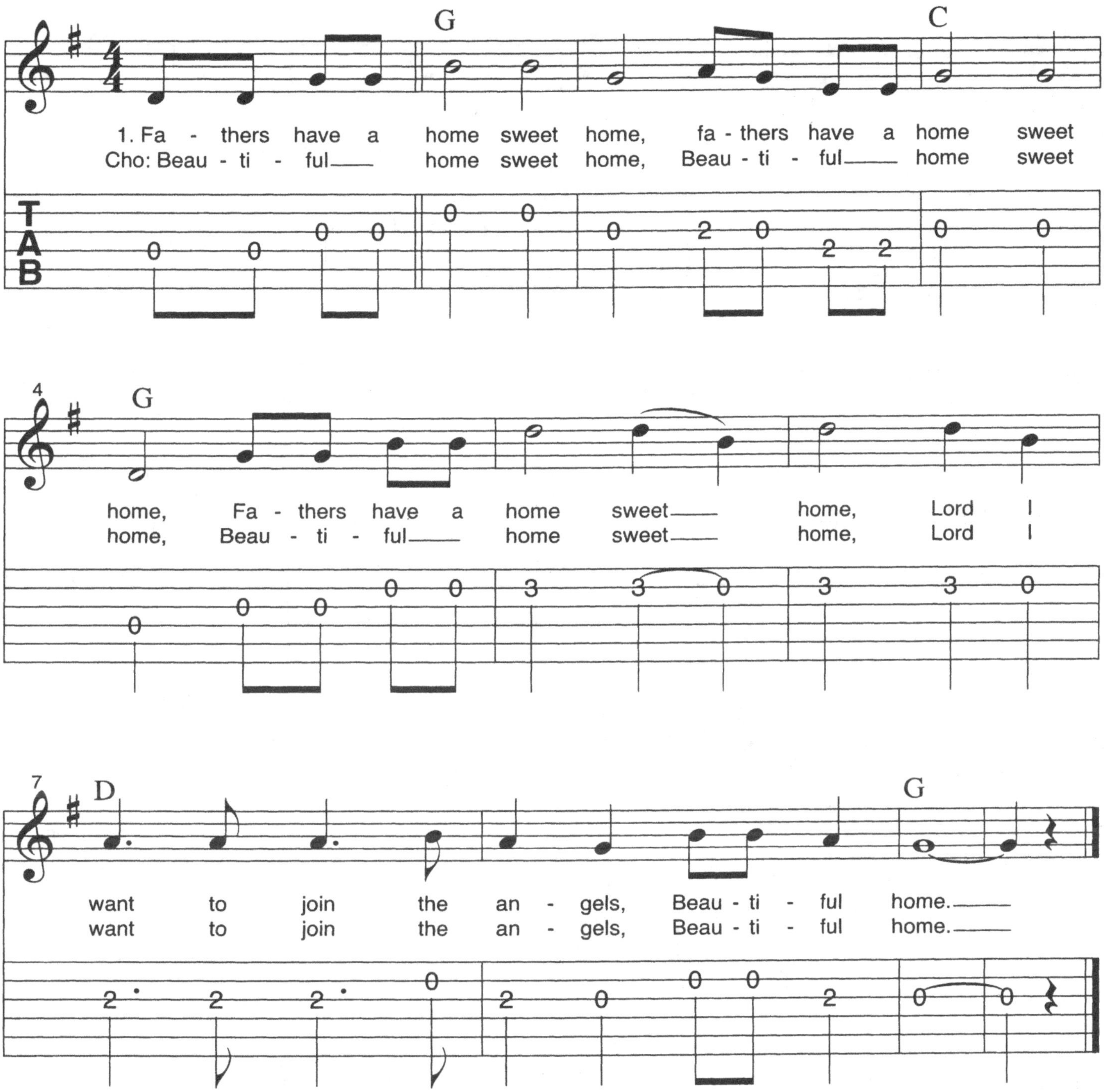

Additional verses:
Mothers, brothers, sisters, etc.

Feast Here Tonight

M: D; F: G or A, capo 5 or 7
CD 1-Track 54

Traditional

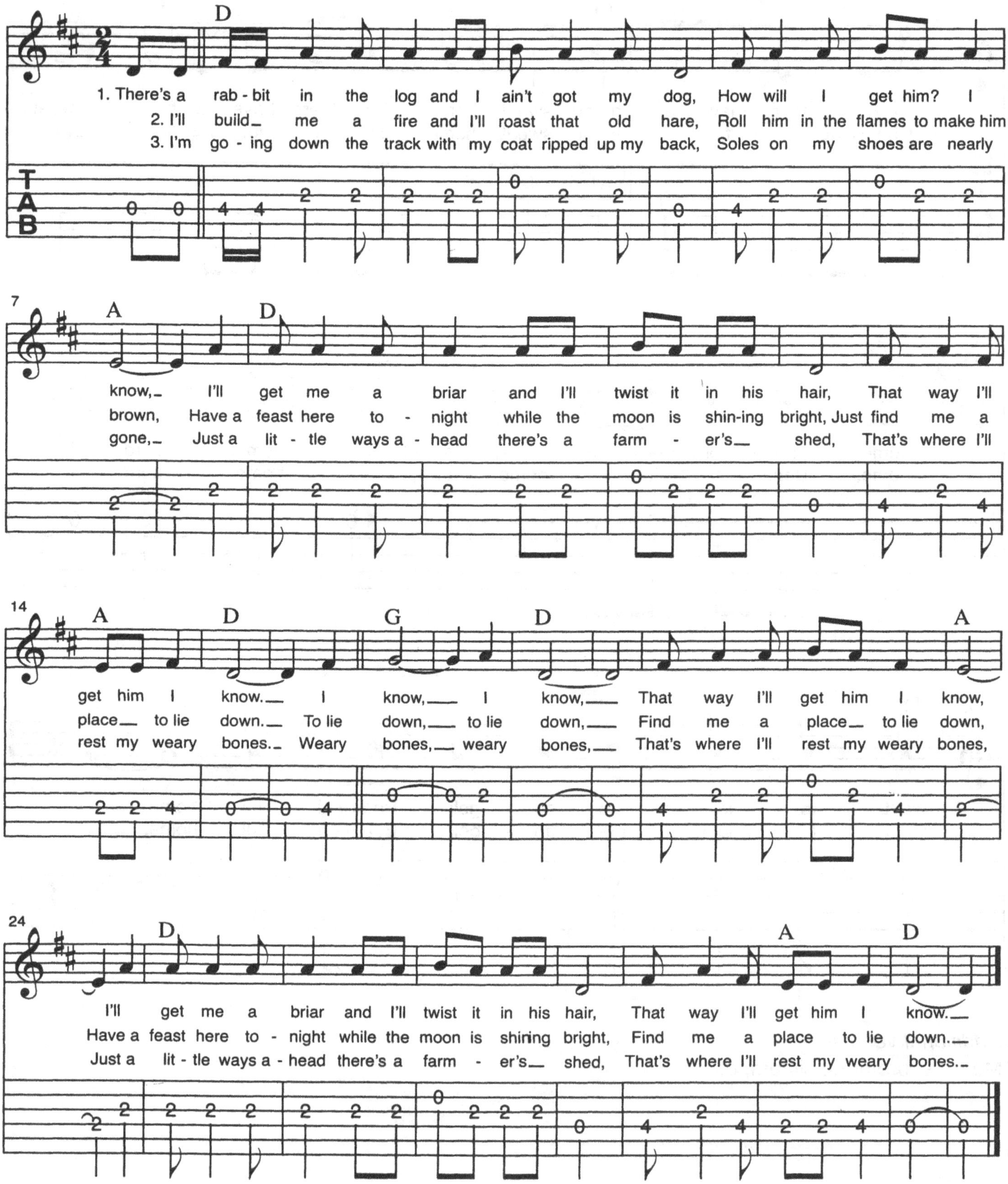

 Monroe Bros., B. Monroe, R. Stanley, Stanley Bros., D. Grisman, Lilly Bros., Scruggs/Watson/Skaggs

The Foggy Mountain Top

M: G; F: C or D, capo 5 or 7
CD 1-Track 55

Traditional

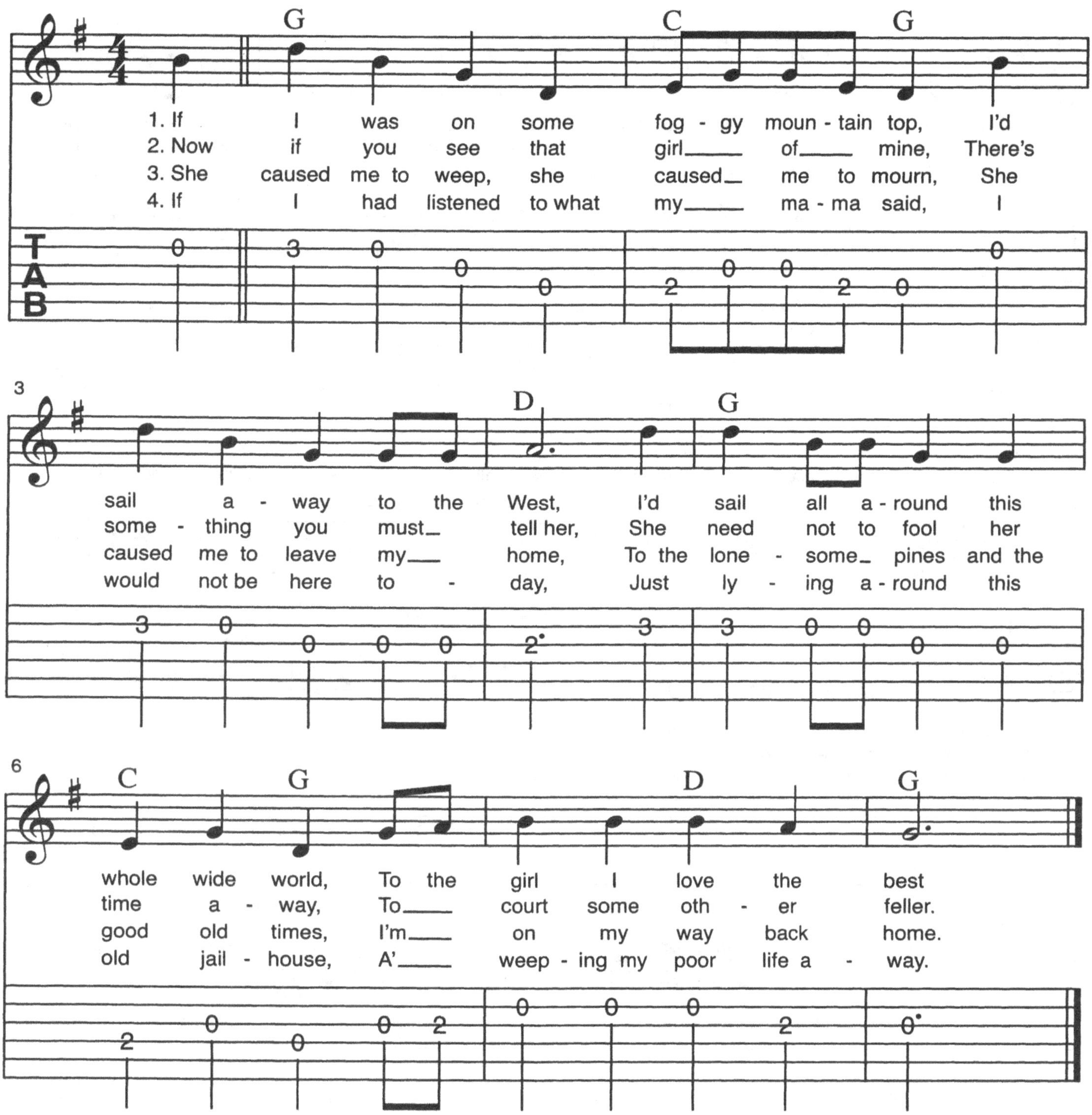

* *Verse 1 often used as chorus*

Footprints in the Snow

M: C; F: F or G, capo 5 or 7
CD 1-Track 56

Harry Wright, ca. 1880

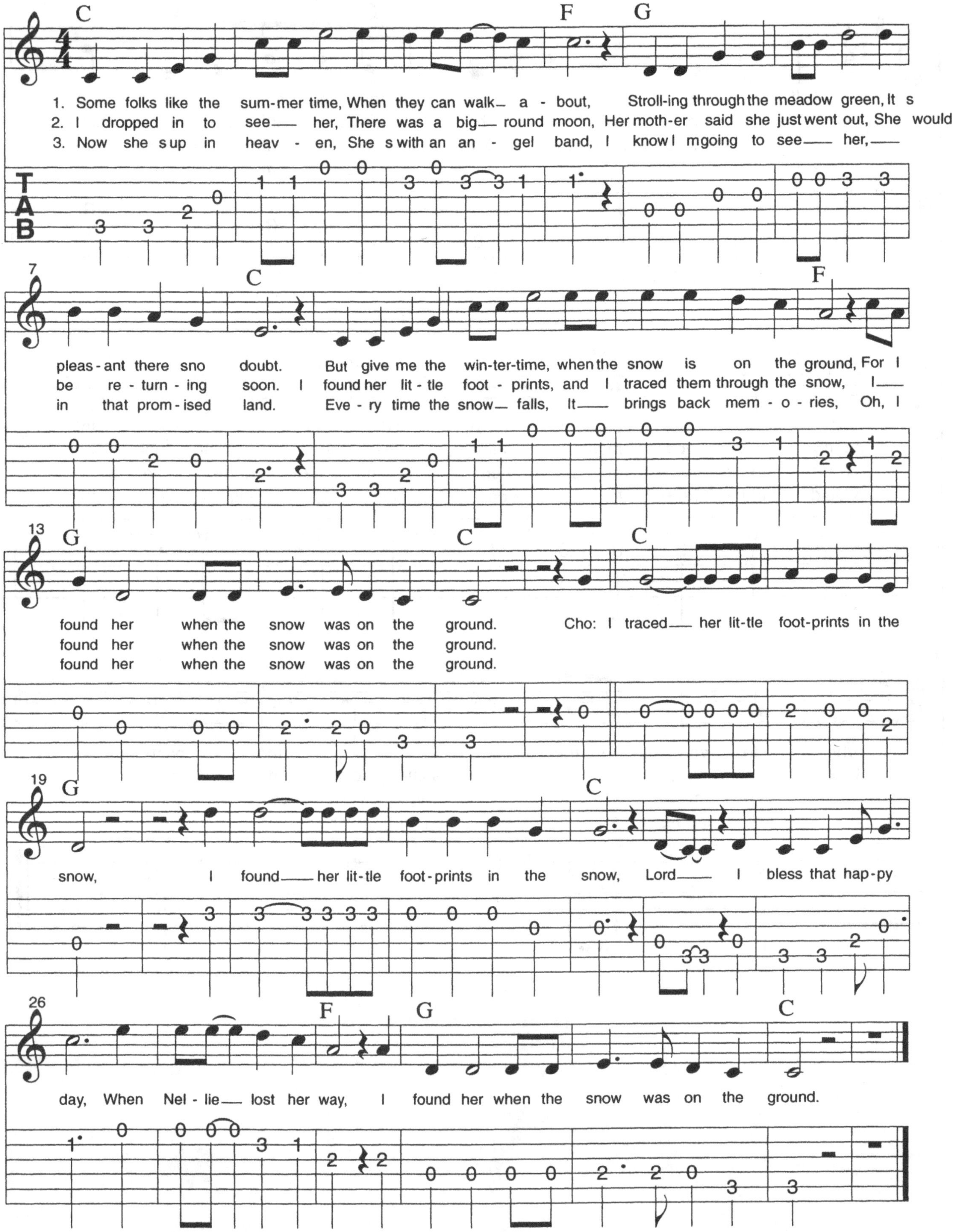

 B. Monroe, Flatt & Scruggs, Stanley Bros., R. Stanley, C. White, Ken. Colonels, D. Watson, B. Kincaid, Muleskinner

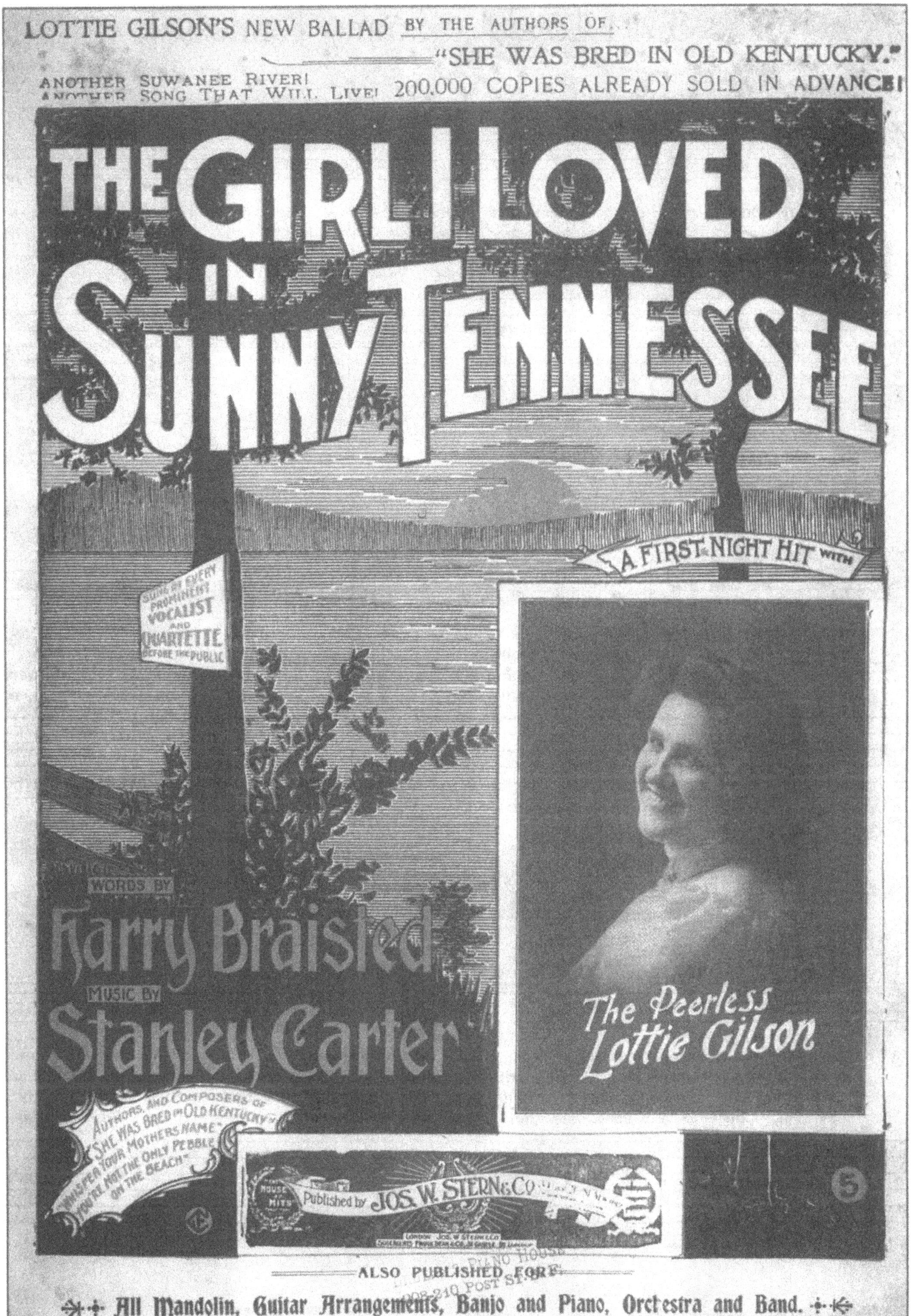

Original 1899 sheet music cover from the collection of Dix Bruce.

The Girl I Loved in Sunny Tennessee

M: G; F: C or D, capo 5 or 7
CD 1-Track 57, medley pt. 1

Braisted & Carter,
ca. 1899

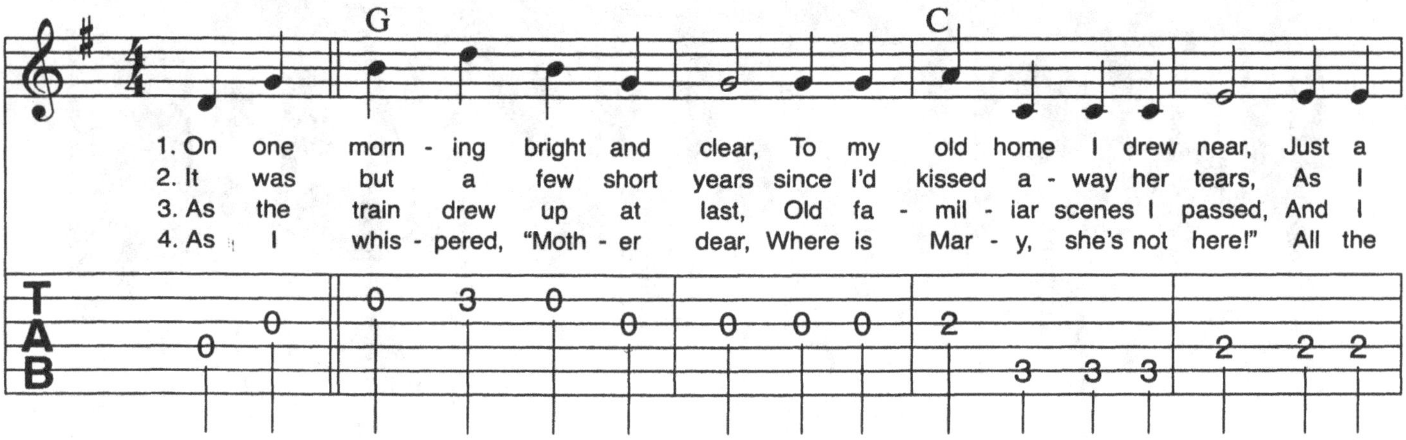

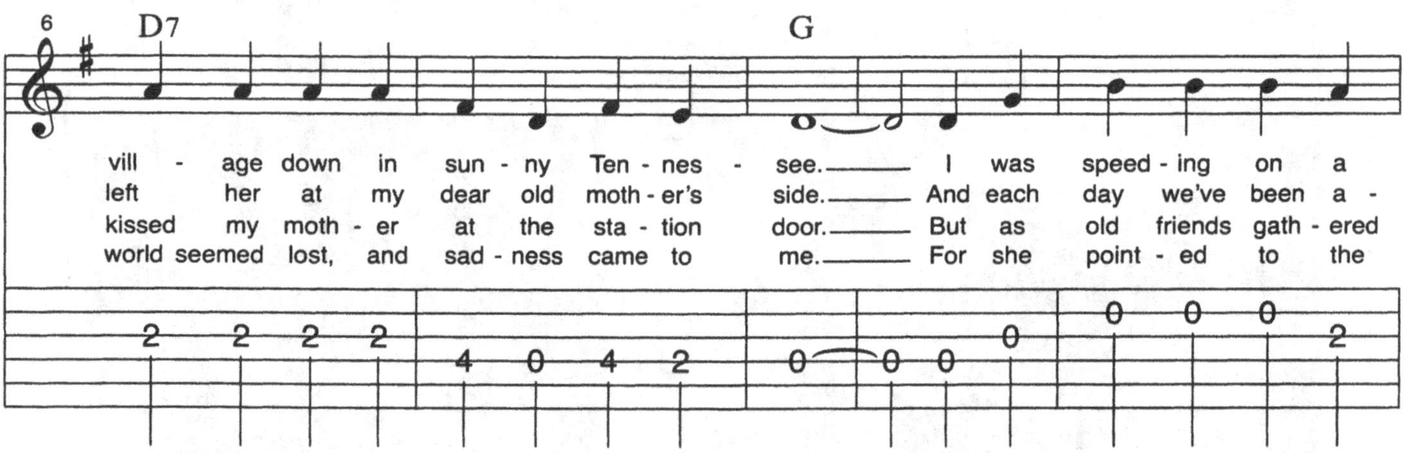

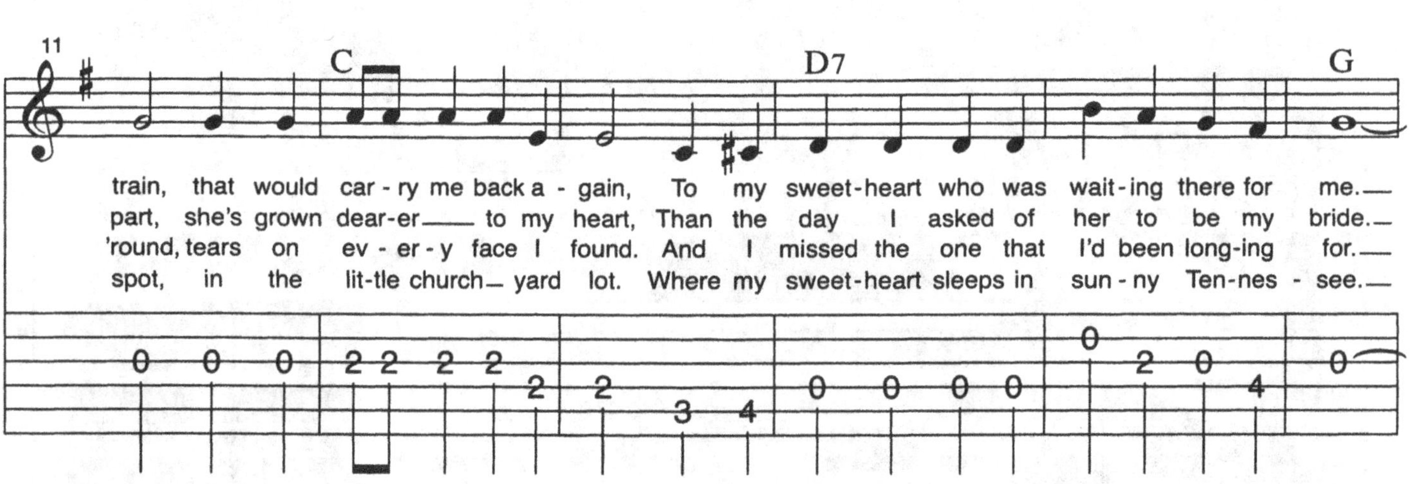

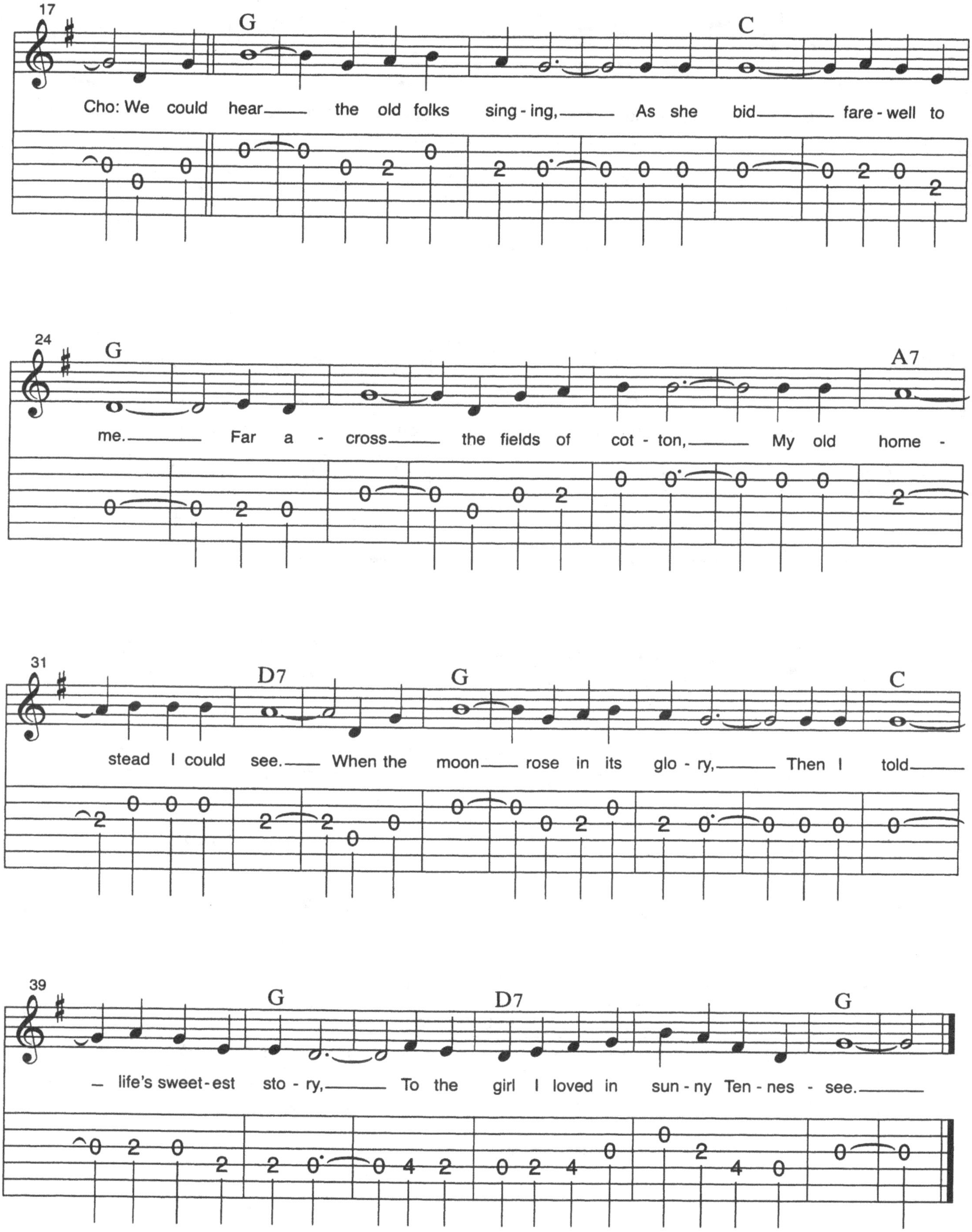
17
G
C
Cho: We could hear the old folks sing-ing, As she bid fare-well to
24
G
A7
me. Far a-cross the fields of cot-ton, My old home-
31
D7
G
C
stead I could see. When the moon rose in its glo-ry, Then I told
39
G
D7
G
life's sweet-est sto-ry, To the girl I loved in sun-ny Ten-nes-see.

Give Me Oil in My Lamp

M: G; F: C or D, capo 5 or 7
CD 1-Track 57, medley pt. 2

Traditional

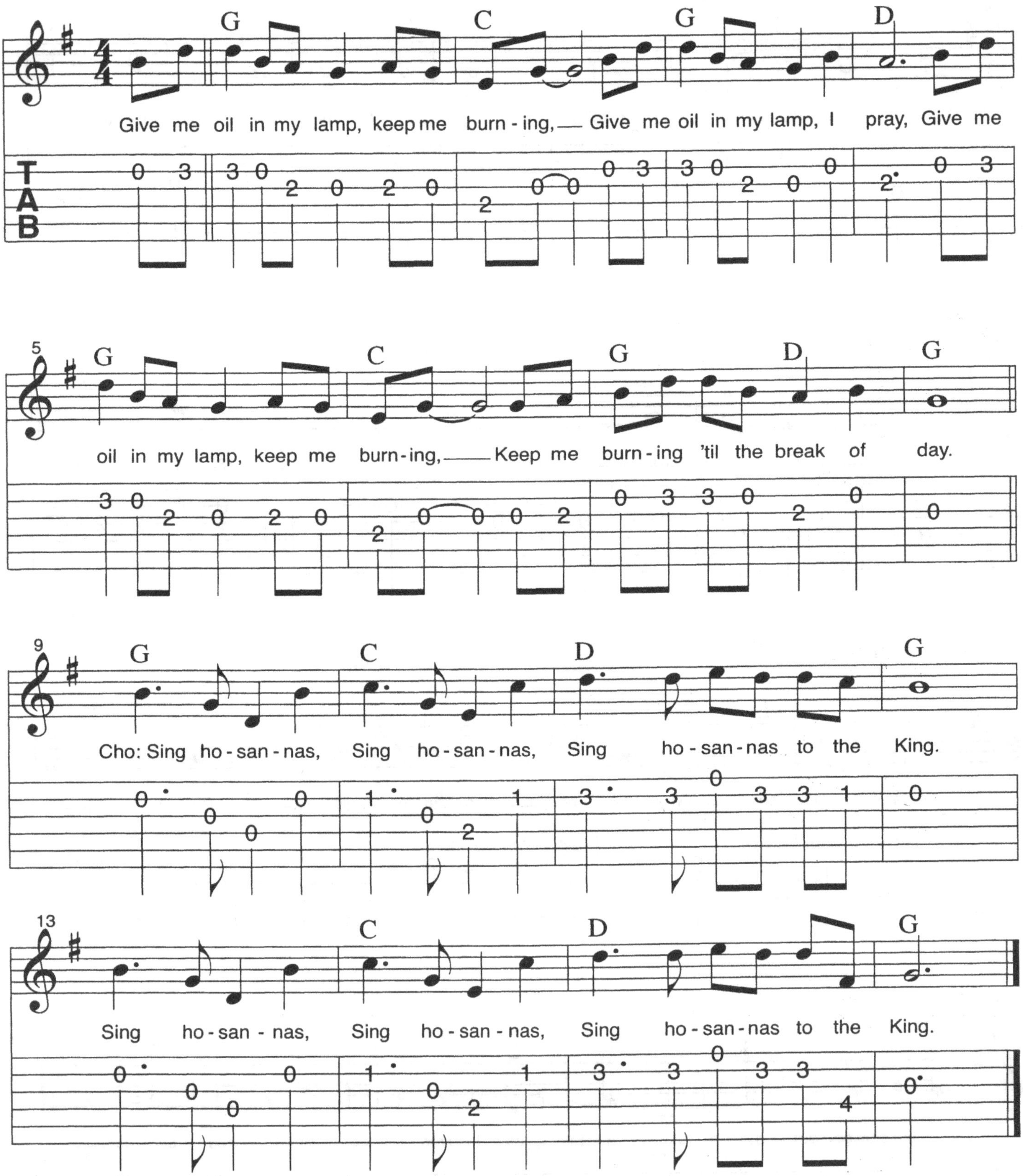

Give Me the Roses While I Live

M: G; F: C or D, capo 5 or 7
CD 1-Track 58

Cornelius & Rowe

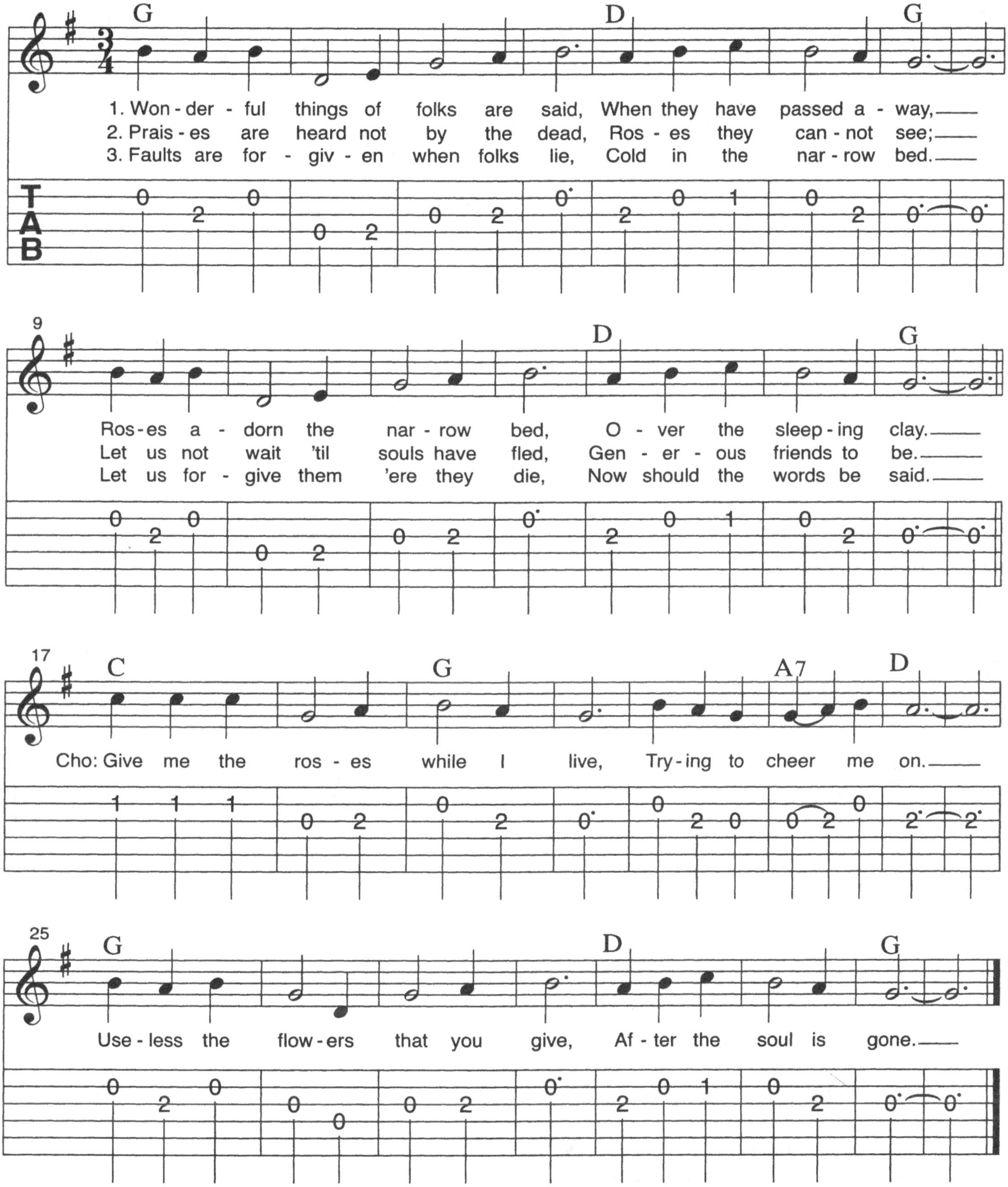

Going Down This Road Feeling Bad

M: G; F: C or D, capo 5 or 7
CD 1-Track 59, medley pt. 1

Traditional

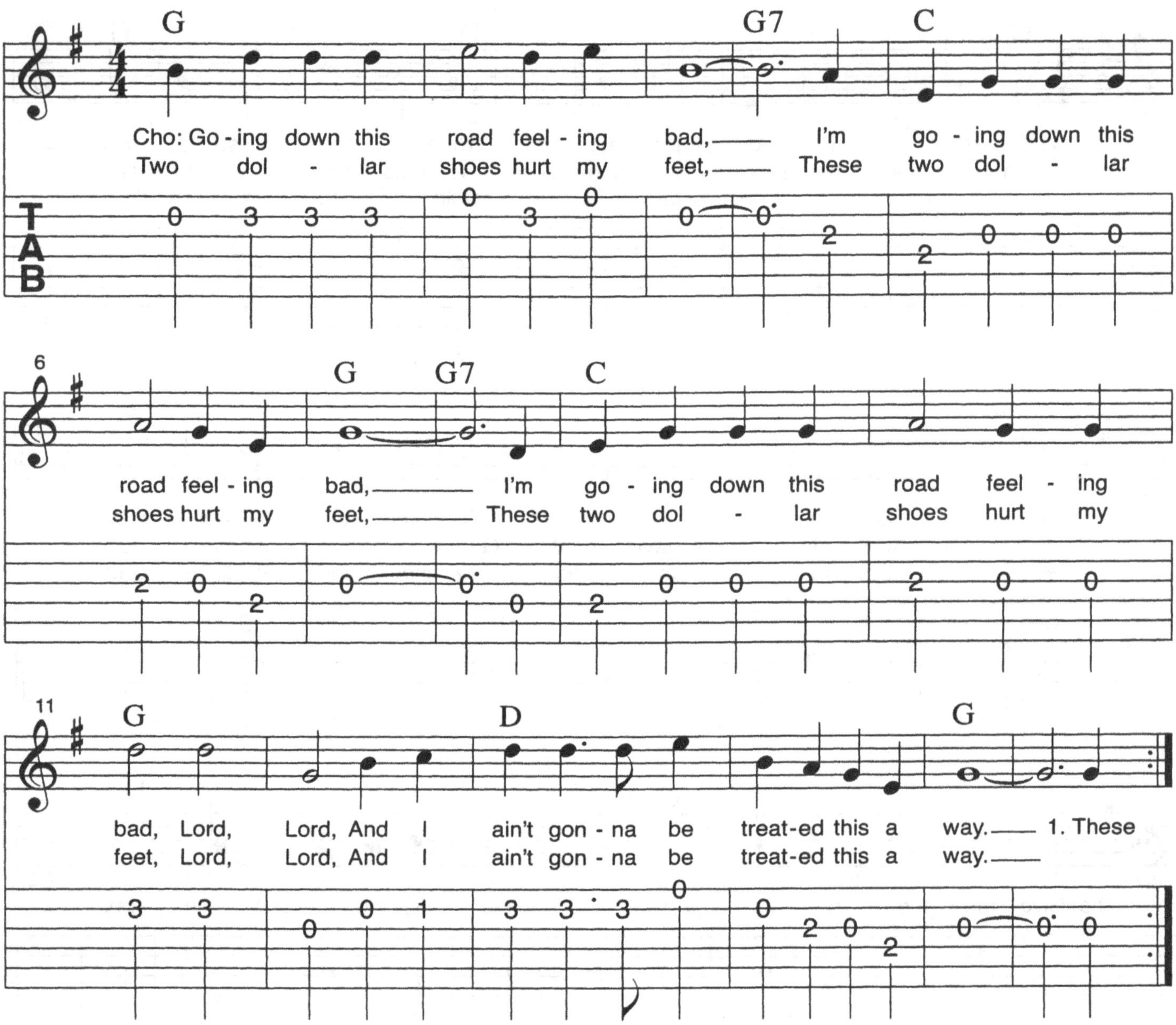


```
G                                   G7
2. They feed me on corn bread and beans,
       C                            G  G7
They feed me on corn bread and beans,
       C                            G
They feed me on corn bread and beans, Lord, Lord,
       D                              G
And I ain't gonna be treated this a way.
```

3. I'm going where the chilly winds don't blow, (etc.)
4. I'm going where the water tastes like wine, (etc.)
5. I'm going where the weather suits my clothes, (etc.)

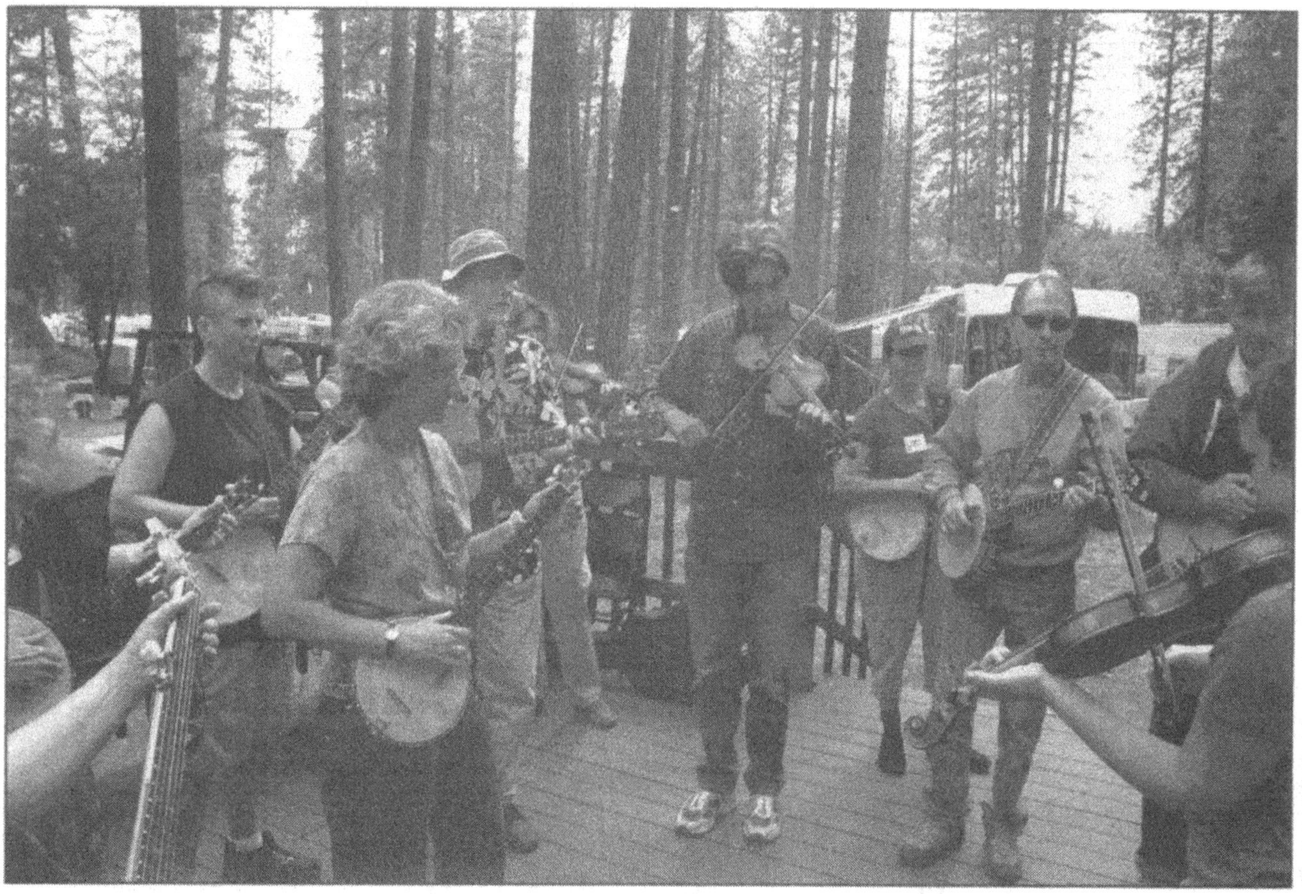

Jam sessions can sometimes be very large! This old time jam — with seven banjos no less — took place at the 2006 California Bluegrass Association's Music Camp in Grass Valley.

Grandfather's Clock

M: G; F: C or D, capo 5 or 7
CD 1-Track 59, medley pt. 2

Henry Clay Work, 1876

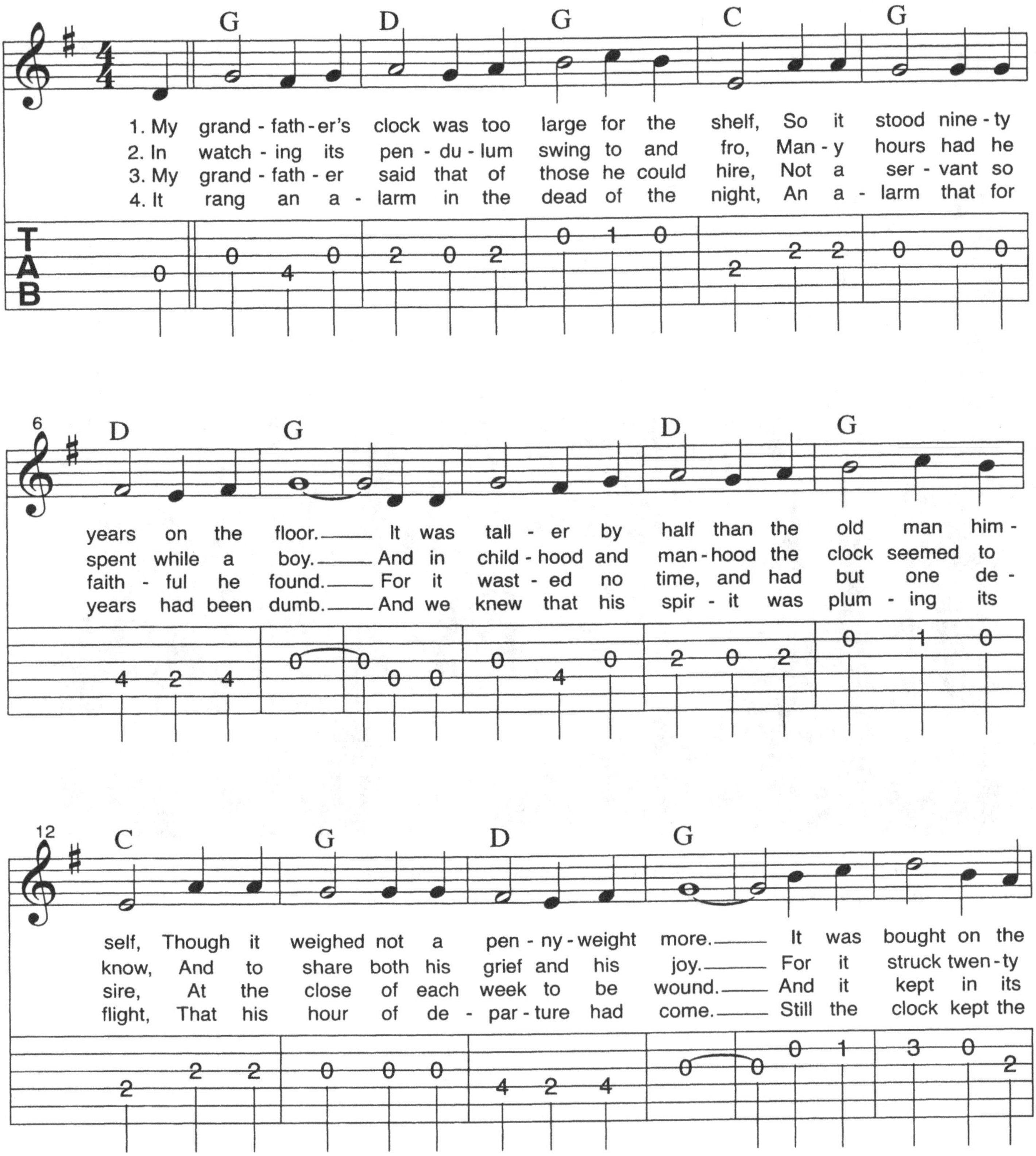

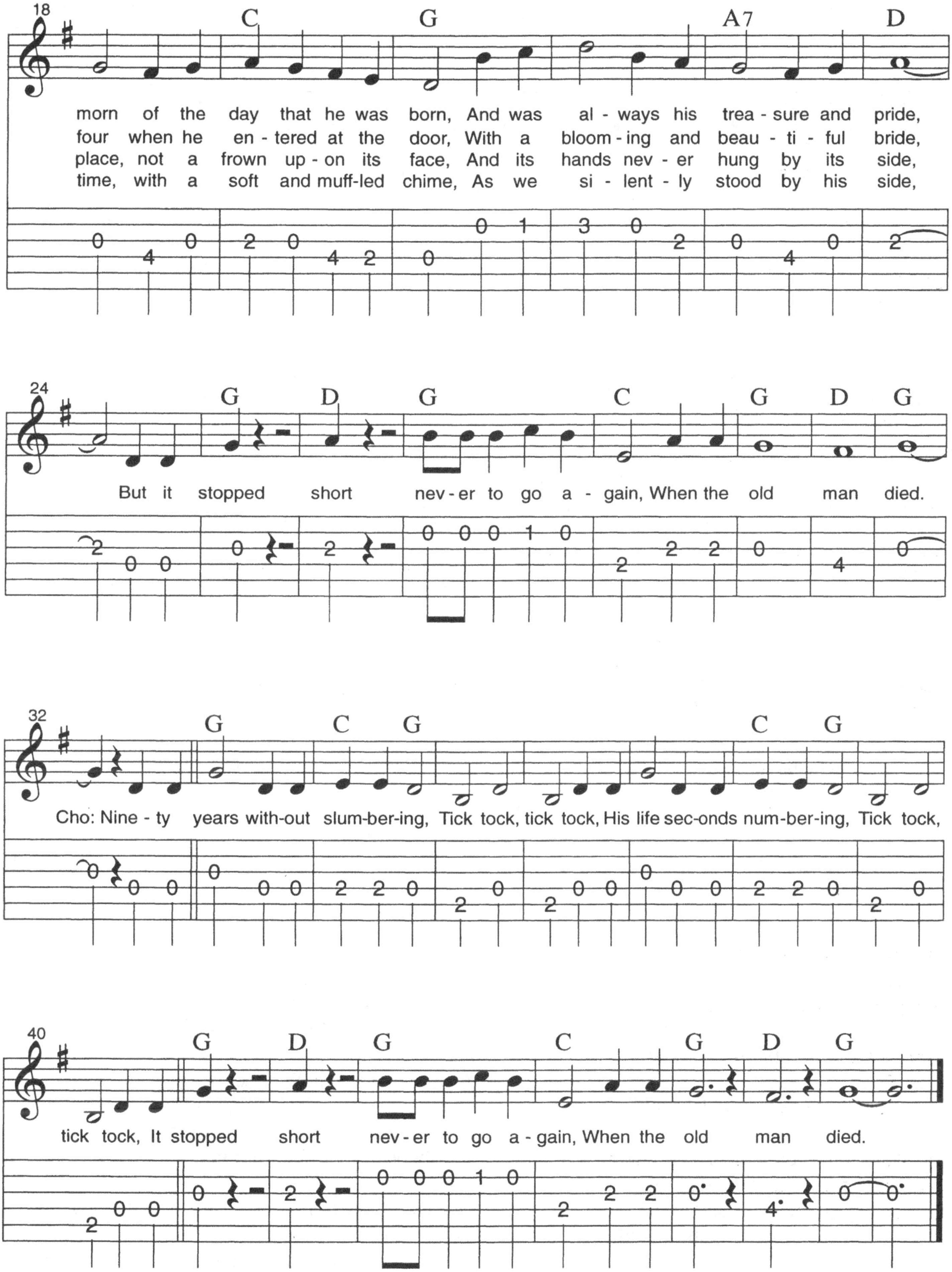
18
C G A7 D
morn of the day that he was born, And was al - ways his trea - sure and pride,
four when he en - tered at the door, With a bloom - ing and beau - ti - ful bride,
place, not a frown up - on its face, And its hands nev - er hung by its side,
time, with a soft and muff-led chime, As we si - lent - ly stood by his side,
24
G D G C G D G
But it stopped short nev - er to go a - gain, When the old man died.
32
G C G C G
Cho: Nine - ty years with-out slum-ber-ing, Tick tock, tick tock, His life sec-onds num-ber-ing, Tick tock,
40
G D G C G D G
tick tock, It stopped short nev - er to go a - gain, When the old man died.

Great Speckled Bird

M: G; F: C or D, capo 5 or 7
CD 1-Track 60

Traditional

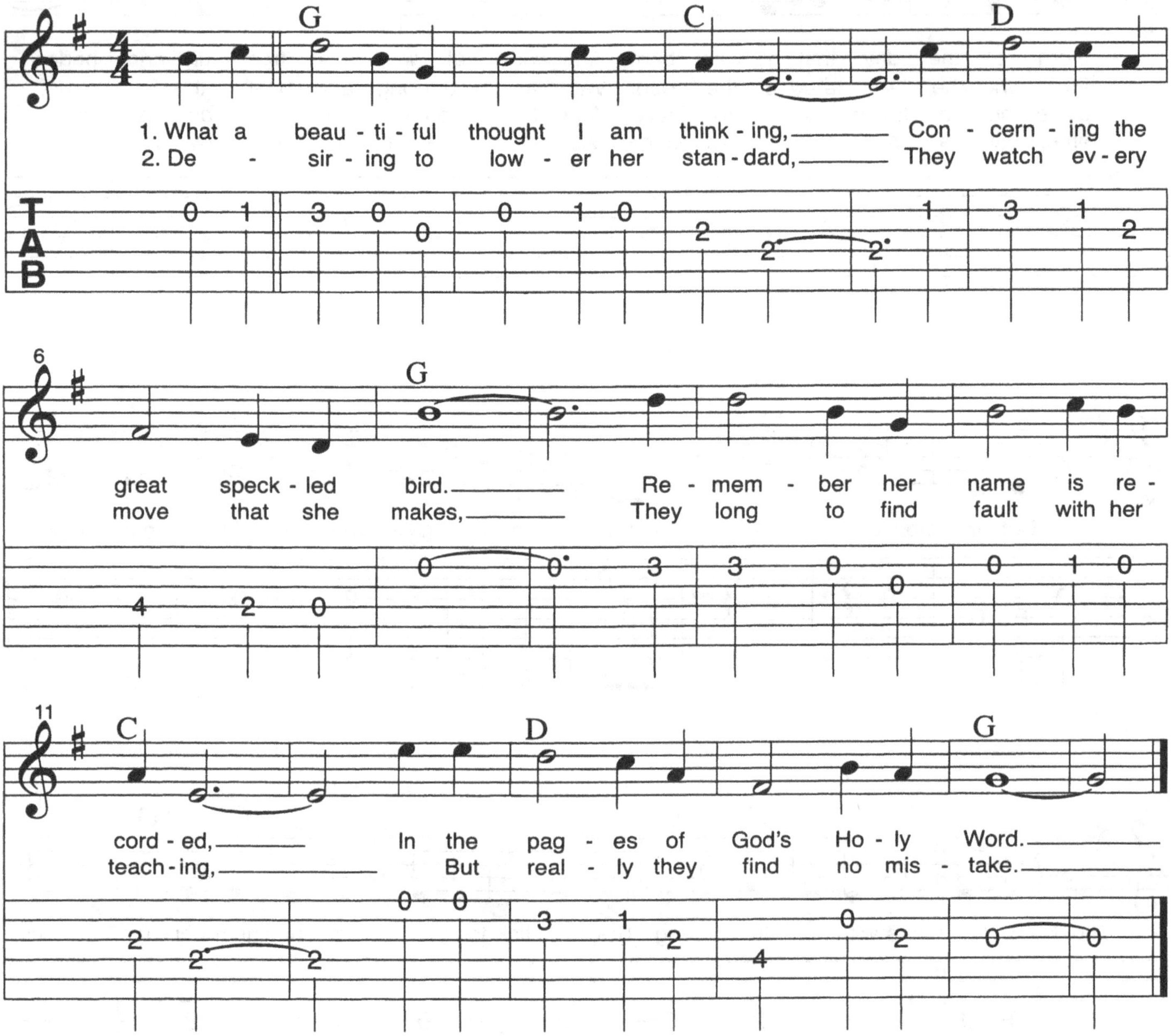

G C
3. I am glad to have learned of her meekness,
D G
I'm proud that my name is in her book,
G C
For I want to be one never fearing,
D G
The face of my Saviour's to look.

4. All the other birds flocking 'round her,
And she is despised by the squad,
But the great speckled bird in the Bible,
Is one with the great church of God.

5. In the presence of all her despisers,
With a song never uttered before,
She will rise and be gone in a moment,
'Til the great tribulation is o'er.

6. When He cometh descending from heaven,
On the clouds as He writes in His word,
I'll be joyfully carried to meet Him,
On the wings of the great speckled bird.

7. She is spreading her wings for a journey,
She's going to leave by and by,
When the trumpet shall sound in the morning,
She'll rise and go up in the sky.

 R. Acuff, M. Wiseman

Green Pastures

M: A; F: D or E, capo 5 or 7
CD 1-Track 61

Traditional

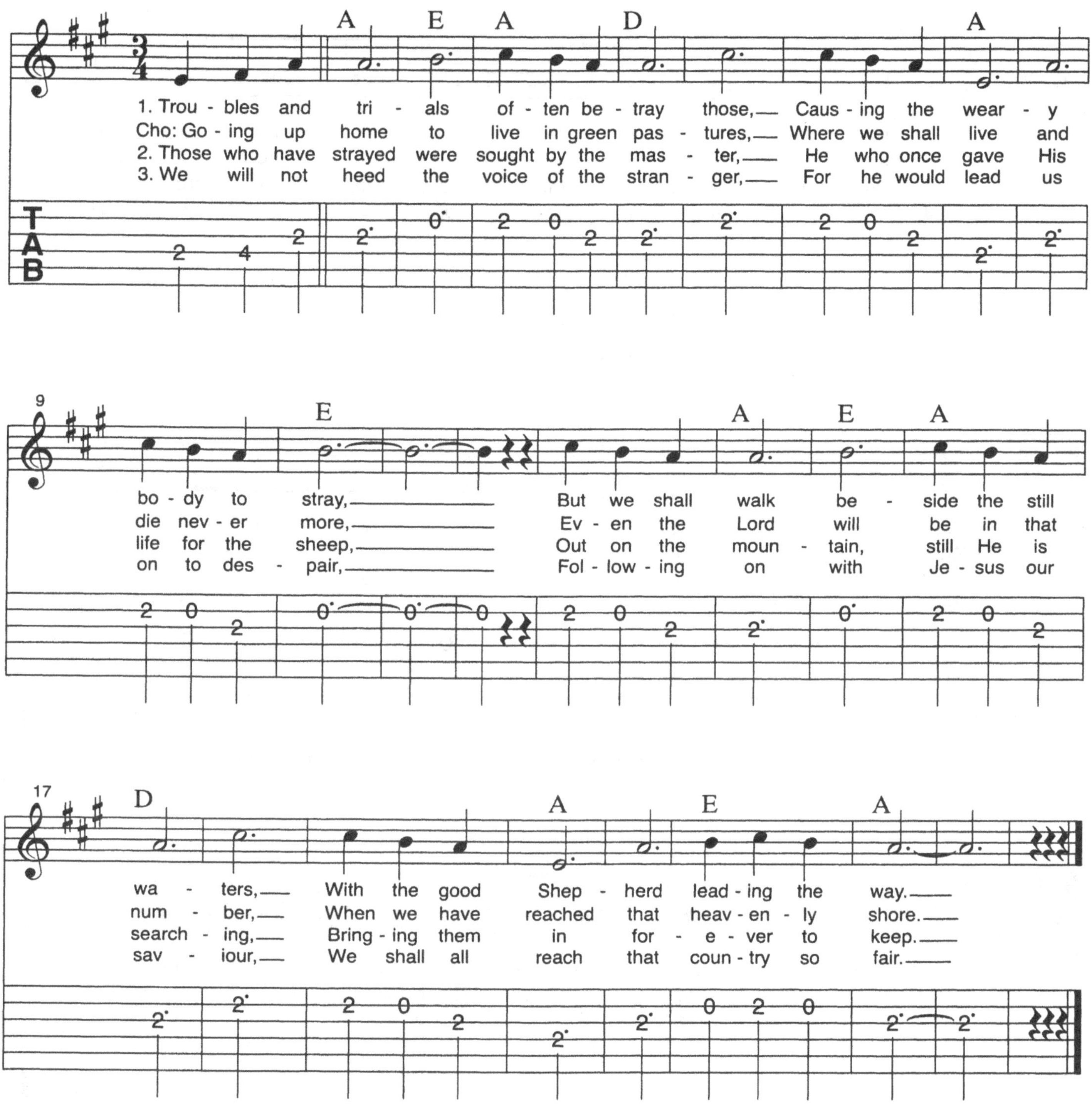

Groundhog

M: *A;* ***F***: *D or E, capo 5 or 7*
CD 1-Track 62

Traditional

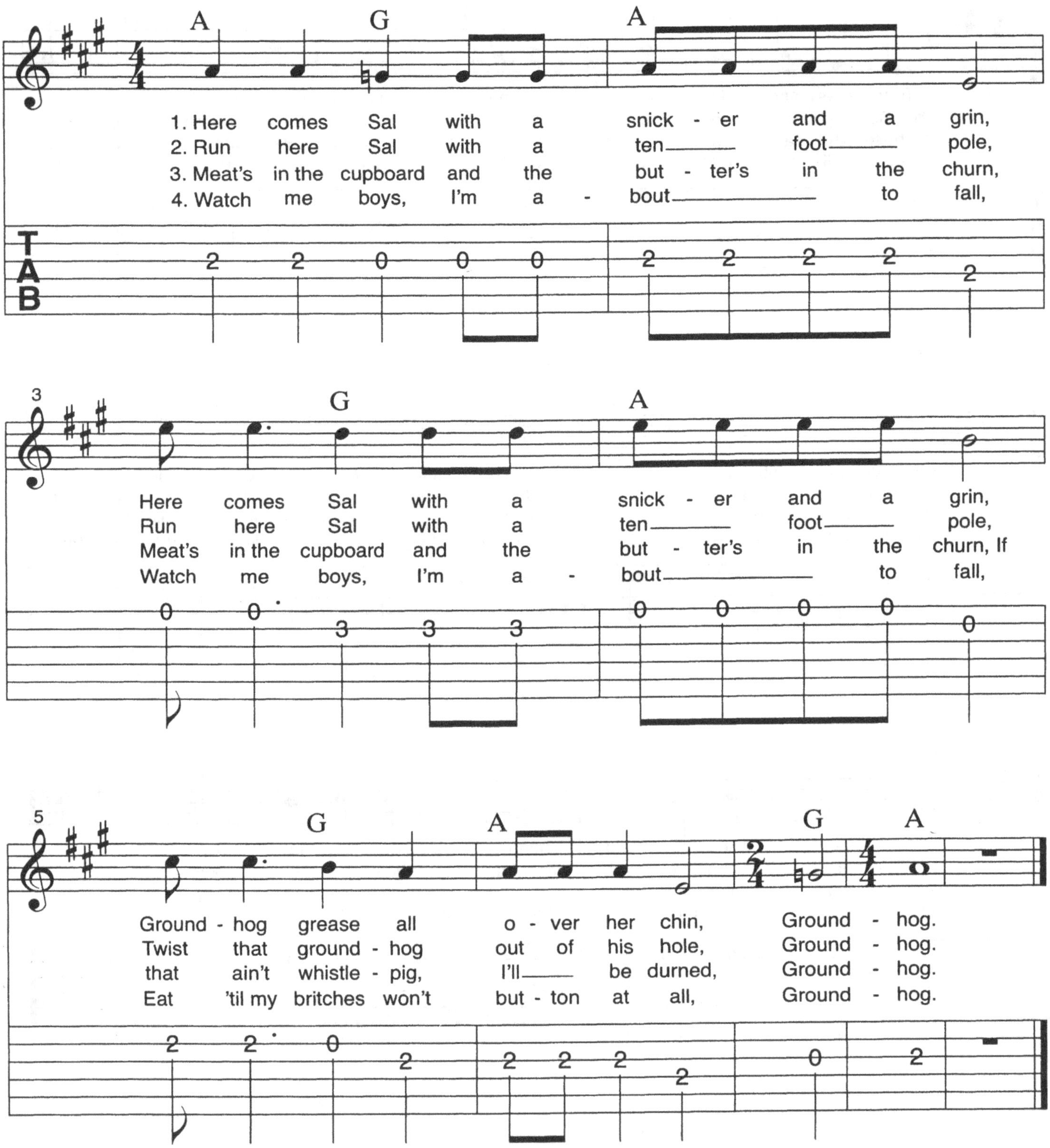

 Stanley Bros., D. Watson, NLCR, Dillards

Hallelujah! I'm Ready

M: C; F: F or G, capo 5 or 7
CD 1-Track 63

Traditional

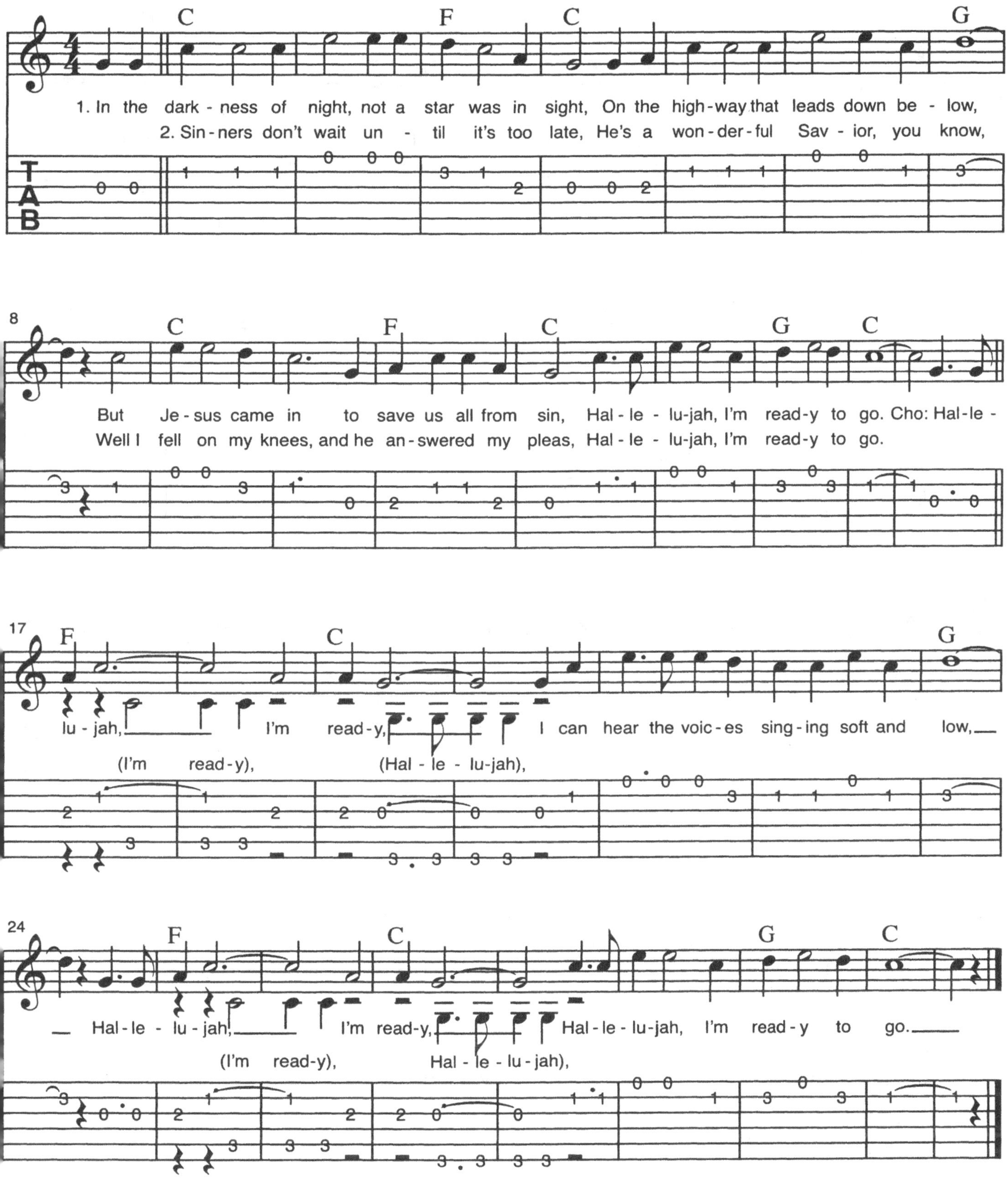

Hand Me Down My Walking Cane

M: G; F: C or D, capo 5 or 7
CD 1-Track 64, medley pt. 1

Traditional

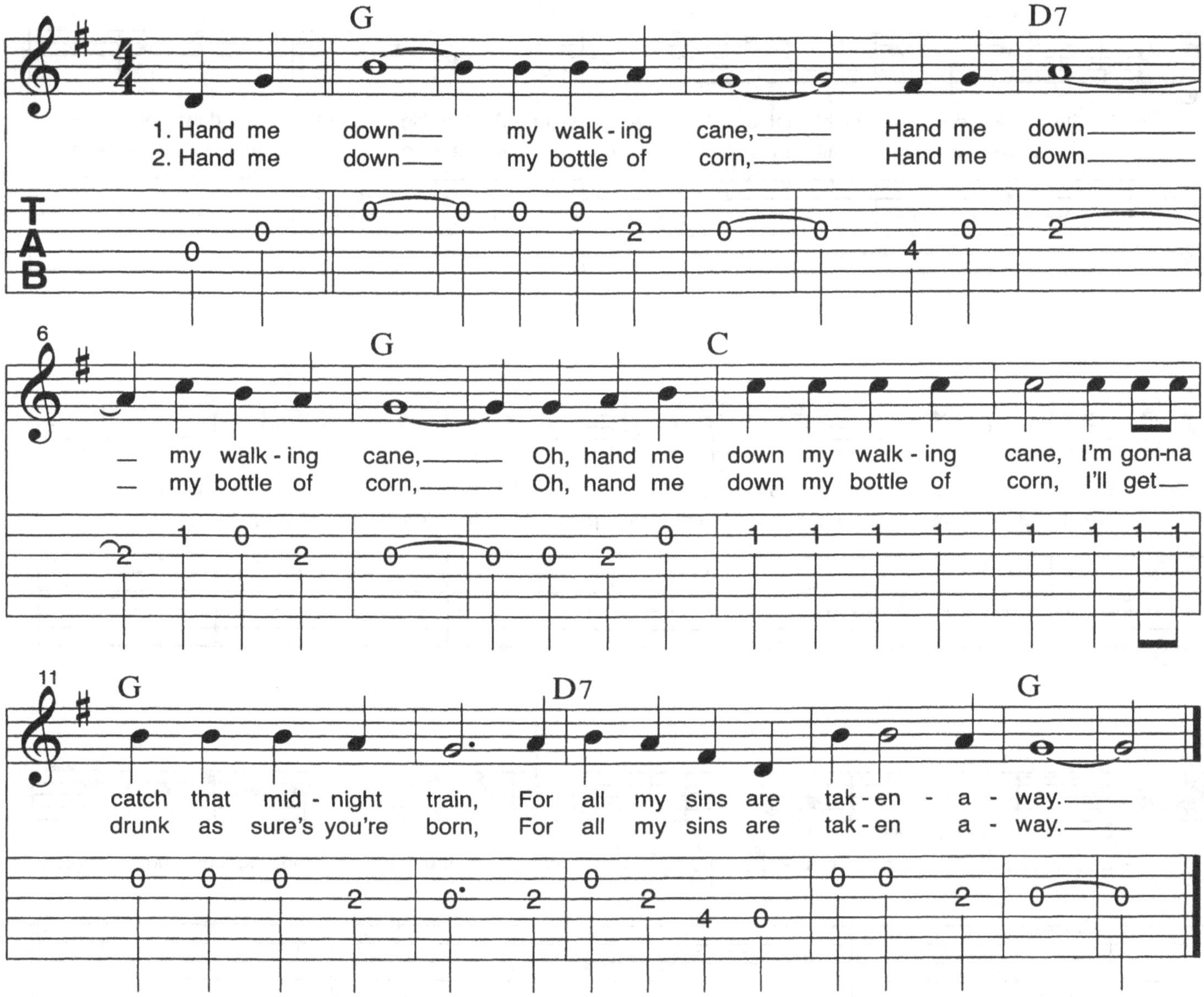

3. Oh, I got drunk and I landed in jail,
Oh, I got drunk and I landed in jail,
Oh, I got drunk and I landed in jail,
With no one to go my bail,
For all my sins are taken away.

(Chords: G / D7 G / C / G / D7 G)

4. The meat is tough, and the beans are bad, (3X)
Oh, my God, I can't eat that,
For all my sins are taken away.

5. The devil chased me 'round a stump, (3X)
I thought he'd catch me at every jump,
For all my sins are taken away.

 Goose Island Ramblers, Osborne Bros., Skillet Lickers, N. Blake

Handsome Molly

M: G; F: C or D, capo 5 or 7
CD 1-Track 64, medley pt. 2

Traditional

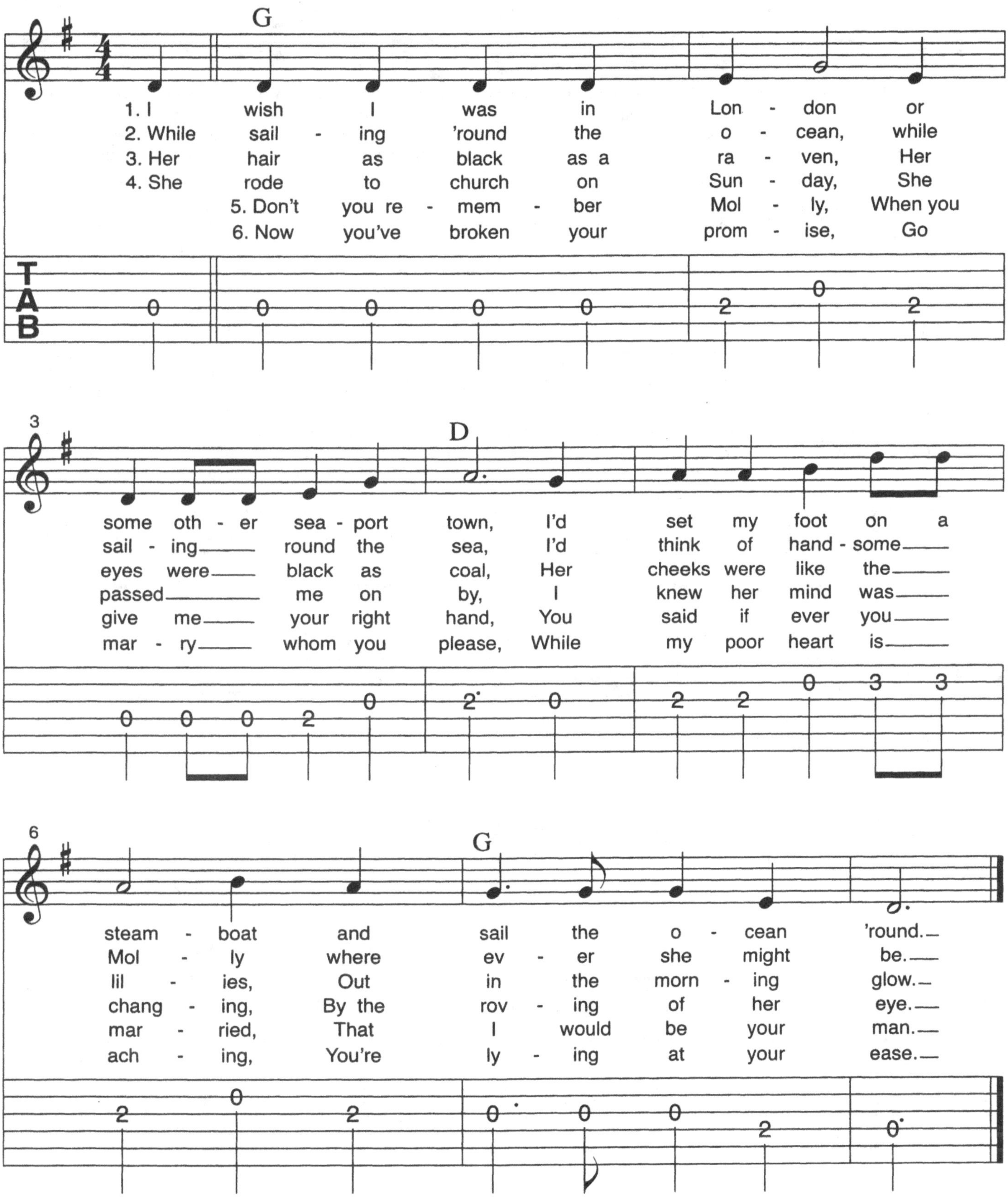

Hard Times, Come Again No More

M: D; F: G or A, capo 5 or 7 — *Foster*
CD 1-Track 65, medley pt. 1

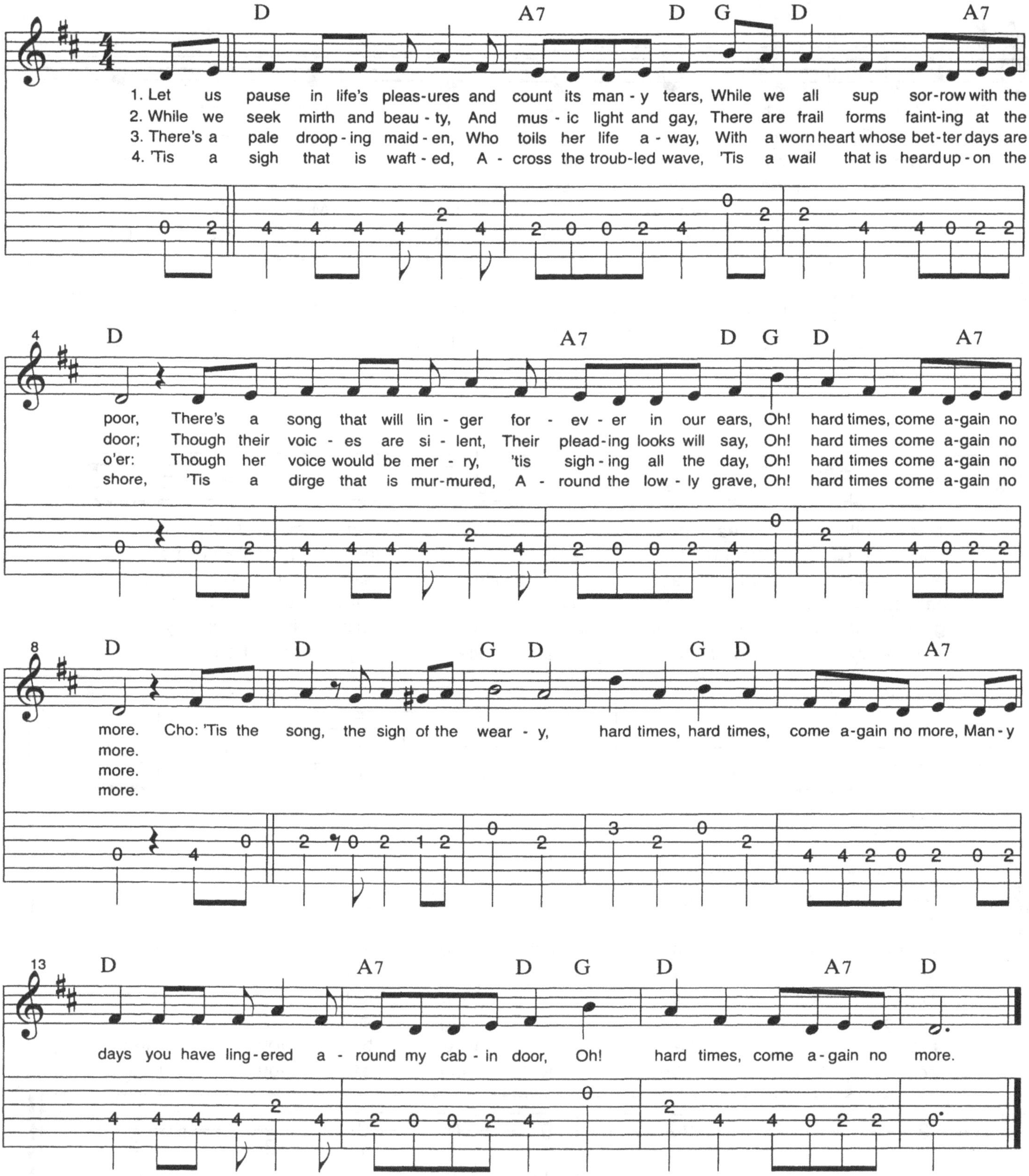

Have Thine Own Way, Lord

M: D; F: G or A, capo 5 or 7
CD 1-Track 65, medley pt. 2

Pollard & Stebbins, 1907

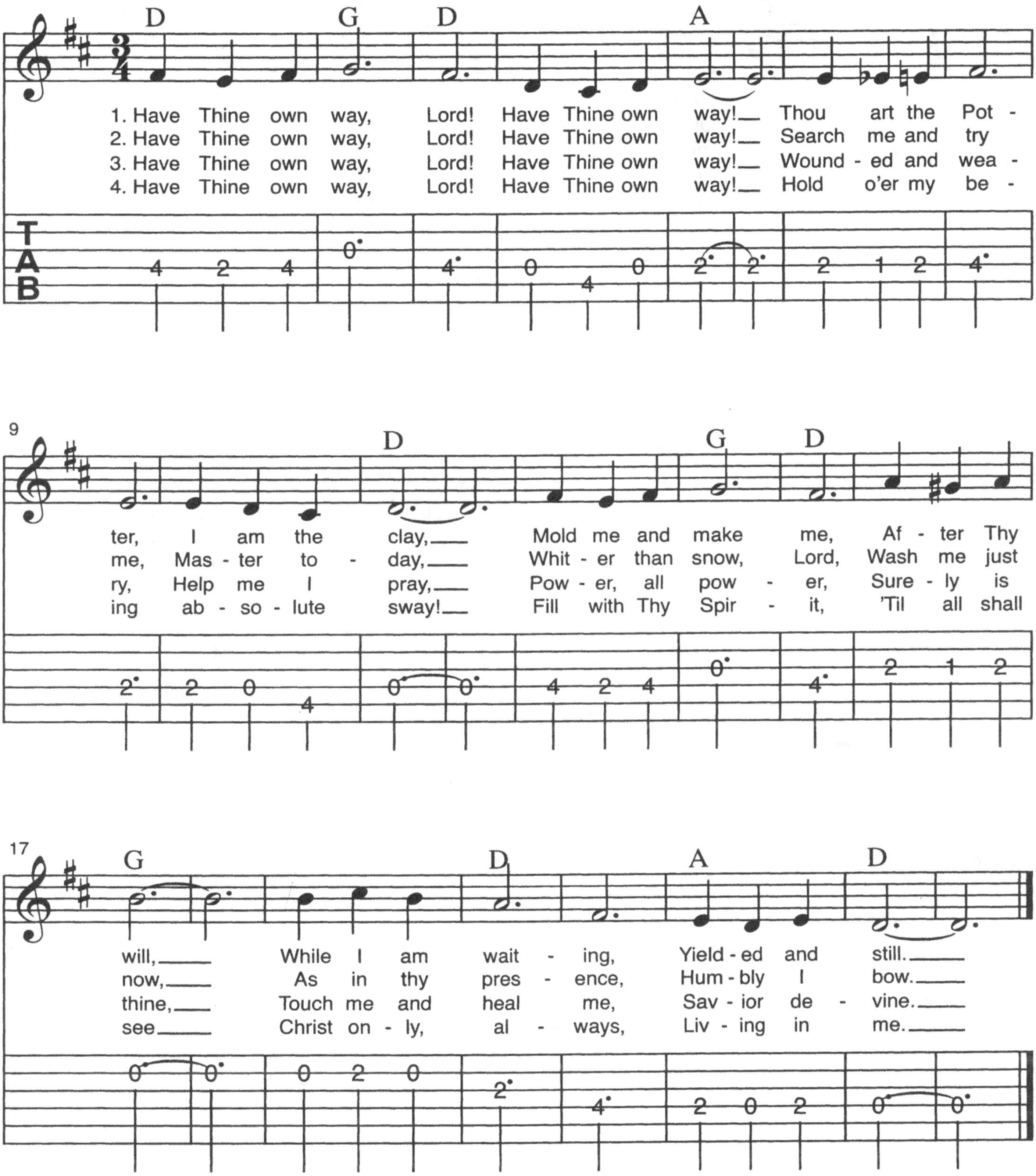

He Was A Friend of Mine

M: G; F: C or D, capo 5 or 7
CD 1-Track 66

Traditional

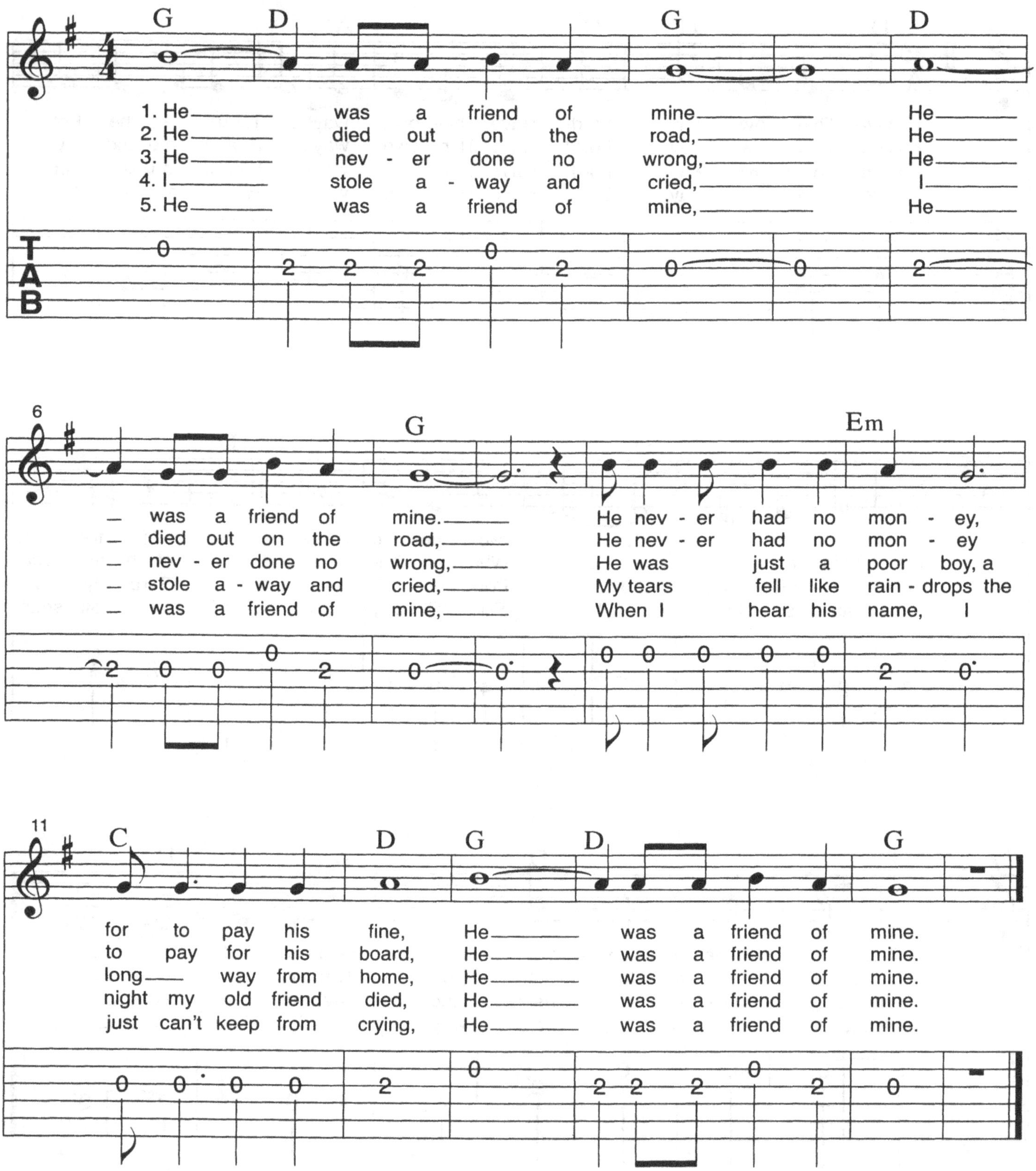

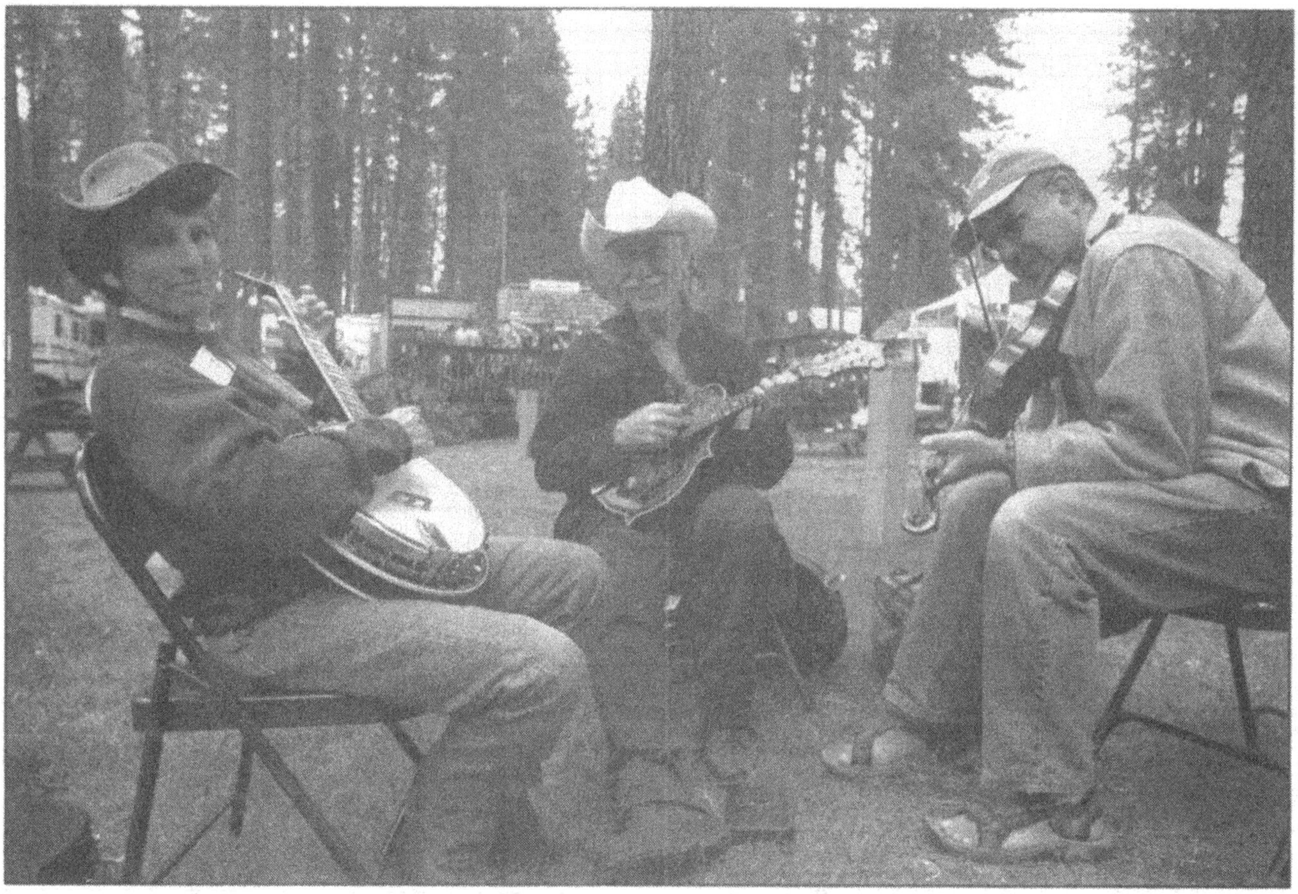

Photo by Bill Evans

Jam sessions can be large or small. No matter the size, they're all lots of fun!

He Will Set Your Fields On Fire

M: A; F: D or E, capo 5 or 7
CD 1-Track 67

Ballew & Brackett

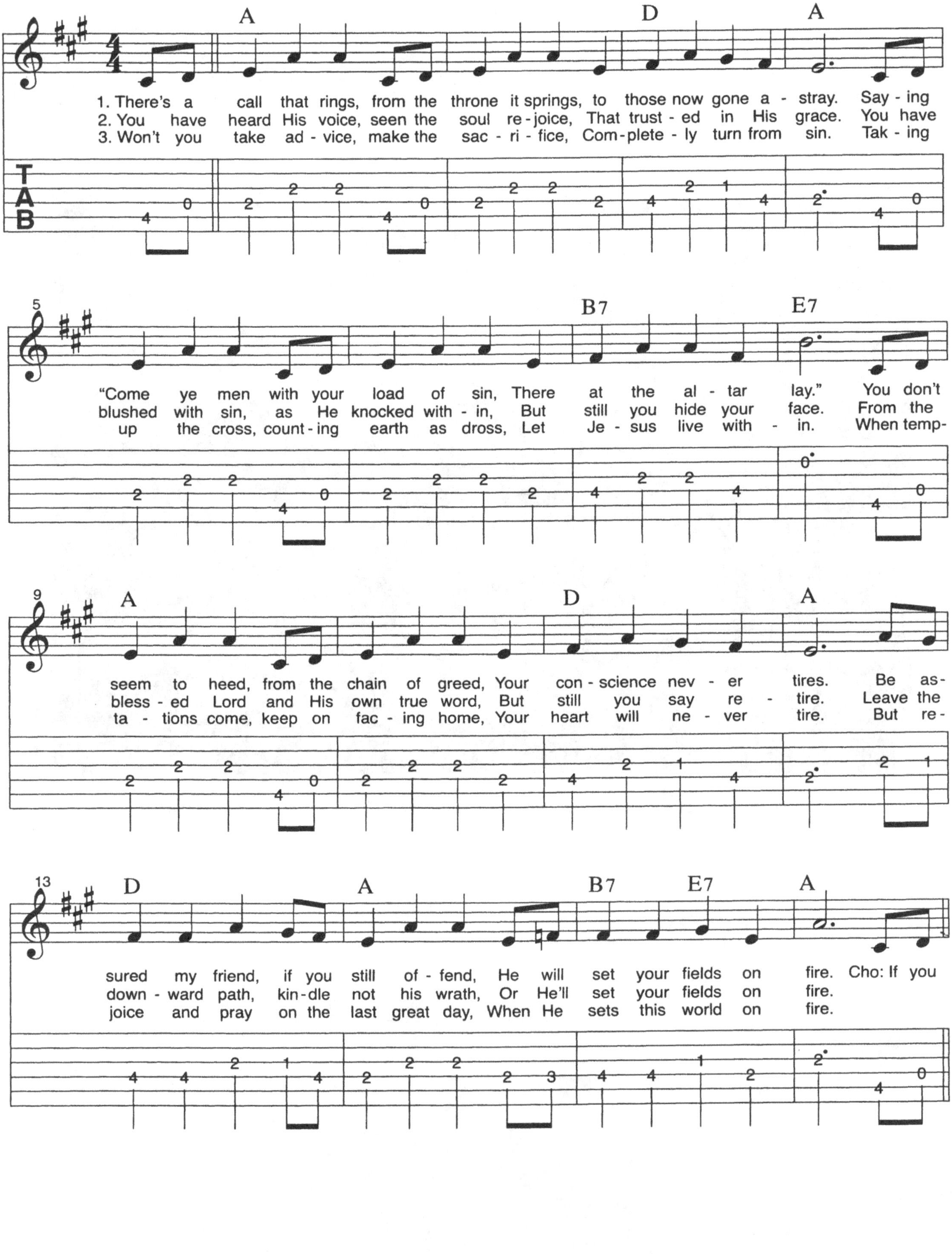

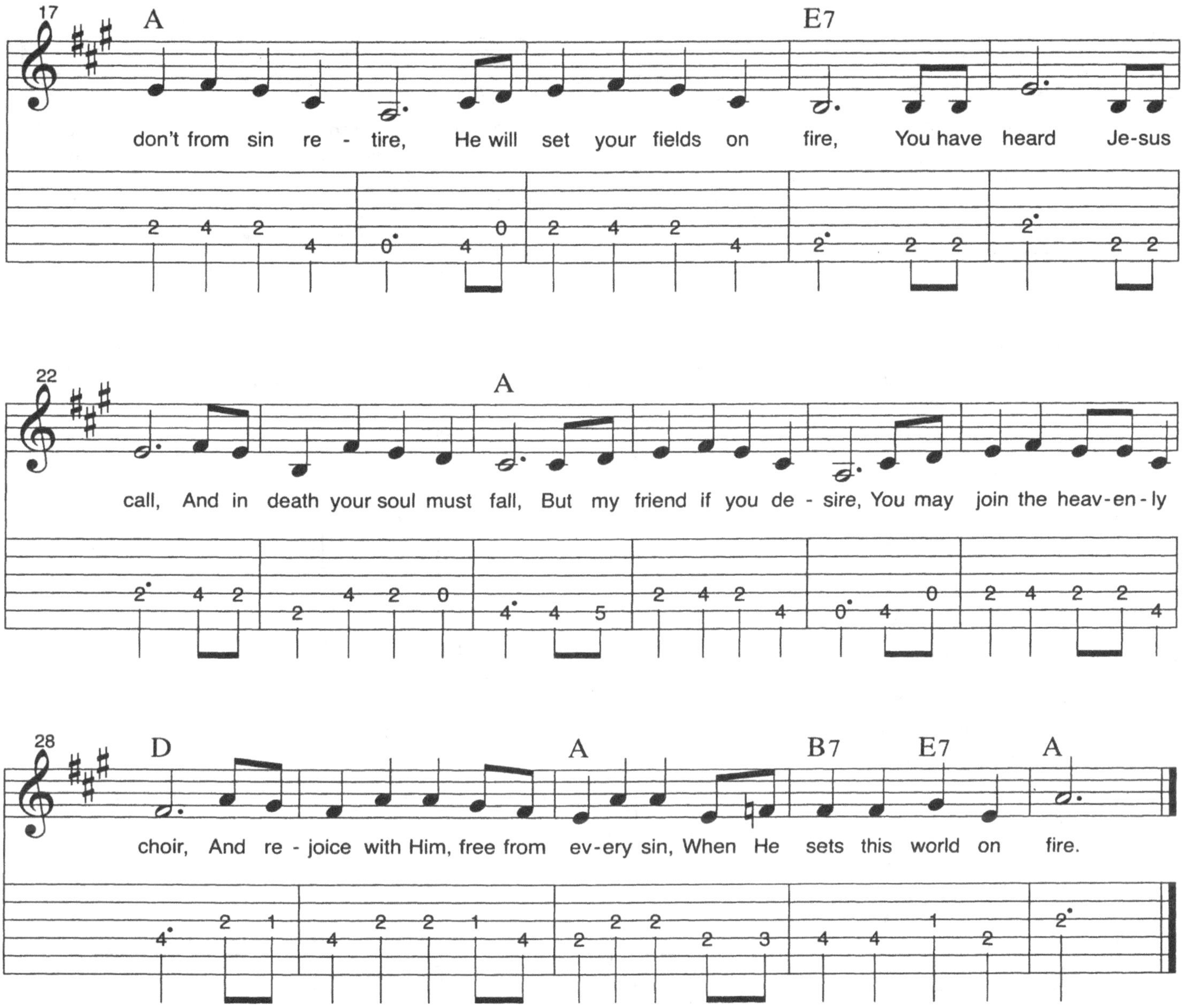
17
A
E7
don't from sin re - tire, He will set your fields on fire, You have heard Je-sus
22
A
call, And in death your soul must fall, But my friend if you de - sire, You may join the heav-en-ly
28
D
A
B7
E7
A
choir, And re - joice with Him, free from ev-ery sin, When He sets this world on fire.

High on a Mountain

M: D; F: G or A, capo 5 or 7
CD 1-Track 68

Ola Belle Reed

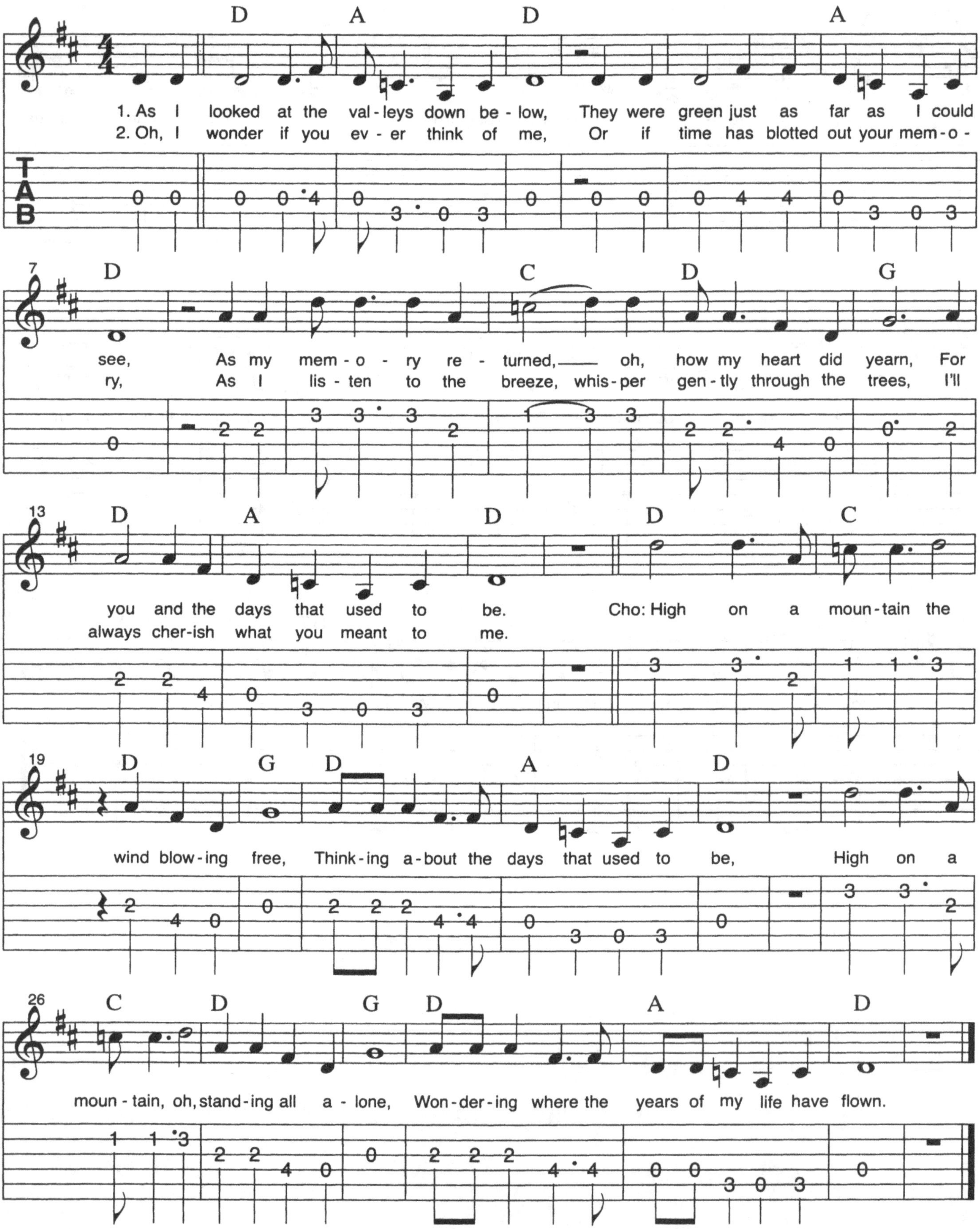

Highway of Sorrow

M: C; F: F or G, capo 5 or 7
CD 1-Track 69

Bill Monroe & Peter Pyle

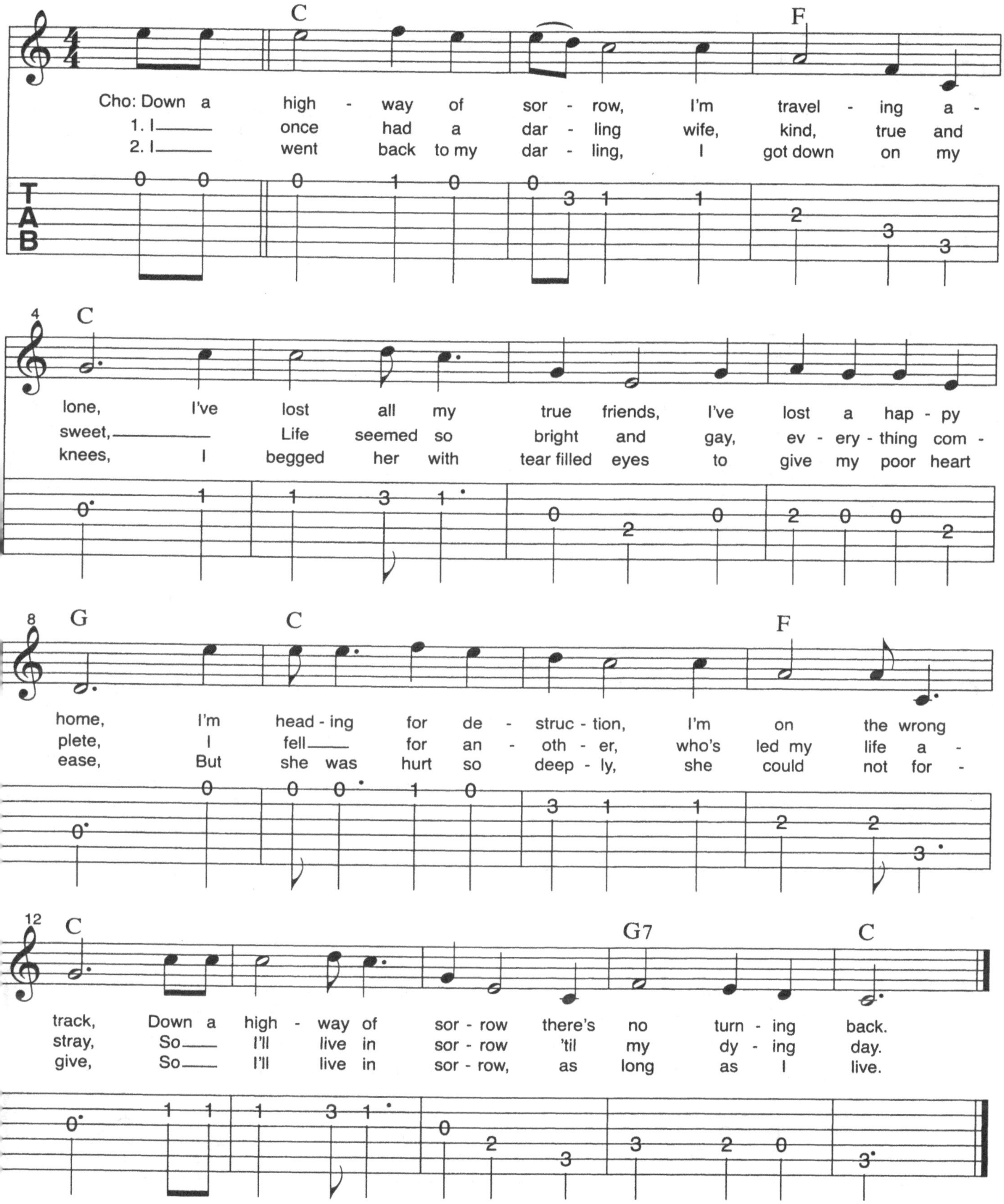

Hills of Roane County

M: G; F: C or D, capo 5 or 7
CD 1-Track 70

Traditional

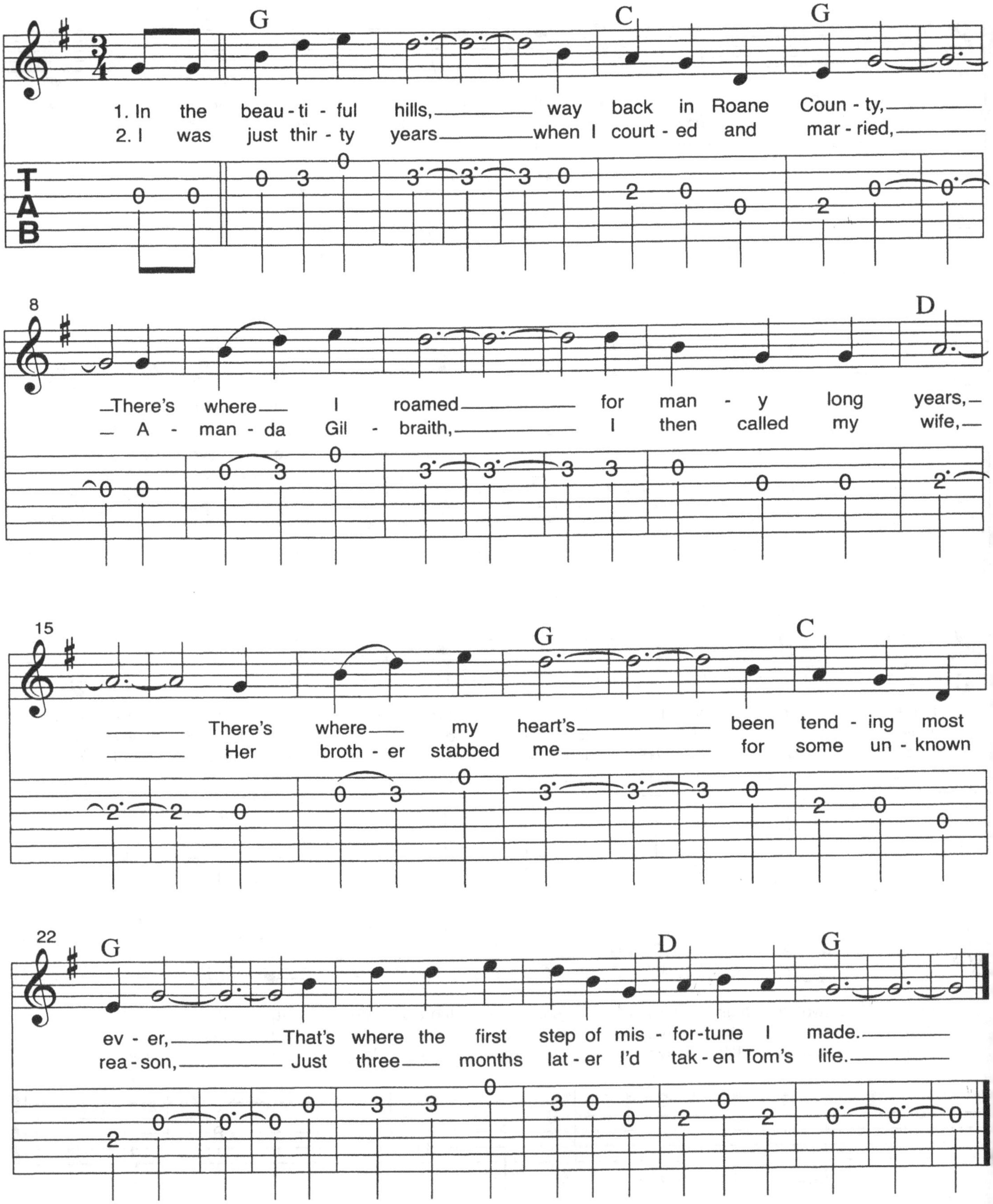

 B. Monroe, Stanley Bros., Blue Sky Boys, Mac Wiseman, T. Rice,

```
                    G          C             G
3. For twenty five years this whole world I rambled,
                                         D
I went to old England to France and to Spain,
                      G          C              G
But I thought of my home way back in Roane County,
                          D            G
I boarded a steamer and came back again.
```

4. I was captured and tried in the village of Kingston,
Not a man in the county would speak one kind word,
When the jury came in with the verdict next morning,
"A lifetime in prison" was the words that I heard.

5. When the train pulled out, poor Mother stood weeping,
And sister she sat, alone with a sigh,
And the last words I heard was, "Willie God bless you,"
Was, "Willie God bless you, God bless you, good bye."

6. Sweet Martha was grave but Corey was better,
There's better and worse, although you can see,
Boys when you write home from the prison in Nashville,
Place one of my songs in your letter for me.

7. In the scorching hot sand of the foundry I'm working,
Toiling and working my poor life away.
They'll measure my grave on the banks of old Cumberland,
Just as soon as I've finished the rest of my days.

8. No matter what happens to me in Roane County,
No matter how long my sentence may be,
I'll love my home way back in Roane County,
It's a' way back down in East Tennessee.

His Eye is on the Sparrow

M: C; F: F or G, capo 5 or 7
CD 1-Track 71

Martin & Gabriel, 1906

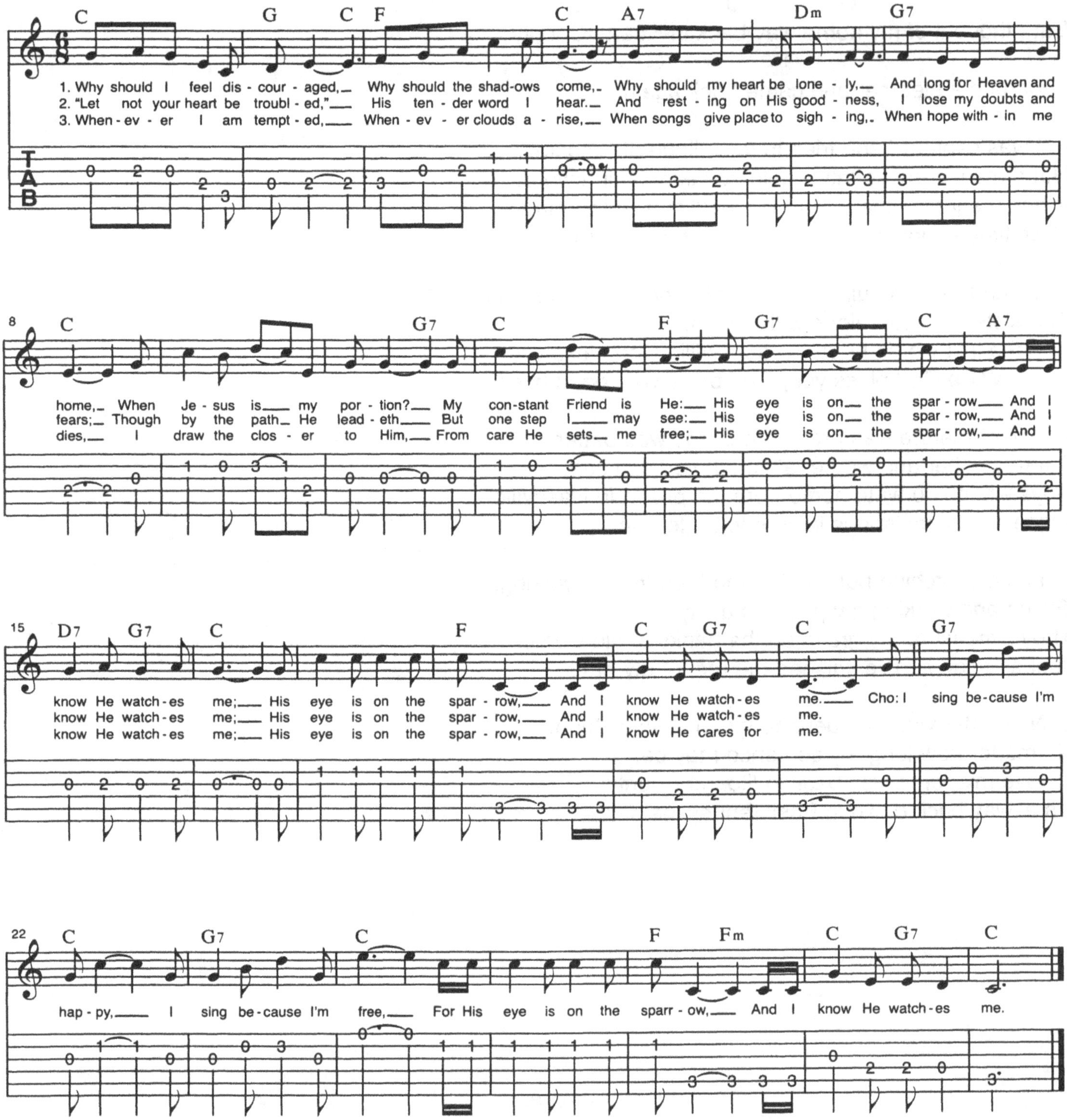

Hold Fast to the Right

M: G; F: C or D, capo 5 or 7
CD 1-Track 72

Traditional

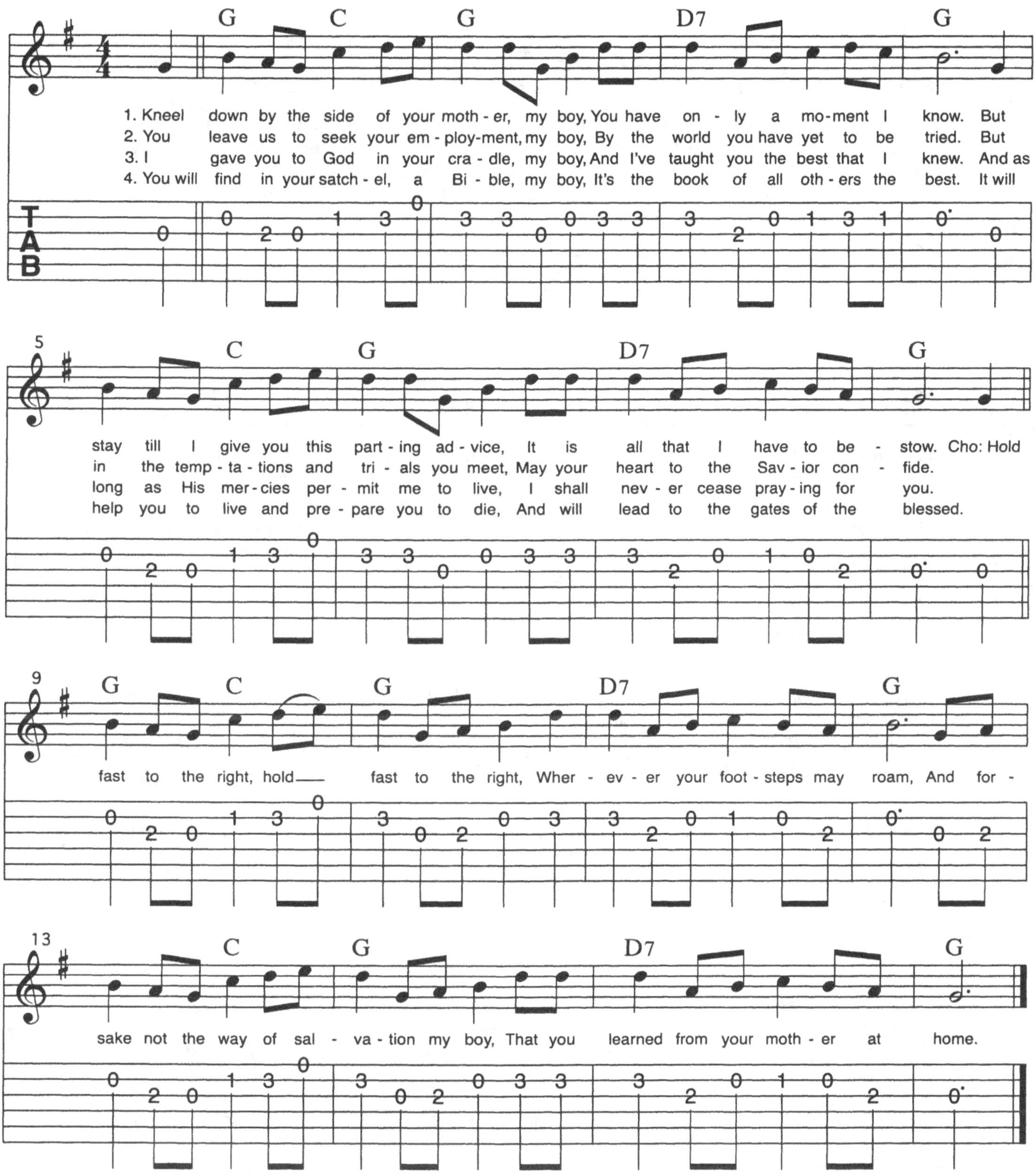

Hold to God's Unchanging Hand

M: F; F: B♭ or C, capo 5 or 7
CD 1-Track 73

Wilson & Eiland

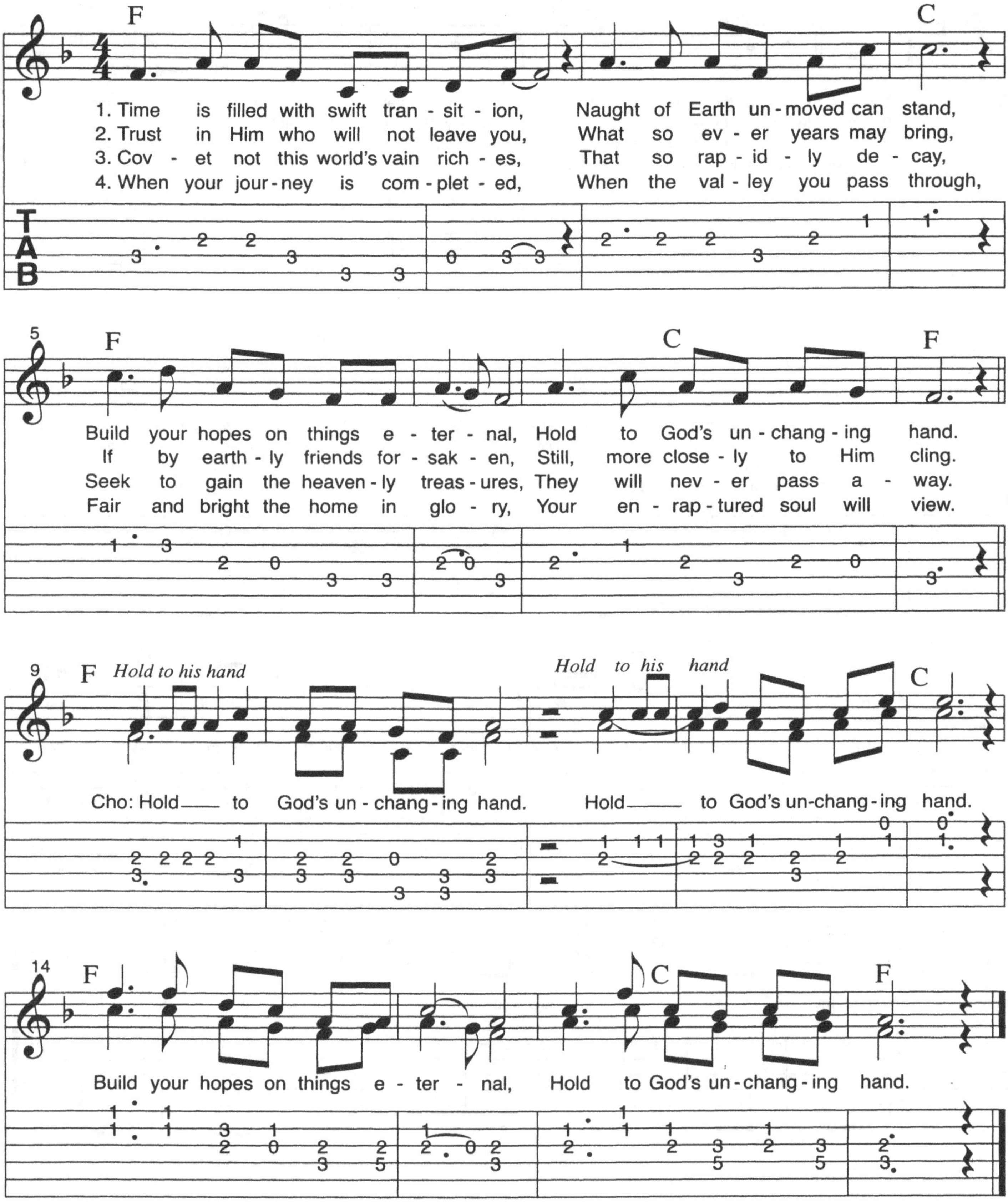

Home Sweet Home

M: D; F: G or A, capo 5 or 7
CD 1-Track 74

Payne & Bishop

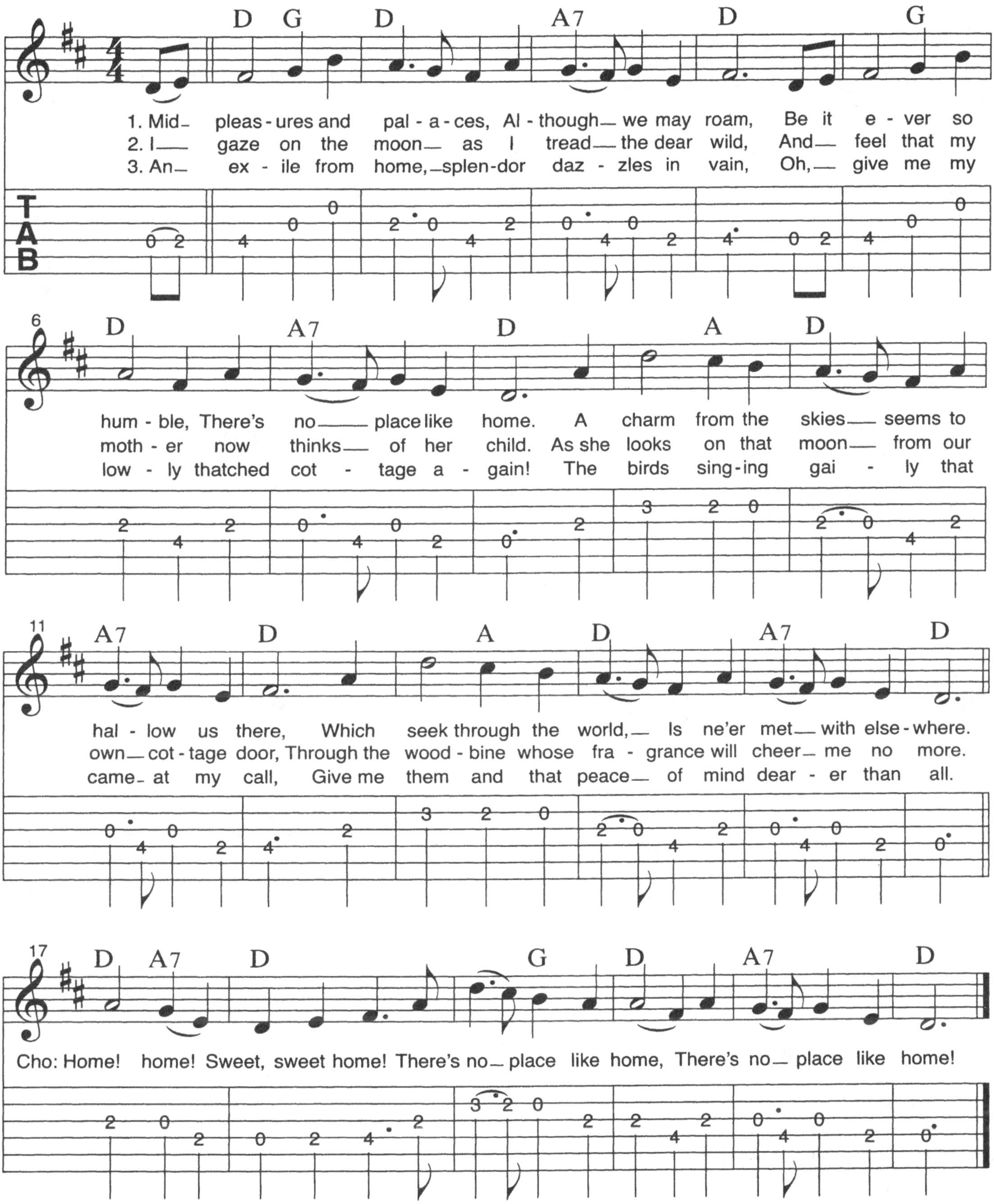

Honey in the Rock

M: G; F: C or D, capo 5 or 7
CD 1-Track 75

Traditional

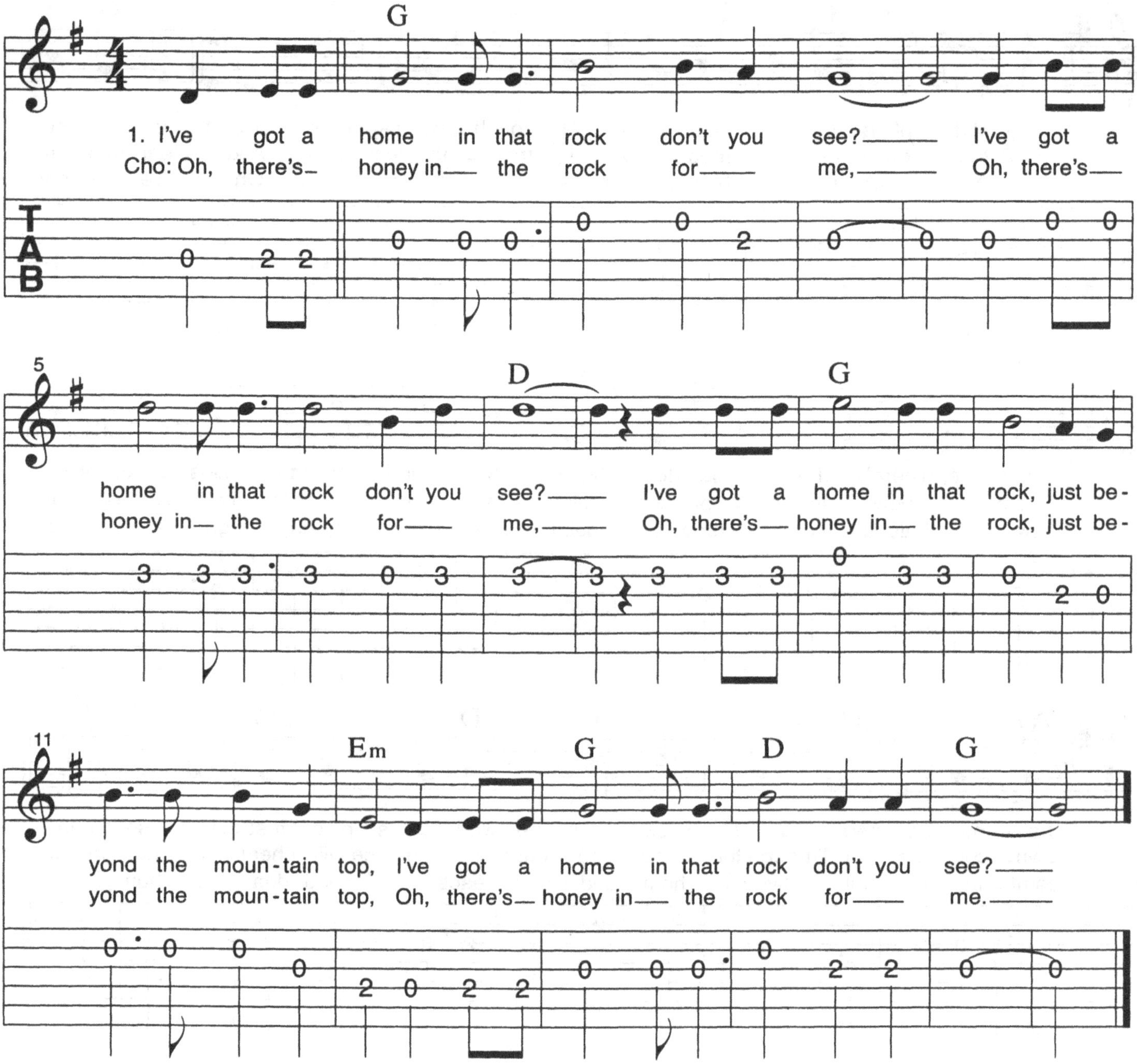


```
                                          G
2. God gave Noah the rainbow sign don't you see?
                                             D
God gave Noah the rainbow sign don't you see?
          G
God gave Noah the rainbow sign,
                                  Em
No more water but the fire next time,
          G                   D          G
God gave Noah the rainbow sign don't you see?
```

3. Oh, I'm climbing up the King's highway, (2X)
Got old Satan on my track,
Never think of looking back,
Oh, I'm climbing up the King's highway.

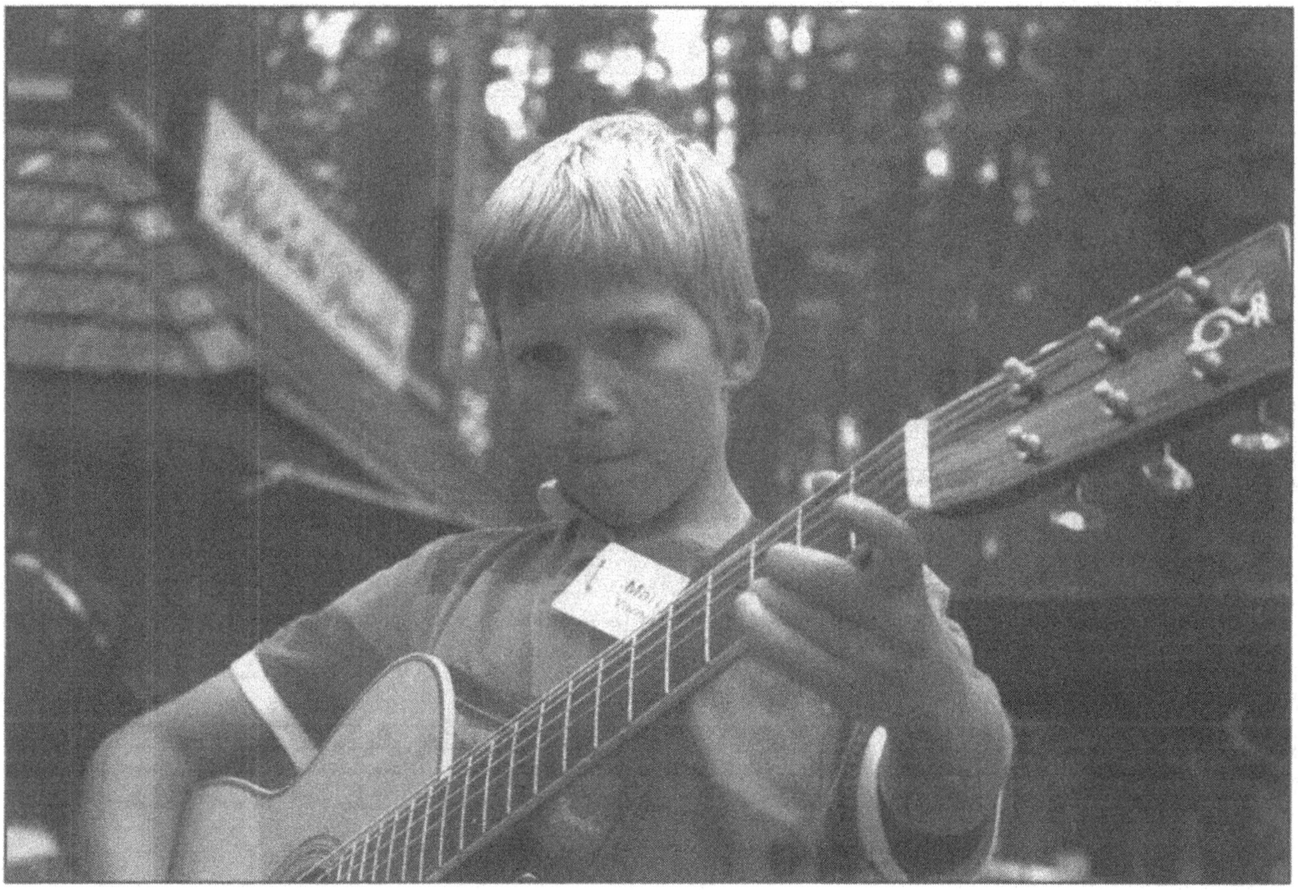

Photo by Bill Evans

Young guitarist Marty Varner is ready for his next jam session!

Hop High Ladies

M: D; F: G or A, capo 5 or 7
CD 1-Track 76

Traditional

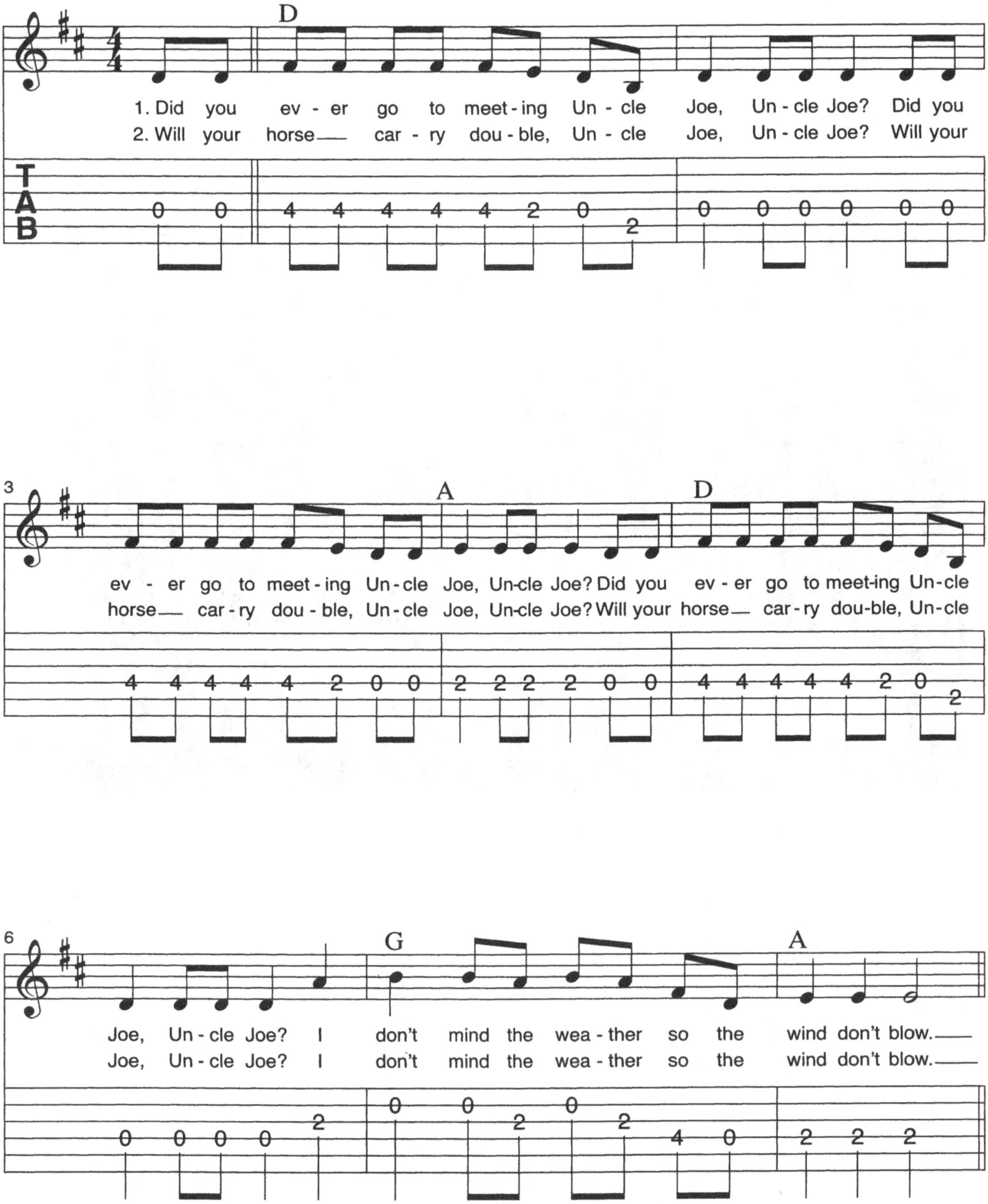

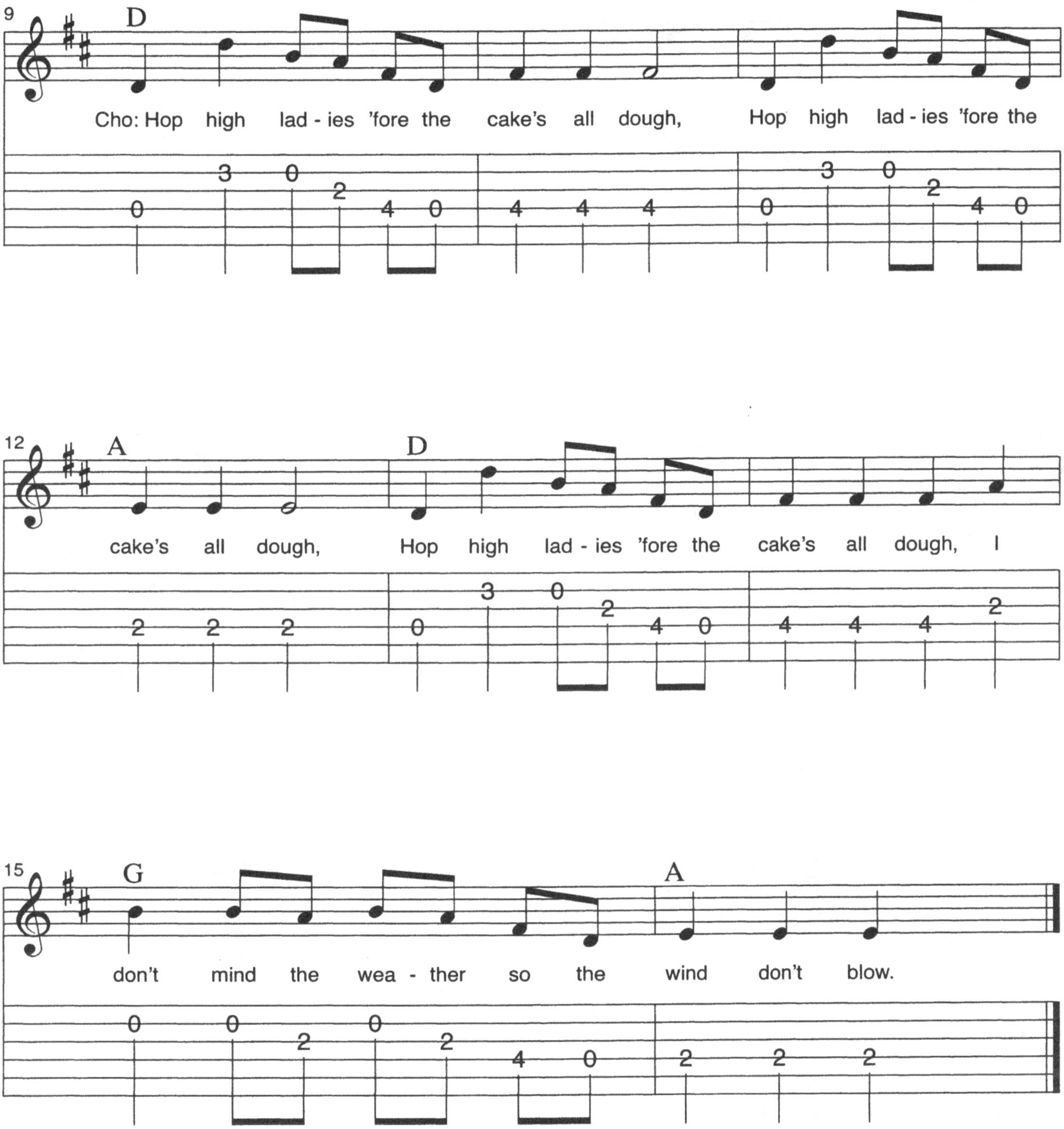
D
Cho: Hop high lad - ies 'fore the cake's all dough, Hop high lad - ies 'fore the
A
D
cake's all dough, Hop high lad - ies 'fore the cake's all dough, I
G
A
don't mind the wea - ther so the wind don't blow.

Hot Corn, Cold Corn

M: C; F: F or G, capo 5 or 7
CD 1-Track 77

Traditional

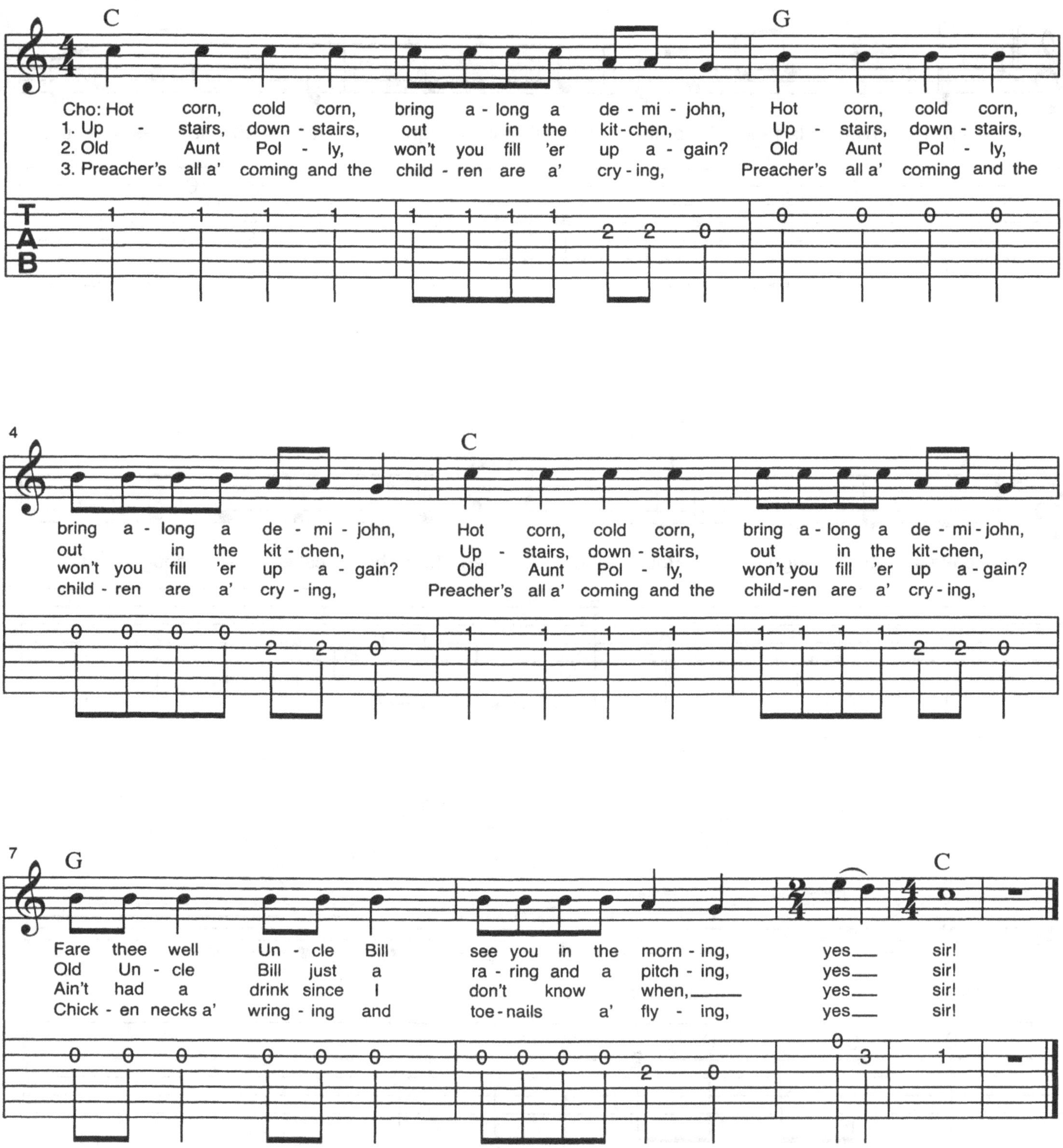

 Flatt & Scruggs, Holy Modal Rounders, Here Today, Grisman, Garcia, Rice, NLCR, Dry Branch Fire Squad, D. Bruce

How Can You Treat Me So?

M: E; F: A or B, capo 5 or 7
CD 1-Track 78

Dix Bruce

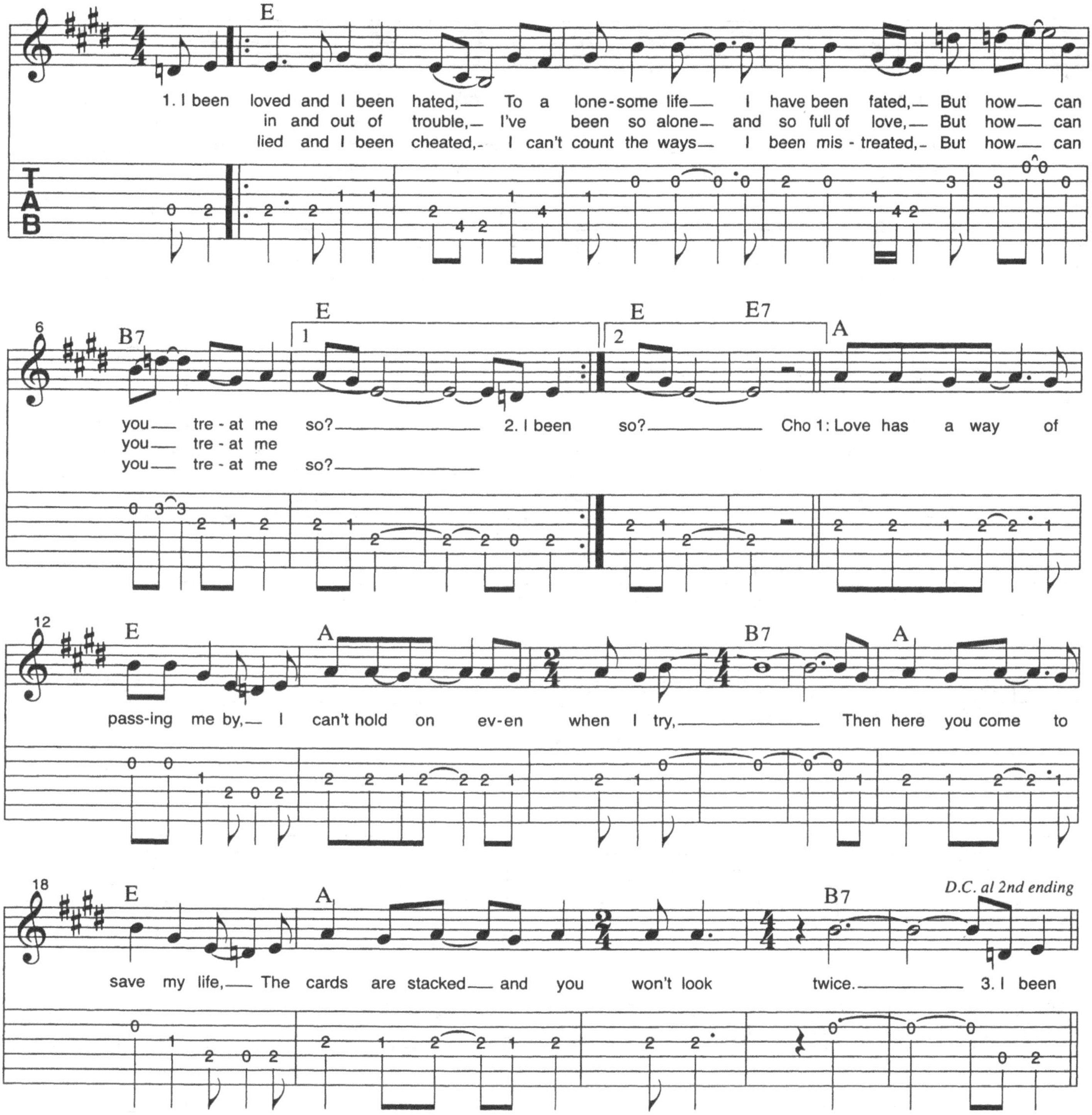

4. I been broke and I been busted, I been robbed by people I trusted,
But how can you treat me so?
I might win and I might lose, I might be in love, I might have the blues,
But how can you treat me so?

(Chords: E over "broke"; B7 over "can", E over "so" in the line "But how can you treat me so?"; E over "win"; B7 over "can", E over "so" in the last line.)

Cho 2: All I ever wanted was you,
I've done my part, baby I been true,
When the whole wide world turned me away,
You opened your arms and you would let me stay.

5. In sickness and in health,
Life can be heaven or it can be hell,
But how can you treat me so?

I Ain't Gonna Work Tomorrow

M: C; F: F or G, capo 5 or 7
CD 1-Track 79

Traditional

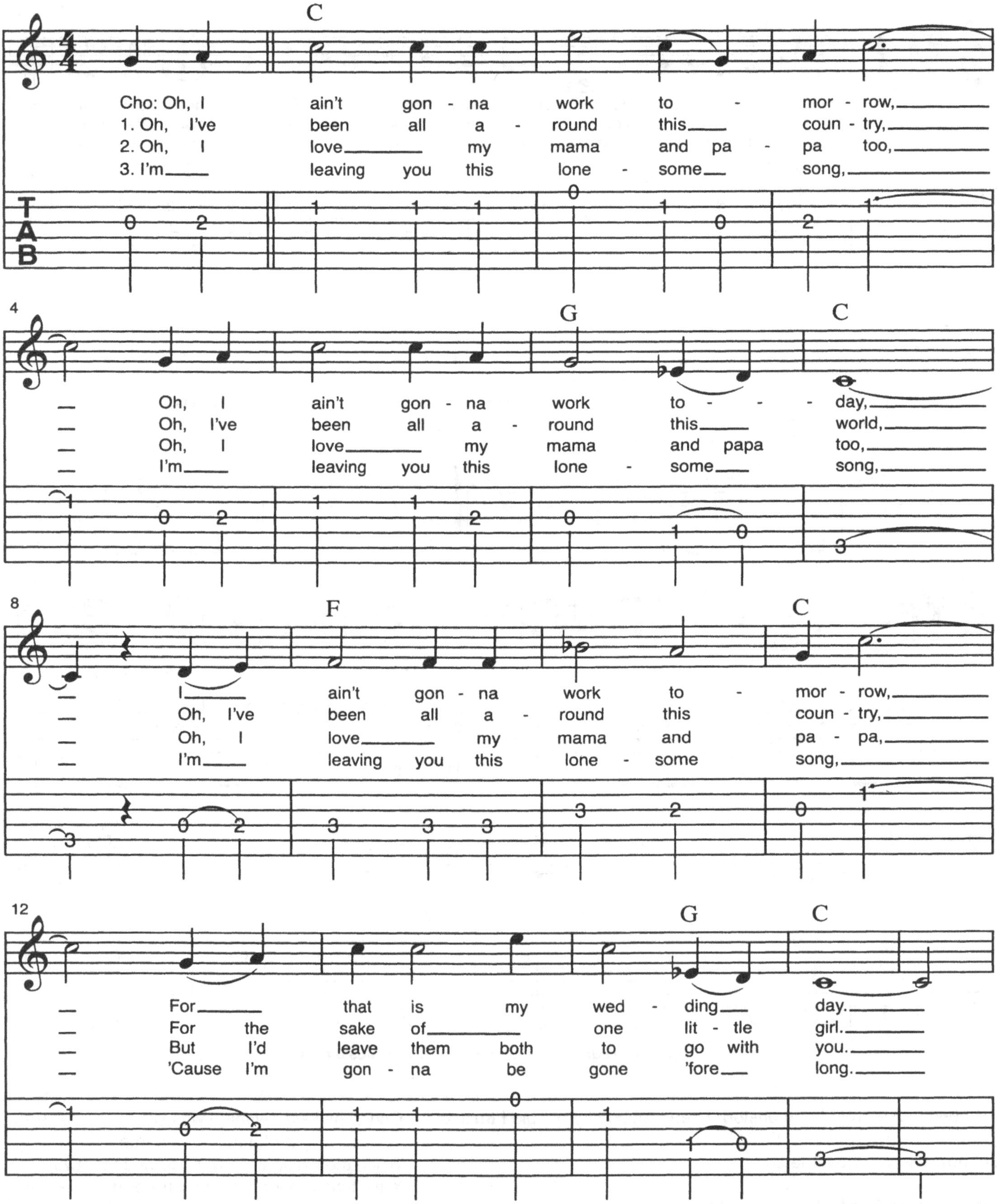

 Carter Fam., Flatt & Scruggs, Country Gentlemen, Louvin Bros.

I Know You Rider

M: A mixolydian; F: D or E mixolydian, capo 5 or 7
CD 1-Track 80

Traditional

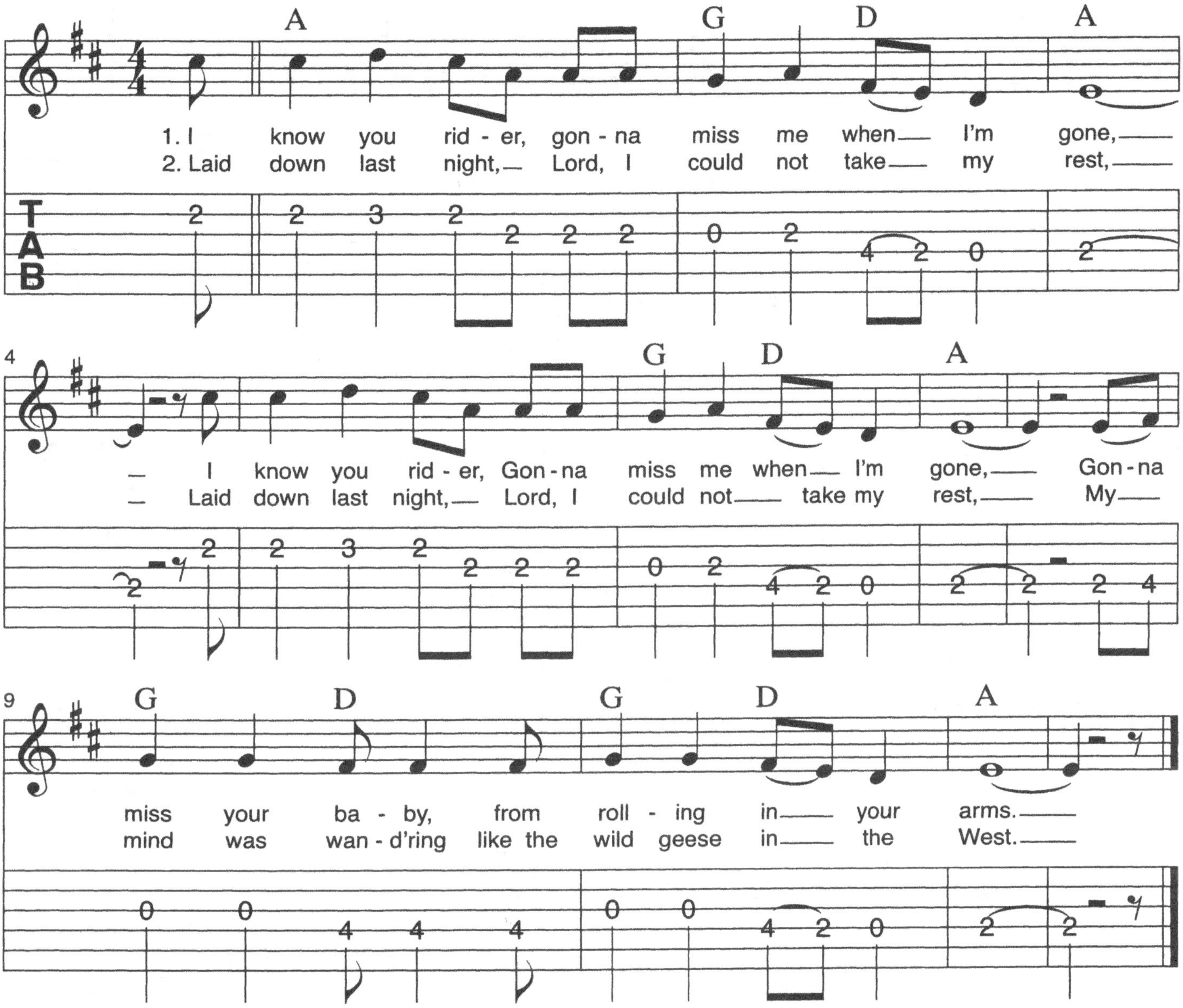

A G D A
3. I'm going down to the river, set in my rockin' chair, (2X)
G D G D A
And if the blues don't find me, gonna rock away from here.

4. I know my baby sure is bound to love me some, (2X)
Throws her arms around me like a circle 'round the sun.

5. The sun's gonna shine in my back door some day, (2X)
The wind's gonna rise and blow my blues away.

6. I wish I was a headlight on a northbound train, (2X)
I'd shine my light through the cold Colorado rain.

7. Just as sure as the bird flies in the sky above, (2X)
Life ain't worth living if you ain't with the one you love.

I Never Will Marry

M: G; F: C or D, capo 5 or 7
CD 1-Track 81, medley pt. 1

Traditional

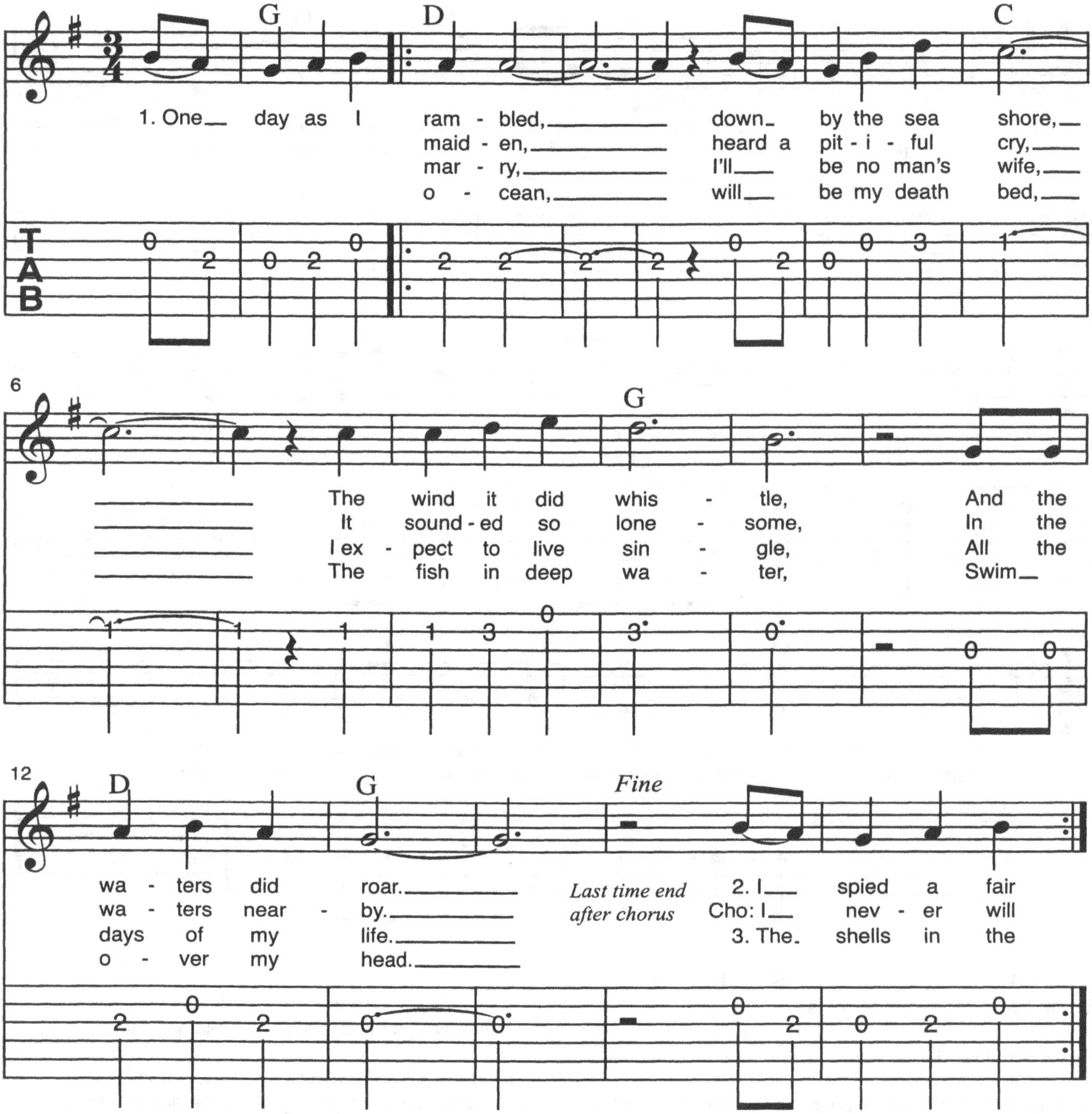


```
G                        D                  C
4. My love's gone and left me, he's the one I adore,
                              G          D          G
He's gone where I never shall see him no more.
```

5. She plunged her dear body, in the water's so deep,
She closed her pretty blue eyes, in the water to sleep.

I Shall Not Be Moved

M: G; F: C or D, capo 5 or 7
CD 1-Track 81, medley pt. 2

Traditional

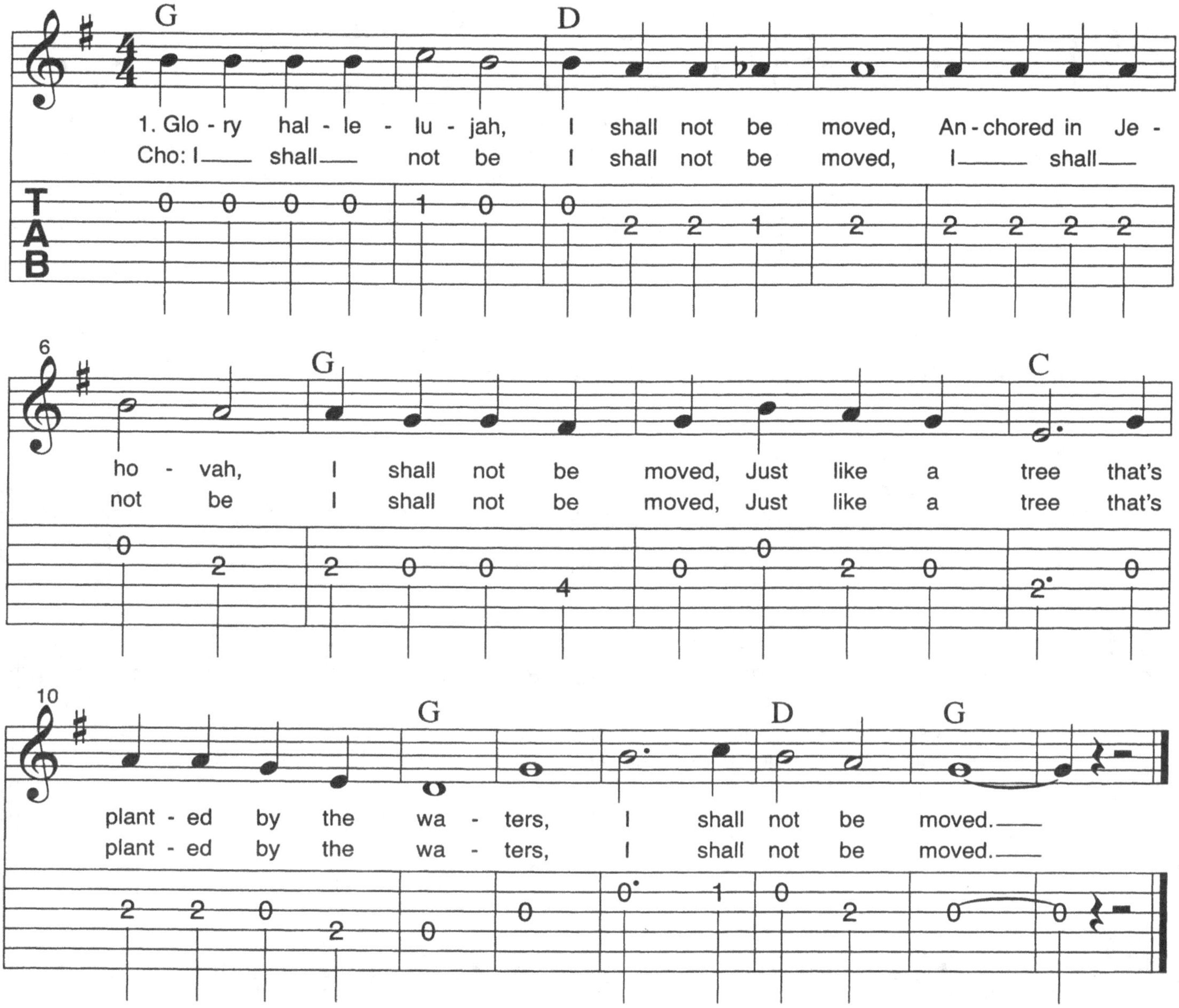


```
G                            D
2. In his love abiding, I shall not be moved,
                             G
And in Him confiding, I shall not be moved.
              C                            G
Just like a tree that's planted by the waters,
          D      G
I shall not be moved.
```

3. Though all Hell assail me, I shall not be moved,
Jesus will not fail me, I shall not be moved. (etc.)

4. Though the tempest rages, I shall not be moved,
On the Rock of Ages, I shall not be moved. (etc.)

I Wonder How the Old Folks Are at Home

M: G; F: C or D, capo 5 or 7
CD 1-Track 82

Lambert & Van der Sloot, 1909

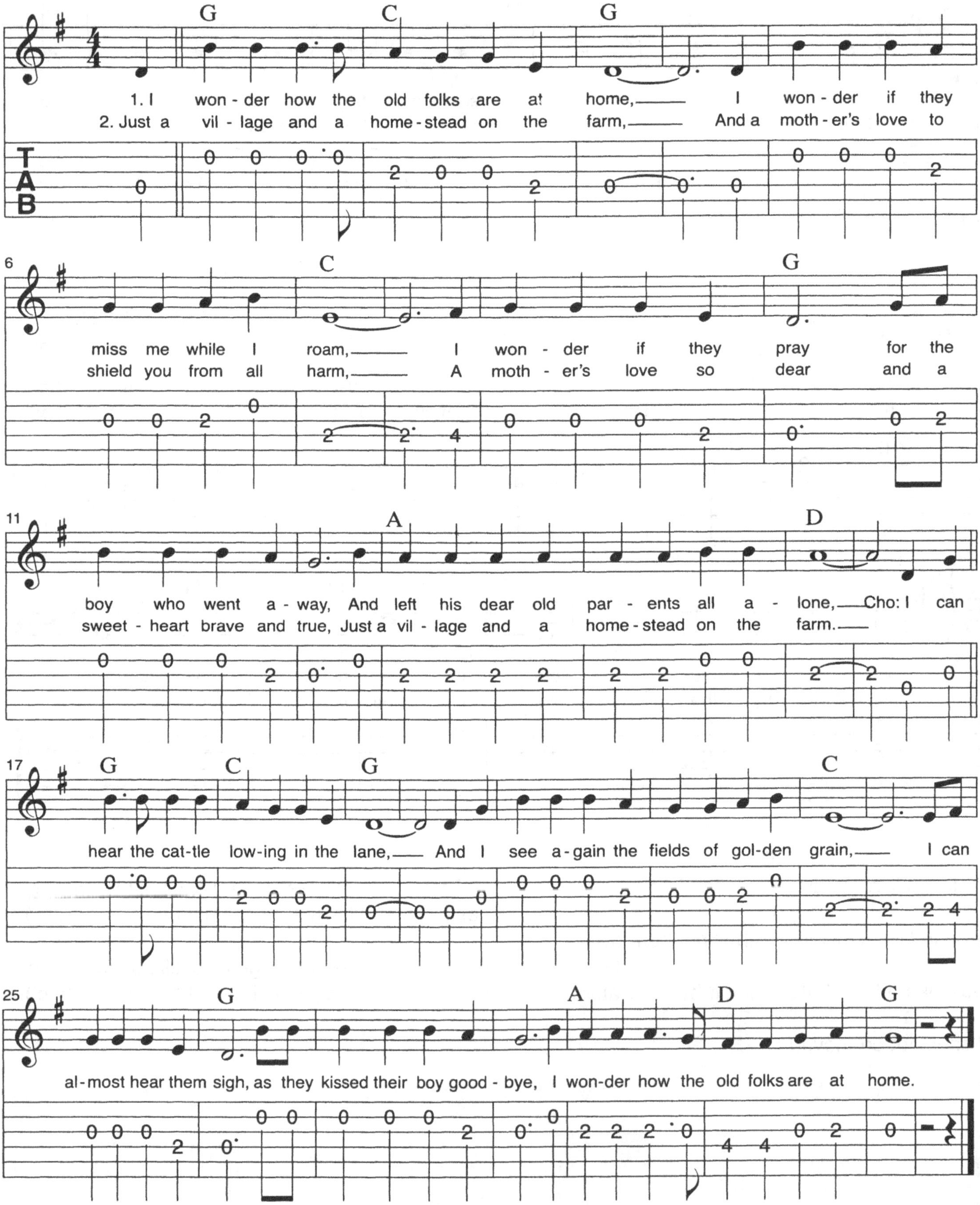

 B. Monroe, R. Stanley, Ken. Colonels, Mac Wiseman, D. Watson, Osborne Bros., Jim & Jesse, Lilly Bros. & D. Stover

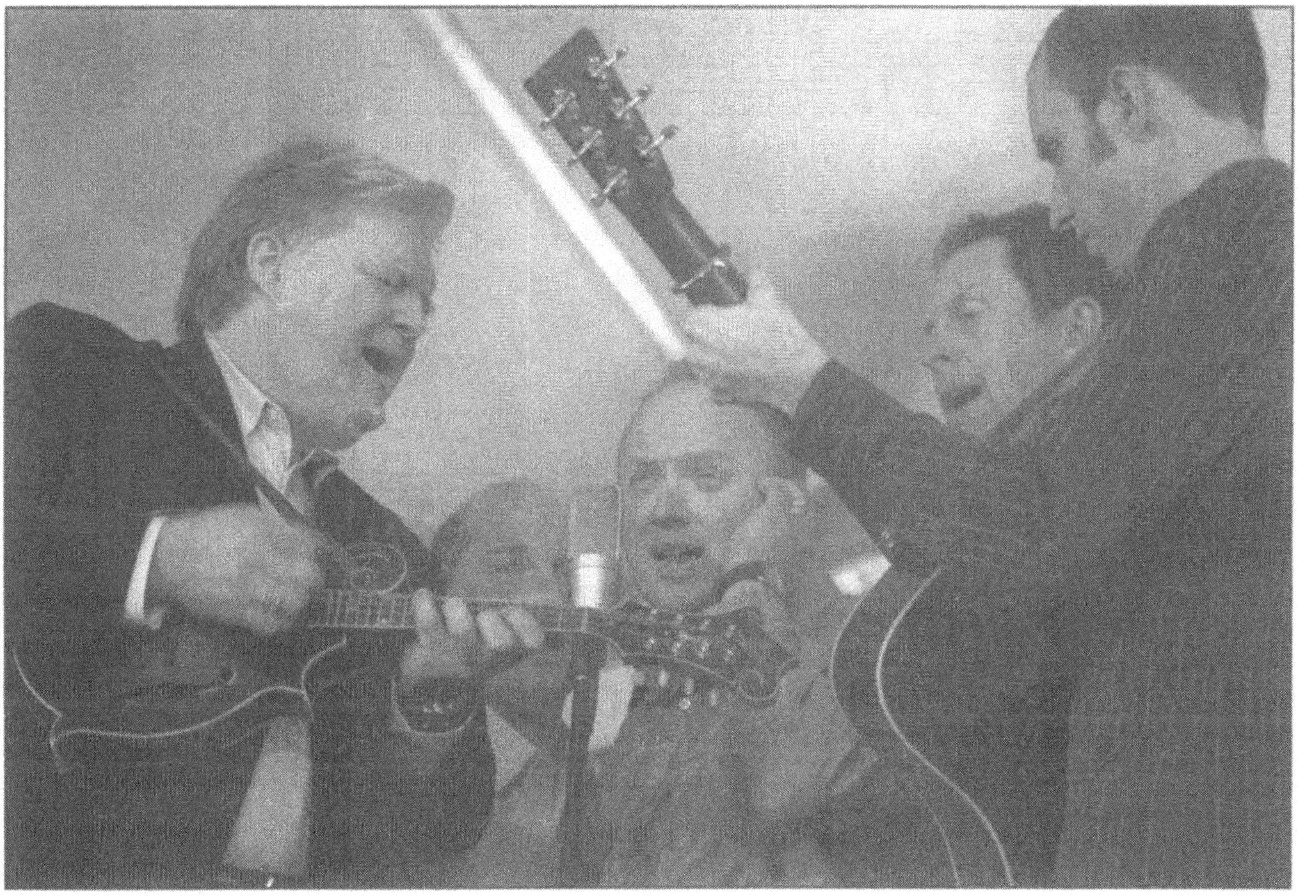

Photo by Bill Evans

Ricky Skaggs, left, and Kentucky Thunder. Band members from left to right are Ricky Skaggs, Darrin Vincent, Jim Mills, Paul Brewster and Cody Kilby.

I'll Be All Smiles Tonight

M: A; F: D or E, capo 5 or 7
CD 1-Track 83

T.B. Ransom, 1879

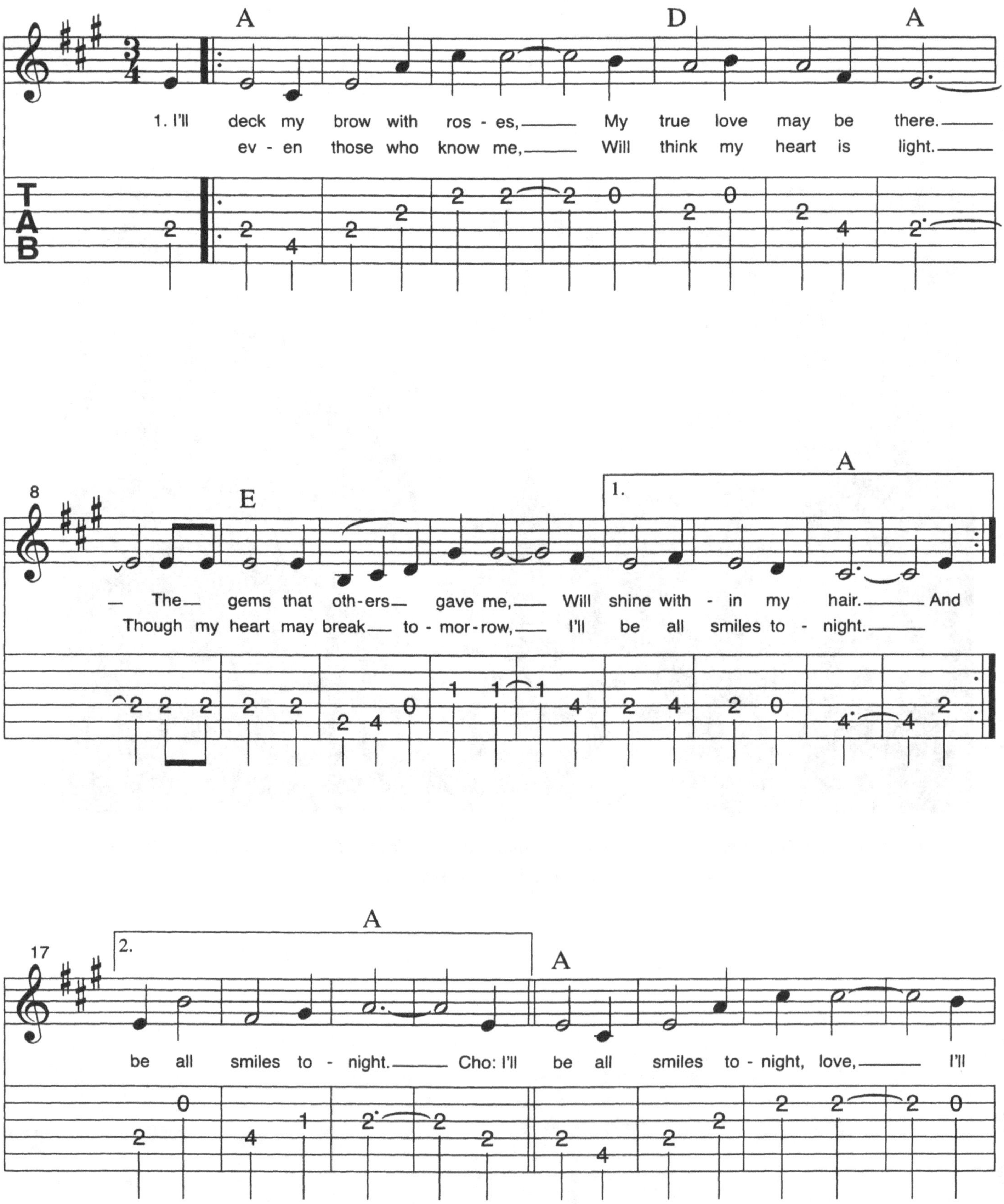

 Carter Fam., B. Clifton, Cox Fam., Louvin Bros., Mac Wiseman

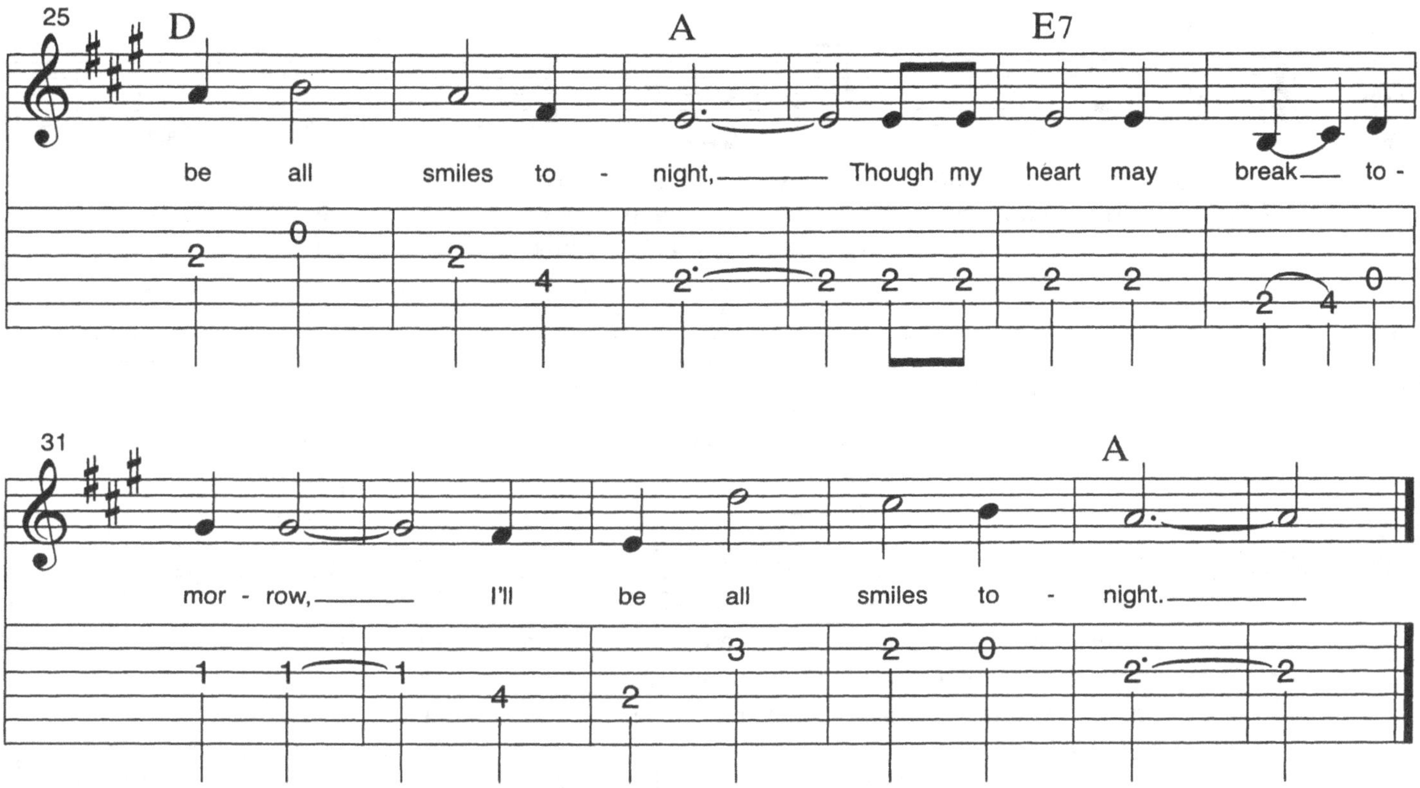


```
     A
2. And when the door he entered,
       D                  A
With a bride upon his arm.
  E
I stood and gazed upon him,
                            A
As though he were some charm.

So, now he smiles on his love,
     D                   A
As once he smiled on me.
     E
He meant not to deceive me,
                           A
There'll be no change in me.
```

(Chorus after each verse)

3. And when the dance commences,
Oh, how I will rejoice,
I'll sing a song he taught me
Without one faltering voice;
When flatterers come around me
They will think my heart is light,
Though my heart will break tomorrow
I'll be all smiles tonight.

4. And when the dance is over,
And all have gone to rest,
I'll think of him, dear mother,
The one that I love best.
He once did love, believe me,
But he's grown cold and strange,
He sought not to deceive me,
False friends have brought this change.

I'll Fly Away

M: G; F: C or D, capo 5 or 7
CD 1-Track 84

A.E. Brumley, 1932

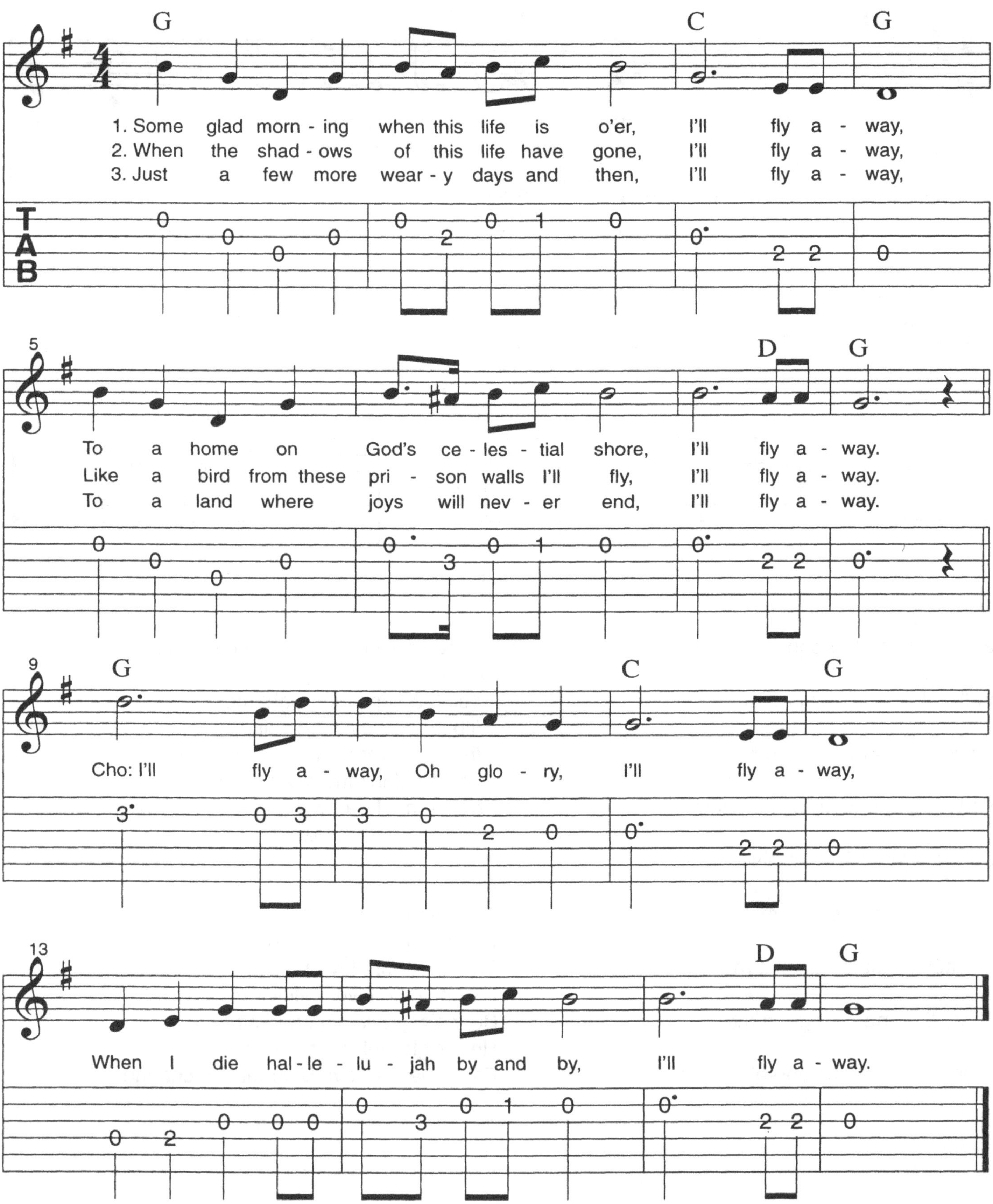

 Stanley Bros., "O Brother" soundtrack, Osborne Bros., Dillards, K. Kallick

I'm Working on a Building

M: D; F: G or A, capo 5 or 7
CD 1-Track 85

Traditional

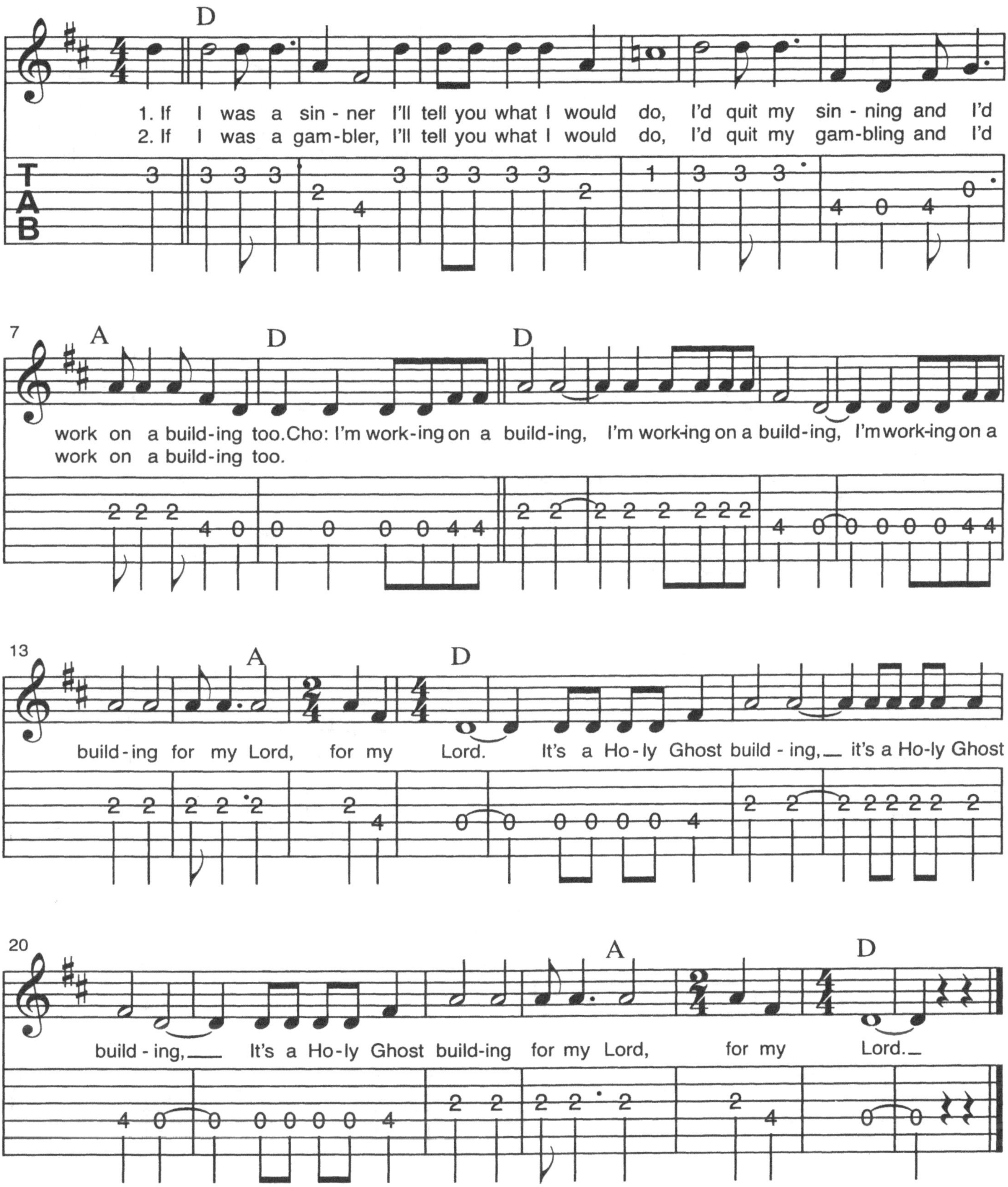

3. If I was a drunkard, I'll tell you what I would do, (etc.)
4. If I was a cheater, I'll tell you what I would do, (etc.)
5. If I was a liar, I'll tell you what I would do, (etc.)
6. If I was a preacher, I'll tell you what I would do, I'd keep on preaching and I'd work on a building too.

Carter Fam., B. Monroe, Stanley Bros., R. Stanley, Ken. Colonels, Hot Rize, Johnson Mtn. Boys, Seldom Scene

In the Garden

M: G; F: C or D, capo 5 or 7
CD 1-Track 86

C.A. Miles, 1912

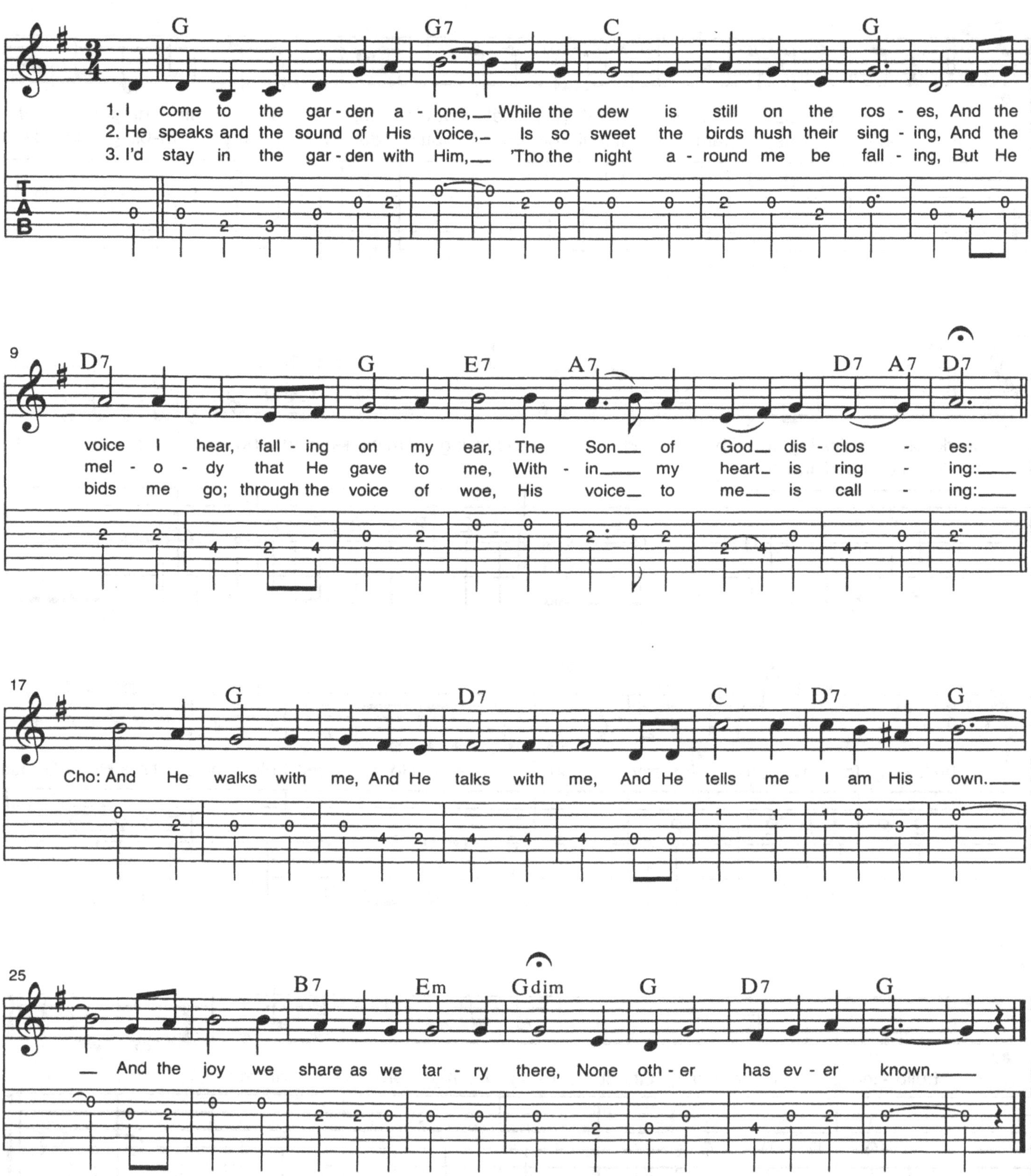

In the Pines

M: D; F: G or A, capo 5 or 7
CD 1-Track 87

Traditional

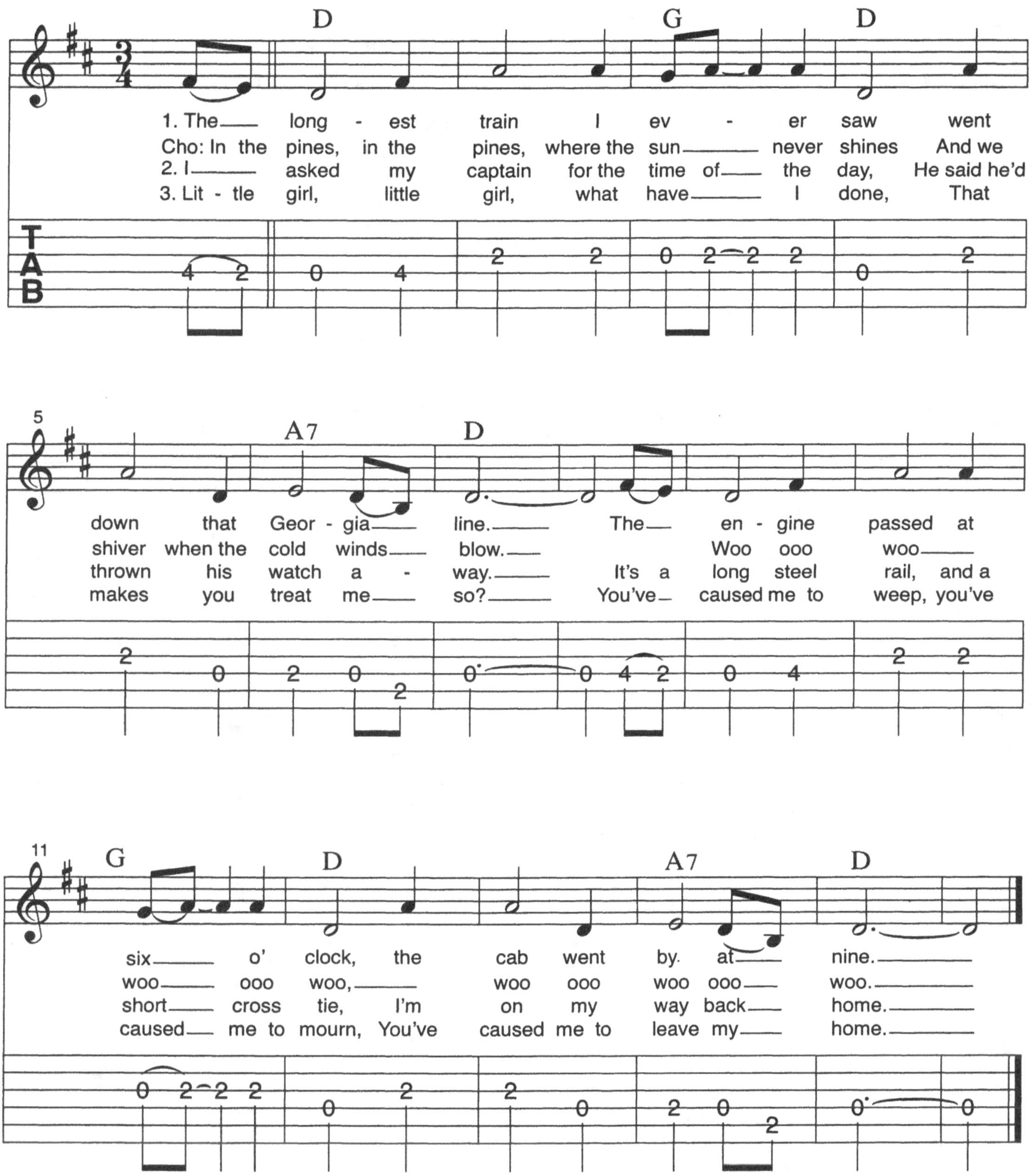

B. Monroe, Jimmy Martin, R. Stanley, C. White, Ken. Colonels, Boone Creek, Grateful Dead, Louvin Bros., Mac Wiseman, Osborne Bros., Seldom Scene

It's Mighty Dark to Travel

M: G; F: C or D, capo 5 or 7
CD 1-Track 88, medley pt. 1

Bill Monroe

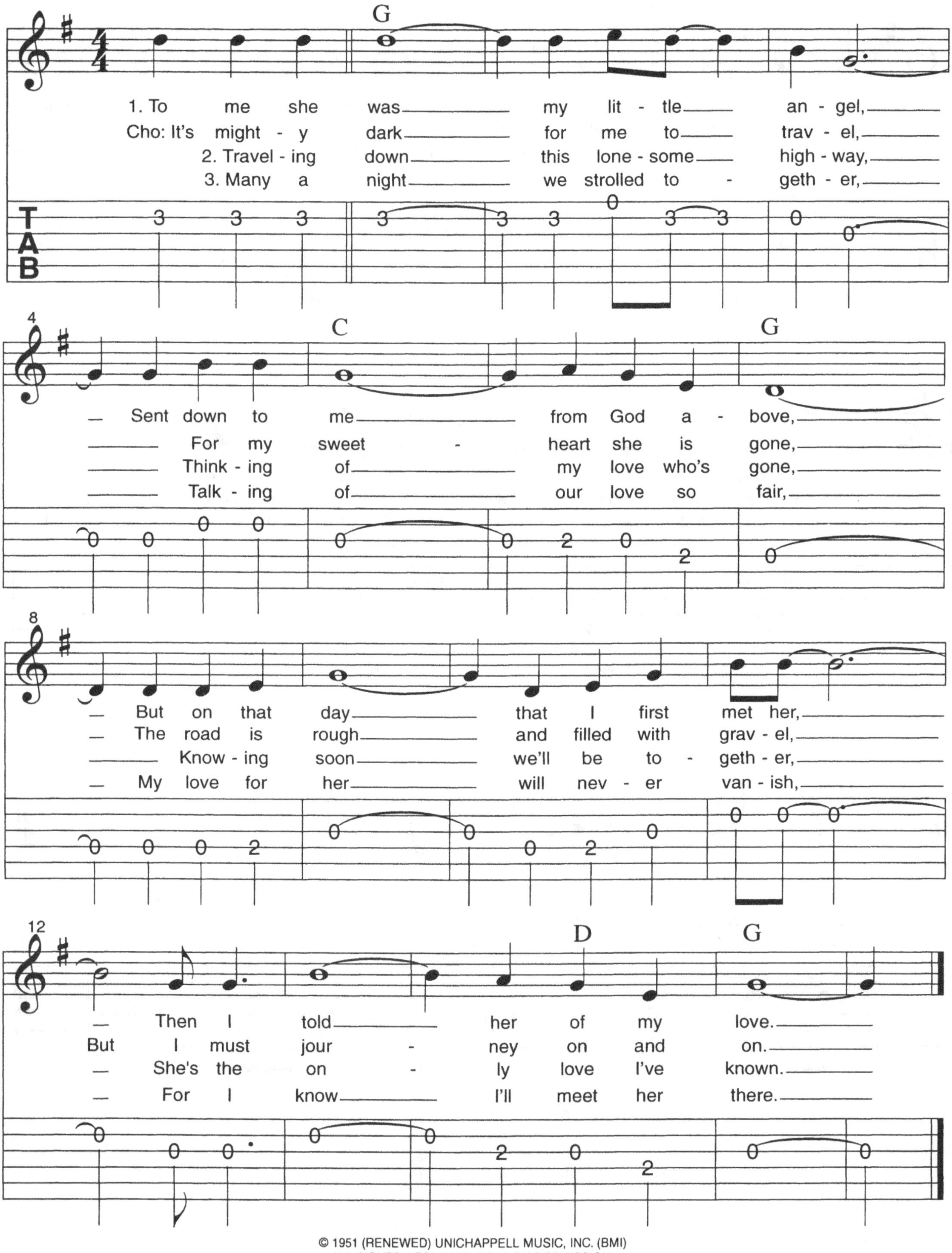

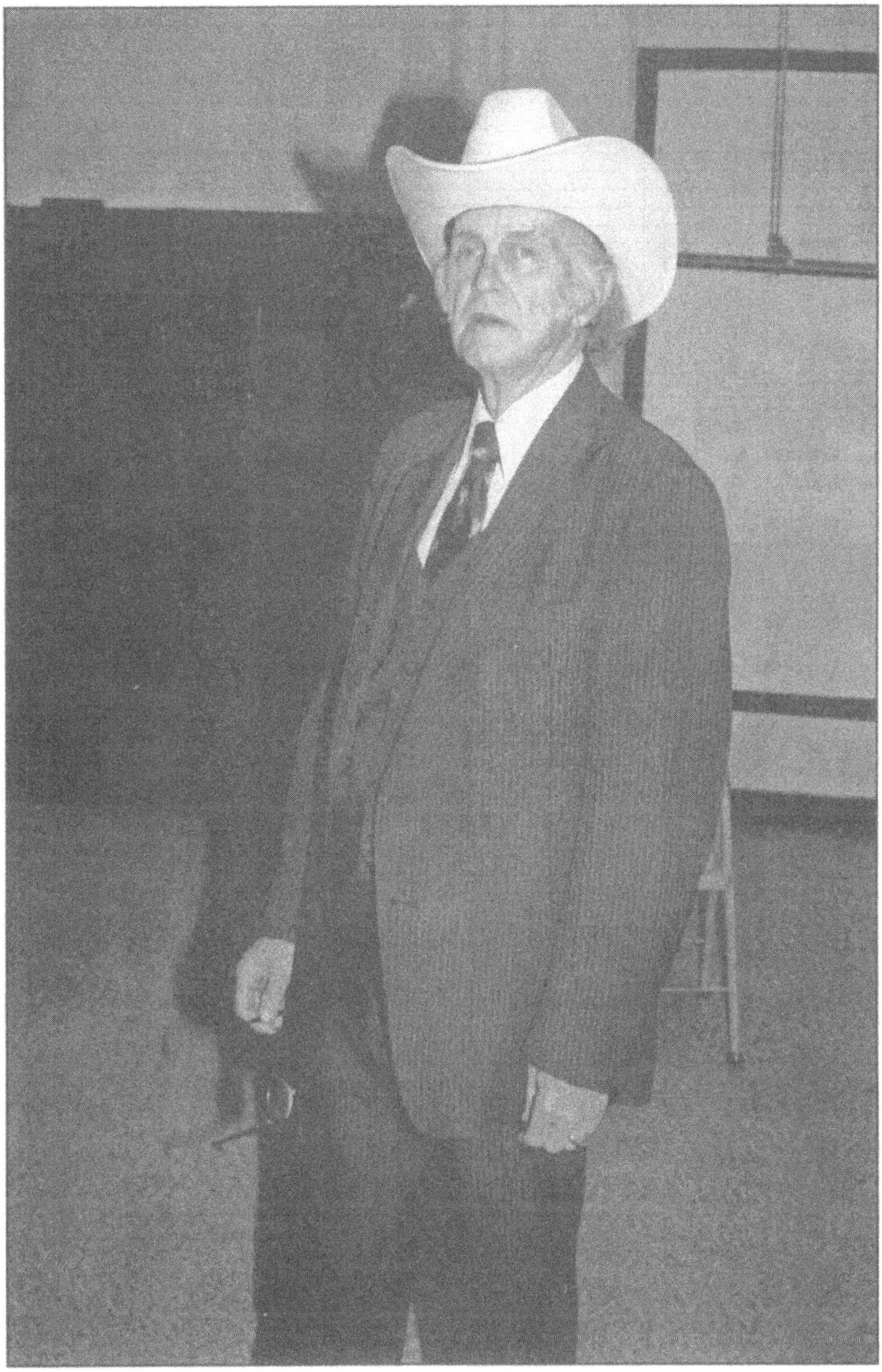

Bill Monroe, the Father of Bluegrass in 1980.

Jesse James

M: G; F: C or D, capo 5 or 7
CD 1-Track 88, medley pt. 2

Garshade, ca. 1882

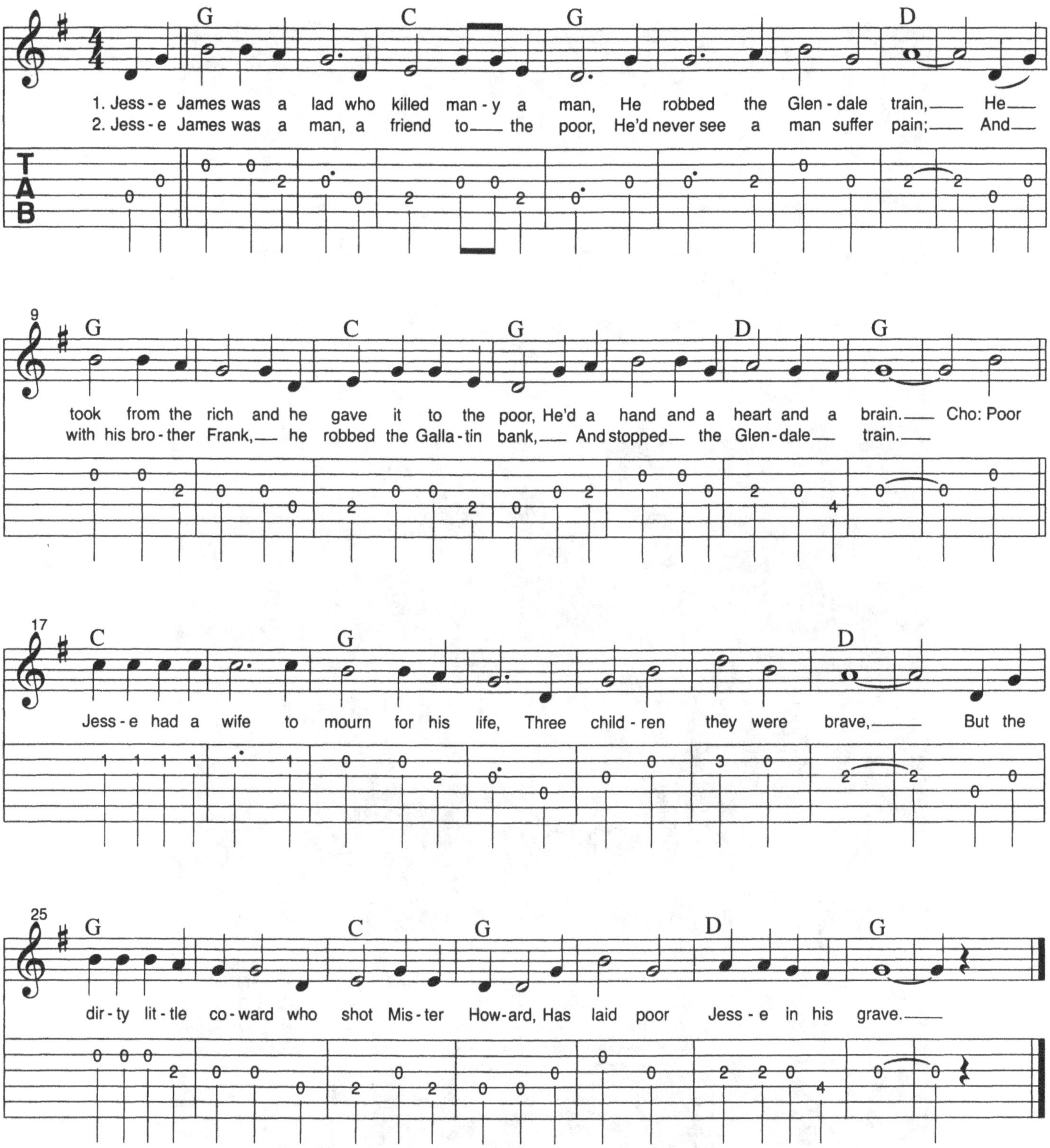

 R. Stanley, Osborne Bros., Fiddlin' John Carson, Country Gentlemen, W. Guthrie

```
            G                                         C                      G
3. It was on a Wednesday night and the moon was shining bright,
                                    D
They robbed the Glendale train,
            G                               C               G
And the people they did say, for many miles away,
                        D                     G
It was robbed by Frank and Jesse James.
```

(Repeat chorus after each verse)

4. It was with his brother Frank that he robbed the Gallatin bank,
And carried the money from the town;
It was in this very place that they had a little chase,
And they shot Captain Sheets to the ground.

5. They went to the crossing, not very far from there,
And there they did the same;
With the agent on his knees, he delivered up the keys,
To the outlaws, Frank and Jesse James.

6. It was Robert Ford, that dirty little coward,
I wonder how he does feel,
He ate Jesse's bread and he slept in Jesse's bed,
Then he laid poor Jesse in his grave.

7. It was on a Saturday night and Jesse was at home
Talking with his family brave,
Robert Ford came along like a thief in the night,
And laid poor Jesse in his grave.

8. The people held their breath when they heard of Jesse's death,
And wondered how he ever came to die.
It was one of the gang, called little Robert Ford,
He shot poor Jesse on the sly.

9. Jesse went to his rest with his hand on his breast,
The devil will be upon his knee,
He was born one day in the county of Clay,
And came from a solitary race.

Jimmie Brown, the Newsboy

M: D; F: G or A, capo 5 or 7
CD 1-Track 89

W.S. Hays, 1875

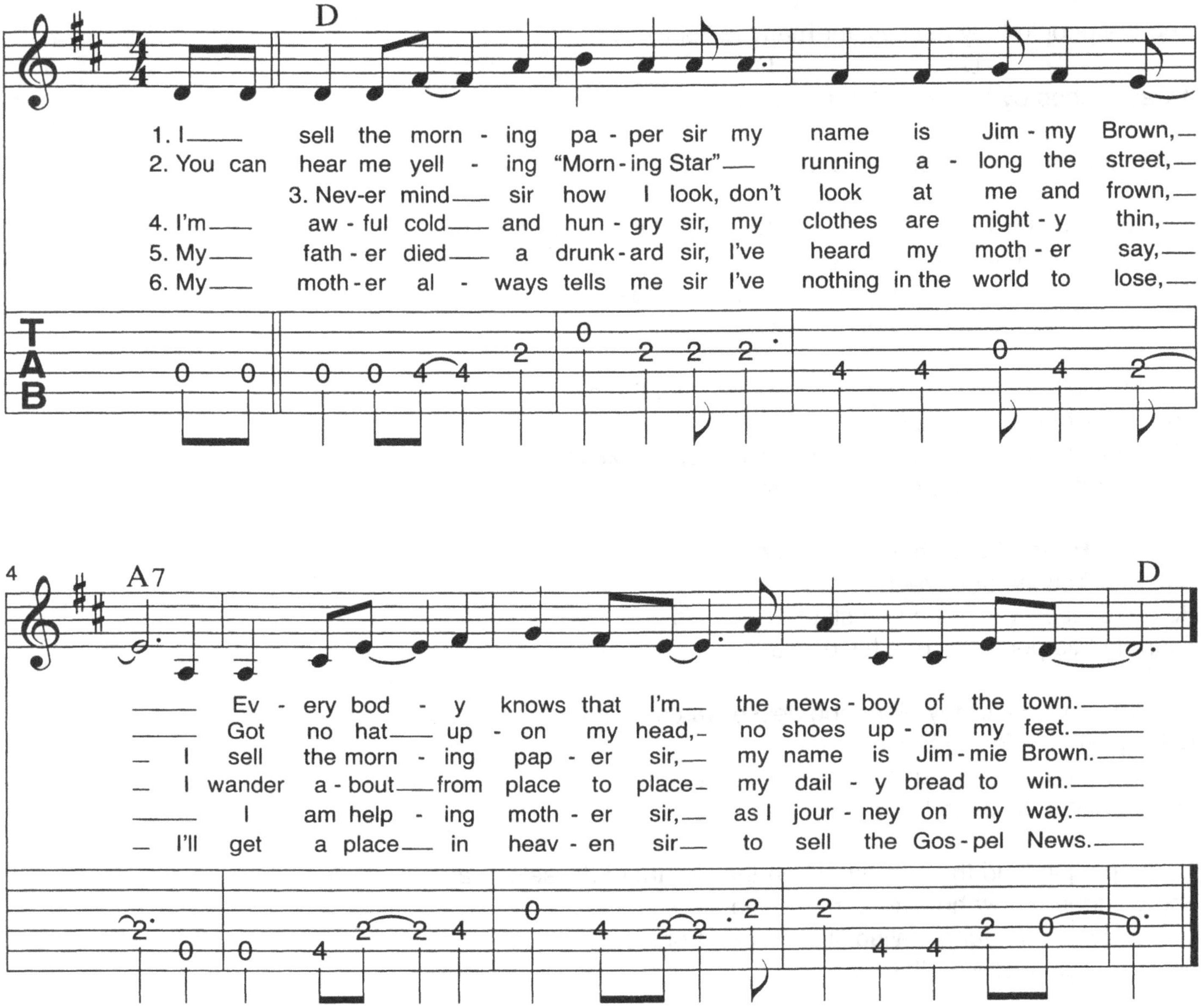

 Carter Fam., Flatt & Scruggs, B. Monroe, C. White, Mac Wiseman

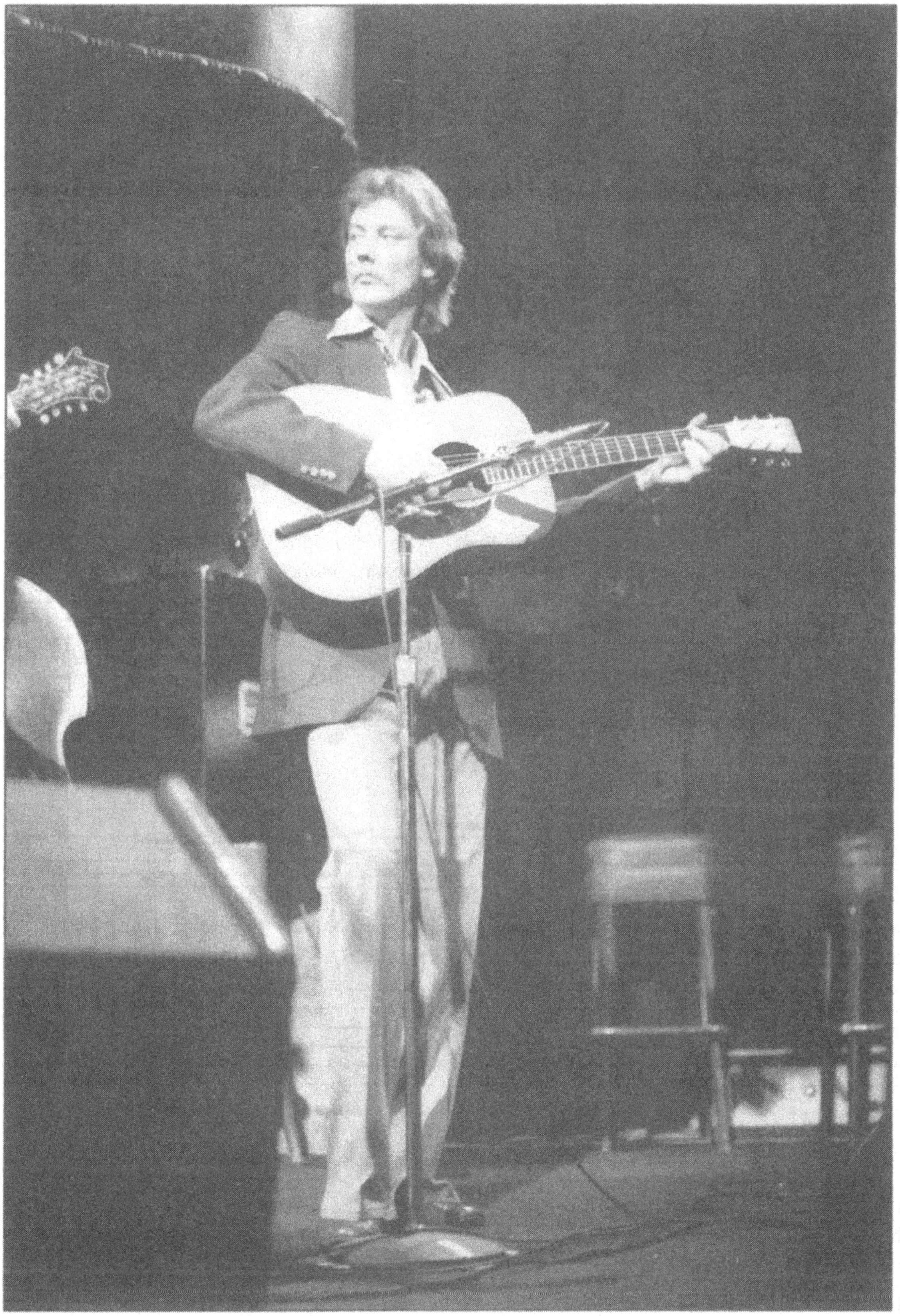

Photo by Dix Bruce

Tony Rice, early 1980s, set new standards of excellence for both lead and rhythm acoustic guitar. He is as well known for his work in bluegrass as with more modern new acoustic groups like The David Grisman Quintet.

John Hardy

M: G; F: C or D, capo 5 or 7
CD 1-Track 90

Traditional

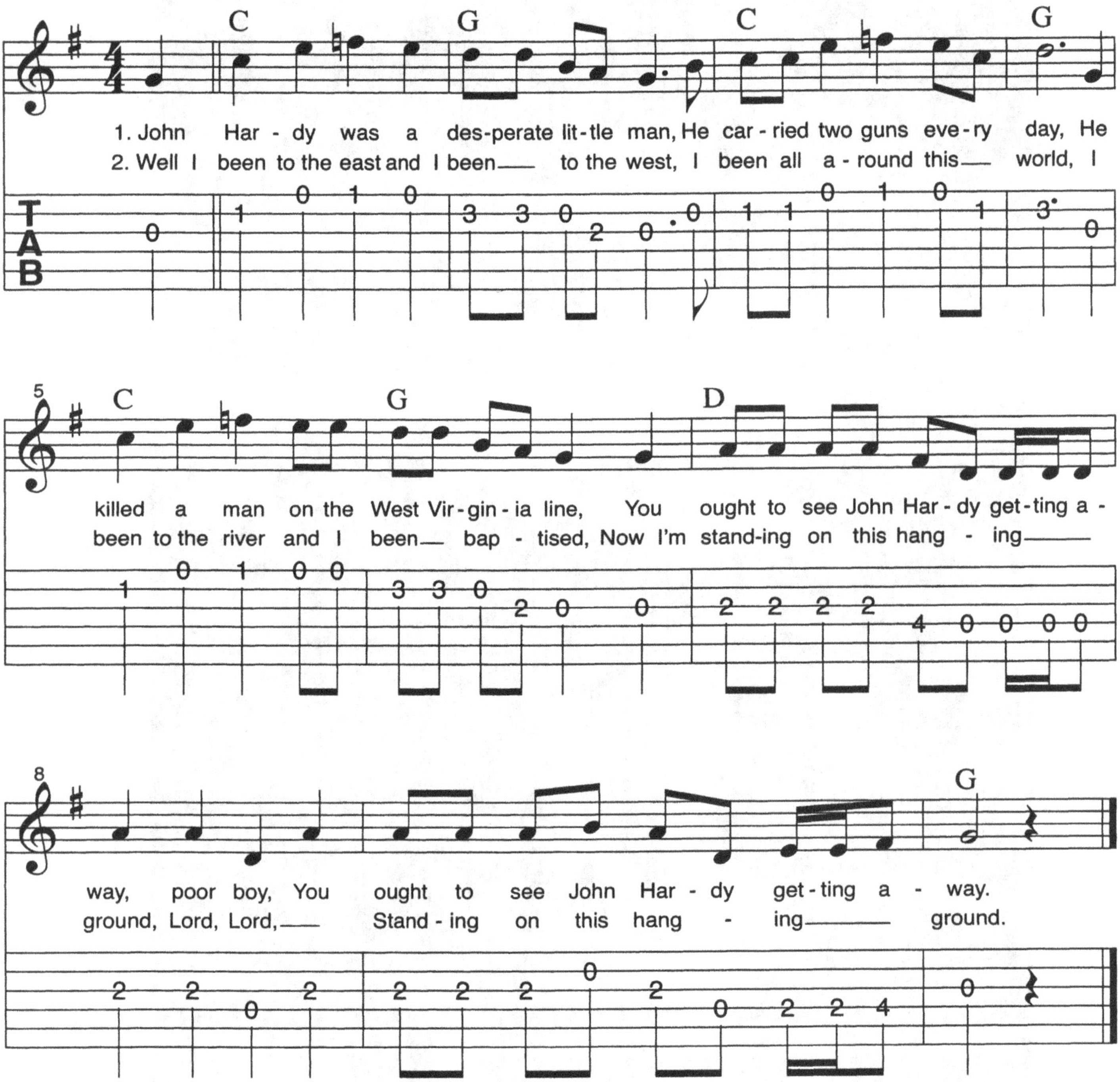

 Carter Fam., Flatt & Scruggs, B. Monroe. Ken. Colonels, Poor Richard's Almanac

C G
3. Hangman, hangman, hold your rope,
C G
Just a little while,
C G
I thought I heard my father's voice,
D
He travelled ten thousand long miles, Lord, Lord,
G
Travelled ten thousand long miles.

4. Did you bring me any silver or gold,
Or money to pay my fee?
Or did you come to see me hung,
Upon this hanging tree, Lord, Lord,
Upon this hanging tree?

5. No, I didn't bring no silver nor gold,
Nor money to pay your fee,
But I did come to see you hung,
Upon that hanging tree, Lord, Lord,
Upon that hanging tree.

6. Hangman, hangman, hold your rope,
Just a little while,
I thought I heard my sweetheart's voice,
She travelled ten thousand long miles, Lord, Lord,
Travelled ten thousand long miles.

7. Oh yes, I brought that silver and gold,
And money to pay your fee,
I have come for to take you home,
And keep you there with me, Lord, Lord,
And keep you there with me.

8. Well, John Hardy run for that old state line,
It was there he thought he'd go free,
But a man walked up and took him by the arm,
Saying "Johnny walk along with me, Lord, Lord,
Johnny walk along with me."

9. Well the first one to visit John Hardy in his cell,
Was a little girl dressed in blue,
She came down to that old jail cell,
Singing "Johnny, I've been true to you, Lord knows,
Johnny I've been true to you."

10. Then the next one to visit John Hardy in his cell,
A little girl dressed in red,
She came down to that old jail cell,
Singing "Johnny, I'd rather see you dead, Lord, Lord,
God knows, Johnny I'd rather see you dead."

11. John Hardy stood in his old jail cell,
The tears running down from his eyes,
He said "I've been the death of many poor boy,
But my six-shooter never told a lie, Lord, Lord,
No my six-shooter never told a lie."

John Henry

M: C; F: F or G, capo 5 or 7
CD 1-Track 91

Traditional

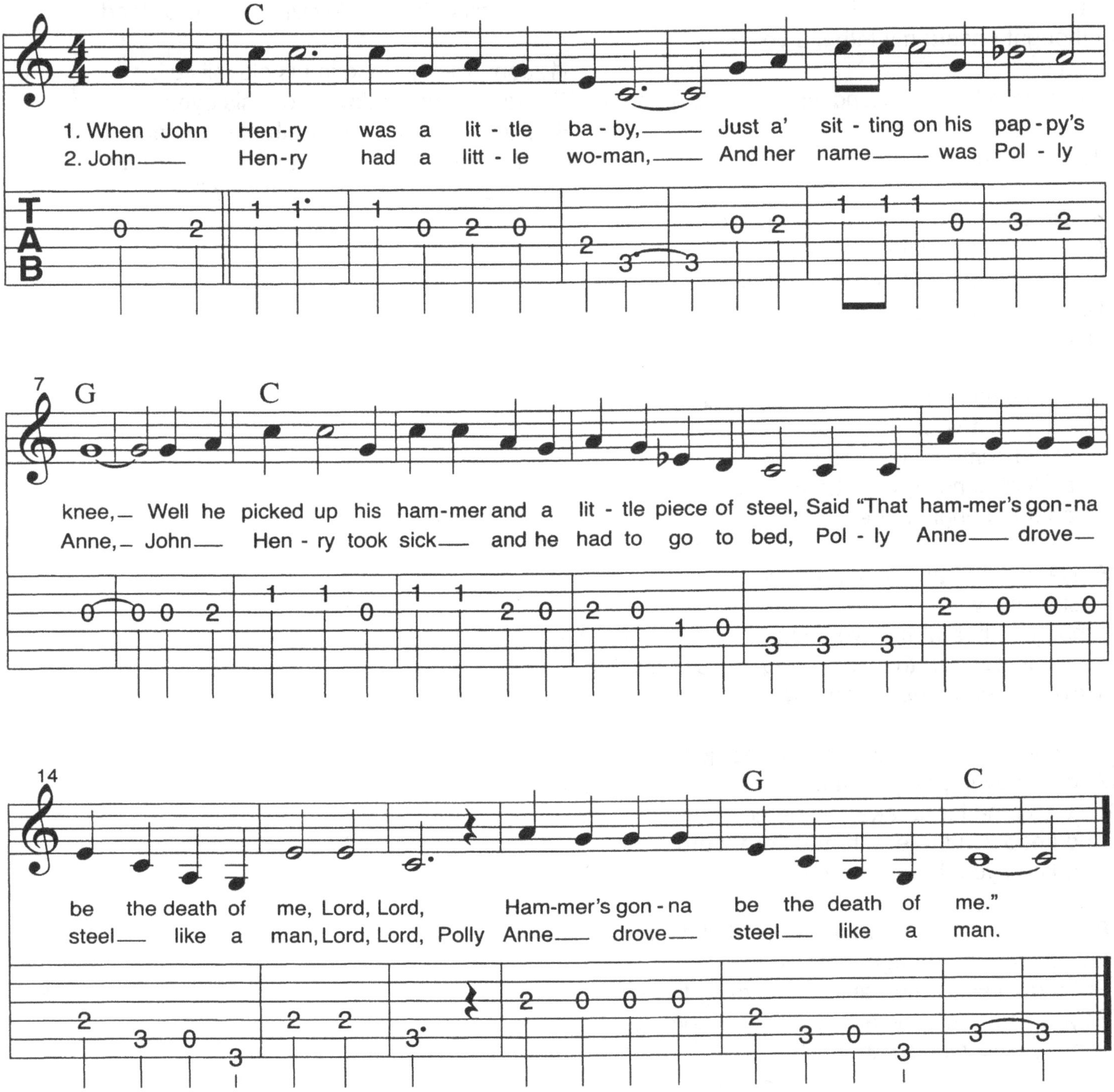

 B. Monroe, Flatt & Scruggs, Stanley Bros., R. Stanley, Jimmy Martin, Ken. Colonels, D. Watson, W. Guthrie, Skillet Lickers, Fiddlin' John Carson, Dry Branch Fire Squad

C
3. Captain said to John Henry,
                                             G
"Gonna bring me a steam drill 'round,
          C
Gonna take that steam drill out on the job,
Gonna drive that steel on down, Lawd, Lawd,
                           G   C
Gonna drive that steel on down."

4. John Henry told his captain,
Said, "A man ain't nothin' but a man,
And before I'd let that steam drill beat me down,
I'll die with this hammer in my hand, Lawd, Lawd,
I'll die with the hammer in my hand."

5. Now the captain told John Henry,
"I believe this mountain's caving in,"
John Henry said to his captain, "Oh my,
It's my hammer just a'sucking wind, Lawd, Lawd,
It's my hammer just a' sucking wind."

6. John Henry told his captain,
"Looky yonder what I see,
Your drill's done broke and your hole's done choke,
And you can't drive steel like me, Lawd, Lawd,
And you can't drive steel like me."

7. John Henry was hammering on the mountain,
And his hammer was striking fire,
He drove so hard 'til he broke his poor heart,
And he laid down his hammer and he died, Lawd, Lawd,
Laid down his hammer and he died.

8. They took John Henry to the graveyard,
And they buried him in the sand,
And every locomotive come roaring by,
Says, "Yonder lies a steel driving man, Lawd, Lawd,
Yonder lies a steel driving man."

Jordan

M: G; F: C or D, capo 5 or 7
CD 1-Track 92

Traditional

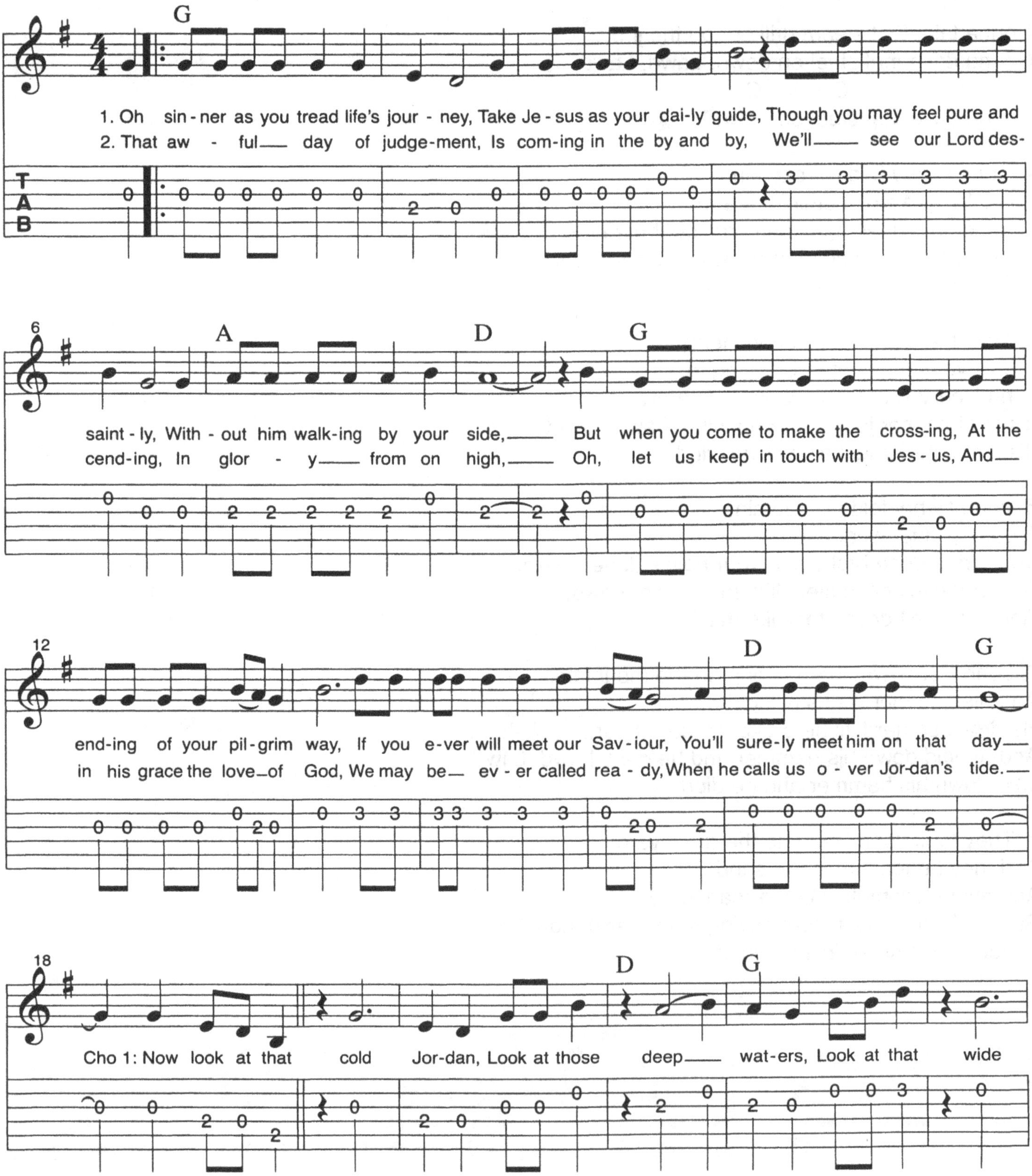

 Stanley Bros., E. L. Harris, Ken. Colonels

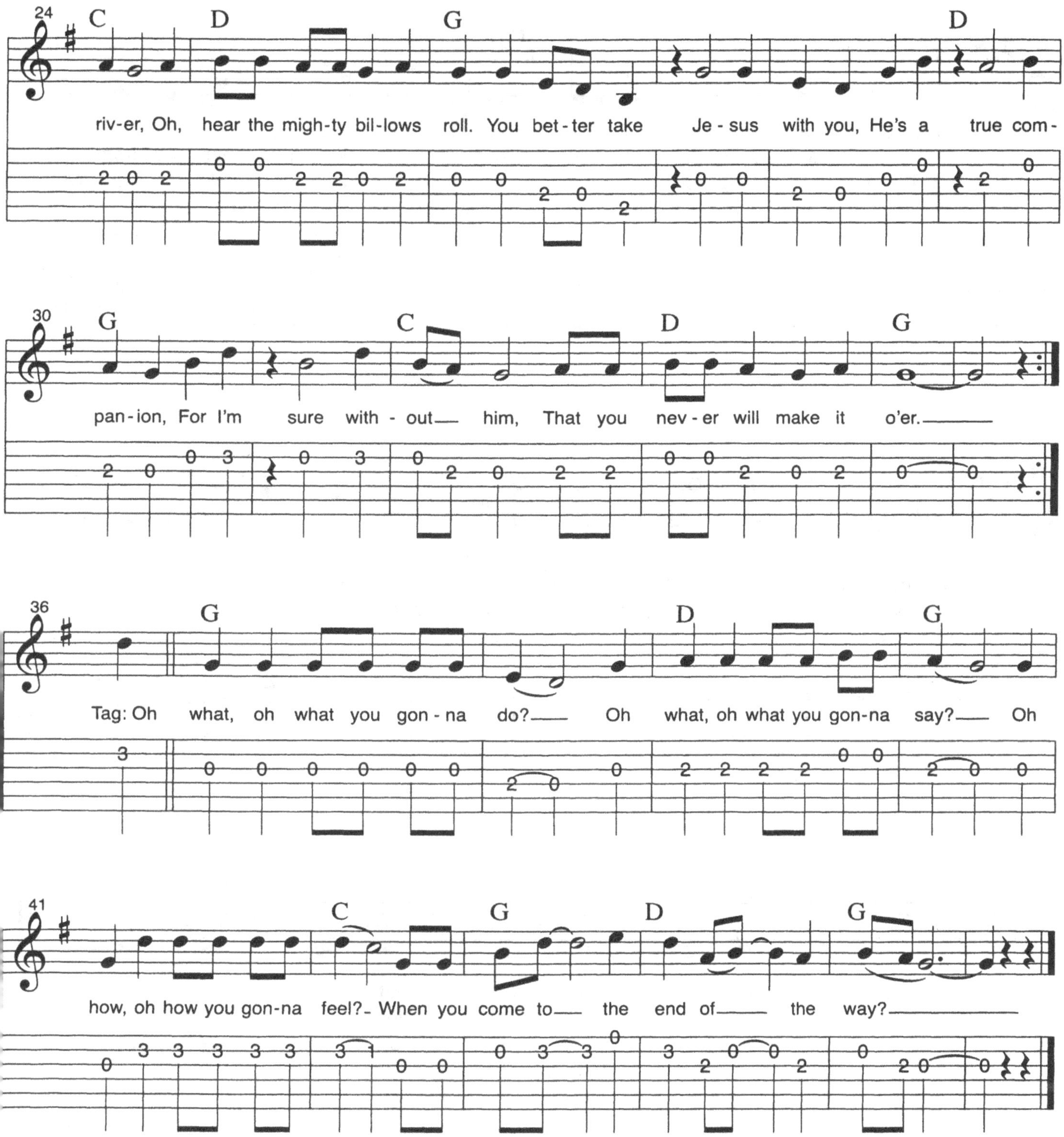
riv-er, Oh, hear the migh-ty bil-lows roll. You bet-ter take Je-sus with you, He's a true com-
pan-ion, For I'm sure with-out him, That you nev-er will make it o'er.
Tag: Oh what, oh what you gon-na do? Oh what, oh what you gon-na say? Oh
how, oh how you gon-na feel? When you come to the end of the way?

Just a Closer Walk with Thee

M: A; F: D or E, capo 5 or 7
CD 1-Track 93

Traditional

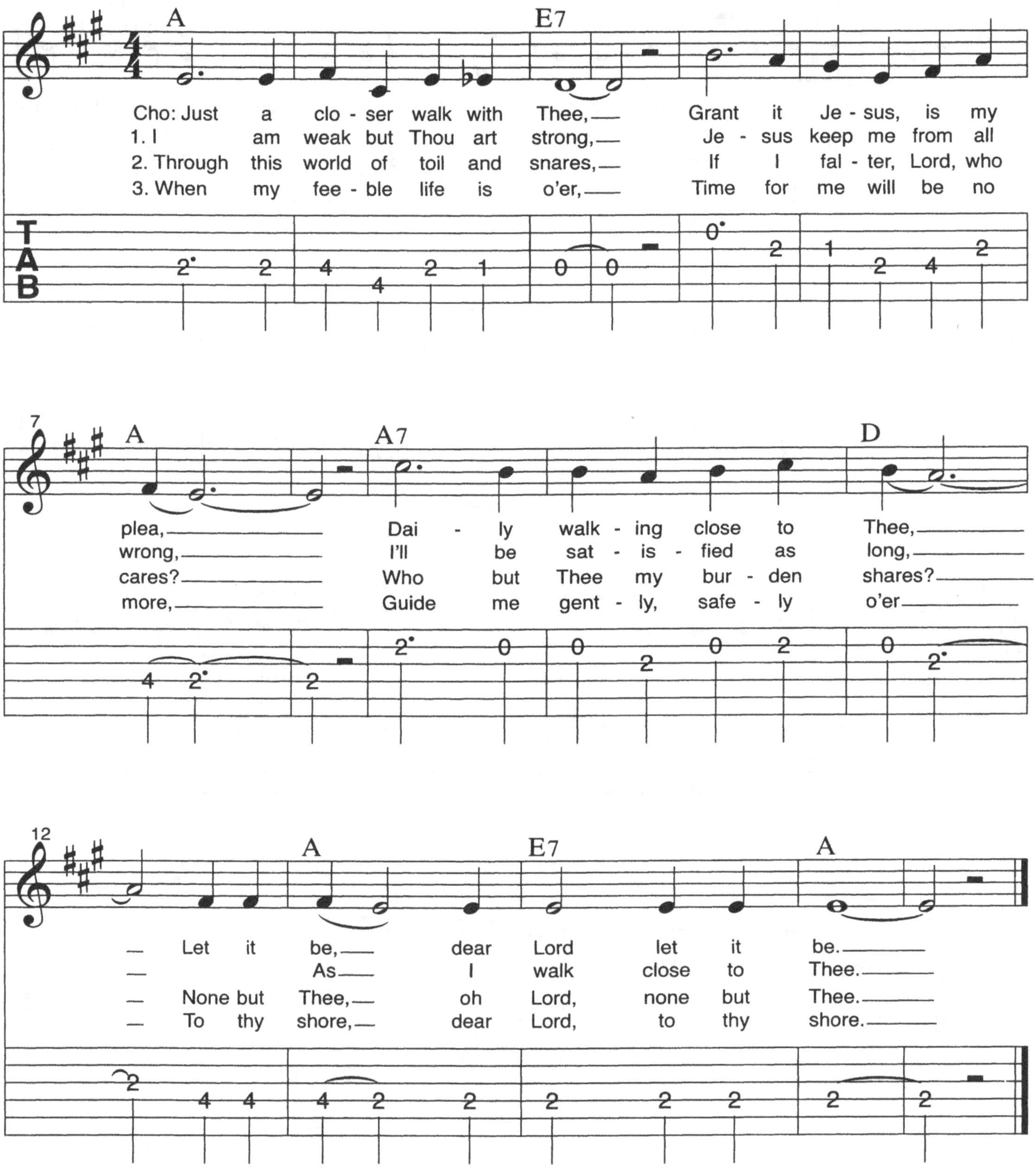

Just as I Am

M: C; F: F or G, capo 5 or 7
CD 1-Track 94

Elliott & Bradbury

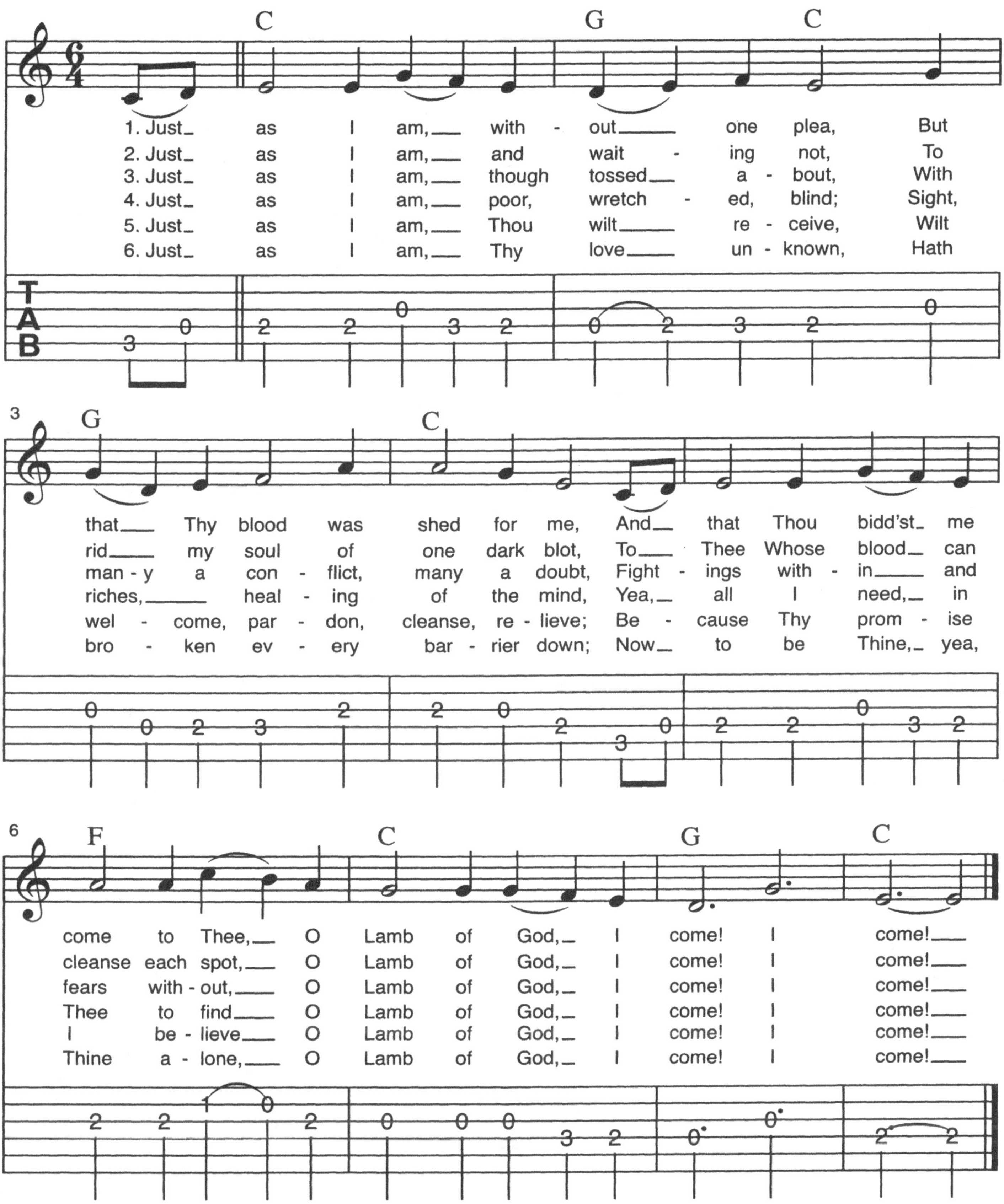

Just Over in the Gloryland

M: A; F: D or E, capo 5 or 7
CD 1-Track 95, medley pt. 1

Acuff & Dean, 1906

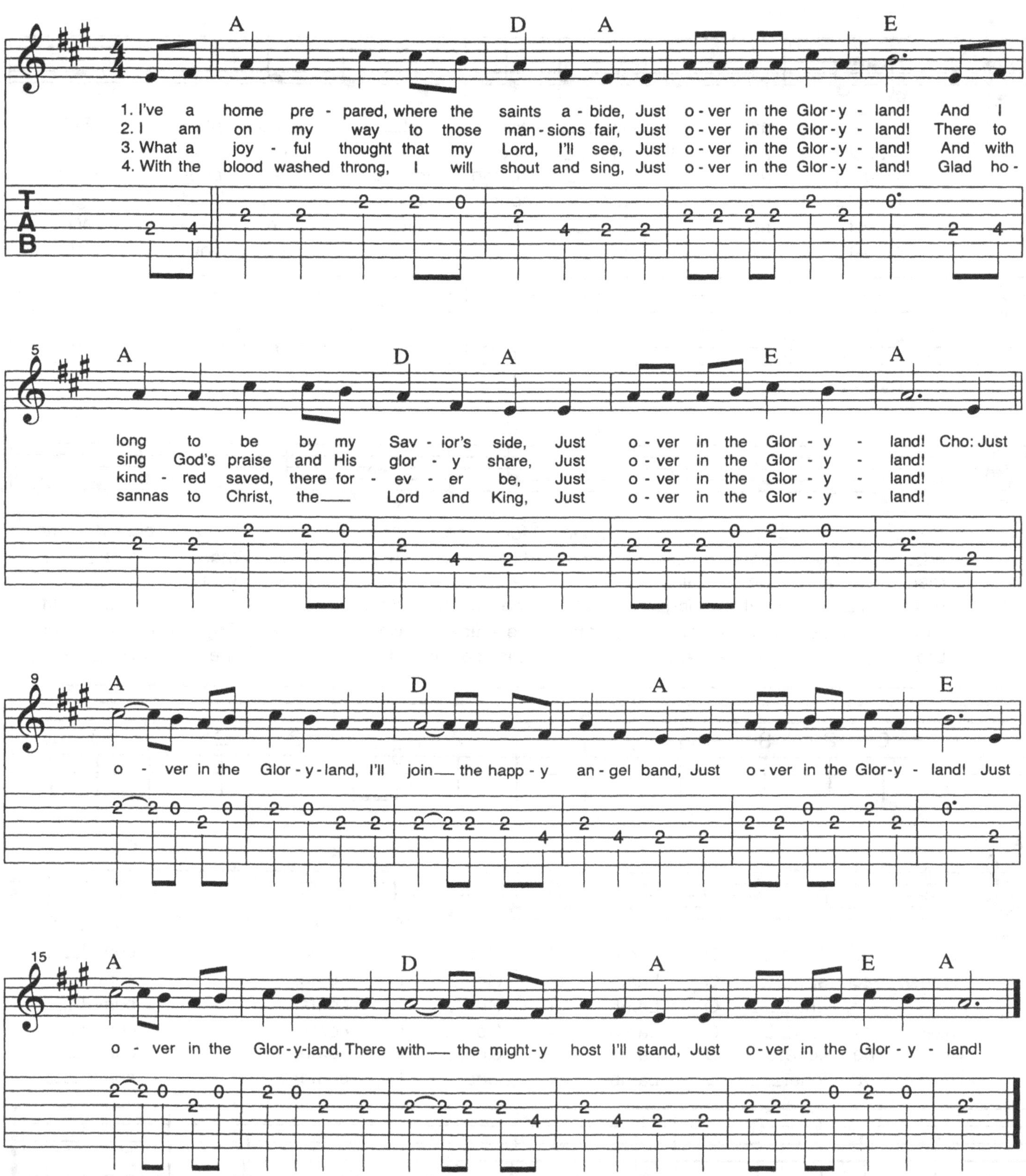

Katy Cline

M: A; F: D or E, capo 5 or 7
CD 1-Track 95, medley pt. 2

Traditional

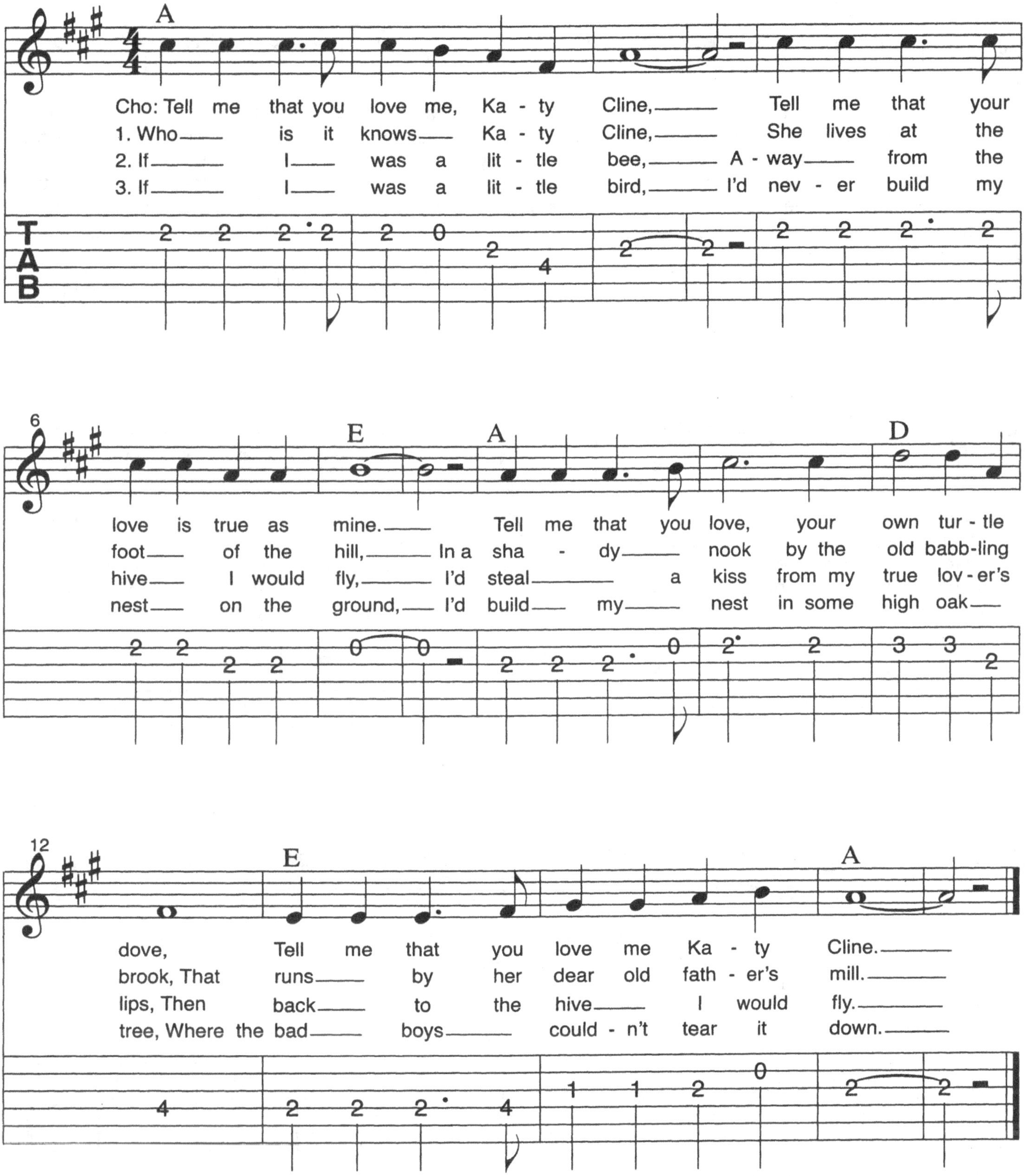

Katy Daley

M: C; F: F or G, capo 5 or 7
CD 1-Track 96

Traditional

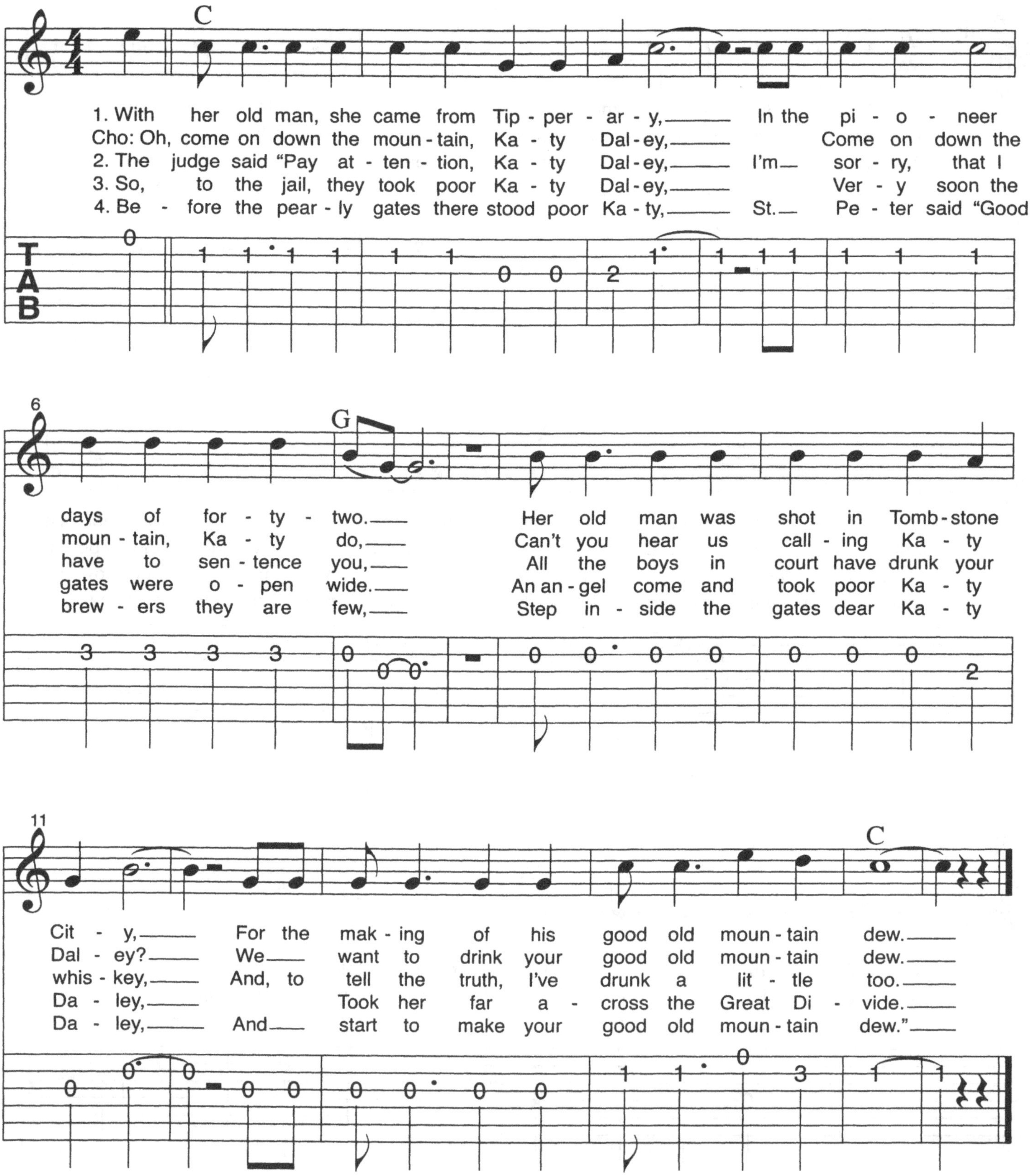

 R. Stanley, Mac Wiseman, Lonesome River Band

Katy Dear

M: D; F: G or A, capo 5 or 7
CD 1-Track 97

Traditional

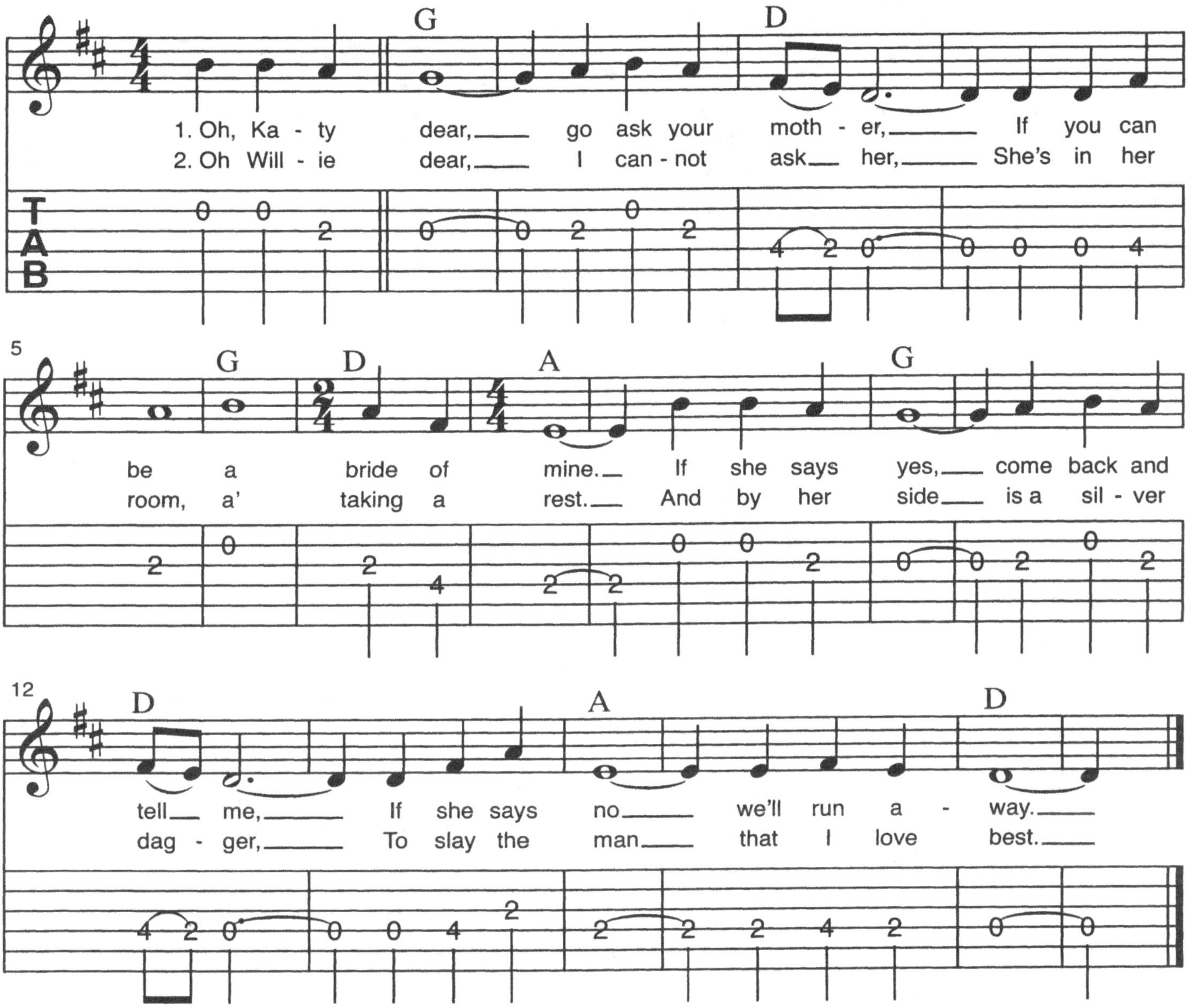

3. Oh, Katy dear, go ask your father,
If you can be a bride of mine.
If he says yes, come back and tell me,
If he says no, we'll run a-way.

(Chords for verse 3: G, D over the first line; G, D, A over the second; G, D over the third; A, D over the fourth.)

4. Oh, Willie dear, I cannot ask him,
He's in his room a' taking a rest,
And by his side, that silver dagger,
To slay the one, that I love best.

5. Then he picked up that silver dagger,
And stove it through his weary heart.
Saying, "Goodbye Katy, goodbye darling,
At last the time has come to part."

6. Then she picked up that bloody dagger,
And stove it through her lilly white breast,
Saying, "Goodbye Willie, goodbye mother,
I'll die with the one that I love best."

Keep on the Sunnyside

M: G; F: C or D, capo 5 or 7
CD 1-Track 98, medley pt. 1

Blenkhorn & Entwisle

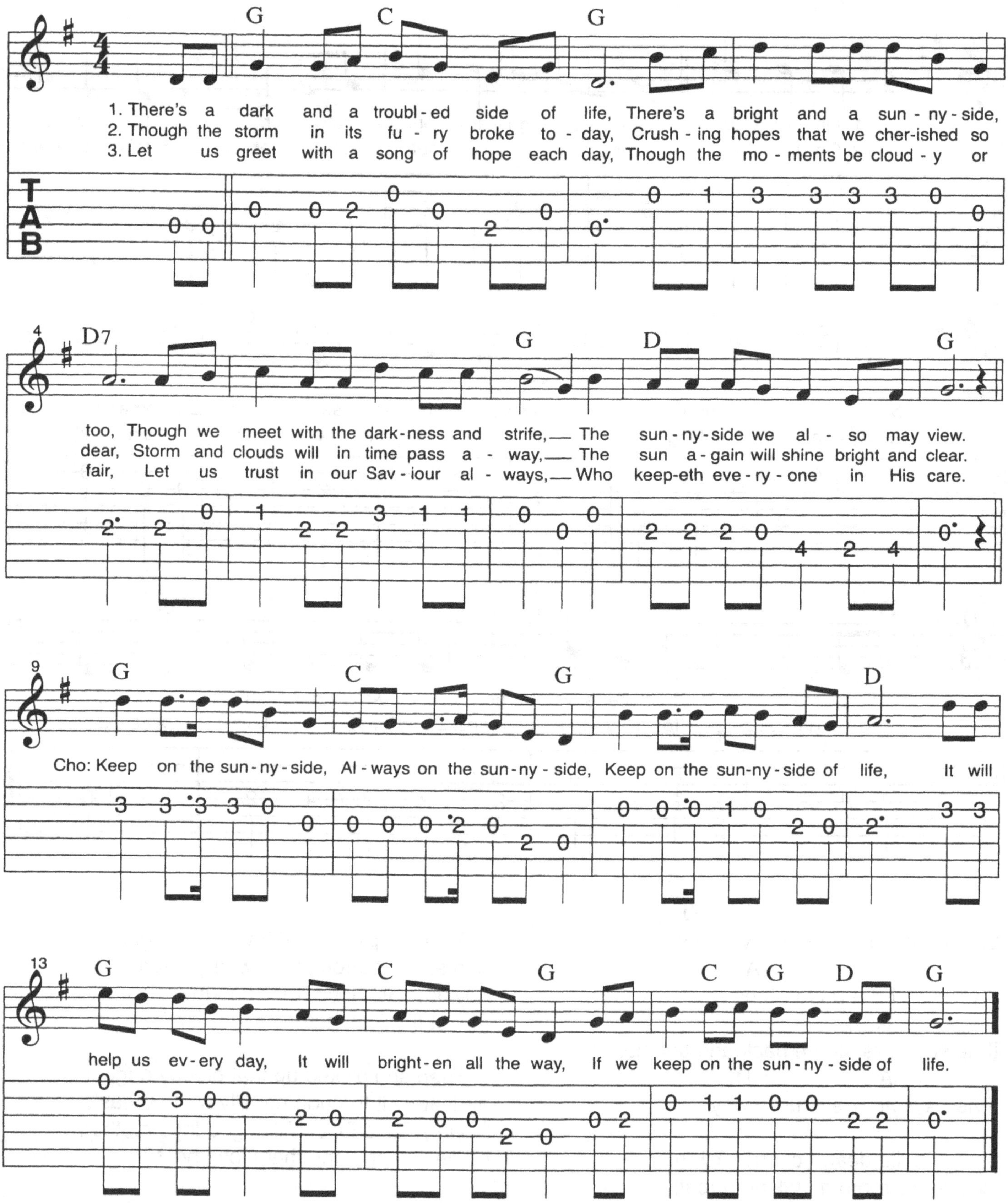

 Carter Fam., Reno & Harrell, Bluegrass Band, D. Watson, Osborne Bros., Flatt & Scruggs, Mac Wiseman, Nitty Gritty Dirt Band

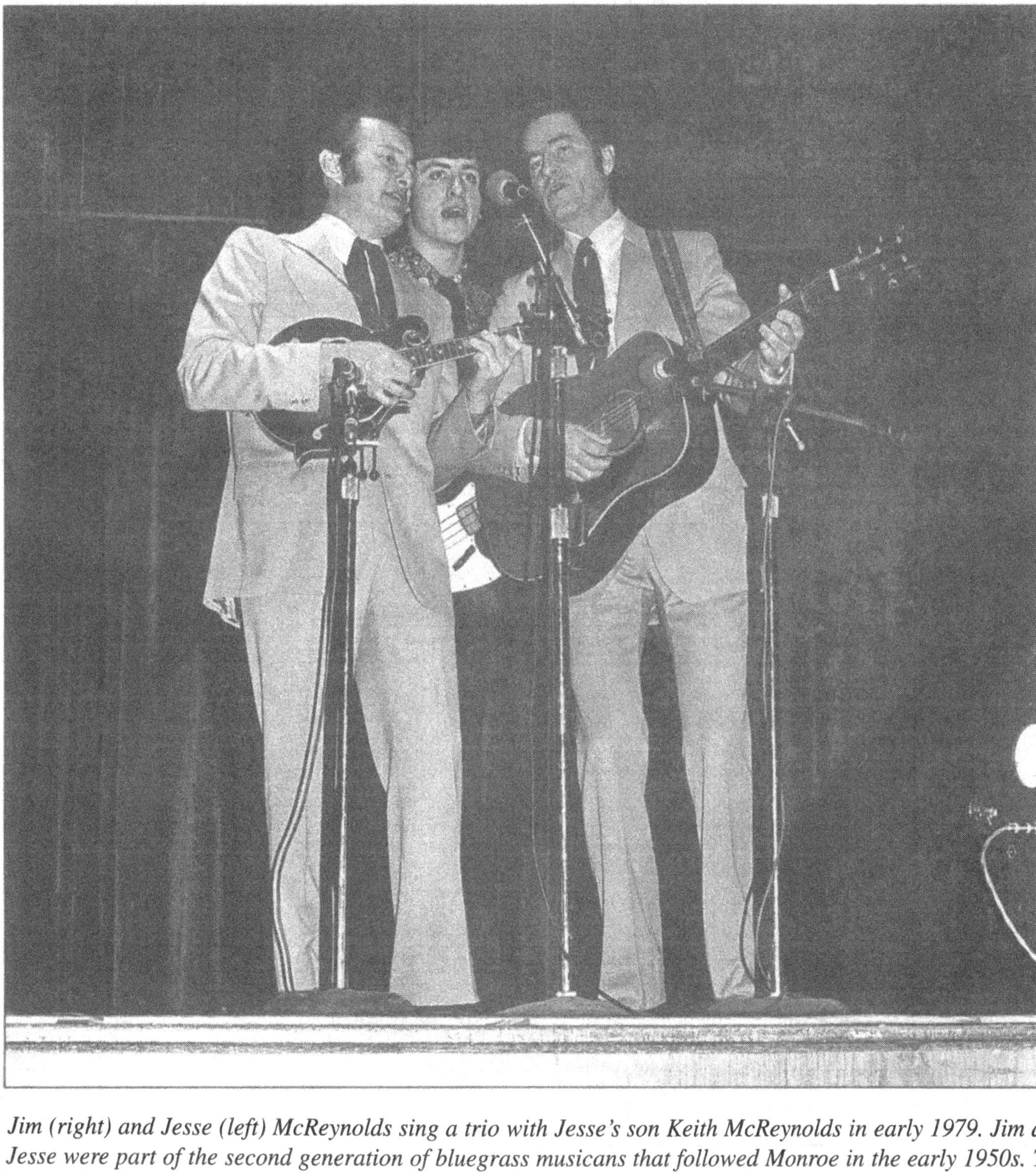

Photo by Dix Bruce

Jim (right) and Jesse (left) McReynolds sing a trio with Jesse's son Keith McReynolds in early 1979. Jim and Jesse were part of the second generation of bluegrass musicans that followed Monroe in the early 1950s. The duo was known for its smooth "brother duet" vocals and for Jesse's phenomenal cross picking on the mandolin.

Knoxville Girl

M: G; F: C or D, capo 5 or 7
CD 1-Track 98, medley pt. 2

Traditional

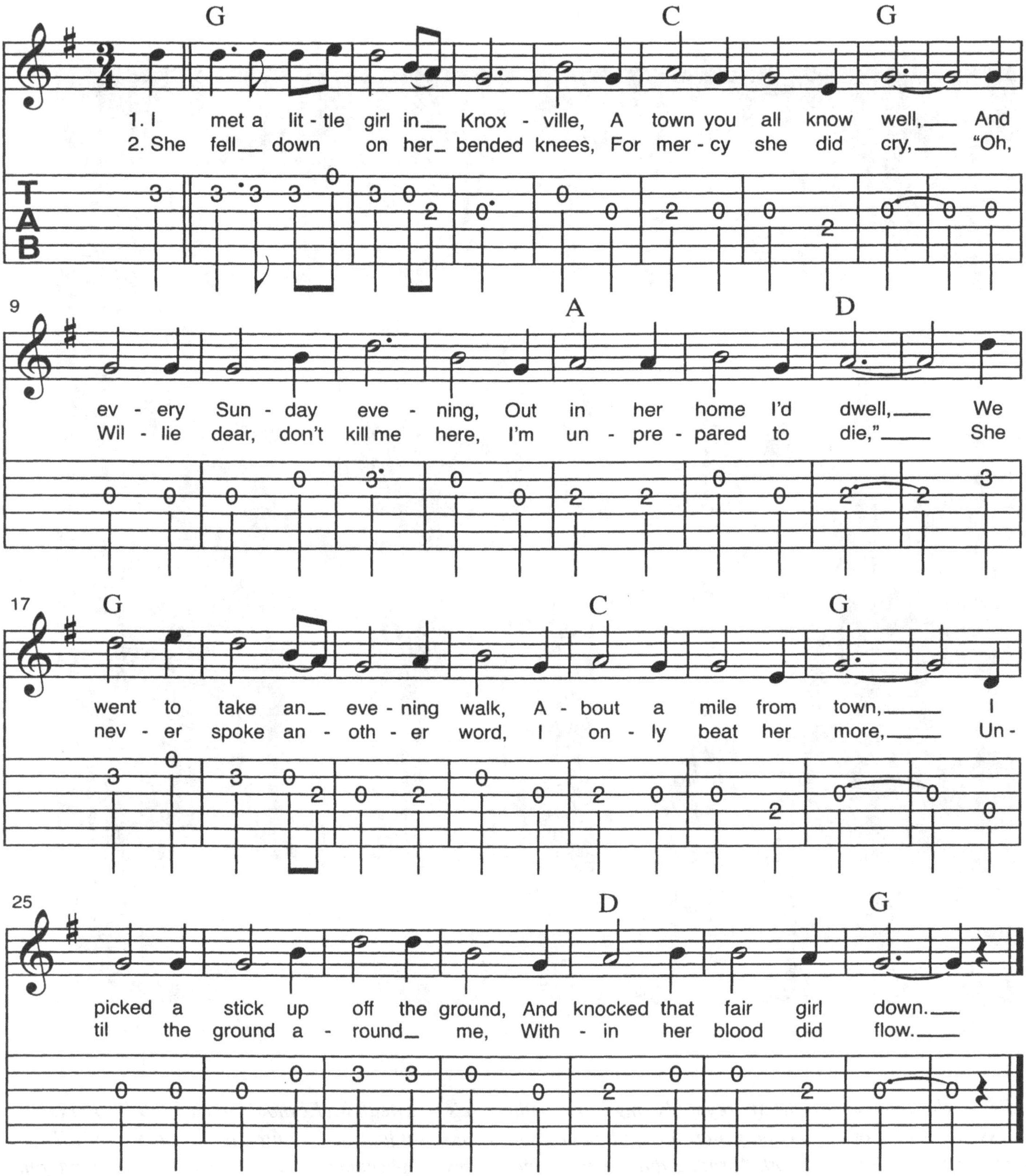

 Louvin Bros., Stanley Bros., Blue Sky Boys, Mac Wiseman, Jimmy Martin, Osborne Bros.

G
3. I took her by her golden curls,
C G
I drug her 'round and 'round,
I threw her into the river,
A D
That flows through Knoxville town,
G
Go down, go down, you Knoxville girl,
C G
With dark and rolling eyes,
Go down, go down, you Knoxville girl,
D G
You'll never be my bride.

4. Starting back to Knoxville,
Got there about midnight,
My mother she was worried,
And woke up in a fright,
Saying, "Son, oh son, what have you done,
To bloody your clothes so?"
I told my anxious mother,
Been bleeding at my nose.

5. I called for me a candle,
To light myself to bed,
I called for me a handkerchief,
To bind my aching head,
Rolled and tumbled the whole night through,
As troubles were for me,
Like flames of Hell around my bed,
And in my eyes could see.

6. They carried me down to Knoxville,
They put me in a cell,
My friends all tried to get me out,
But none could go my bail,
I'm here to waste my life away,
Down in this dirty old jail,
Because I murdered that Knoxville girl,
The girl I loved so well.

Late Last Night

M: C; F: F or G, capo 5 or 7
CD 2-Track 1

Traditional

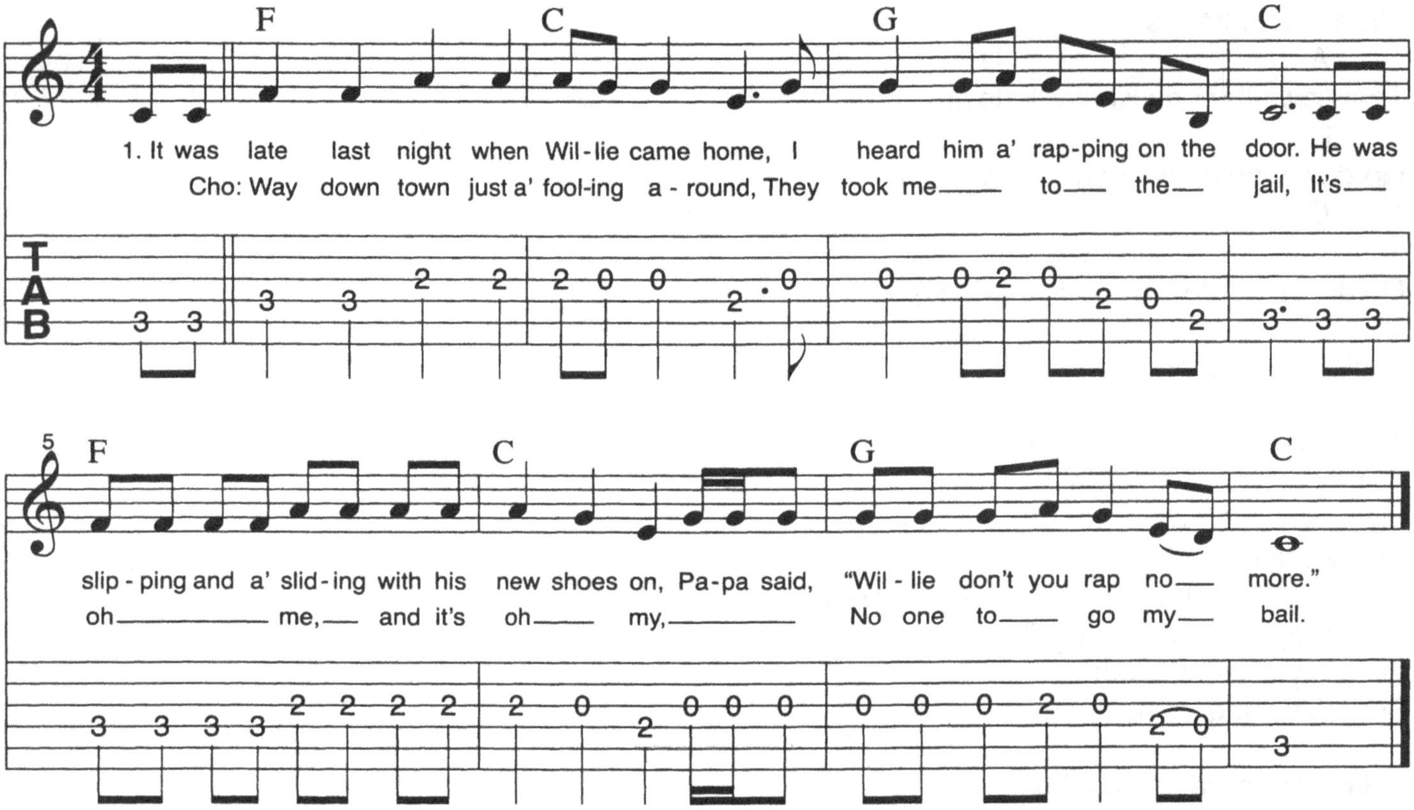


```
  F                        C
2. Wish I was over at my sweet Sally's house,
G                         C
Sitting in that big armed chair,
 F                       C
One arm around this old guitar,
 G                         C
Other one around my dear.
```

3. This one old shirt is about all I got,
And a dollar is all I crave,
I brought nothing with me into this old world,
Ain't gonna take nothing to my grave.

4. I like the hills of West Virginia,
I like the hills of Tennessee,
North, south, east or west,
It's home, sweet home to me.

 D. Watson, Stanley Bros., R. Stanley, T. Rice, Dry Branch Fire Squad, Nitty Gritty Dirt Band

Leave it There

M: D; F: G or A, capo 5 or 7
CD 2-Track 2

C.A. Tindley, 1916

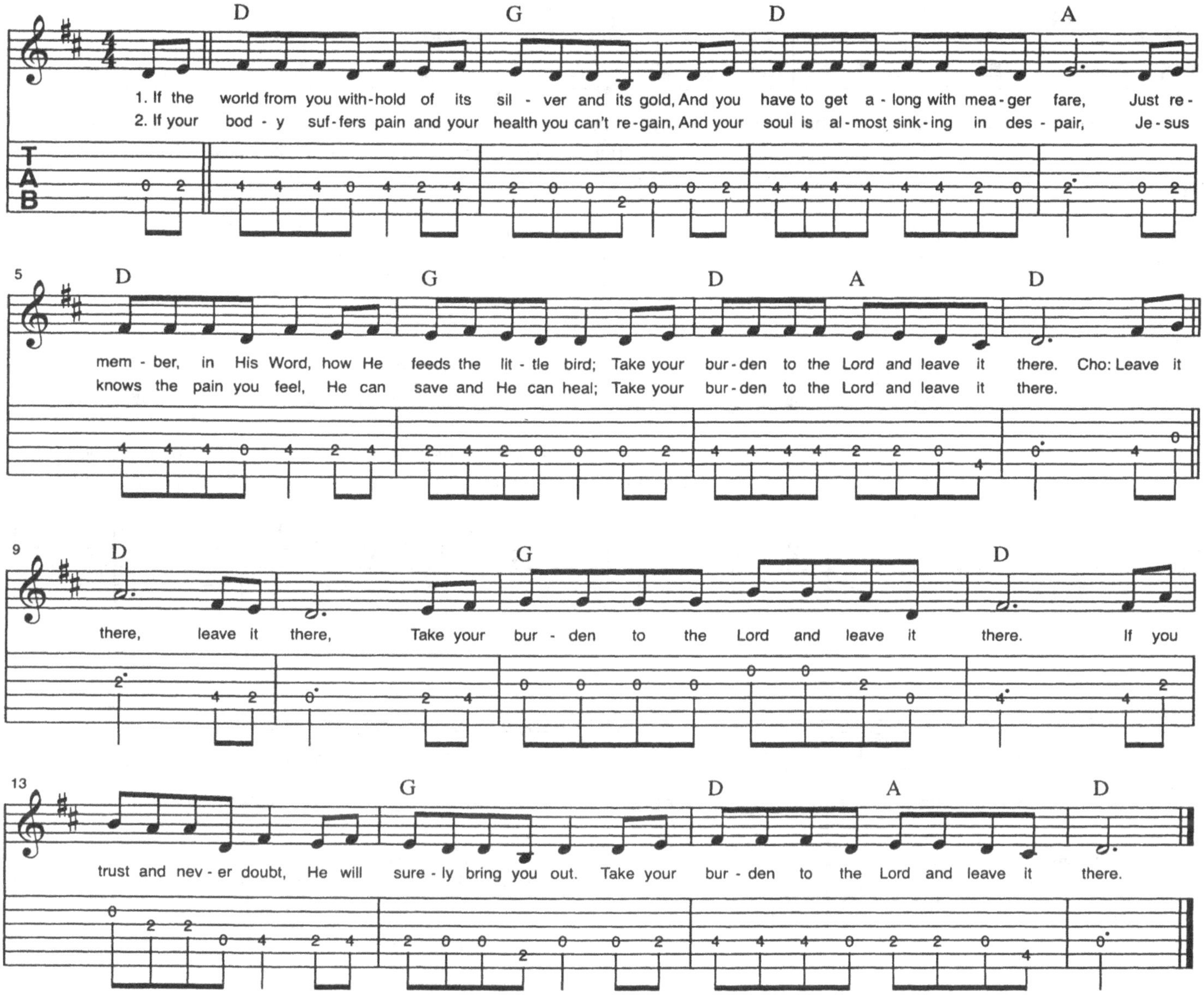


```
       D                                    G
3. When your enemies assail and your heart begins to fail,
         D                                  A
Don't forget that God in heaven answers prayer;
        D                              G
He will make a way for you and will lead you safely through,
          D           A               D
Take your burden to the Lord and leave it there.
```

4. When your youthful days are gone and old age is stealing on,
And your body bends beneath the weight of care;
He will never leave you then, He'll go with you to the end,
Take your burden to the Lord and leave it there.

5. If your mother leaves you here, grief and sorrow you must bear,
And you feel the only friend you have is gone,
But whenever you feel alone, He will take you in his arms,
Take your burden to the Lord and leave it there.

Let Me Rest at the End of My Journey

M: G; F: C or D, capo 5 or 7
CD 2-Track 3

Traditional

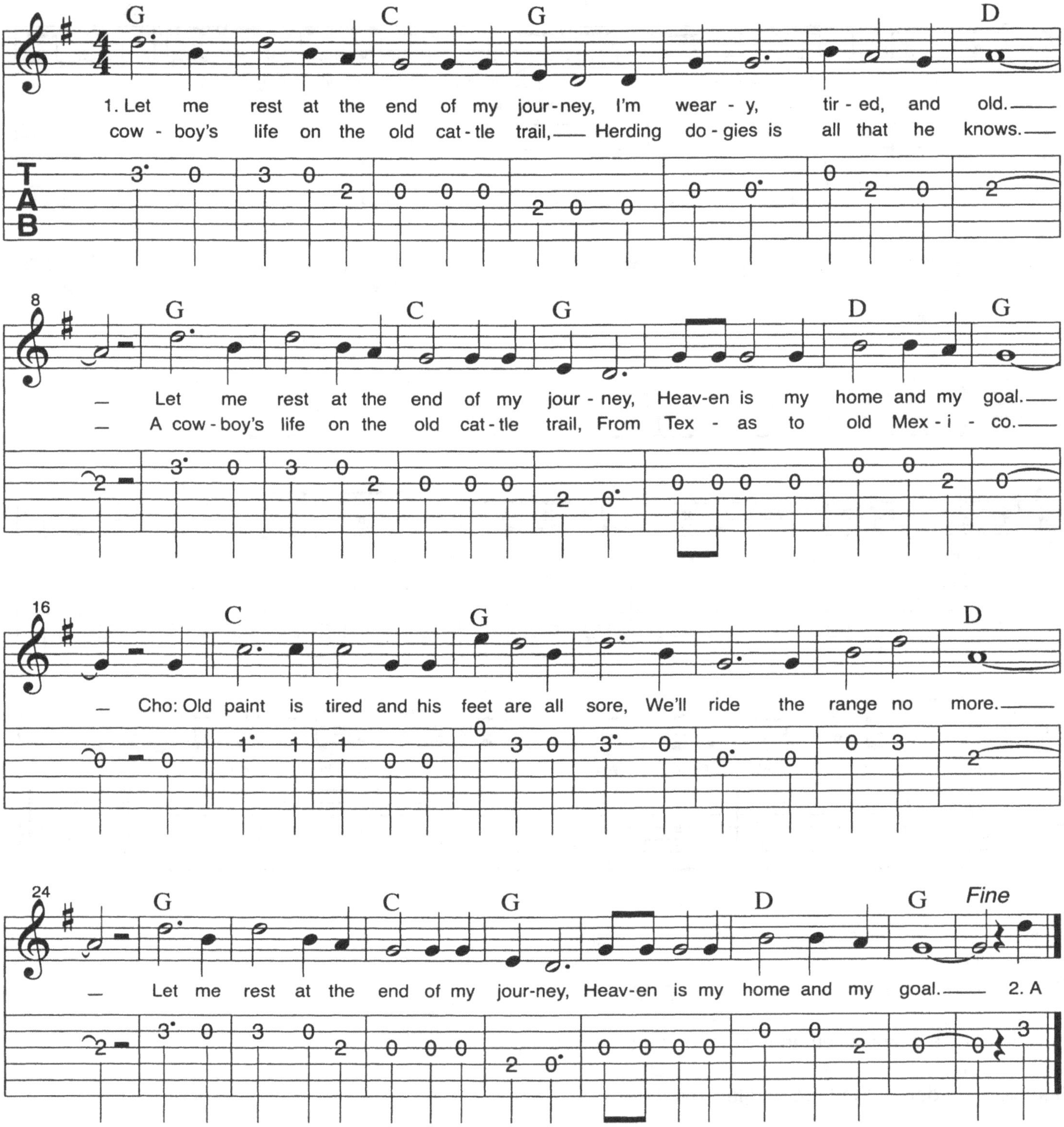

The Letter Edged in Black

M: D; F: G or A, capo 5 or 7
CD 2-Track 4

Hattie Nevada, 1897

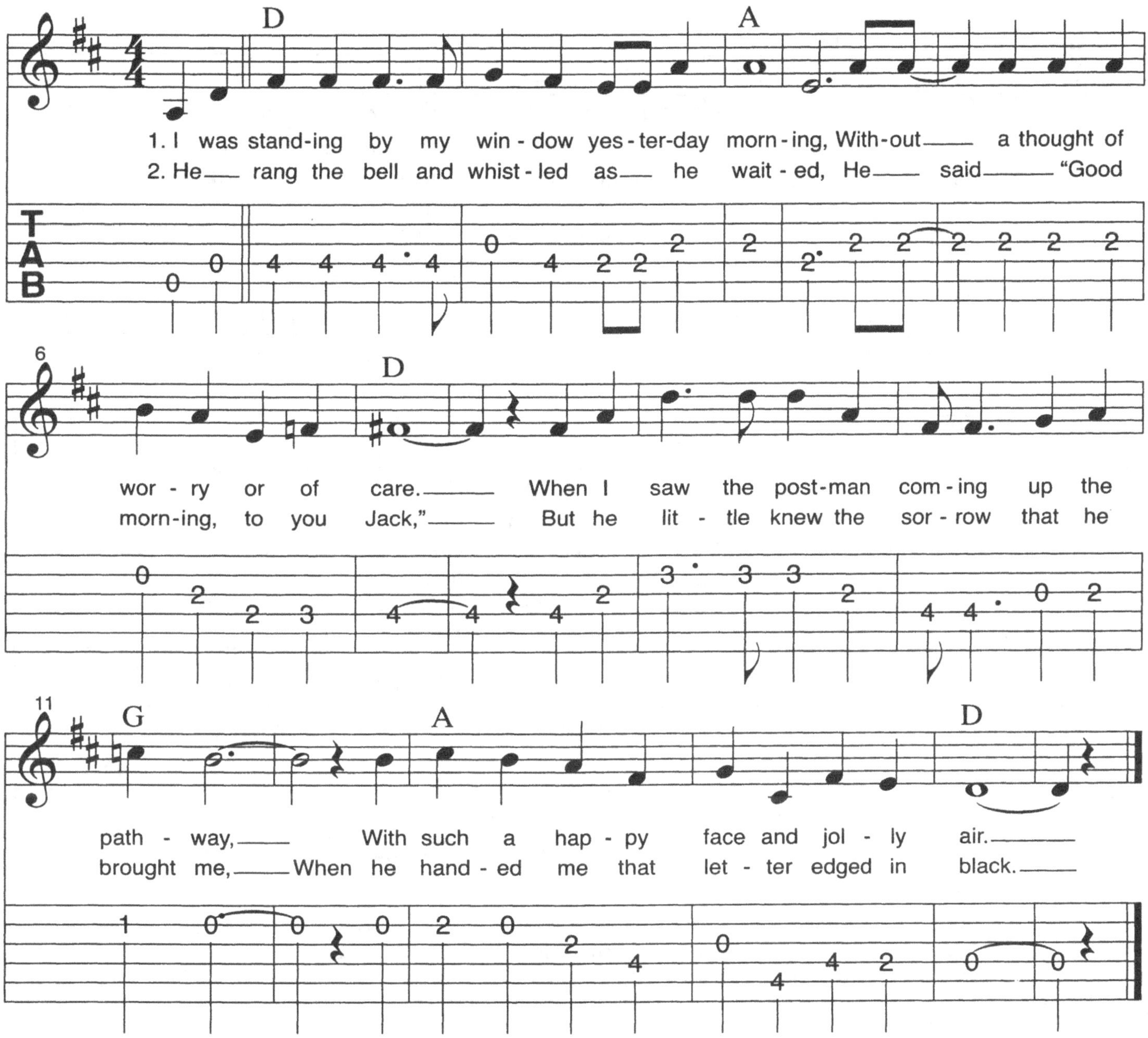

D A
3. With trembling hands, I took that letter from him,
D
I broke the seal and this is what it said:
G
"Come home my boy, your dear old father wants you,
A D
Come home my boy, your dear old mother's dead."

4. "Those angry words I wished I'd never spoken,
You know I didn't mean them don't you Jack?
I bow my head in sadness and in sorrow,
While I'm writing you this letter edged in black."

5. "The last words that your mother ever uttered,
Were 'Tell my boy, I want him to come back,'
May the angels bear me witness I am asking,
Your forgiveness in this letter edged in black."

(Repeat verse 2)

Life's Railway to Heaven

M: D; F: G or A, capo 5 or 7
CD 2-Track 5

Abbey & Tillman, 1890

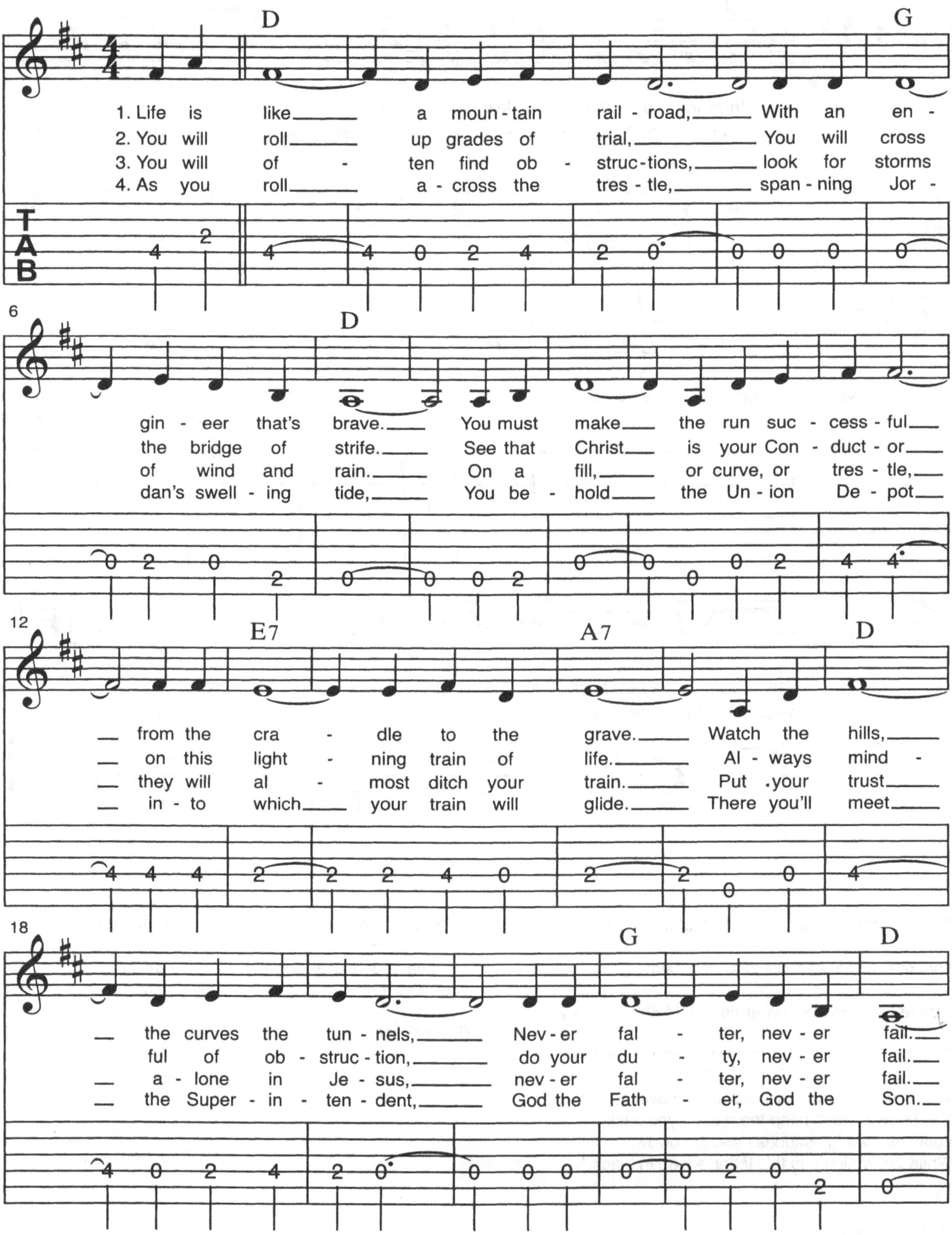

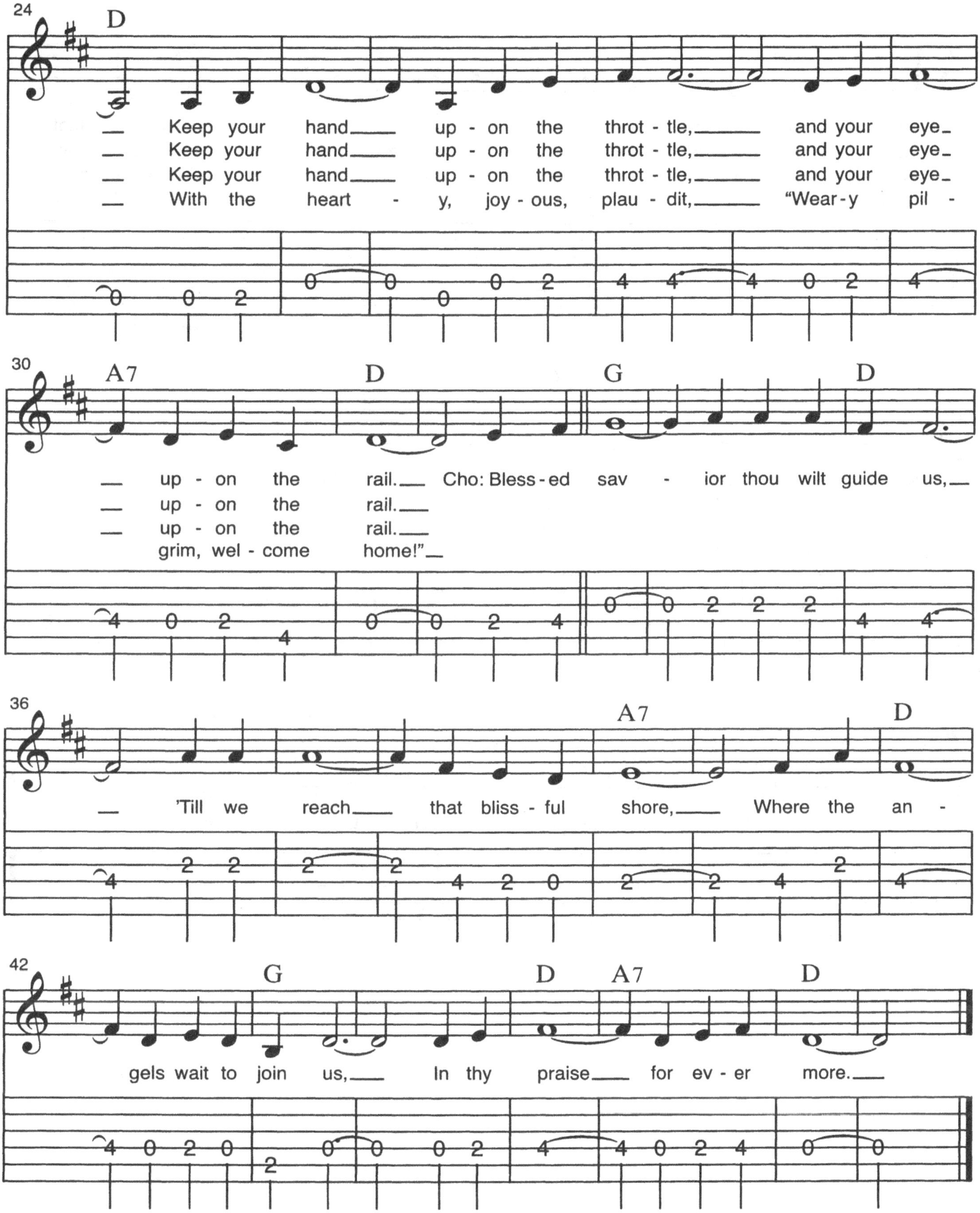
24
D
Keep your hand up - on the throt - tle, and your eye
Keep your hand up - on the throt - tle, and your eye
Keep your hand up - on the throt - tle, and your eye
With the heart - y, joy - ous, plau - dit, "Wear - y pil -
30
A7 D G D
up - on the rail. Cho: Bless - ed sav - ior thou wilt guide us,
up - on the rail.
up - on the rail.
grim, wel - come home!"
36
A7 D
'Till we reach that bliss - ful shore, Where the an -
42
G D A7 D
gels wait to join us, In thy praise for ev - er more.

Li'l Liza Jane

M: C; F: F or G, capo 5 or 7
CD 2-Track 6

Traditional

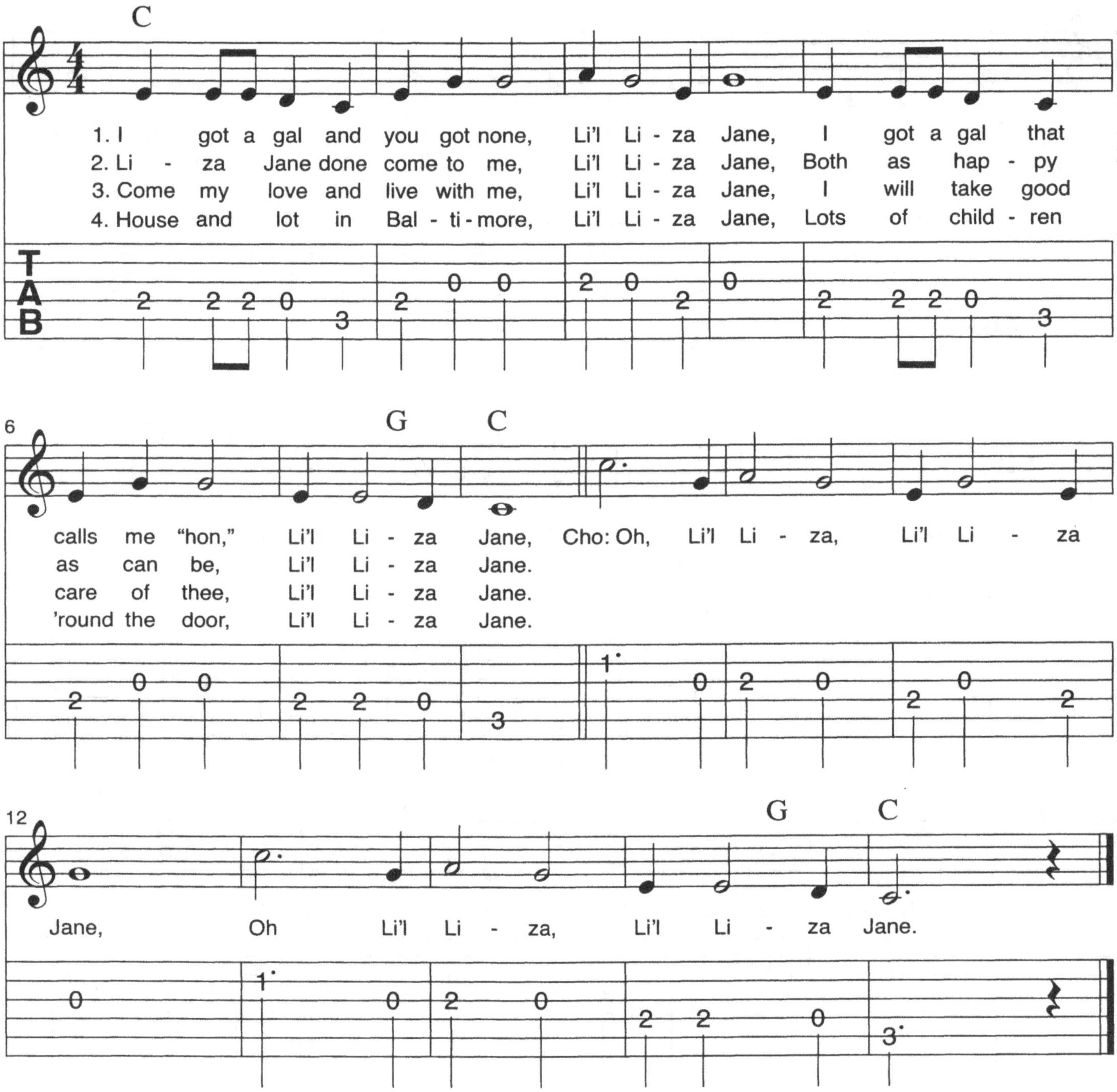

Little Annie

M: C; F: F or G, capo 5 or 7
CD 2-Track 7

Traditional

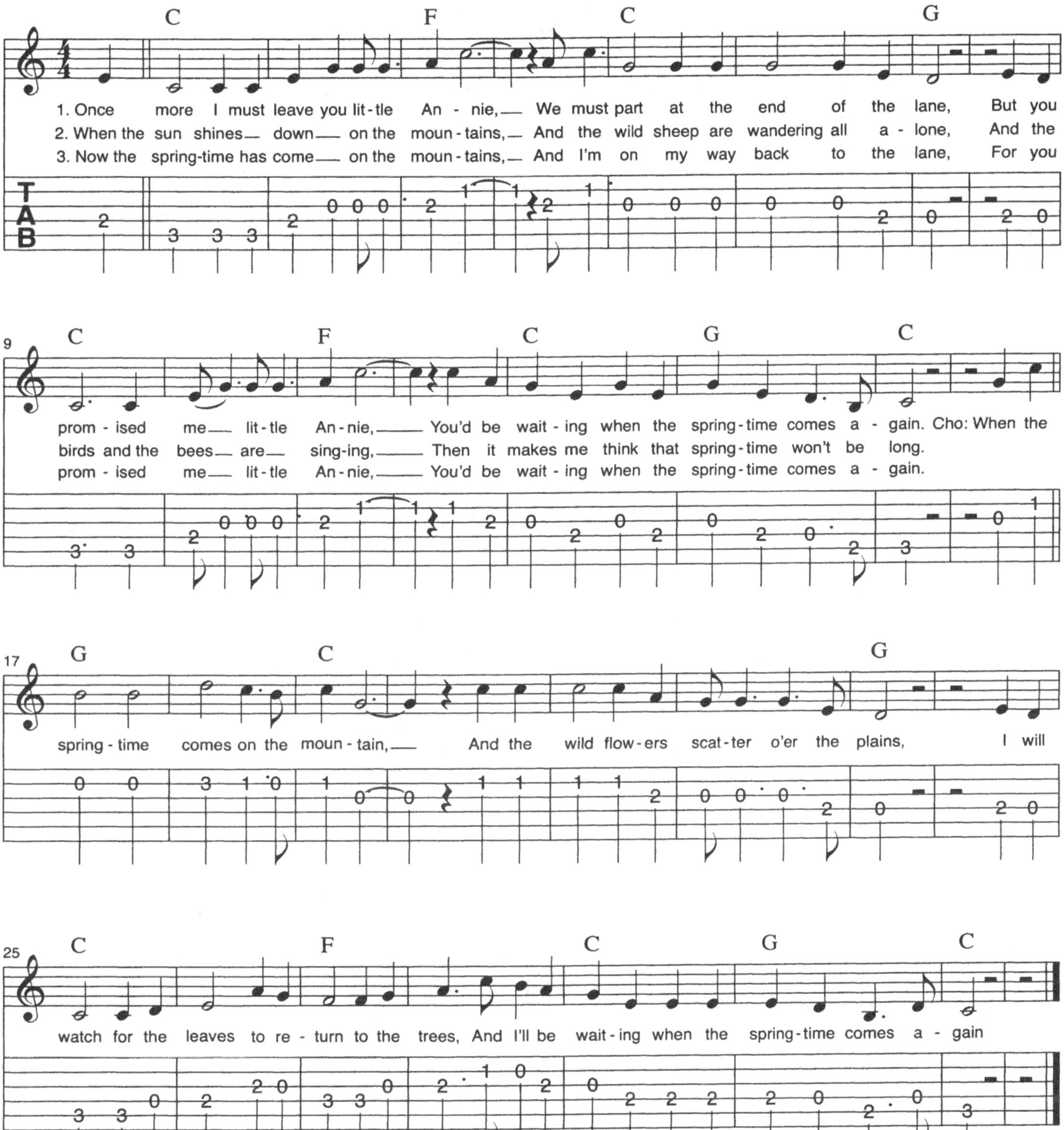

Little Bessie

M: G; F: C or D, capo 5 or 7
CD 2-Track 8

Crandall & Porter, 1875

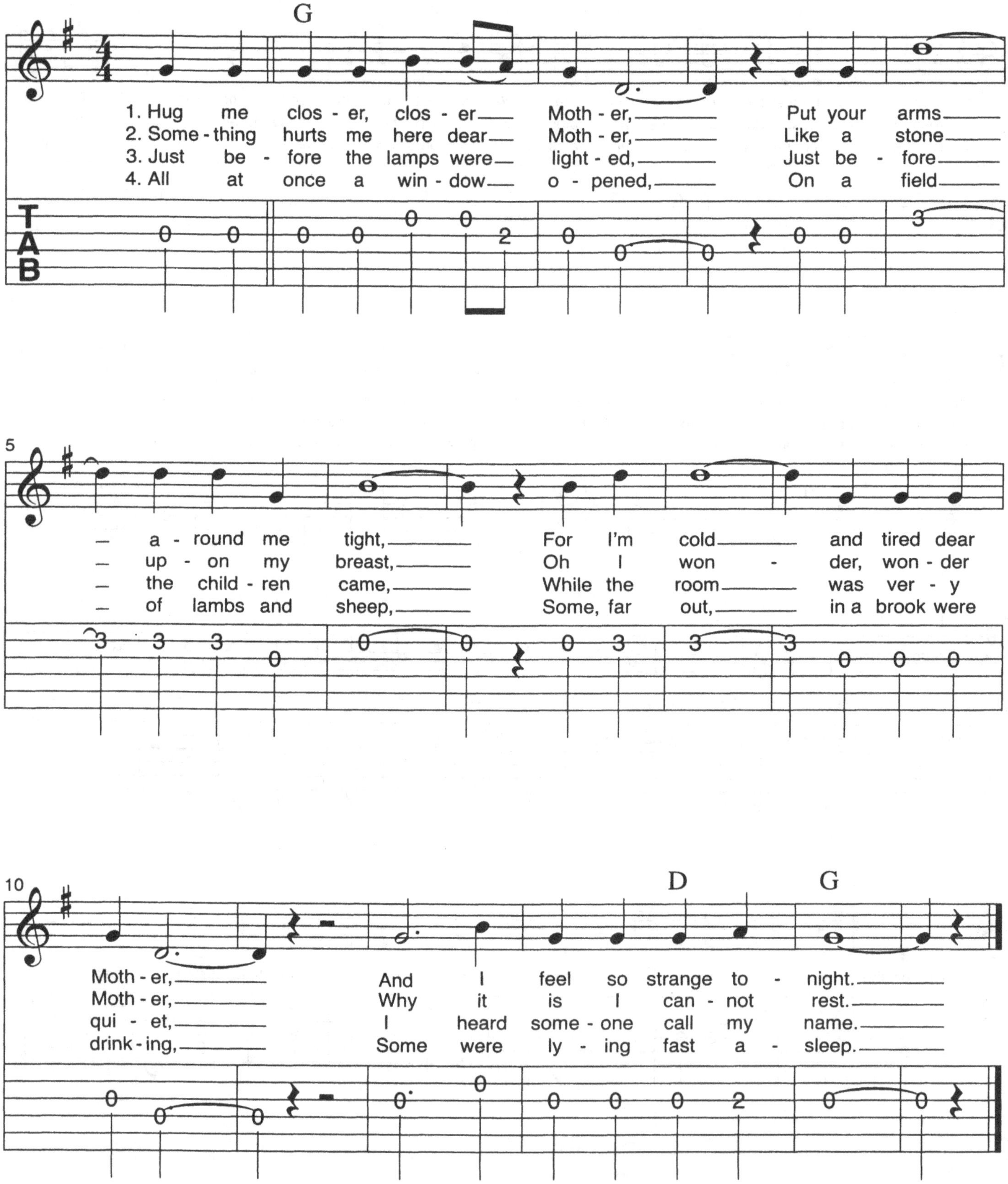

 Country Gentlemen, Stanley Bros., R. Stanley, Blue Sky Boys, Dixon Bros., N. Blake, R. Skaggs

G
5. In a moment I was looking,
On a world so bright and fair,
Which was filled with little children,
D G
And they seemed so happy there.

6. They were singing, oh, so sweetly,
Sweetest songs I'd ever heard.
They were singing sweeter, Mother,
Than a darling little bird.

7. Come up here little Bessie,
Come up here and live with me,
Where little children never suffer,
Suffer through eternity.

8. Then I thought of all you told me,
Of that bright and happy land,
I was going when you called me,
When you came and kissed my hand.

9. I felt so sorry when you called me,
And from this world I soon must go,
Go to sleep and never suffer,
Then dear Mother don't be crying so.

10. And the mother pressed her closer,
To her own dear burning breast,
To the heart so near broken,
Lay the heart so near its rest.

11. At the solemn hour of midnight,
In the darkness calm and deep,
Lying on her mother's bosom,
Little Bessie fell asleep.

12. Far up yonder past the portals,
That are shining very fair,
Little Bessie now is tended,
By her Savior's loving care.

Little Birdie

M: G; F: C or D, capo 5 or 7
CD 2-Track 9

Traditional

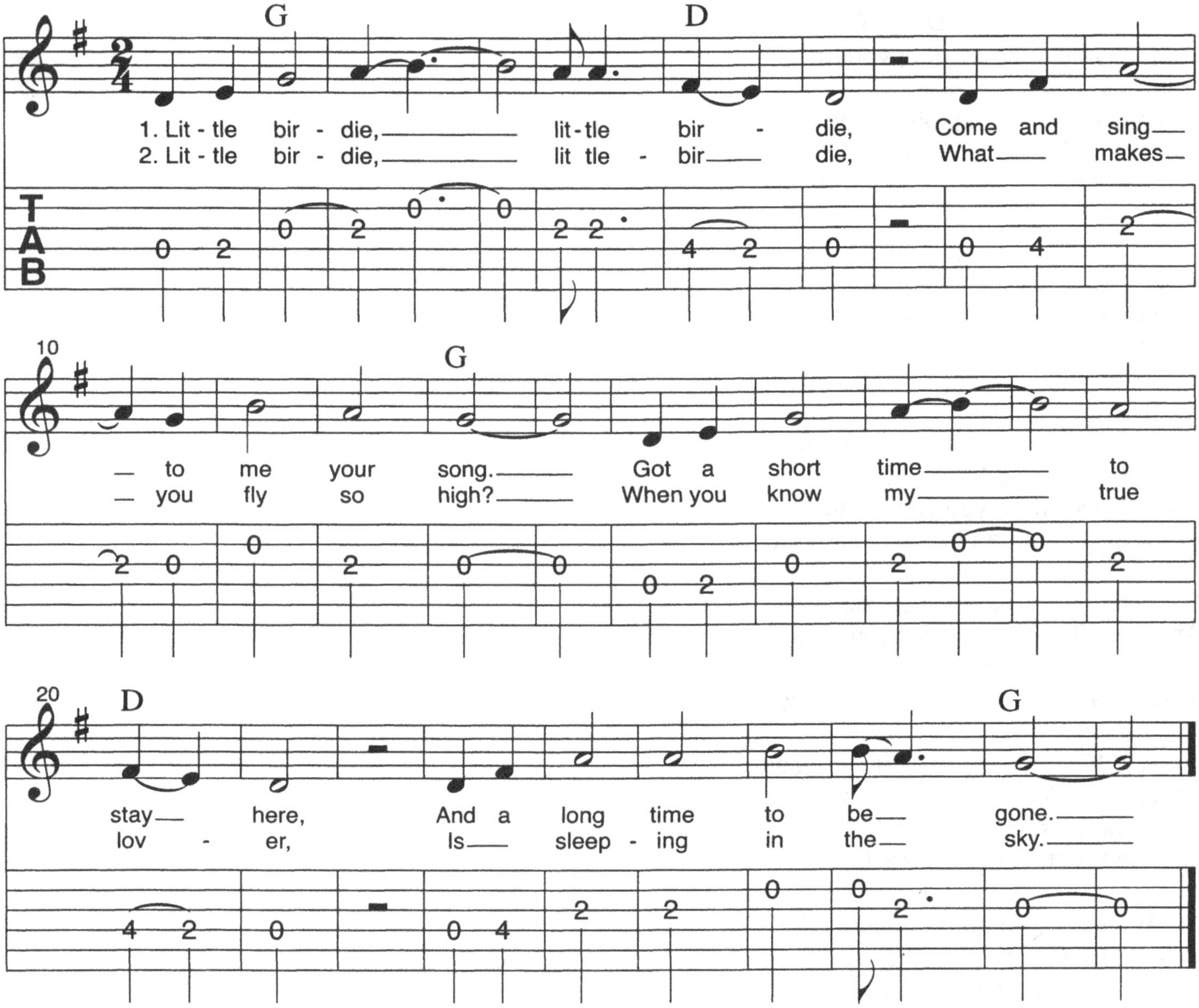

G D
3. I'm a long way from old Dixie,
G
And my old Kentucky home,
D
Now my parents are both dead and gone,
G
Have no place to call my home.

4. Now I'd rather be a sailor,
'Way out upon the sea,
Then to be at home a married man,
With a baby on my knee.

5. For the married man, he sees trouble,
And the single boy sees none,
I expect to live single,
'Til my days on earth are done.

6. Now I'd rather be in some dark hollow,
Where the sun don't ever shine,
Then to see you love another,
When you promised to be mine.

 Flatt & Scruggs, Stanley Bros., R. Stanley, R. Allen & F. Wakefield, Greenbriar Boys, NLCR, Cox Family, M. Seeger, King Wilkie

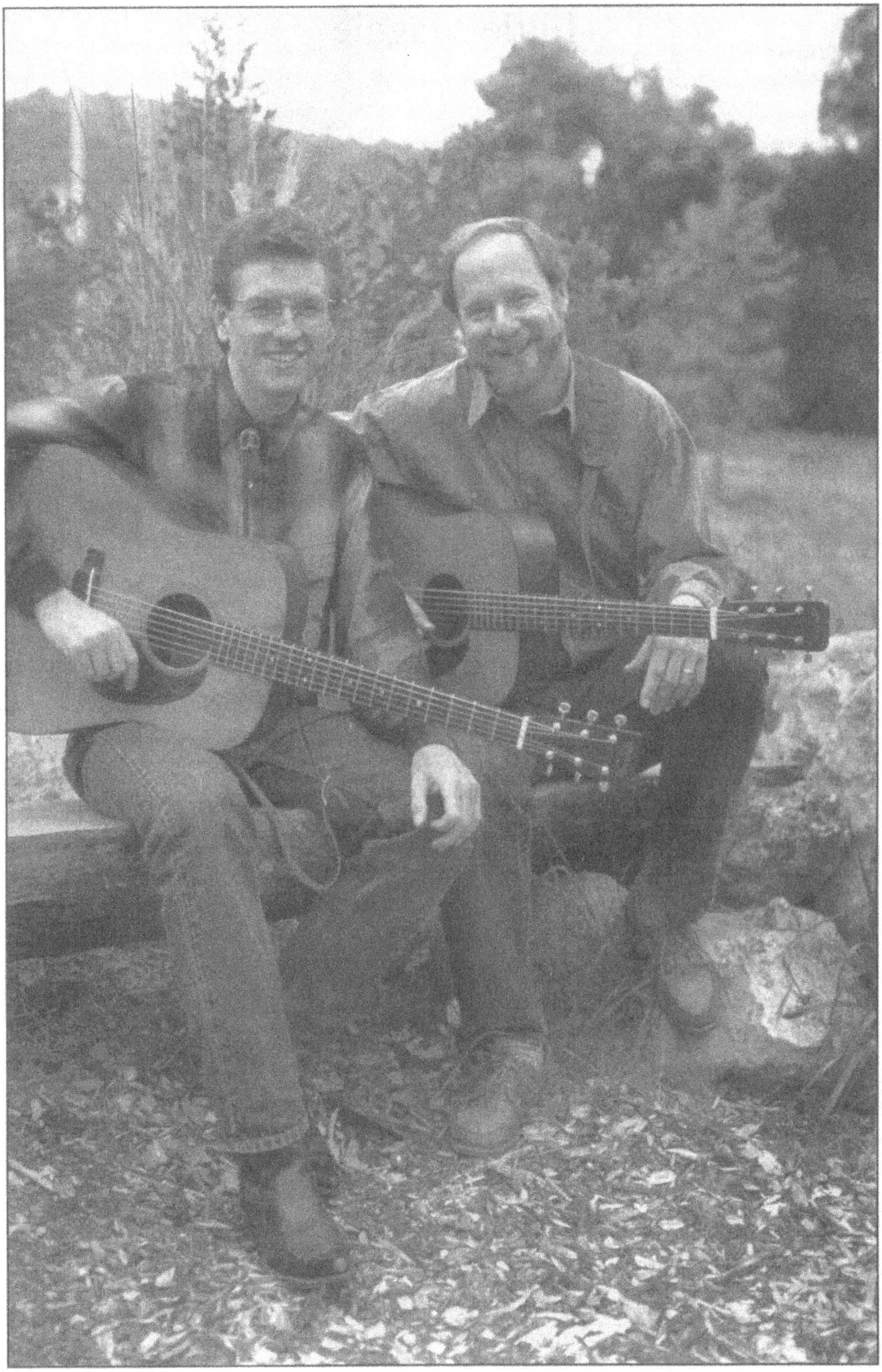

Photo by Amy Stenberg

Jim Nunally (left) and Dix Bruce have performed and recorded together since 1994. Their concerts showcase brother-style vocal harmonies and lots of hot guitar playing delivered with good humor and dazzling digital dexterity. Jim also plays with The Jaybirds and David Grisman's Bluegrass Experience.

Little Maggie

M: G; F: C or D, capo 5 or 7
CD 2-Track 10, medley pt. 1

Traditional

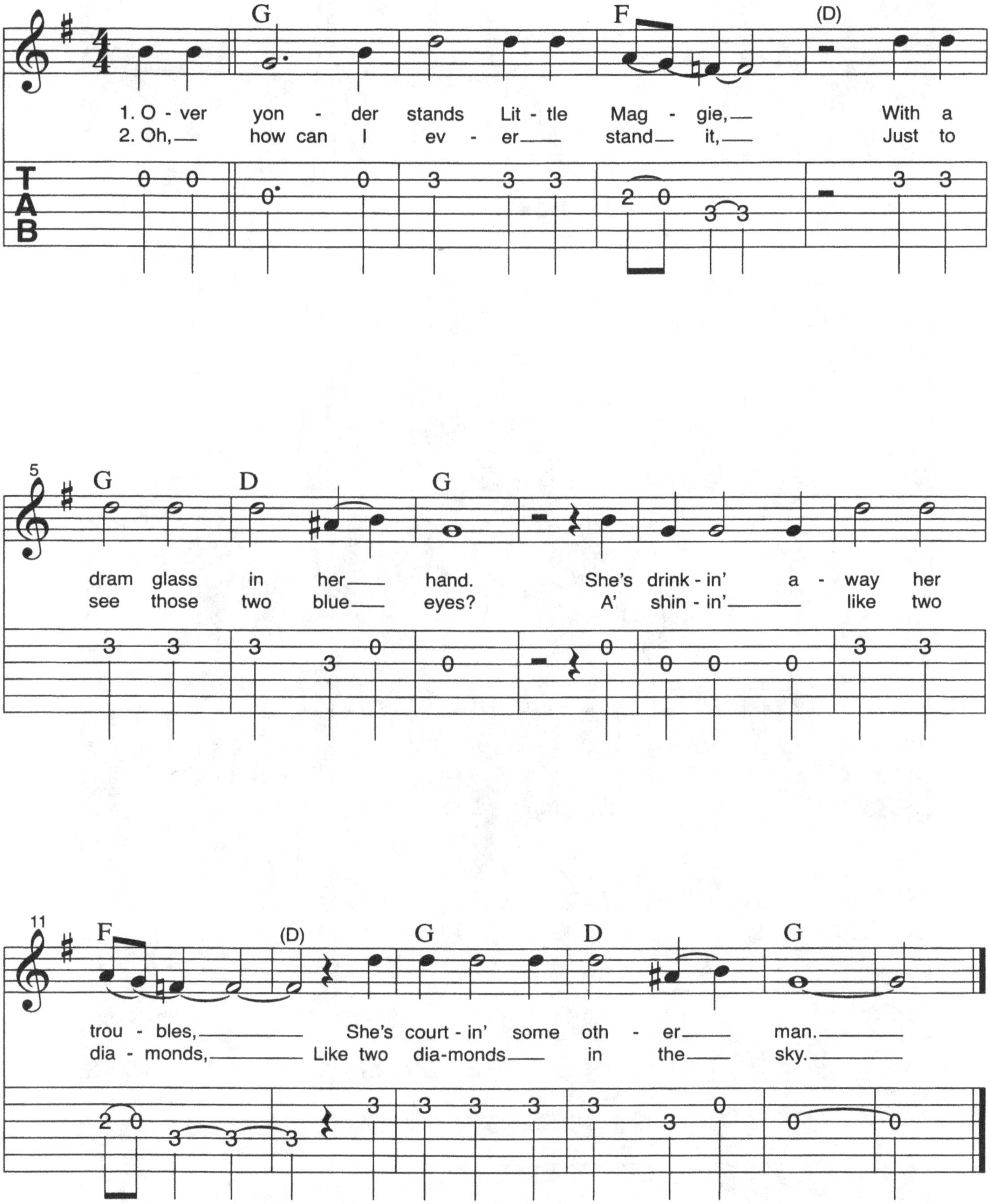

 Stanley Bros., R. Stanley, B. Monroe, Flatt & Scruggs, J. Martin, R. Allen & F. Wakefield, Grayson & Whitter, R. Skaggs, T. Adams

```
     G                           F  (D)
3. Last time I saw little Maggie,
            G               D            G
She was sitting on the banks of the sea.
                        F       (D)
With a forty-four around her,
        G      D      G
And a banjo on her knee.
```

4. Lay down your last gold dollar,
Lay down your gold watch and chain.
Little Maggie's gonna dance for daddy,
Listen to that old banjo ring.

5. Pretty flowers were made for blooming,
Pretty stars were made to shine.
Pretty girls were made for loving,
Little Maggie was made for mine.

6. March me down to the station,
With my suitcase in my hand.
I'm going away for to leave you,
I'm going to some far distant land.

7. I'd rather be in some dark hollow,
Where the sun don't never shine.
Then to know you're another man's darling,
And no longer a darling of mine.

8. Sometimes I have a nickel,
And sometimes I have a dime.
Sometimes I have ten dollars,
Just to pay little Maggie's fine.

9. Go away, go away little Maggie,
Go and do the best that you can.
I'll get me another woman,
You can get you another man.

Little Old Log Cabin in the Lane

M: G; F: C or D, capo 5 or 7
CD 2-Track 10, medley pt. 2

W.S. Hays, 1871

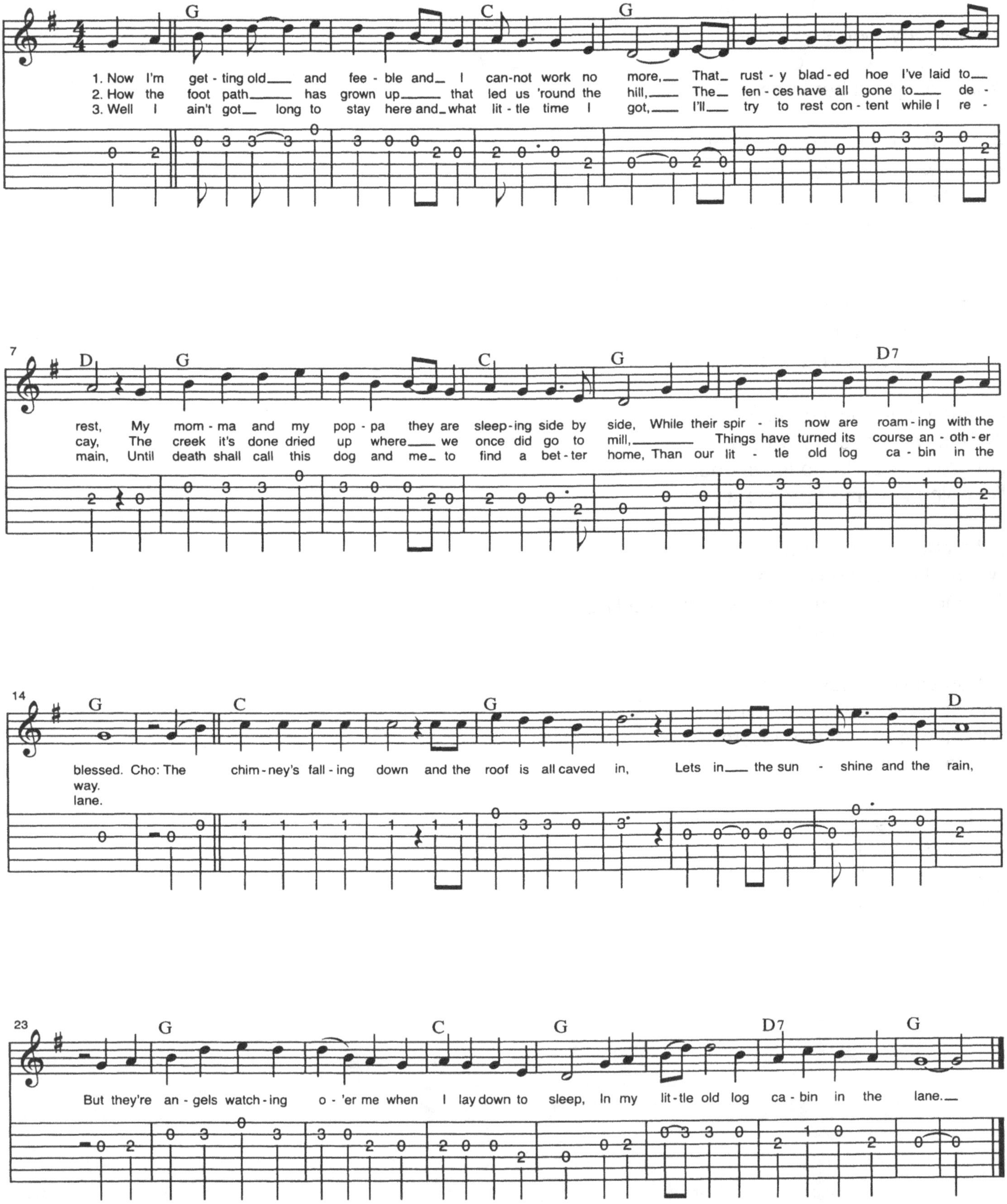

Little Rosewood Casket

M: C; F: F or G, capo 5 or 7
CD 2-Track 11

Goullaud & White, 1870

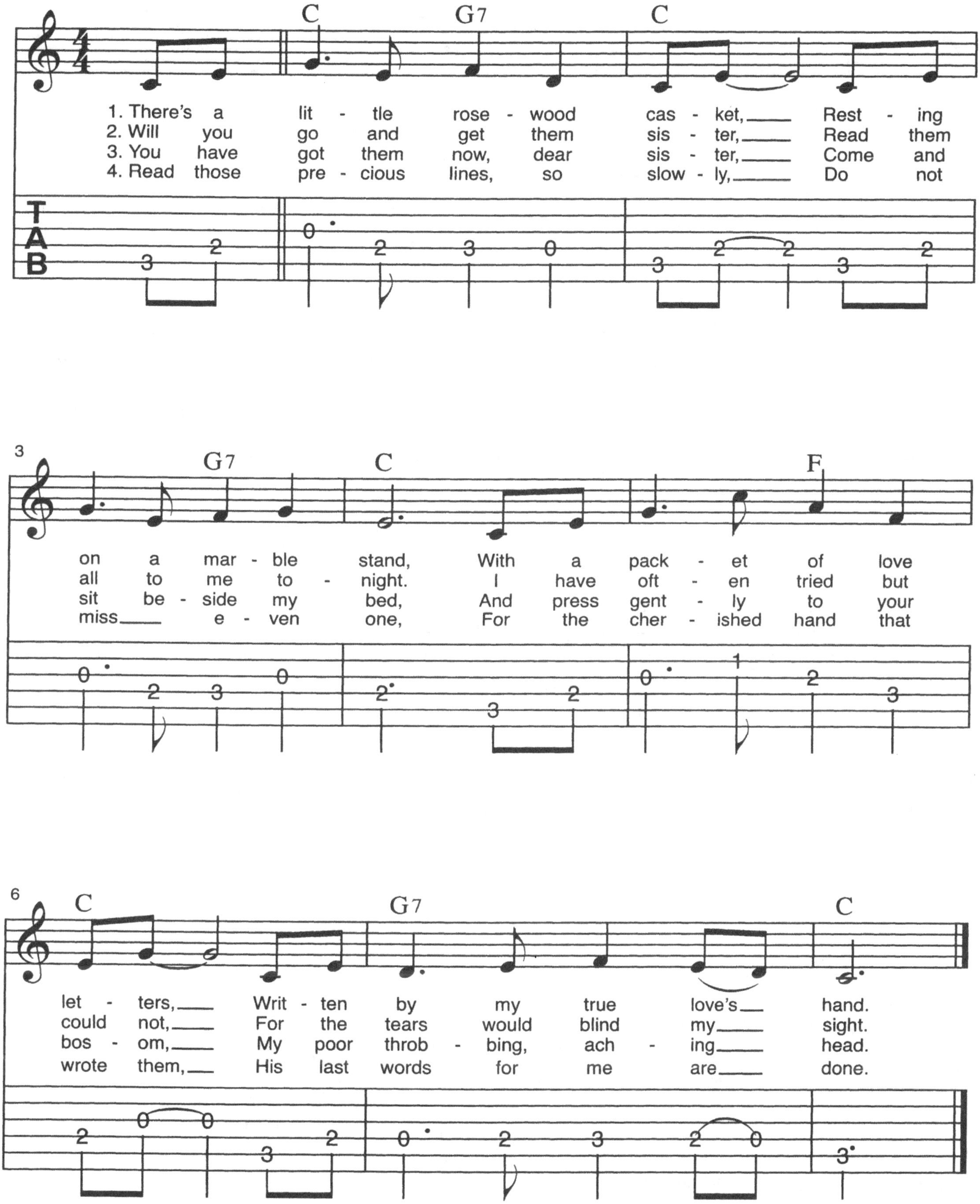

Little Sadie

M: Em; F: Am, capo 5
CD 2-Track 12

Traditional

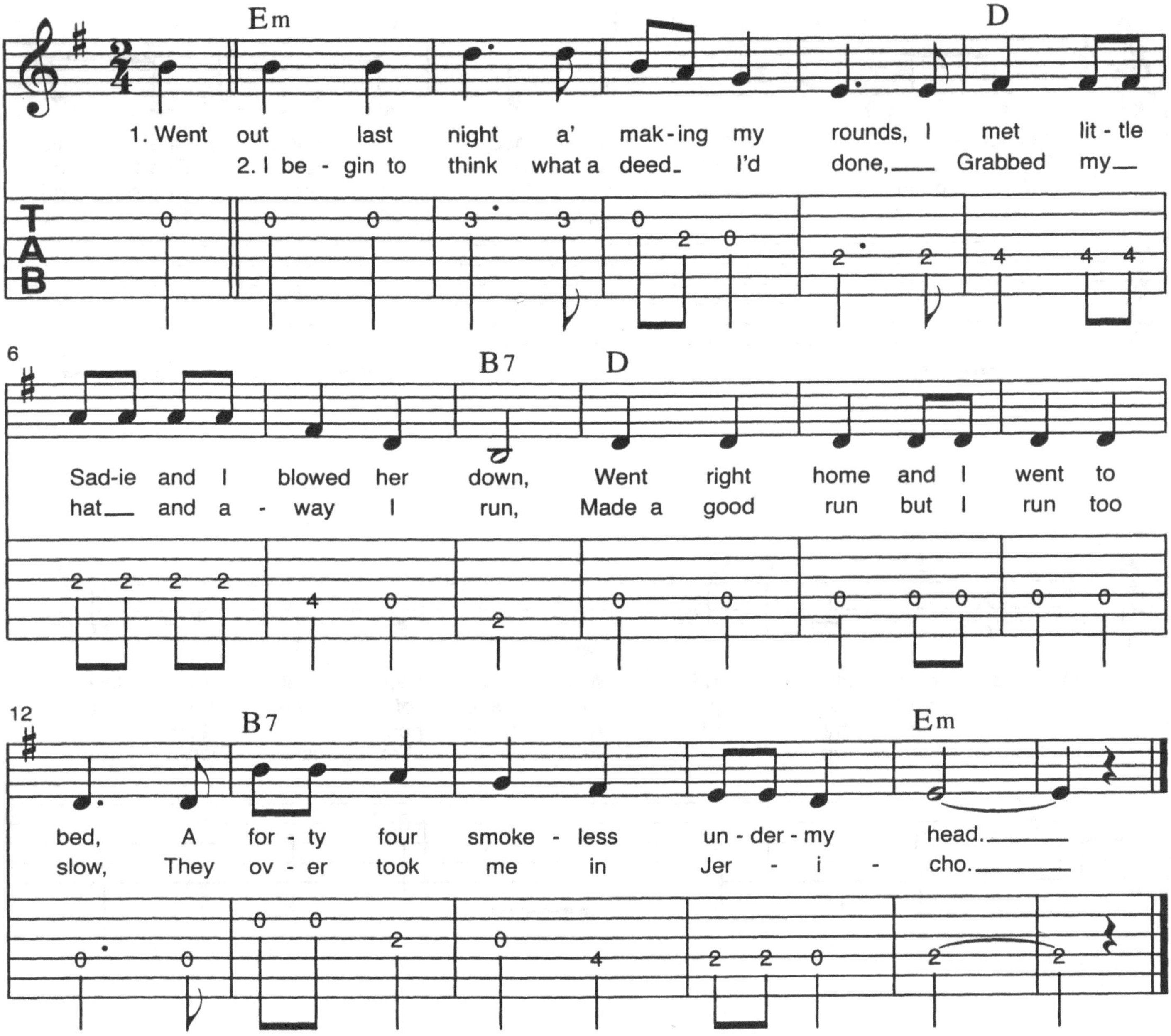

Em
3. Standing on the corner reading a bill,
D B7
Up stepped the sheriff from Thomasville,
D
Says, "Young man is your name Brown?
B7 Em
Remember the night you blowed Sadie down?"

4. Oh, yes sir, my name is Lee,
I murdered little Sadie in the first degree,
First degree and the second degree,
If you got any papers will you read 'em to me?

5. Took me downtown, they dressed me in black,
They put me on the train and they took me back,
Had no one for to go my bail,
Crammed me back in the county jail.

6. Judge and the jury, took their stand,
Judge had his papers in his right hand,
Forty one days, forty one nights,
Forty one years to wear the ball and the stripes.

 D. Watson, T. Rice, Grisman, Garcia, Rice, D. Grisman, T. O'Brien

Little Willie

M: G; F: C or D, capo 5 or 7
CD 2-Track 13

Traditional

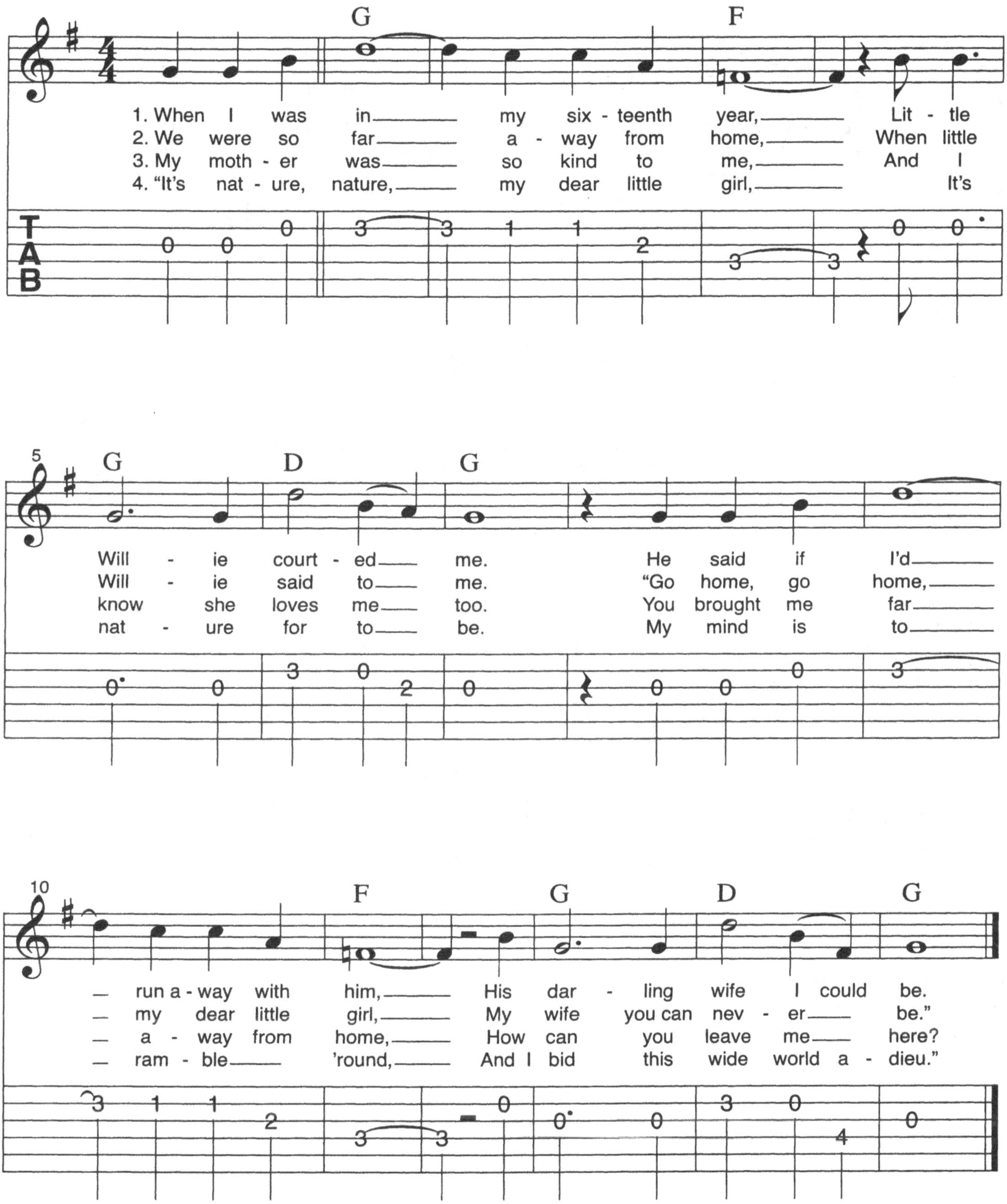

Lonesome Valley

M: G; F: C or D, capo 5 or 7
CD 2-Track 14, medley pt. 1

Traditional

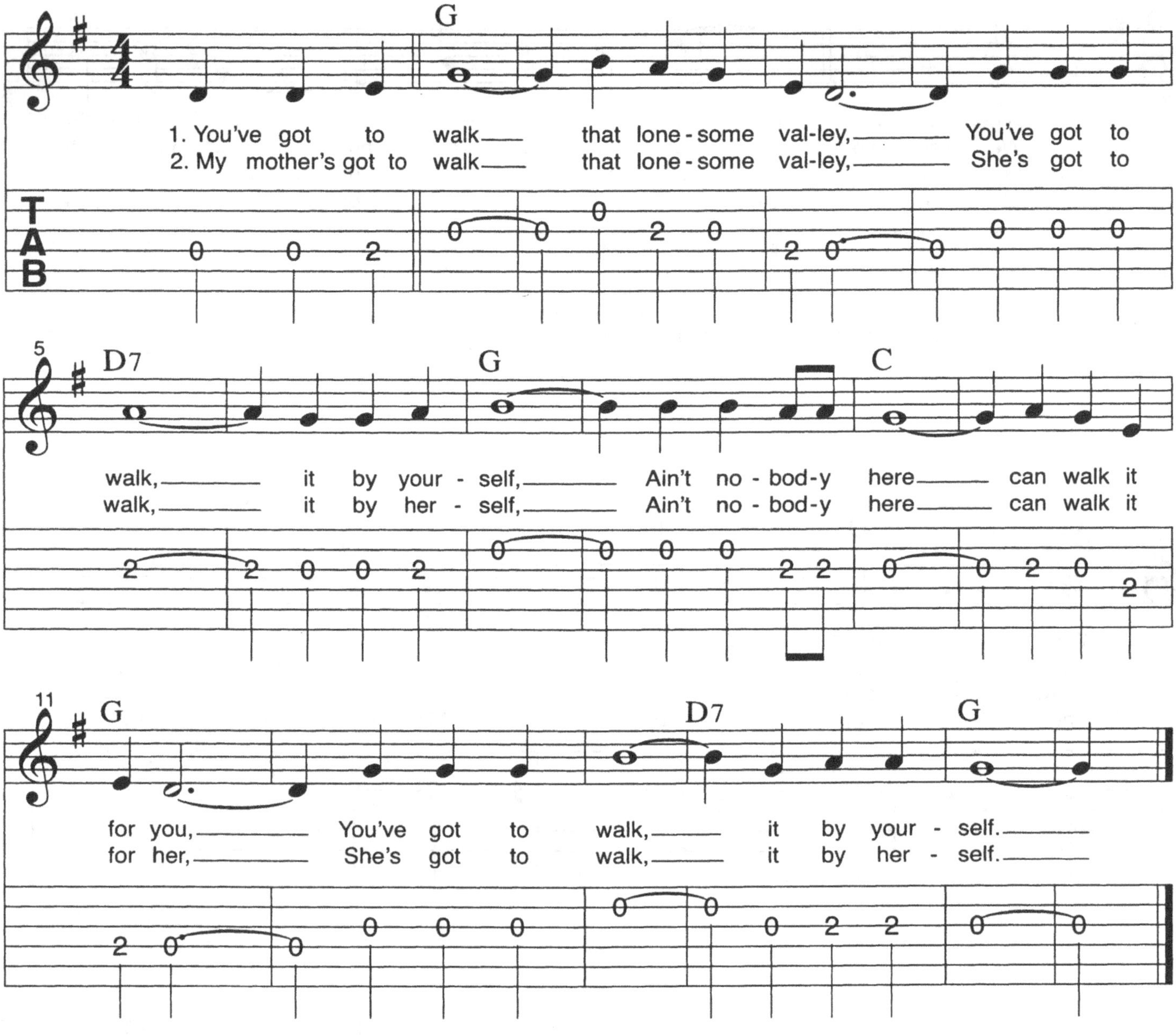

My sister's got to walk, etc.
My brother's got to walk, etc.
My father's got to walk, etc.
All sinners got to walk, etc.

Long Journey Home

M: G; F: C or D, capo 5 or 7
CD 2-Track 14, medley pt. 2

Traditional

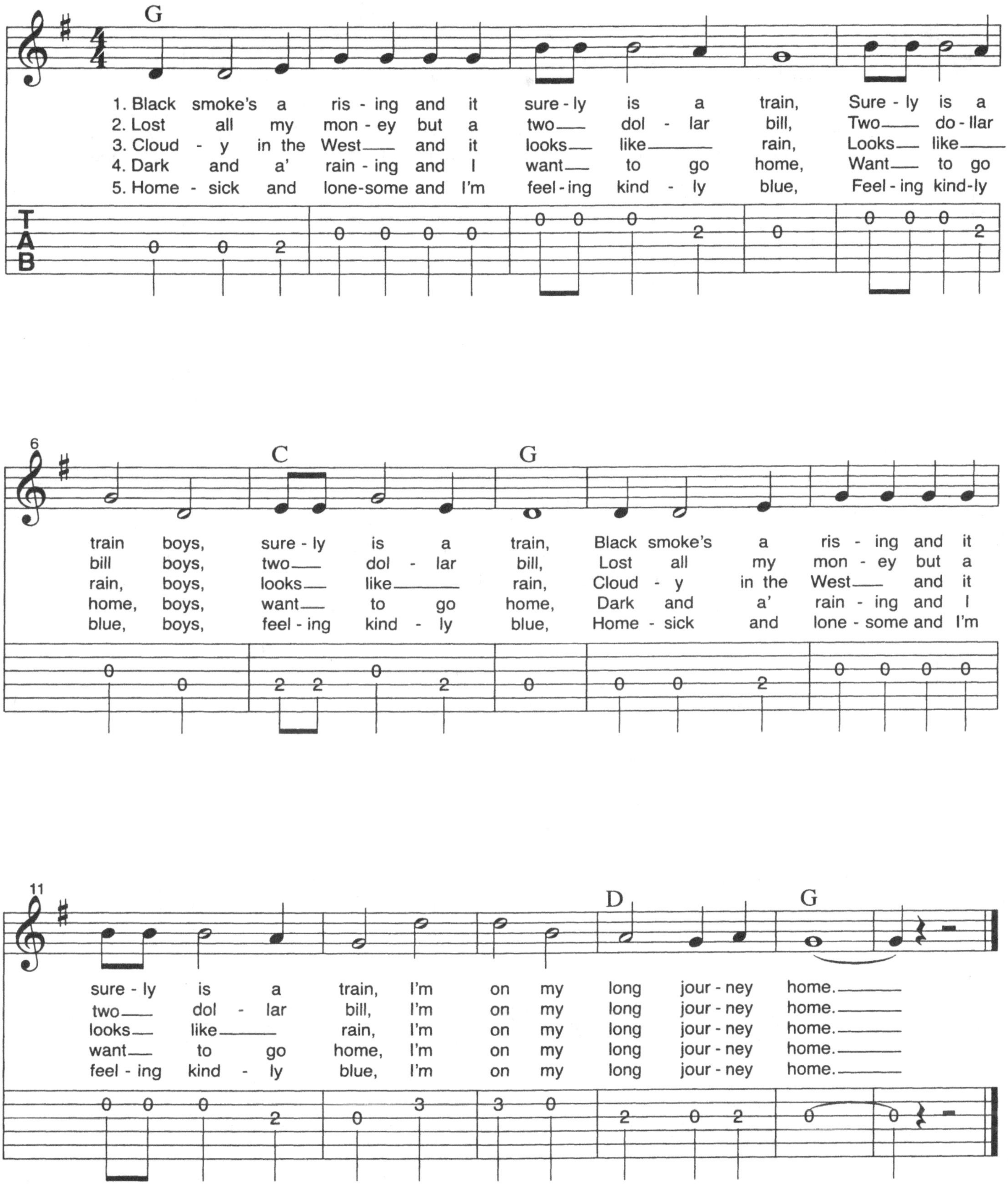

Lord, I'm Coming Home

M: G; F: C or D, capo 5 or 7
CD 2-Track 15

Wm. J. Kirkpatrick, 1892

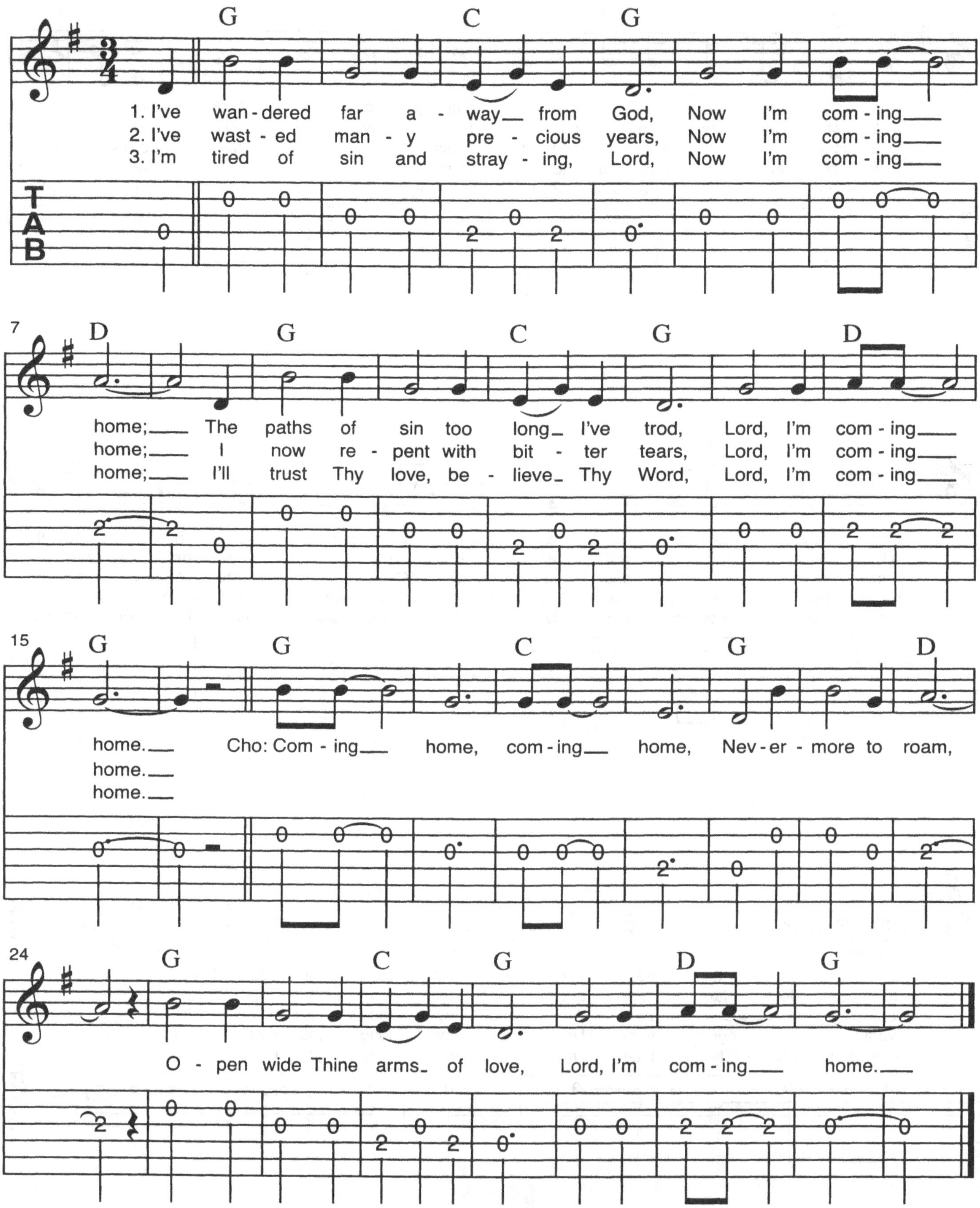

 Stanley Bros., Country Gentlemen, Jim & Jesse, J. Martin, Louvin Bros., Mac Wiseman

G C G
4. My soul is sick, my heart is sore,
D
Now I'm coming home;
G C G
My strength renew, my hope restore,
D G
Lord, I'm coming home.

5. My only hope, my only plea,
Now I'm coming home;
That Jesus died, and died for me.
Lord, I'm coming home.

6. I need His cleansing blood, I know,
Now I'm coming home;
O wash me whiter than the snow,
Lord, I'm coming home.

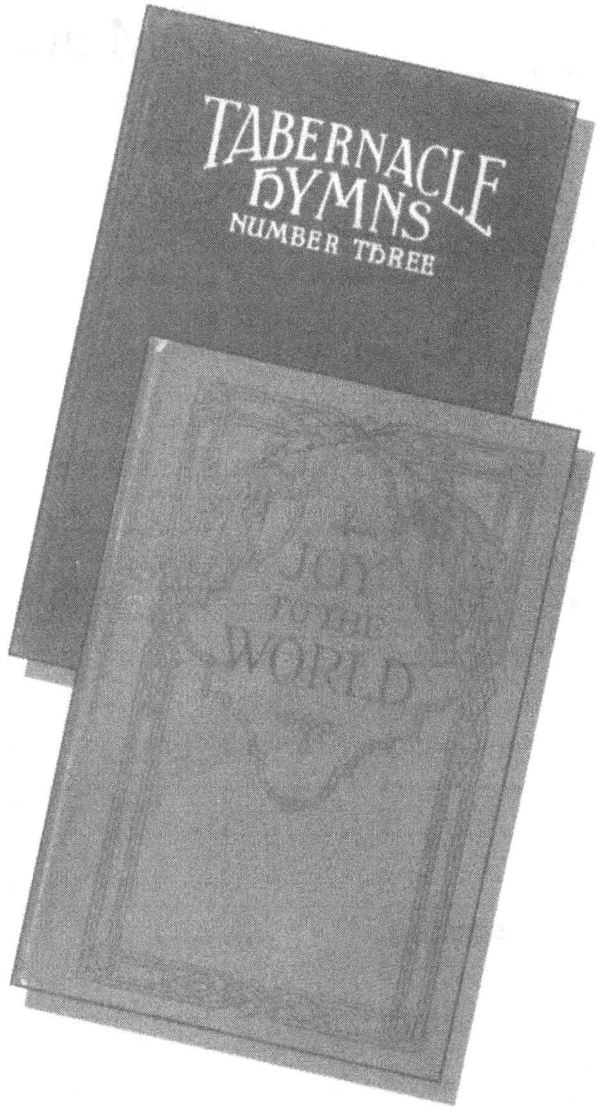

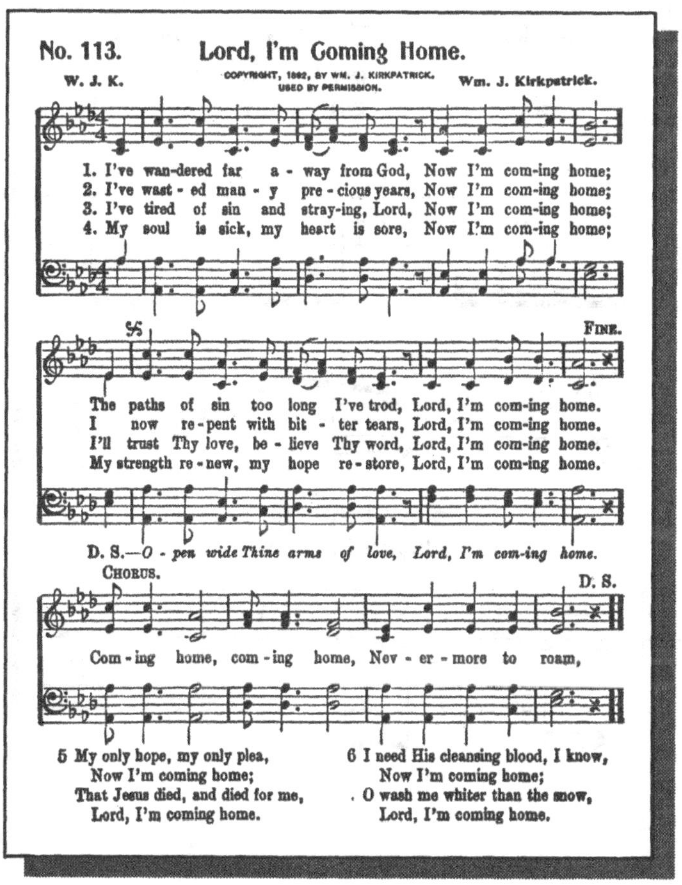

Old Baptist hymnals are a great source of old time and bluegrass gospel songs. These two, "Tabernacle Hymns" and "Joy to the World," date from the early 1900s and both include the song "Lord, I'm Coming Home," among many other gospel greats.

Mama Don't Allow

M: C; F: F or G, capo 5 or 7
CD 2-Track 16

Traditional

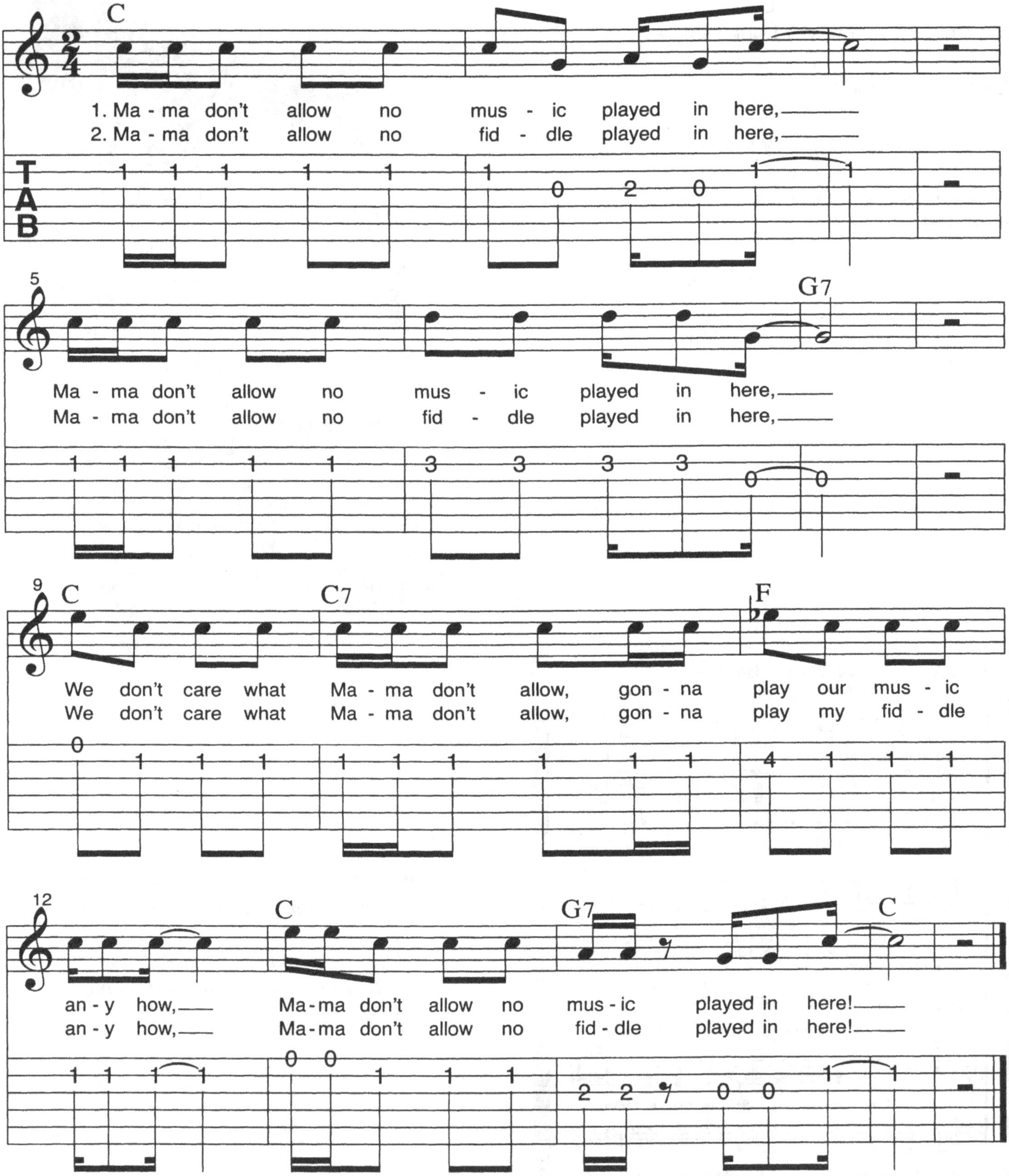

Mama don't allow no banjo playing here, etc.
Guitar, mandolin, Dobro, etc.

Man of Constant Sorrow

M: D; F: G or A, capo 5 or 7
CD 2-Track 17

Dick Burnett, ca. 1912

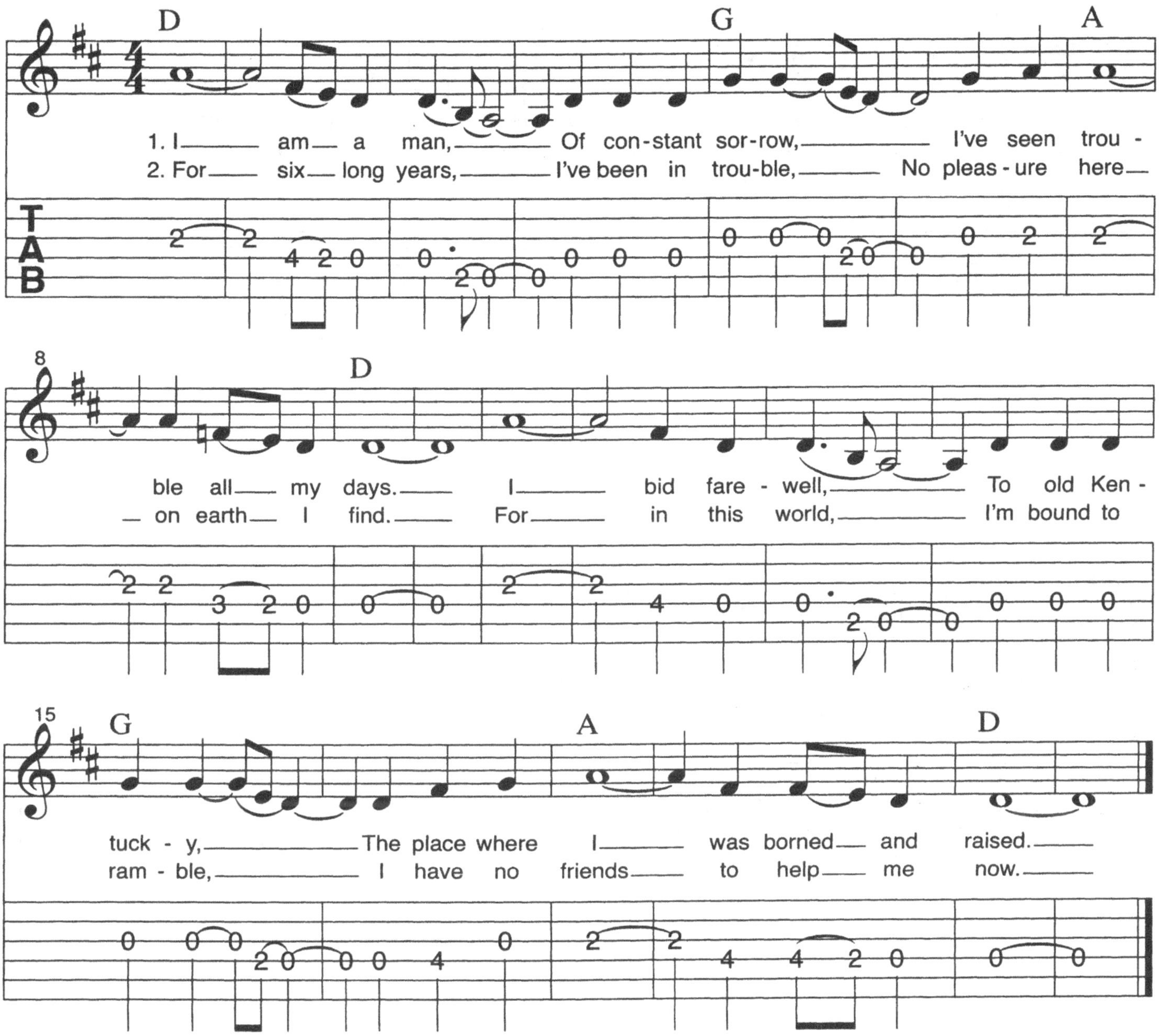

D G
3. It's fare thee well, my own true lover,
A D
I never expect to see again.
G
For I'm bound to ride, that northern railroad,
A D
Perhaps I'll die upon this train.

4. You can bury me, in some deep valley,
For many years where I may lay.
Then you may learn, to love another,
While I am sleeping in my grave.

5. Maybe your friends think, I'm just a stranger,
My face you never will see no more.
But there is one promise that is given,
I'll meet you on God's golden shore.

Stanley Bros., R. Stanley, "O Brother" soundtrack, Grisman, Garcia, Rice, Blue Highway, Bluegrass Band, Dillards, P. Rowan

The Maple on the Hill

M: G; F: C or D, capo 5 or 7
CD 2-Track 18

G.L. Davis, 1880

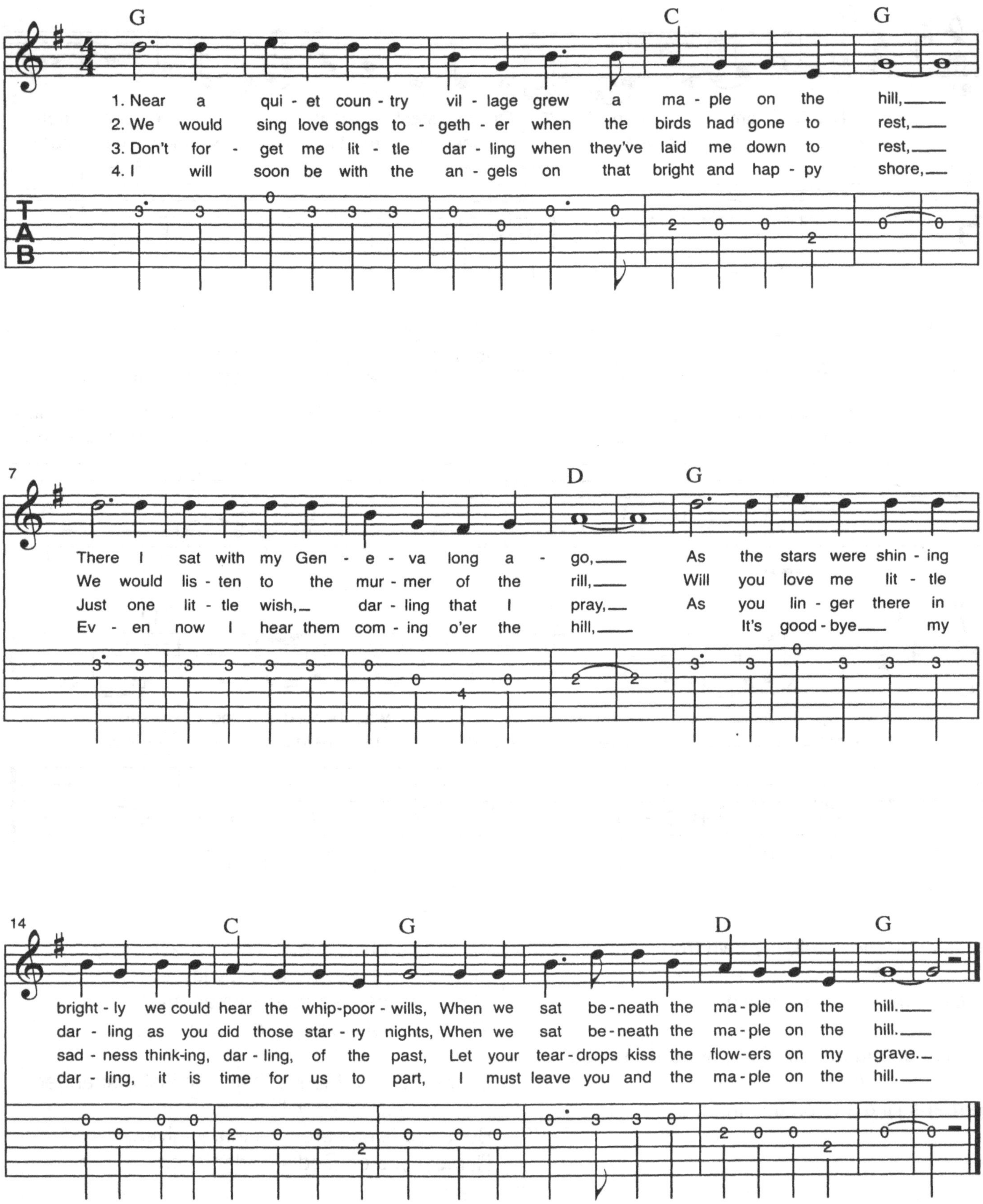

 Stanley Bros., R. Stanley, Dixon Brothers, Mac Wiseman, J.E. Mainer

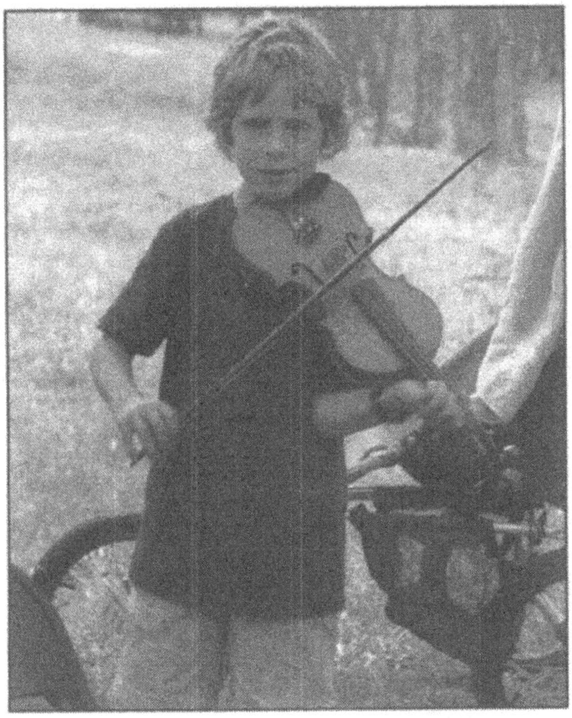

Photo by Bill Evans

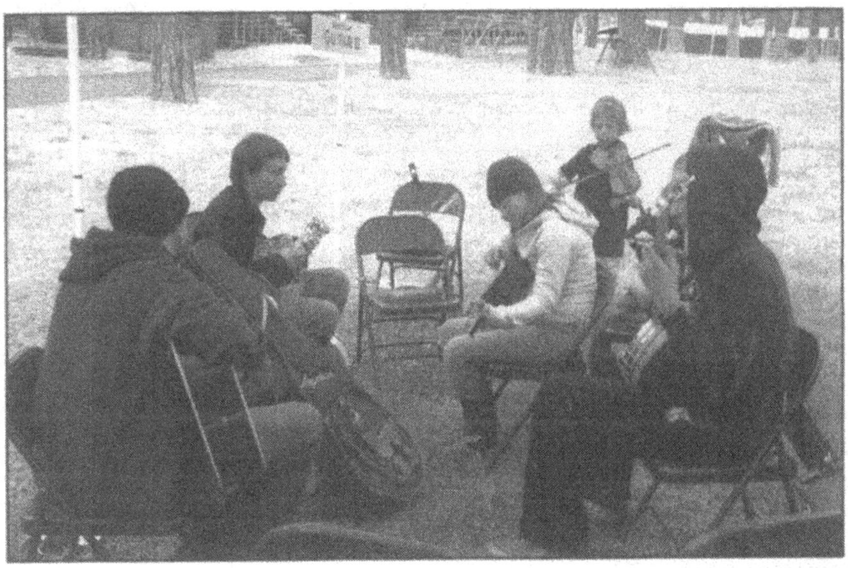

Photo by Bill Evans

One of the great things about playing old time and bluegrass music is that you can have fun playing with others even if you are still a beginner. Playing in a parking lot session is something that brings together musicians of all ages.

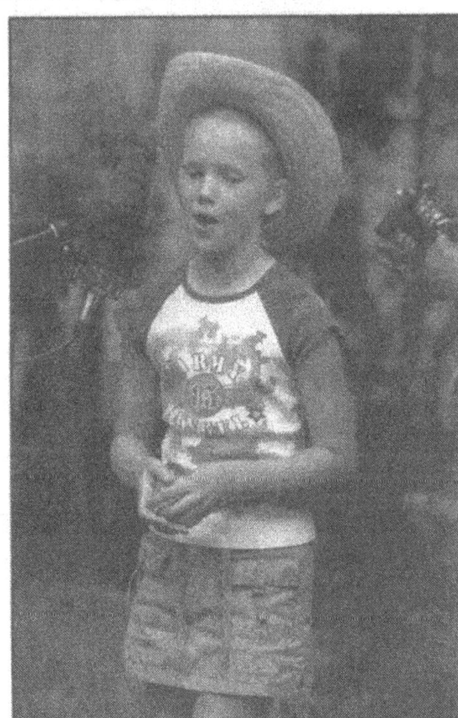

Photo by Tom Tworek

Methodist Pie

M: D; F: G or A, capo 5 or 7
CD 2-Track 19, medley pt. 1

Traditional

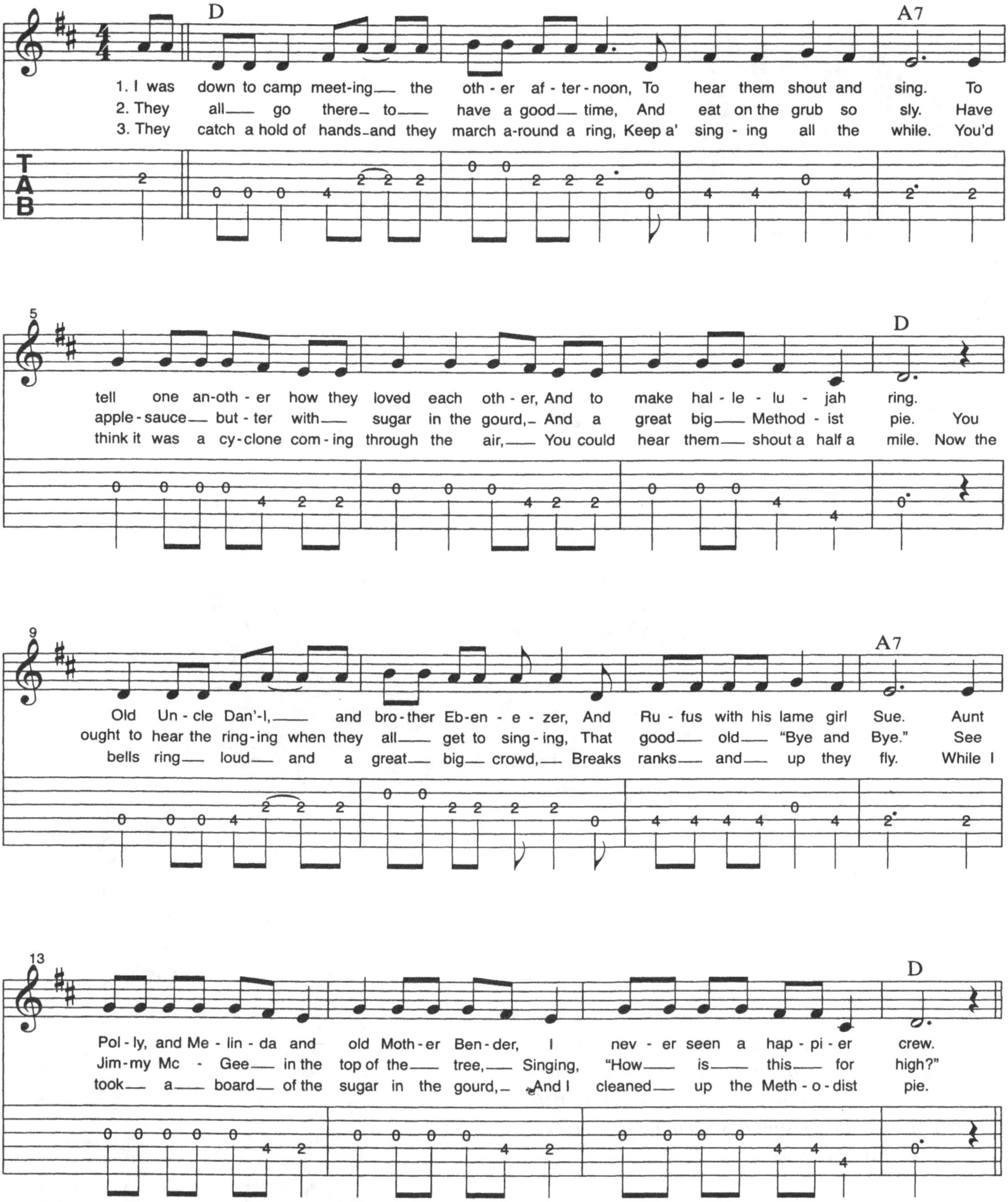

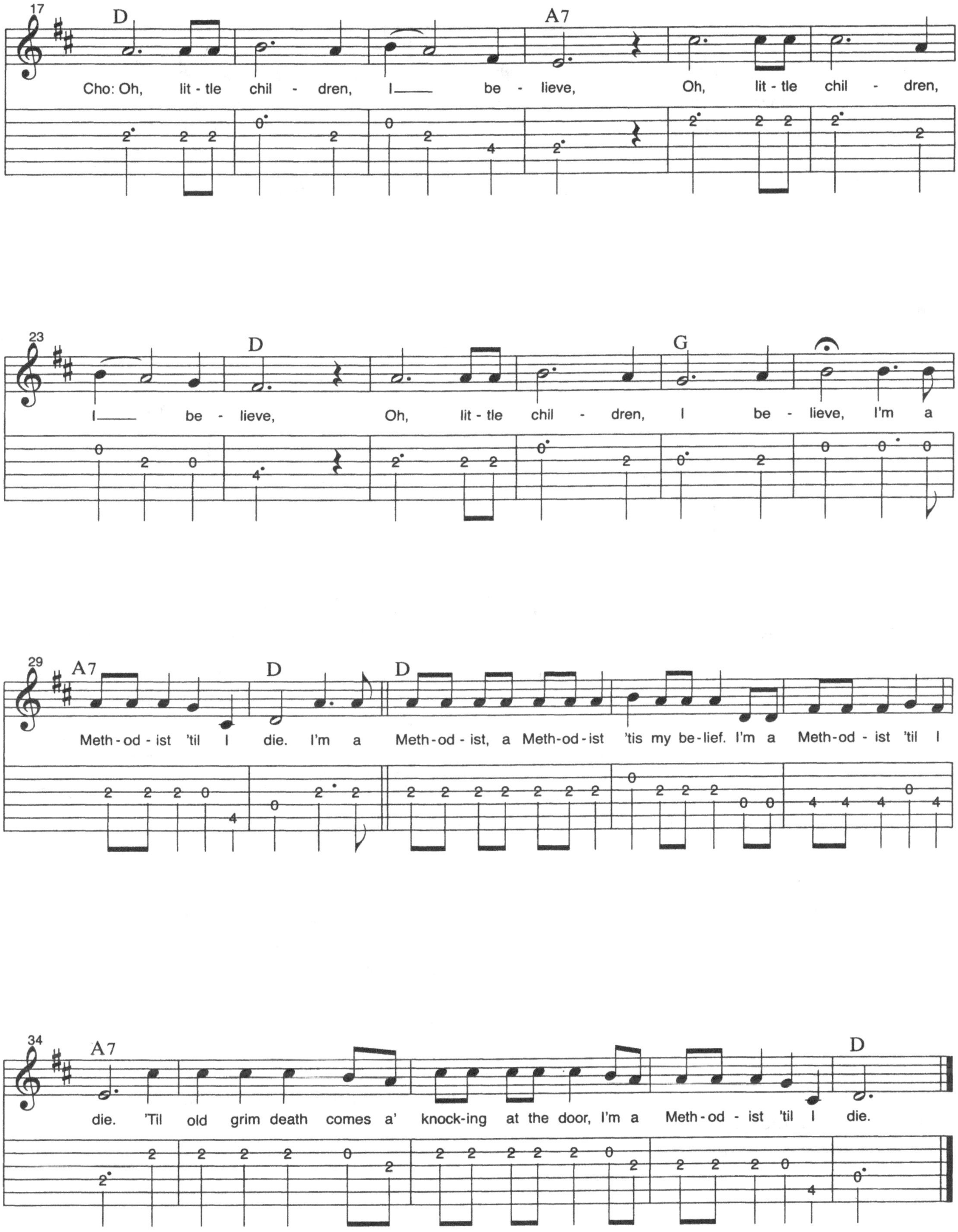
17
D
A7
Cho: Oh, lit - tle chil - dren, I be - lieve, Oh, lit - tle chil - dren,
23
D
G
I be - lieve, Oh, lit - tle chil - dren, I be - lieve, I'm a
29
A7
D
D
Meth - od - ist 'til I die. I'm a Meth - od - ist, a Meth - od - ist 'tis my be - lief. I'm a Meth - od - ist 'til I
34
A7
D
die. 'Til old grim death comes a' knock - ing at the door, I'm a Meth - od - ist 'til I die.

Midnight on the Stormy Deep

M: D; F: G or A, capo 5 or 7
CD 2-Track 19, medley pt. 2

Traditional

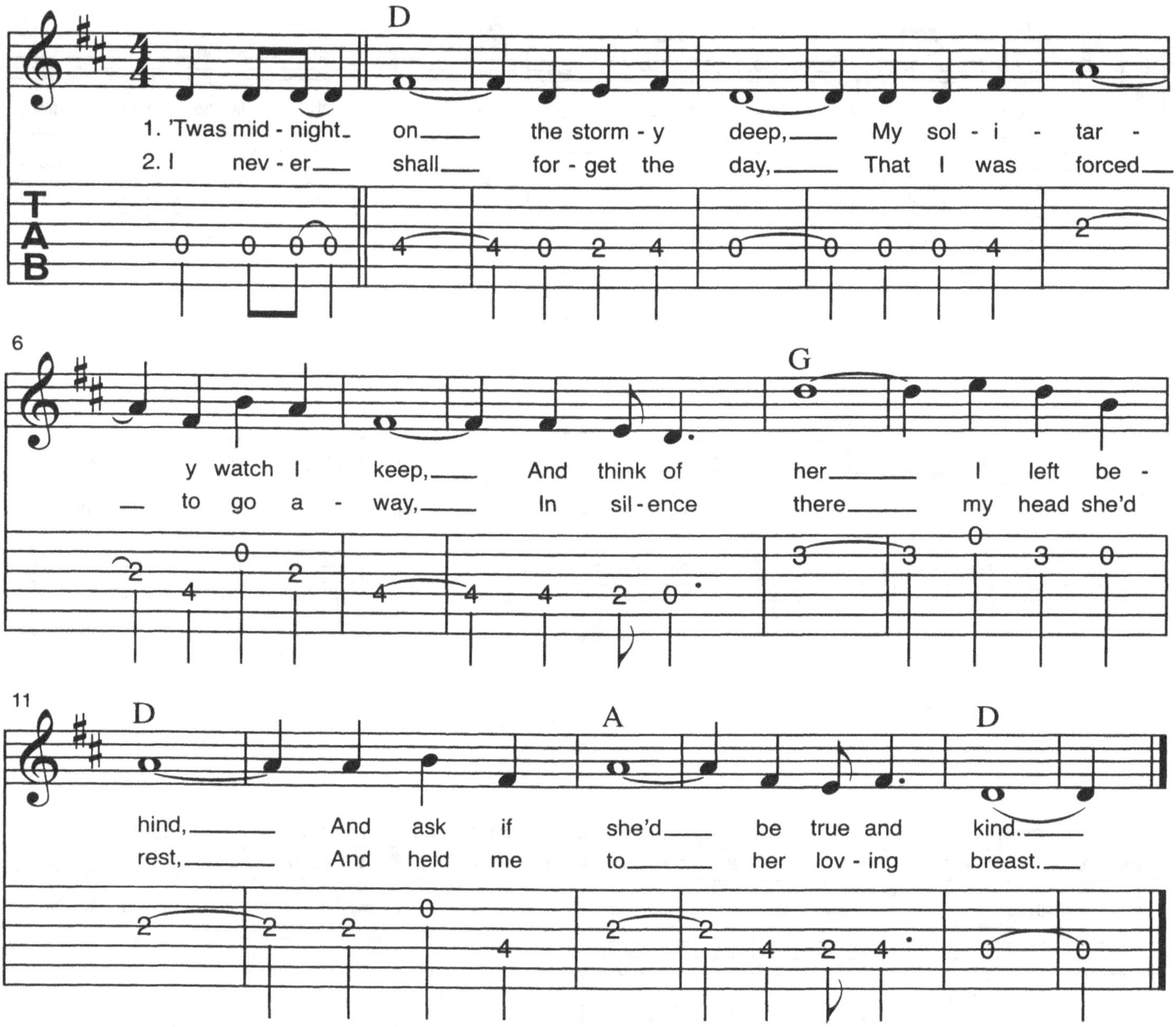

D
3. Oh Willy don't go back to sea,
There's other girls as good as me,
G D
But none can love you true as I,
A D
Pray don't go where the bullets fly.

4. The deep, deep sea may us divide,
And I may be some other's bride,
But still my thoughts will oft times stray,
To thee when thou are far away.

5. I never have proved false to thee,
The love I gave is true and kind,
But you have proved untrue to me,
I can no longer call thee mine.

6. Then fare thee well, I'd rather make,
My home upon some icy lake,
Where the southern sun refuses to shine,
Then to trust a love so false as thine.

 B. Monroe, D. Watson, Dry Branch Fire Squad, P. Rowan, T. Rice

Milwaukee Blues

M: C; F: F or G, capo 5 or 7
CD 2-Track 20

Traditional

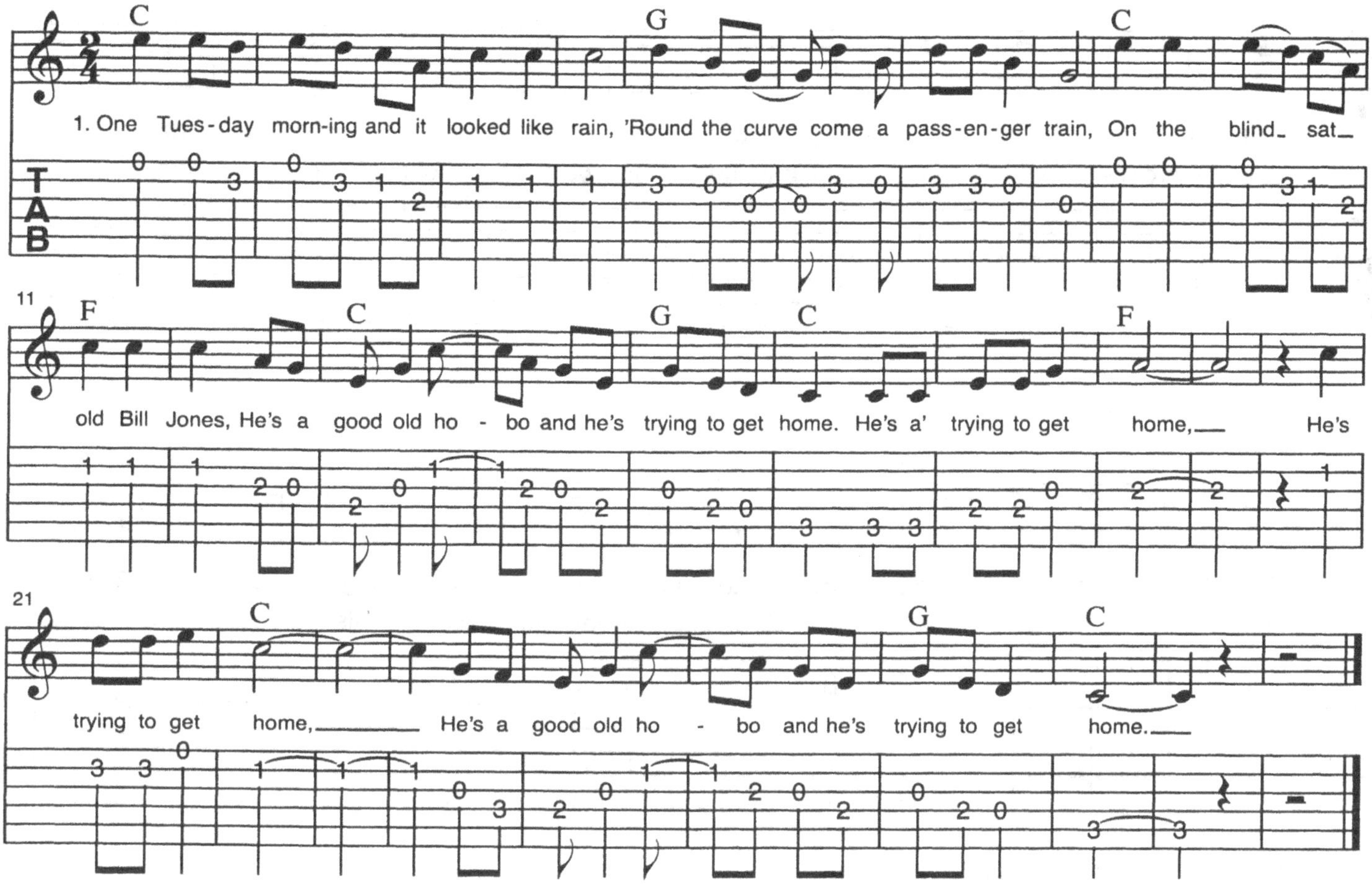

C
2. Way down in Georgia on a tramp,
G
The roads are getting muddy and the leaves are getting damp,
C F
Got to catch a freight train, leave this town
C G C
Cause they don't 'low no hoboes a' hanging around.
F C
Hanging around, hanging around,
G C
They don't 'low no hoboes a' hanging around.

3. Left Atlanta one morning 'fore day,
The brakeman said, "You'll have to pay.'
Had no money so I pawned my shoes,
I want to go west, I've got the Milwaukee blues.
Got the Milwaukee blues, got the Milwaukee blues,
I want to go west, I got the Milwaukee blues.

4. Old Bill Jones said before he died,
"Fix the road so the 'boes can ride.
When they ride, they will ride the rods,
Put all their trust in the hands of God.
In the hands of God, in the hands of God,
Put all their trust in the hands of God.

5. Old Bill Jones said before he died,
There's two more roads he'd like to ride.
Fireman said, "What can it be?"
"The Southern Pacific and the Santa Fe.
Santa Fe, yes, the Santa Fe,
The Southern Pacific and the Santa Fe."

Molly and Tenbrooks

M: G; F: C or D, capo 5 or 7
CD 2-Track 21

Traditional

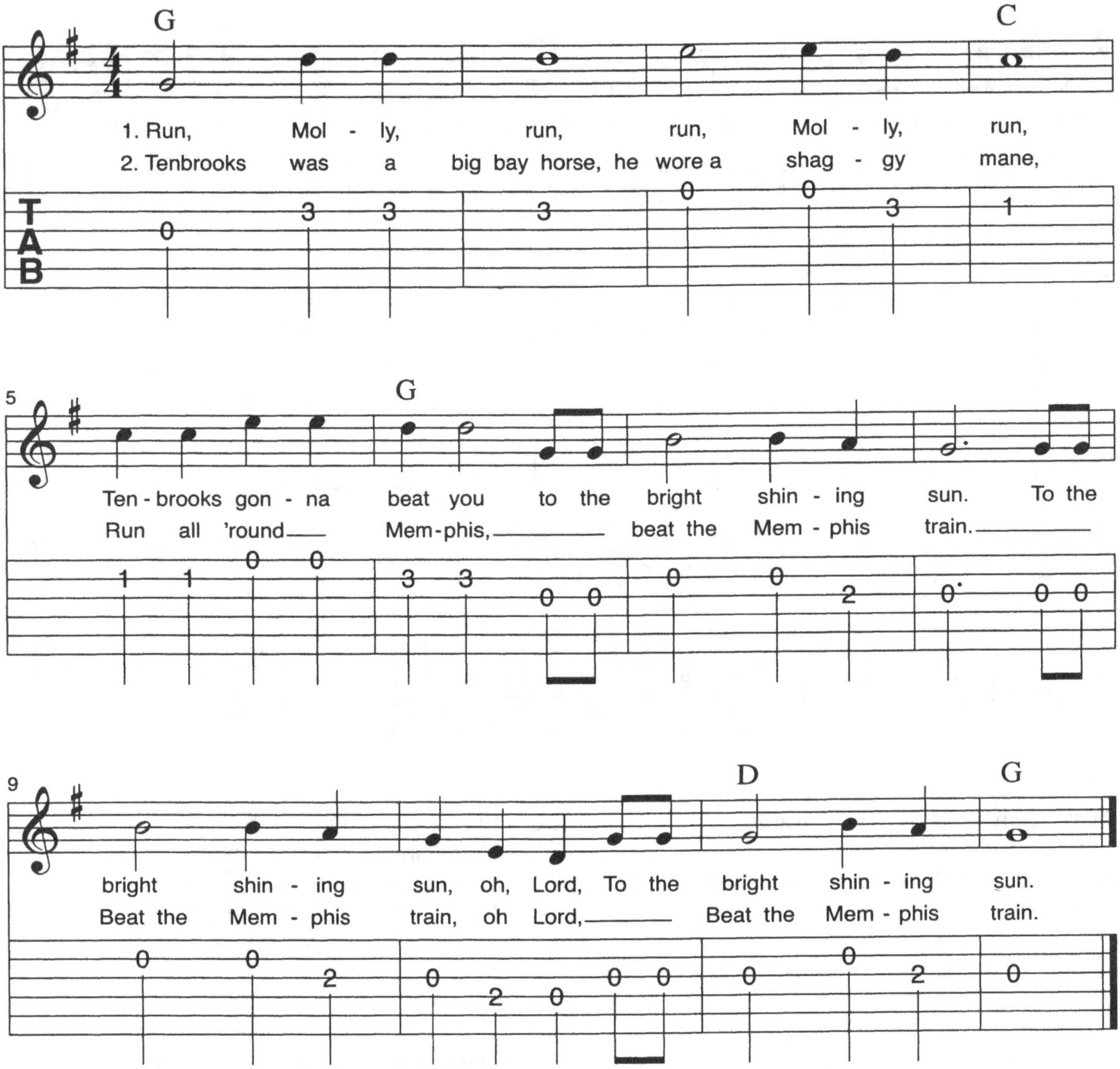

B. Monroe, Stanley Bros., J.D. Crowe, Country Gentlemen, E. Taylor, Bluegrass Band, Country Gazette, Jimmy Martin, J. Val, Osborne Bros., Bluegrass Album BandB. Monroe, Seldom Scene, D. Grisman Carter Fam., Bluegrass Album Band, D. Watson, K. Kallick

```
   G                                                C
3. Tenbrooks said to Molly, "What makes your head so red?"
                  G               D          G
"Running in the hot sun with a fever in my head.
                                D          G
Fever in my head, oh Lord, fever in my head."
```

4. Molly said to Tenbrooks, "You're looking mighty squirrel,"
Tenbrooks said to Molly, "I'm leaving this old world." (etc.)

5. Out in California where Molly done as she pleased,
She come back to old Kentucky, got beat with all ease. (etc.)

6. The women's all a' laughing, the children all a' crying,
Men folks all a' hollering, old Tenbrooks a' flying. (etc.)

7. Kuyper, Kuyper, you're not riding right,
Molly's a beatin' old Tenbrooks clear out of sight. (etc.)

8. Kuyper, Kuyper, Kuyper, my son,
Give Tenbrooks the bridle and let old Tenbrooks run. (etc.)

9. Go and catch old Tenbrooks and hitch him in the shade,
We're gonna bury old Molly in a coffin ready made. (etc.)

My Home's Across the Blue Ridge Mountains

M: D; F: G or A, capo 5 or 7 *Traditional*
CD 2-Track 22

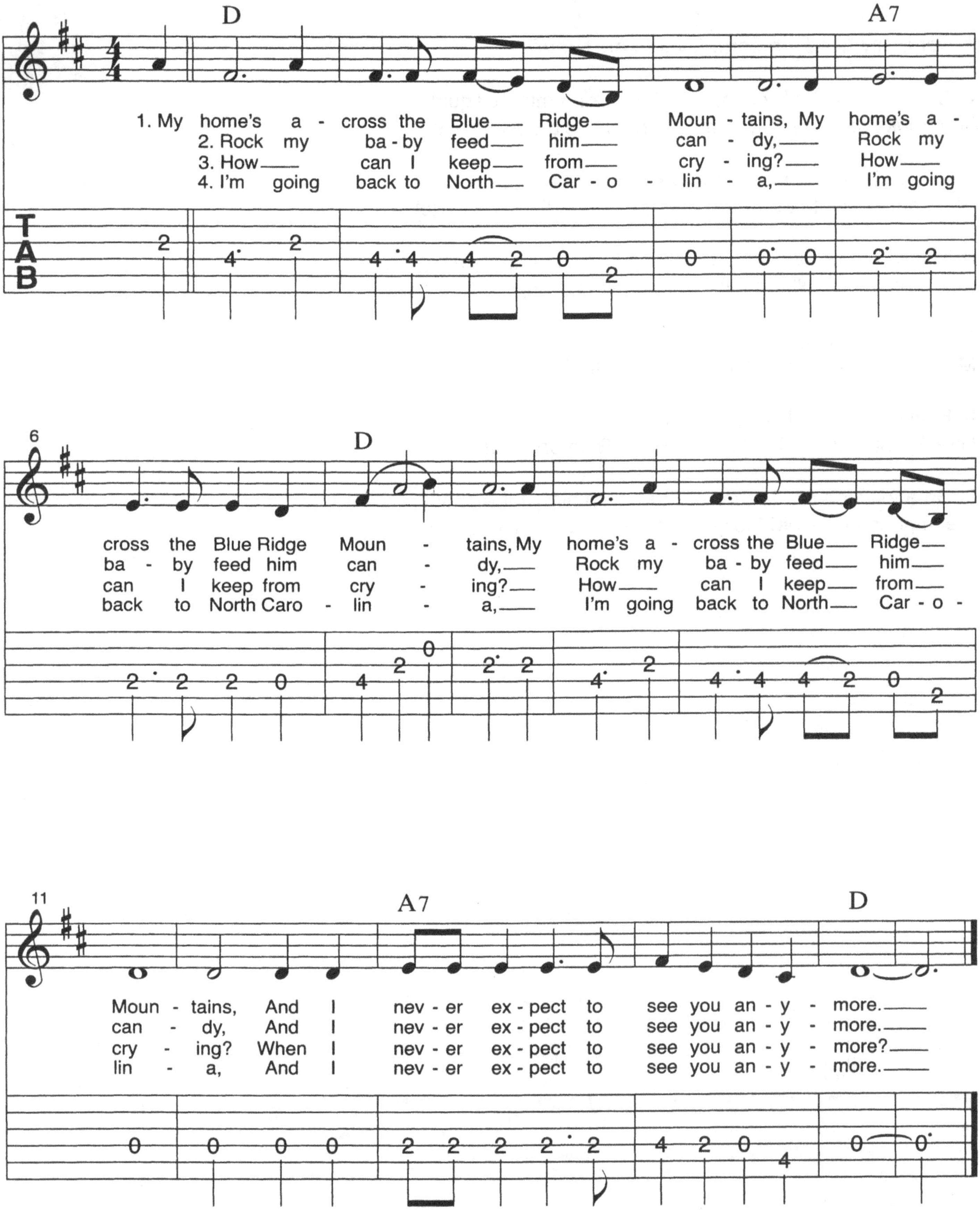

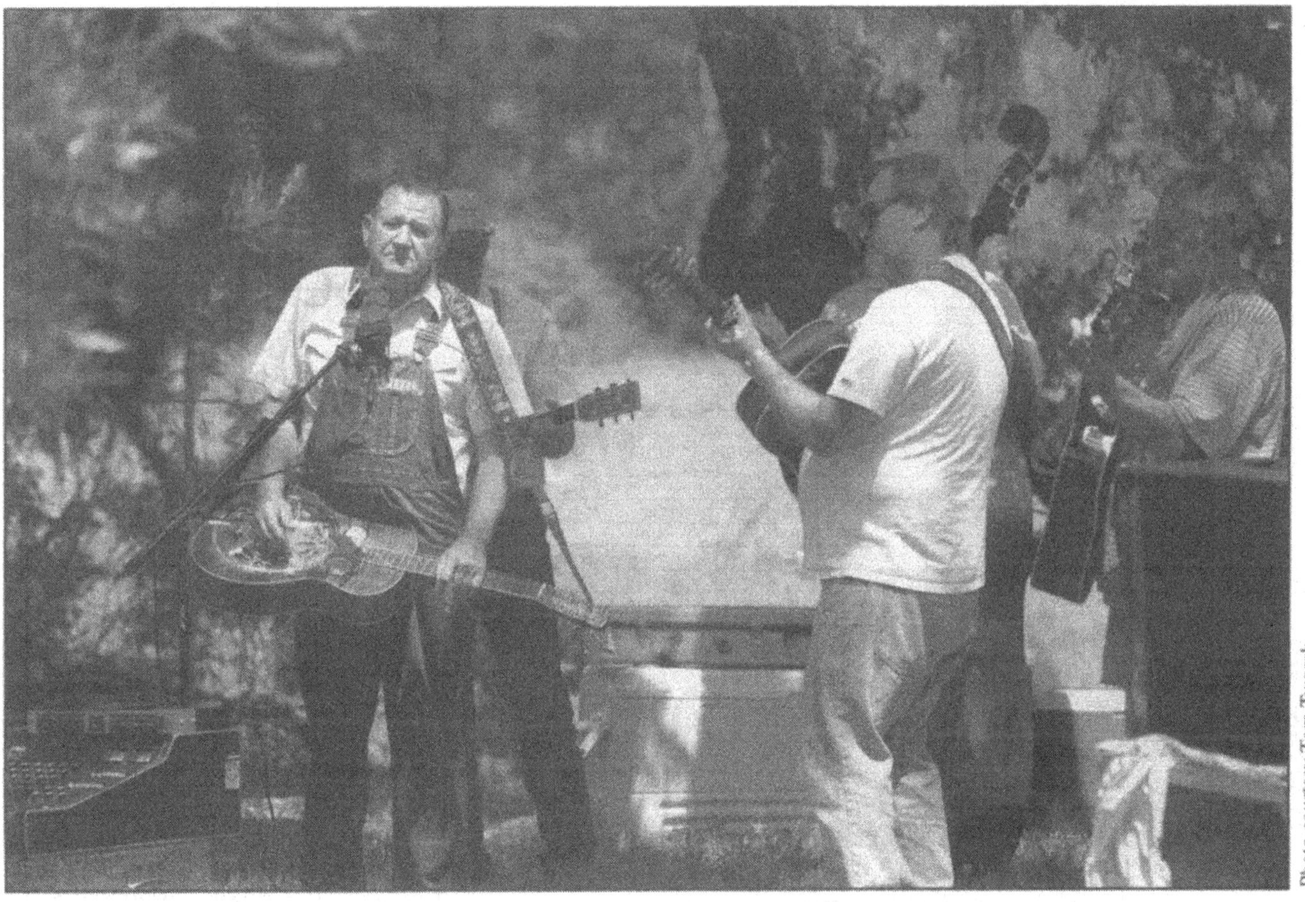
Photo courtesy Tom Tworek

Ernie Hunt (left) jamming with photographer Tom Tworek (center) in a beautiful outdoor setting.

My Little Georgia Rose

M: G; F: C or D, capo 5 or 7
CD 2-Track 23

Bill Monroe

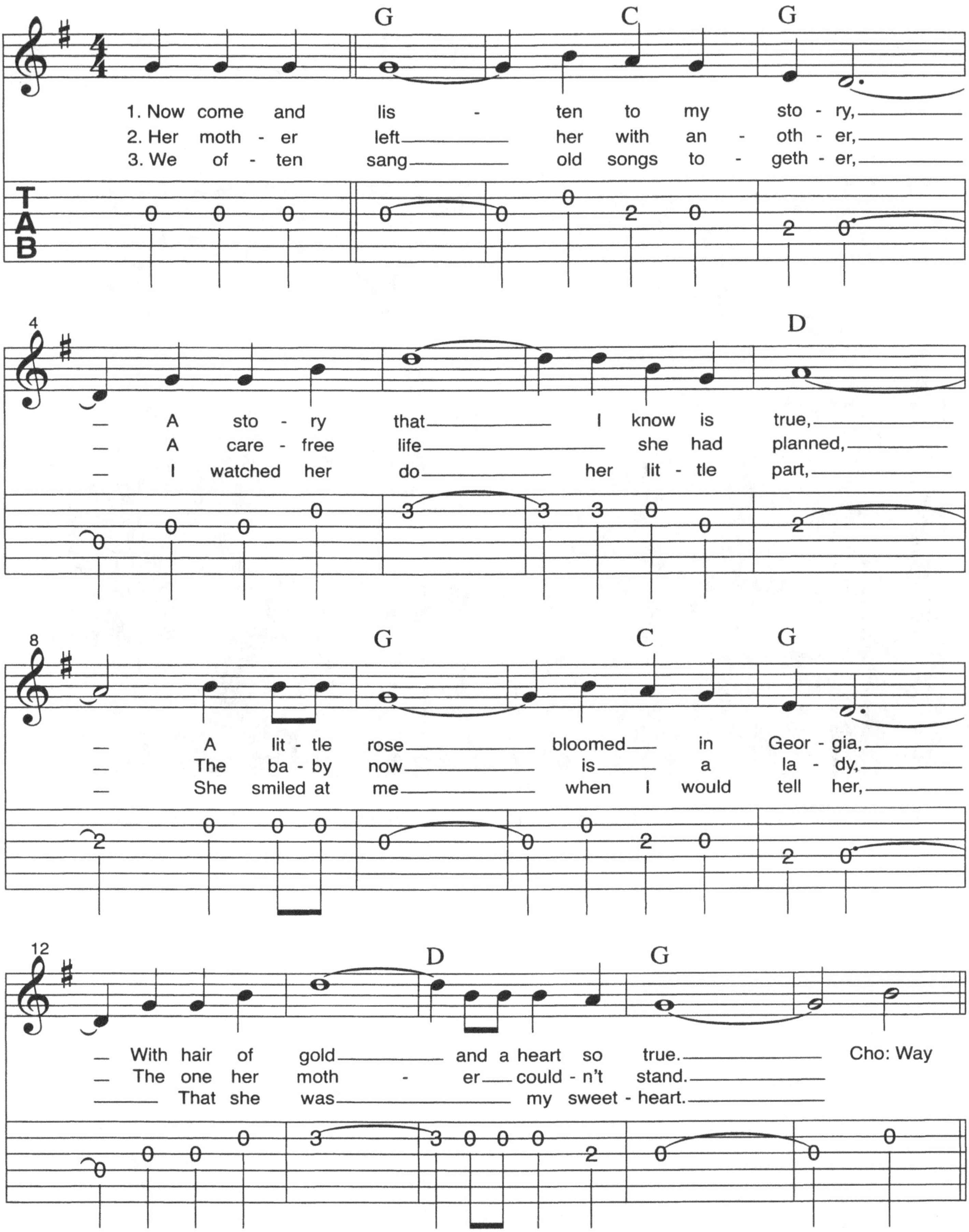

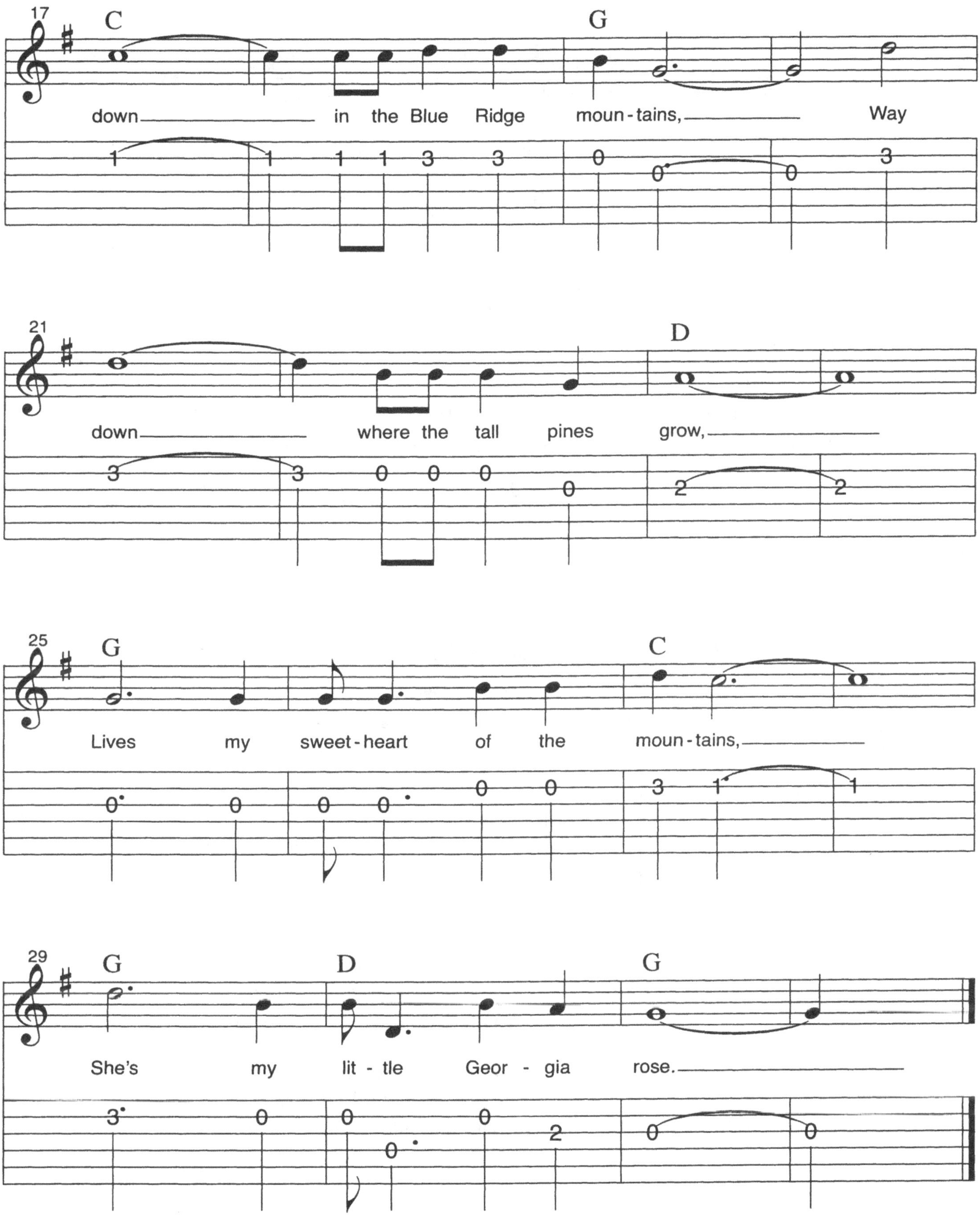
17
C
G
down in the Blue Ridge moun-tains, Way
21
D
down where the tall pines grow,
25
G
C
Lives my sweet-heart of the moun-tains,
29
G
D
G
She's my lit-tle Geor-gia rose.

New River Train

M: G; F: C or D, capo 5 or 7
CD 2-Track 24, medley pt. 1

Traditional

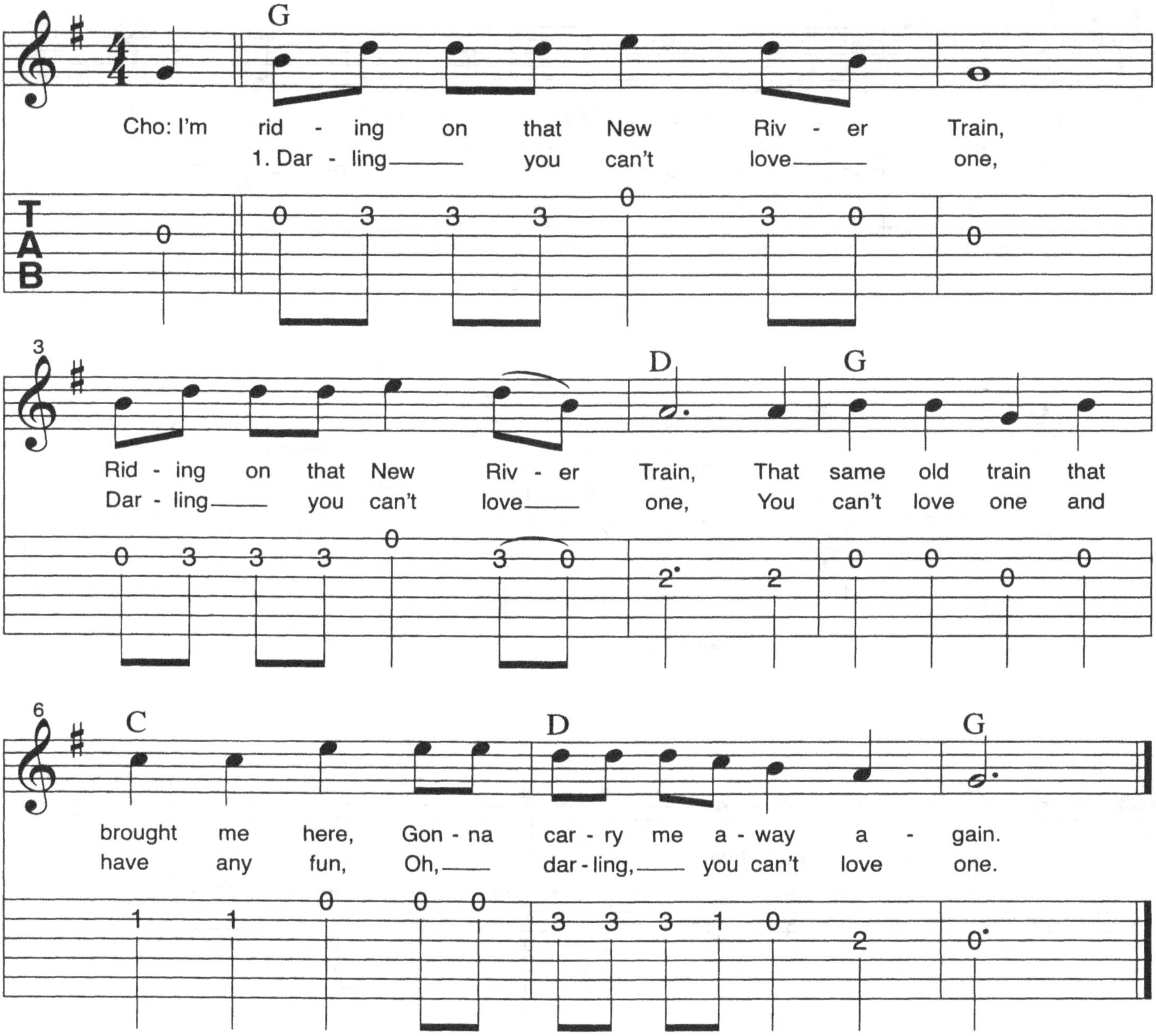

G
2. Darling, you can't love two,
D
Darling, you can't love two,
G C
You can't love two and your little heart be true,
D G
Oh, darling, you can't love two.

3. Darling, you can't love three, (2X)
You can't love three and still love me,
Oh, darling, you can't love three.

4. Darling, you can't love four, (2X)
You can't love four and love me anymore,
Oh, darling, you can't love four.

Nine Pound Hammer

M: G; F: C or D, capo 5 or 7
CD 2-Track 24, medley pt. 2

Traditional

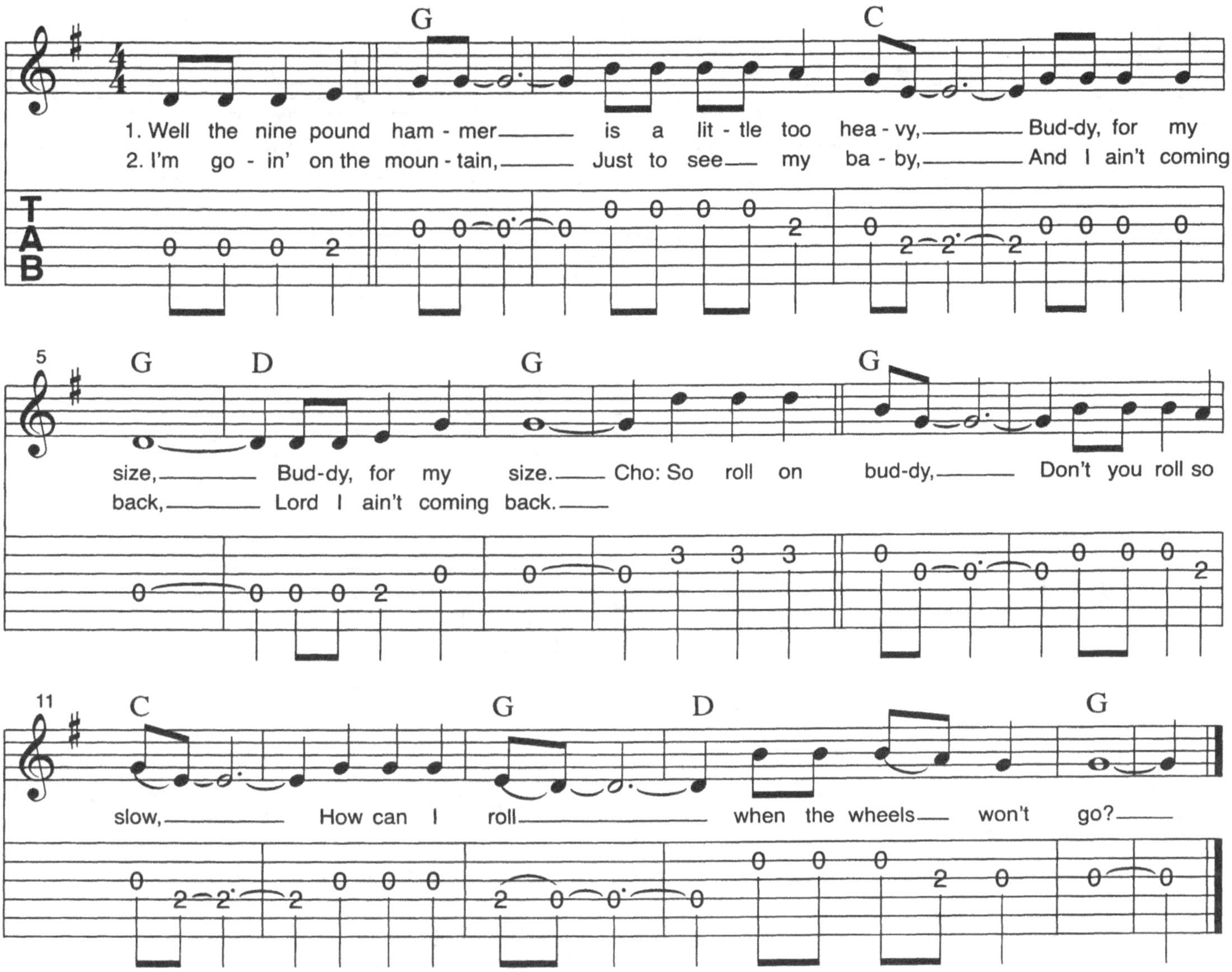

G C
3. There ain't no hammer, in this tunnel,
G D G
That can ring like mine, that can ring like mine.

4. This nine pound hammer, it killed John Henry,
But it won't kill me, no it won't kill me.

5. It's a long way to Harlan, it's a long way to Hazard,
Just to get a little brew, just to get a little brew.

6. I'm working all day, down under ground,
Black as night, it's black as night.

Monroe Bros., B. Monroe, Flatt & Scruggs, Stanley Bros., R. Stanley, Osborne Bros., T. Rice, D. Watson, R. Allen & F. Wakefield, D. Grisman, Ken. Colonels, C. White, Blue Sky Boys, Jim & Jesse

Nobody's Business

M: G; F: C or D, capo 5 or 7
CD 2-Track 25

Traditional

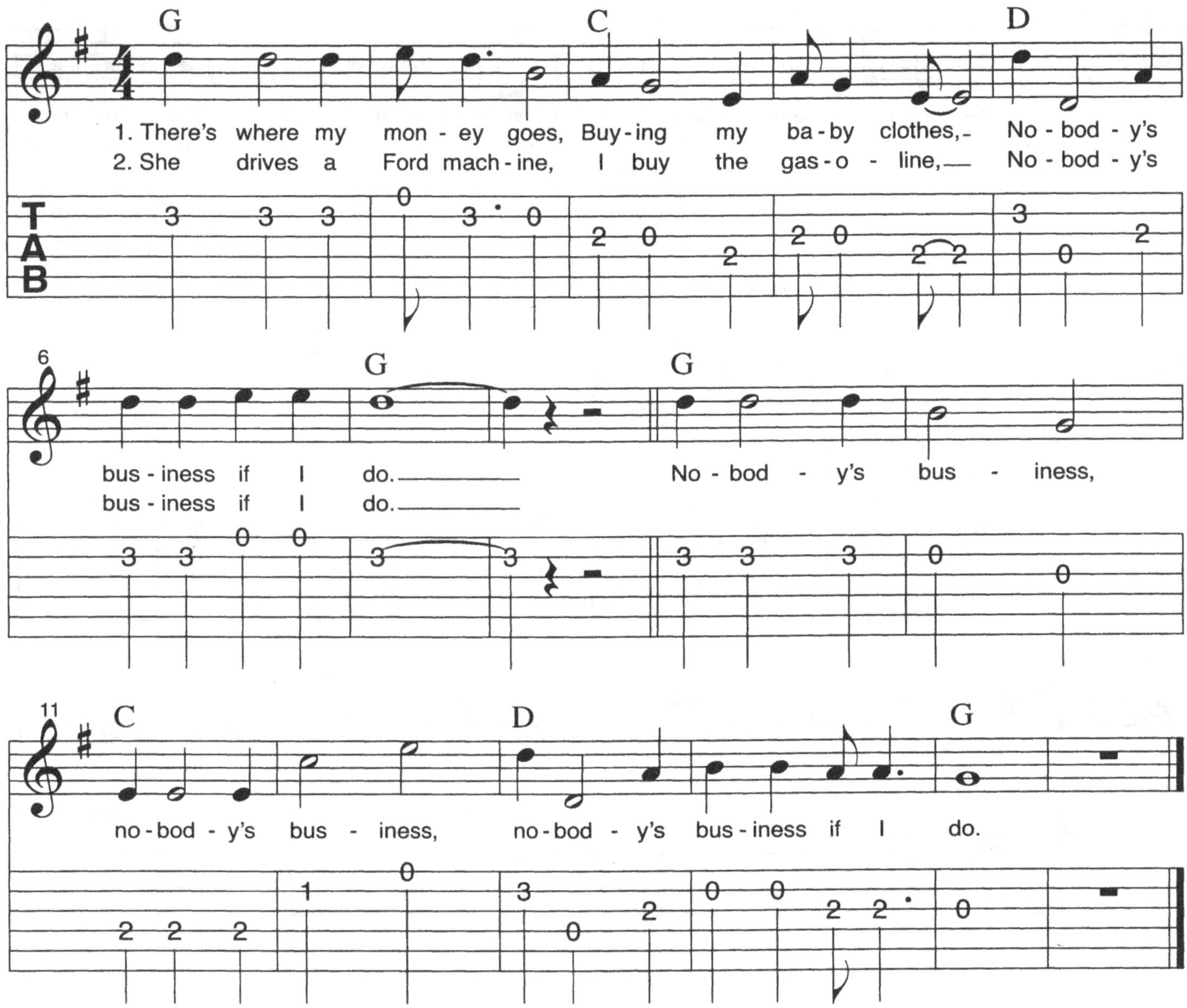

G
3. She's worth her weight in gold,
C
She likes to rock & roll,
D G
Nobody's business if I do,
G C
Cho: Nobody's business, Nobody's business,
D G
Nobody's business if I do,

4. My wife's from Alabam,
Way out in no man's land,
Nobody's business if I do, (etc.)

5. Sliced ham and pickled feet,
Ham and eggs and sausage meat,
Nobody's business if I do, (etc.)

6. She rides the limousine,
I crank the old machine,
Nobody's business if I do, (etc.)

 Stanley Bros., N. Blake, Country Gentlemen, L. Sparks, D. Reno

Oh Death

M: Em; F: Am, capo 5
CD 2-Track 26

Traditional

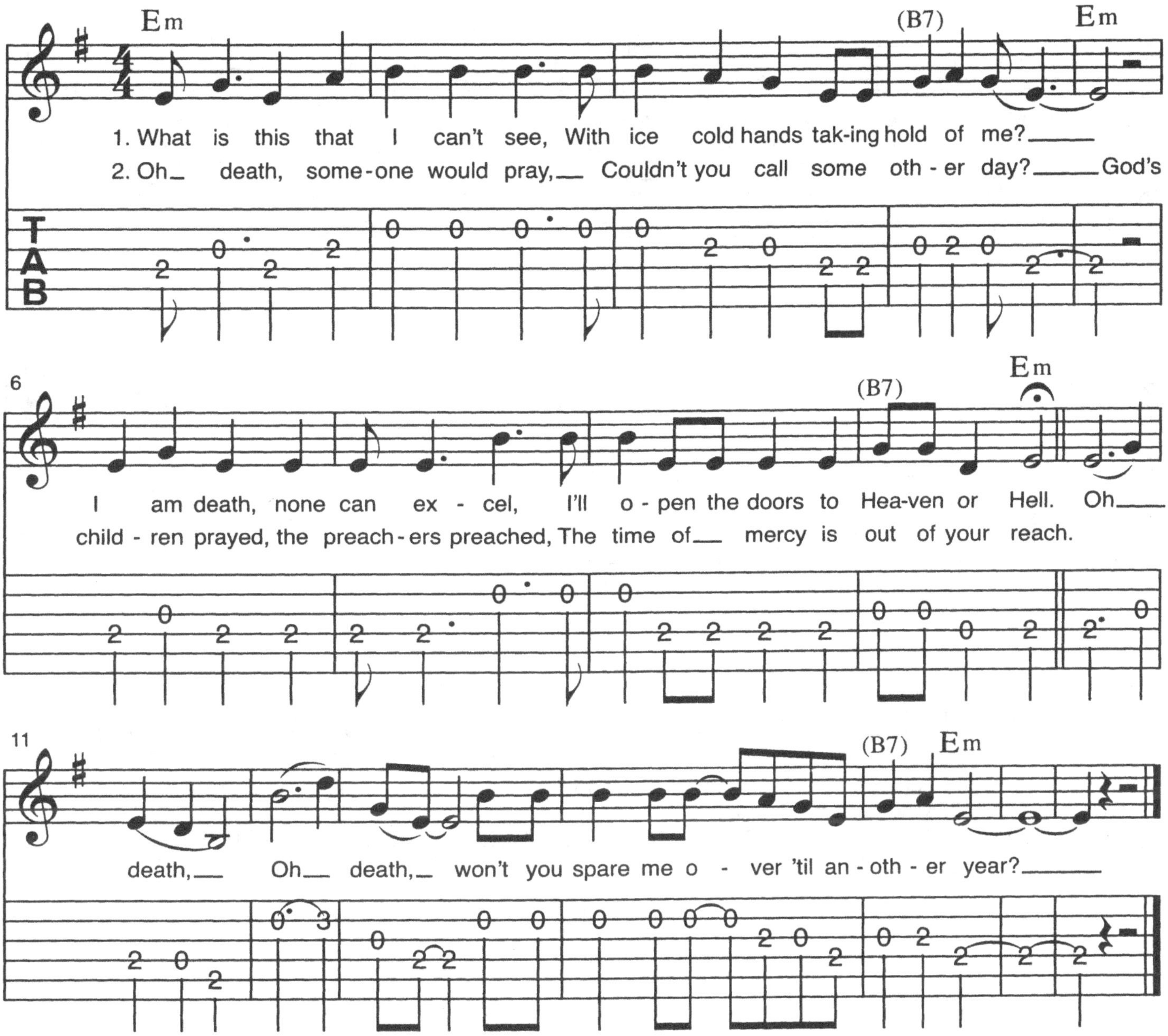

Em
3. I'll fix your feet so you can't walk,
B7 Em
I'll lock your jaws so you can't talk,
I'll close your eyes so you can't see,
B7 Em
This very hour come go with me. *(Repeat chorus)*

4. Death, I come to take the soul,
Leave the body and leave it cold,
To drop the flesh off of the frame,
The earth and worms both have a claim.

5. My mother come to my bed,
Place a cold towel upon my head,
My head is warm, my feet are cold,
Death is moving upon my soul.

6. Oh death, how you treat me,
You close my eyes so I can't see.
You hurt my body, you make me cold,
You've run the life right out of my soul.

7. Oh death, please consider my age,
Please don't take me at this stage,
My wealth is all at your command,
If you will move your icy hand.

8. Old, the young, the rich or poor,
All alike with me, you know,
No wealth, no land, no silver, no gold,
Nothing satisfies me but your soul.

Stanley Bros., R. Stanley, "O Brother" soundtrack, NLCR, Carter Fam.

Oh! Didn't He Ramble

M: G; F: C or D, capo 5 or 7
CD 2-Track 27, medley pt. 1

Will Handy, 1902

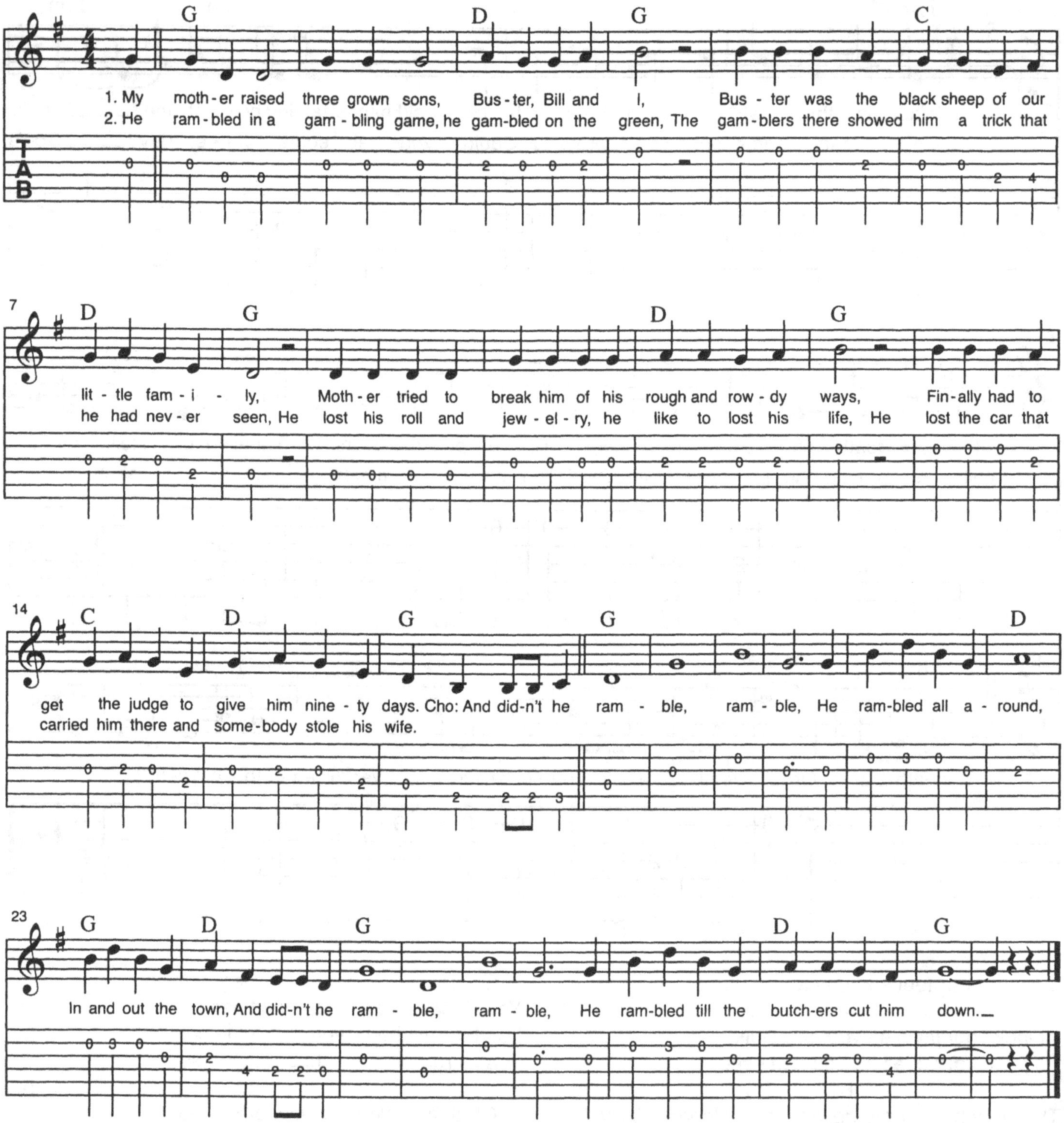

```
         G                           D            G
3. He rambled in a swell hotel, his appetite was stout,
                          C                 D                   G
And when he refused to pay the bill, the landlord kicked him out.
                                                    D               G
He reached a brick to smack him with, and when he went to stop,
                            C                    D            G
The landlord kicked him over the fence, right in a barrel of slop.
```

(Repeat chorus after each verse)

4. He rambled through the tunnel once, on board a moving train.
Another train came rumbling in, and rammed him out again.
It rammed him just a block, and then, they caught him on the fly,
And with a ton of dynamite, they rammed him to the sky.

5. He rambled to an Irish wake, on one St. Patrick's night.
They asked him what he'd like to drink, they meant to treat him right.
But like the old Kilkenny cats, their backs began to arch.
When he called for orange phosphate, on the seventeenth of March.

6. He rambled to the races, to make a gallery bet.
He backed a horse named Hydrant, and Hydrant's running yet.
He would have had to walk back home, his friends all from him hid.
By luck he met old George Sedam, it's a damn good thing he did.

Old Dan Tucker

M: G; F: C or D, capo 5 or 7
CD 2-Track 27, medley pt. 2

Traditional

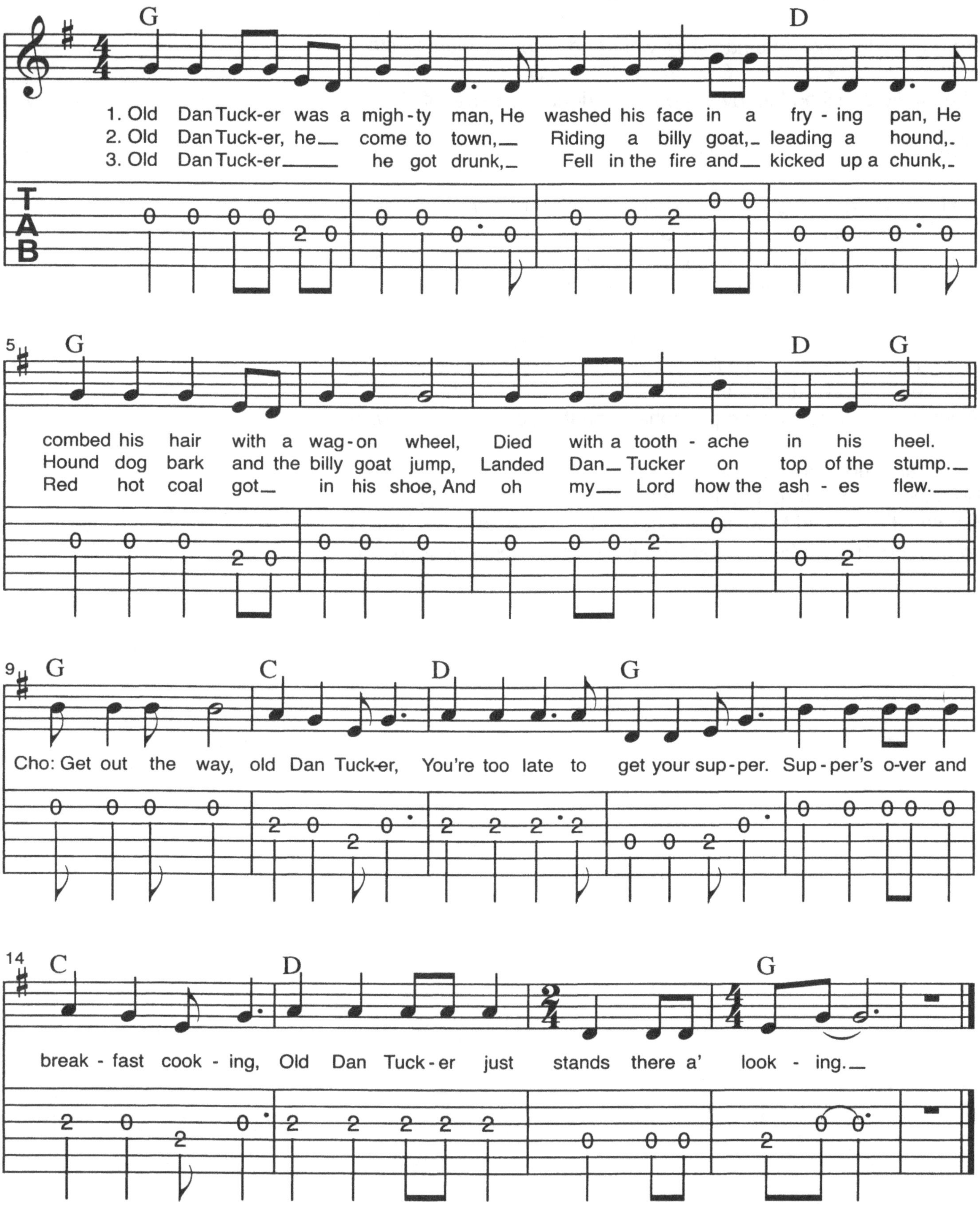

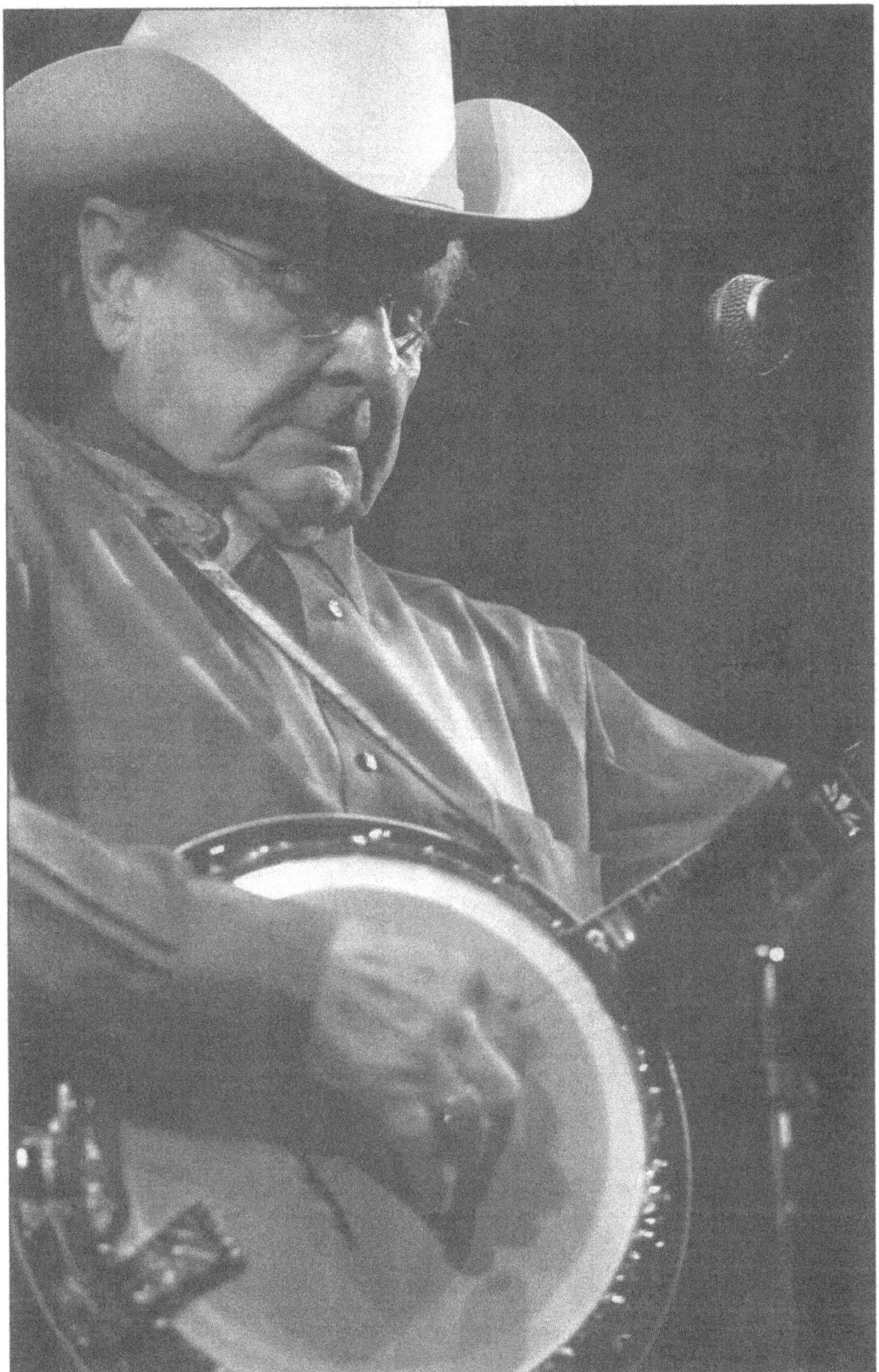

Ralph Stanley began his professional music career with his brother Carter as The Stanley Brothers. Apart from Bill Monroe, the Stanley sound is probably the most influential in bluegrass and old time music.

Old Home Place

M: G; F: C or D, capo 5 or 7
CD 2-Track 28

Webb & Jayne

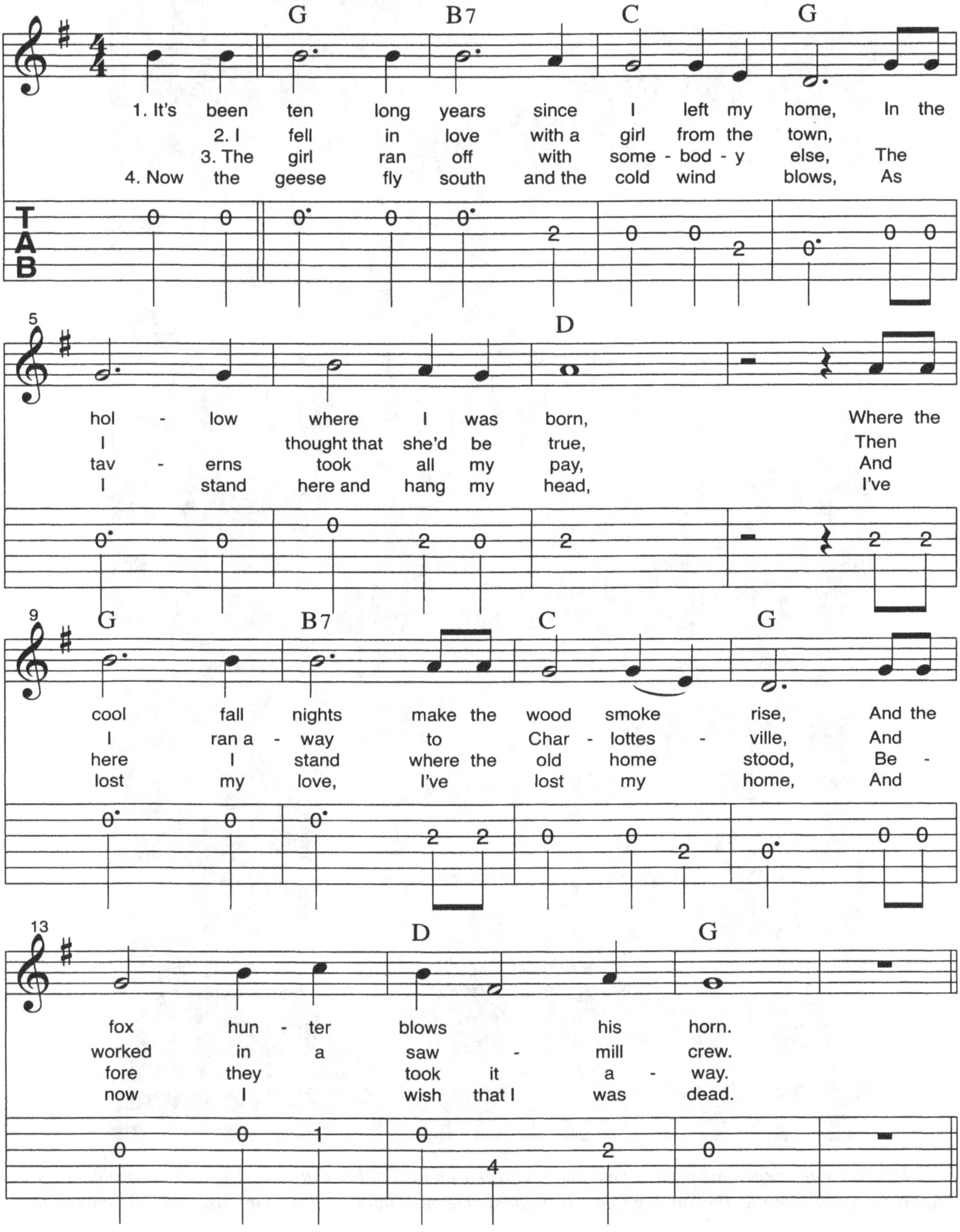

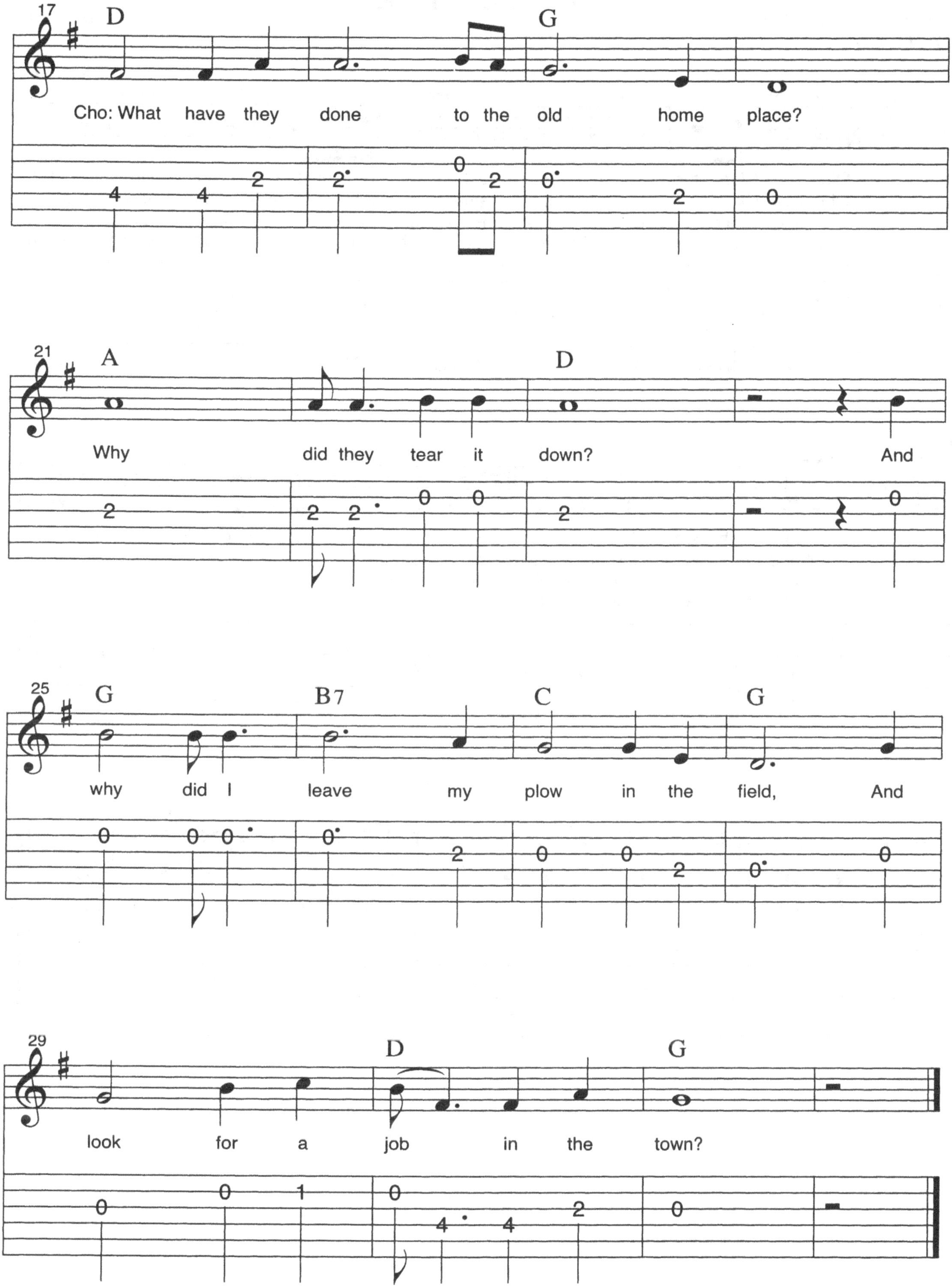
17
D
G
Cho: What have they done to the old home place?
21
A
D
Why did they tear it down? And
25
G
B7
C
G
why did I leave my plow in the field, And
29
D
G
look for a job in the town?

Old Joe Clark

M: D; F: G or A, capo 5 or 7
CD 2-Track 29

Traditional

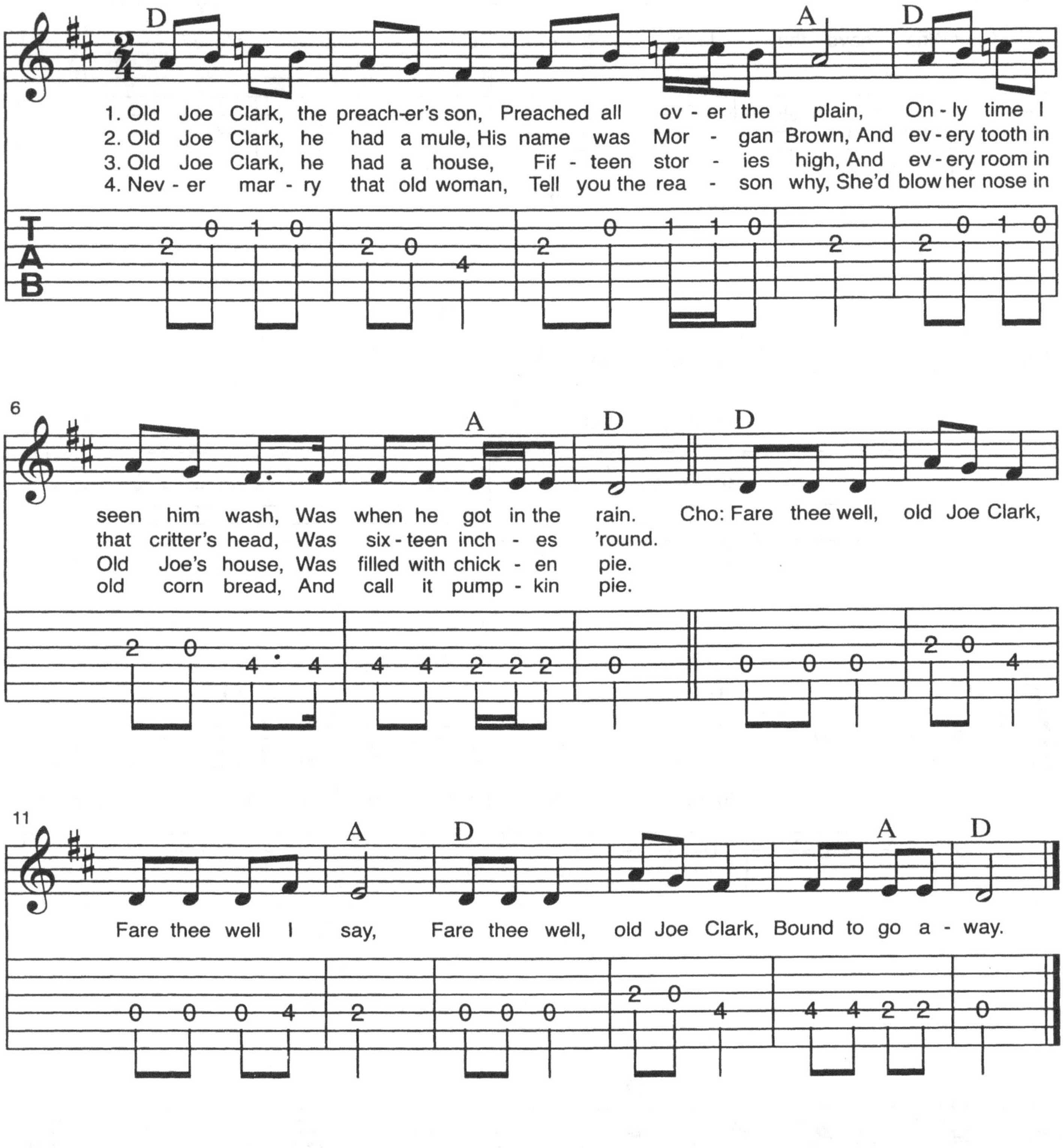

 Flatt & Scruggs, B. Monroe, Goose Island Ramblers, Ken. Colonels, C. White, Skillet Lickers, Red Allen, D. Dillard, T. Adams, T. Trischka, A. Munde

Old Man at the Mill

M: G; F: C or D, capo 5 or 7
CD 2-Track 30

Traditional

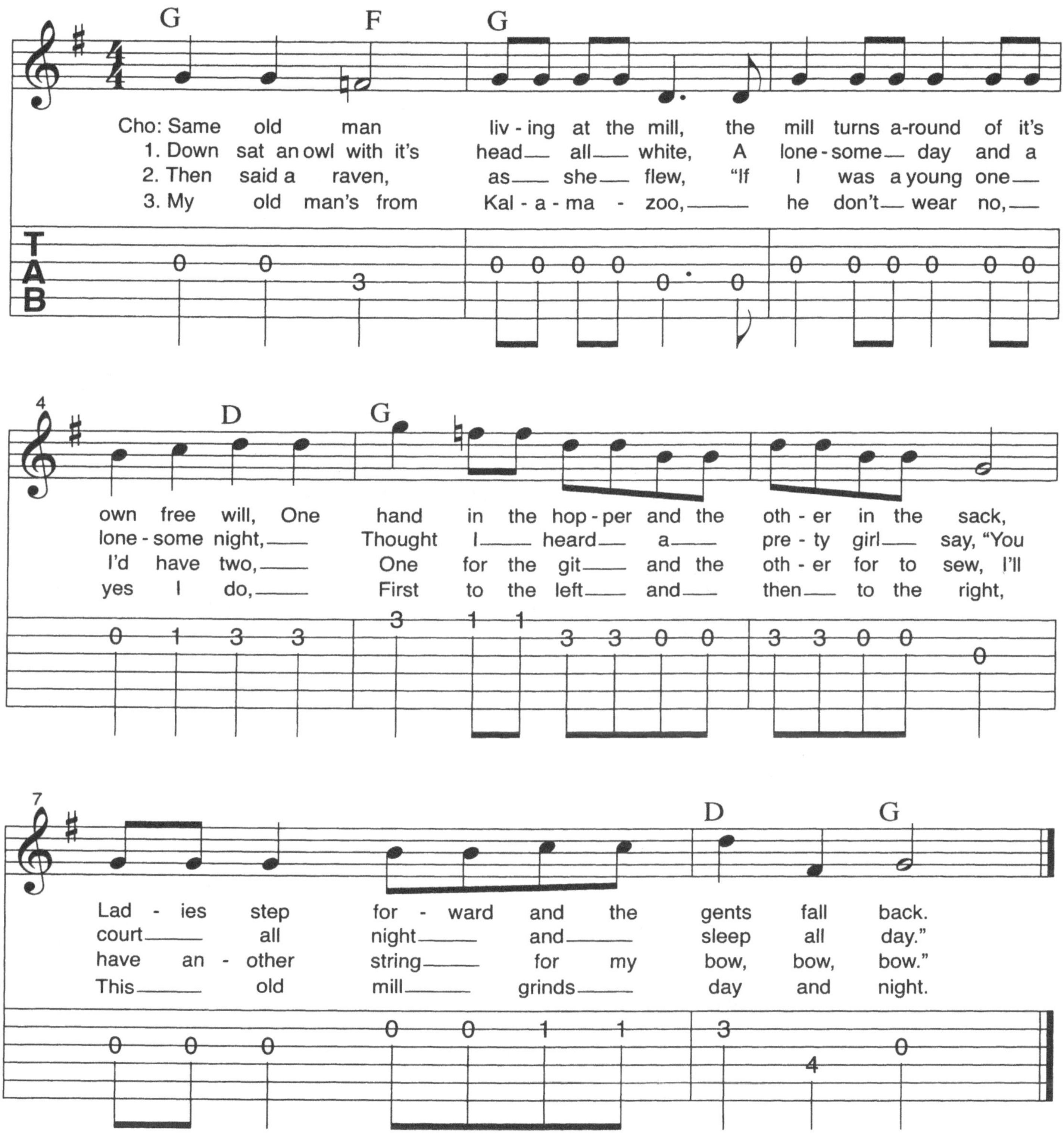

Old Paint

M: G; F: C or D, capo 5 or 7
CD 2-Track 31

Traditional

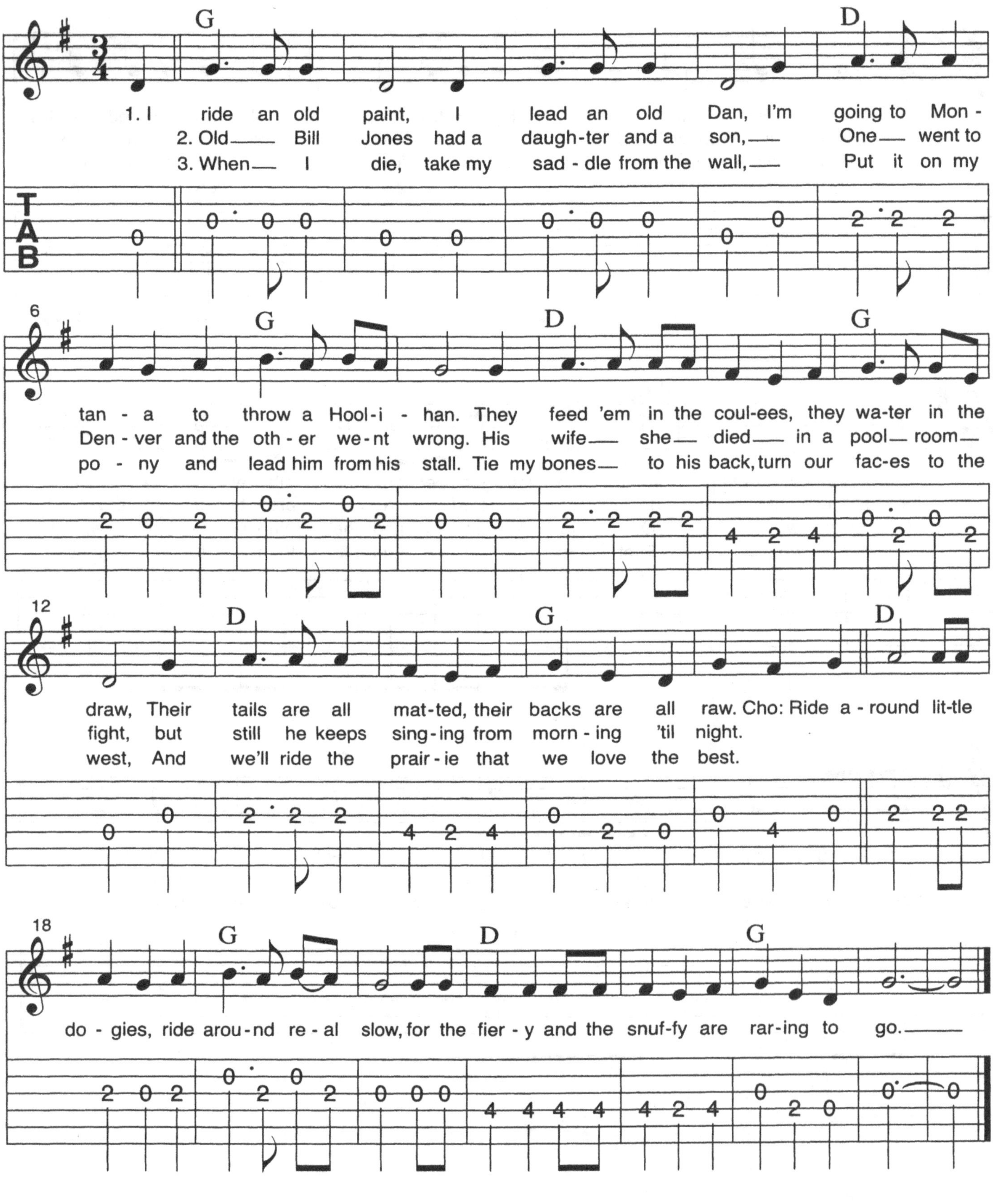

The Old Rugged Cross

M: A; F: D or E, capo 5 or 7
CD 2-Track 32

Geo. Bennard, 1913

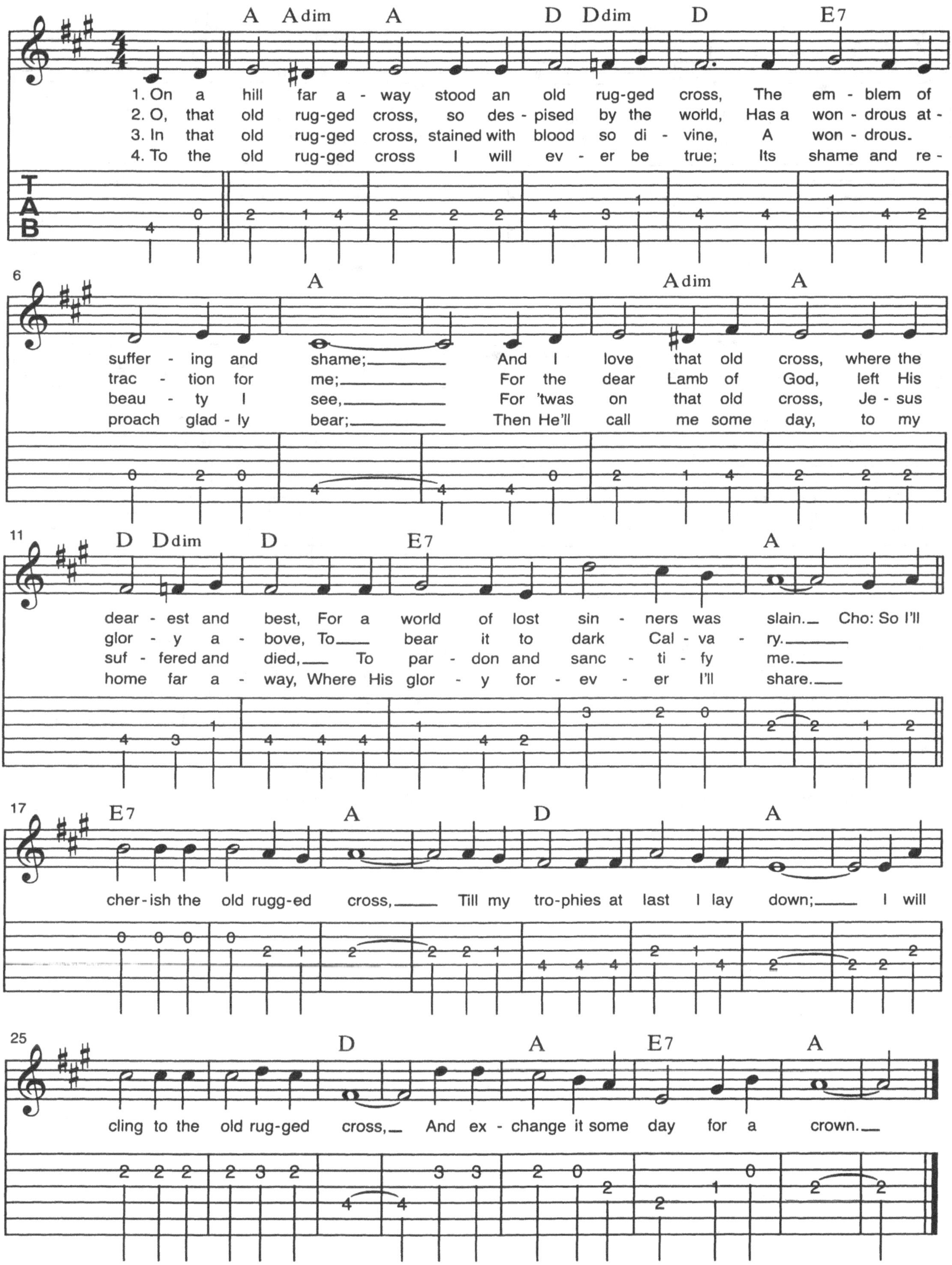

Old Time Religion

M: G; F: C or D, capo 5 or 7
CD 2-Track 33

Traditional

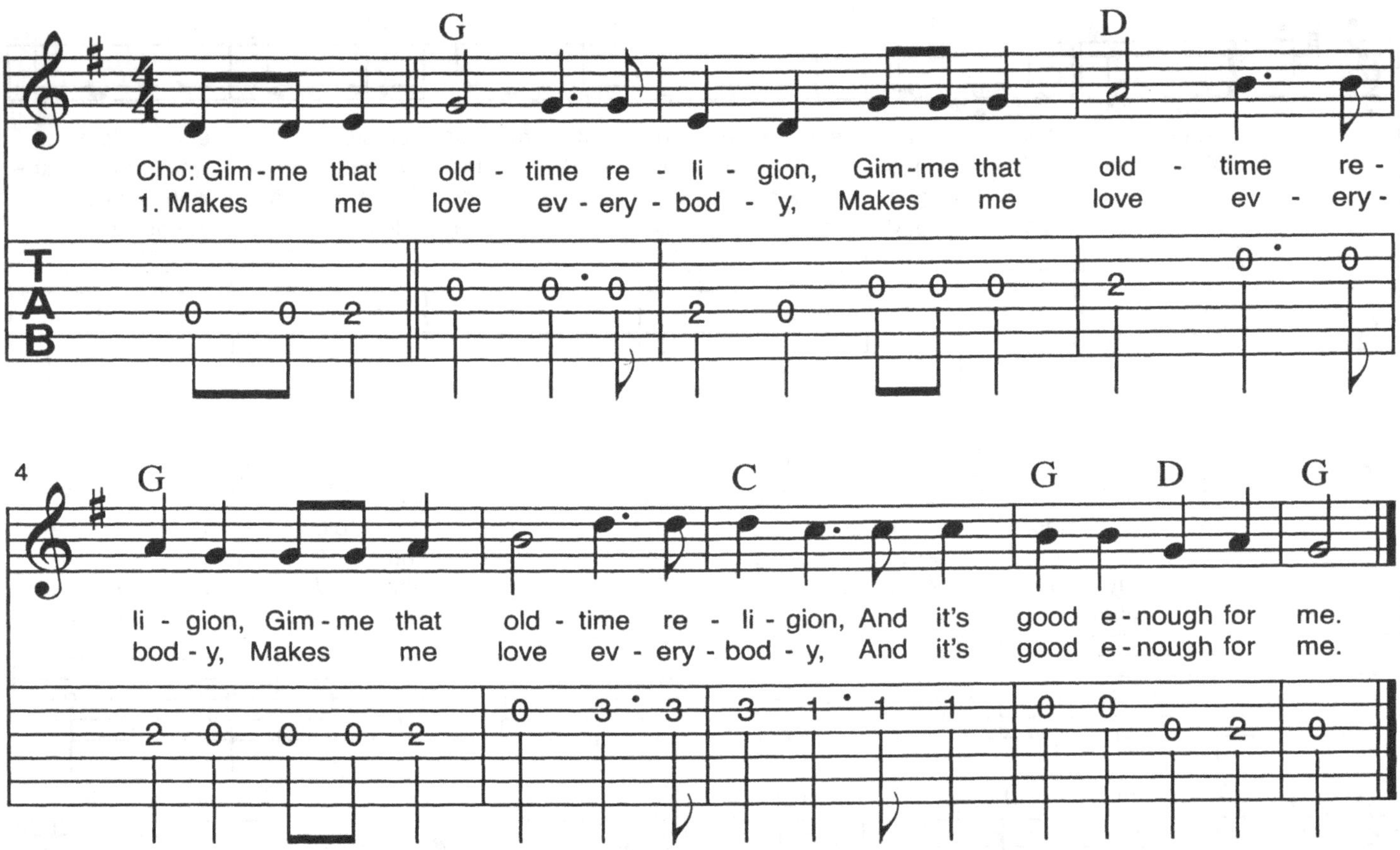


```
          G
2. It was good for our mothers,
          D             G
It was good for our mothers,
                        C
It was good for our mothers,
           G       D          G
And it's good enough for me.
```

3. It has saved all our fathers, (3X, etc.)
4. It will save all our children, (3X, etc.)
5. It was good for Paul and Silas, (3X, etc.)
6. It was good for the Prophet Daniel, (3X, etc.)
7. It was good for the Hebrew children, (3X, etc.)
8. It was tried in the fiery furnace, (3X, etc.)
9. It will do when I'm a'dying, (3X, etc.)
10. It will take us all to heaven, (3X, etc.)

On and On

M: G; F: C or D, capo 5 or 7
CD 2-Track 34

Bill Monroe

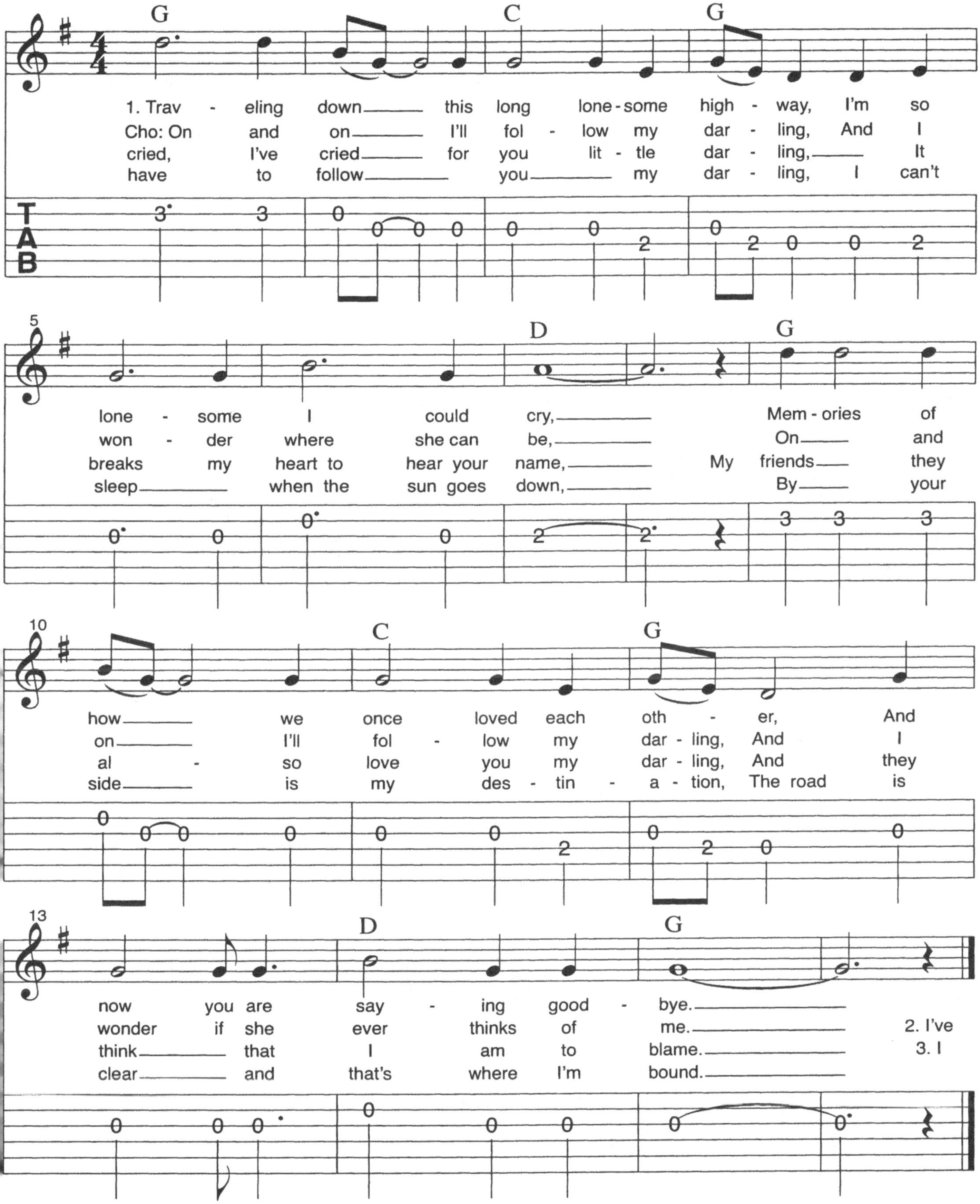

Over the Hills to the Poorhouse

M: G; F: C or D, capo 5 or 7
CD 2-Track 35

Traditional

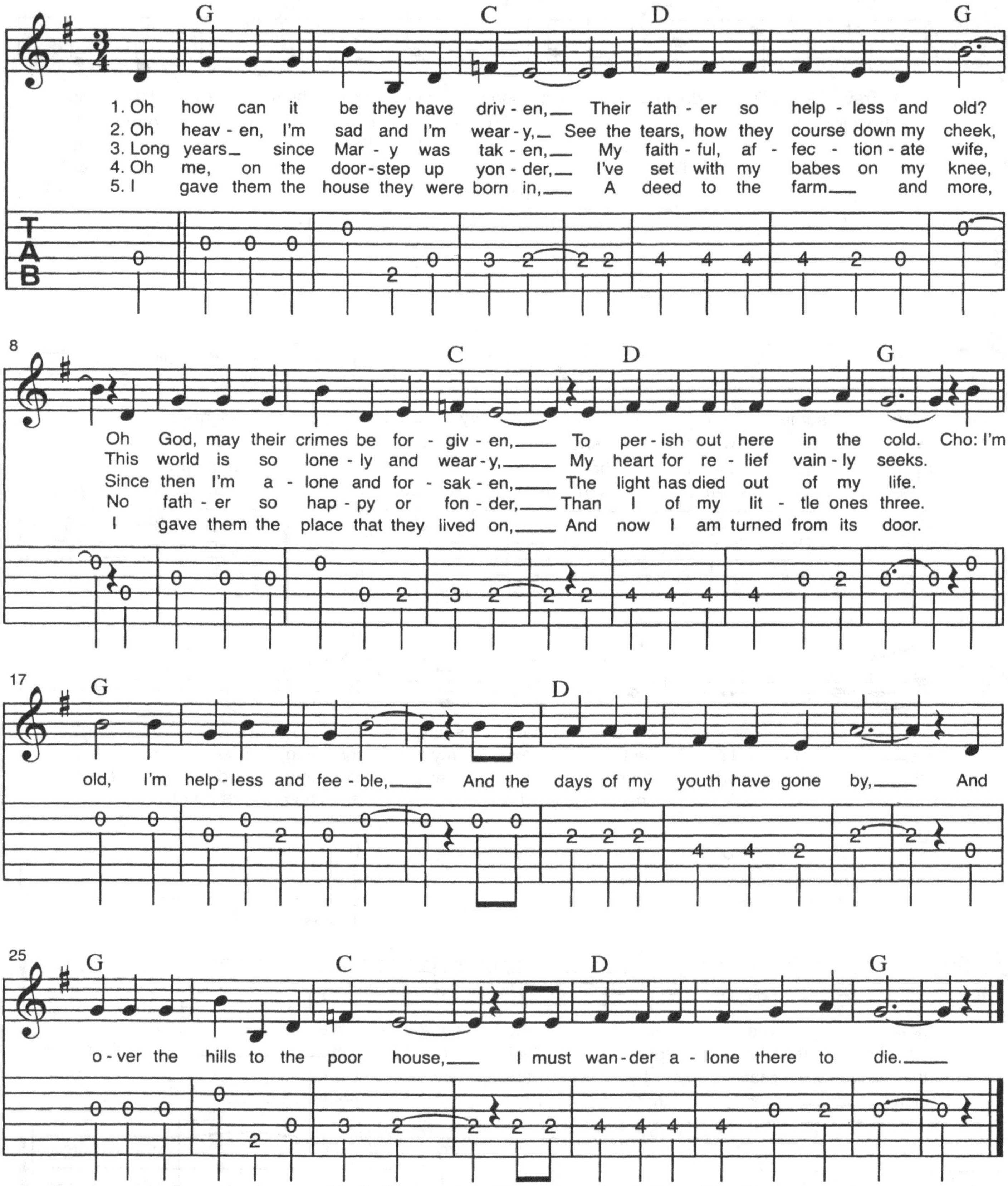

 Flatt & Scruggs, R. Allen & F. Wakefield, Country Gentlemen

Pass Me Not

M: G; F: C or D, capo 5 or 7
CD 2-Track 36

Crosby & Doan, ca. 1870

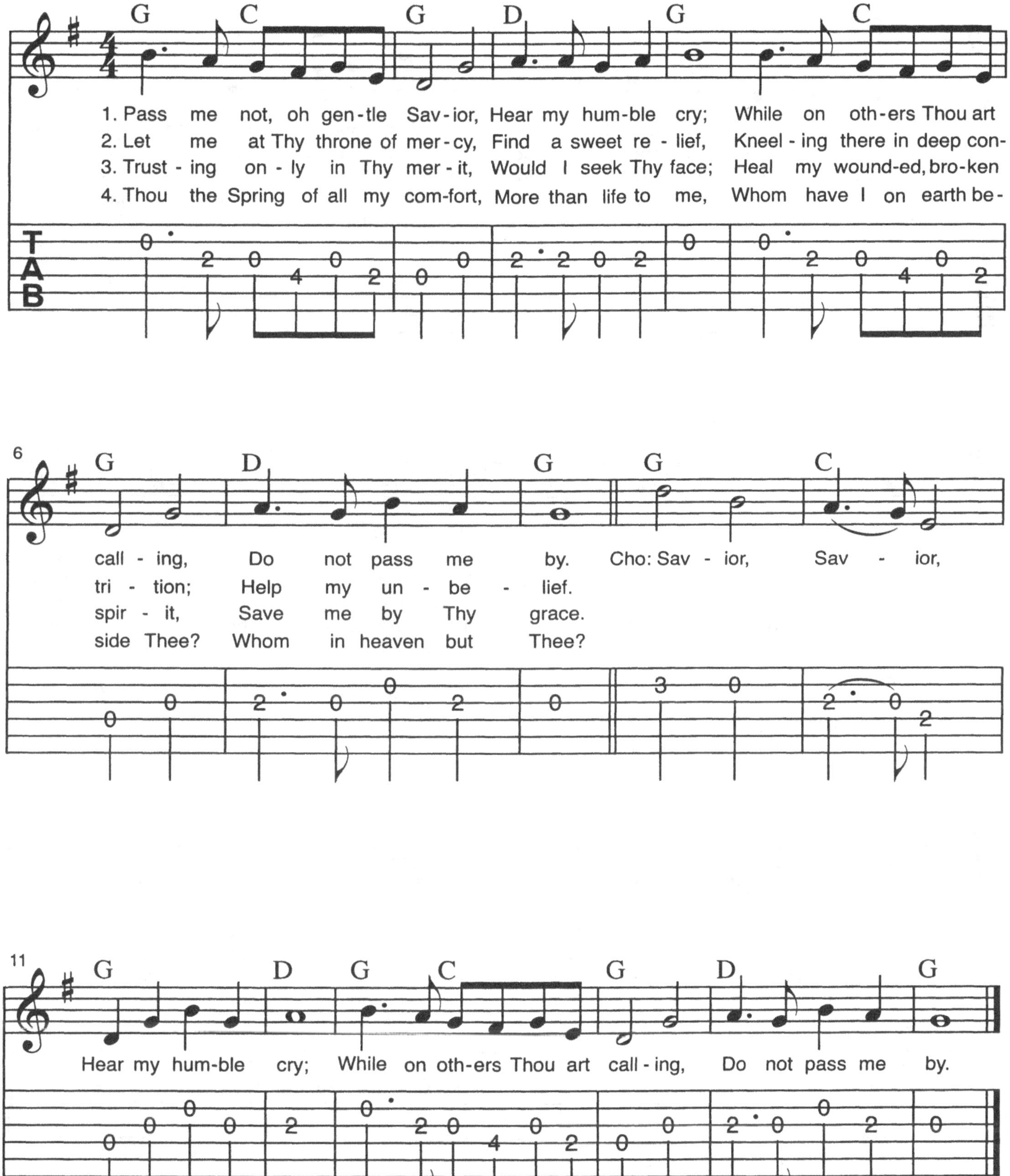

Paul and Silas

M: G; F: C or D, capo 5 or 7
CD 2-Track 37

Traditional

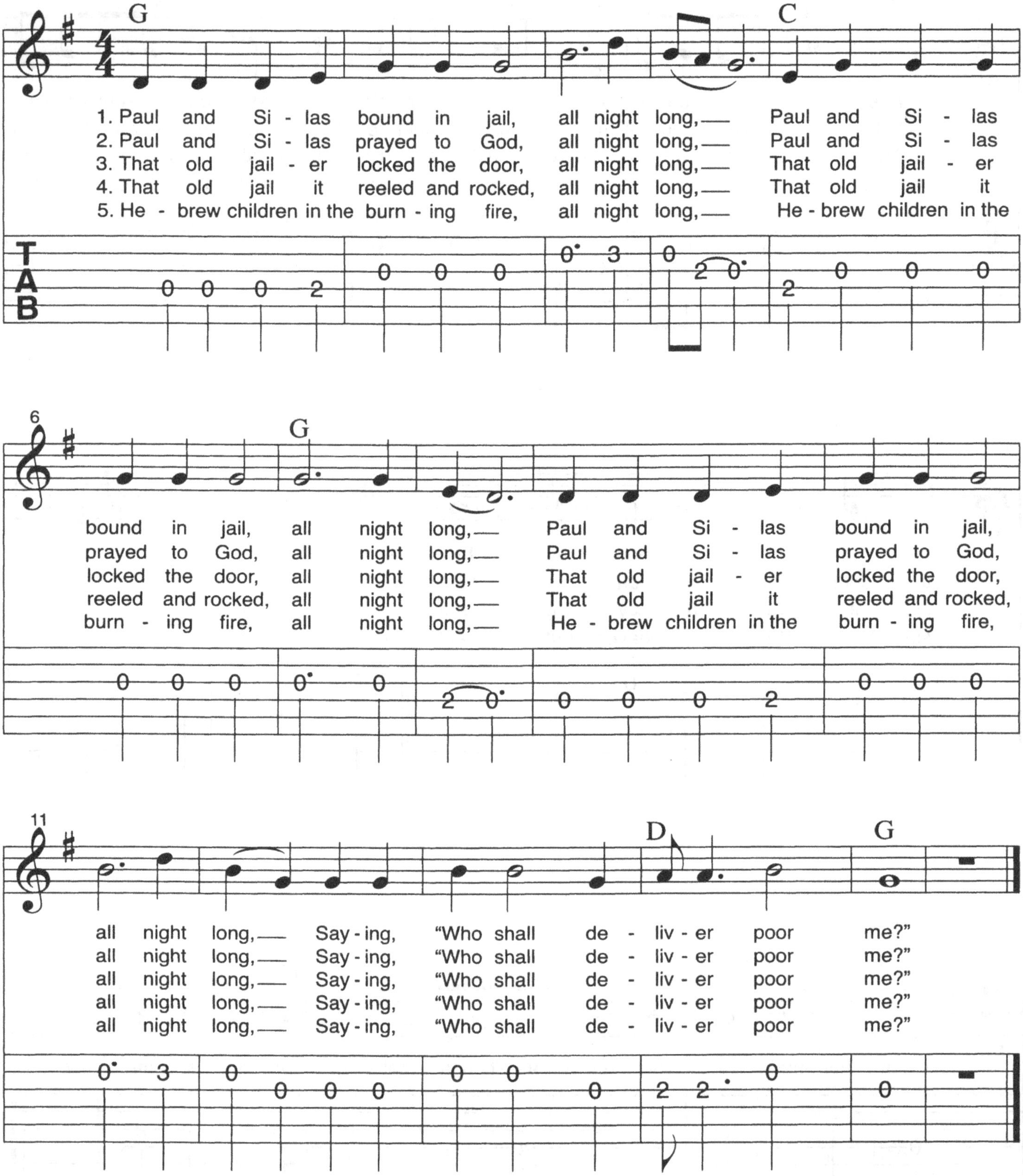

 Flatt & Scruggs, Stanley Bros., F. Wakefield, Country Gentlemen

Pig in a Pen

M: G; F: C or D, capo 5 or 7
CD 2-Track 38

Traditional

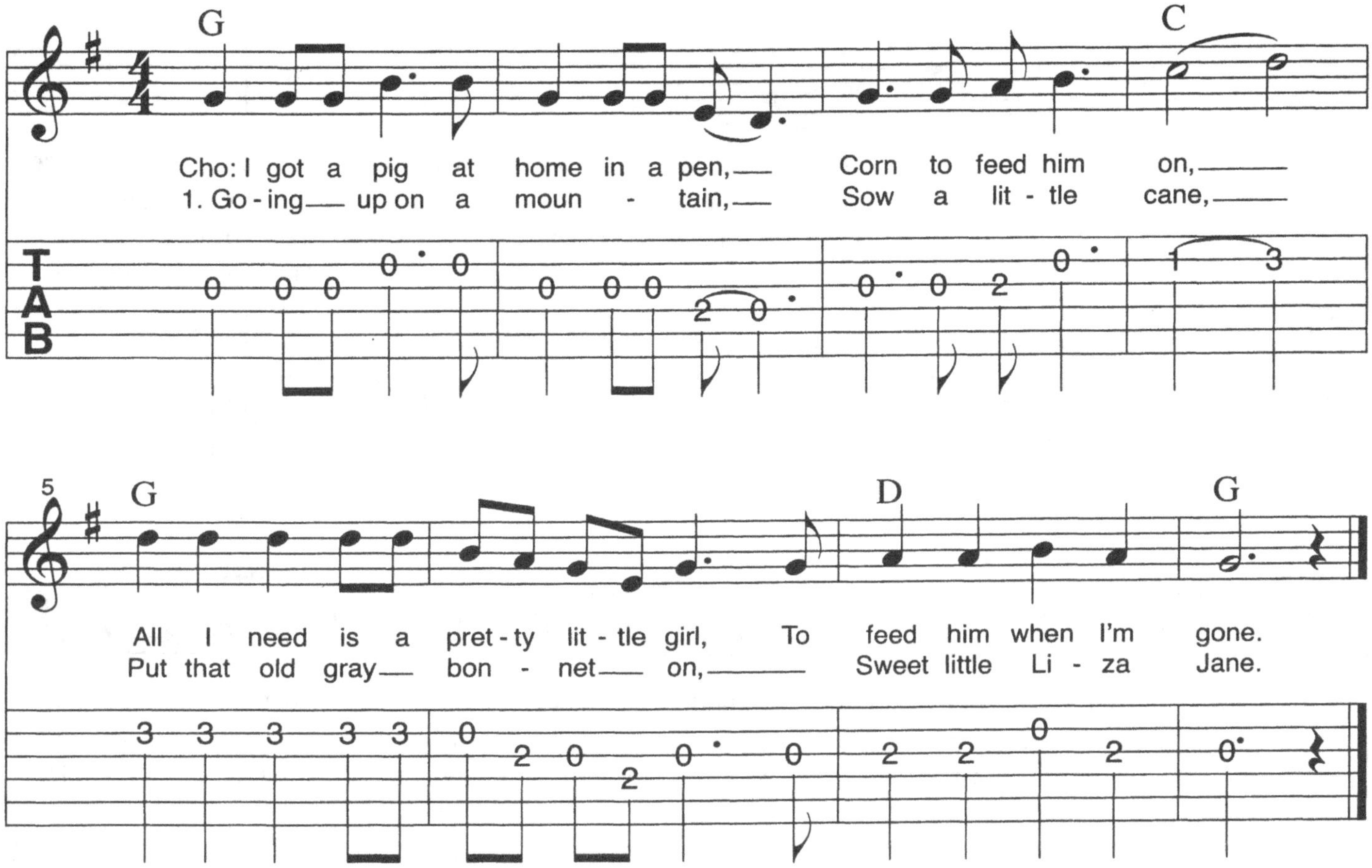

G
2. Going up on a mountain,
C
To sow a little cane,
G
Raise a barrel of sorghum,
D G
Sweet little Liza Jane.

3. Black smoke arising,
Surely is a train,
Put that old gray bonnet on,
Little Liza Jane.

4. Bake them biscuits baby,
Bake 'em good and brown,
When you get them biscuits baked,
I'm Alabama bound.

Poor Ellen Smith

M: G; F: C or D, capo 5 or 7
CD 2-Track 39

Traditional

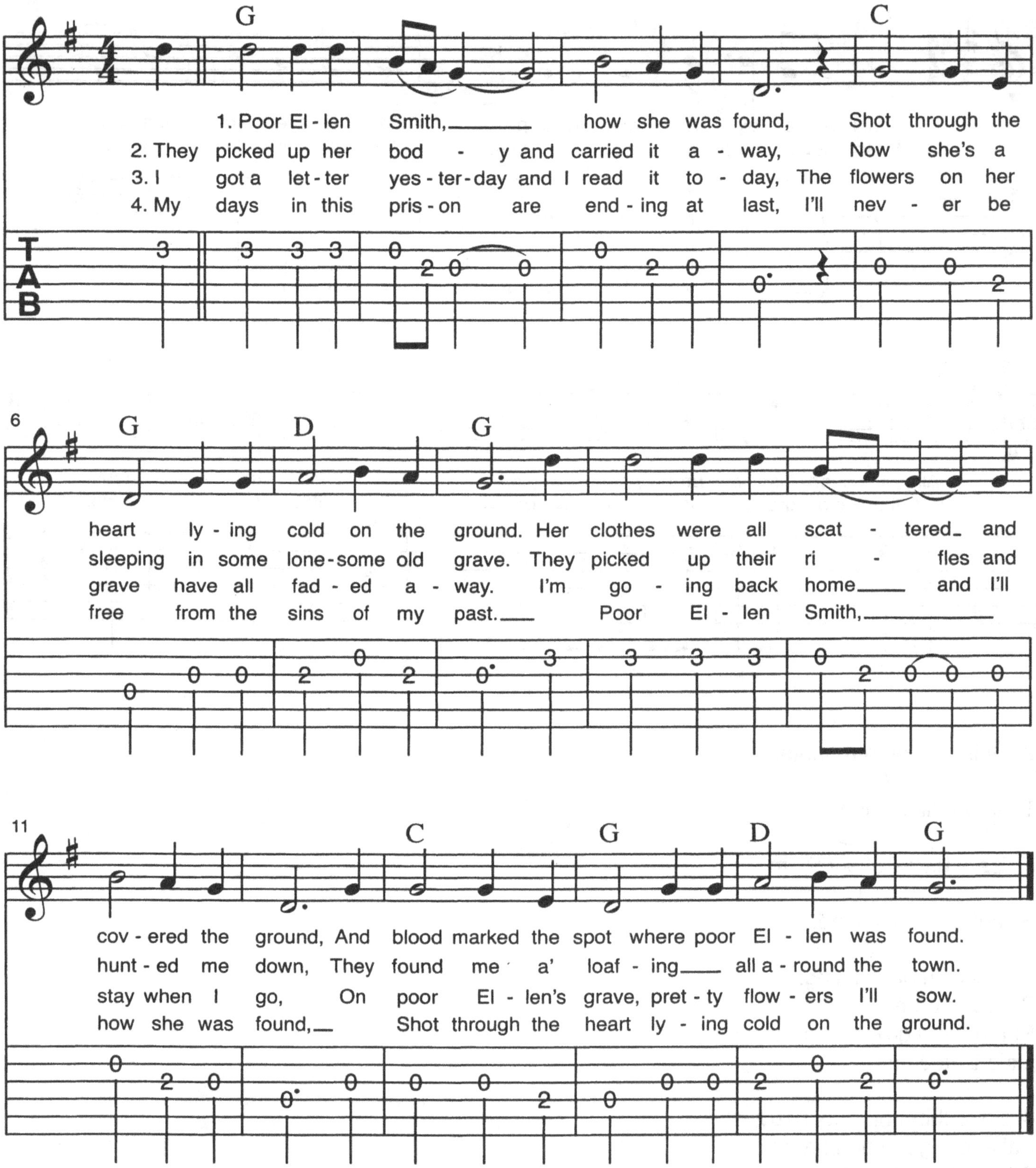

J. Martin, Stanley Bros., Flatt & Scruggs, NLCR, E. Taylor, Country Gentlemen, Reno & Harrell, J. Val, Mac Wiseman, N. Blake, Bluegrass Intentions

Precious Memories

M: G; F: C or D, capo 5 or 7
CD 2-Track 40

J.B.F. Wright

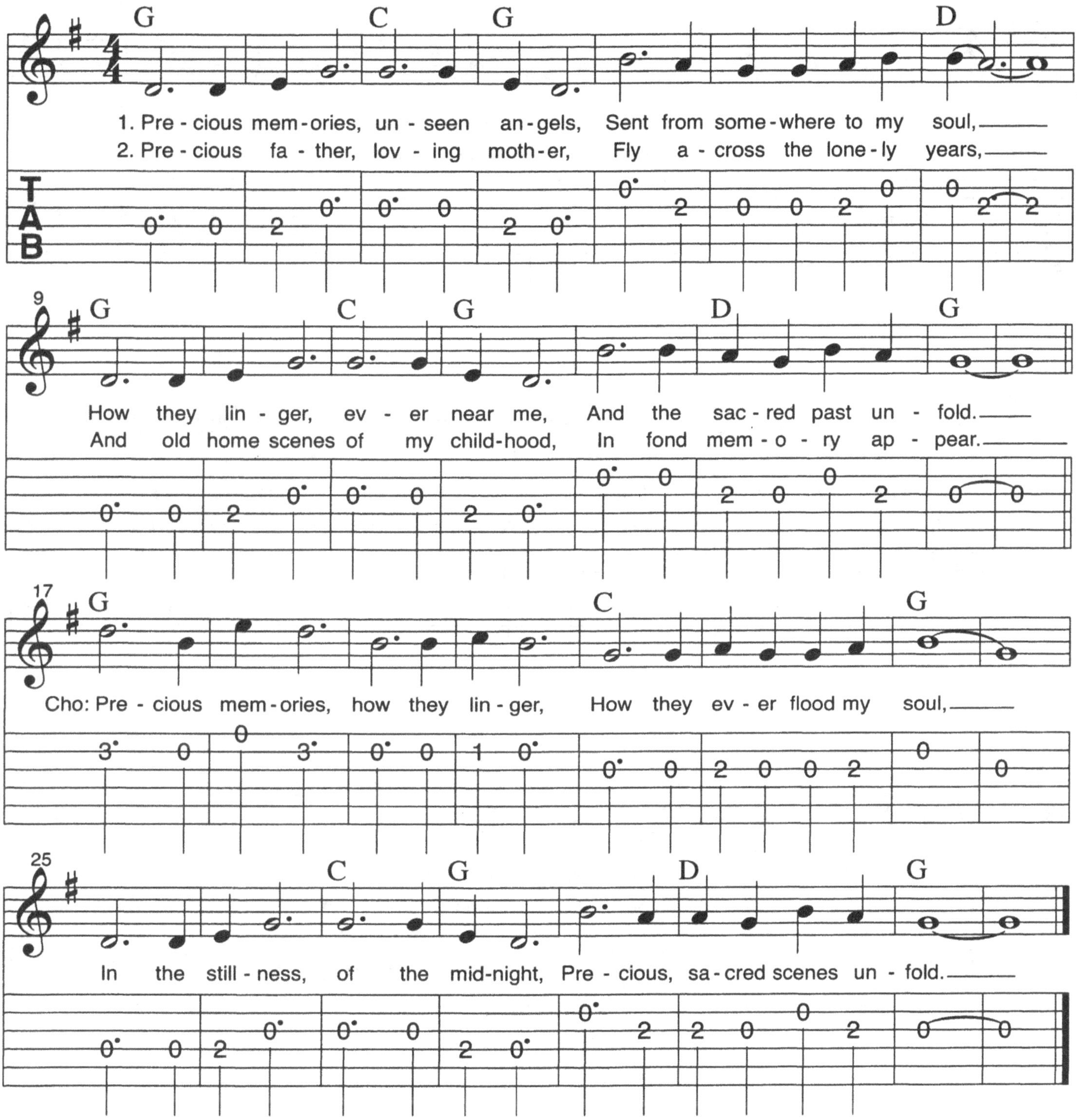

G C G
3. In the stillness of the midnight,
D
Echoes from the past I hear;
G C G
Old time singing, gladness bringing,
D G
From that lovely land somewhere.

4. I remember mother praying,
Father, too on bended knee;
Sun is sinking, shadows falling,
But their prayers still follow me.

5. As I travel on life's pathway,
Know not what the years may hold;
As I ponder, hope grows fonder,
Precious memories flood my soul.

Pretty Polly

M: G; F: C or D, capo 5 or 7
CD 2-Track 41

Traditional

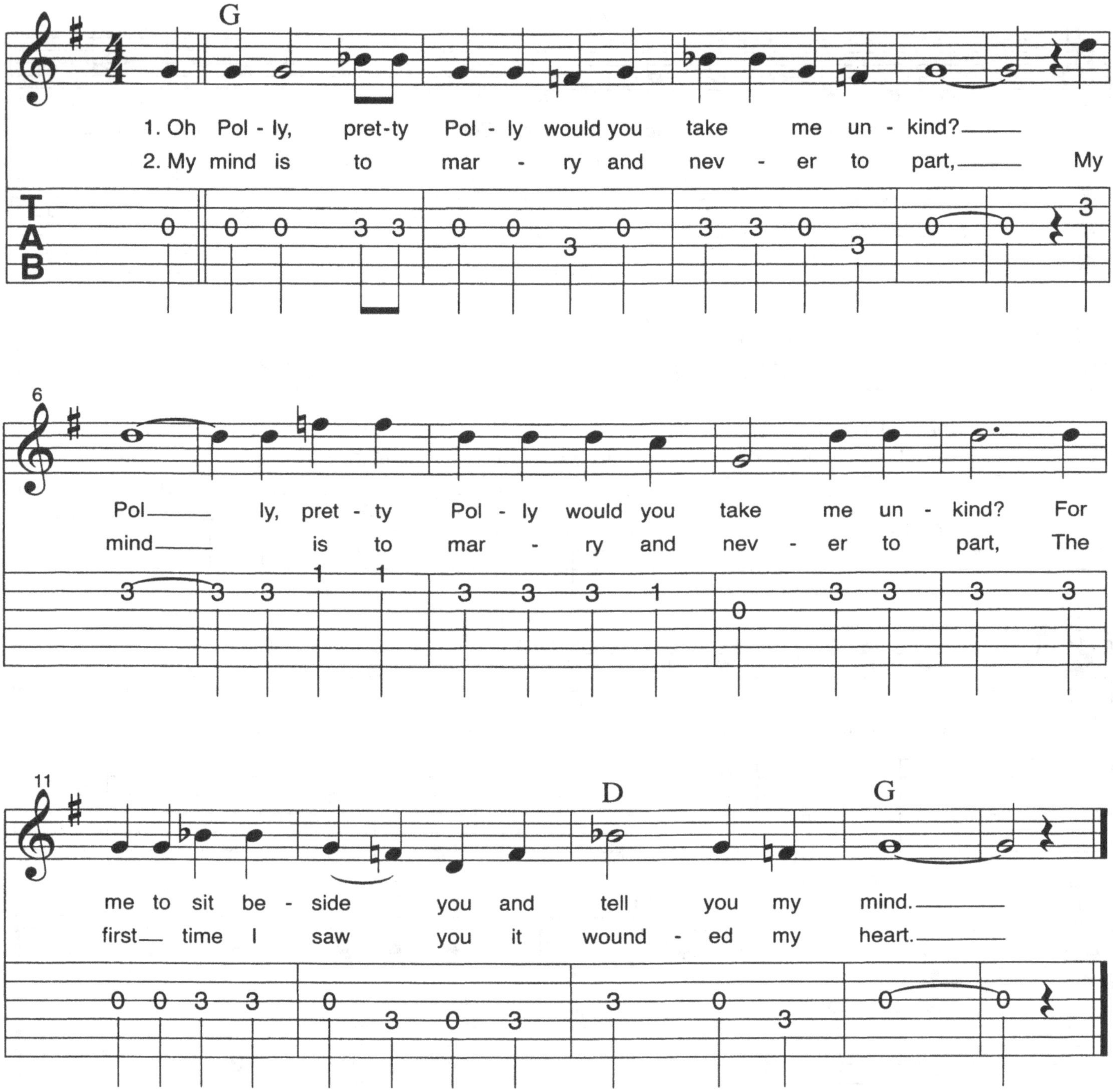

 Stanley Bros., R. Stanley, Dillards, C. White, D. Grisman, NLCR, D. Watson, D. Boggs

G
3. Oh, Polly, pretty Polly, come and go along with me,
Polly, pretty Polly, come and go along with me,
D G
Before we get married some pleasure to see.

4. He led her over mountains and valleys so deep,
He led her over mountains and valleys so deep,
Polly mistrusted and then began to weep.

5. Saying, "Willie, oh Willie, I'm afraid of your ways,
"Willie, oh Willie, I'm afraid of your ways,
The way you've been rambling, you'll lead me astray."

6. Well Polly, pretty Polly, your guess is about right,
Polly, pretty Polly, your guess is about right,
I dug on your grave the best part of last night.

7. Then he led her a little farther and what did they spy?
Led her a little farther and what did they spy?
A new-dug grave with a spade lying by.

8. She knelt down before him a' pleading for her life,
Knelt before him a' pleading for her life,
"Let me be a single girl if I can't be your wife."

9. Now Polly, pretty Polly, that never can be,
Polly, pretty Polly, that never can be,
Your past reputation's been trouble to me.

10. He stabbed her in the heart and her blood it did flow,
He stabbed her in the heart and her blood it did flow,
And into the grave pretty Polly did go.

11. Then he went down to the jail house and what did he say?
He went to the jail house and what did he say?
"I've killed pretty Polly and tried to get away."

12. Now gentlemen and ladies, I bid you farewell,
Gentlemen and ladies, I bid you farewell,
For killing pretty Polly my soul must go to hell.

Put My Little Shoes Away

M: G; F: C or D, capo 5 or 7
CD 2-Track 42

Mitchell & Pratt, 1873

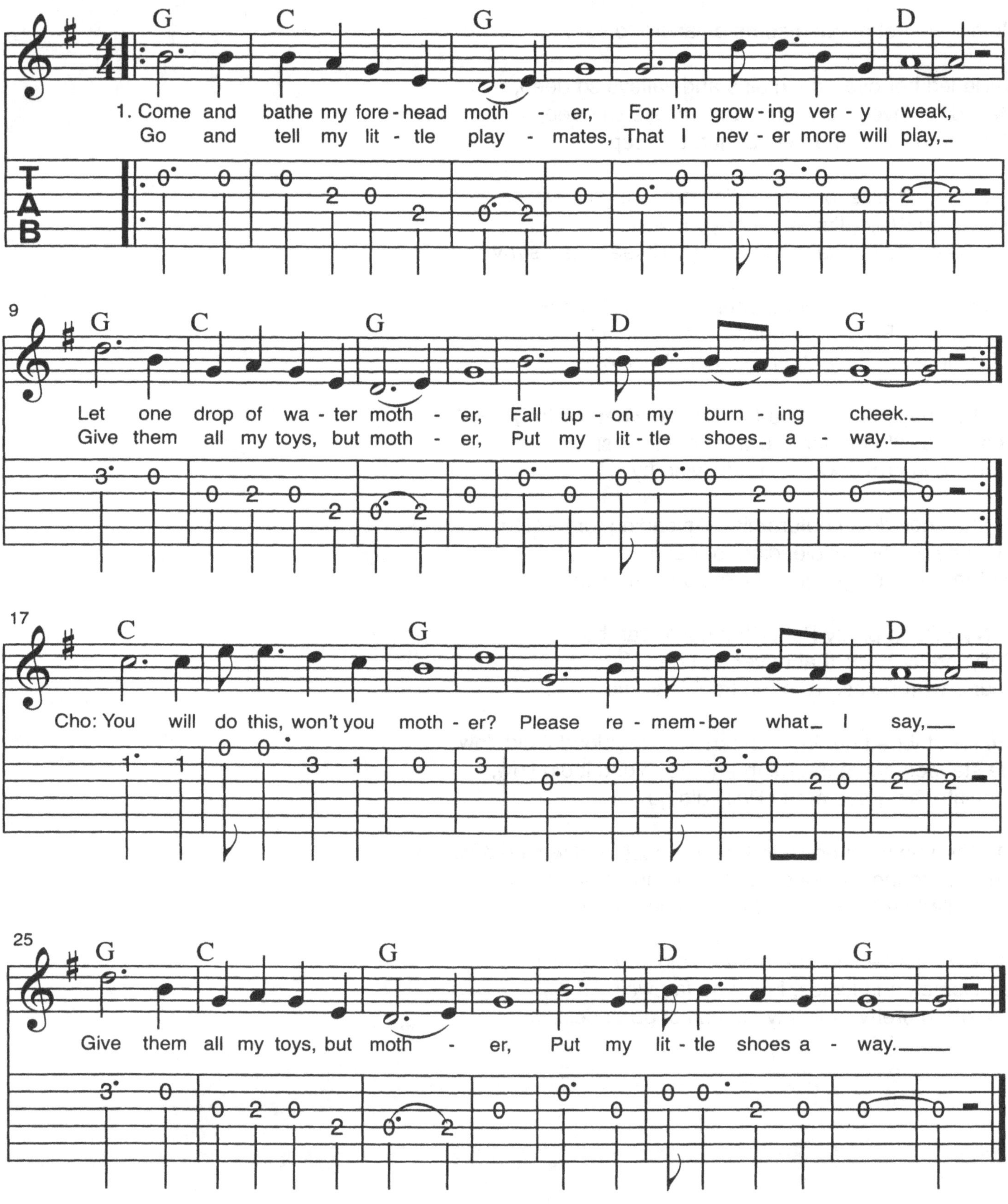

 B. Monroe, Jimmy Martin

    G   C   G
3. Santa Claus, he brought them to me,
                                D
With a lot of other things,
G   C   G
And I think he brought an angel,
         D   G
With a pair of golden wings.
G   C   G
I will be an angel, Mother,
                                   D
By perhaps another day,
G   C   G
You will do this for me, Mother,
          D   G
Put my little shoes away.

4. Soon the baby will be larger,
Then they'll fit his little feet,
Won't he look so nice and cunning,
When he walks upon the street?
I'm going to leave you, Mother,
So remember what I say,
You will do this for me, Mother,
Put my little shoes away.

5. Now I'm growing tired, dear Mother,
Soon I'll say to you "Good Day,"
Always remember what I told you,
Put my little shoes away.
I'm about to leave you, Mother,
So remember what I say,
You will do this for me, Mother,
Put my little shoes away.

Railroad Bill

M: C; F: F or G, capo 5 or 7
CD 2-Track 43

Traditional

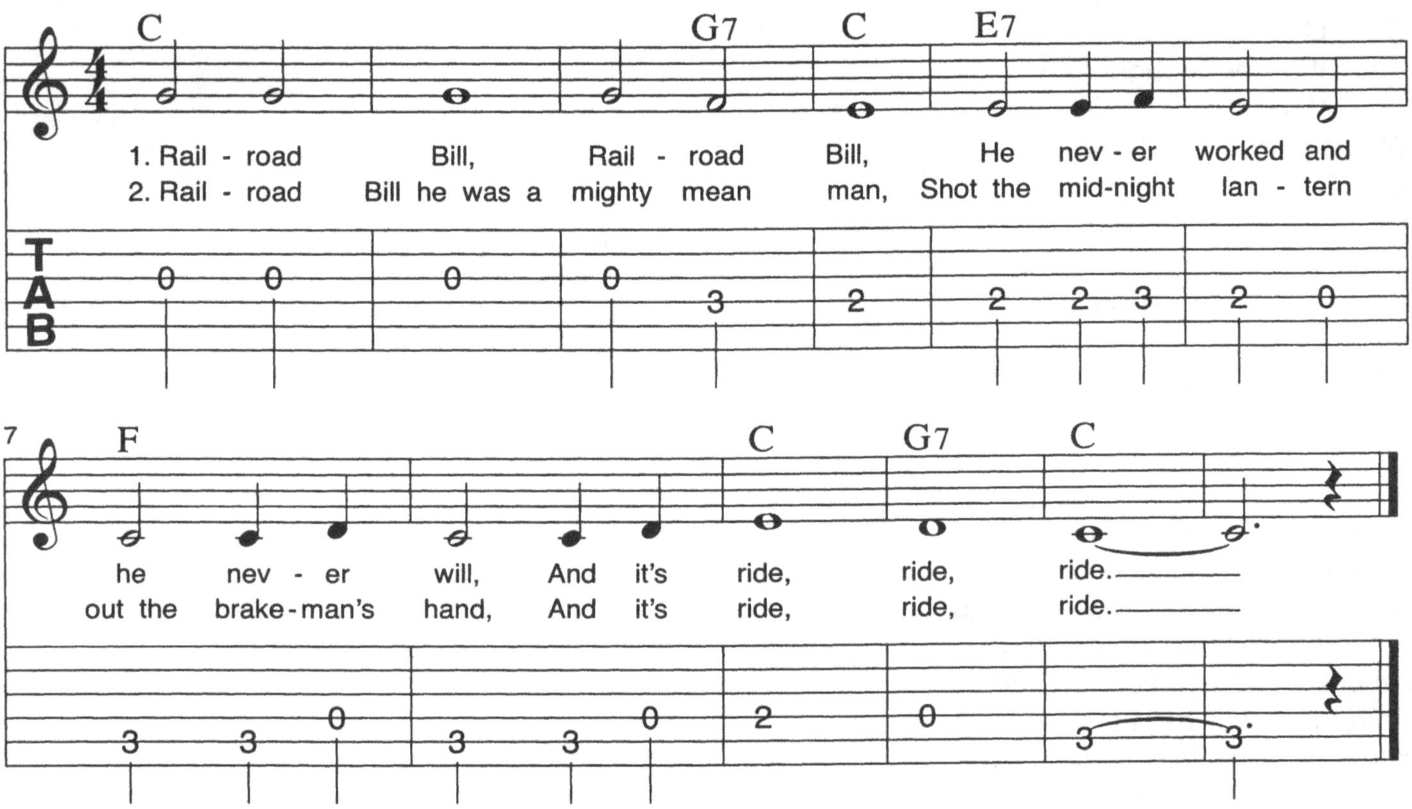

C G7 C
3. Railroad Bill took my wife,
E7 F
Said if I didn't like it, he would take my life,
C G7 C
And it's ride, ride, ride.

4. Going on a mountain, going way out west,
Thirty-eight special sticking out of my vest,
And it's ride, ride, ride.

5. Gonna buy me a pistol, long as my arm,
Kill everybody that's ever done me harm,
And it's ride, ride, ride.

6. I've got a thirty-eight special on a forty-five frame,
How can I miss him when I got dead aim,
And it's ride, ride, ride.

7. Honey, babe, do you think that I'm a fool,
Think that I'd quit you with the weather still so cool,
And it's ride, ride, ride.

 D. Bruce & J. Nunally, D. Watson, E. Baker, Skillet Lickers

Rain and Snow

M: Am dorian; F: Dm or Em dorian, capo 5 or 7
CD 2-Track 44

Traditional

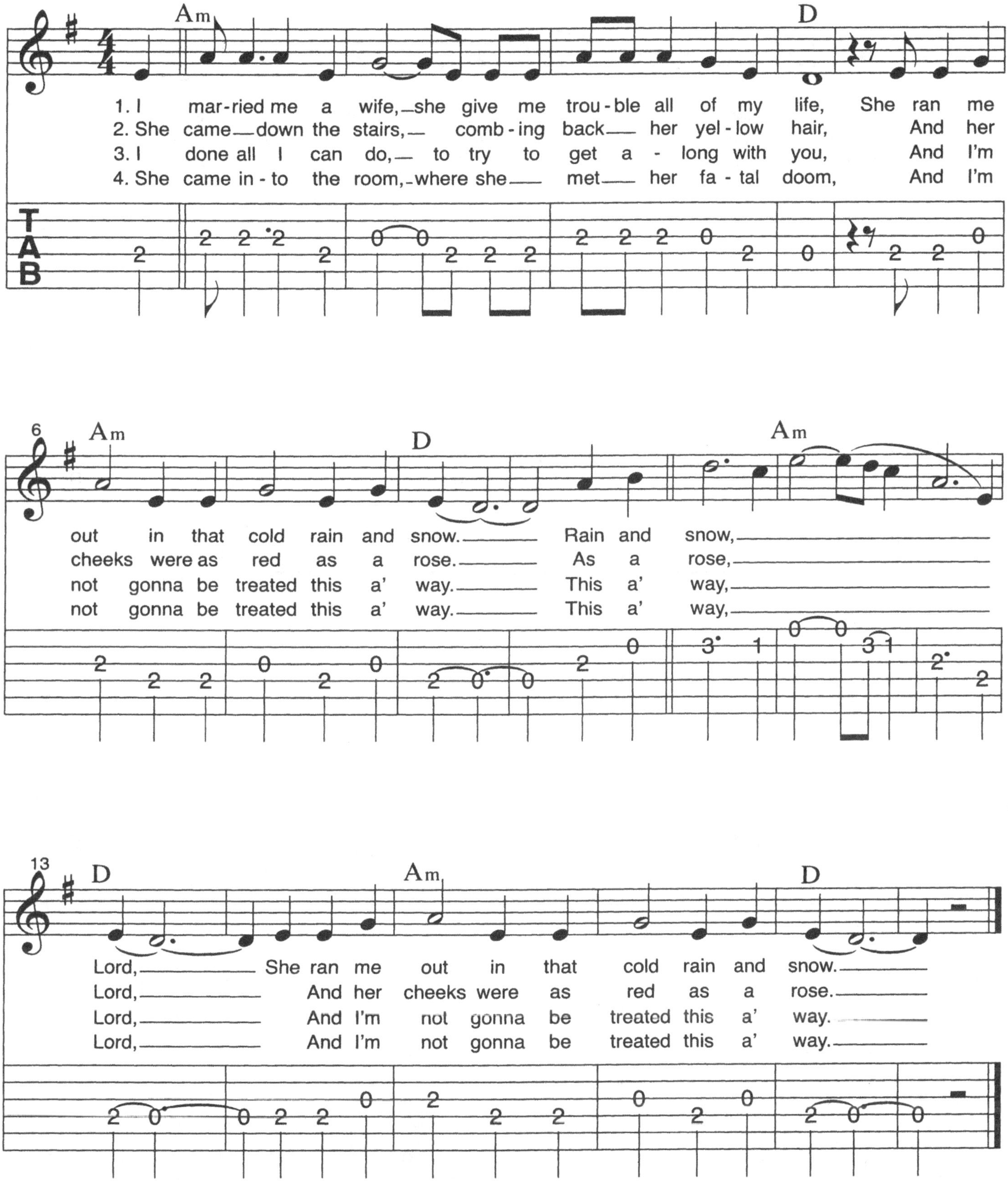

Rank Strangers to Me

M: G; F: C or D, capo 5 or 7
CD 2-Track 45

Albert E. Brumley

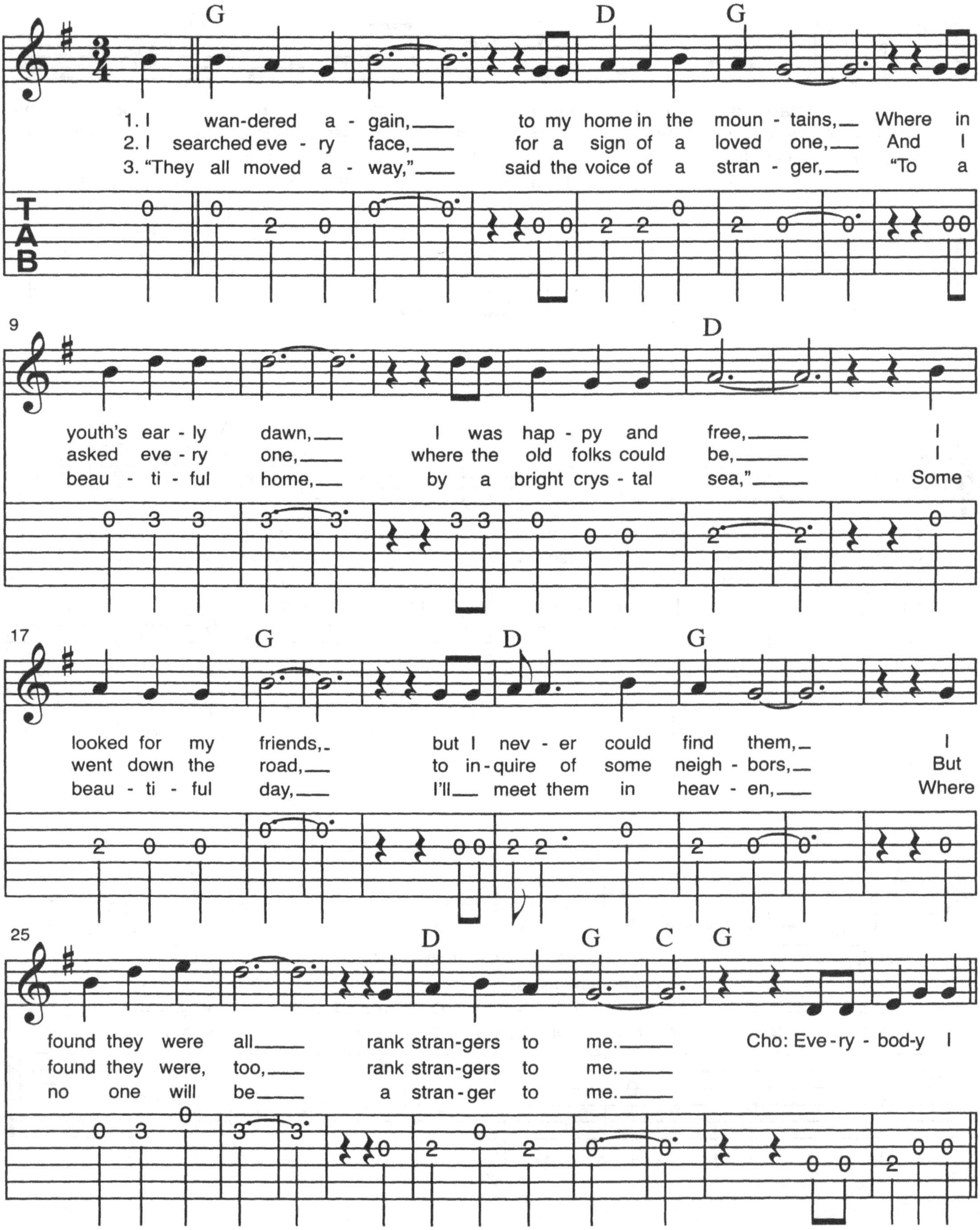

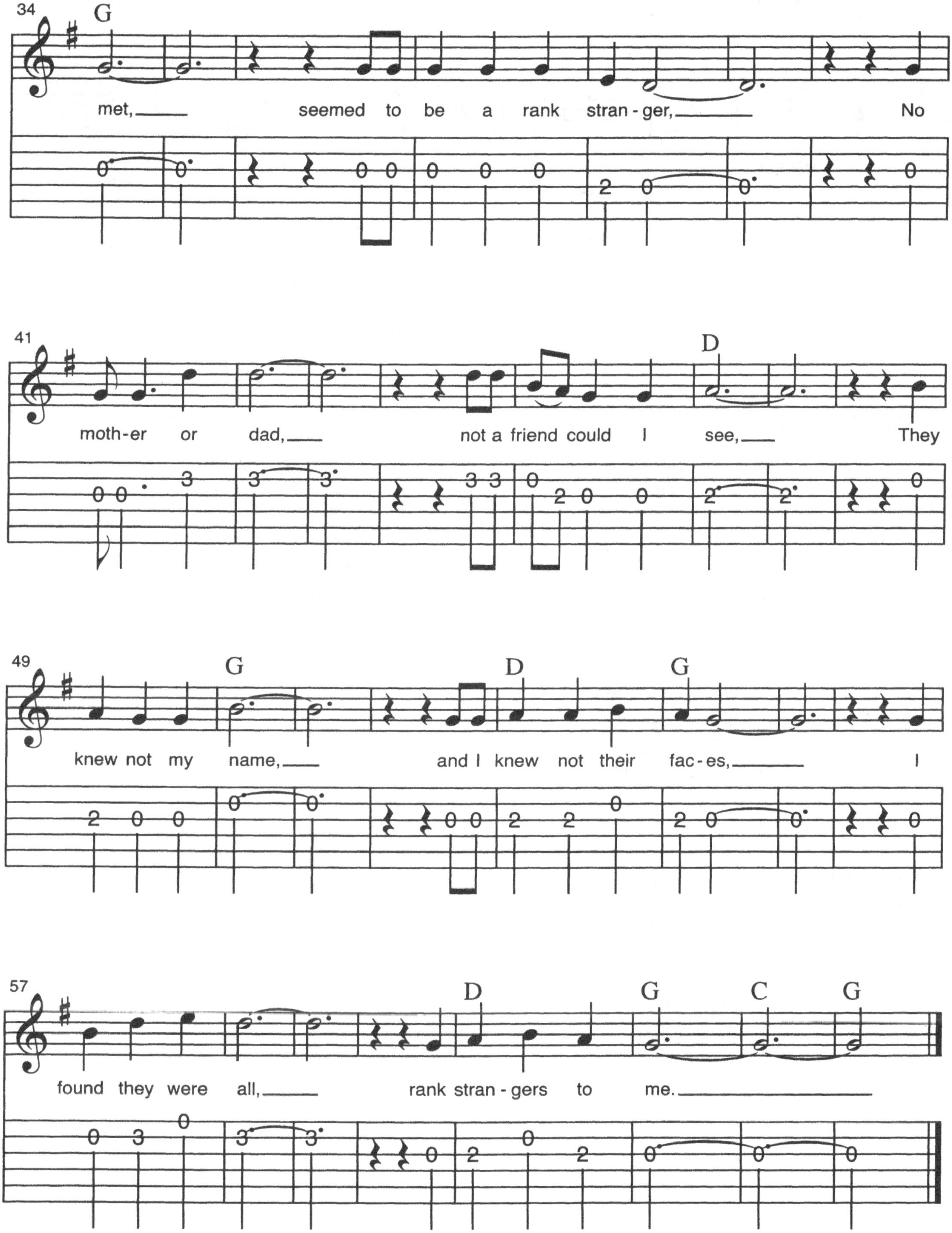

34
G
met, seemed to be a rank stran - ger, No
41
D
moth-er or dad, not a friend could I see, They
49
G D G
knew not my name, and I knew not their fac - es, I
57
D G C G
found they were all, rank stran - gers to me.

Red Rocking Chair

M: G; F: C or D, capo 5 or 7
CD 2-Track 46

Traditional

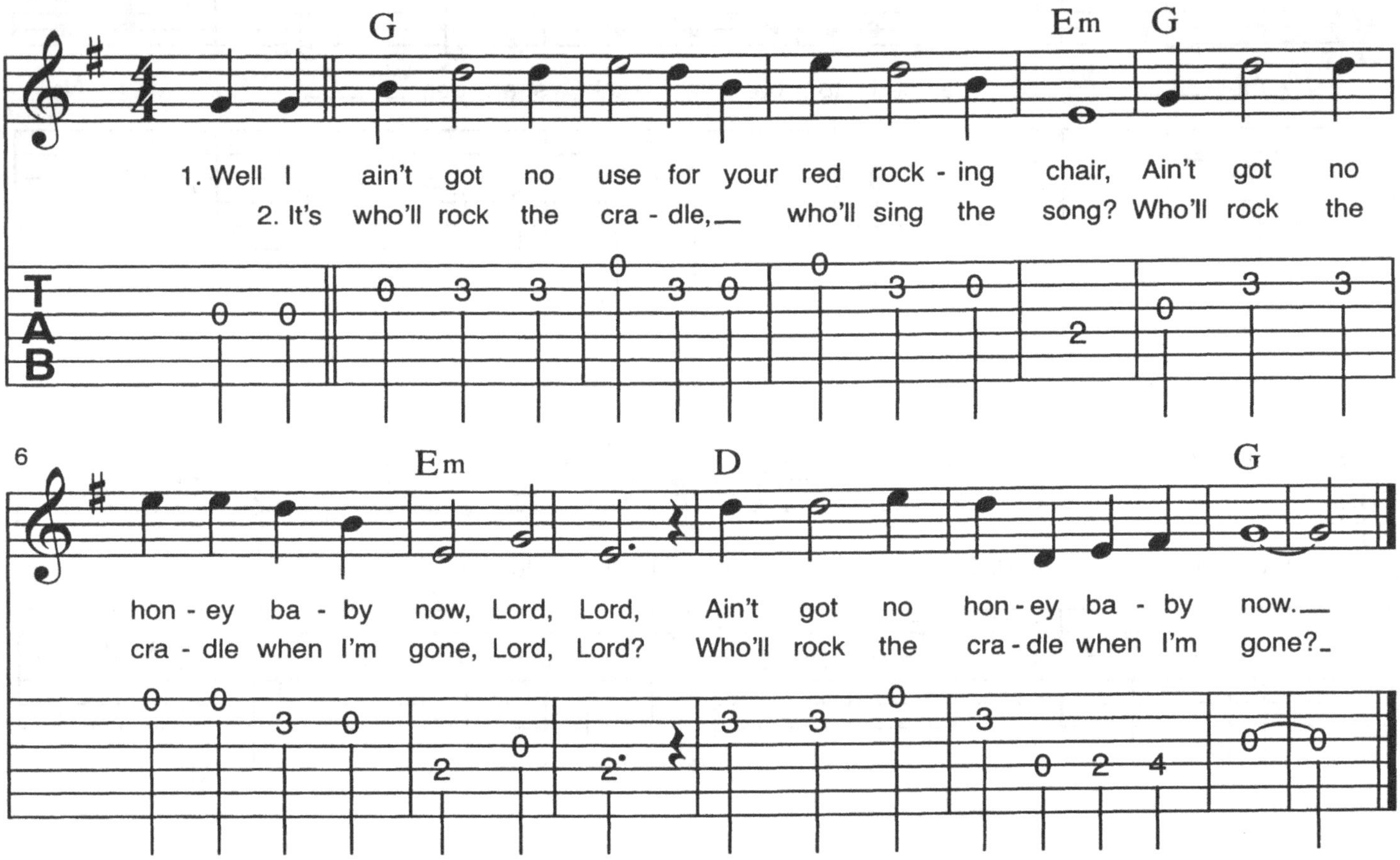


```
    G                              Em
3. I'll rock the cradle, I'll sing the song,
G                                Em
I'll rock the cradle when you're gone, Lord, Lord,
D                               G
I'll rock the cradle when you're gone.
```

4. It's all I can do, all I can say,
Ain't gonna be treated this a' way, Lord, Lord,
Ain't gonna be treated this a' way.

5. It's all I can do, all I can say,
Sing it to you mama next pay day, Lord, Lord,
Sing it to you mama next pay day.

C. Monroe, Country Gentlemen, D. Watson, Reno & Harrell, Dry Branch Fire Squad, J.D. Crowe, Mac Wiseman, Muleskinner, Kruger Bros.

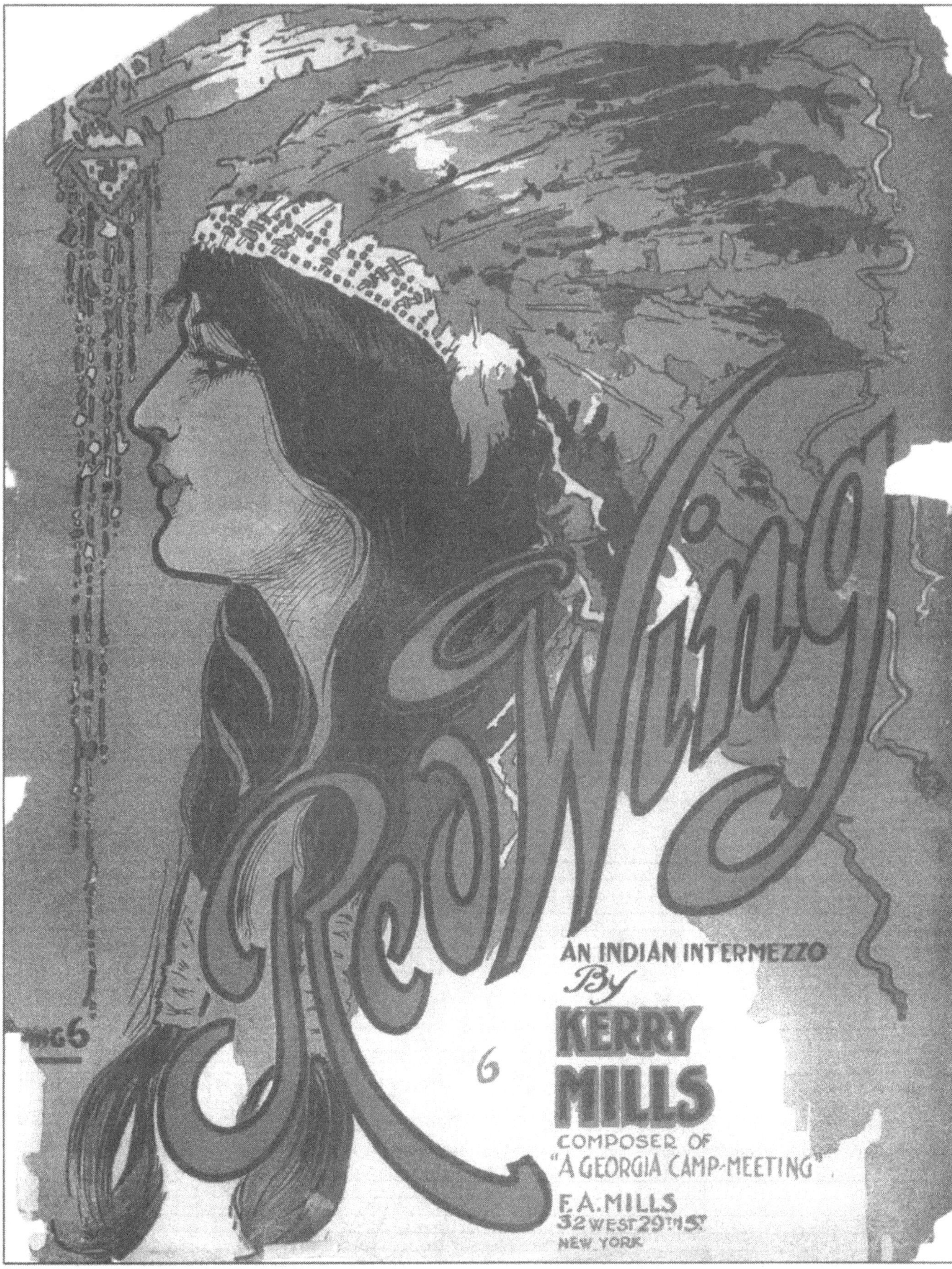

Original 1907 sheet music cover from the collection of Dix Bruce.

Red Wing

M: C; F: F or G, capo 5 or 7
CD 2-Track 47

Chattaway & Mills, 1907

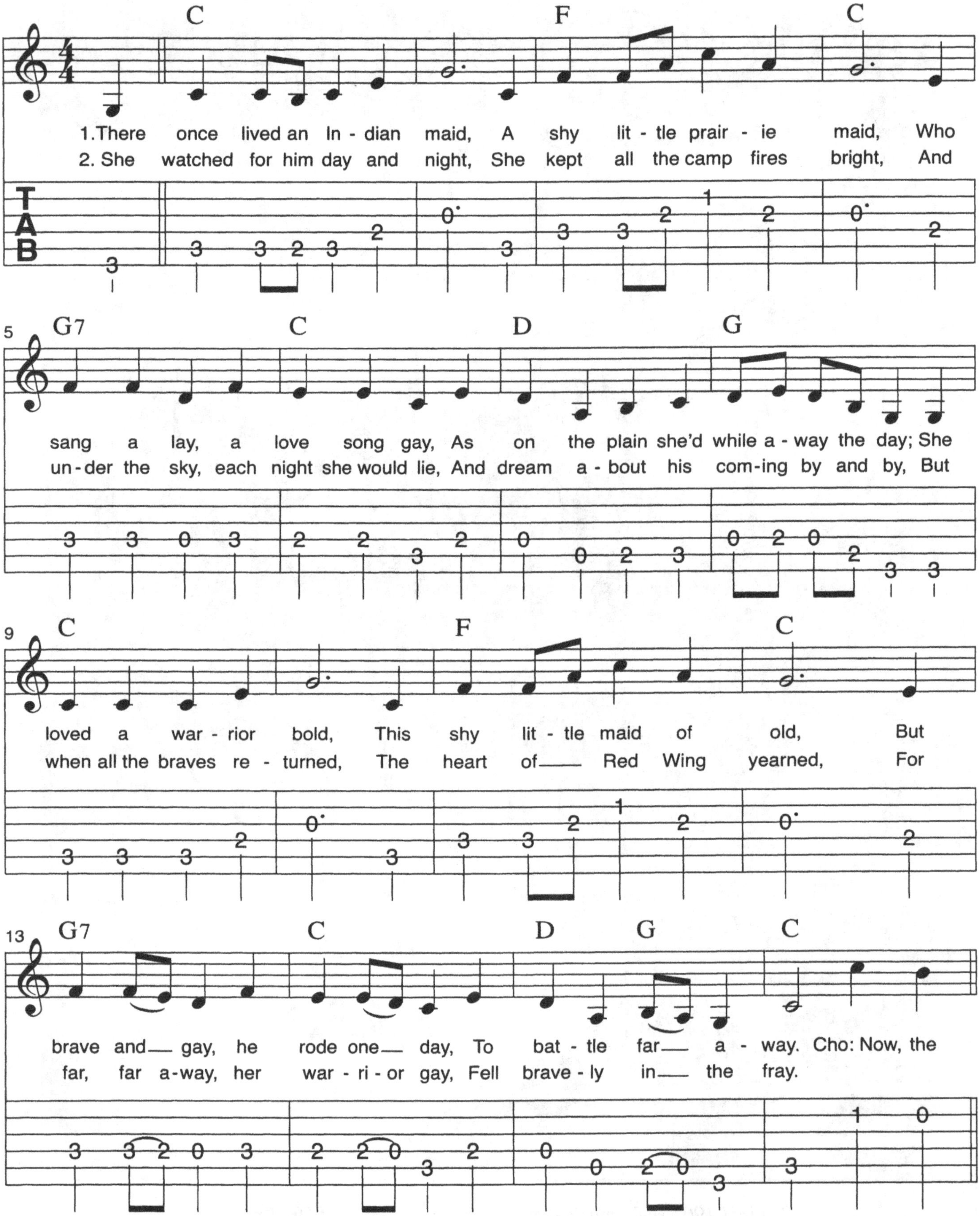

 N. Blake, Osborne Bros., R. Smiley, J. McEuen, A. Munde, L. Flatt & B. Monroe,

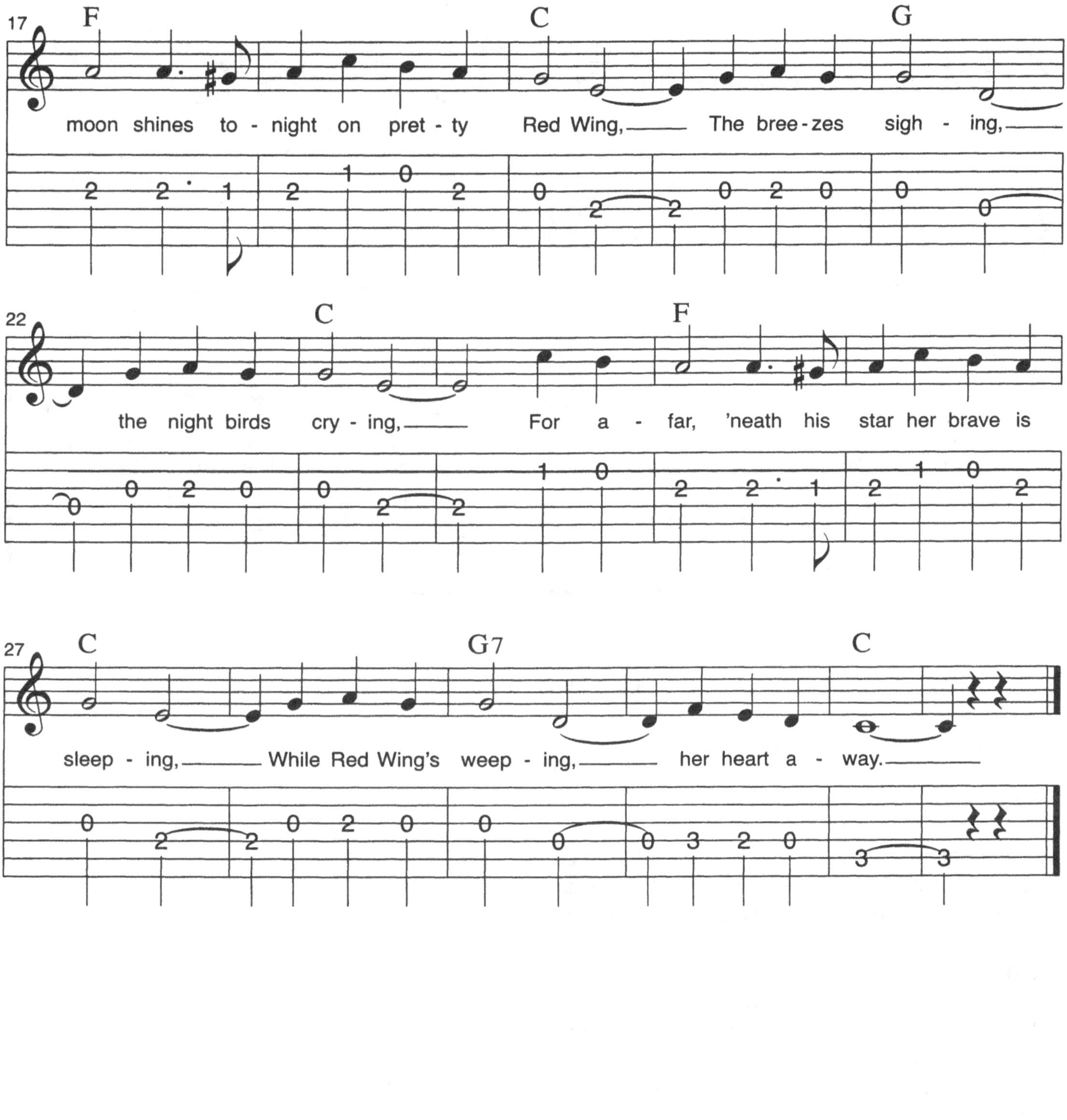

F C G
moon shines to - night on pret - ty Red Wing, The bree - zes sigh - ing,
C F
the night birds cry - ing, For a - far, 'neath his star her brave is
C G7 C
sleep - ing, While Red Wing's weep - ing, her heart a - way.

Reuben's Train

M: D; F: G or A, capo 5 or 7
CD 2-Track 48

Traditional

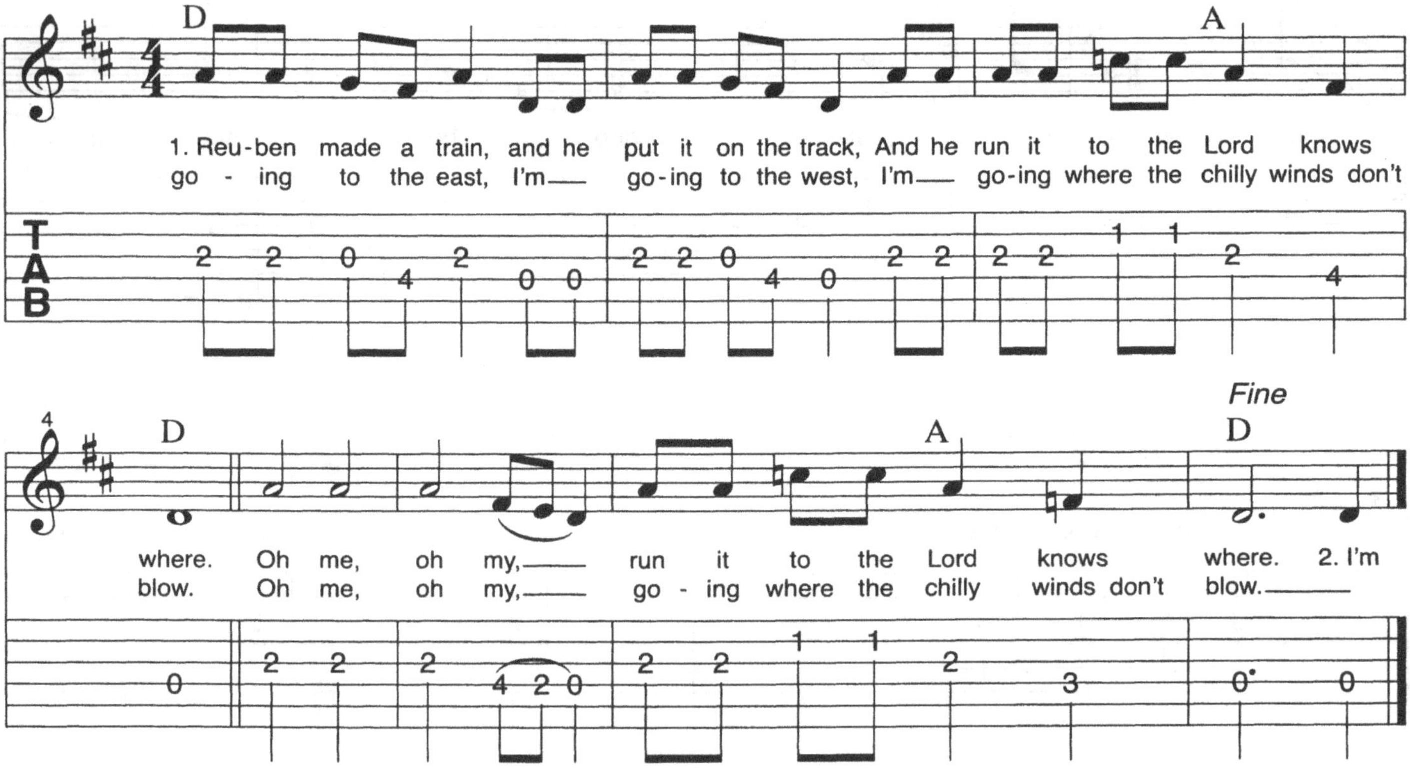

D
3. If that train's running right, see my woman tomorrow night.
A D
I'm nine hundred miles away from home.
A D
Oh me, oh my, nine hundred miles away from home.

4. You ought to been uptown, to see that train come down,
You could hear the whistle blow a hundred miles.
Oh me, oh my, hear the whistle blow a hundred miles.

5. Last night I lay in jail, had no money to go my bail,
Lord, how it sleeted and it snowed.
Oh me, oh my, Lord how it sleeted and it snowed.

6. Oh, the train that I ride, is a hundred coaches long,
You can hear the whistle blow a hundred miles.
Oh me, oh my, you can hear the whistle blow a hundred miles.

7. I got myself a blade, laid Reuben in the shade,
I'm starting me a graveyard of my own.
Oh me, oh my, starting me a graveyard of my own.

 Flatt & Scruggs, D. Watson, Holy Modal Rounders, T. Rice, D. Bruce and J. Nunally

Rocky Top

M: G; F: C or D, capo 5 or 7
CD 2-Track 49

Boudeleau & Felice Bryant

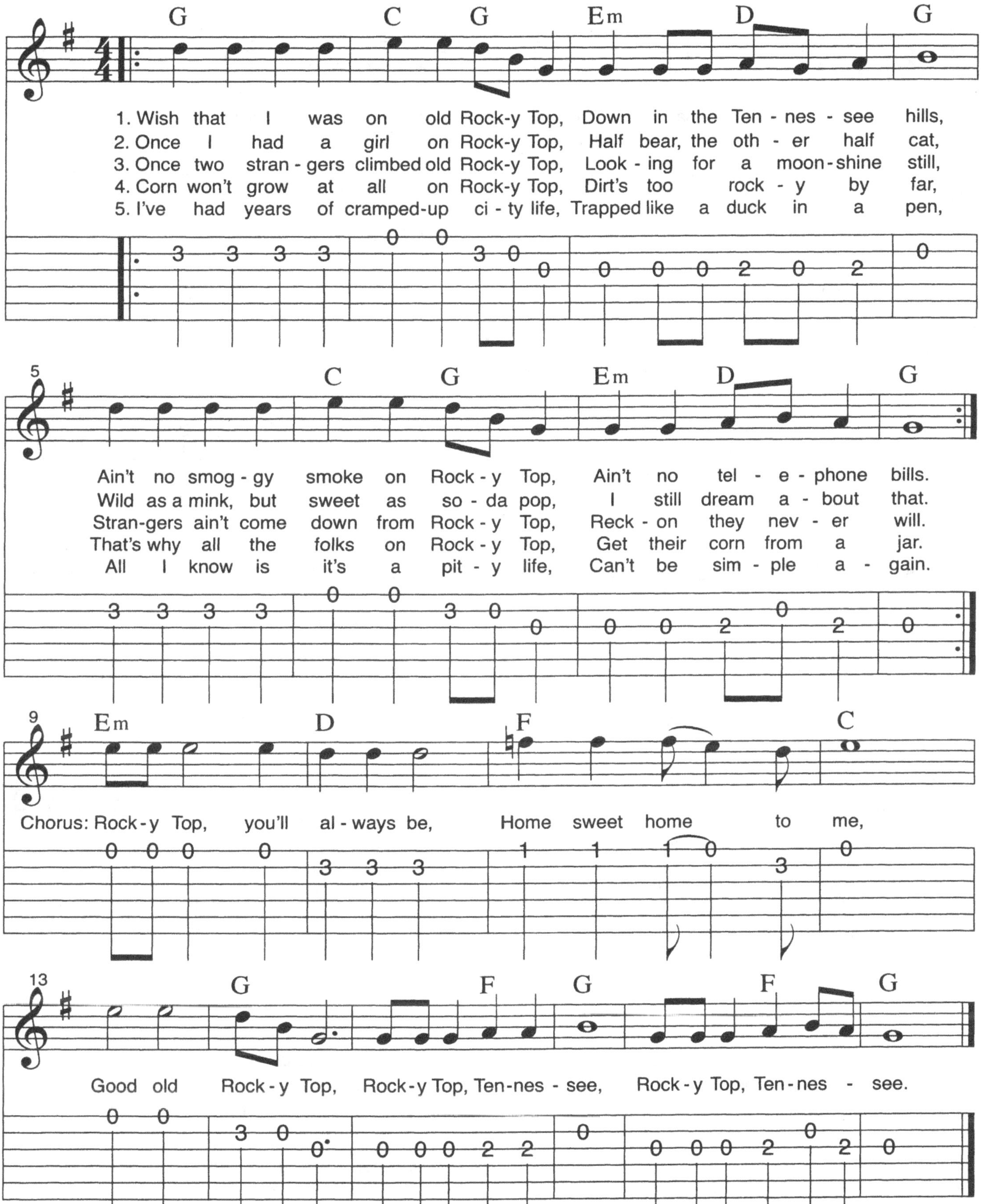

Roll in My Sweet Baby's Arms

***M:** A; **F:** D or E, capo 5 or 7*
CD 2-Track 50

Traditional

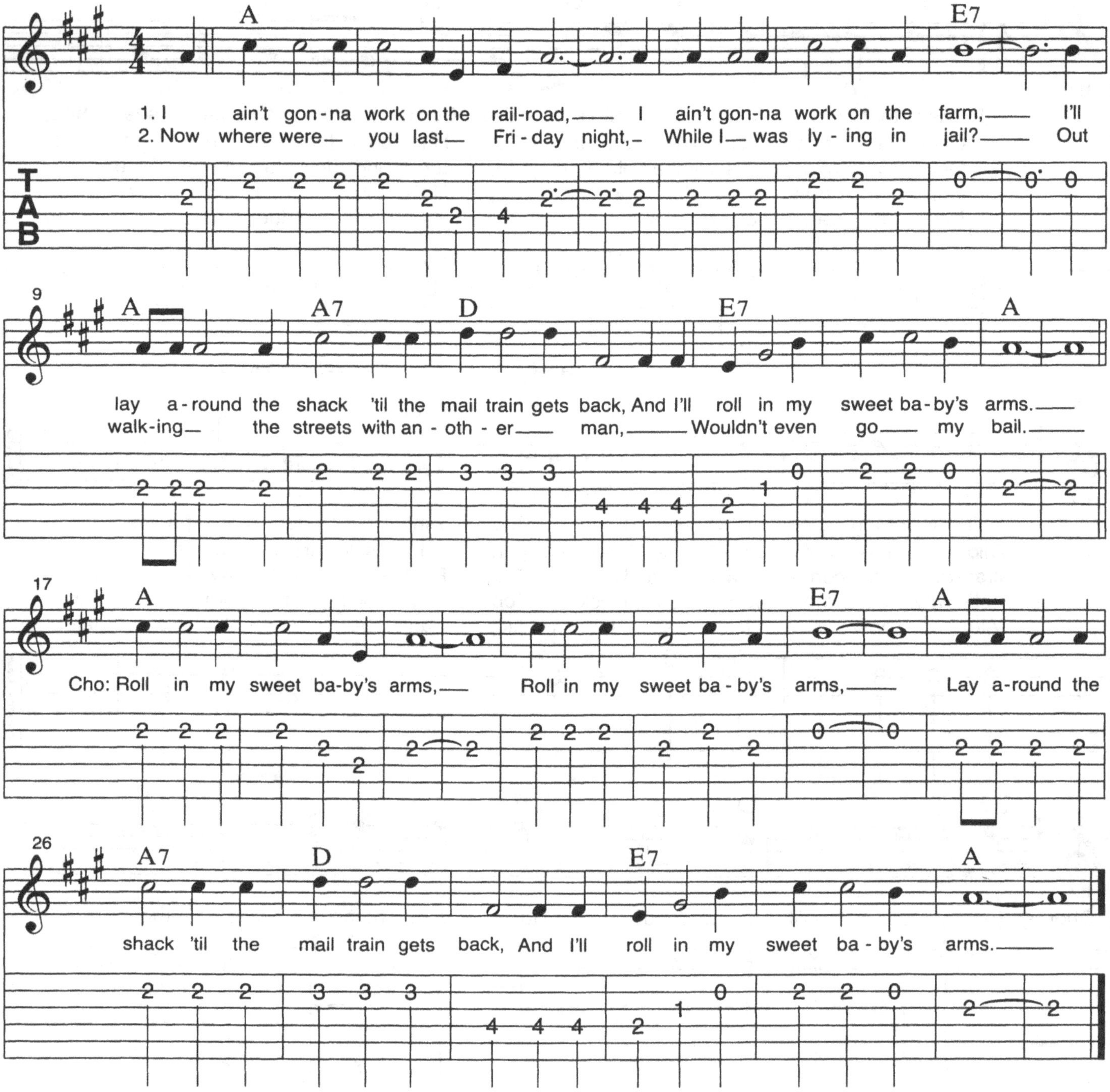


```
A
3. I know your parents don't like me,
                                    E7
They drove me away from your door,
   A        A7          D
If I had my life to live over,
    E7                    A
I'd never go there any more.
```

4. Mama's a beauty operator,
Sister can weave and spin,
Pappa's got an interest in an old cotton mill,
My, how the money rolls in!

5. Sometimes there's a change in the weather,
Sometimes there's a change in the sea,
Sometimes there's a change in my own true love,
But there's never a change in me.

 Monroe Bros., Flatt & Scruggs, B. Monroe, R. Stanley, J.D. Crowe, Bluegrass Band, D. McCoury, Scruggs/Watson/Skaggs, Lilly Bros.

Roll on Buddy

M: G; F: C or D, capo 5 or 7
CD 2-Track 51

Traditional

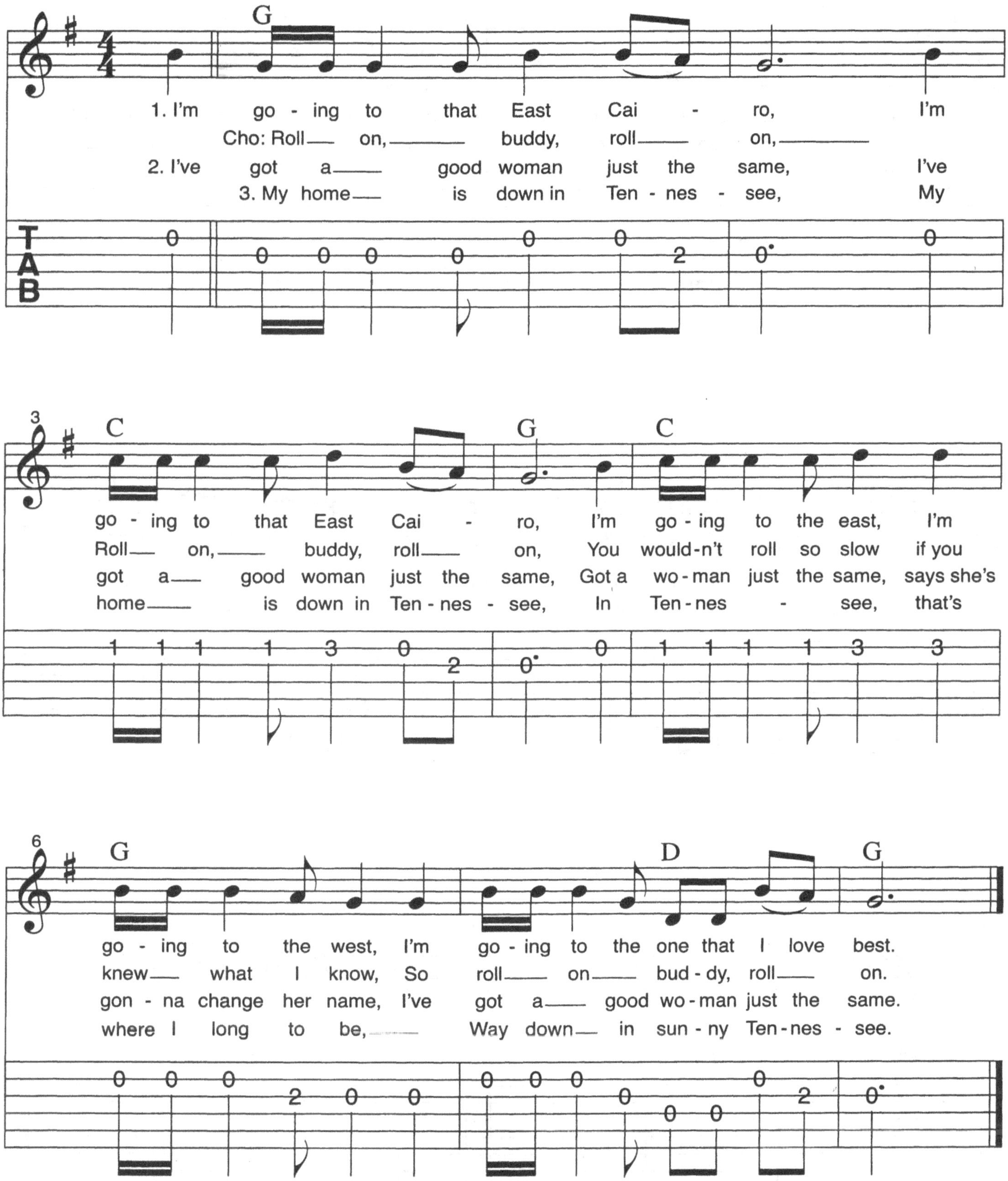

Roving Gambler

M: G; F: C or D, capo 5 or 7
CD 2-Track 52

Traditional

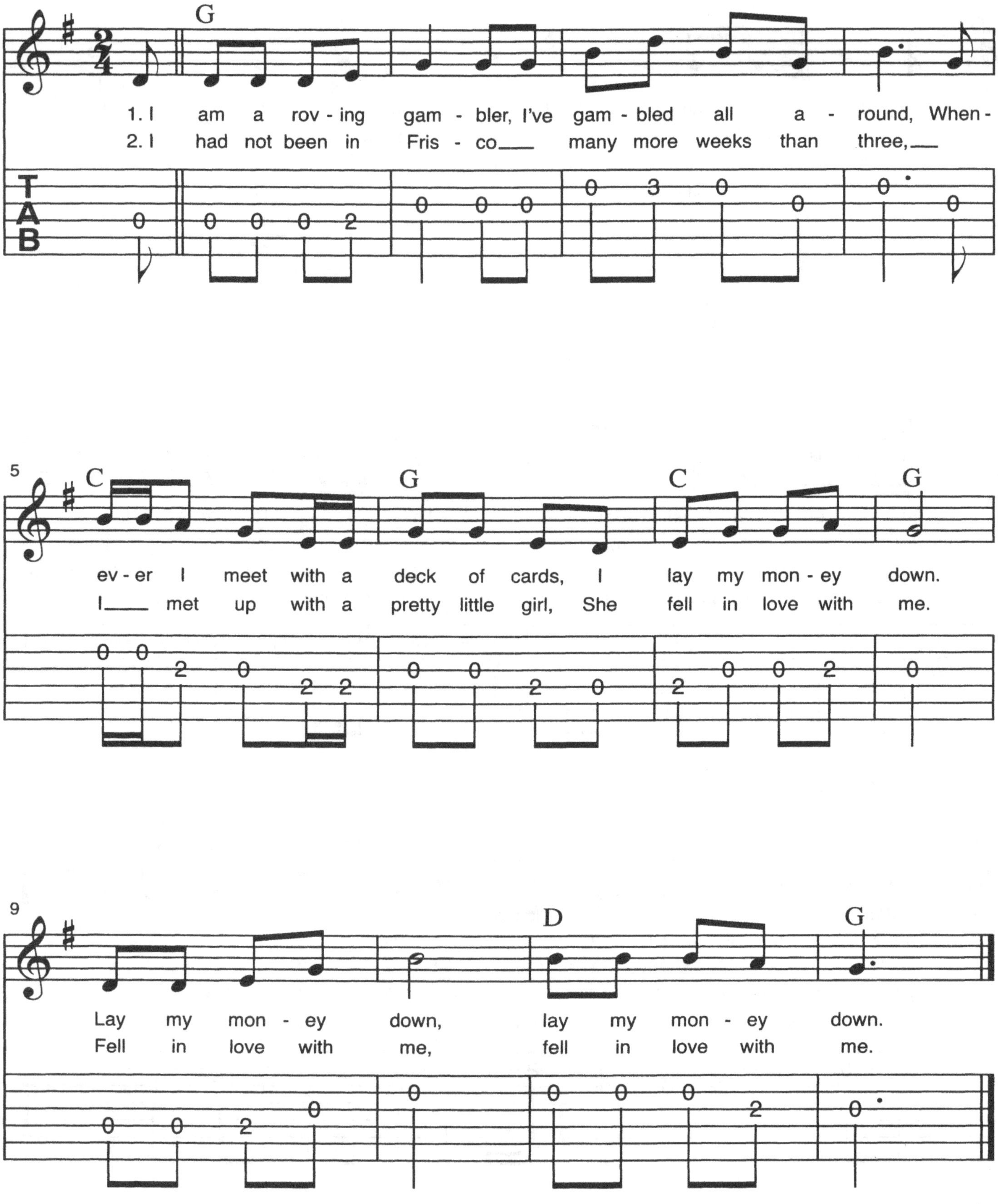

 Stanley Bros., Country Gentlemen, P. Rowan, D. Watson, B. Clifton, Mac Wiseman

G
3. She took me in her parlor, she cooled me with her fan,
C G
She whispered low in her mother's ear,
C G
"I love this gambling man.
D G
Love this gambling man, love this gambling man."

4. Oh daughter, oh dear daughter, how can you treat me so?
Leave your dear old mother,
And with a gambler go,
With a gambler go, with a gambler go?

5. Oh mother, oh dear mother, you cannot understand,
If you ever see me a'coming back,
I'll be with the gambling man,
With the gambling man, with the gambling man.

6. I left her in Frisco and I ended up in Maine,
I met up with a gambling man,
We got in a poker game,
Got in a poker game, got in a poker game.

7. We put our money in the pot and dealt the cards around,
I saw him deal from the bottom of the deck,
So I shot that gambler down,
Shot the gambler down, shot the gambler down.

8. Now I'm up in prison, got a number for my name,
Jailer said as he locked the door,
"You've gambled your last game,
Gambled your last game, gambled your last game."

Sailor on the Deep Blue Sea

M: D; F: G or A, capo 5 or 7
CD 2-Track 53

Traditional

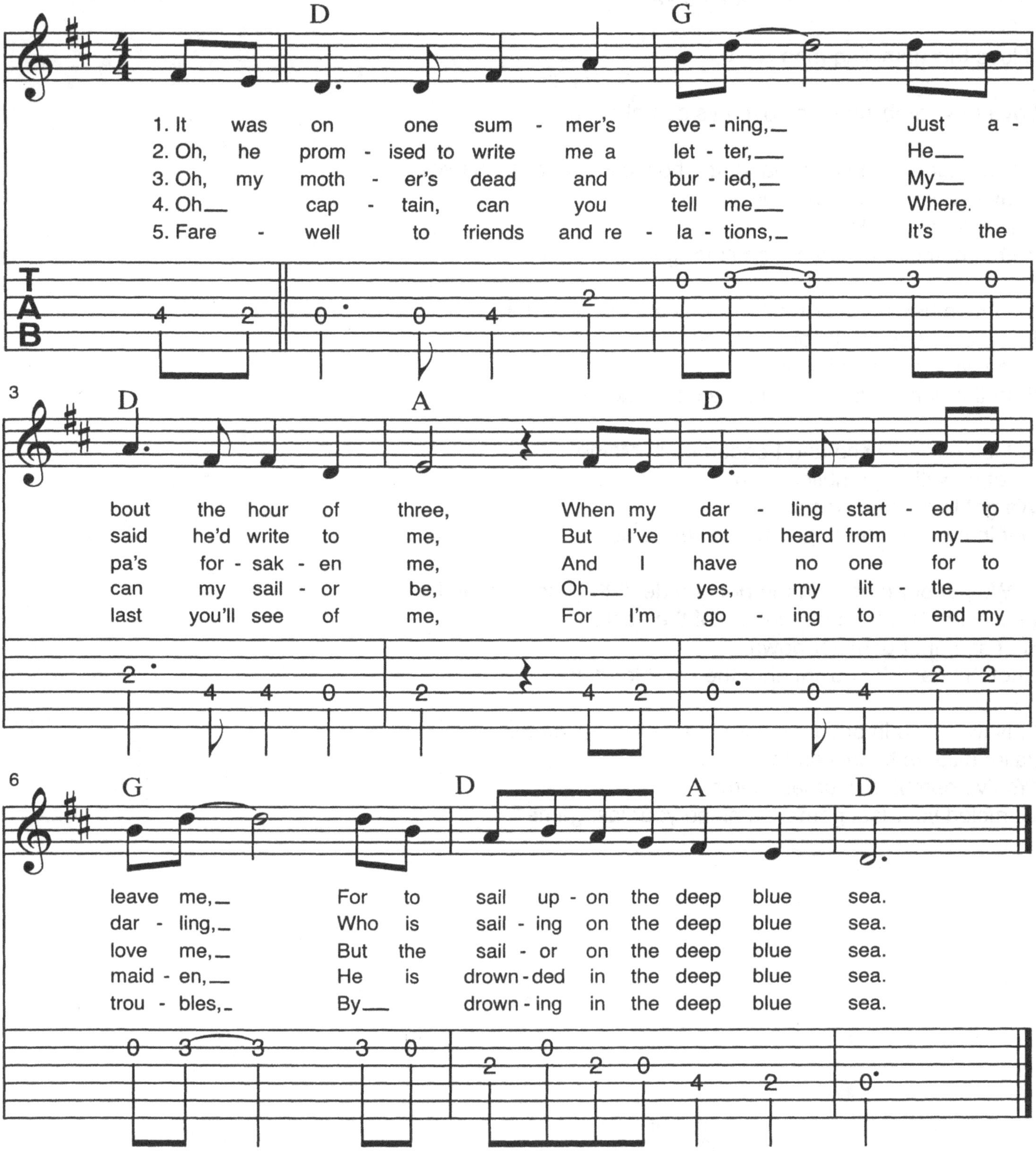

Sally Goodin

M: A capo 2; F: D or E, capo 7 or 9
CD 2-Track 54

Traditional

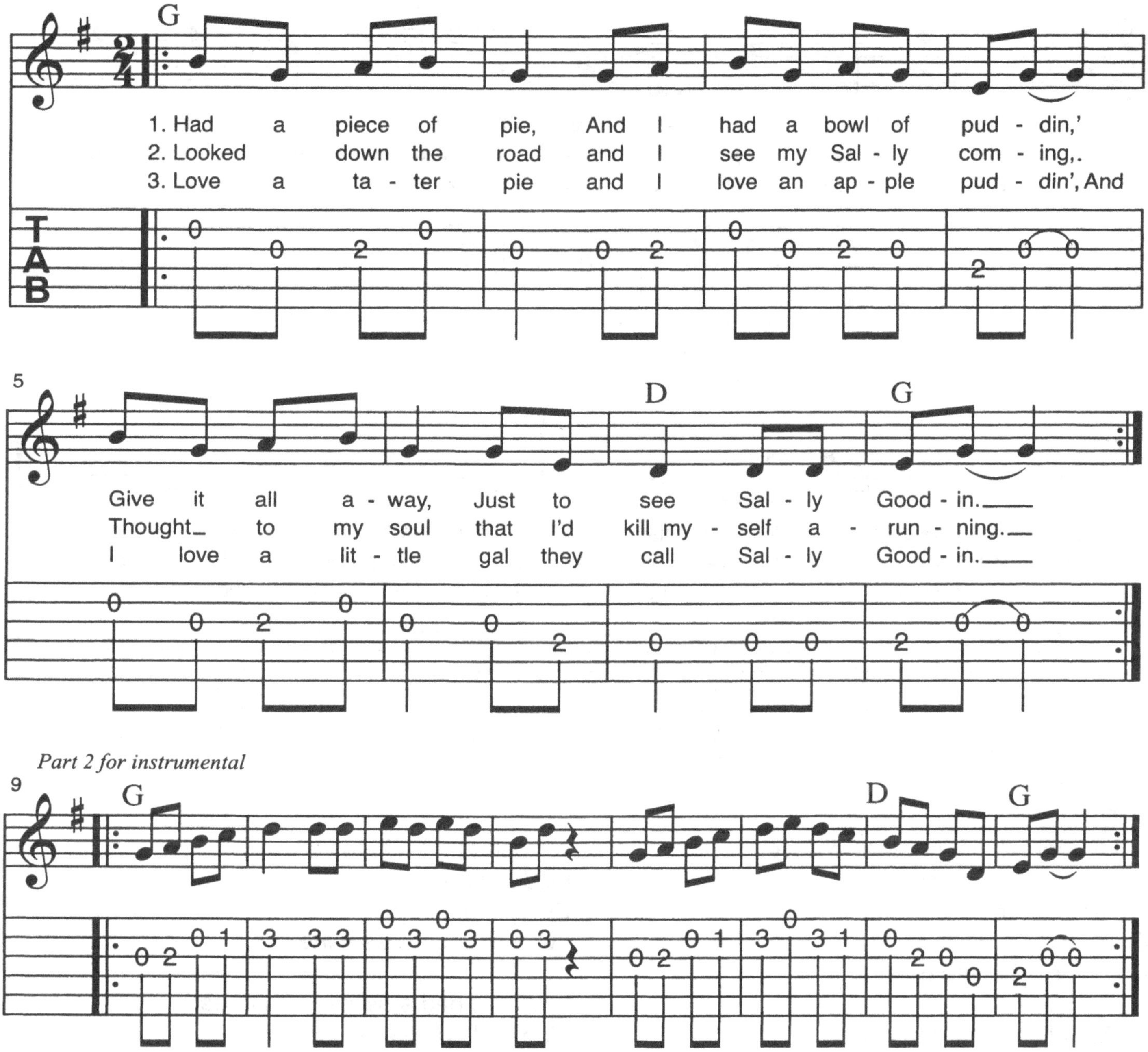

G
4. I dropped the tater pie and I left the apple puddin',
D G
Went across the mountain to see my Sally Goodin.

5. Sally is my dooxy and Sally is my daisy,
When Sally says she hates me I think I'm going crazy.

6. Little dog'll bark and the big dog'll bite you,
Little gal'll court you and a big gal'll fight you.

7. Raining and a' pouring and the creek's running muddy,
I'm so drunk I can't stand steady.

8. I'm goin up the mountain and marry little Sally,
Raise corn on the hillside and the devil in the valley.

Flatt & Scruggs, B. Monroe, R. Stanley, C. White, Hot Rize, NLCR, A. Munde, J. Hickman

Shady Grove

M: C; F: F or G, capo 5 or 7
CD 2-Track 55

Bluegrass style

Traditional

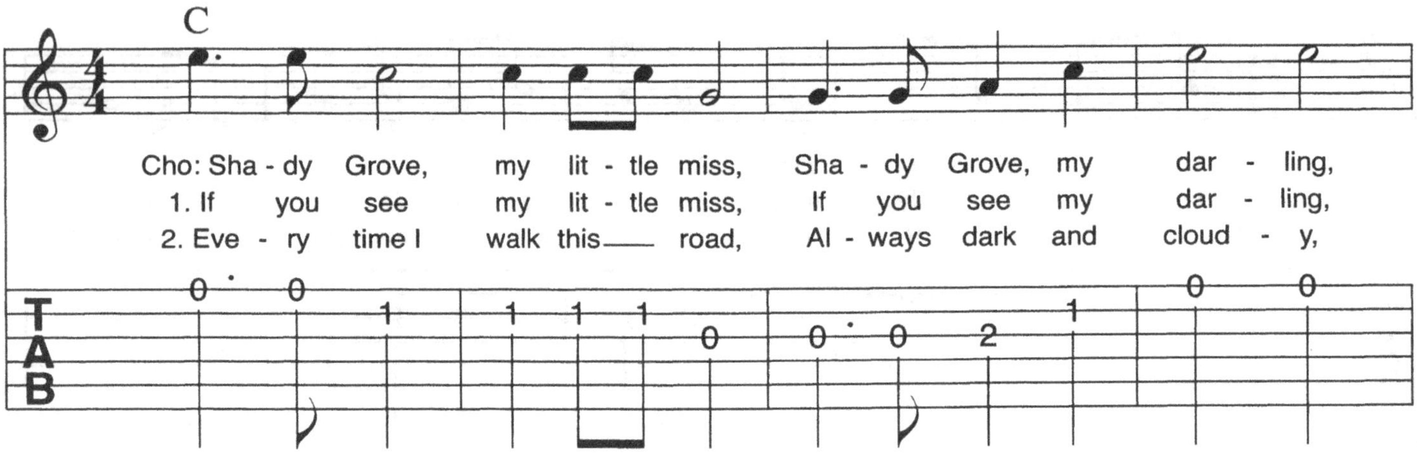

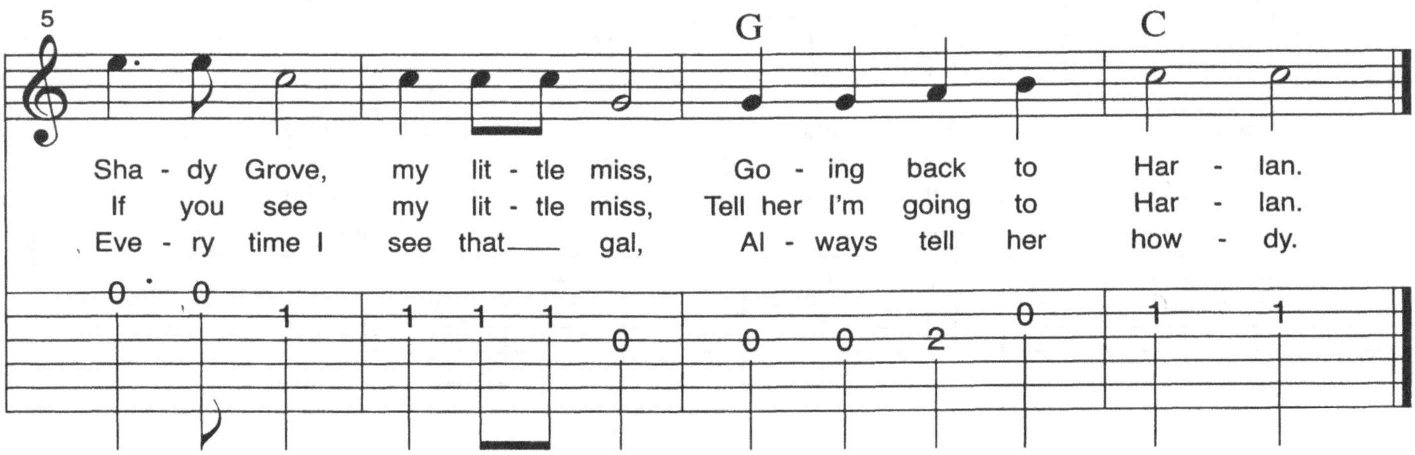

C
4. Fly around, my pretty little dove,
Fly around, my daisy,
Fly around, my pretty little love,
G C
Bound to drive me crazy.

5. Wish I was in Shady Grove,
Sitting in a rocking chair,
And if those blues would bother me,
I'd rock away from there.

6. All I want is a pig in a pen,
Corn to feed him on,
Pretty little girl to stay at home,
Feed him when I'm gone.

7. Wish I had a banjo string,
Made of golden twine,
Every tune I'd play on it,
I wish that girl was mine.

8. Wish I had a needle and thread,
Fine as I could sew,
I'd sew that pretty girl to my side,
And down the road I'd go.

9. Some come here to fiddle and dance,
Some come here to tarry,
Some here to fiddle and dance,
I come here to marry.

 B. Monroe, Garcia & Grisman, Ken. Colonels, Hot Rize, D. Watson, Grisman, Garcia, Rice

Shady Grove

Old Time style

***M**: Em modal; **F**: Am or Bm modal, capo 5 or 7*
CD 2-Track 56

Traditional

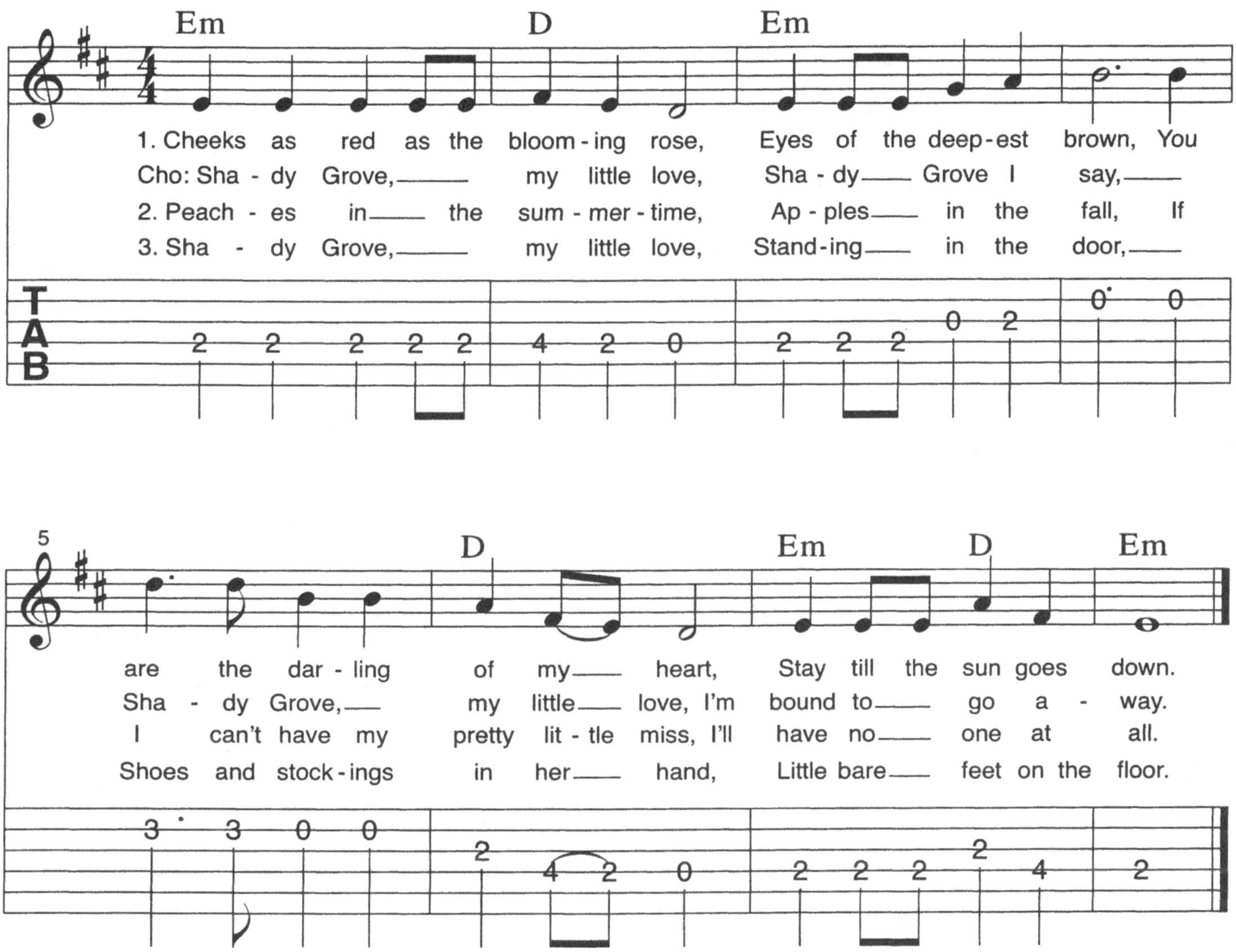

Shall We Gather at the River

M: C; F: F or G, capo 5 or 7
CD 2-Track 57

Robert Lowry

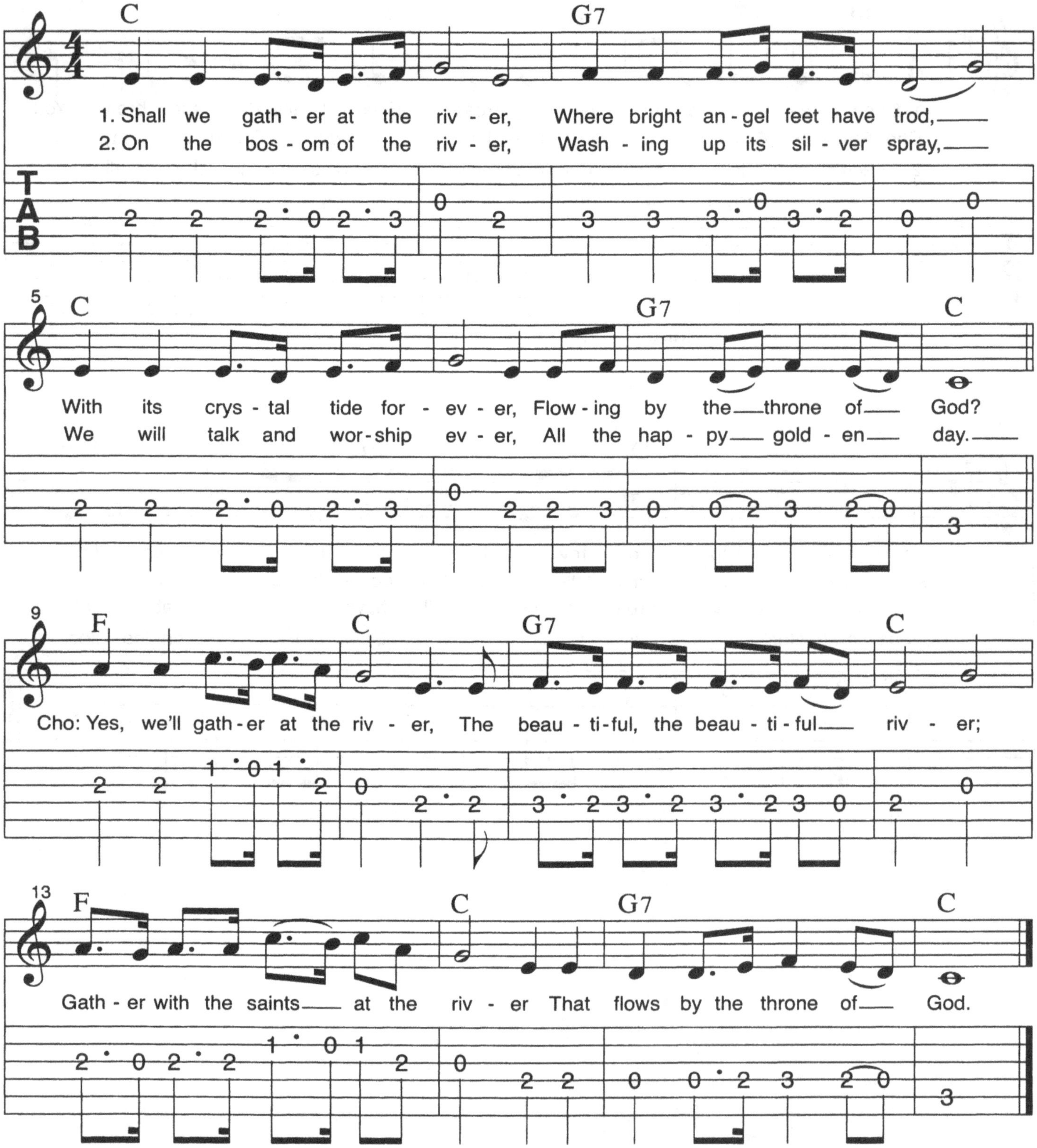

C
3. 'Ere we reach the shining river,
G7
Lay we every burden down;
C
Grace our spirits will deliver,
G7 C
And provide a robe and crown.

4. At the smiling of the river,
Mirror of the Savior's face,
Saints, whom death will never sever,
Lift their songs of saving grace.

5. Soon we'll reach the shining river,
Soon our pilgrimage will cease;
Soon our happy hearts will quiver,
With the melody of peace.

A Short Life of Trouble

M: C; F: F or G, capo 5 or 7
CD 2-Track 58

Traditional

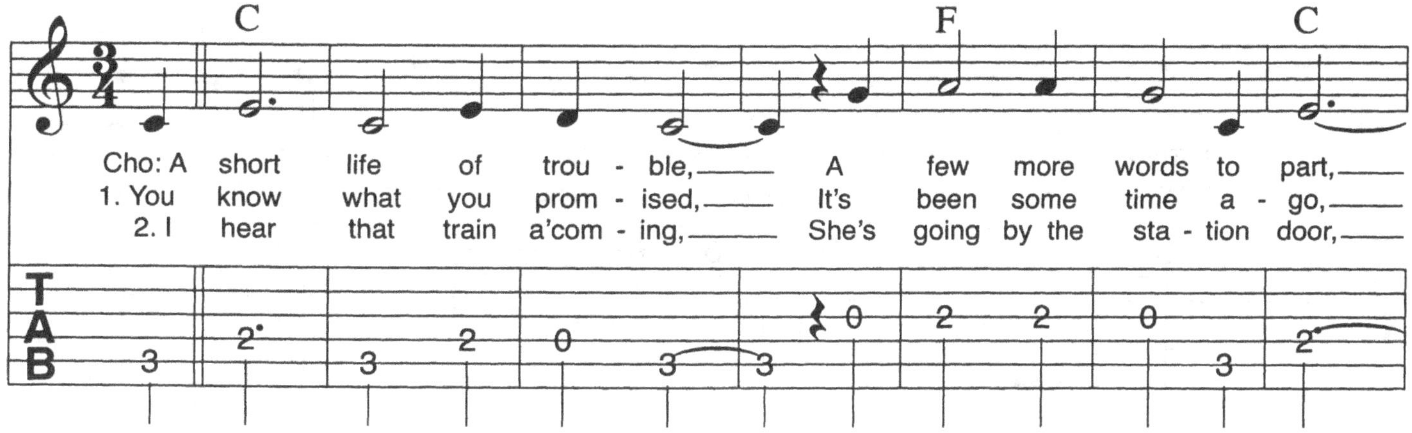

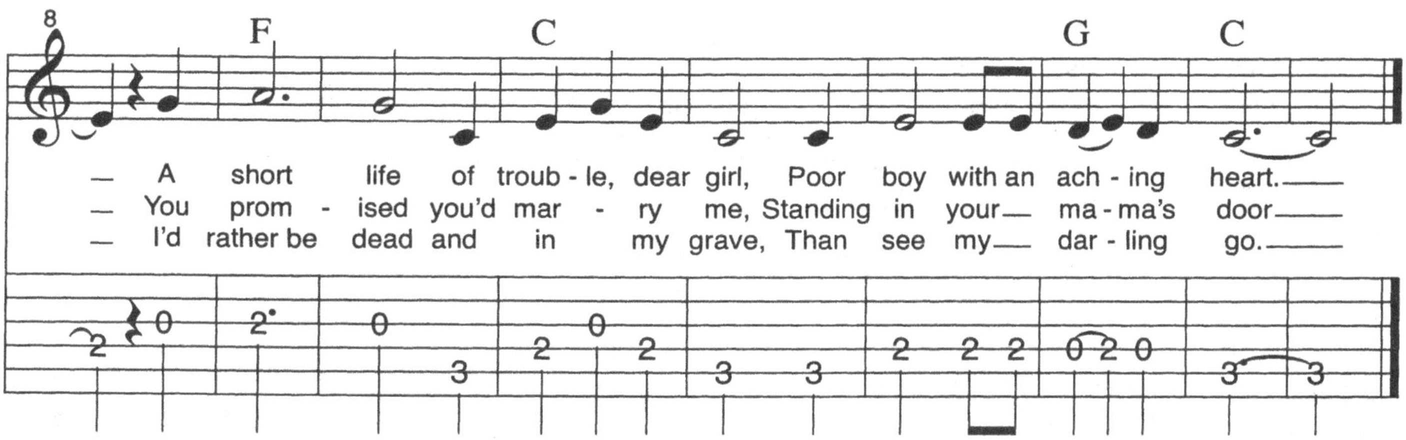


```
C
3. Now you've broken your promise,
     F              C
Go marry whom you may,
F                       C
For this old world's so big and so wide,
          G          C
I'll ramble back some day.
```

4. Now you've gone and left me,
I don't know what I'll do,
I'd give the world and half of my life,
Just to be married to you.

5. I see my coffin coming,
My shroud and all is on,
To take me to some lonesome graveyard,
And let the grave be my home.

6. And when my days have ended,
Will you come sow some flowers,
To show to the people 'round you,
The heart you've broken lies there.

Shortenin' Bread

M: D; F: G or A, capo 5 or 7
CD 2-Track 59

Traditional

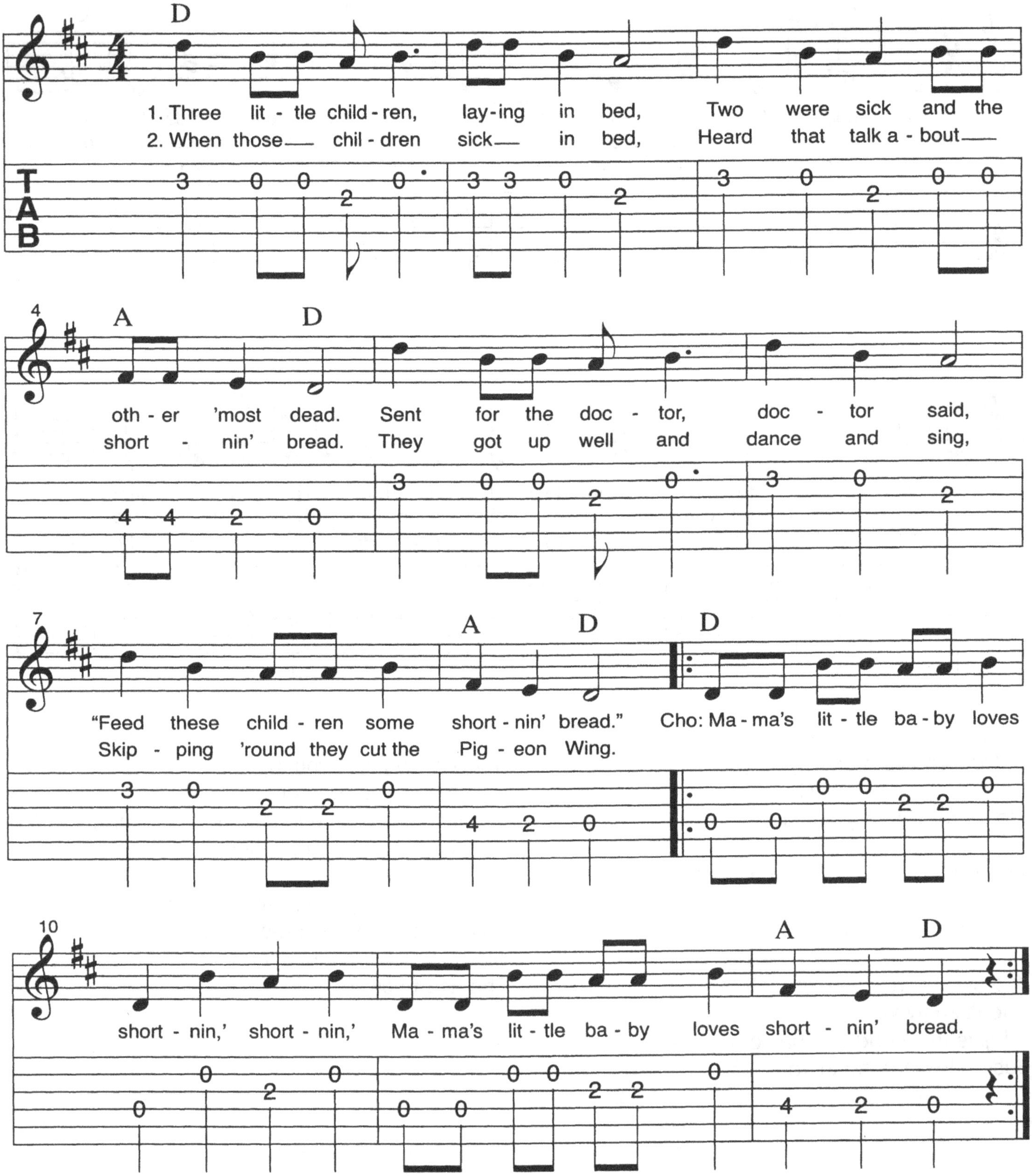

Silver Threads Among the Gold

M: G; F: C or D, capo 5 or 7 *Rexford & Danks, 1901*
CD 2-Track 60

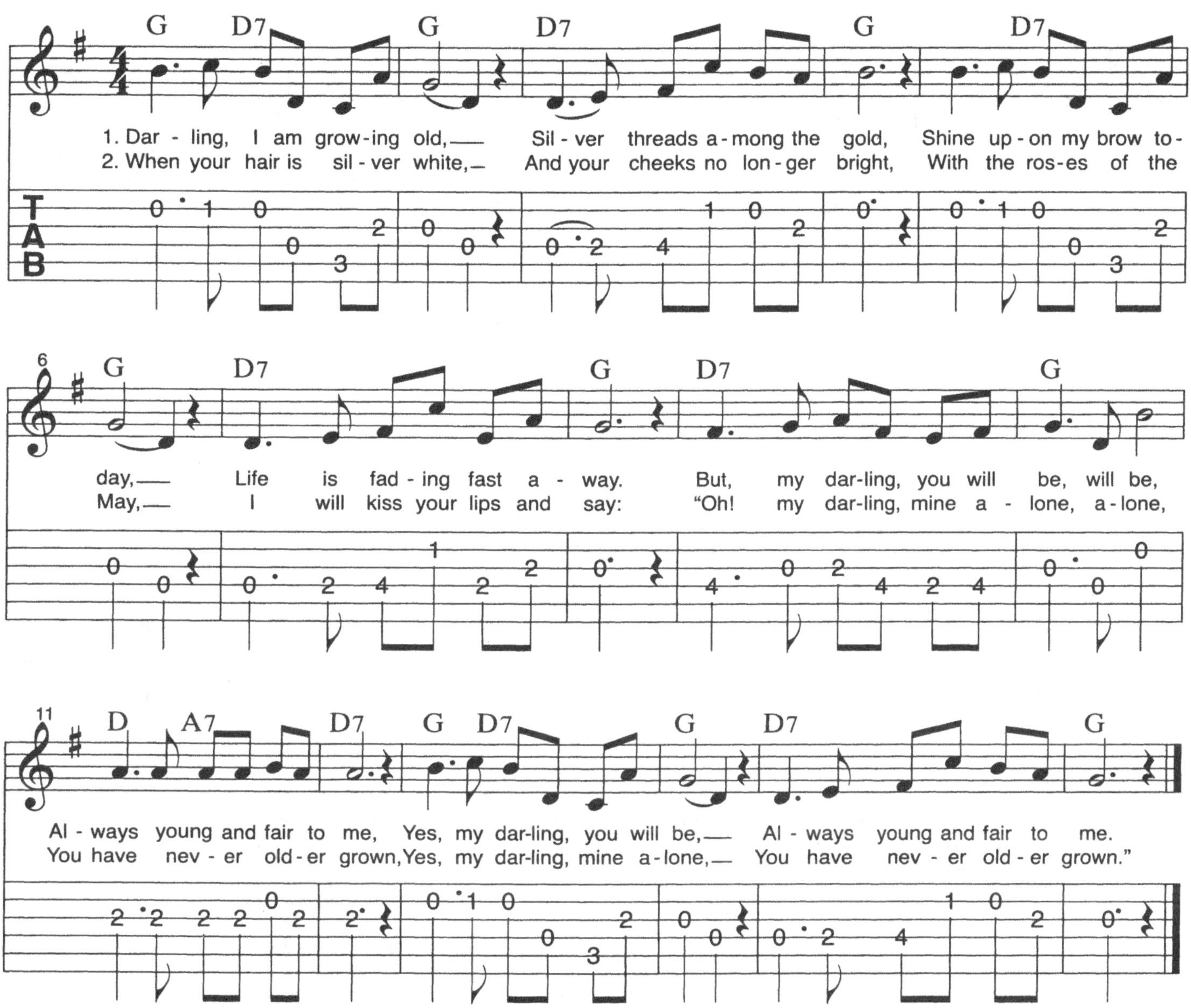

G D7 G
3. Love can never more grow old.
D7 G
Locks may lose their brown and gold,
G D7 G
Cheeks may fade and hollow grow,
D7 G
But the hearts that love will know.
D7 G
Never, never, winter's frost and chill,
D A7 D7
Summer warmth is in them still;
G D7 G
Never winter's frost and chill,
D7 G
Summer warmth is in them still.

4. Love is always young and fair.
What to us is silver hair?
Faded cheeks or steps grown slow,
To the heart that beats below?
Since I kissed you, mine alone, alone,
You have never older grown;
Since I kissed you, mine alone,
You have never older grown.

Sitting on Top of the World

M: G; F: C or D, capo 5 or 7
CD 2-Track 61

Traditional

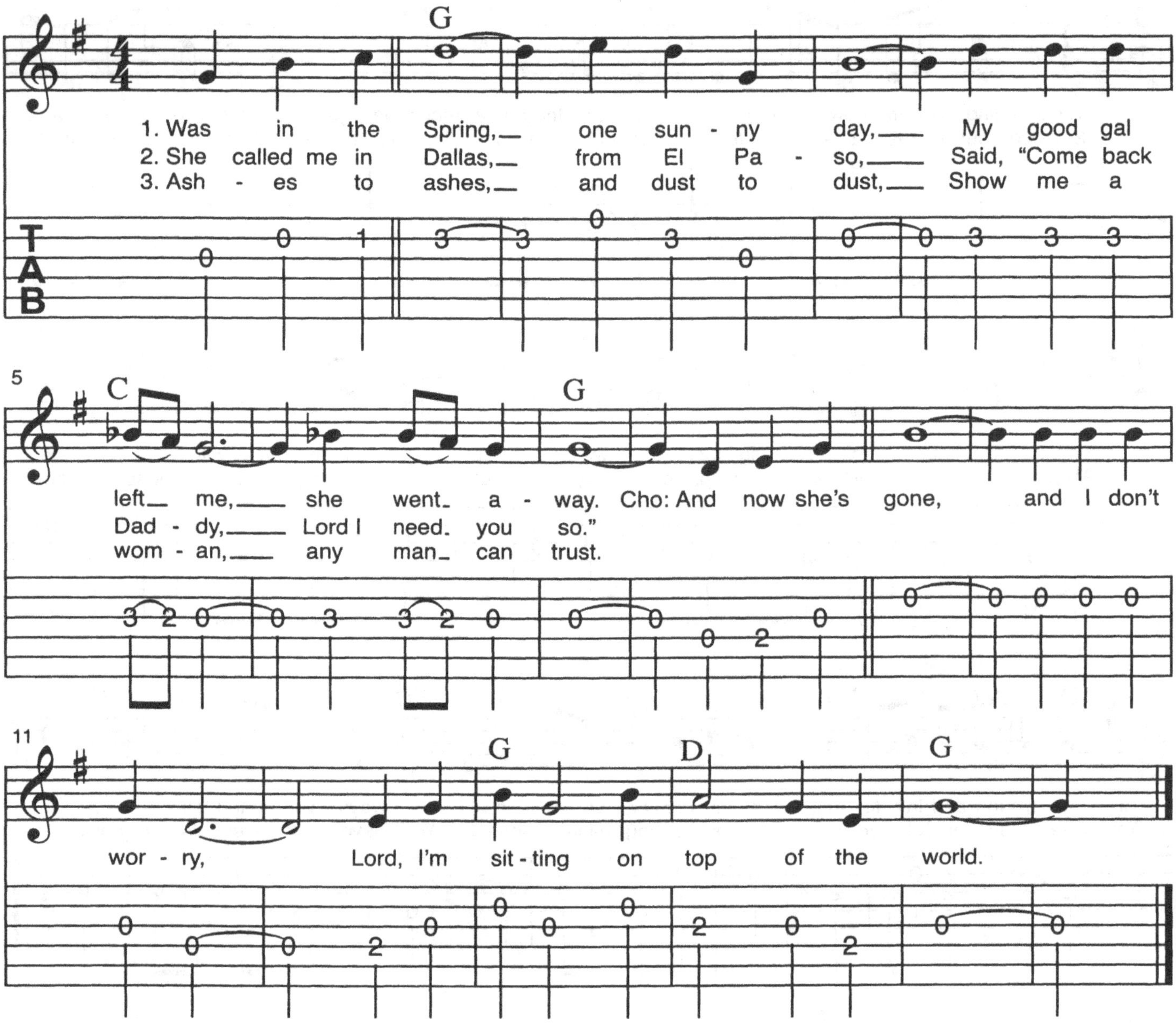

G
4. Mississippi River, long, deep and wide,
C G
The woman I'm loving's, on the other side.
Chorus: But now she's gone, and I don't worry,
D G
Lord, I'm sitting on top of the world.

5. You don't like my peaches, don't you shake my tree,
Get out of my orchard, let my peaches be. (Chorus)

6. Don't you come here running, poking out your hand,
I'll get me a woman, like you got your man. (Chorus)

 B. Monroe, R. Stanley, D. Watson, F. Wakefield, D. Bruce & J. Nunally, Nitty Gritty Dirt Band

Softly and Tenderly

M: G; F: C or D, capo 5 or 7
CD 2-Track 62

W.L. Thompson

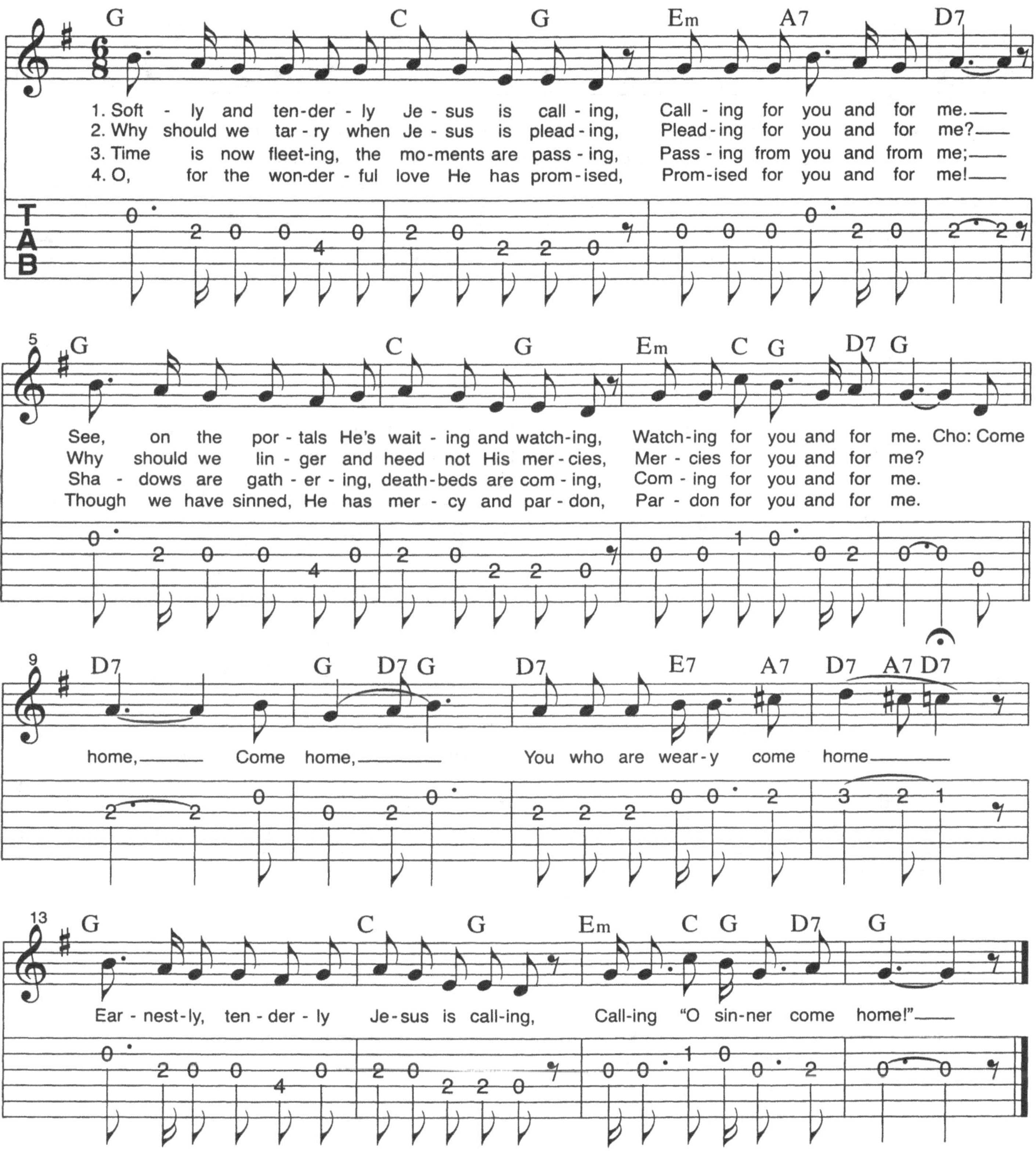

Somebody Touched Me

M: G; F: C or D, capo 5 or 7
CD 2-Track 63

Traditional

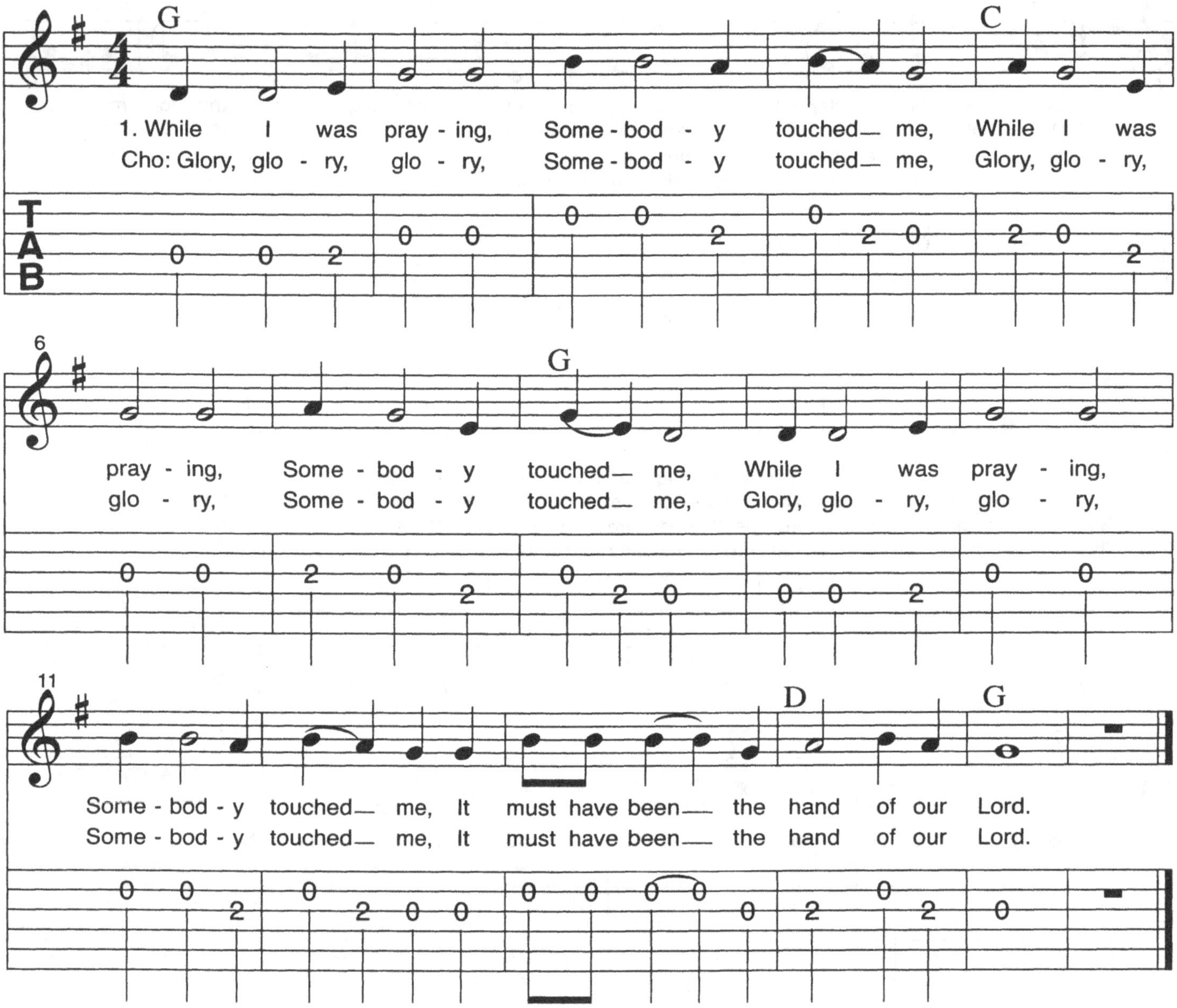


```
   G
2. While I was preaching, somebody touched me,
C                                   G
While I was preaching, somebody touched me,
While I was preaching, somebody touched me,
                            D        G
It must have been the hand of our Lord.
```

3. While I was singing, somebody touched me, etc.

 B. Monroe, Stanley Bros., R. Stanley, Dillards, D. Watson

Standing in the Need of Prayer

M: G; F: C or D, capo 5 or 7
CD 2-Track 64

Traditional

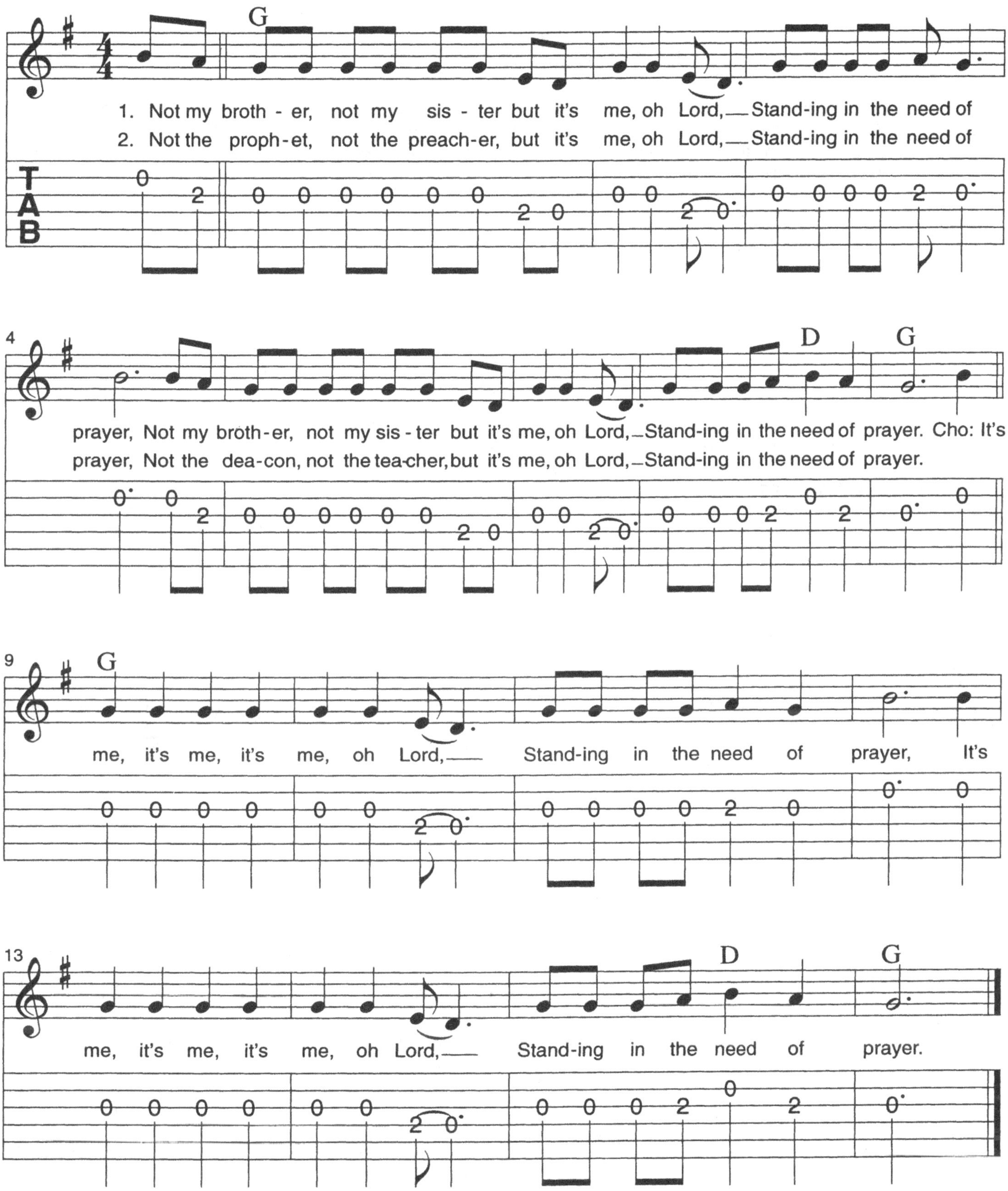

Sugar Hill

M: G; F: C or D, capo 5 or 7
CD 2-Track 65

Traditional

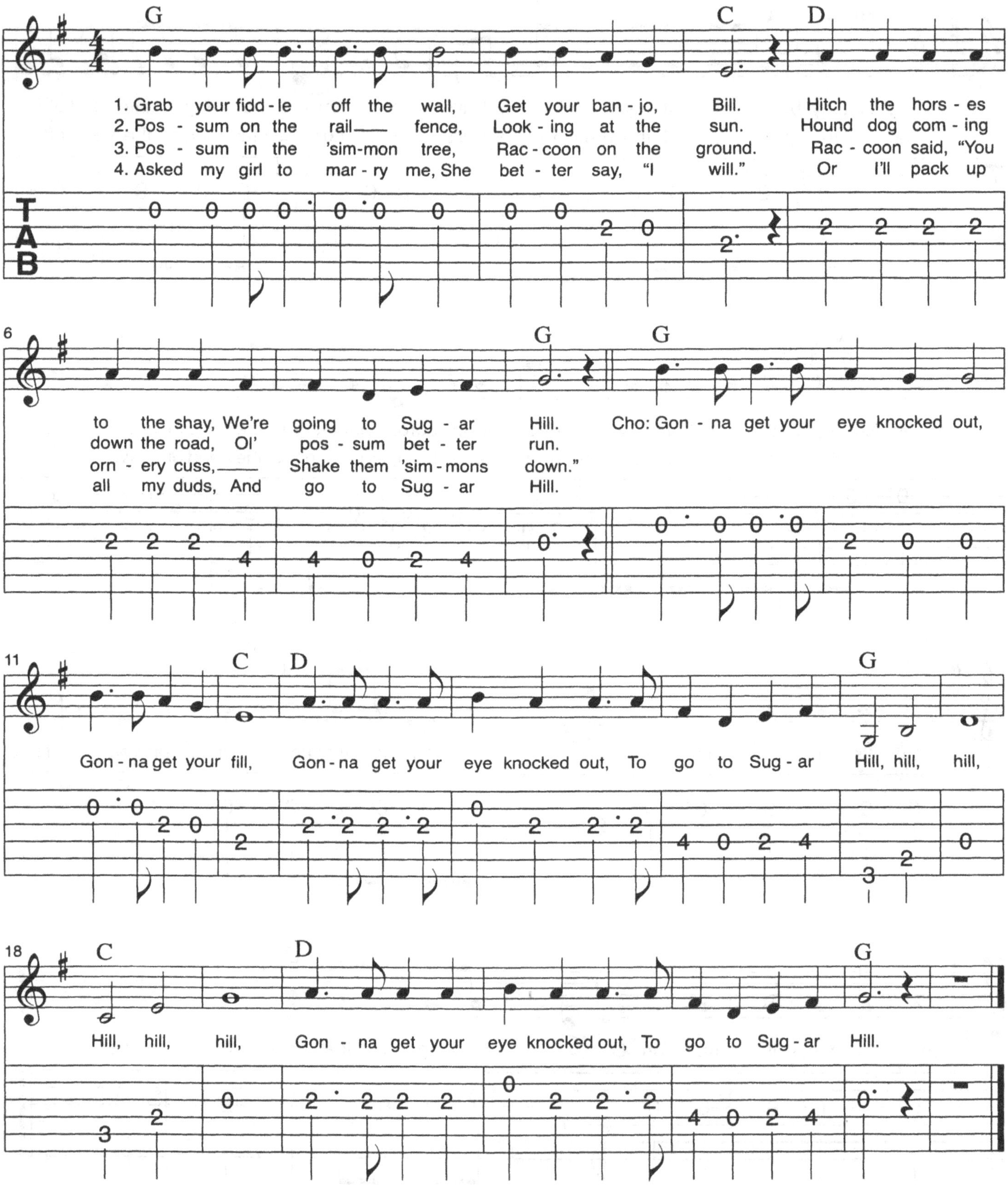

Sweet By and By

M: G; F: C or D, capo 5 or 7
CD 2-Track 66

Bennett & Webster

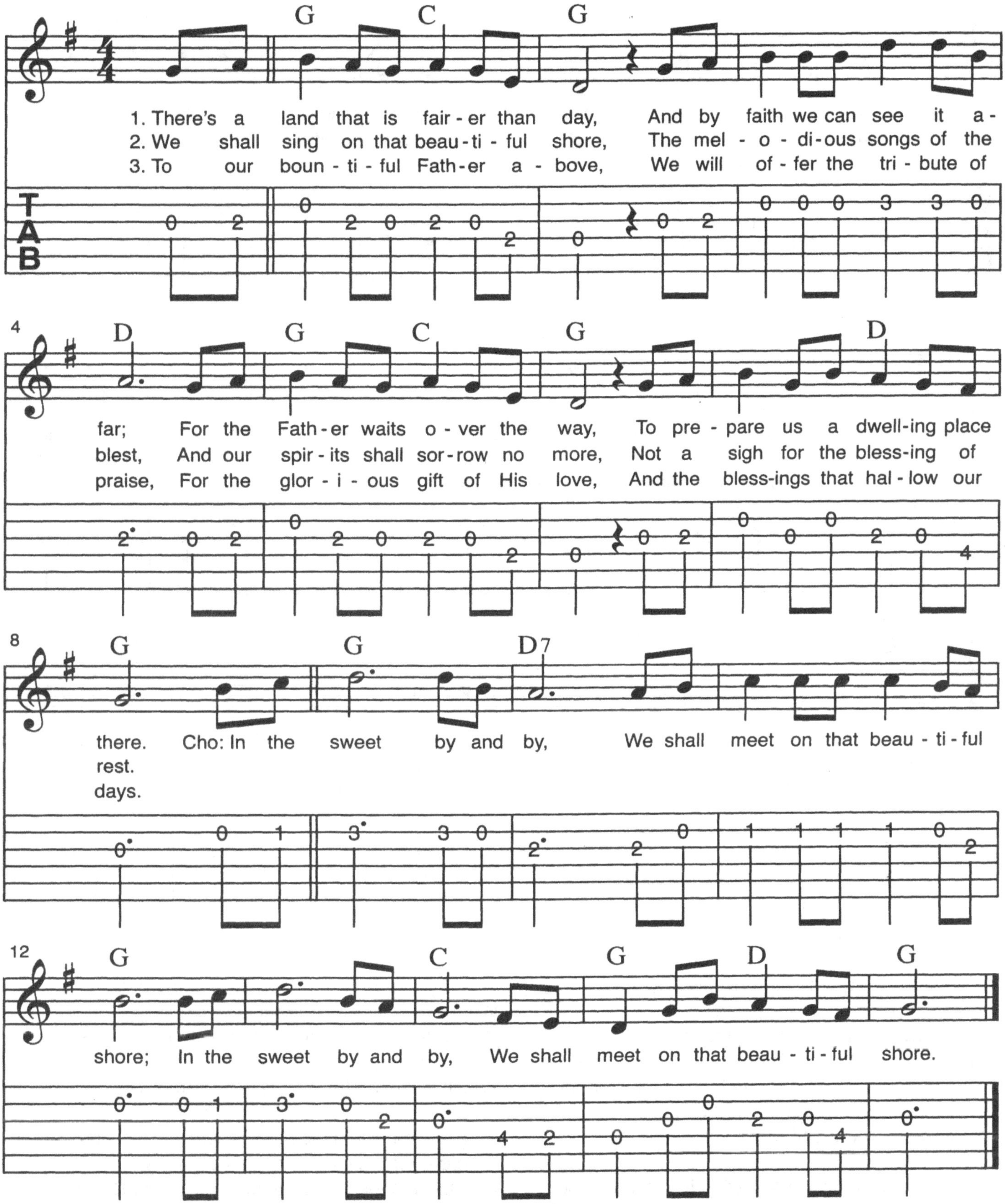

Sweet Sunny South

M: G; F: C or D, capo 5 or 7
CD 2-Track 67

W.L. Bloomfield, 1853

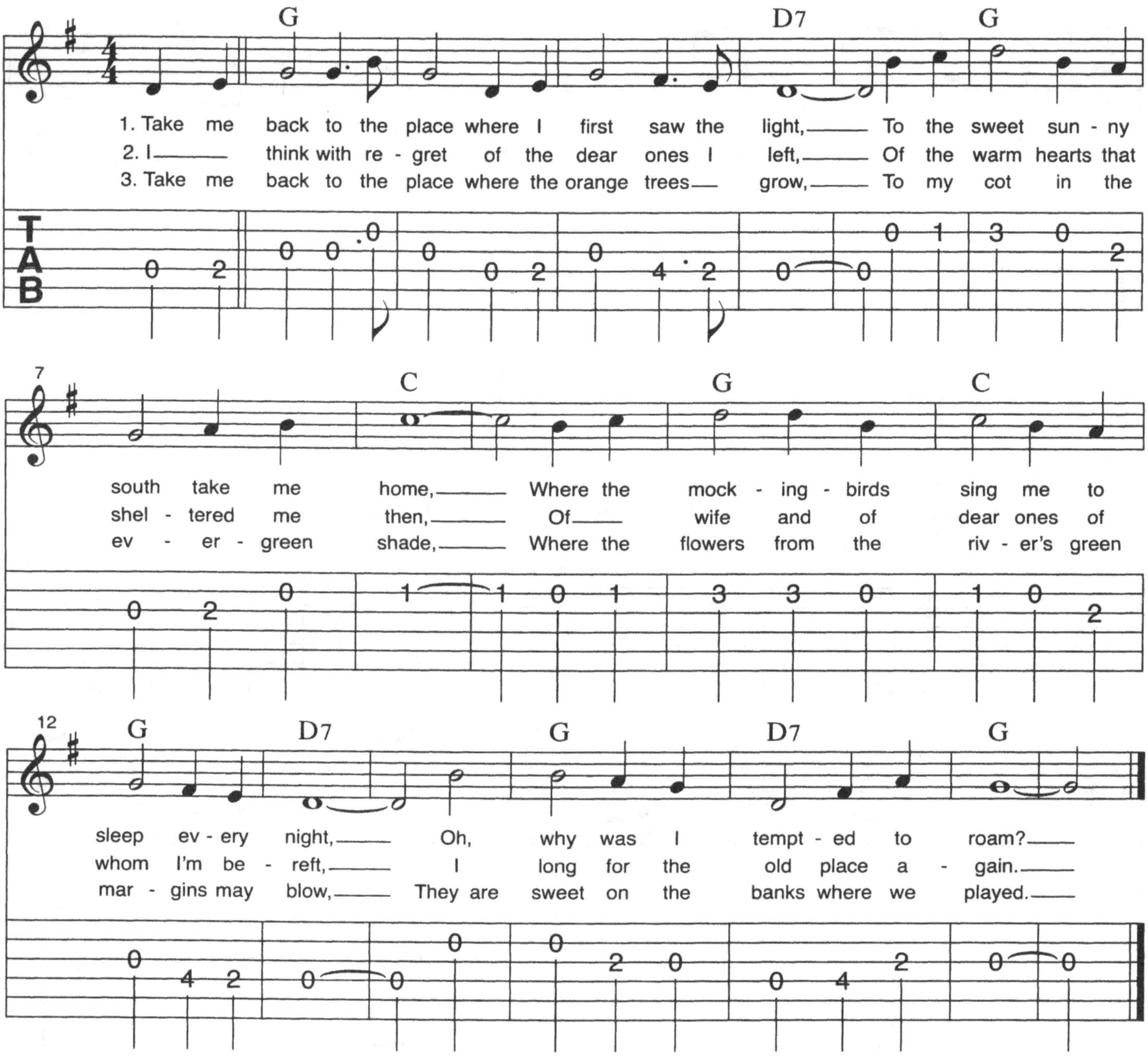

G D7
4. The path to our cottage they say has grown green,
G C
And the place is quite lonely around,
G C G D7
I know that the smiles and the forms I have seen,
G D7 G
Now lie deep in the soft mossy ground.

5. Take me back, let me see what is left that I know,
Could it be that the old house is gone?
The dear friends of my childhood indeed must be few,
And I must lament all alone.

6. But yet I'll return to the place of my birth,
Where my children have played 'round the door,
Where they pulled the white blossoms that garnished the earth,
Which will echo their footsteps no more.

7. Take me back to the place where my little ones sleep,
Where poor massa lies buried close by,
O'er the graves of my loved ones, I long to weep,
And among them to rest when I die.

 C. Poole, Grisman, Garcia, Rice, K. Hall, Bluegrass Album Band, T. O'Brien

Swing Low, Sweet Chariot

M: G; F: C or D, capo 5 or 7
CD 2-Track 68

Traditional

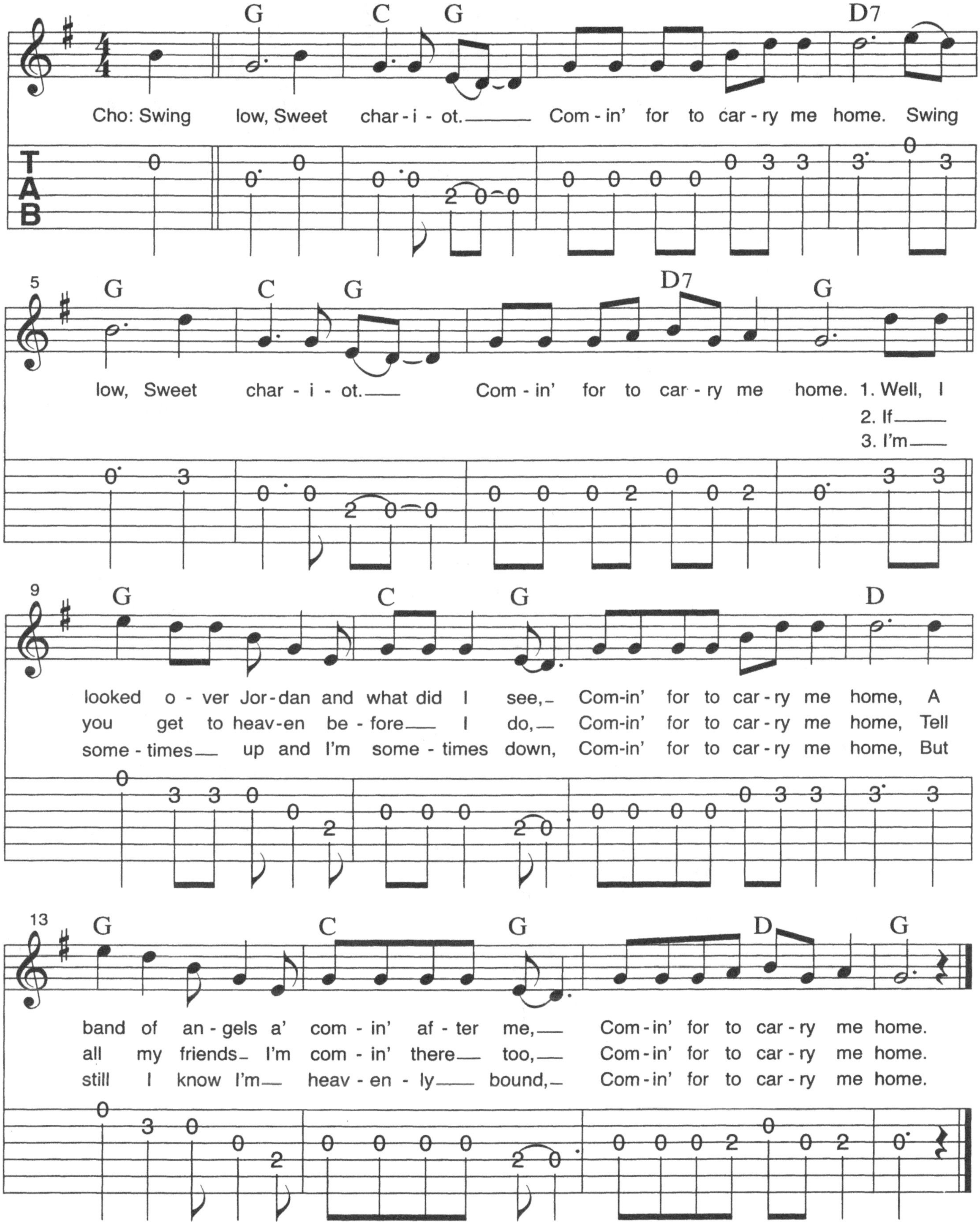

B. Monroe, Stanley Bros., R. Allen & F. Wakefield, Louvin Bros.

Take This Hammer

M: G; F: C or D, capo 5 or 7
CD 2-Track 69

Traditional

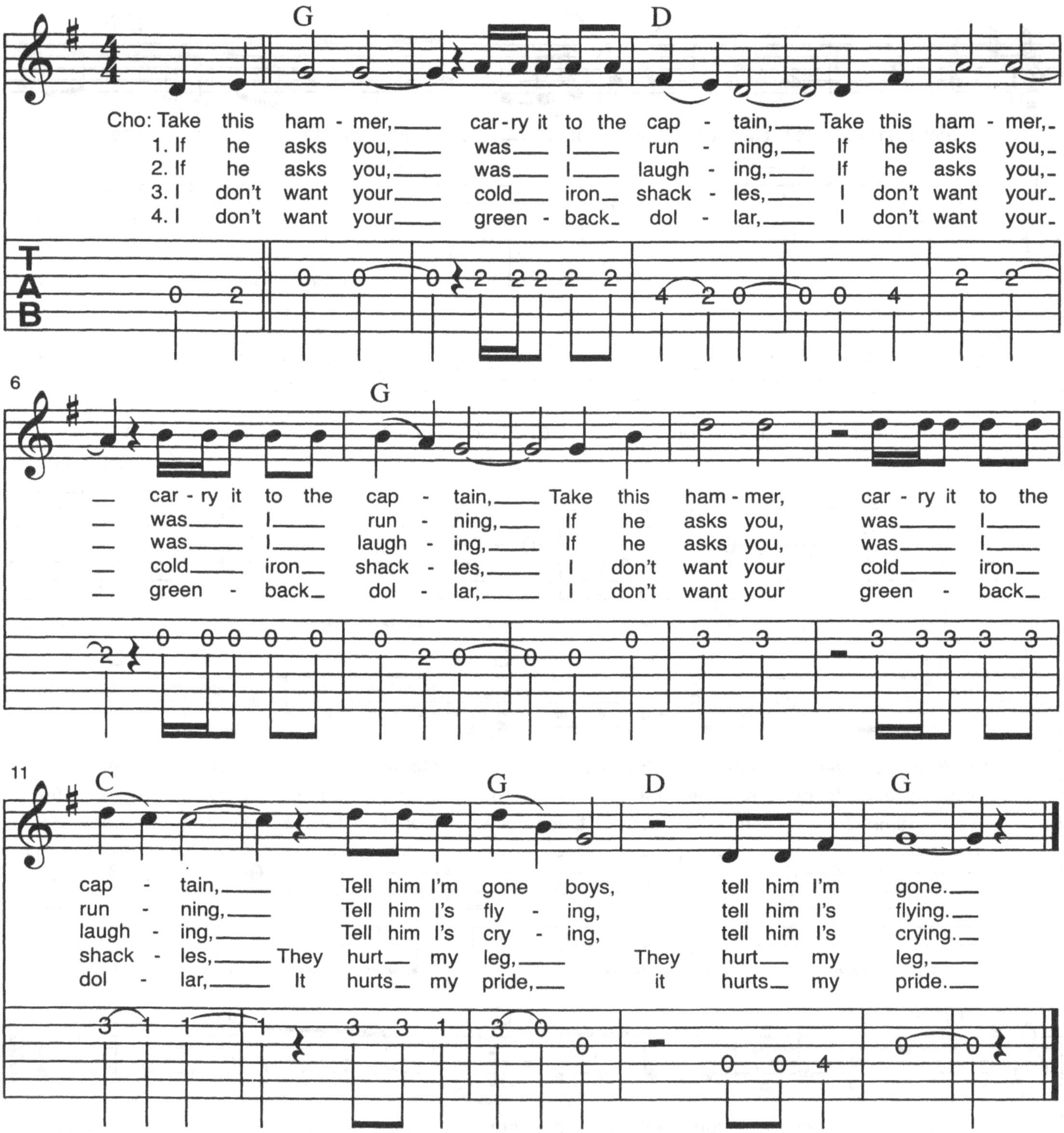

 Flatt & Scruggs, C. White, J.D. Crowe, Country Gentlemen, Osborne Bros.

Talk About Sufferin'

M: Em; F: Am or Bm, capo 5 or 7
CD 2-Track 70

Traditional

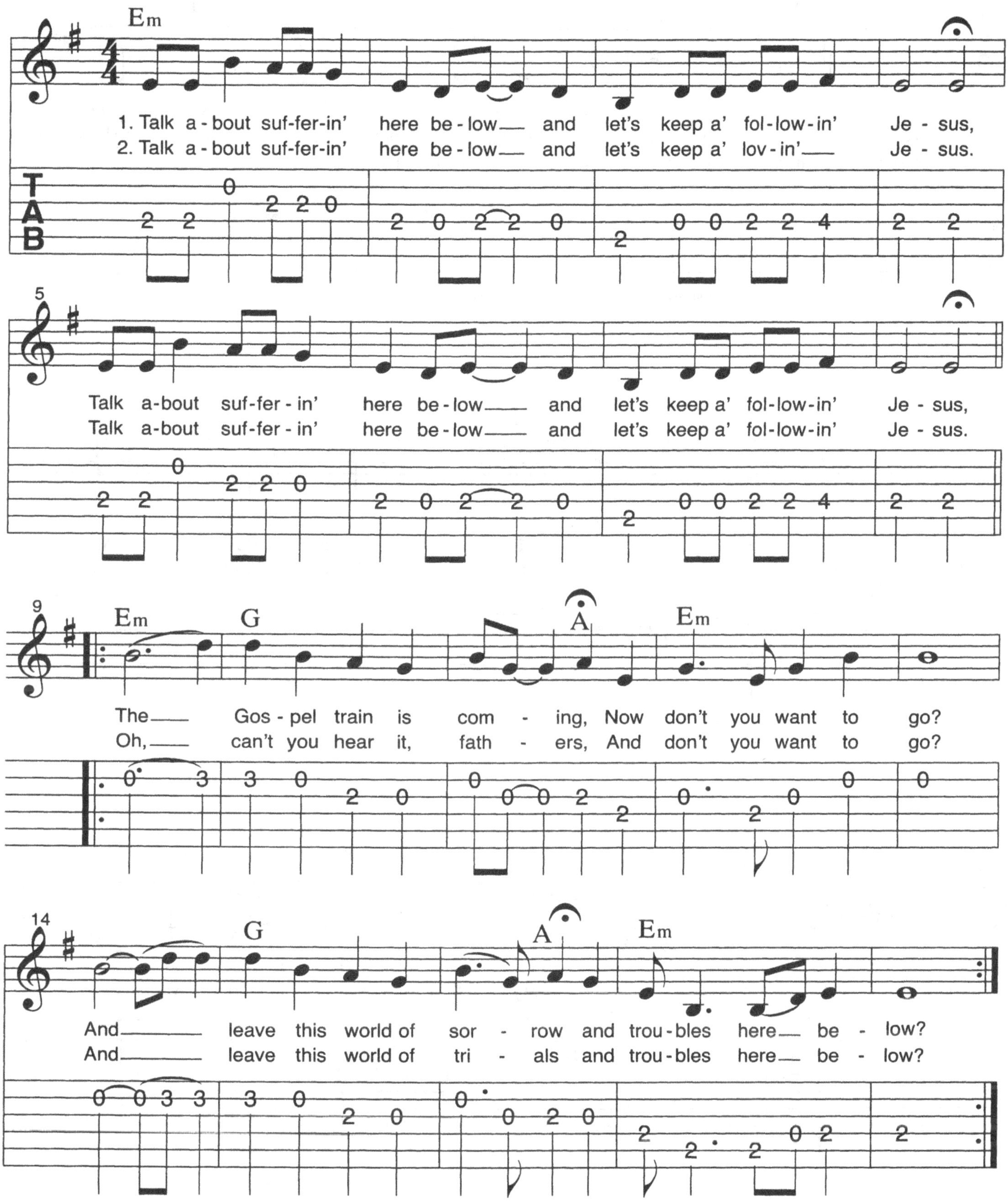

Oh, can't you hear it Mother, Sister, etc.

There's More Pretty Girls Than One

M: C; F: F or G, capo 5 or 7
CD 2-Track 71

Traditional

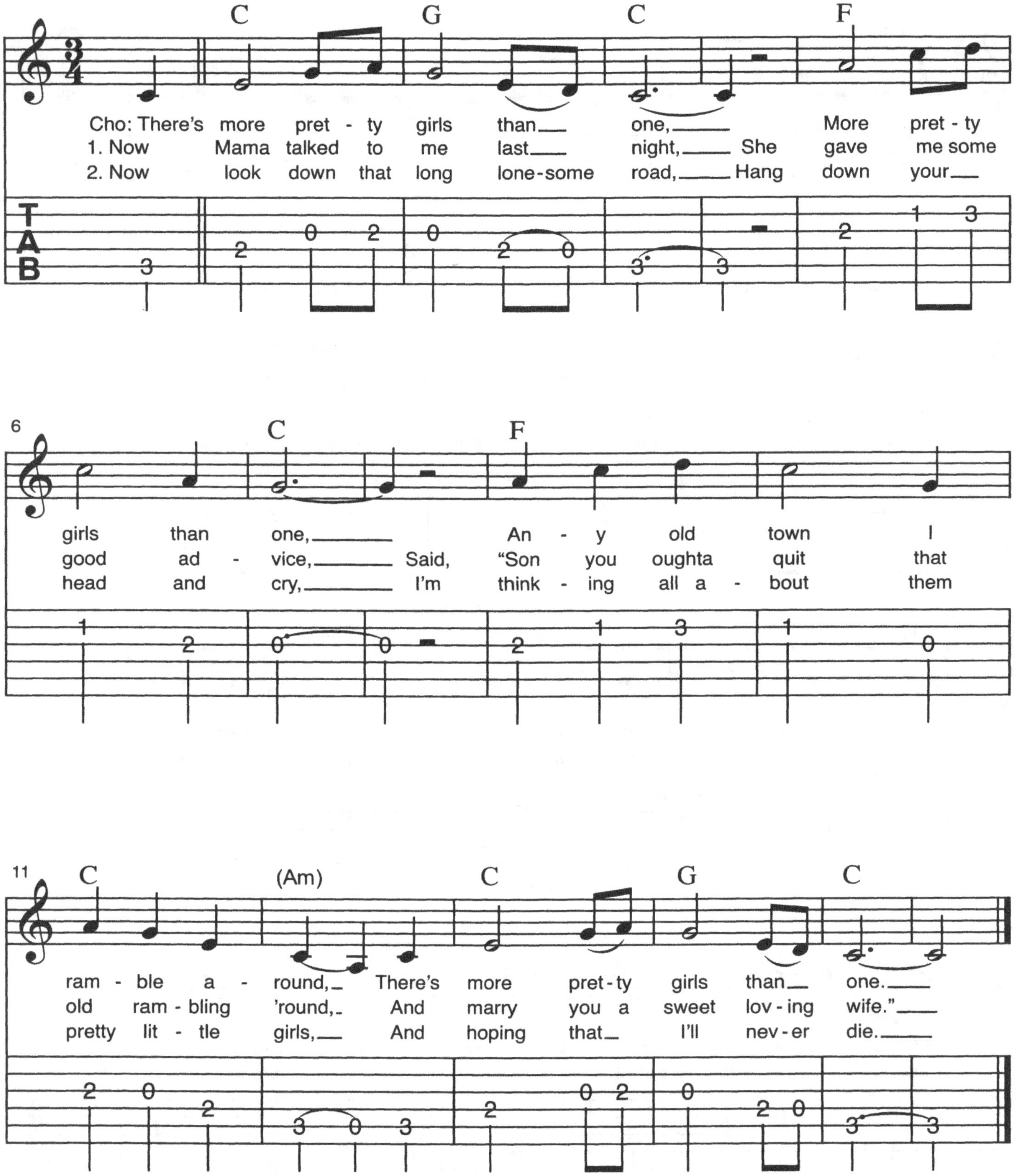

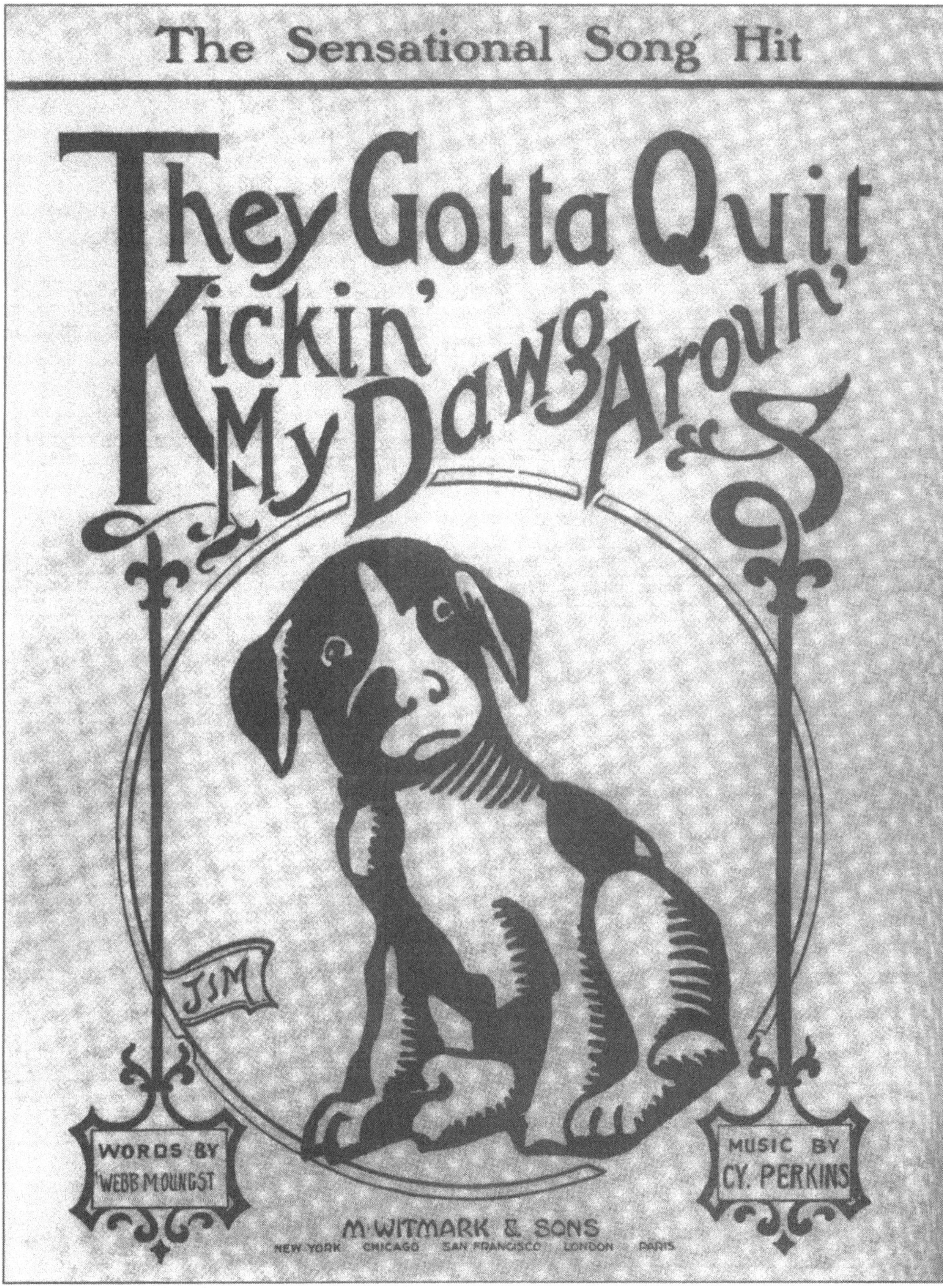

Original 1912 sheet music cover from the collection of Dix Bruce.

They Gotta Quit Kicking My Dawg Around

M: G; F: C or D, capo 5 or 7
CD 2-Track 72

Oungst &
Perkins, 1912

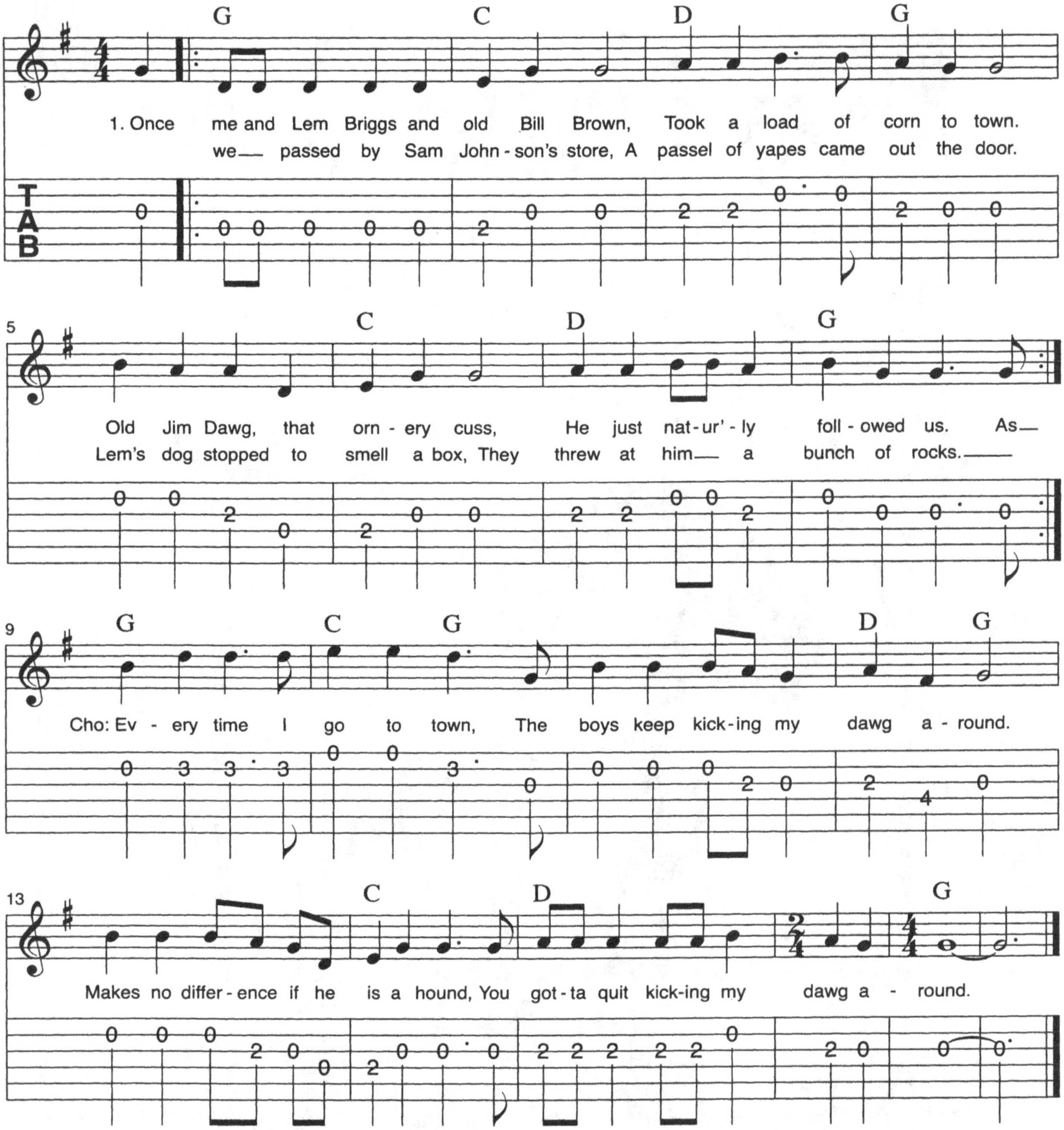

```
          G                C
2.  They tied a tin can to his tail,
D                       G
Drove him past the county jail.
                       C
That plum natur'ly made me sore,
D                       G
Lem, he cussed and Bill he swore.
G                            C
Me and Lem Briggs and old Bill Brown,
D                  G
Lost no time in jumping down.
                             C
We whipped those guys upon the ground,
    D                          G
For kickin' that old hound dog around.
```

3. Well, they say that a dog can't hold no grudge,
Once when I got too much budge,
Those town ducks tried to do me up,
But, they didn't count on old Lem's pup.
He saw his duty there and then,
He lit into those gentlemen,
He sure messed up the courthouse square,
With rags and meat and hunks of hair.

This Little Light of Mine

M: C; F: F or G, capo 5 or 7
CD 2-Track 73

Traditional

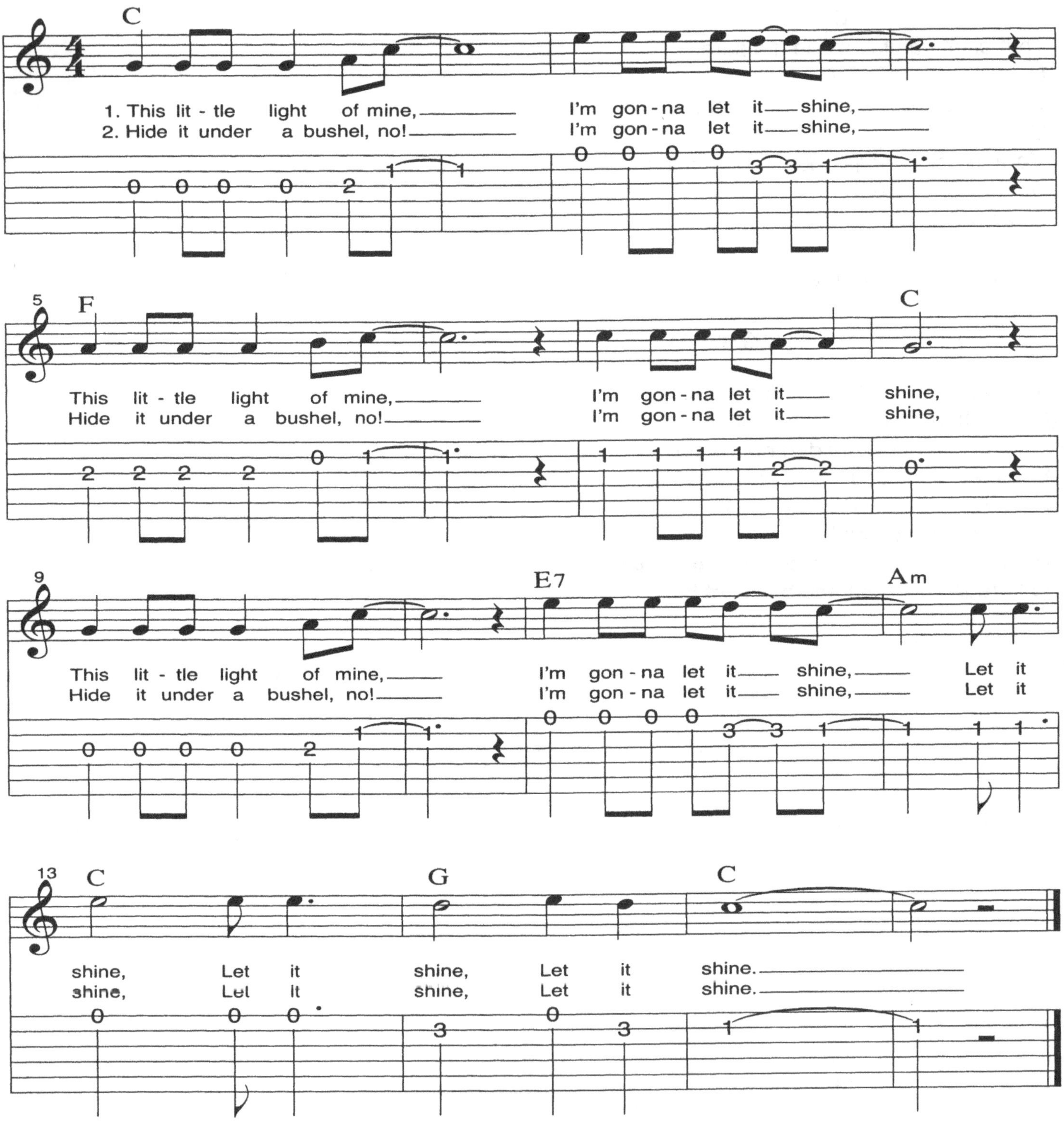

C
3. Won't let Satan blow it out,
I'm gonna let it shine,
F
Won't let Satan blow it out,
C
I'm gonna let it shine,

Won't let Satan blow it out,

E7 Am
I'm gonna let it shine,
C G C
Let it shine, let it shine, let it shine.

4. Let it shine 'til Jesus comes,
I'm gonna let it shine,
Let it shine 'til Jesus comes,
I'm gonna let it shine,
Let it shine, let it shine, Let it shine 'til Jesus comes,
I'm gonna let it shine, let it shine.

This Train

M: G; F: C or D, capo 5 or 7
CD 2-Track 74

Traditional

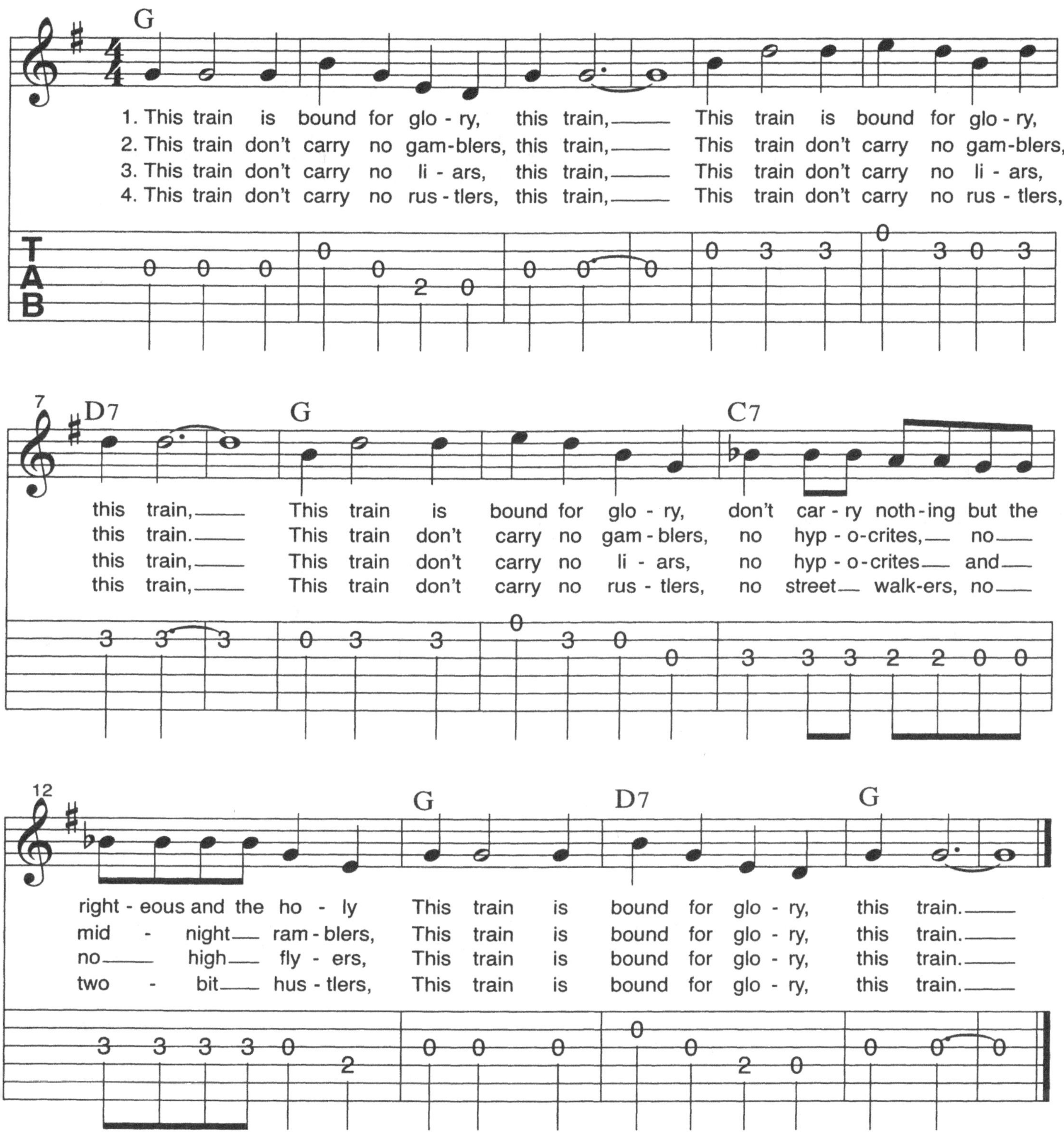

This World is Not My Home

M: G; F: C or D, capo 5 or 7
CD 2-Track 75

Traditional

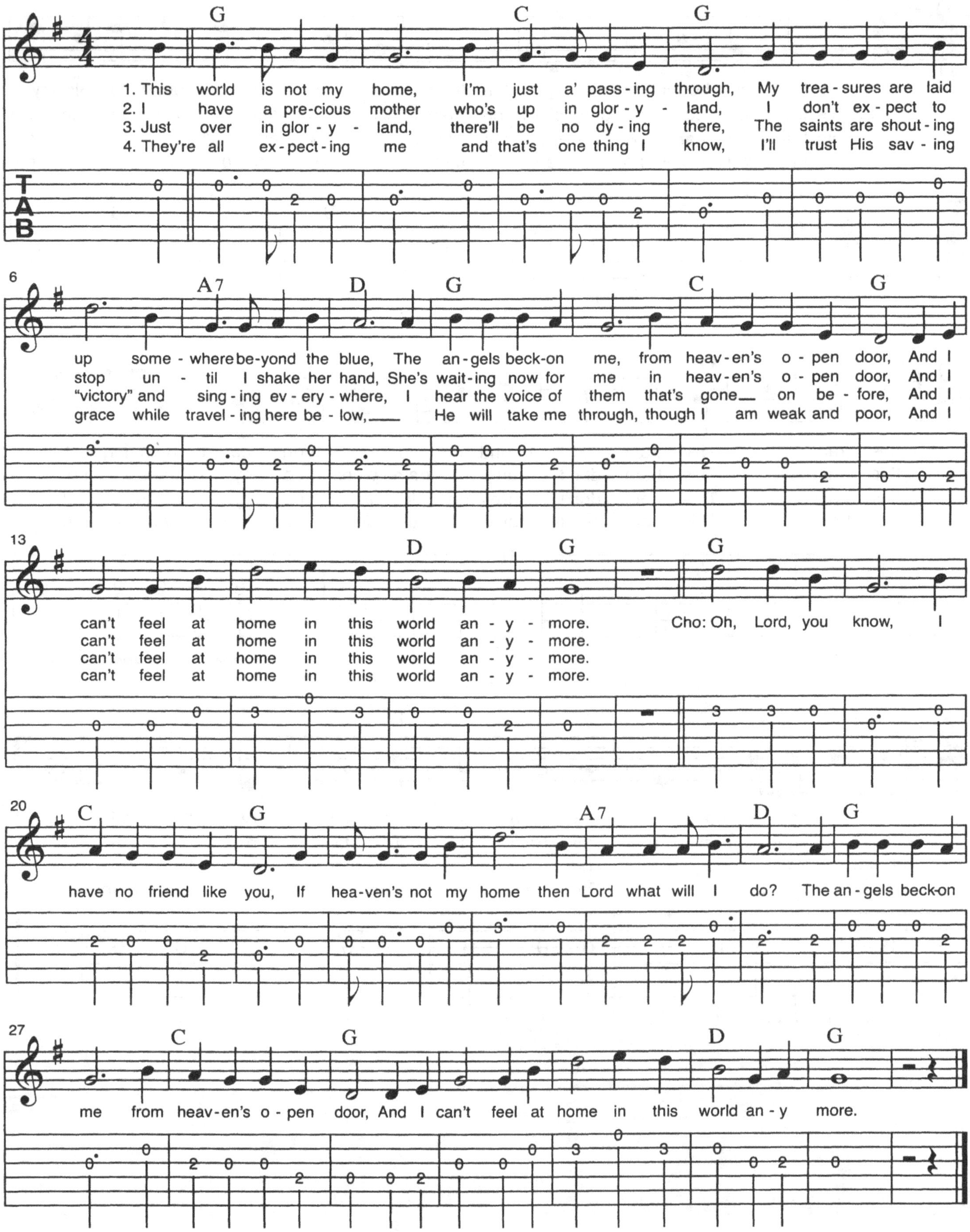

 Monroe Bros., B. Monroe, Stanley Bros., Jimmy Martin, Blue Highway, NLCR

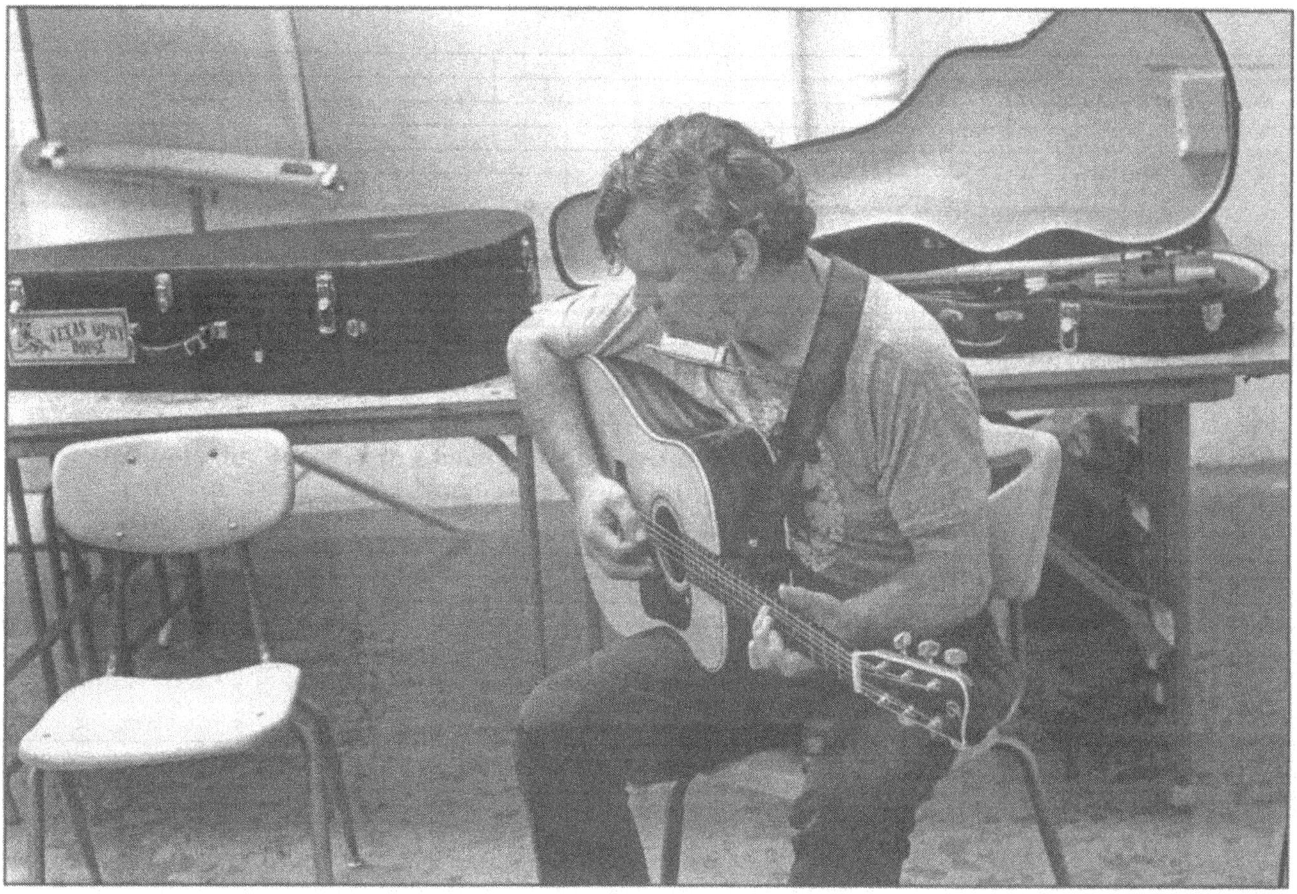

Photo courtesy Dix Bruce

The great Doc Watson, shown here ca. 1975. His virtuosity expanded the role of the guitar in traditional American music and elevated it to equal status as a lead instrument with the fiddle and banjo. Up to that time the guitar had played mostly a supporting rhythmic role. Doc Watson revolutionized the role of the guitar in folk, old time, bluegrass, and country music.

Train, Train, Train

M: G; F: C or D, capo 5 or 7
CD 2-Track 76

by Dix Bruce

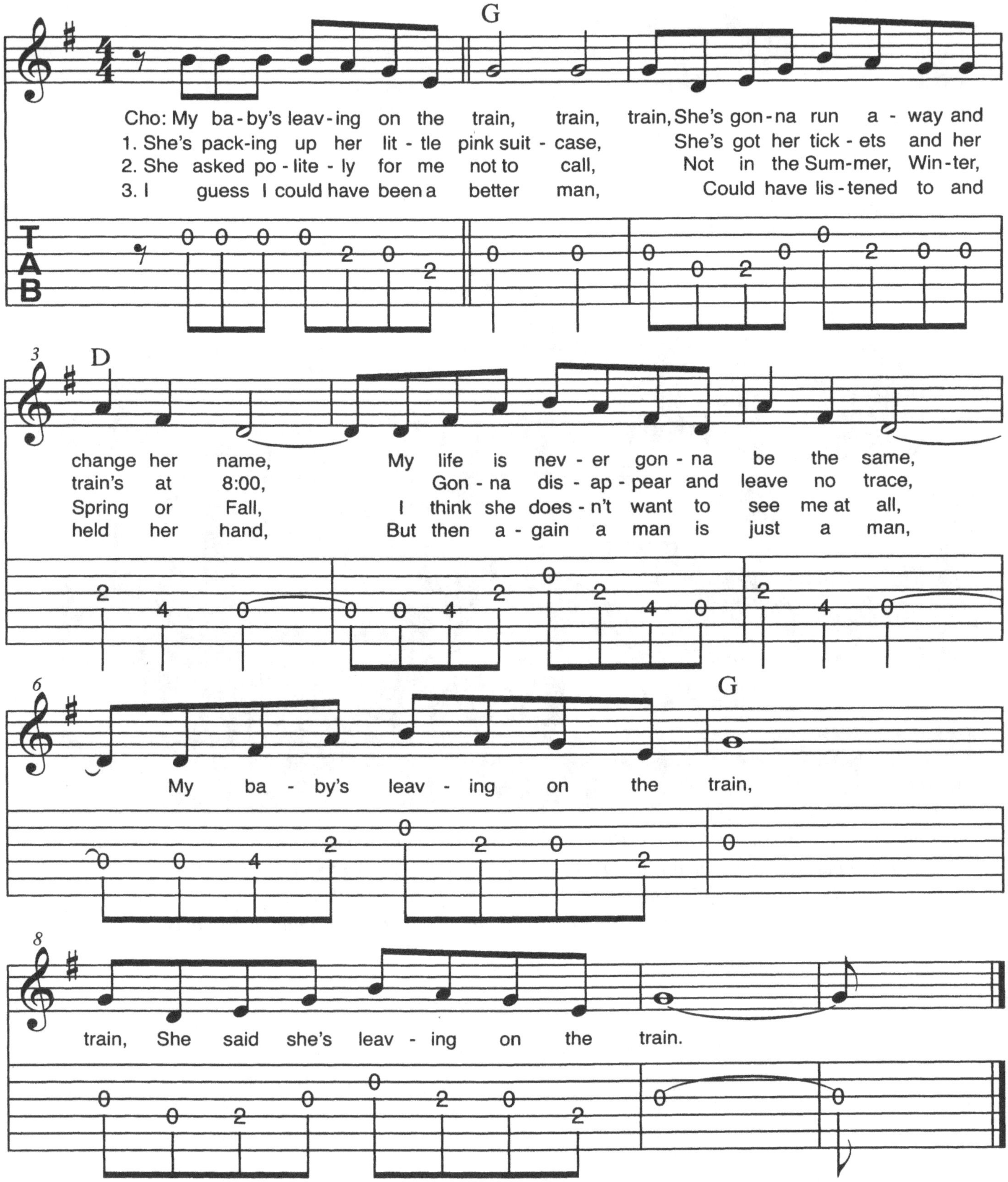

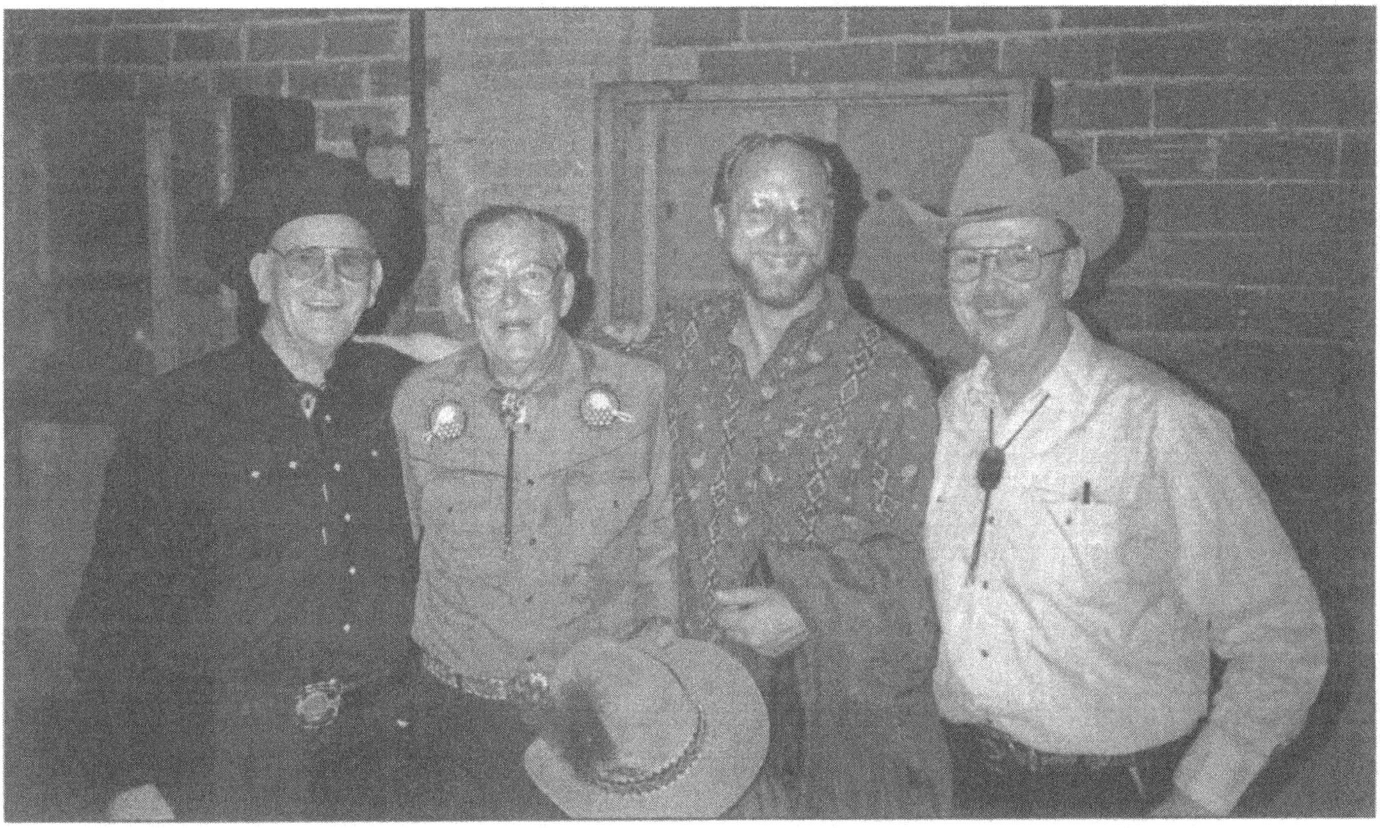

Photo by Rick March

The Goose Island Ramblers with Dix Bruce 1999:
left to right: Wendy Whitford, George Gilbertsen, Dix Bruce, Bruce Bollerud

The Train That Carried My Girl From Town

M: D; F: G or A, capo 5 or 7
CD 2-Track 77

Traditional

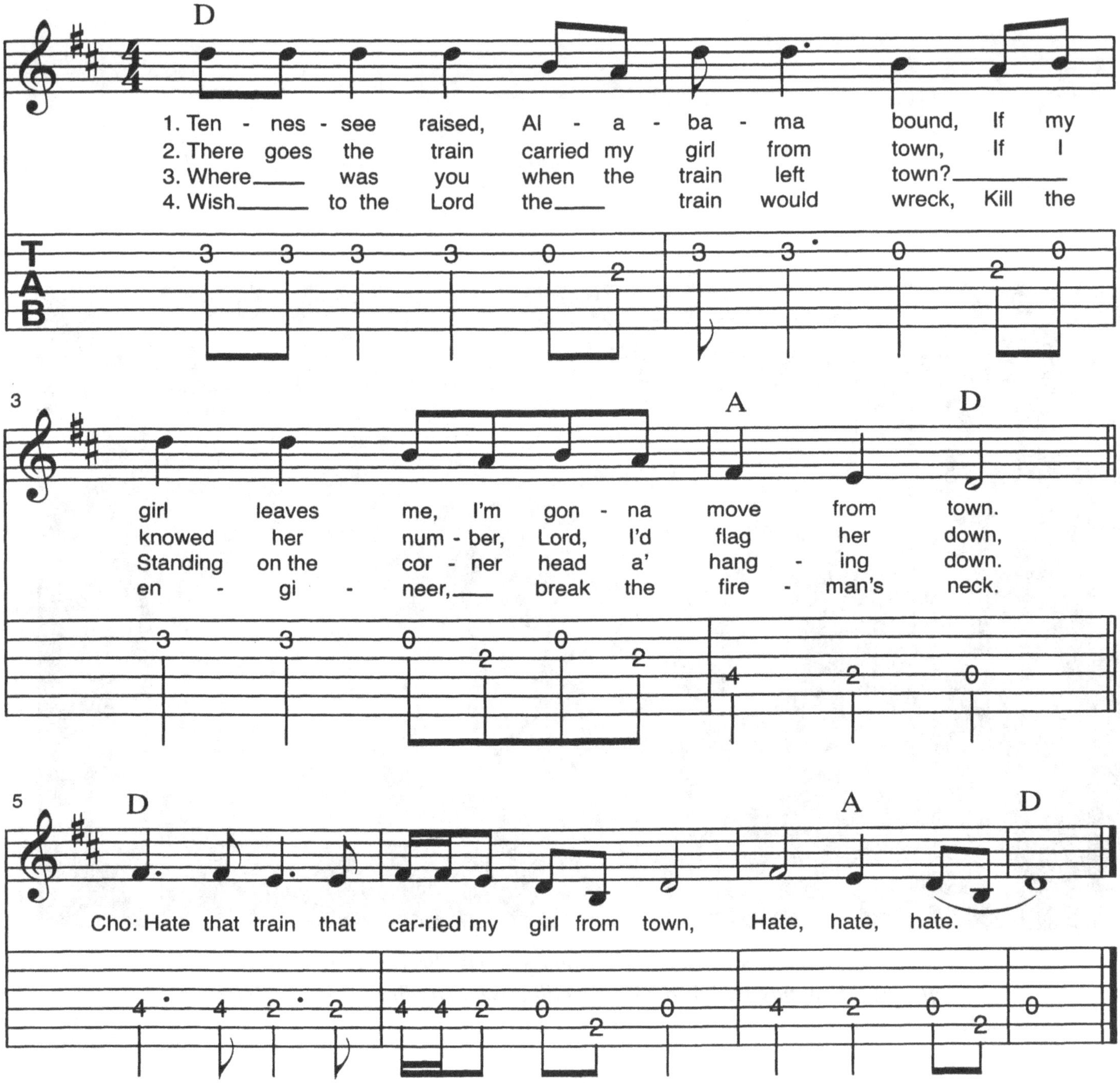

D
5. Hello central, give me 6-0-9,
A D
Just wanna talk to that brown of mine.
Cho: Hate that train that carried my girl from town.
A D
Hate, hate, hate, hate.
(Repeat chorus after each verse)

6. Rations on the table, coffee's getting cold,
Some old rounder stole my jelly roll.

7. If I had a gun I'd let the hammer down,
Lord, I'd shoot that rounder took my girl from town.

8. There goes my girl, somebody call her back,
She put her hands in my money sack.

9. Ashes to ashes and dust to dust,
Show me a woman a man can trust.

The Unclouded Day

M: G; F: C or D, capo 5 or 7
CD 2-Track 78

J.K. Alwood, 1890

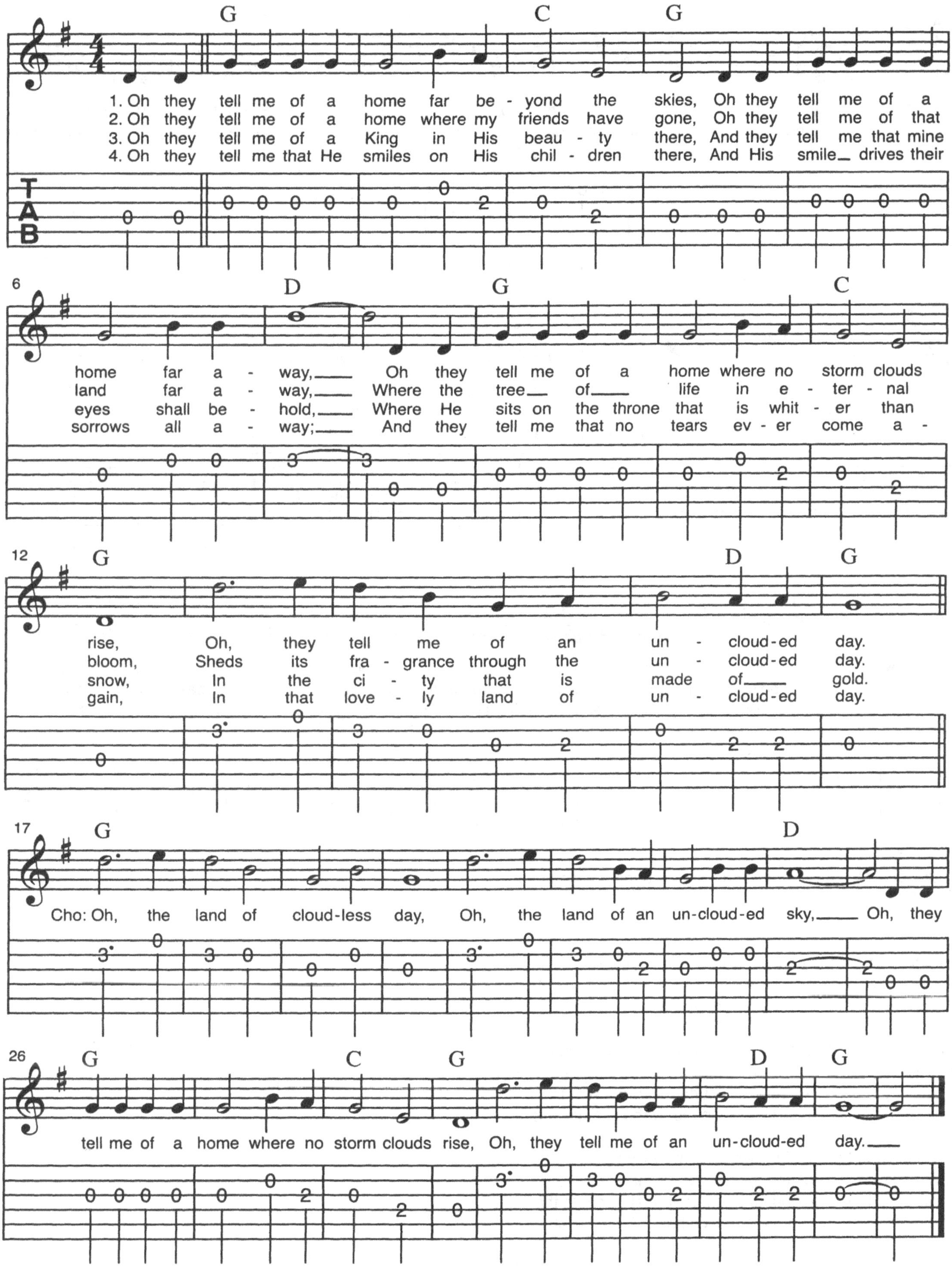

Wabash Cannonball

M: G; F: C or D, capo 5 or 7
CD 2-Track 79

Woode & Fulmer, 1881

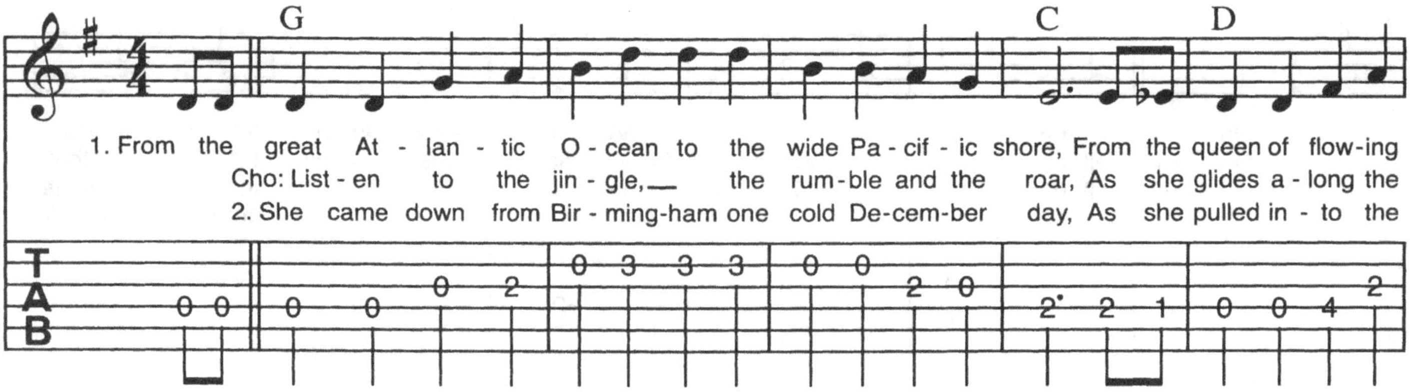

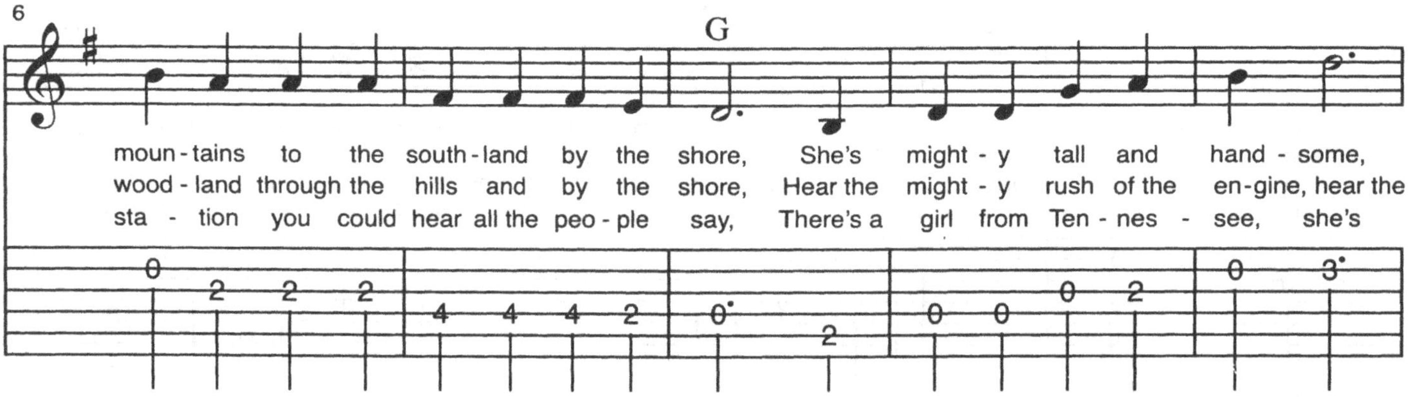

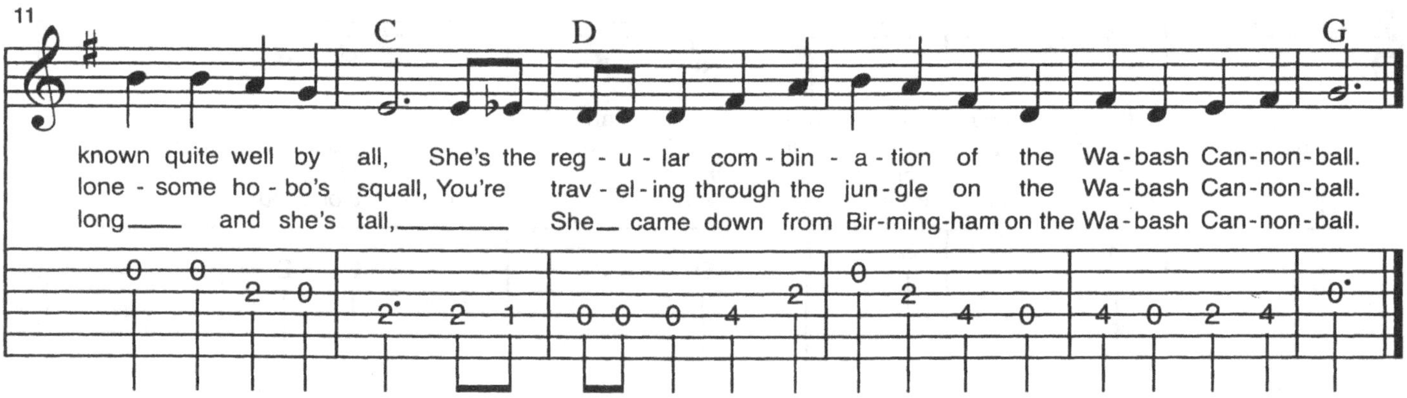

G C
3. Our eastern states are dandy, so the people always say,
D G
From New York to St. Louis, and Chicago by the way,
C
From the hills of Minnesota, where the rippling waters fall,
D G
No changes can be taken, on the Wabash Cannonball.

4. Here's to Daddy Claxton, may his name forever stand,
And always be remembered in the courts thoughout the land,
His earthly race is over and the curtains 'round him fall,
We'll carry him home to victory on the Wabash Cannonball.

5. I have rode the I.C. Limited, also the Royal Blue,
Across the eastern countries on mail car number two,
I have rode those highball trains from coast to coast that's all,
But I have found no equal to the Wabash Cannonball.

Carter Fam., R. Acuff, Flatt & Scruggs, B. Monroe, Mac Wiseman, Louvin Bros., Osborne Bros., Claire Lynch, Nitty Gritty Dirt Band

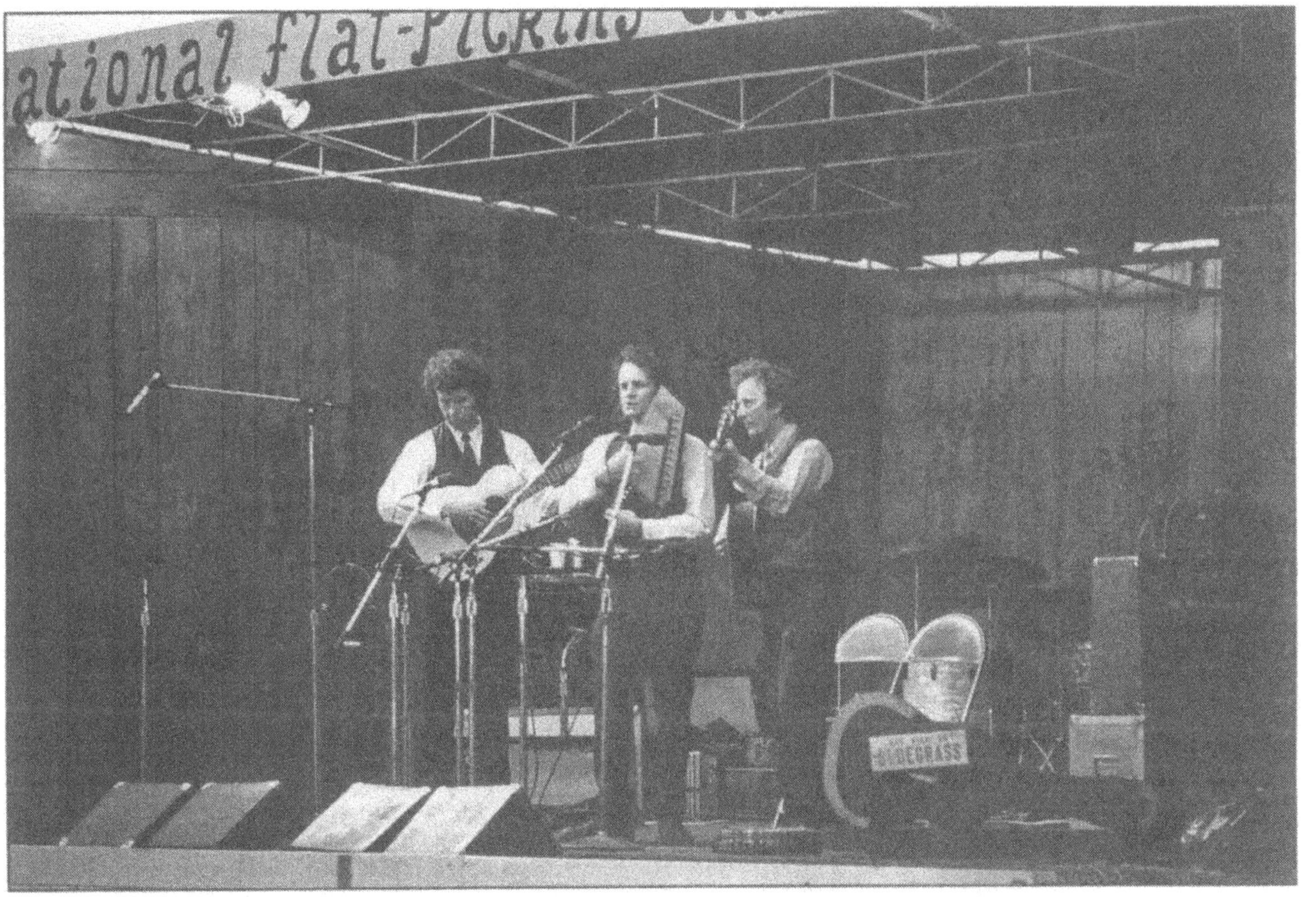

Photo courtesy Dix Bruce

The New Lost City Ramblers (left to right: Tracy Schwartz, Mike Seeger, John Cohen) inspired generations of old time and bluegrass players by recording and performing a wide range of American music from the early 1900s. Photo from 1976.

Walk in Jerusalem Just Like John

M: F; F: B♭ or C, capo 5 or 7
CD 2-Track 80

Traditional

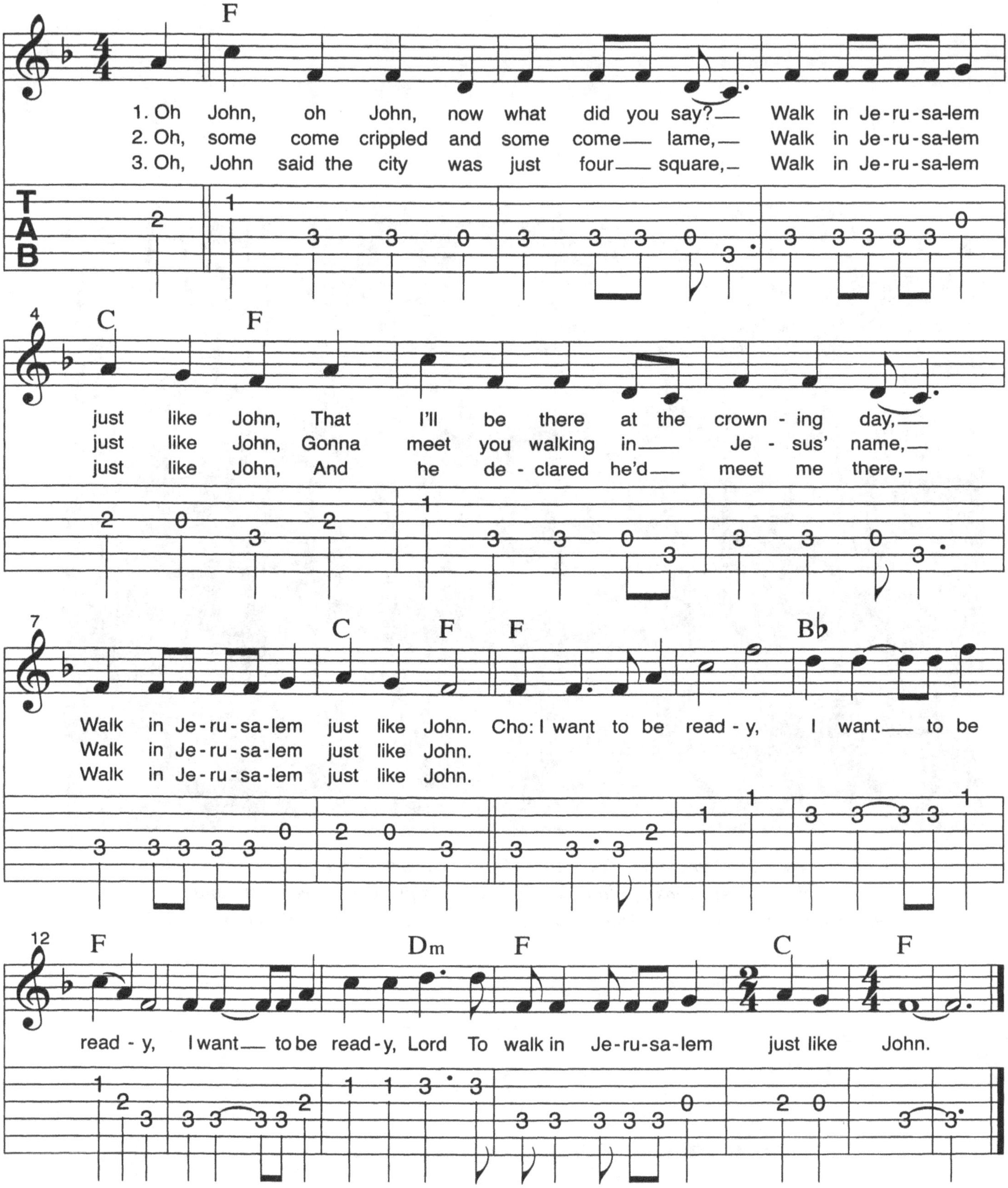

 B. Monroe, D. Watson, Newgrass Revival, Country Gentlemen

              F
4. When Peter was preaching at the Pentacost,
                            C   F
Walk in Jerusalem just like John,
He was endowed with the Holy Ghost,
                            C   F
Walk in Jerusalem just like John.
F   B♭   F
Cho: I want to be ready, I want to be ready,
                               Dm
I want to be ready, Lord
    F   C   F
To walk in Jerusalem just like John.

5. If you get there before I do,
Walk in Jerusalem just like John,
Tell all my friends I'm a'coming too,
Walk in Jerusalem just like John.

Walking in My Sleep

M: C; F: F or G, capo 5 or 7
CD 2-Track 81

Traditional

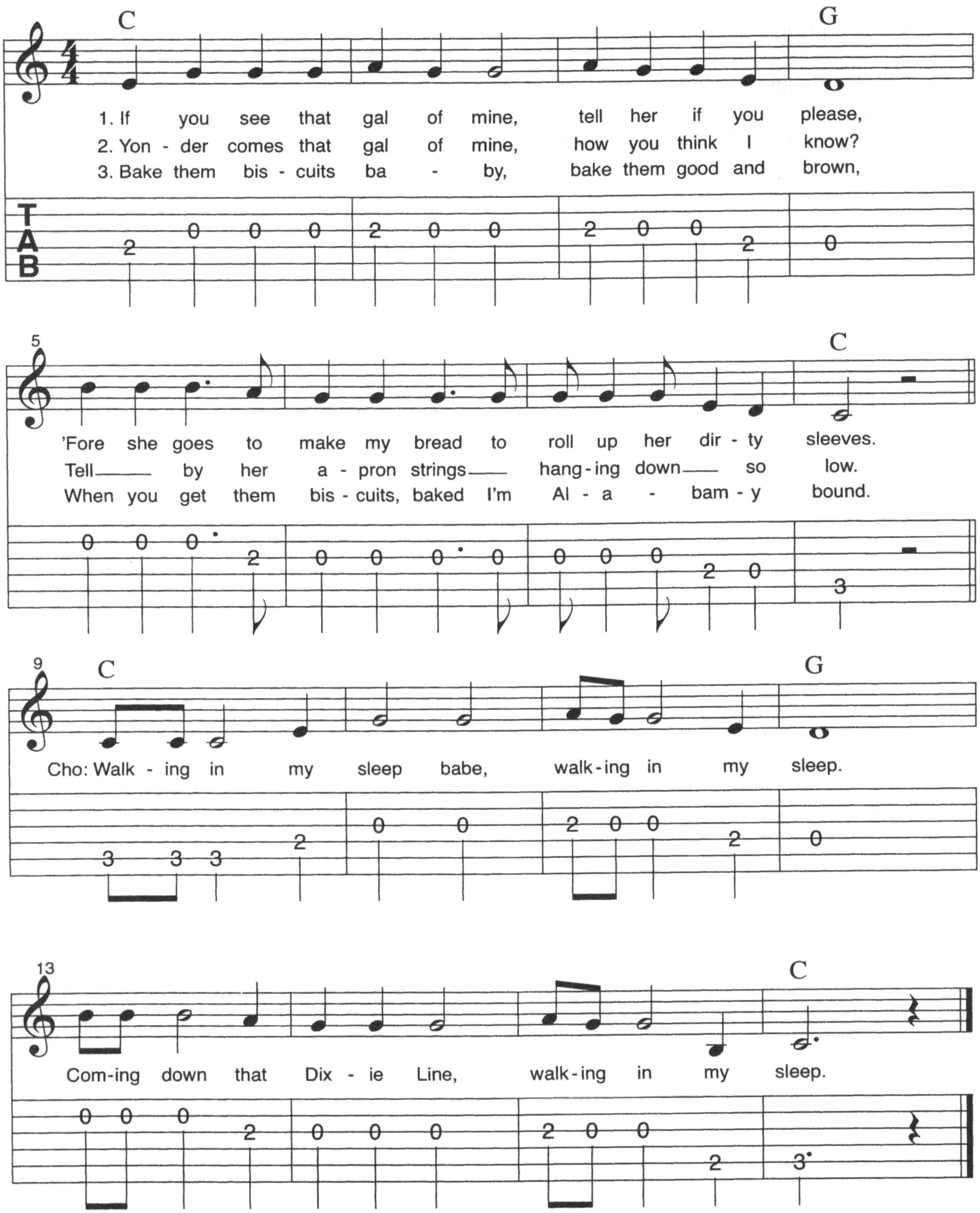

The Wayfaring Stranger

***M**: Dm; **F**: Gm or Am, capo 5 or 7*
CD 2-Track 82

Traditional

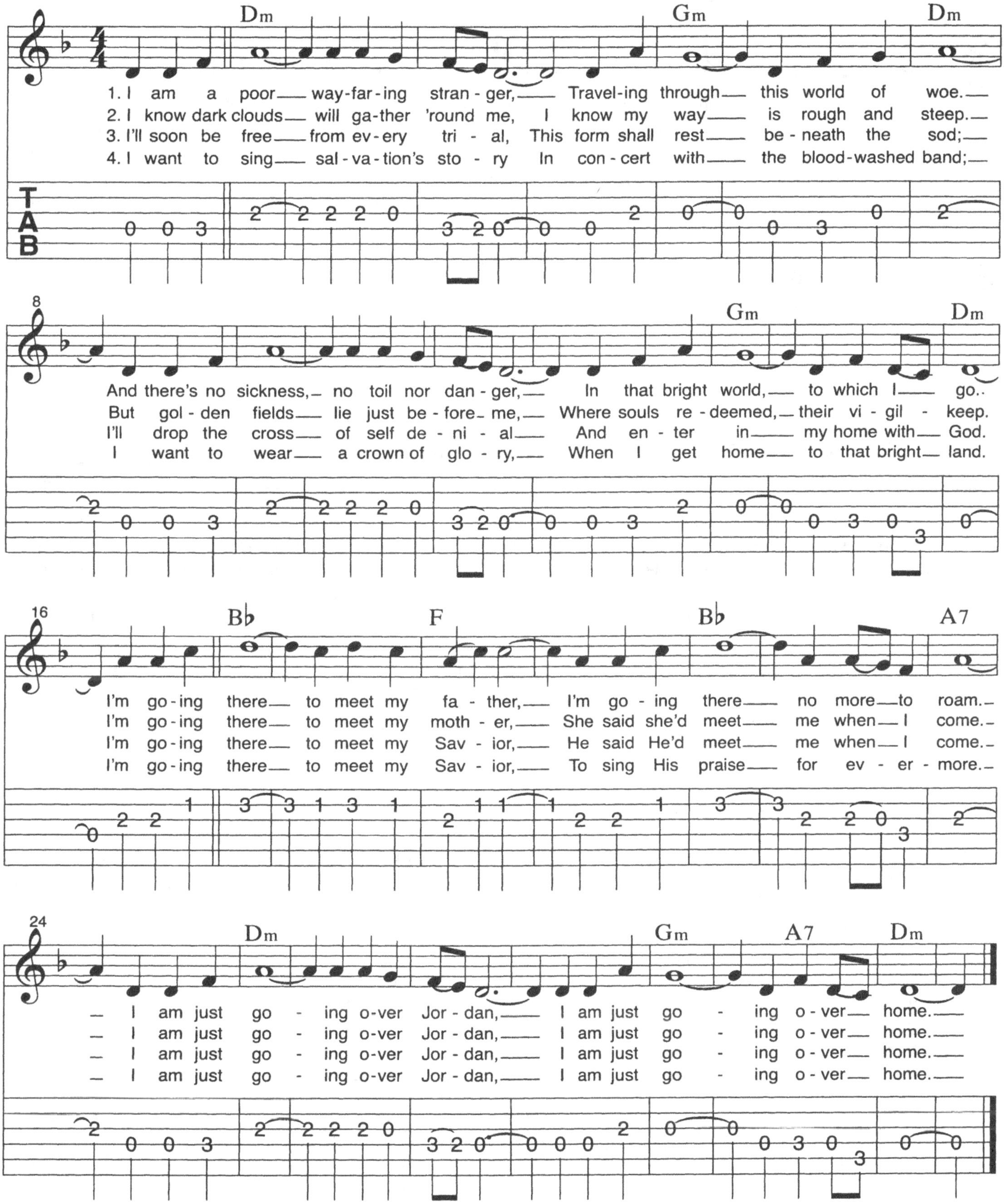

Were You There When They Crucified My Lord?

M: G; F: C or D, capo 5 or 7
CD 2-Track 83, medley pt. 1

Traditional

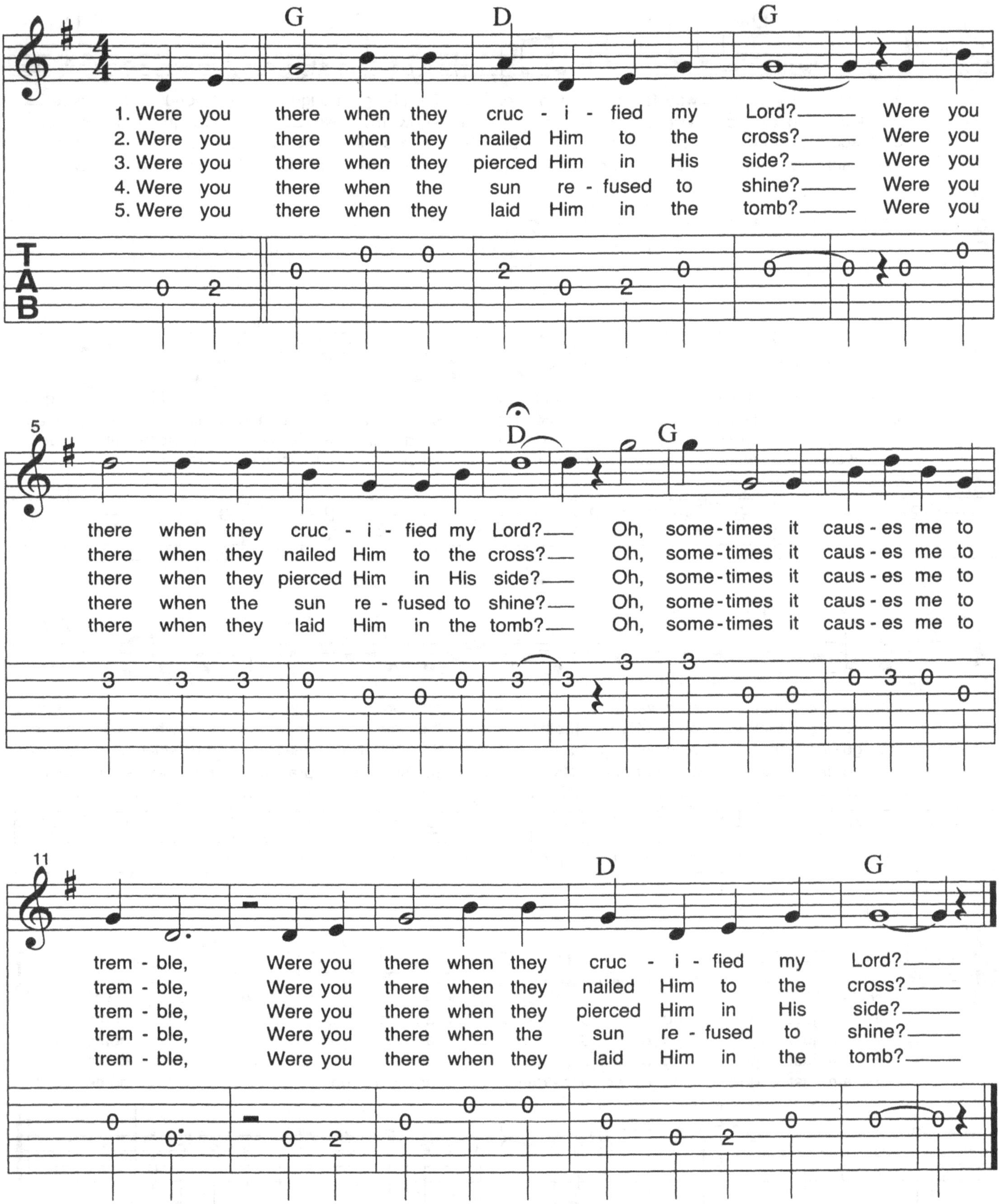

 B. Monroe, Blue Sky Boys, Dry Branch Fire Squad, Seldom Scene, R. Skaggs

What a Friend We Have in Jesus

M: G; F: C or D, capo 5 or 7
CD 2-Track 83, medley pt. 2

Converse & Scriven, ca. 1868

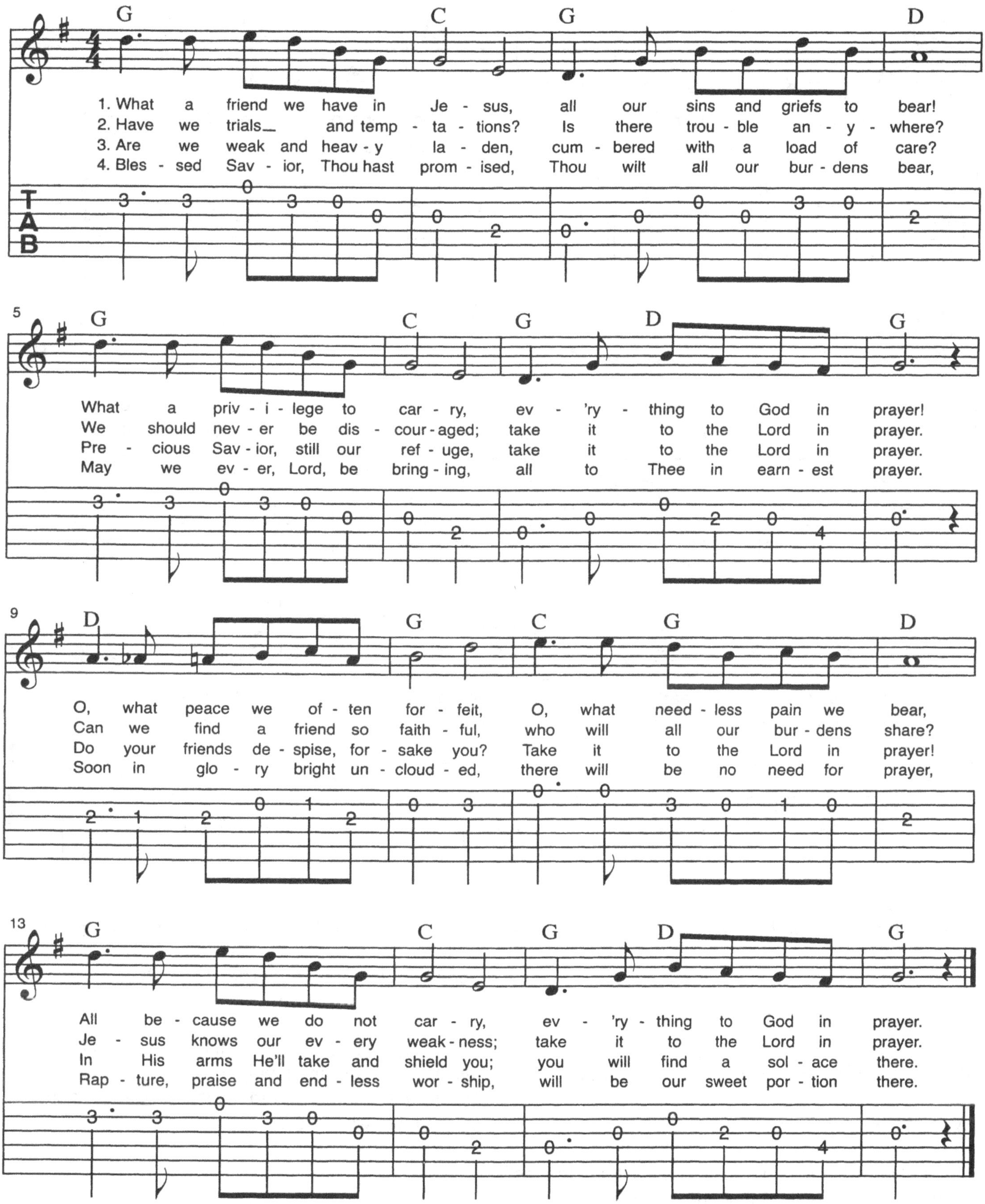

When I Die

M: G; F: C or D, capo 5 or 7
CD 2-Track 84

Dix Bruce

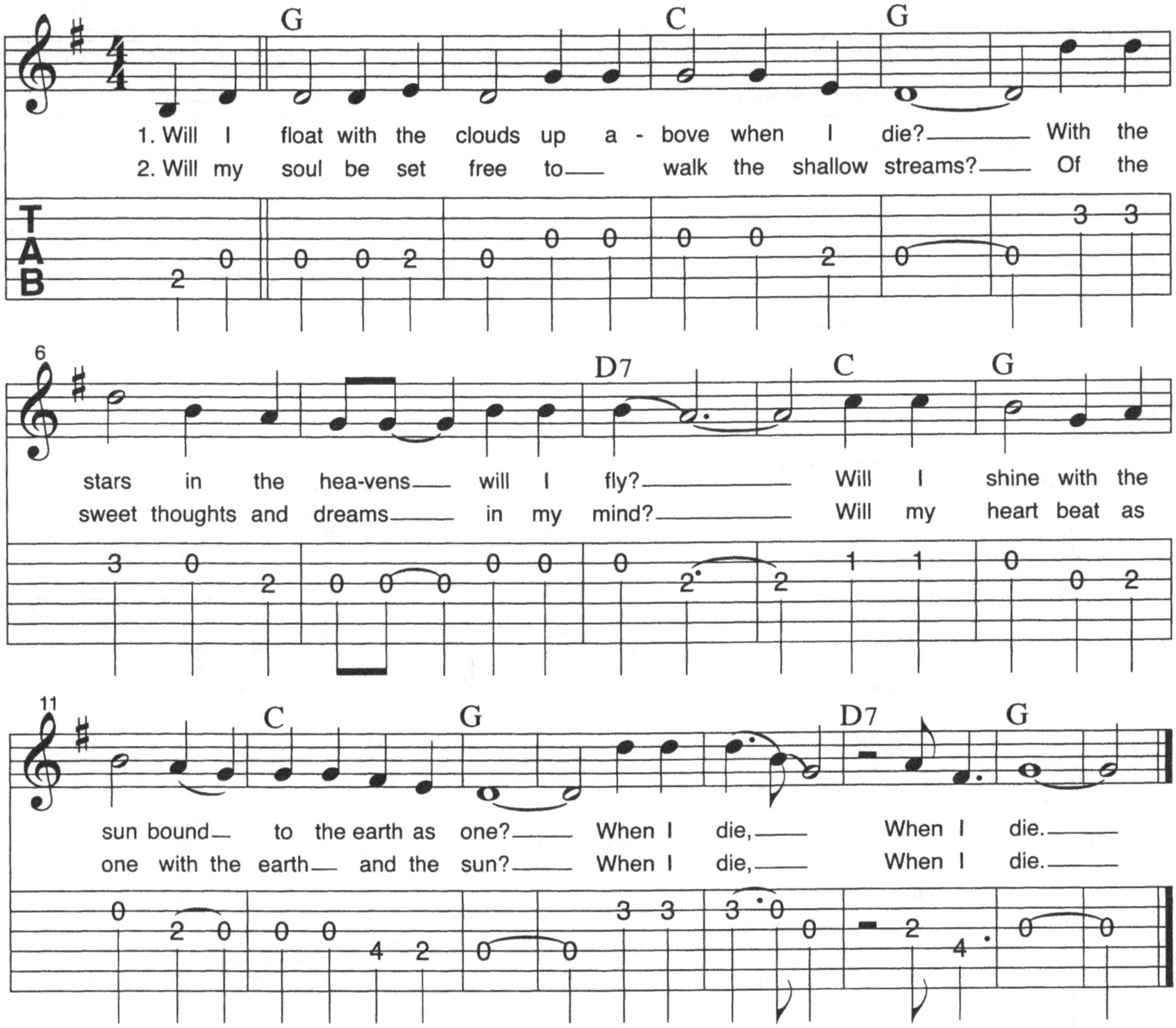


```
G                                             C
3. Will I roam through the fields down the mountains,
         G
cross the land?
                                   D
Wade the rivers down to the ocean sand?
C   G                       C         G
Will I touch trusted friends in a whisper of the wind?
            D      G
When I die, when I die.
```

4. Can I be with my family, can I visit with my friends?
As they spend the short time they were lent?
Will they quietly know that I really did not go?
When I die, when I die.

5. Will the ones that I love someday join me up above?
Will we laugh, will we sing, will we cry?
Together will we be through all eternity?
When I die, when I die.

6. Will I grow in the hearts of those I have known?
Will they think of me fondly now and then?
Will I live on and on when my life on earth is done?
When I die, when I die.

When I Lay My Burden Down

M: G; F: C or D, capo 5 or 7
CD 2-Track 85

Traditional

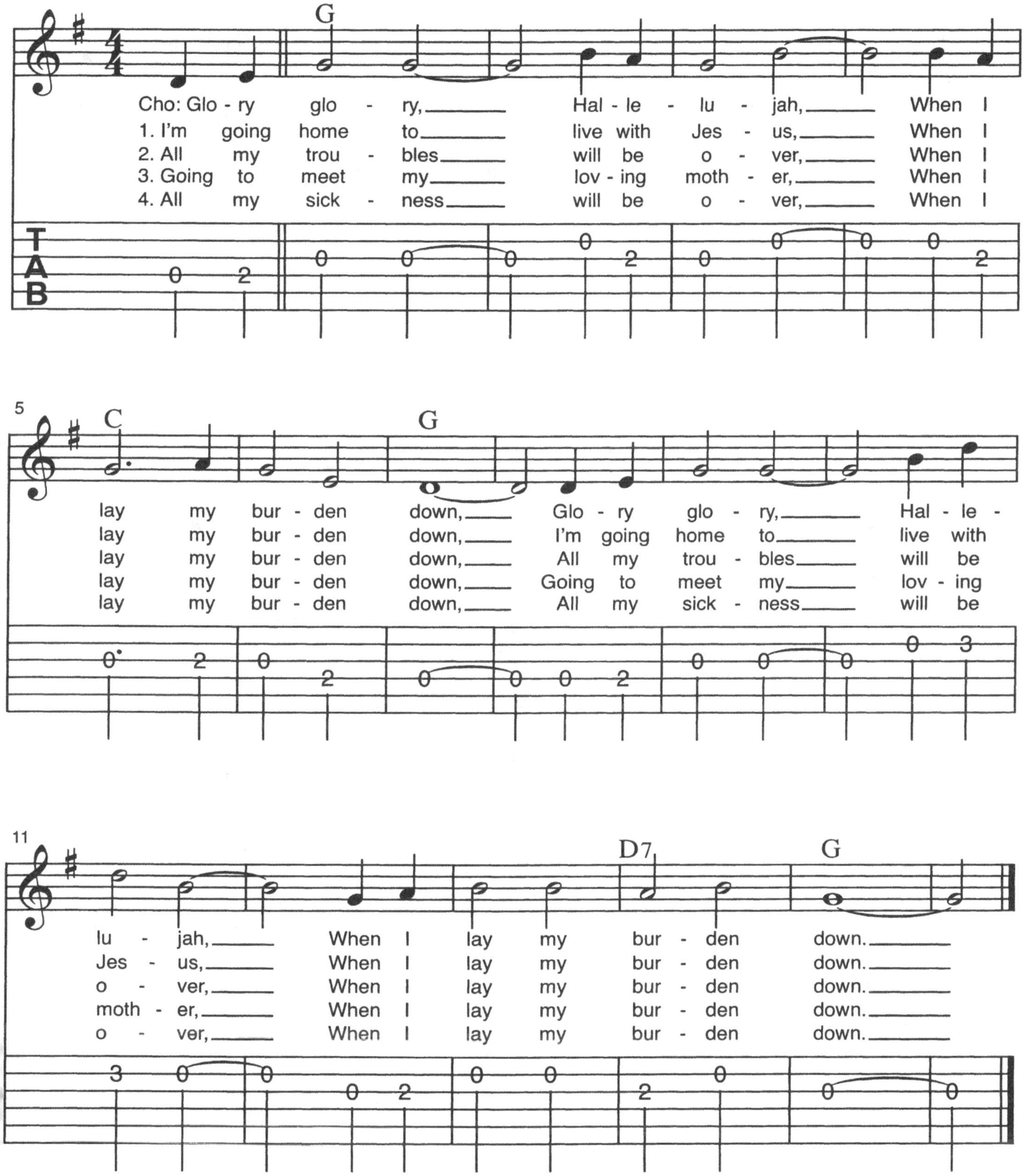

When My Race is Run

M: G; F: C or D, capo 5 or 7
CD 2-Track 86

Dix Bruce

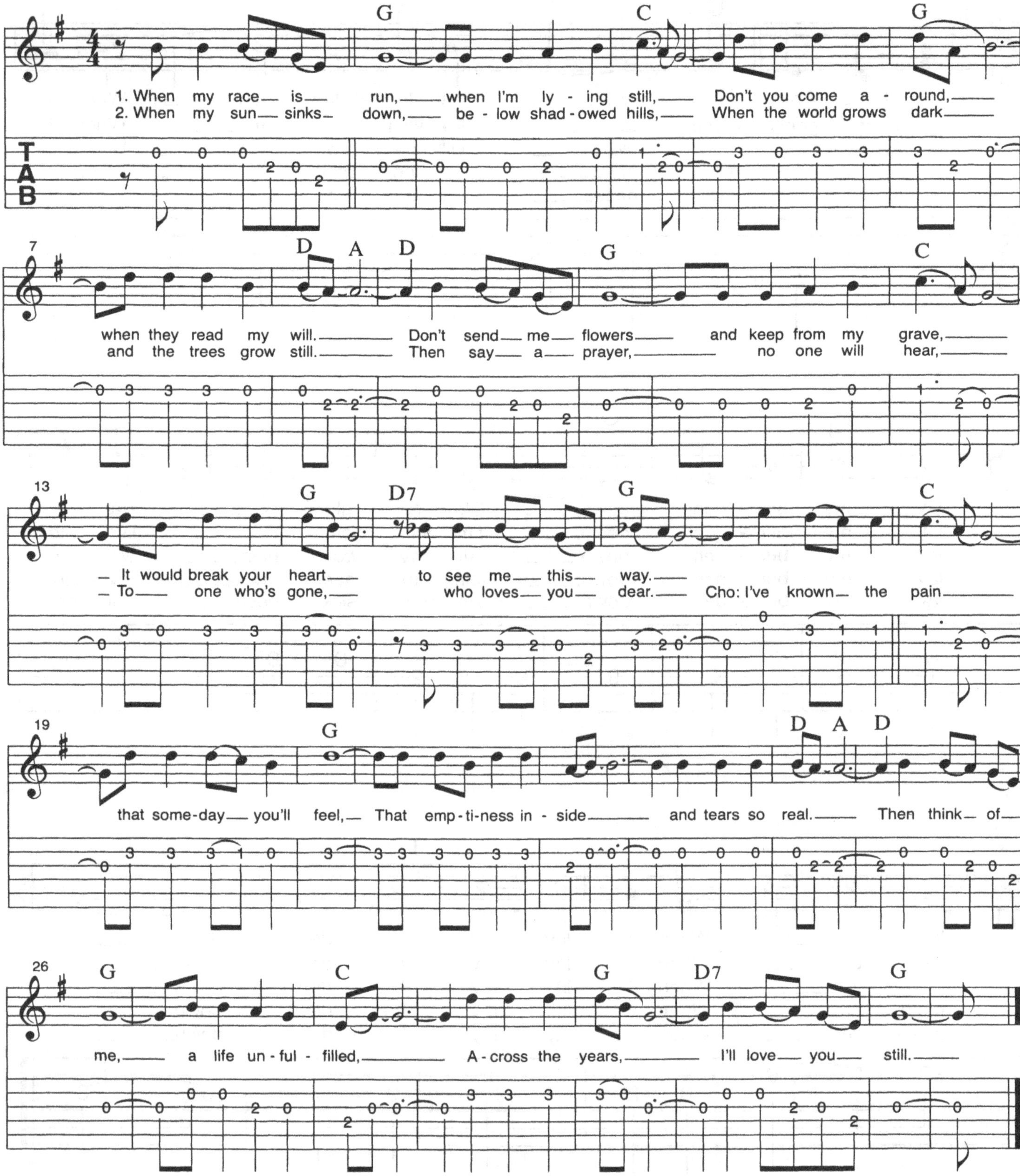

When the Roll is Called Up Yonder

M: G; F: C or D, capo 5 or 7
CD 2-Track 87, medley pt. 1

J.M. Black, 1893

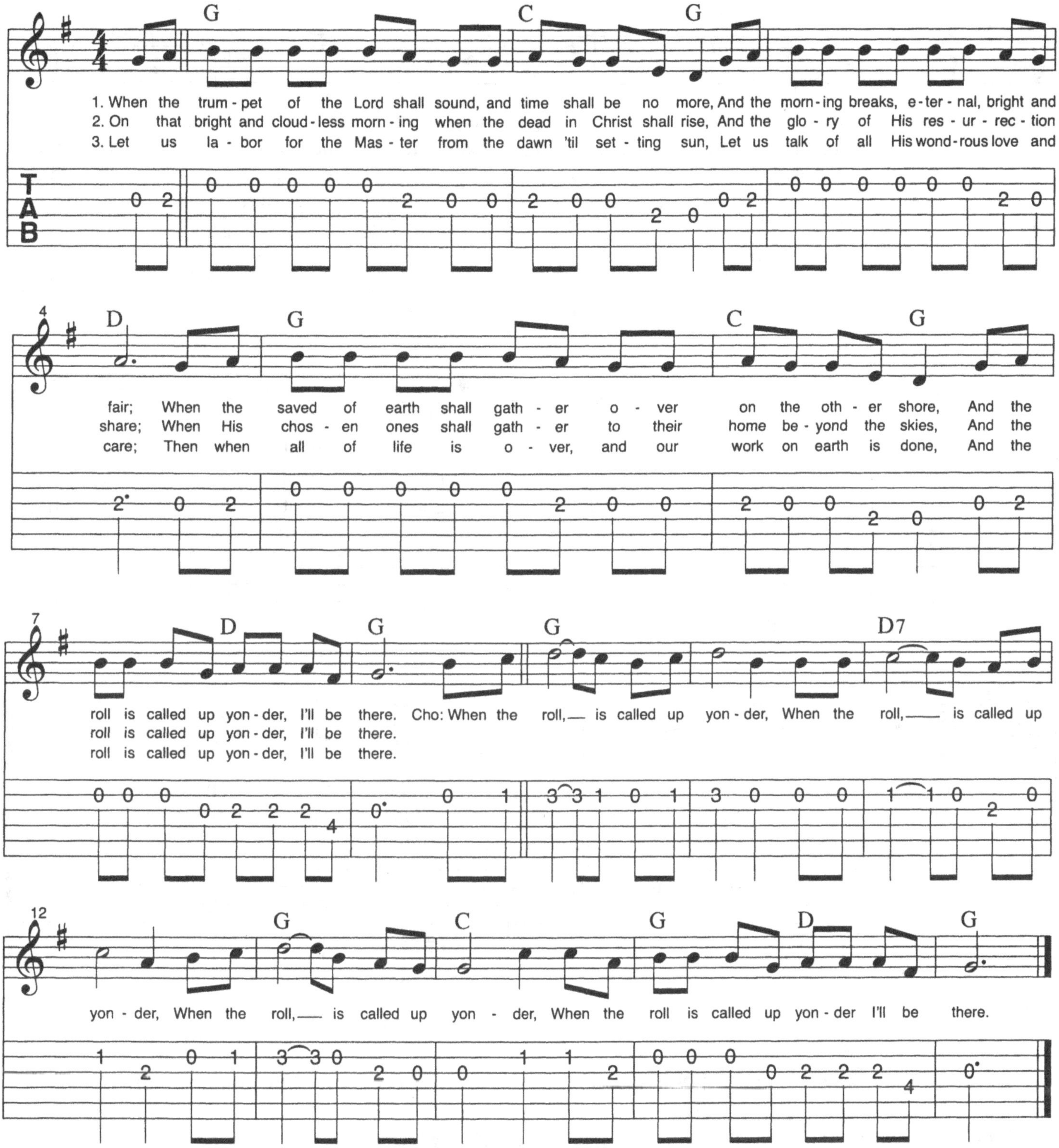

When the Saints Go Marching In

M: G; F: C or D, capo 5 or 7
CD 2-Track 87, medley pt. 2

Traditional

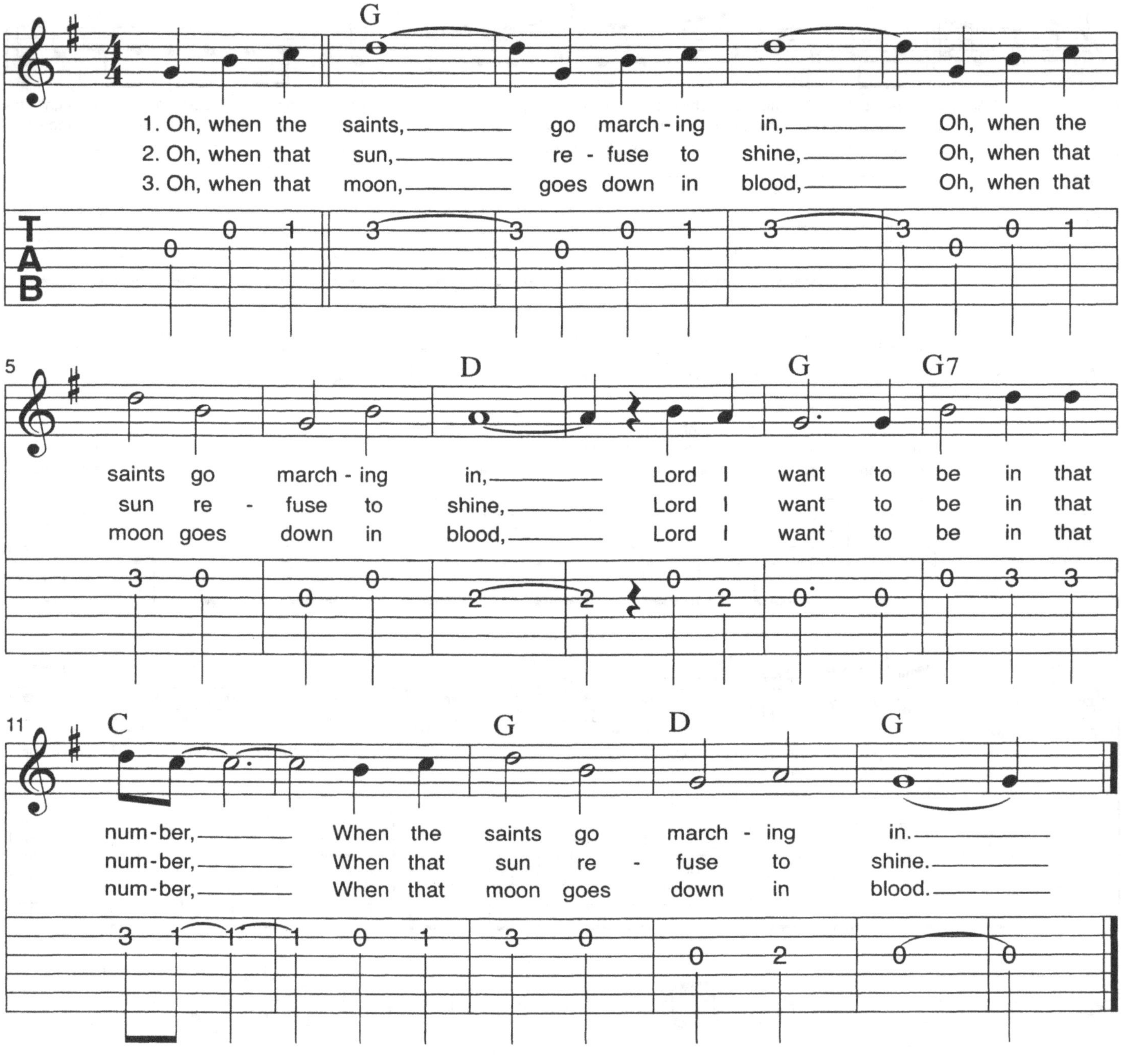

G
4. Oh, when they crown Him King of kings,
D
Oh, when they crown Him King of kings,
G G7 C
Lord I want to be in that number,
G D G
When they crown Him King of kings.

5. Oh, when they gather 'round the throne, (etc.)

6. Oh, while the happy ages roll, (etc.)

 Monroe Bros., B. Monroe, Flatt and Scruggs, Lilly Bros., Fiddlin' J. Carson

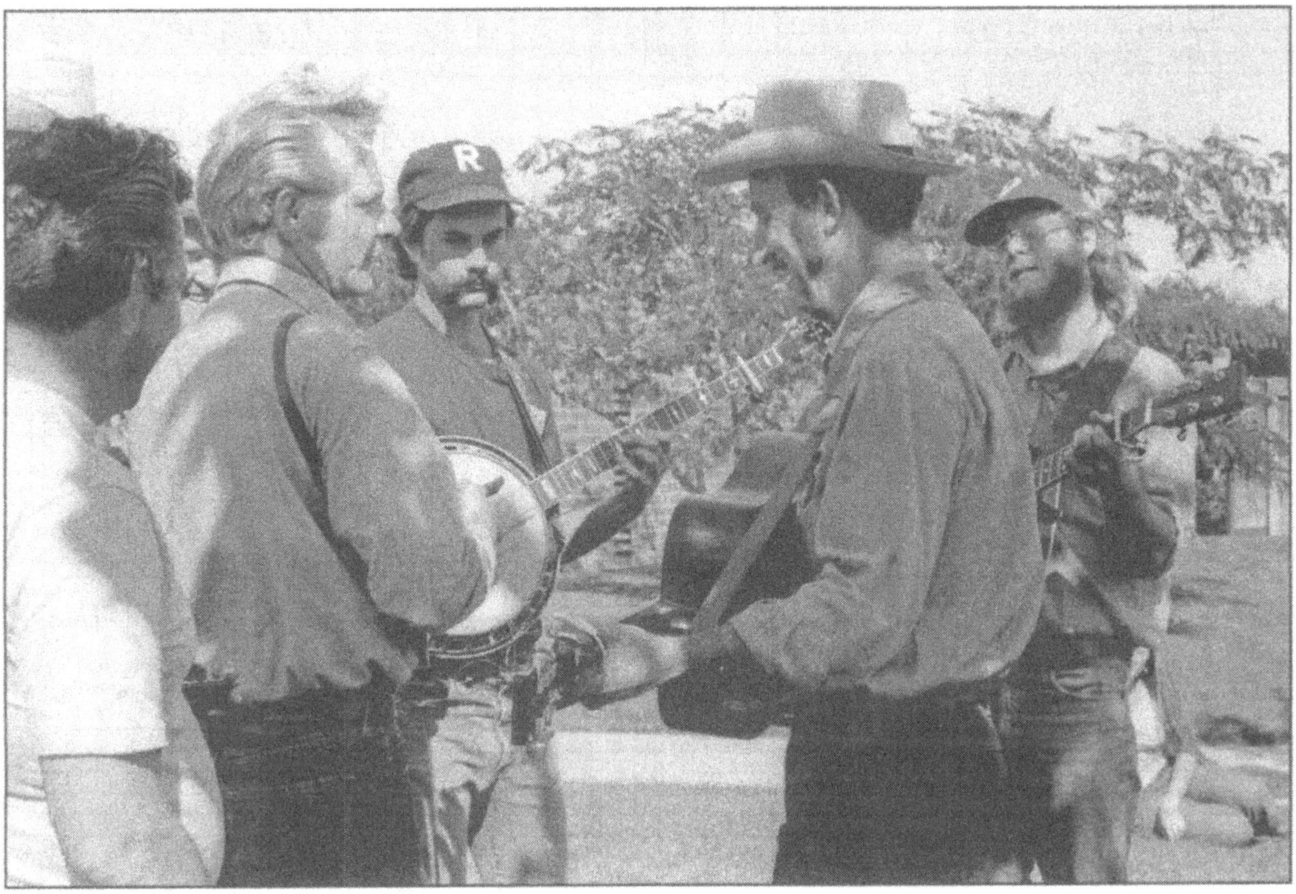

Photo courtesy Dix Bruce

Vern Williams (second from left) and Ray Park (second from right) jam with fans after a concert, ca. 1977.

When the Work's All Done This Fall

M: C; F: F or G, capo 5 or 7
CD 2-Track 88

Traditional

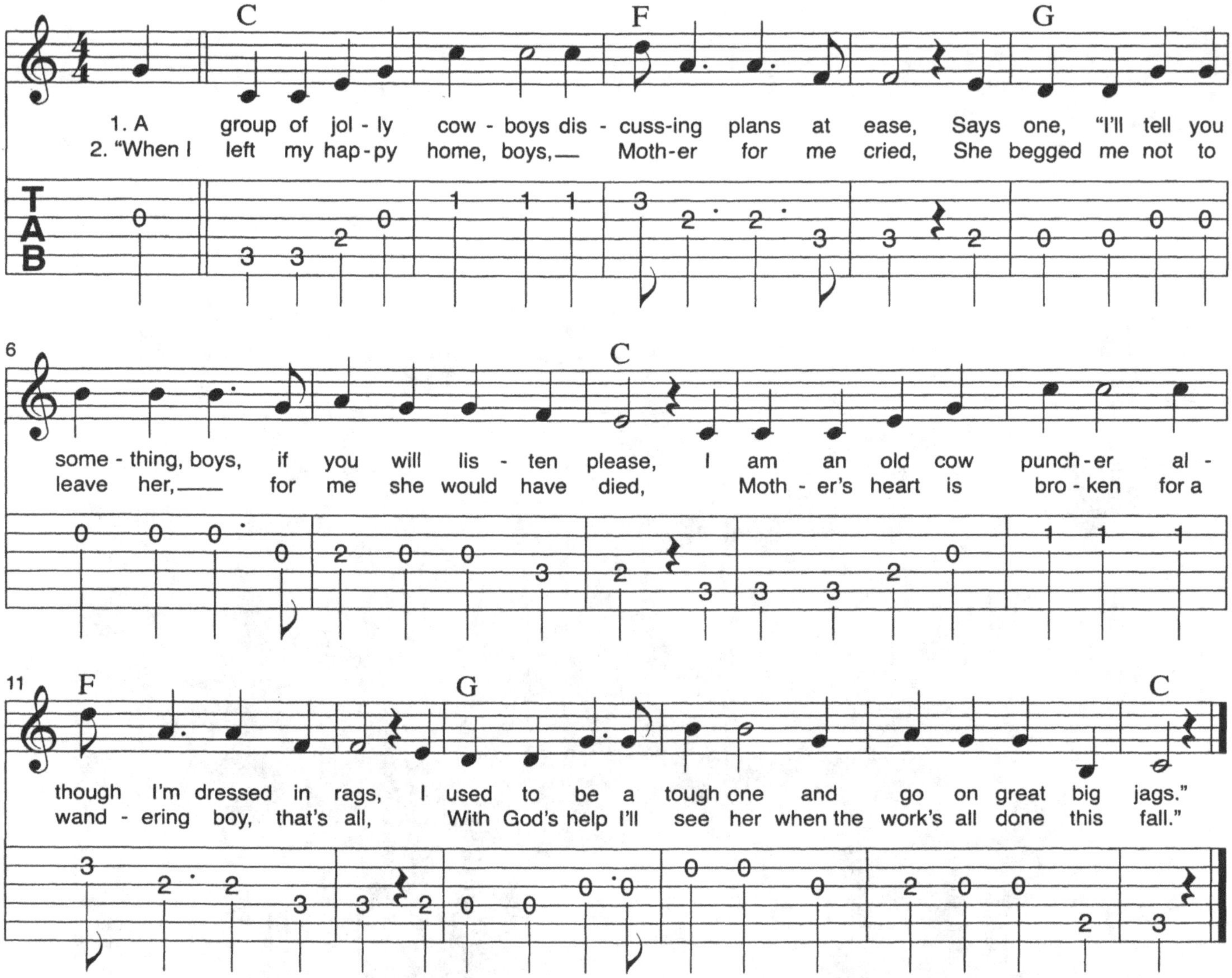

 D. Watson, Goose Island Ramblers, B. Clifton, N. Blake, M. Wiseman

          C   F
3. Well, after the roundup's over, and the shipping's done,
    G   C
I'm going right home boys, before my money's gone,
                                                 F
I have changed my ways, boys, no more will the temptors call,
  G   C
I want to see my mother, when the work's all done this fall."

4. That very night the cowboy, went out to stand his guard,
The night was dark and cloudy, and storming very hard,
The cattle all got freightened, and rushed in wild stampede,
The cowboy tried to head them, while riding at full speed.

5. While riding in the darkness, so wildly did he shout,
He tried his best to turn them, and head the herd about,
His saddle pony stumbled, and on the boy did fall,
He won't see his mother, when the work's all done this fall.

6. His body was so mangled, the boys all thought him dead,
They picked him up so gently, and laid him on the bed,
He opened wide his blue eyes, and looking all around
He motioned for his comrades, to sit near him on the ground.

7. "Well, send my mother my wages, the wages that I've earned,
I won't live to see her, the last steer I have turned,
I'm going to a new range, I've heard the Master's call,
And I won't see my mother, when the work's all done this fall."

8. "Hey George, you take my pistol, Jack you take my bed,
Jim you take my saddle, after I am dead,
Boys, speak of me kindly, when you look upon them all,
For I won't see my mother, when the work's all done this fall."

9. Well, Charlie was buried at daybreak, no tombstone at his head,
Nothing but a little board, and this is what it said,
"Charlie died at daybreak, and he died from the fall,
He won't see his mother, when the work's all done this fall."

When You And I Were Young Maggie

M: F; F: B♭ or C, capo 5 or 7
CD 2-Track 89

Johnson &
Butterfield, ca. 1866

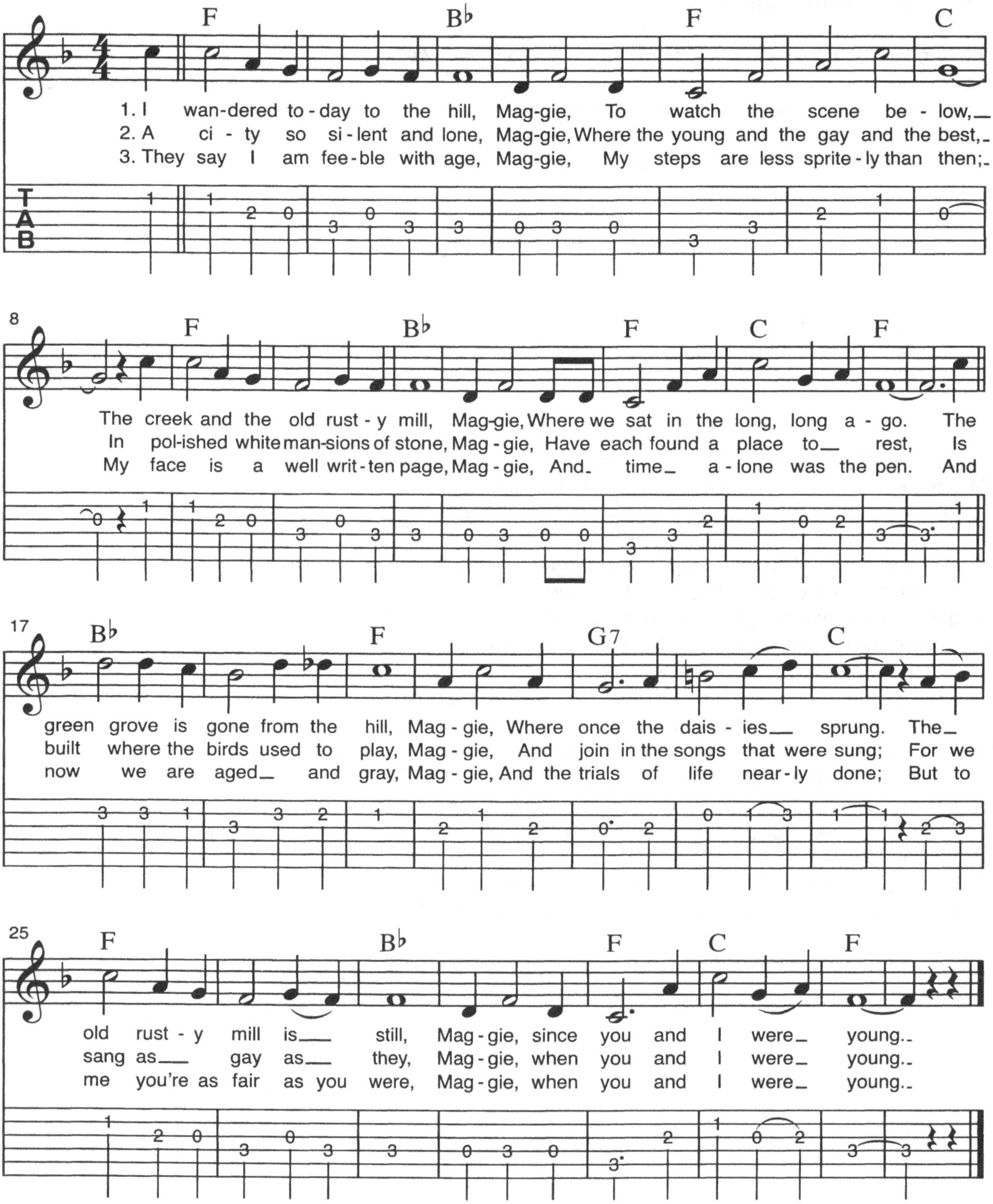

 Stanley Bros., Reno & Smiley, Fiddlin' John Carson, Mac Wiseman, D. Grisman, B. Waller

Where the Soul Never Dies

M: E; F: A or B, capo 5 or 7
CD 2-Track 90

Wm. Golden

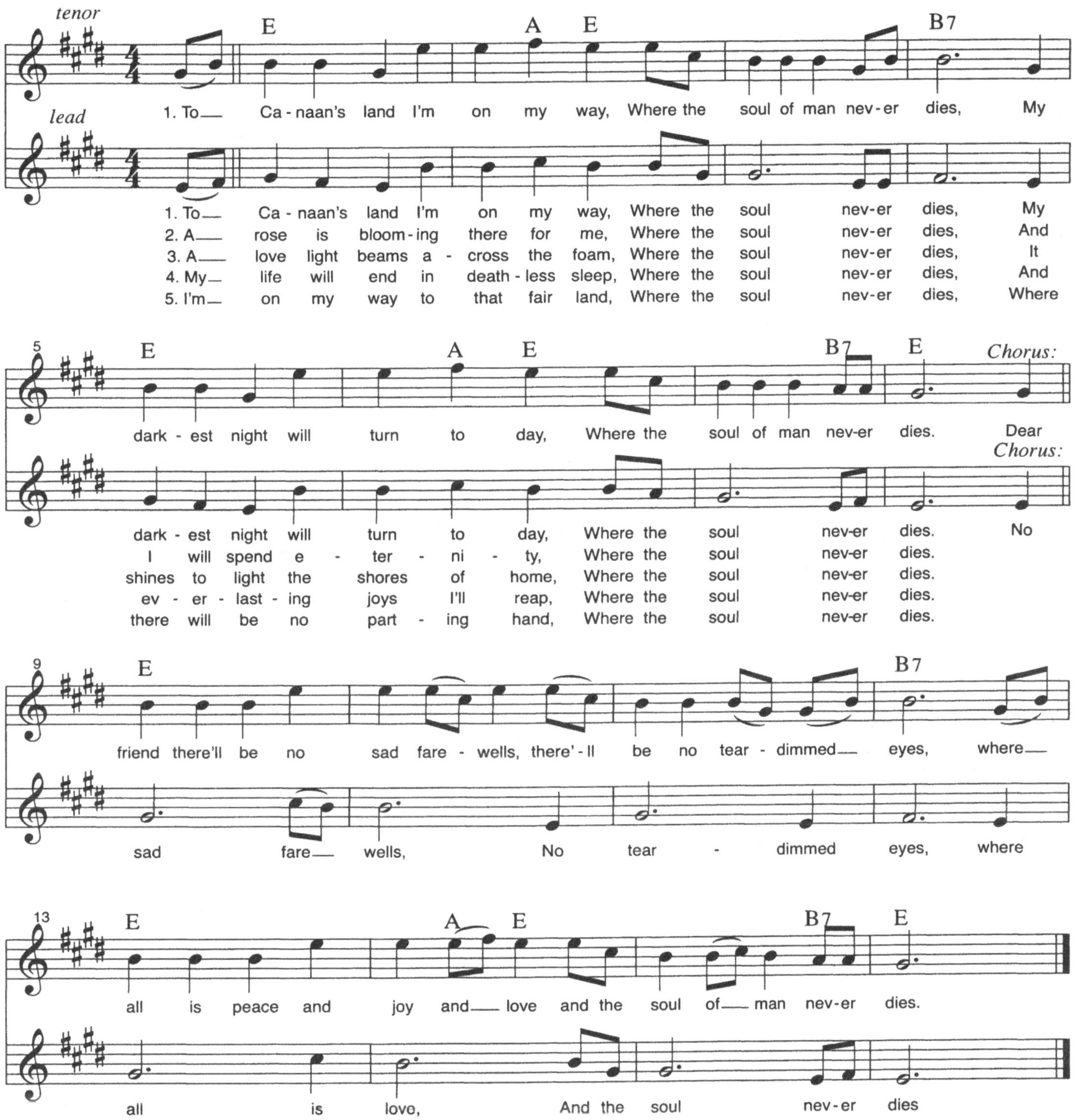

(Note: Tablature on page following.)

Where the Soul Never Dies

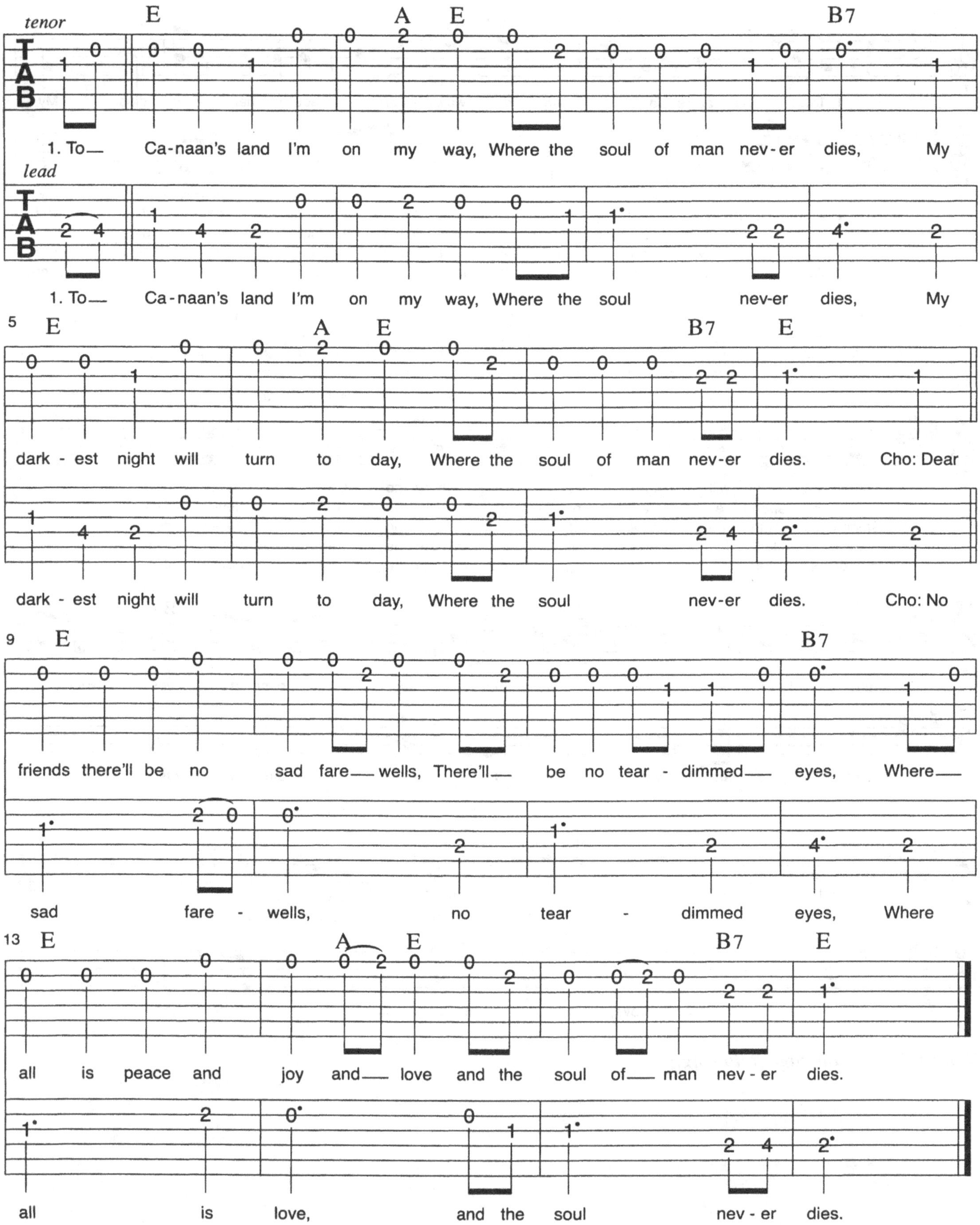

Whitehouse Blues

M: G; F: C or D, capo 5 or 7
CD 2-Track 91, medley pt. 1

Traditional

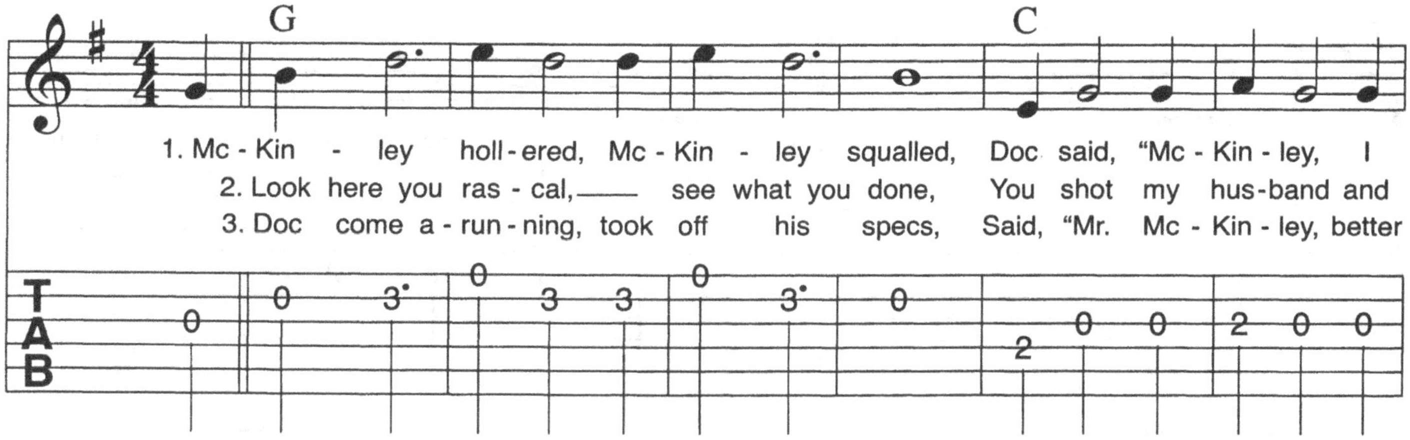

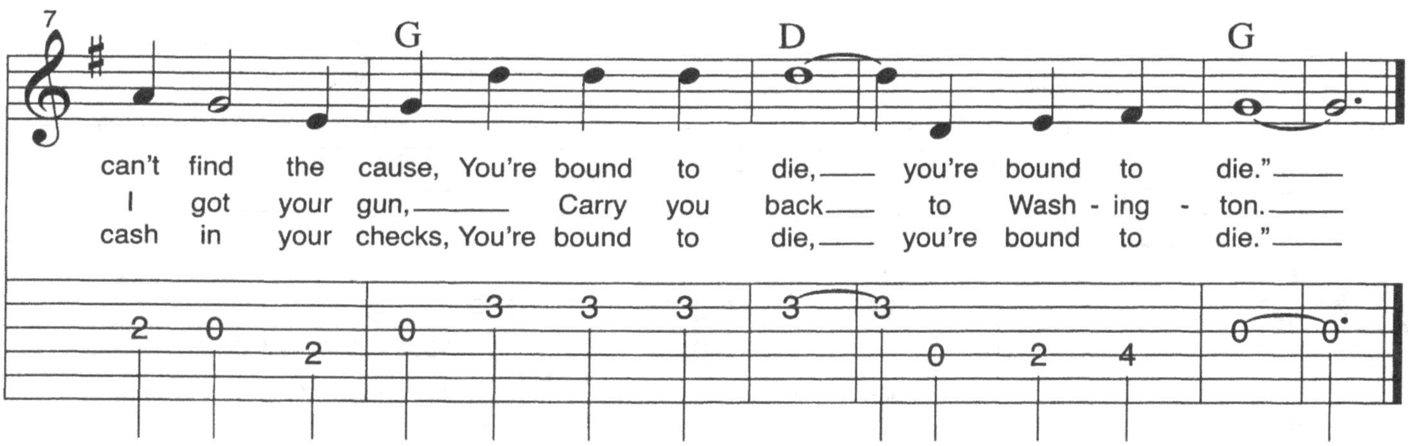

G
4. Roosevelt's in the White House, doing his best,
C G
McKinley's in the graveyard taking his rest,
D G
He's long gone, long gone.

5. Roosevelt's in the White House, drinking out of a silver cup,
McKinley's in the graveyard, he's never gonna wake up,
He's long gone, long gone.

6. Hush up little children, now don't you fret,
You're bound to draw a pension from your papa's death,
He's long gone, long gone.

7. Jumped on a horse, he threw down his reins,
He said to the horse, "You gotta outrun the train,
From Buffalo to Washington."

8. Nixon's in the Whitehouse, making a mess,
Johnson's in the graveyard, taking his rest,
He's long gone, long gone.

Who Broke the Lock?

M: G; F: C or D, capo 5 or 7
CD 2-Track 91, medley pt. 2

Traditional

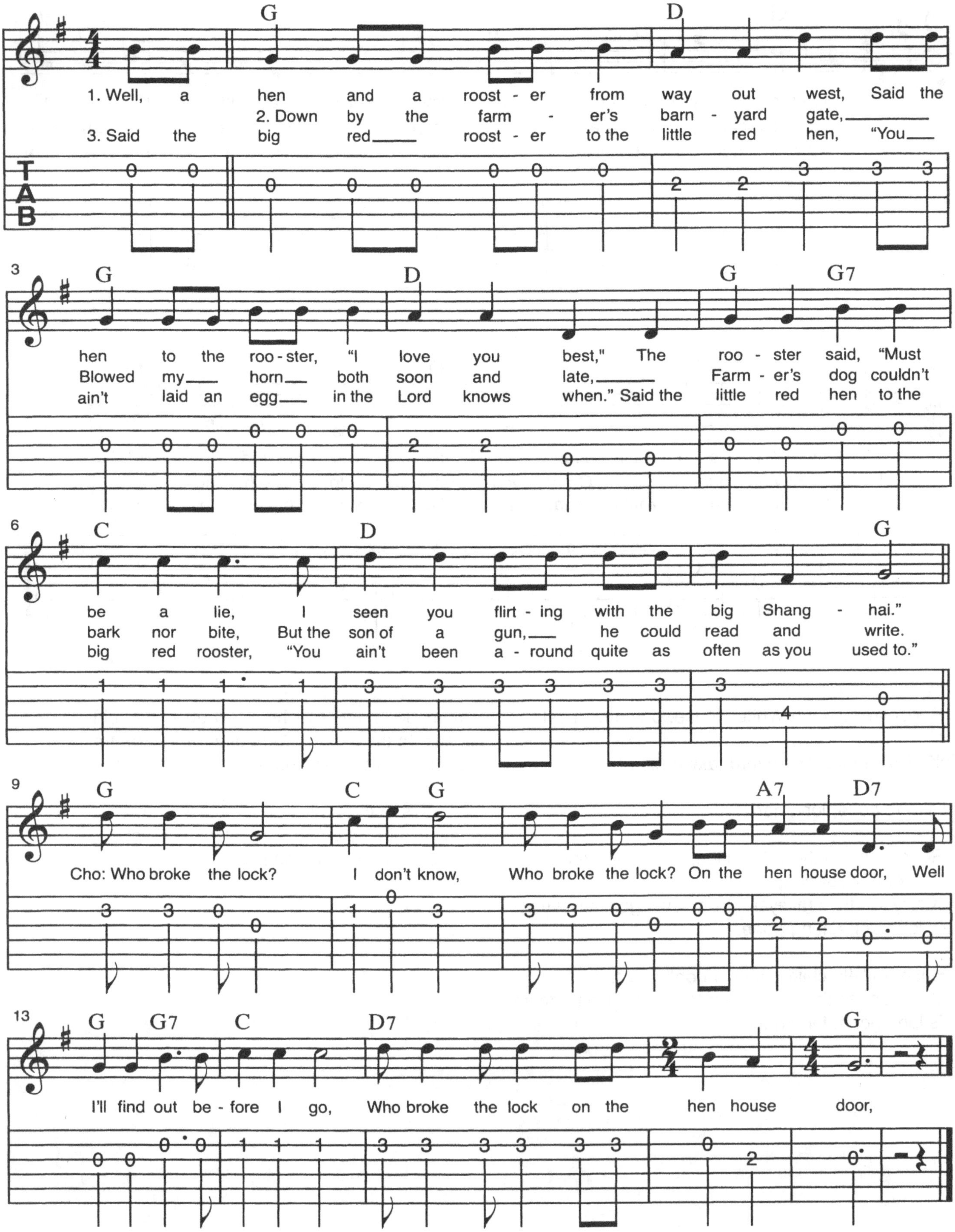

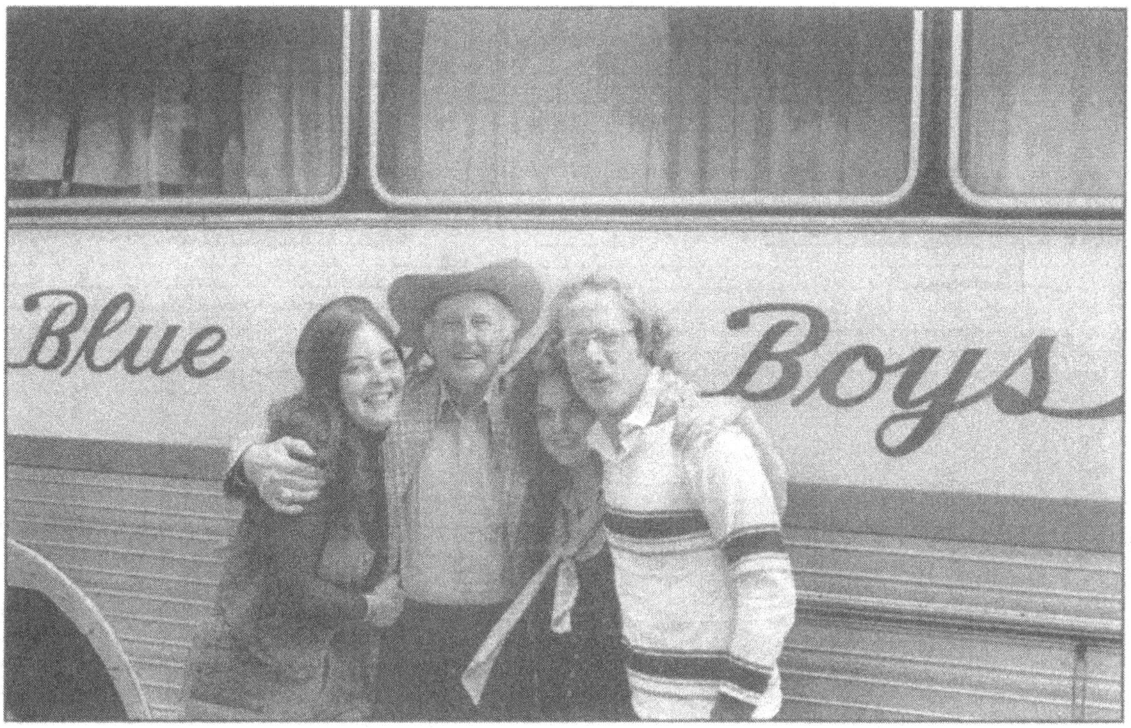

Left to right: Kathy Kallick, Bill Monroe, Julia LaBella, Dix Bruce. San Francisco, late 1970s.

Who Will Sing for Me?

M: A; F: D or E, capo 5 or 7
CD 2-Track 92

Traditional

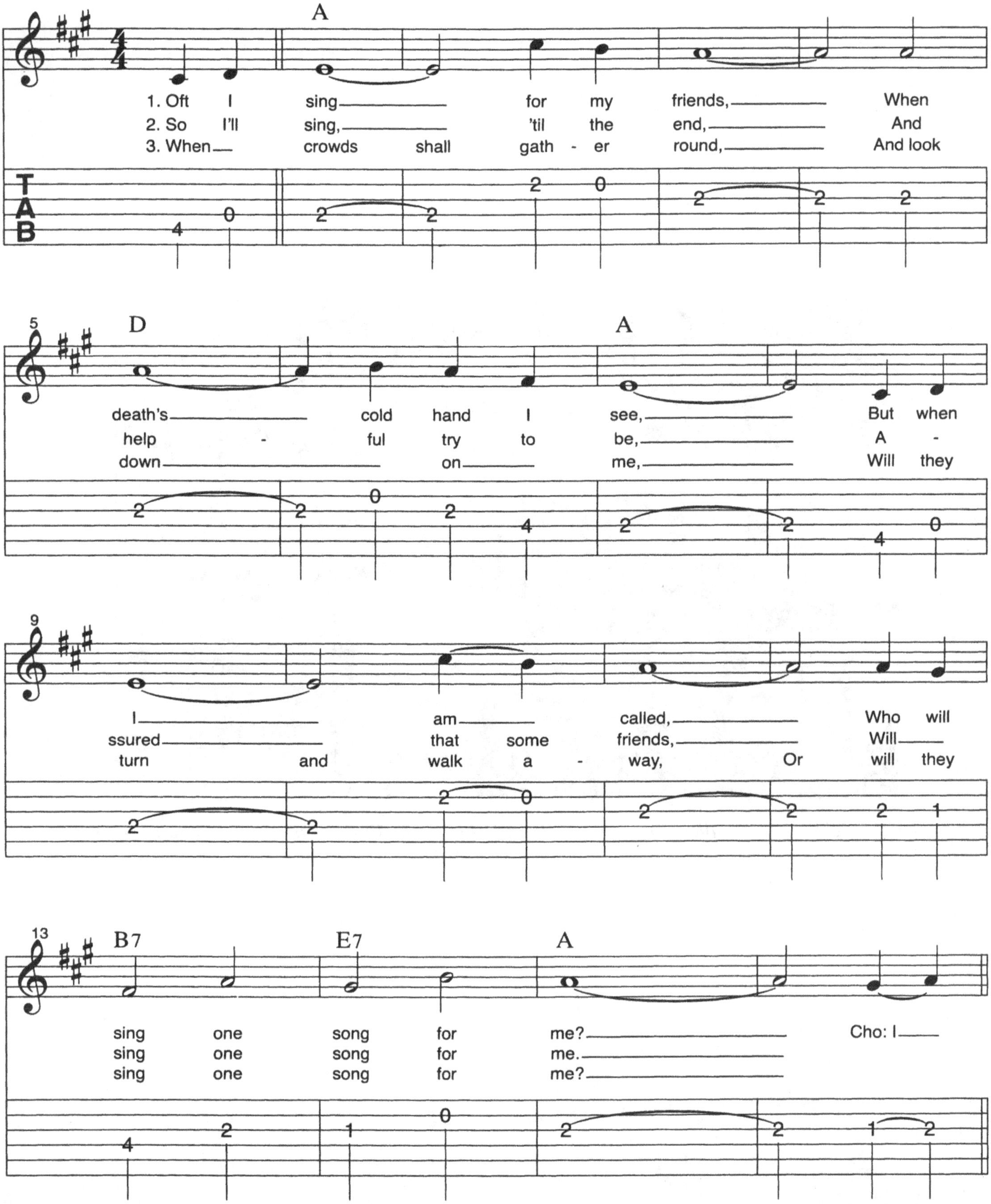

 Flatt & Scruggs, Stanley Bros., R. Stanley, Scruggs/Watson/Skaggs, Jimmy Martin, E.L. Harris

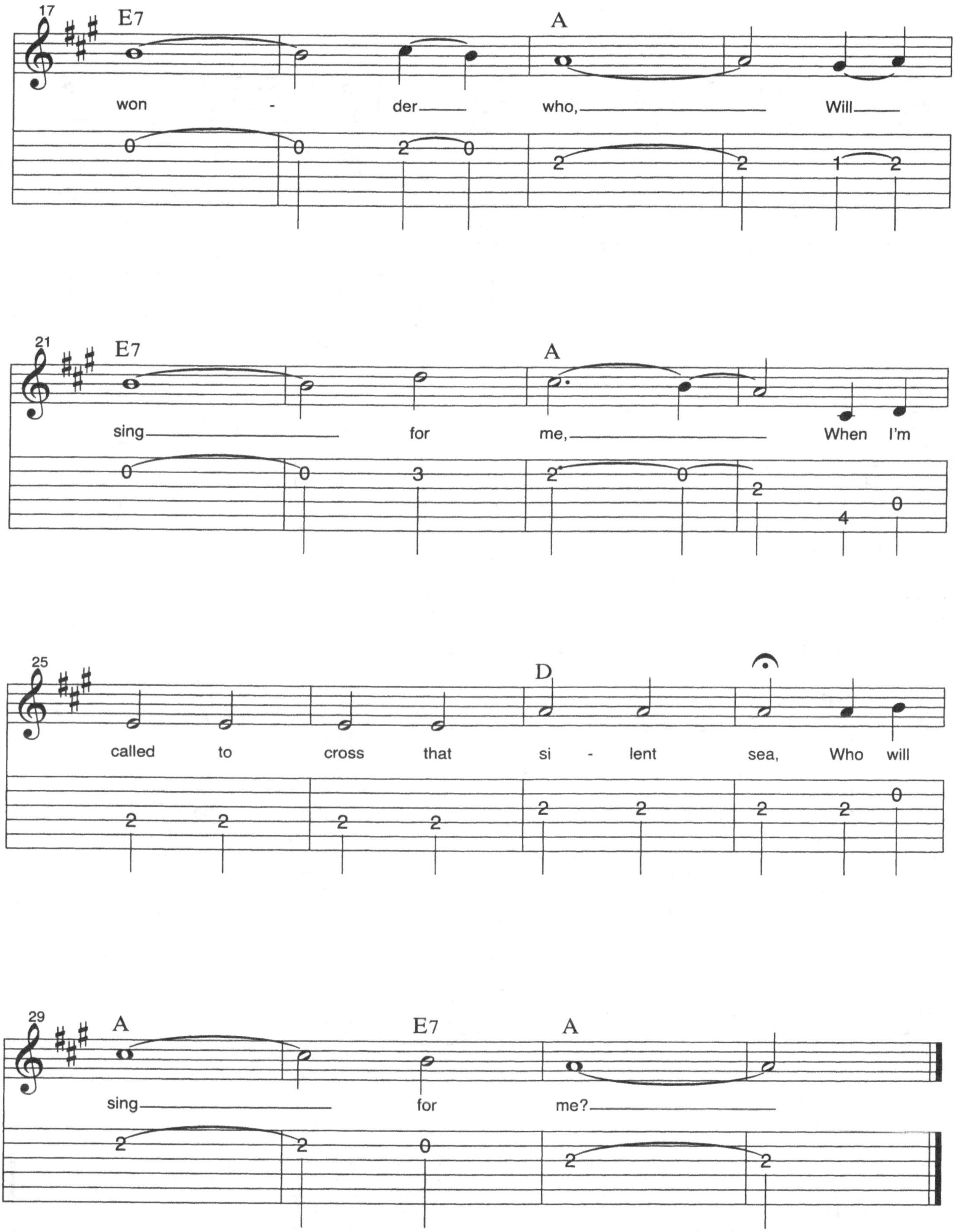
17
E7
A
won - der who, Will
21
E7
A
sing for me, When I'm
25
D
called to cross that si - lent sea, Who will
29
A
E7
A
sing for me?

Wild Bill Jones

M: G; F: C or D, capo 5 or 7
CD 2-Track 93

Traditional

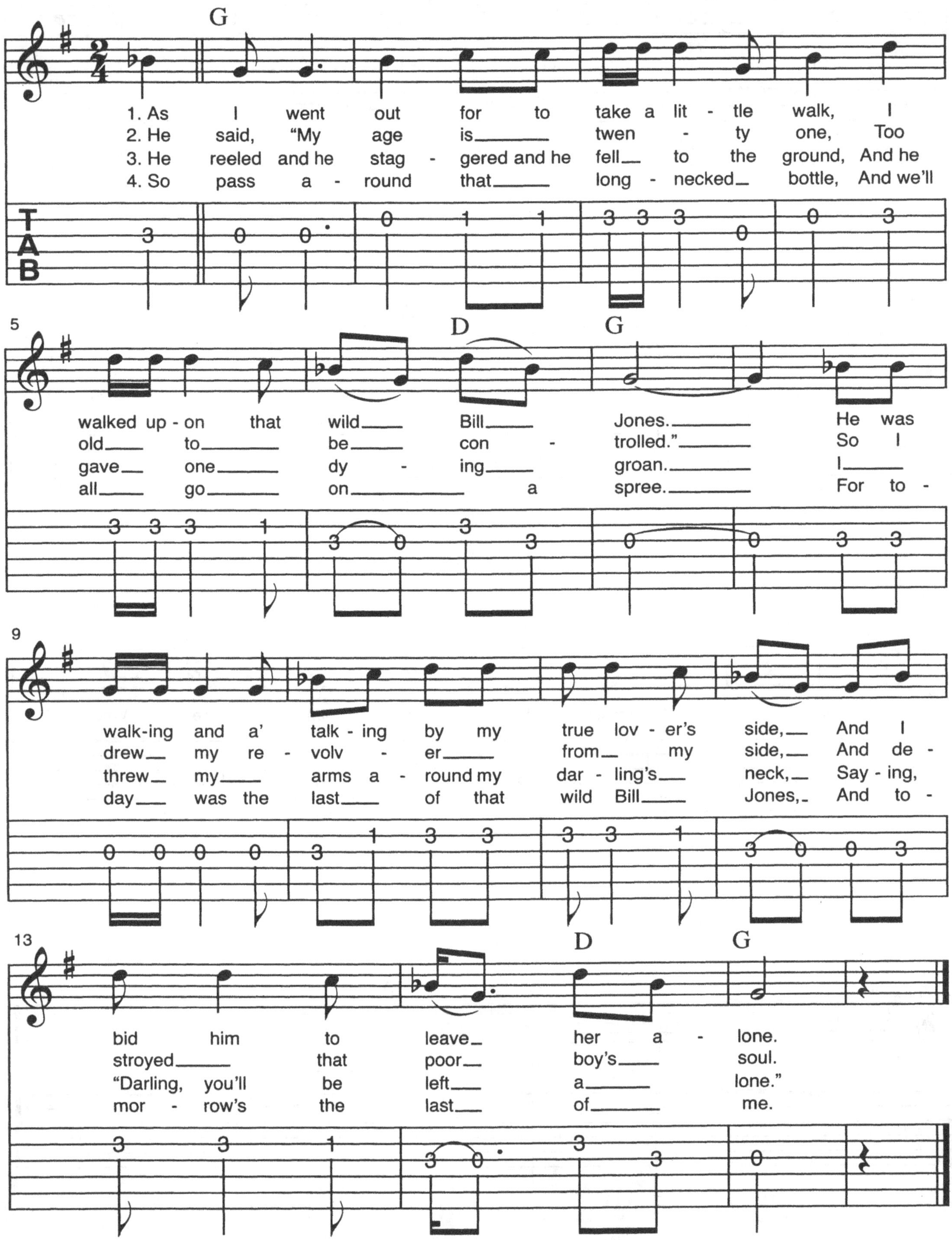

 Stanley Bros., R. Stanley, Ken. Colonels, Hot Rize, D. Boggs, J.E. Mainer, J. Stecher, Alison Krauss

Wildwood Flower

M: C; F: F or G, capo 5 or 7
CD 2-Track 94

Traditional

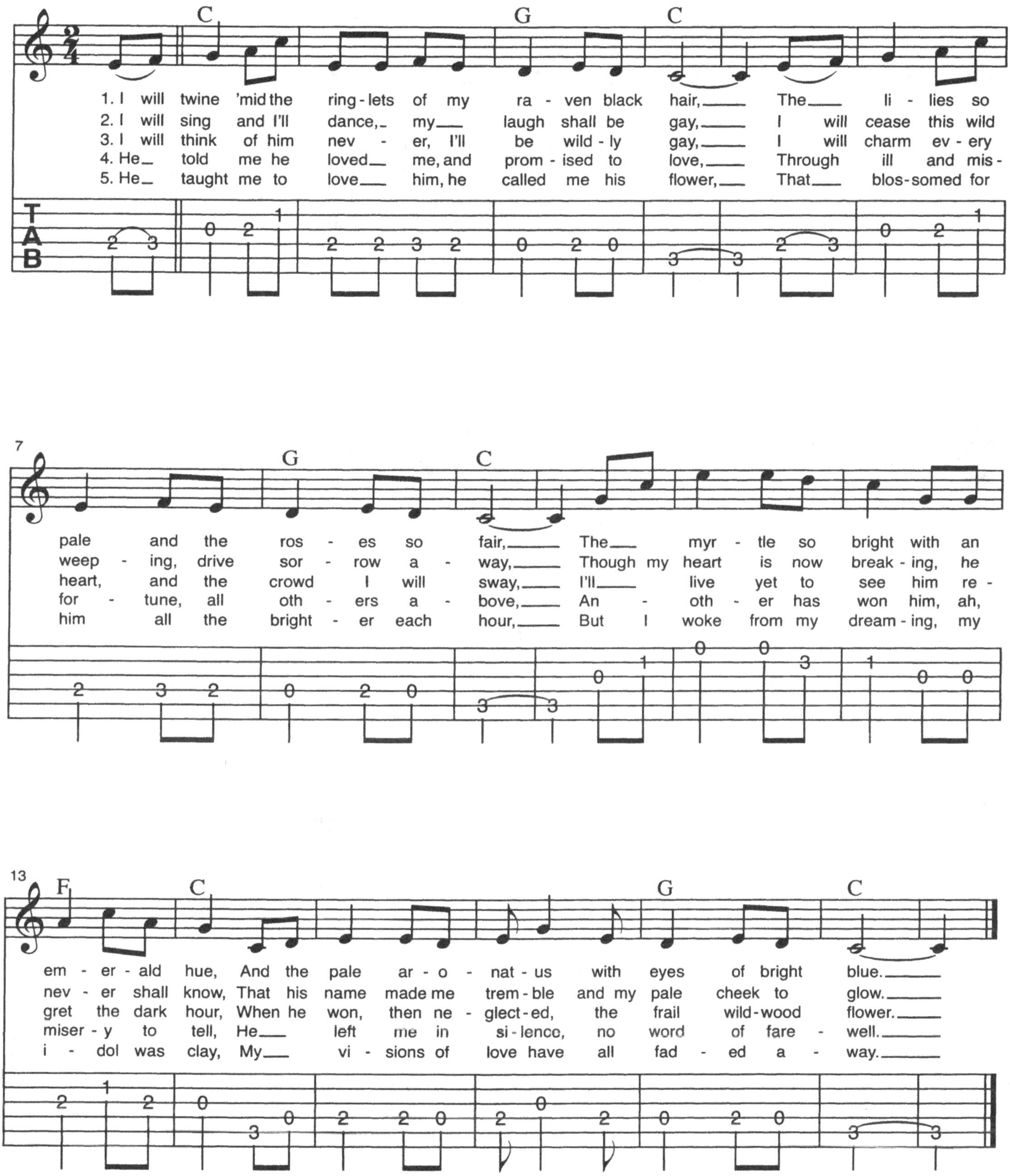

Will the Circle Be Unbroken?

M: G; F: C or D, capo 5 or 7
CD 2-Track 95, medley pt. 1

Traditional

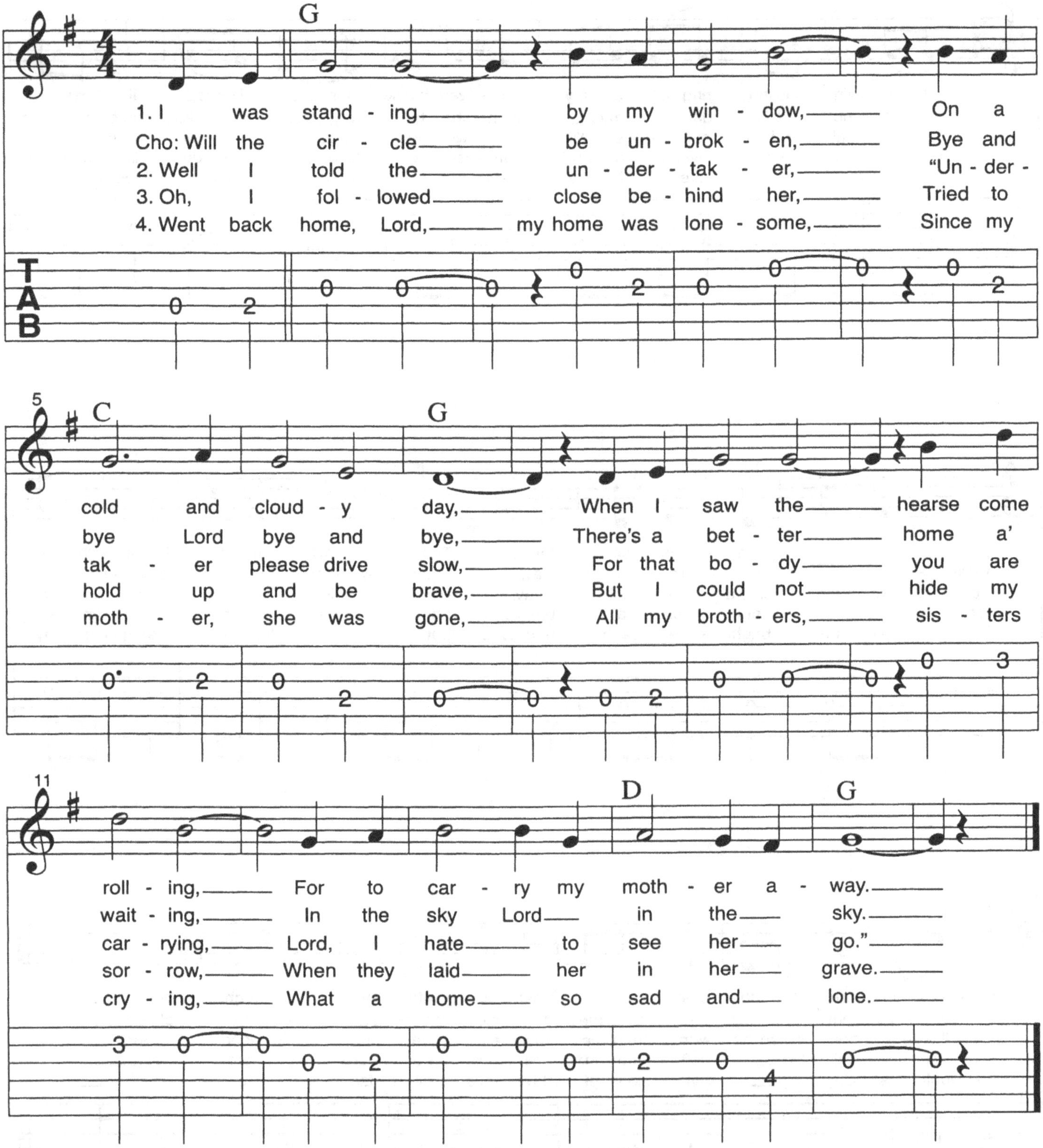

 Carter Fam., Monroe Bros., D. Watson, Stanley Bros., Nitty Gritty Dirt Band

Will There Be Any Stars in My Crown?

M: G; F: C or D, capo 5 or 7
CD 2-Track 95, medley pt. 2

Sweney & Hewitt, ca 1897

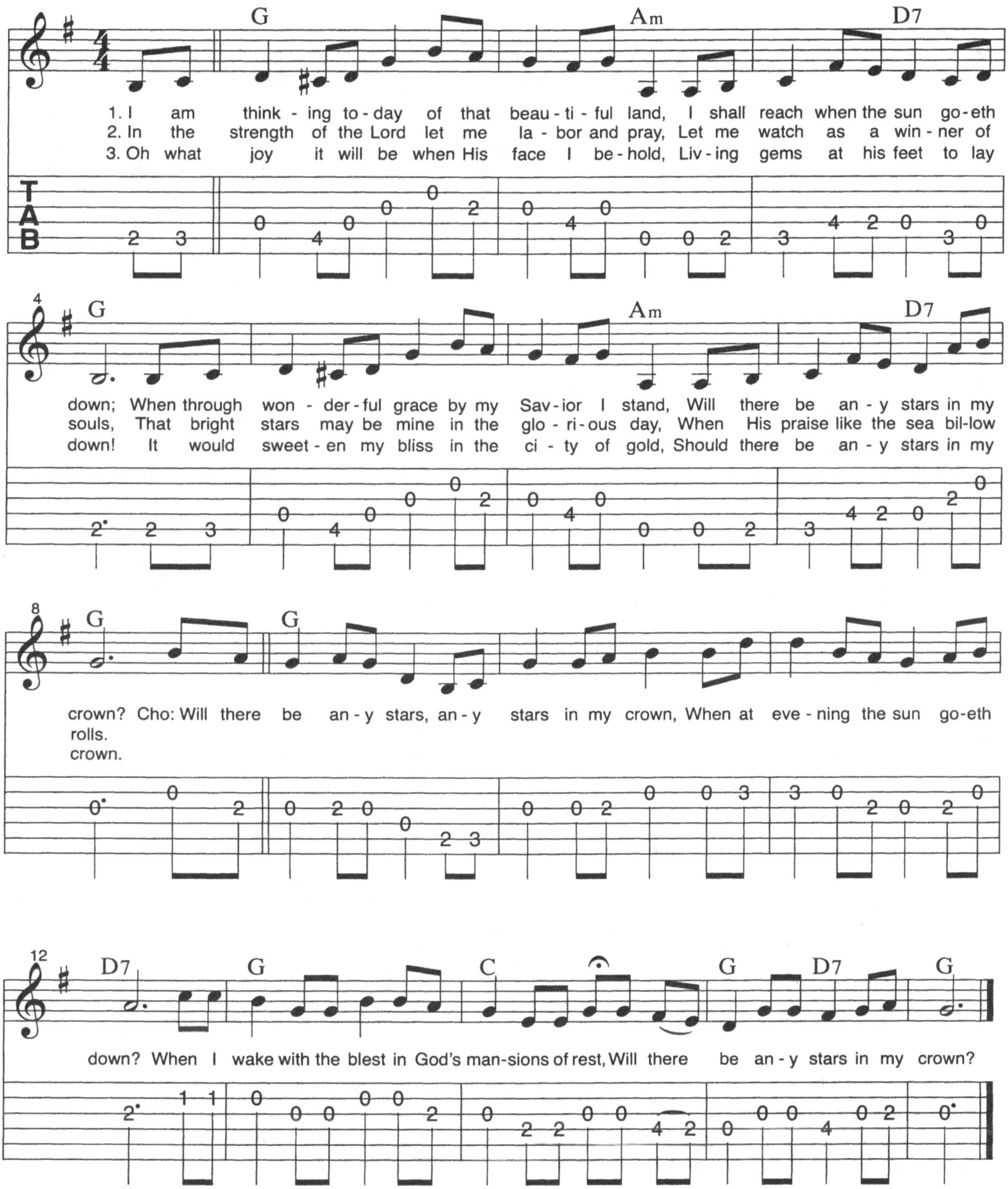

Willie My Darling

M: G; F: C or D, capo 5 or 7
CD 2-Track 96

Traditional

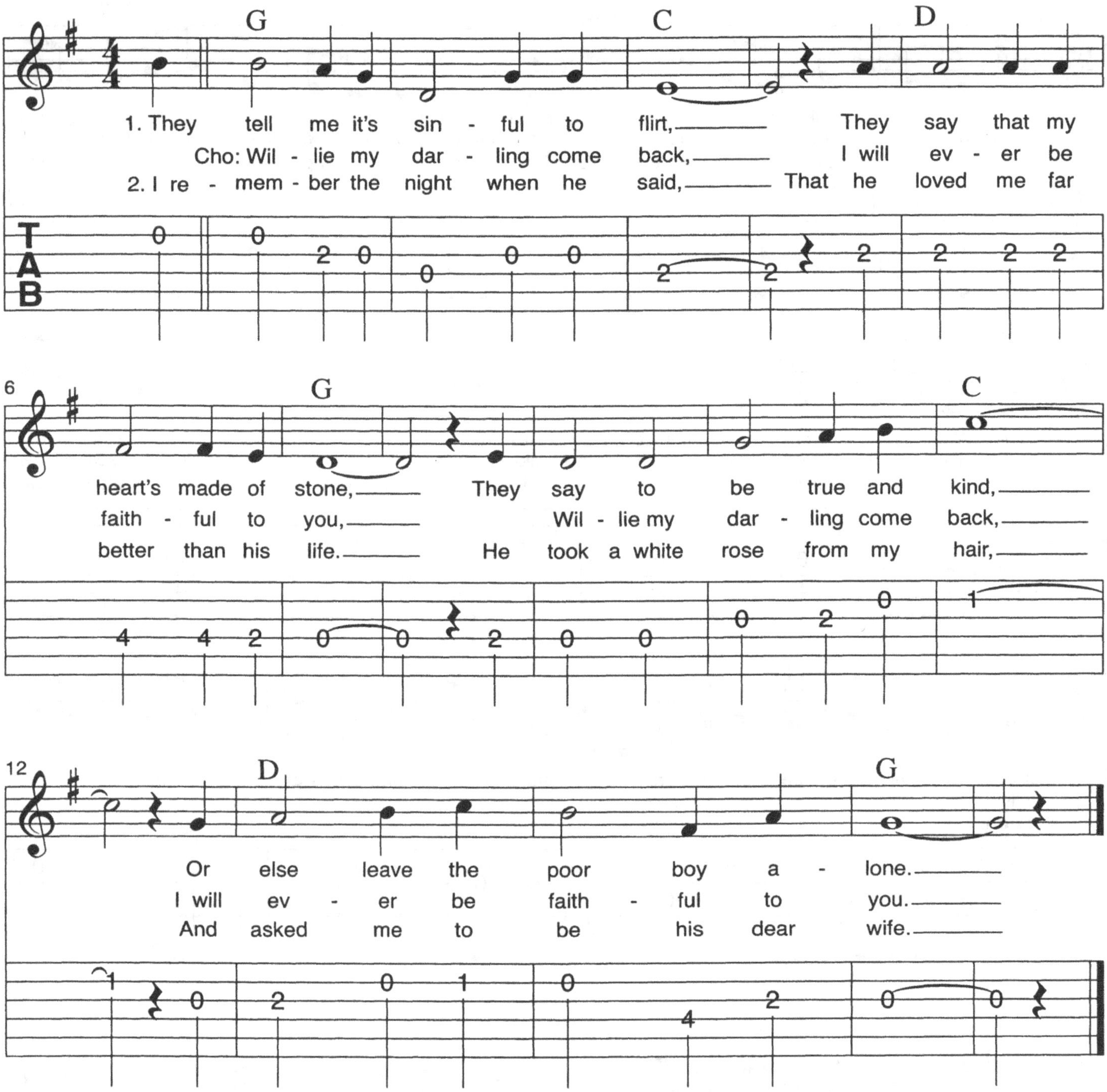

G C
3. "Well, Willie," I said with a smile,
D G
"I'm afraid that I'll have to say no,
C
'Cause Papa and Mama aren't willing,"
D G
Then he said, "Goodbye, I must go."

4. Next morning poor Willie was found,
He was drowned in the pond by the mill.
In the cold, icy waters so deep,
That flowed from the brink of the hill.

5. His blue eyes forever were closed,
And damp were his curls so fair.
And close to his pale lips he held,
The white rose that he took from my hair.

Worried Man Blues

M: C; F: F or G, capo 5 or 7
CD 2-Track 97, medley pt. 1

Traditional

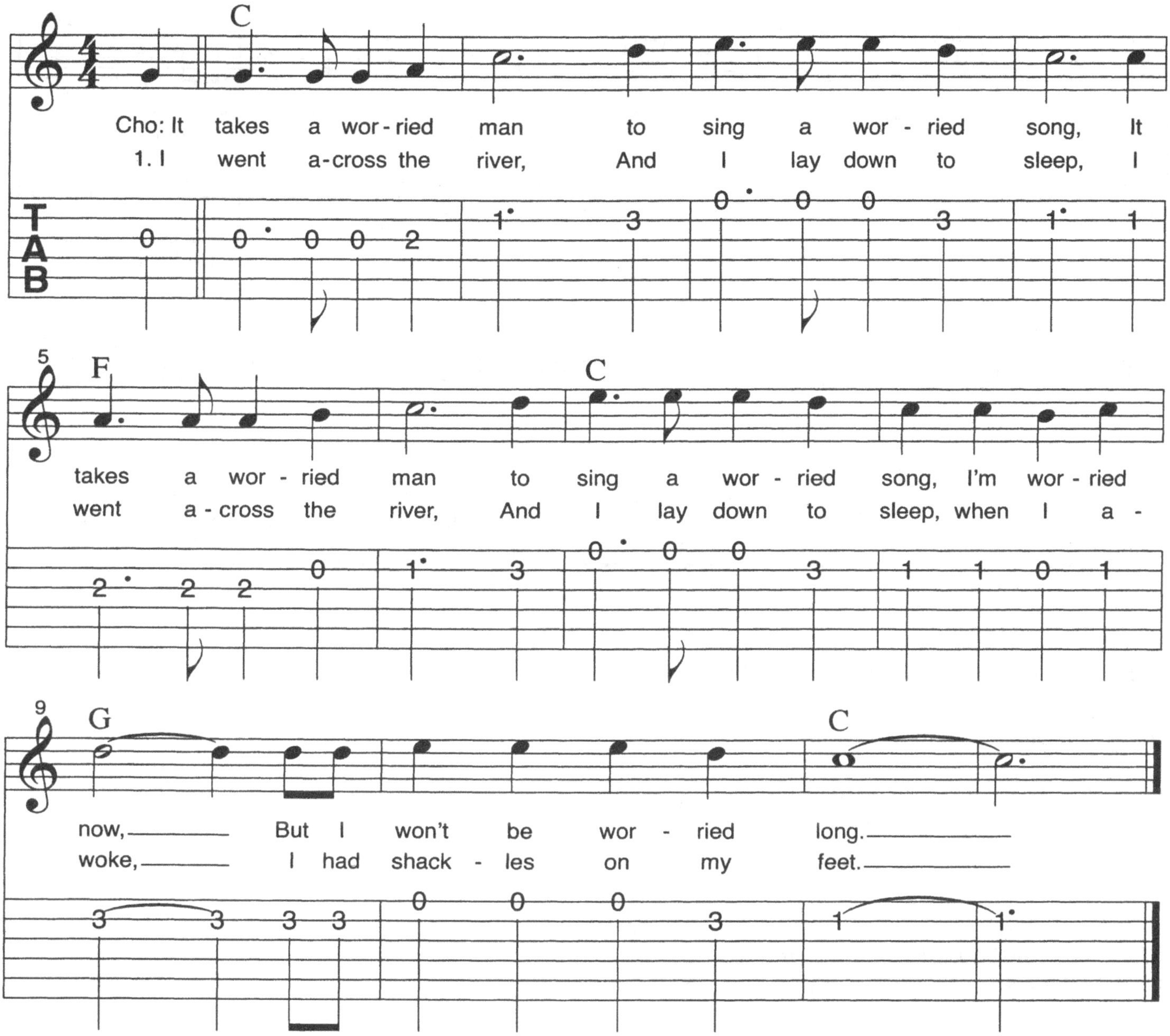


```
C
2. Twenty nine links of chain around my leg,
F                               C
Twenty nine links of chain around my leg,
            G                          C
And on each link an initial of my name.
```

3. I asked the judge, what might be my fine,
I asked the judge, what might be my fine,
Twenty one years on the R.C. Mountain Line.

4. If anyone should ask you, who composed this song,
If anyone should ask you, who composed this song,
Tell them 'twas I, and I sing it all day long.

5. I looked down the track, as far as I could see,
I looked down the track, as far as I could see,
A little hand was waving after me.

Carter Fam., Flatt & Scruggs, Stanley Bros., NLCR, Blue Sky Boys, Reno & Harrell, Jim & Jesse, Osborne Bros., W. Guthrie

The Wreck of the Old 97

M: C; F: F or G, capo 5 or 7
CD 2-Track 97, medley pt. 2

Traditional

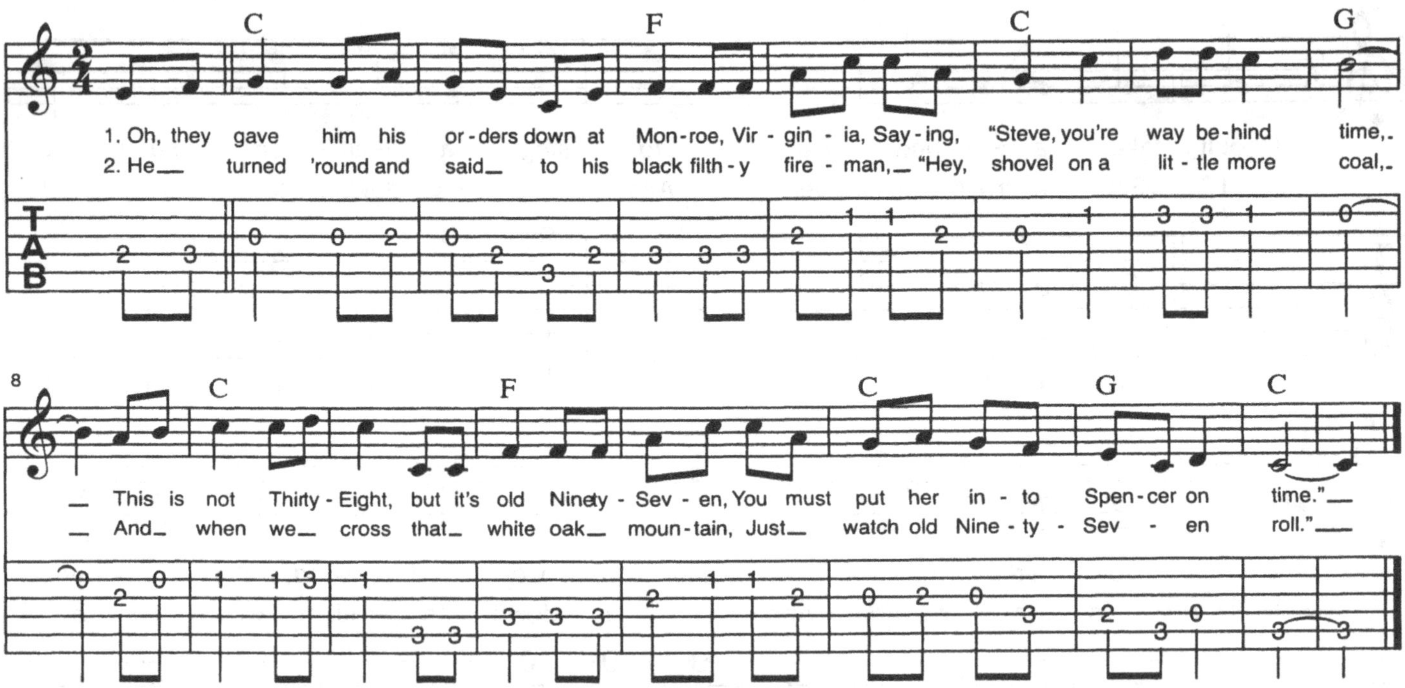


```
   C                           F
3. It's a mighty rough road from Lynchburg to Danville,
    C                          G
And lying on a three mile grade,
      C                        F
It was on that grade that he lost his average,
    C          G       C
You see what a jump he made.
```

4. He was going down the grade making ninety miles an hour,
When his whistle broke into a scream,
He was found in the wreck with his hand on the throttle,
And scalded to death by the steam.

5. Well, a telegram came to Washington City,
And this is how it read:
"The brave engineer that run old Ninety-Seven,
Is lying in old Danville dead."

6. Now all you ladies, heed, take warning,
From this time on and learn,
Never speak harsh words to your true loving husband,
He may leave you and never return.

 Skillet Lickers, Flatt & Scruggs, Bluegrass Band, Mac Wiseman, NLCR, N. Blake, W. Guthrie

You're a Flower Blooming in the Wildwood

M: G; F: C or D, capo 5 or 7
CD 2-Track 98

Traditional

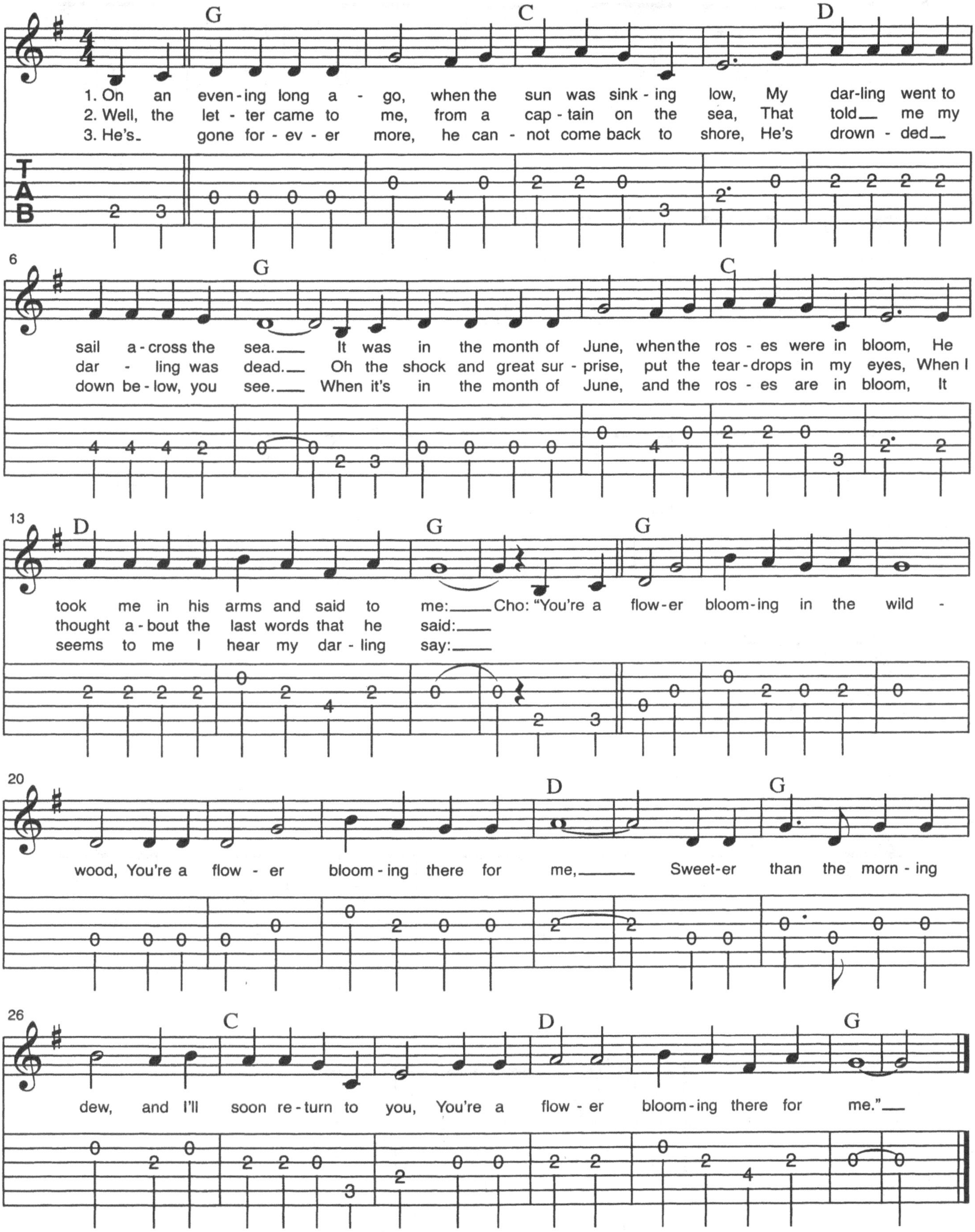

Guitar Chords

Major Chords

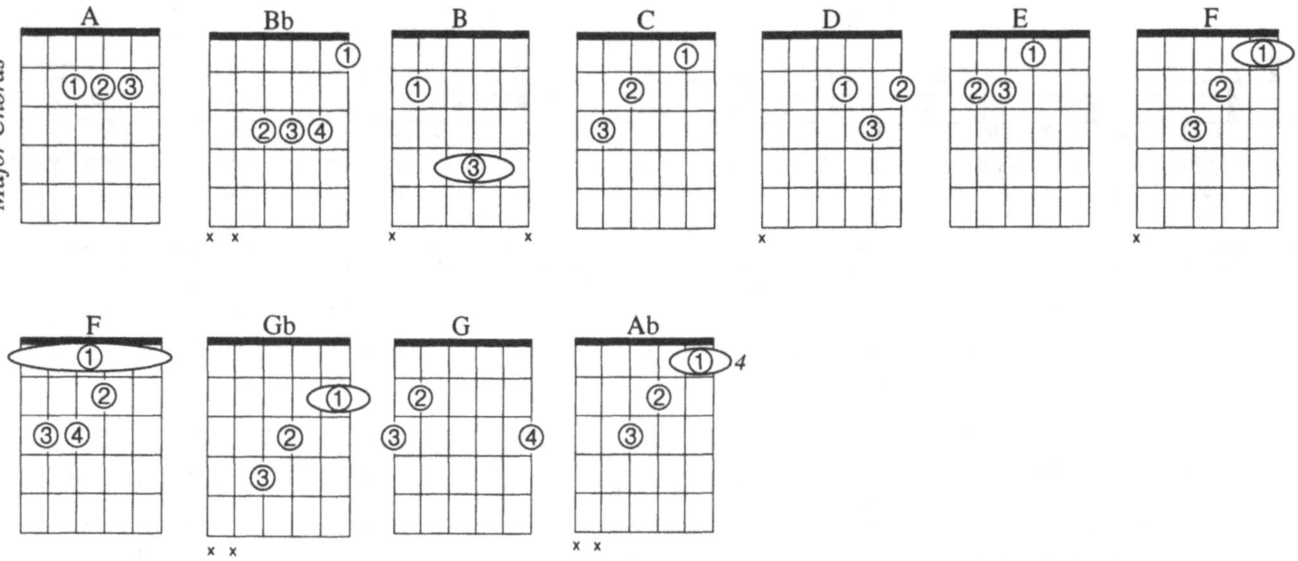

Dominant Seven Chords

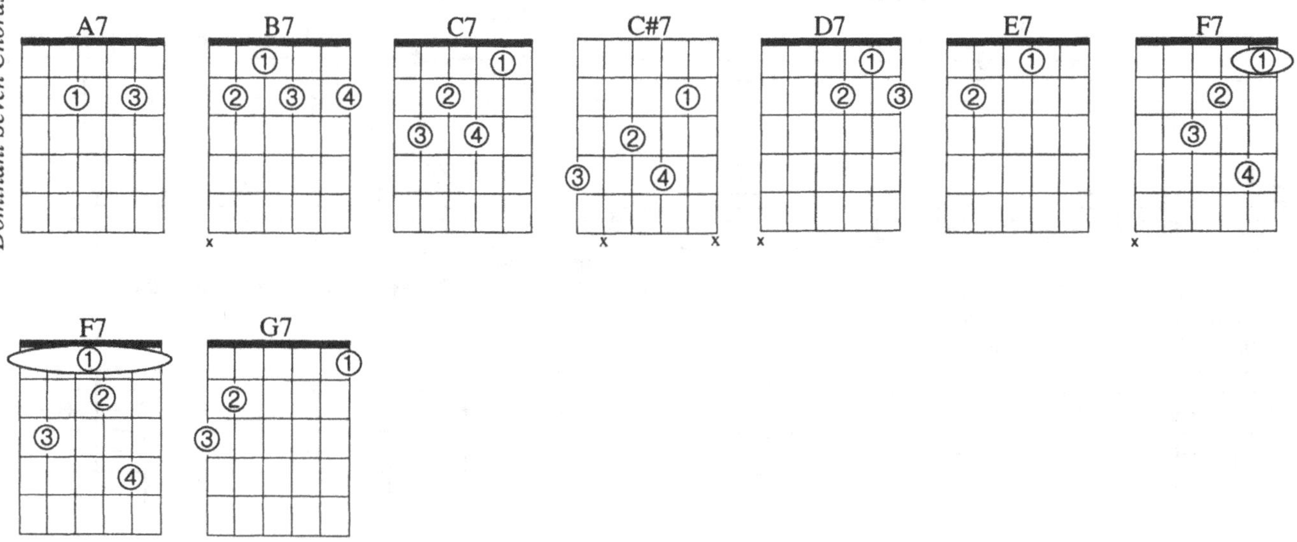

Minor Chords

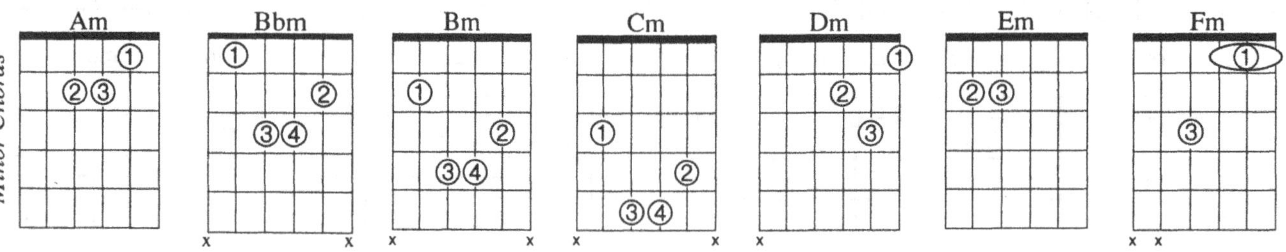

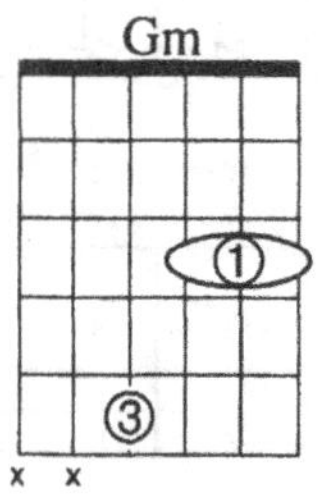

Diminished Chords

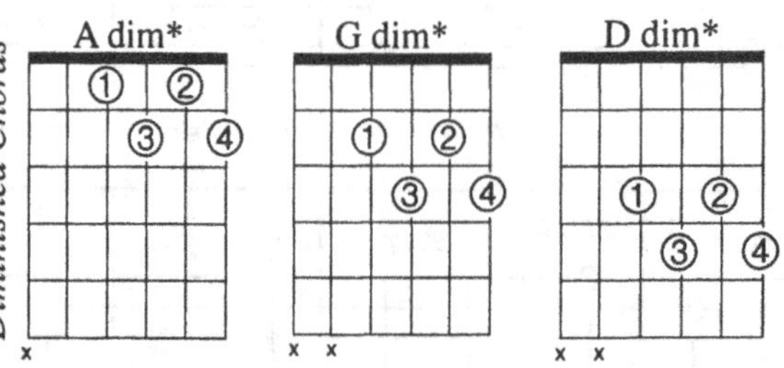

* Also F#, C & Eb dim

* Also Bb, Db & E dim

* Also F, Ab & B dim

Notes on Selected Songs

For a complete alphabetical listing of all the songs in this book, see the Table of Contents on page 2.

A

All the Good Times, p. 8: An eloquent description of the despair lost love can bring.

Amazing Grace, p. 9: Probably the greatest hit of spiritual music, it appeals to people with a wide variety of beliefs.

Angel Band, p. 10: I love the comforting message of "Angel Band." Quite a different point of view from "He Will Set Your Fields on Fire." (p. 94)

Angelina Baker, p. 11: Probably the source for the instrumental "Angelina Baker." This vocal version is quite happy and peppy considering that the story is about a slave who's sweetheart has "gone away," no doubt sold to another owner. Like many songs of the pre-Civil War period, this one idealized slave and plantation life. "Darling Nellie Gray" (p. 54) has a very similar story but is much more somber in tone.

Angels Rock Me To Sleep, p. 12: Another comforting image of death.

Are You From Dixie?, p. 14: One of a vast repertoire of songs that idealize the sunny south including "Sweet Sunny South," (p. 234) "My Old Kentucky Home," "Blue Ridge Mountain Blues," (p. 26) "The Girl I Loved in Sunny Tennessee." (p. 76) These types of songs, some from the mid-1800s, some as recent as the latest pop country hit, have resonated across the US and throughout the world. Of course we're not all from the south but we all have a mother, maybe a sweetheart, or a warm concept of home. That might explain the enduring popularity of these types of songs.

Are You Washed in the Blood of the Lamb?, p. 16: This one, along with many other great old time gospel songs, comes from my worn Baptist hymnal "Tabernacle Hymns." You can still find these for a dollar or two or three in used books stores.

Arkansas Traveller, p. 17: You probably sang this as "Bringing Home a Baby Bumble Bee" as a kid. My dream is to play "Arkansas Traveller" for Bill Clinton. It's probably been done.

As I Went Down in the Valley to Pray: See "Down in the Valley to Pray." (p. 65)

Aunt Dinah's Quilting Party, p. 18: Sometimes titled "Seeing Nellie Home."

Away in a Manger, p. 19: One of my favorites since childhood. Peaceful and reassuring. Makes a good bluegrass Christmas song.

B

Banks of the Ohio, p. 20: I love the melody to this grisly but popular murder ballad. There must be hundreds of versions of it with a variety of different lyrics. On some the chorus is, "Only say that you'll be mine/And in no other's arms entwine." In the version in this book the third verse makes little sense. Suddenly we're talking about the sea instead of the Ohio River. No matter, it's still a powerful song and a good example of the "folk process" where lyrics are repeated, misheard, changed, repeated, etc.

Beautiful Life, A, p. 21: Who could argue with the sentiments expressed in this song? It's usually performed in an intricate vocal quartet arrangement. Like several other similar songs, I've simplified the arrangement in this book for clarity and the sake of space. Listen to one of the original recordings to hear the vocal arrangement.

Beautiful Star of Bethlehem, p. 22: One of the prettiest Christmas songs and one often performed by bluegrass bands.

Bile Them Cabbage Down, p. 24: There are several songs with similar verses about one mammal in a tree, the other on the ground imploring him to "shake some 'simmins (persimmons) down." Wendy Whitford of the Goose Island Ramblers always sang "Shake them *cinnamons* down."

Black Eyed Susie, p. 25: Compare this song with "Blue Eyed Verdie" and some of the verses in "Pig in a Pen," (p. 199) among other songs with similar lyrics.

Blue Ridge Mountain Blues, p. 26: This song is unusual in that subsequent choruses have alternate lyrics. Some singers also fit in lyrics that include "Want to see my old dog Trey."

Bluebirds are Singing for Me, The, p. 27: Usually performed with a "call-and-response" chorus with repeated or echoed lines: "There's a bluebird singing" / *"There's a bluebird singing"* / "In the Blue Ridge Mountains" / *"In the Blue Ridge Mountains,"* etc.

Bound to Ride, p. 28: When I hear this song, I imagine a young bachelor riding the train, far away from home and sweetheart, eating saltine crackers because they're so cheap. I remember in my own youth when Kraft Macaroni and Cheese could be had for $.25 a package. Tough to prepare and eat in a moving vehicle though.

Bright Morning Stars, p. 29: Often performed a capella. This arrangement is shown with accompanying chords.

Bring Back to Me My Wandering Boy, p. 30: Bill Monroe's version of this song is called "Out in the Cold World."

Buffalo Gals, p. 31: Another one we sang as kids. Of course that was during "The Enlightenment" when most public schools had art and music classes.

Bully of the Town, The, p. 32: A great song then and now! We've still got bullies coming out of the woodwork and heroes ready to take 'em on. A G diminished chord can be substituted for the Gb chord.

Bury Me Beneath the Willow, p. 34: One of the first folk or old time songs players learn. A "must know."

C

C-H-I-C-K-E-N, p. 36: Originally a pop song from 1902.

Can't You Hear Me Callin'?, p. 38: Also the title of a comprehensive biography of Monroe, *Can't You Hear Me Callin': The Life of Bill Monroe, Father of Bluegrass* by Richard D. Smith (Warner Books). The chorus is often sung as "I loved you best," but "Bess" was Monroe's long time companion and bass player Bessie Lee Mauldin. You decide how to sing it.

Careless Love, p. 39: A standard in the folk, bluegrass, and jazz repertoires. I first heard the "in the family way" lyrics when I discovered them while doing research for this book. The song makes much more sense in this light.

Children Go Where I Send Thee, p. 40: Reminiscent of "The Twelve Days of Christmas" with the numbers and repetitions of characters. Listen to the CD to hear how the chorus grows upon repetition. Great bluegrass Christmas song.

Church in the Wildwood, The, p. 41: I remember my grandmother Nellie Bruce singing this to us grandkids. The chorus is often performed with multiple parts. My grandmother would crack us up singing the bass part, which was a chant below the melody on the chorus: "Oh come, come, come, come…"

Cindy, p. 42: Another I learned in grade school music class. I was pleasantly surprised to discover it in the bluegrass repertoire.

Cold Jordan: See "Jordan." (p. 132)

Columbus Stockade: See "Columbus Stockade Blues." (p. 43)

Columbus Stockade Blues, p. 43: This one makes a great hard country or rockabilly song.

Come All Ye Fair and Tender Ladies: See "Fair and Tender Ladies." (p. 70)

Coo Coo, The: See "Cuckoo, The" (p. 49)

Cotton-Eyed Joe, p. 44: A standard for fiddlers in all types of country and old time music.

Crawdad Song, The, p. 46: Makes a wonderful kids' bluegrass song.

Cripple Creek, p. 47: Most often played as an instrumental but when it is sung, the lyrics are usually only sung on part one. Also known as "Shootin' Creek."

Cuckoo, The, p. 49: I love the verses, melancholy mood, and varied verses of "The Cuckoo," alternately titled "The Coo Coo."

D

Daniel Prayed, p. 50: I'd heard "Daniel Prayed" for years but really got into it when I transcribed a Doc Watson recording with three vocal parts, lead, tenor, and bass, for my Doc Watson and Clarence Ashley book (MB97056) published by Mel Bay. It's a wonderful old time gospel trio arrangement. Check it out. The version in this book is simplified and written with just the lead voice. The Watson/Ashley book is packed with songs that have become "greatest hits" of old time and bluegrass.

Danny Boy, p. 52: Often played as an instrumental, this song's lyrics are haunting and beautiful. War takes its toll on all those involved in it but surely mothers bear the greatest burden.

Darling Corey, p. 53: Notice the close similarity in lyrics between "Darling Corey" and "Little Maggie." (p. 156) Many of the songs in *The Parking Lot Picker's Songbook*, and indeed in the greater traditional American music repertoire, share lines, whole verses, or themes with other songs. Credit the "folk process" of hearing songs, adding verses, swapping lyrics or melodies, mixing the whole thing up and serving it new as each individual singer adapts a song.

Darling Nellie Gray, p. 54: One of the most powerful songs I've ever heard. When Jim Nunally and I perform it, an older listener invariably comes up to tell us they'd learned the song in grade school, but had never heard verse four. "Darling Nellie Gray" has been a popular song for generations, for obvious reasons, published again and again, but that particular verse, the one that gave the lyric its power and the song its meaning, was censored. Many people mistakenly assume this is a Stephen Foster composition when in fact it was composed by B.R. Hanby. I hear a similarity in the movement and tone of the melody between this and Bob Wills' classic "Faded Love."

Darling Will You Ever Think of Me?, p. 56: I wanted to include a few of my own compositions in *The Parking Lot Picker's Songbook*. Here's one that I hope you'll enjoy.

Deep Elem Blues, p. 57: I first learned this when I played in Frank Wakefield's band in the late 1970s. It's a comical look at the bad part of town.

Diamonds in the Rough, p. 58: Worth learning for the metaphor alone. Performed in both 4/4 (as written) and 6/8 (on CD).

Didn't He Ramble: See "Oh, Didn't He Ramble." (p. 184)

Do Lord, p. 60: The C♯7 and F♯m chords in measure eleven are enclosed in parenthesis noting that they are optional. In the process of collecting the songs for this book, I consulted several hymnals. To my surprise I found that the harmonies in my old Baptist hymnal often included these somewhat "modern" sounding chords, the three dominant and the six minor.

Don't Let Your Deal Go Down, p. 61: This arrangement combines elements from different old time and more modern bluegrass sources. Compare these lyrics with "Storms are on the Ocean."

Don't You Hear Jerusalem Moan?, p. 63: A fun and funny song that's slightly "crooked" with an extra vocal phrase. And, could we ever have enough songs that make fun of preachers and authority in general? Here's another set of lyrics:

1) Well I went to church last Sunday morning/Don't you hear Jerusalem moan?/ Heard all them sinners just a moaning and a groaning/Don't you hear Jerusalem moan?

2) I'm gonna get down on my knees today,
Don't you (etc.)
Let Jesus wash my sins away, (etc.)

3) There's many souls lost here in sin,
Don't you go and talk to them, (etc.)

Down Among the Budded Roses, p. 64: One I learned from Wendy Whitford and the Goose Island Ramblers and a "true" song with a perfect image that says it all. As the others are coming into the bloom of life, the singer's own life seems over due to a lost love. Compare with "Wildwood Flower" (p. 275) and "Little Rosewood Casket." (p. 159)

Down in the Valley to Pray, p. 65: This song is performed as "Down to the River to Pray" in the film "O Brother Where Art Thou?"

Down in the Willow Garden, p. 66: I'm not sure what "burglar's wine" is, unless it's a mickey. Some people sing "burgundy wine."

Down the Road, p. 67: Country Gazette performed this with an added chorus: "Down the road, down the road, Got a little pretty girl down the road." Flatt & Scruggs left the chorus out. You can fill in your own name in the lyric "Old man (or woman) __________ (insert your name here)"

Down to the River to Pray: See "Down in the Valley to Pray." (p. 65)

E

East Virginia Blues, p. 69: This is a truly epic story and there are several versions of it that are sung in old time and bluegrass circles. Compare it with "Katy Dear." (p. 139) The lyrics to "East Virginia Blues" vary according to version. For example, in verse two, some versions have white lilies on her breast and in verse #4, the second and third lines are also sung "Where she lies on her bed of rest, For in her hand she holds a dagger," The order and number of verses varies widely.

End of My Journey: See "Let Me Rest at the End of My Journey." (p. 146)

F

Fair and Tender Ladies, p. 70: Lots of great songs came to bluegrass from the folk revival of the 1960s. These types of songs were often performed by the more "modern" bluegrass groups like the Osborne Brothers and the Country Gentlemen.

Fathers Have a Home Sweet Home, p. 71: Often performed with lead, tenor, and bass vocal parts.

Feast Here Tonight, p. 72: Sometimes called "Rabbit in a Log," this song is a classic. The definitive version was recorded by the Monroe Brothers.

Footprints in the Snow, p. 74: Bill Monroe's version sets the bluegrass standard for this song.

G

Girl I Left in Sunny Tennessee, The: See "Girl I Loved in Sunny Tennessee, The" (p. 76)

Girl I Loved in Sunny Tennessee, The, p. 76: The original source of this song is a sentimental pop song from 1899. It's often called "The Girl I *Left* in Sunny Tennessee."

Give Me Oil in My Lamp, p. 78: From the Baptist canon.

Give Me the Roses While I Live, p. 79: A popular theme in several different traditional and old time songs. It's as true today as it was a hundred or more years ago. Don't let someone slip away without them knowing of your love or admiration. It can happen in the blink of an eye.

Going Down This Road Feeling Bad, p. 80: Also known as "Lonesome Road Blues" and the basis of Earl Scruggs' instrumental of the same name. It's sometimes performed with an Em chord in measure twelve over the lyrics "Lord/And I."

Going Up Cripple Creek: See "Cripple Creek." (p. 47)

Going Up Home to Live in Green Pastures: See "Green Pastures." (p. 95)

Grandfather's Clock, p. 82: Long a hit with banjo pickers and guitar fingerpickers, this one also makes a wonderful vocal with its eerie story.

Green Pastures, p. 85: Another Stanley standard with a beautiful, peaceful view of the great beyond.

Groundhog, p. 86: Red Allen repeats the word "groundhog" twice more as a kind of chorus.

H

Hallelujah! I'm Ready, p. 87: A few of the songs in *The Parking Lot Picker's Songbook* are written with basic two part vocal arrangements. In the case of this "call and response" duet, I've omitted the tablature stems to make it easier to read. You can hear the arrangement on the accompanying CD.

Hand Me Down My Walking Cane, p. 88: Long a favorite among folkies, Norman Blake does a great old time version of this song.

Handsome Molly, p. 89: Every generation updates traditional music. My favorite update of "Handsome Molly" is a kind of Latin-Reggae romp by the Extended Playboys. Try to find that on your iTunes! In one of Doc Watson's earlier versions of "Handsome Molly" he sings "I wish I was in London/or some other *depot* town."

Hard Times, Come Again No More, p. 90: This is still a very popular song among folk singers, especially at group sings.

He Was a Friend of Mine, p. 92: I first heard a version of this on a Byrds' LP where it was rewritten about John F. Kennedy's assassination. Since that time in the mid-1960s, I've heard it performed in several folk contexts including bluegrass and traditional blues.

He Will Set Your Fields on Fire, p. 94: Talk about your fire and brimstone! This one is usually performed with an intricate, multi-voice arrangement.

High on a Mountain, p. 96: One incredible song by Ola Belle Reed. The image, melody, modal chord movement, story, and tone of it all make it a classic and a "must-know" song.

Highway of Sorrow, p. 97: Bill Monroe had a reputation as a gruff, tough and stubborn curmudgeon. When I interviewed him in the early 1980s, I found this to not be the case, exactly. While reserved and private, he also showed a great sense of humor and a playful streak. He was expansive on many subjects from his own legacy to his thoughts about rock and jazz as well as his views on life. It's amazing to me that he revealed himself as much as he did in compositions like "Highway of Sorrow," "It's Mighty Dark to Travel," (p. 122) and "Can't You Hear Me Calling." (p. 38) He was truly a great artist.

Hills of Roane County, p. 98: For me, a cryptic verse like: "Sweet Martha was grave but Corey was better/There's better and worse, although you can see," kicks this song into greatness. It's mysterious, beautiful, unknowable.

His Eye is on the Sparrow, p. 100: From "Tabernacle Hymns." Singer and actress Ethel Waters sang "His Eye is on the Sparrow" beautifully and soulfully as part of the Billy Graham Crusades in the 1950s and 1960s.

Hold Fast to the Right, p. 101: In this case I believe "right" refers to the "correct way" as opposed to any far-flung node in the political spectrum.

Hold to God's Unchanging Hand, p. 102: Soothing words for modern life.

Home Sweet Home, p. 103: This song has been a hit for well over a hundred years. Jim Nunally and I play it quite often and audiences still love it.

Hop High Ladies, p. 106: Also know as "Mrs. McCleod's Reel."

Hot Corn, Cold Corn, p. 108: Wonderful goofy song that seems to have something to do with John Barleycorn.

How Can You Treat Me So?, p. 109: I had Bill Monroe's voice in mind as I wrote this one.

I

I am a Man of Constant Sorrow: See "Man of Constant Sorrow." (p. 167)

I Know You Rider, p. 111: Originally a blues, this one has been adapted by rock groups and "modern" bluegrass bands, most notably The Seldom Scene.

I Ride an Old Paint: See "Old Paint." (p. 192)

I Shall Not Be Moved, p. 113: From the gospel repertoire and popular in old time gospel, jazz, bluegrass, and folk circles. It was an important and symbolic marching song during the civil rights movement of the 1950s and 1960s.

I Wonder How the Old Folks Are at Home, p. 114: Good old pop song from 1909. Popularized in bluegrass by Mac Wiseman.

I'll Be All Smiles Tonight, p. 116: I first heard this from Wendy Whitford of the Goose Island Ramblers. It's a wonderful take on the woman's point of view of a breakup. It's sung by both men and women. See also "Little Rosewood Casket" (p. 159) and "Wildwood Flower." (p. 275)

I'll Fly Away, p. 118: Everybody's favorite gospel/bluegrass song.

I'm Ready: See "Hallelujah! I'm Ready." (p. 87)

I'm Sitting on Top of the World: See "Sitting on Top of the World." (p. 228)

I'm Standing in the Need of Prayer: See "Standing in the Need of Prayer." (p. 231)

In the Garden, p. 120: From "Tabernacle Hymns."

In the Pines, p. 121: Another great bluesy standard of bluegrass and old time music.

It's Mighty Dark to Travel, p. 122: Bill Monroe overheard the phrase "it's mighty dark to travel" in a barber shop as someone mentioned that they had a long way to travel in the dark of night. Monroe turned the phrase into a bluegrass standard.

J

Jesse James, p. 124: If you're gonna be an outlaw, you'd better have somebody write a sympathetic folk song about you. This song is all about primitive attempts at "spin." Woody Guthrie wrote a similar but politically charged song about "Pretty Boy Floyd."

Jimmie Brown, the Newsboy, p. 126: A sentimental parlor tune from the late 1800s. Like much of their repertoire, the Carter Family adapted it to fit their style in the late 1920s. Flatt & Scruggs version from the early 1950s brought this great song into the bluegrass repertoire.

John Hardy, p. 128: See "Jesse James" (p. 142) above. Hardy didn't get quite the treatment in song that Jesse did. I say, pay the extra few bucks, get a good songwriter.

John Henry, p. 130: There must be over a hundred different versions of "John Henry." It's been so popular over the years because it so dramatically tells the story of automation and human against machine.

Jordan, p. 132: The chorus to "Jordan" is often performed with the bass voice taking the lead on the first clause of each phrase of the chorus. Bass solo: "Now look at that," ensemble joins in "cold Jordan," etc.

Just a Closer Walk with Thee, p. 134: This one is popular in many musical genres from gospel and blues to dixieland and bluegrass.

Just as I Am, p. 135: You mature youngsters may remember this theme from the televised Billy Graham crusades of the 1950s and beyond. Willie Nelson recorded a beautiful instrumental version for his *Red Headed Stranger* LP.

Just Over in the Gloryland, p. 136: Another song whose popularity spans many musical genres from gospel and blues to dixieland and bluegrass.

K

Katy Dear, p. 139: Compare the lyrics of this "Romeo and Juliet"-type tale with "East Virginia Blues" (p. 69) and "Silver Dagger."

Keep on the Sunnyside, p. 140: An old song the Carter Family adopted as their theme song. What better advice for life?

Knoxville Girl, p. 142: A murder ballad similar to "Banks of the Ohio" (p. 20) but perhaps even more gory and disturbing.

L

Late Last Night, p. 144: Also known as "Way Down Town," I first heard this from Doc Watson on the *Will the Circle be Unbroken* project from the early 1970s. That historic three LP set introduced traditional music and traditional and bluegrass musicians to the rock-oriented youth culture of the era.

Leave it There, p. 145: I heard this on a 1920s recording by Washington Phillips and it really grabbed me. Not only is it filled with great sentiment, I realized I recognized it from somewhere. Turns out it was from the old Baptist hymnal "Tabernacle Hymns."

Let Me Rest at the End of My Journey, p. 146: One of many cowboy-themed songs that ended up in the bluegrass repertoire.

Letter Edged in Black, The, p. 147: When I was a callow youth learning this repertoire from the older generation, songs like "The Letter Edged in Black" struck me as overly sentimental and dramatic. I was more drawn to the hot and fast material. I guess it was because I hadn't yet experienced the loss of a parent. Now, as I've gotten older and lived more of life, I've come to love these songs and appreciate their eloquence in dealing with the life and death issues that we all face.

Life is Like a Mountain Railway: See "Life's Railway to Heaven." (p. 148)
Life's Railway to Heaven, p. 148: Even if you're not religious, this song is an apt description of the journey of life.
Li'l Liza Jane, p. 150: Another folk song they taught us in grade school.
Little Annie, p. 151: I first heard this great song from Vern Williams, California's most important contribution to old time bluegrass. "Little Annie" marks the beginning of the massive "Little" section, ironically the largest section in this book, which spans the old time musical horizon from "Annie" to "Willie." (One could argue that "Li'L Liza Jane" belongs here as well, but it's in the "Li'l" section, not the "Little.") For size, the "Old" section is a close rival.
Little Bessie, p. 152: As I mentioned above in "The Letter Edged in Black," my perception of these songs has changed with my age. Being the father of a beautiful twenty-one year old daughter (as of 2005), I find it impossible to sing "Little Bessie" without breaking down in tears.
Little Birdie, p. 154: This arrangement is simplified from the way it's typically performed. Singers usually stretch out syllables like the first "birdie..." an extra measure or longer. The band has to pay attention to the singer!
Little Georgia Rose: See "My Little Georgia Rose." (p. 178)
Little Maggie, p. 156: As with "Little Birdie," (p. 154) singers often stretch lyrics beyond their written time values.
Little Old Log Cabin in the Lane, p. 158: If you can find it, listen to Fiddlin' John Carson's version. It was one of the first "country" or "hillbilly" recordings made in the early 1920s. It's just him singing, with his fiddle, and it's haunting.
Little Rosewood Casket, p. 159: Not about what you might think it's about. Compare with "I'll Be All Smiles Tonight" (p. 116) and "Wildwood Flower." (p. 275)
Little Sadie, p. 160: Both this and "Little Willie" (p. 161) are epic story songs where a lot goes on. Both have similarities to "Banks of the Ohio," (p. 20) "Knoxville Girl," (p. 142) and "Pretty Polly." (p. 202) May not be suitable for younger listeners.
Little Willie, p. 161: A brutal and graphic song but a true representation of real events.
Lonesome Reuben: See "Reuben's Train." (p. 214)
Lonesome Road Blues: See "Going Down This Road Feeling Bad." (p. 80)
Long Journey Home, p. 163: Check out the Monroe Brothers definitive version.
Lord, I'm Coming Home, p. 164: After hearing this for years by artists like the Stanley Brothers and loving it, I discovered "Lord, I'm Coming Home" in one of my worn old hymnals.

M

Mama Don't Allow, p. 166: A well-known and loved song that pops up in a variety of musical styles including jazz and country. It's a proven crowd pleaser.
Man of Constant Sorrow, p. 167: The most famous version of this song is from the film "O Brother, Where Art Thou?" sung by the mythical Soggy Bottom Boys. Their version is based on one recorded by the Stanley Brothers which features a repeat of each verse's last line as in "I have no friends to help me now/He has no friends to help him now."
McKinley: See "White House Blues." (p. 269)
Methodist Pie, p. 170: Another tongue-in-cheek look at religion.
Midnight on the Stormy Deep, p. 172: The classic recording of this song is by Bill Monroe in the mid-1960s. Peter Rowan sings it in duet with Monroe.
Milwaukee Blues, p. 173: If you don't know the music of Charlie Poole, run to the store right now and buy one of the new CD box sets. He's one of the true pioneers of old time and bluegrass music with a repertoire and style that influenced all that came after him. Charlie Poole made great, entertaining music. In the last verse, "Santa Fe" rhymes with "be."
Molly and Tenbrooks, p. 174: One of the all-time hits of bluegrass based on much earlier sources.
More Pretty Girls Than One: See "There's More Pretty Girls Than One." (p. 238)
Mrs. McCleod's Reel: See "Hop High Ladies." (p. 106)
My Home's Across the Blue Ridge Mountains, p. 176: Sometimes sung as "My Home's Across the Smoky Mountains."
My Little Georgia Rose, p. 178: The true story behind this Bill Monroe composition can be found in his biography "*Can't You Hear Me Callin': The Life of Bill Monroe, Father of Bluegrass* by Richard D. Smith (Warner Books).
My Walking Cane: See "Hand Me Down My Walking Cane." (p. 88)
My Wandering Boy: See "Bring Back to Me My Wandering Boy." (p. 30)

N

Nellie Gray: See "Darling Nellie Gray." (p. 54)
New River Train, p. 180: Another classic from the Monroe Brothers.
Nine Pound Hammer, p. 181: You gotta learn this one! It's one of the ten or twenty songs played by ALL Parking Lot Pickers.
Nobody's Business, p. 182: There are a variety of versions of this basic song in bluegrass, old time, blues, and jazz. It may be even more well-known in blues than in bluegrass. As far as I know, the Stanley Brothers brought it into the bluegrass lexicon.

O

Oh Death, p. 183: Another great song featured in the film "O Brother, Where Art Thou?" It's usually sung unaccompanied, with no instrumental backup, in a *rubato* (loose, drawn out rhythm) style. It's written here with backup chords, so you can hear the tonality, and in standard rhythm. The B7s in parenthesis are optional. Be sure to listen to Ralph Stanley's recording.
Oh! Didn't He Ramble, p. 184: Another old pop song appropriated by Charlie Poole. Also popular with Dixieland jazz bands.
Old Dan Tucker, p. 186: One they taught us in grade school.
Old Joe Clark, p. 190: Check out the less than proper lyrics. Good taste is timeless! Fiddlers usually play this in the key of A.

Old Man at the Mill, p. 191: Also known as "Same Old Man," I first heard this old time song in a bluegrass context by the Dillards. The flatted seven chord, in this case an F natural, gives the song it's modal flavor.

Old Paint, p. 192: It always gets back to just a cowboy and his horse. See also "Let Me Rest at the End of My Journey." (p. 146)

Old Rugged Cross, The, p. 193: The A diminished chord in measure one is a little unusual in old time and bluegrass music. Though it comes straight out of the hymnal, in practice it's often played as an Ab chord.

On and On, p. 195: Another very popular Monroe-penned classic of life on the road without your sweetheart.

Out in the Cold World: See "Bring Back to Me My Wandering Boy." (p. 30)

Over the Hills to the Poorhouse, p. 196: A pre-Social Security song that may have renewed resonance in the next few years, especially for baby boomer bluegrass musicians. It's a true song, if slightly dramatic.

P

Pass Me Not, p. 197: Beautiful melody, comforting lyrics.

Pig in a Pen, p. 199: Different versions of this song feature different combinations of the same basic lyrics. And you'll find verses from "Pig in a Pen" in a variety of other songs.

Poor Ellen Smith, p. 200: Sometimes this song is performed with the one line chorus "Nobody knows how I loved Ellen, nobody knows."

Poor Nellie Gray: See "Darling Nellie Gray." (p. 54)

Poor Wayfaring Stranger: See "Wayfaring Stranger." (p. 225)

Precious Memories, p. 201: I love the dreamy imagery and moving poetry of this song. It's often mistaken for a gospel song though there's nothing overtly religious about it.

Pretty Polly, p. 202: Another murder ballad done so well by Ralph Stanley.

Put My Little Shoes Away, p. 204: The lyric "Won't he look so nice and cunning" always confused me. Webster's Dictionary of 1913 explains, "Pretty or pleasing; as, a cunning little boy."

R

Rabbit in a Log: See "Feast Here Tonight." (p. 72)

Railroad Bill, p. 206: I learned this one from my brother-in-law Rick March when he was teaching me to fingerpick.

Rain and Snow, p. 207: This song has a kind of nebulous tonal center rocking between the Am and the D chord. That gives it a modal feel and the unresolved lyrics add to the song's sense of mystery.

Rank Strangers to Me, p. 208: One of the Stanley Brothers all-time hits that's become a bluegrass standard. The chorus is typically performed in a "call and response" format.

Red Rocking Chair, p. 210: Slightly unusual in that it has an Em or six minor chord in it.

Red Wing, p. 212: One of the most widely known tunes in American music. It's a pop song from the early 1900s, part of a group of songs that idealized native Americans. Because of its popularity, the melody to "Red Wing" has been adapted again and again to other sets of lyrics. An anonymous writer used it as the basis for "Charlie Chaplin," a children's old time song about the famous tramp, and Woody Guthrie used it for his labor song "Union Maid." The main theme of "Red Wing" is based on Schumann's "The Happy Farmer" from 1849.

Reuben's Train, p. 214: This one shows up with many alternate titles including "Train 45," "Lonesome Reuben," and just plain old "Reuben."

Roll in My Sweet Baby's Arms, p. 216: You gotta know this one if you're going to play bluegrass. Especially for bluegrass bakers.

Roll on Buddy, p. 217: Another great one from the Monroe Brothers song bag. By the way, did you get one of the Monroe Brothers CD box sets yet?

Roving Gambler, p. 218: Another from the folk bag that's slipped into the bluegrass repertoire. Listen to the Country Gentlemen's version.

S

Sally Goodin, p. 221: Probably best known as a fiddle tune, "Sally Goodin" also has some funny lyrics, which are usually sung over the first part. The second part is played instrumentally.

Same Old Man: See "Old Man at the Mill." (p. 191)

Seeing Nellie Home: See "Aunt Dinah's Quilting Party." (p.18)

Shady Grove, Bluegrass style, p. 222: "Shady Grove" is performed with a variety of arrangements and lyrics. Here's a version often played by bluegrass bands. An old time version follows. Lyrics are shared between the two and you'll notice one verse that's also in "Pig in a Pen." (p.199)

Shady Grove, Old Time style, p. 223: See "Shady Grove, Bluegrass style." (p. 222)

Shall We Gather at the River, p. 224: Learned in church from "Tabernacle Hymns."

She's My Little Georgia Rose: See "My Little Georgia Rose." (p. 178)

Short Life of Trouble, A, p. 225: Kind of a depressed look at life brought on by a failed love. The theme of verse six is common in traditional music: "You broke my heart, it killed me, plant some flowers on my grave so everybody'll know what a rat you are." Like that would happen!

Shortening Bread, p. 226: A very popular traditional song that fits well into the old time/bluegrass format.

Silver Threads Among the Gold, p. 227: A sentimental old parlor song dating from the late 1800s if not earlier. I've collected several different sheet music versions of the song. Similar to "When You and I Were Young, Maggie," (p. 266) "Silver Threads" has beautiful, moving, and poetic lyrics about true love that seem all the more meaningful as I age.

Sitting on Top of the World, p. 228: From the blues repertoire.

Softly and Tenderly, p. 229: This one reminds me a bit of "Just as I Am," (p. 135) "Angel Band," (p. 10) and some of the other songs in this collection that offer a reassuring view of the inevitable.

Somebody Touched Me, p. 230: A great old gospel rouser.

Standing in the Need of Prayer, p. 231: Ditto "Somebody Touched Me." (p. 230)

Sugar Hill, p. 232: I learned this from the Goose Island Ramblers. Guitarist Wendy Whitford usually sang, "Shake them cinnamons down" instead of "Shake them 'simmons down."

Swing Low, Sweet Chariot, p. 235: Another popular song that appears in many different genres from gospel to blues to country.

T

Take Me Home: See "Sweet Sunny South." (p. 234)

Take This Hammer, p. 236: Similar in theme to "Nine Pound Hammer" (p. 181) and other mining songs, "Take This Hammer" has the added edge of forced labor and confinement. I love the verse: "If he asks you was I running/Tell him I's flying."

Take Your Burden to the Lord and Leave it There: See "Leave it There." (p. 145)

Talk About Sufferin', p. 237: This is another song that's typically performed a capella. It's written here with accompaniment chords and fermatas.

Tenbrooks and Molly: See "Molly and Tenbrooks." (p. 174)

That's the Way to Spell Chicken: See "C-H-I-C-K-E-N." (p. 36)

There's More Pretty Girls Than One, p. 238: This song is also performed in 4/4. Check out Tony Rice and Ricky Skaggs' version on "Skaggs and Rice," one of the most beautiful duo recordings ever set to wax.

They Gotta Quit Kicking My Dawg Around, p. 240: Another from the Goose Island Ramblers and a pop song from the early 1900s. I've collected the original sheet music, or at least most of it. The cover of my copy is missing.

This Little Light of Mine, p. 242: From Sunday school.

This Train, p. 243: Another one learned in grade school.

This World is Not My Home, p. 244: *The Parking Lot Picker's Songbook* includes a lot of songs about death. I guess that's because, like love, it's a universally mysterious subject we all have difficulty dealing with. "This World is Not My Home" speaks to the fact that we're not here for a very long time; we're only passing through.

Train, Train, Train, p. 246: A new song by Dix Bruce. Never recorded by anybody. You could be the first!

Train 45: See "Reuben's Train."

Train That Carried My Girl From Town, The, p. 248: I suppose the singer's hate of the train, its engineer and fireman, is some what misplaced, but that's what makes the song interesting.

'Twas Midnight on the Stormy Deep: See "Midnight on the Stormy Deep." (p. 172)

Two Dollar Bill: See "Long Journey Home." (p. 163)

U

Unclouded Day, The, p. 249: This song would not be near as interesting if it had been titled "The Clear Day."

W

Wabash Cannonball, p. 250: This is one of the true classics of American folk music. There must be hundreds of variations. Some singers use the lyrics "rumor and roar" in the chorus. One of my favorite songs loosely based on "Wabash Cannonball" is Chuck Berry's "Promised Land."

Walk in Jerusalem Just Like John, p. 252: You'll notice the similarity of the last verse to one in "Swing Low, Sweet Chariot." (p. 235)

Walking in My Sleep, p. 254: "Walking in My Sleep" is a great old time song with wonderfully entertaining lyrics like verse one: "If you see that gal of mine tell her if you please/'Fore she goes to make my bread to roll up her dirty sleeves." That's art, man!

Way Downtown: See "Late Last Night." (p. 144)

Wayfaring Stranger, The, p. 255: A beautiful standard played many different ways in a variety of genres.

What a Friend We Have in Jesus, p. 257: Learned in Sunday school from "Tabernacle Hymns."

When I Die, p. 258: Here's one I wrote. I was walking through the woods one day and suddenly felt the presence of my dear departed grandmother, the one who used to sing "The Church in the Wildwood" (p. 41) to me. The song puts words to my thoughts about the incident.

When I Lay My Burden Down, p. 259: Note the similarity of this melody to that of "Will the Circle Be Unbroken." (p. 276)

When My Race is Run, p. 260: Another of mine. I'll show her! Wait 'til I'll die!

When Springtime Comes Again: See "Little Annie." (p. 151)

When the Roll is Called Up Yonder, p. 261: One more from the old Baptist hymnal.

When the Saints Go Marching In, p. 262: You're probably most familiar with this as a New Orleans jazz tune.

When the Work's All Done This Fall, p. 264: A cowboy song that's worked its way into the old time and bluegrass repertoire.

When You And I Were Young Maggie, p. 266: Another moving take on love and aging similar to "Silver Threads Among the Gold" (p. 227) and "Sweet Sunny South." (p. 234)

Where the Soul Never Dies, p. 267: I just had to write out both parts to this great duet. On the verses, the tenor sings the same lyrics as the lead adding "of man" into the phrase "Where the soul never dies." On the chorus the voices are in counterpoint to one another. You can hear it on the CD. I split the TAB from the music so each would fit on one page.

Whitehouse Blues, p. 269: Doctors are better now, especially with their bedside manner. The last verse made the rounds in the late 1960s.

Who Broke the Lock?, p. 270: Learned from Wendy Whitford of the Goose Island Ramblers.

Who Will Sing for Me?, p. 272: Another ponderous song about death.

Wild Bill Jones, p. 274: Another good "bully" song.

Wildwood Flower, p. 275: This song, probably the best known of all guitar melodies, has wonderful and poetic lyrics which so beautifully express the feelings of the composer. Compare the sentiments to "I'll Be all Smiles Tonight," (p. 116) and "Little Rosewood Casket." (p. 159) The Carter Family sings lyrics that are a bit different here and there. They may have "mis-heard" the names of some of the flowers mentioned.

Will the Circle Be Unbroken?, p. 276: One of the greatest hits of old time and bluegrass music.

Willie My Darling, p. 278: Beautiful song with bang-up, unexpected tear-jerker-ending. A classic of the "anti-flirting" genre.

Working on a Building: See "I'm Working on a Building." (p. 119)

Worried Man Blues, p. 279: You may have heard the hit version of this in the early 1960s. It goes back much further than that, probably to slavery times.

Wreck of the Old 97, The, p. 280: You will need to know several train wreck songs if you intend to play bluegrass. Here's a good one that also happens to be quite popular.

Y

You're a Flower Blooming in the Wildwood, p. 281: Lost love and death. A perfect summation of the main themes of this collection of songs. Not a word about taxes, politics, gas prices, or cell phones. If you ask me, the writers of all these songs knew what was important.

You're Drifting Too Far From the Shore: See "Drifting Too Far From the Shore." (p. 68)

You've Got to Walk That Lonesome Valley: See "Lonesome Valley." (p. 162)

Index by Artist

Polly, p. 202; Sailor on the Deep Blue Sea, p. 220; Sally Goodin, p. 221; This World is Not My Home, p. 244; Worried Man Blues, p. 279; The Wreck of the Old 97, p. 280

New Tradition, The

Old Rugged Cross, p. 193

Nitty Gritty Dirt Band

Diamonds in the Rough, p. 58; Don't You Hear Jerusalem Moan, p. 63; Keep on the Sunnyside, p. 140; Late Last Night, p. 144; Life's Railway to Heaven, p. 148; Nine Pound Hammer, p. 181; Sitting on Top of the World, p. 228; Wabash Cannonball, p. 250; Will the Circle Be Unbroken, p. 276

Nunally, Jim & Bruce, Dix

Banks of the Ohio, p. 20; The Bluebirds are Singing for Me, p. 27; Crawdad Song, p. 46; Darling Nellie Gray, p. 54; Darling Will You Ever Think of Me?, p. 56; Home Sweet Home, p. 103; How Can You Treat Me So?, p. 109; Railroad Bill, p. 206; Sitting on Top of the World, p. 228; When I Die, p. 258; When My Race is Run, p. 260; Wildwood Flower, p. 275

O'Brien, Tim

Little Sadie, p. 160; Sweet Sunny South, p. 234

"O Brother Where Art Thou?" Soundtrack

I'll Fly Away, p. 118; Man of Constant Sorrow, p. 167; Oh Death, p. 183

Old & In the Way

Angel Band, p. 10; Drifting Too Far From the Shore, p. 68; On and On, p. 195; Pig in a Pen, p. 199

Osborne Bros.

Amazing Grace, p. 9; Aunt Dinah's Quilting Party, p. 18; The Cuckoo, p. 49; Down in the Willow Garden, p. 66; Fair and Tender Ladies, p. 70; Hand Me Down My Walking Cane, p. 88; I'll Fly Away, p. 118; I Wonder How the Old Folks Are at Home, p. 114; In the Pines, p. 121; Jesse James, p. 124; Keep on the Sunnyside, p. 140; Knoxville Girl, p. 142; Little Rosewood Casket, p. 159; Little Willie, p. 161; Molly and Tenbrooks, p. 174; Rank Strangers to Me, p. 208; Red Wing, p. 212; Rocky Top, p. 215; Take This Hammer, p. 236; The Unclouded Day, p. 249; Wabash Cannonball, p. 250; What a Friend We Have in Jesus, p. 257; Worried Man Blues, p. 279

Paisley, Bob

Down Among the Budded Roses, p. 64

Parton, Dolly

Hold Fast to the Right, p. 101; Sweet By and By, p. 233; The Wayfaring Stranger, p. 255; What a Friend We Have in Jesus, p. 257

Poole, Charlie

Don't Let Your Deal Go Down, p. 61; Girl I Left in Sunny Tennessee, p. 76; Milwaukee Blues, p. 173; Oh! Didn't He Ramble, p. 184; Sweet Sunny South, p. 234

Poor Richard's Almanac

John Hardy, p. 128

Red Clay Ramblers

Milwaukee Blues, p. 173

Reed, Ola Belle

High on a Mountain, p. 96

Reischman, John & the Jaybirds

Katy Dear, p. 139

Reno, Don

Nobody's Business, p. 182

Reno & Harrell

Keep on the Sunnyside, p. 140; Poor Ellen Smith, p. 200; Red Rocking Chair, p. 210; Whitehouse Blues, p. 269; Worried Man Blues, p. 279

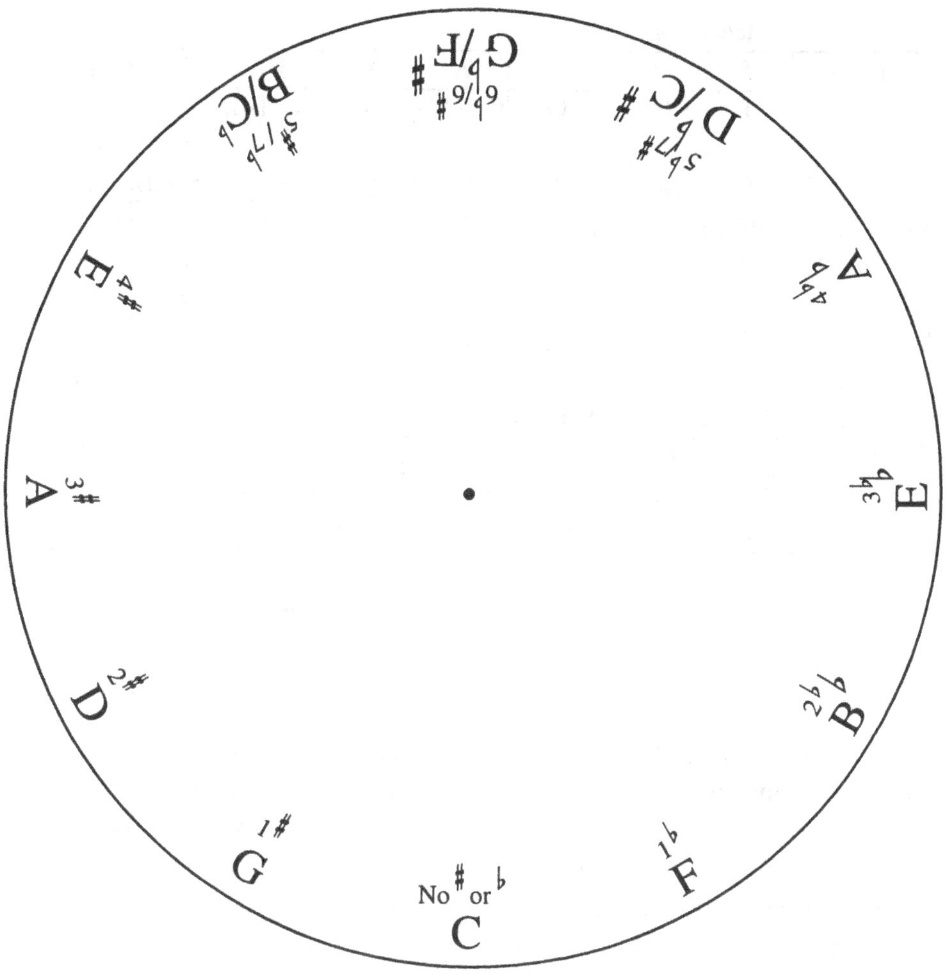

MUSIX TRANSPOSER WHEEL

Copy this page onto card stock or download and print it from the "Downloads" section of www.musixnow.com. Carefully cut out both wheels. Punch a small hole at the dot in the middle of each. Attach the smaller wheel to the larger wheel with a paper fastener making sure both wheels can spin independently. To transpose, follow directions on inner wheel.

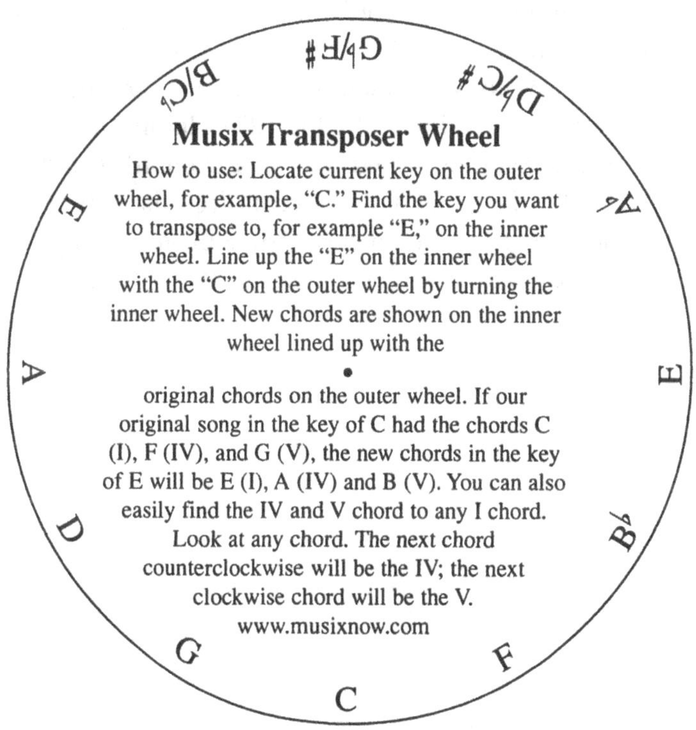

Capo Chart

Chord held

Actual Sound of Chord

Capo on Fret #

	1	2	3	4	5	6	7	8	9	10	11	12
C	C#/Db	D	D#/Eb	E	F	F#/Gb	G	G#/Ab	A	A#/Bb	B	C
C#/Db	D	D#/Eb	E	F	F#/Gb	G	G#/Ab	A	A#/Bb	B	C	C#/Db
D	D#/Eb	E	F	F#/Gb	G	G#/Ab	A	A#/Bb	B	C	C#/Db	D
D#/Eb	E	F	F#/Gb	G	G#/Ab	A	A#/Bb	B	C	C#/Db	D	D#/Eb
E	F	F#/Gb	G	G#/Ab	A	A#/Bb	B	C	C#/Db	D	D#/Eb	E
F	F#/Gb	G	G#/Ab	A	A#/Bb	B	C	C#/Db	D	D#/Eb	E	F
F#/Gb	G	G#/Ab	A	A#/Bb	B	C	C#/Db	D	D#/Eb	E	F	F#/Gb
G	G#/Ab	A	A#/Bb	B	C	C#/Db	D	D#/Eb	E	F	F#/Gb	G
G#/Ab	A	A#/Bb	B	C	C#/Db	D	D#/Eb	E	F	F#/Gb	G	G#/Ab
A	A#/Bb	B	C	C#/Db	D	D#/Eb	E	F	F#/Gb	G	G#/Ab	A
A#/Bb	B	C	C#/Db	D	D#/Eb	E	F	F#/Gb	G	G#/Ab	A	A#/Bb
B	C	C#/Db	D	D#/Eb	E	F	F#/Gb	G	G#/Ab	A	A#/Bb	B

You can use this Capo Chart to determine what the actual sound of a capoed chord will be. For example, let's say you've moved your capo around and find that you can sing a song most comfortably when you play an A chord capoed at the fifth fret. Since you're capoed, what you're playing no longer sounds like an A. What chord are you really playing? Another guitarist could simply place his or her capo at the fifth fret and copy your chords but anyone else playing a non-capoed instrument, say a mandolin or bass, would need more specific information. You can find that information in the Capo Chart.

Look in the chart above and find the A chord in the first column on the left. Now follow over to the right to the column labeled "5." This will tell you that an A chord capoed at the fifth fret will have the actual sound of a D chord. As a rule of thumb, if the song begins, and more importantly ends, on the D chord, you're most likely in the key of D. Anyone playing along with you will have to play in the same actual key of D.

You can also use the Capo Chart to determine other chord/capo combinations for the same key. Let's look at the example above. You've chosen to play an A chord capoed at the fifth fret with an actual sound of a D chord, likely in the key of D. How else could you capo and what chords could you play and still be in the key of D? Start by looking under the different capo position columns (1, 2, 3, etc.) to find the D. Moving from the left, the first we find is under the "2" column, "C" row. That means that if we play a C chord capoed at the second fret, the resulting sound will be a D chord. Another combination is under the "7" column, "G" row. If we play a G chord capoed at the seventh fret, the actual sound will be a D. Using these different chord/capo combinations can give you an great range of interesting timbres on the guitar. When playing with more than one guitarist, try each capoing at a different position.

Audio Track Listing

Audio #1

1. All the Good Times :41
2. Amazing Grace :35
3. Angel Band :59
4. Angelina Baker :37
5. Angels Rock Me to Sleep :44
6. Are you From Dixie? 1:04
7. Are You Washed in the Blood of the Lamb? :38
8. Arkansas Traveller :25
9. Aunt Dinah's Quilting Party :37
10. Away in a Manger :34
11. Banks of the Ohio :56
12. Beautiful Life, A :47
13. Beautiful Star of Bethlehem 1:17
14. Bile Them Cabbage Down
    Black Eyed Susie medley :39
15. Blue Ridge Mountain Blues :36
16. Bluebirds are Singing for Me :43
17. Bound to Ride :19
18. Bright Morning Stars :28
19. Bring Back My Wandering Boy :43
20. Buffalo Gals :23
21. Bully of the Town :36
22. Bury Me Beneath the Willow :50
23. C-H-I-C-K-E-N :40
24. Can't You Hear Me Callin'? :41
25. Careless Love :42
26. Children Go Where I Send Thee :50
27. Church in the Wildwood :42
28. Cindy :19
29. Columbus Stockade Blues :43
30. Cotton-Eyed Joe :22
31. Cowboy Jack :26
32. Crawdad Song, The :23
33. Cripple Creek :24
34. Crying Holy :37
35. Cuckoo, The :25
36. Daniel Prayed :51
37. Danny Boy 1:33
38. Darling Cory – Darling Nellie Gray 1:40
39. Darling Will You Ever Think of Me :43
40. Deep Elem Blues :27
41. Diamonds in the Rough :39
42. Do Lord :36
43. Don't Let Your Deal Go Down :35
44. Don't This Road Look Rough and Rocky? 1:02
45. Don't You Hear Jerusalem Moan? :29
46. Down Among the Budded Roses :53
47. Down in the Valley to Pray :33
48. Down in the Willow Garden :41
49. Down the Road :17
50. Drifting too Far from the Shore :51
51. East Virginia Blues :38
52. Fair and Tender Ladies :38
53. Fathers Have a Home Sweet Home :46
54. Feast Here Tonight :32
55. Foggy Mountain Top :24
56. Footprints in the Snow :44
57. Girl I Loved in Sunny Tennessee, The
    Give Me Oil in My Lamp medley 1:49
58. Give Me the Roses While I Live :38
59. Going Down this Road Feeling Bad
    Grandfather's Clock 1:24
60. Great Speckled Bird :36
61. Green Pastures :59
62. Groundhog :17
63. Hallelujah! I'm Ready :37
64. Hand Me Down My Walking Cane
    Handsome Molly :52
65. Hard Times Come Again No More
    Have Thine Own Way, Lord medley 1:40
66. He was a Friend of Mine :37
67. He Will Set Your Fields On Fire 1:05
68. High on a Mountain 1:00
69. Highway of Sorrow :34
70. Hills of Roane County :37
71. His Eye is on the Sparrow 1:22
72. Hold Fast to The Right :42
73. Hold to God's Unchanging Hand :56
74. Home Sweet Home :57
75. Honey in the Rock :26
76. Hop High Ladies :25
77. Hot Corn, Cold Corn :30
78. How Can You Treat Me So? :50
79. I Ain't Gonna Work Tomorrow :19
80. I Know You Rider :43
81. I Never Will Marry
    I Shall Not Be Moved medley 1:13
82. I Wonder How the Old Folks are at Home :41
83. I'll Be all Smiles Tonight 1:01
84. I'll Fly Away :36
85. I'm Working on a Building :40
86. In the Garden :55
87. In the Pines :53
88. It's Mighty Dark to Travel – Jesse James medley 1:18
89. Jimmie Brown, the Newsboy :24
90. John Hardy :24
91. John Henry :26
92. Jordan 1:00
93. Just a Closer Walk With Thee :42
94. Just as I Am :30
95. Just Over in the Gloryland – Katy Cline medley 1:03
96. Katy Daley :36
97. Katy Dear :27
98. Keep on the Sunny Side – Knoxville Girl medley 1:23

Audio #2

1. Late Last Night :38
2. Leave it There :51
3. Let Me Rest at the End of My Journey :47
4. Letter Edged in Black :28
5. Life's Railway to Heaven 1:00
6. Li'l Liza Jane :22
7. Little Annie :41
8. Little Bessie :25
9. Little Birdie :22
10. Little Maggie
    Little Old Log Cabin in the Lane medley 1:03
11. Little Rosewood Casket :29
12. Little Sadie :28
13. Little Willie :26
14. Lonesome Valley – Long Journey Home medley :45
15. Lord I'm Coming Home 1:01
16. Mama Don't Allow :21
17. Man of Constant Sorrow :35
18. Maple on the Hill :29
19. Methodist Pie
    Midnight on the Stormy Deep medley 1:15
20. Milwaukee Blues :26
21. Molly and Tenbrooks :28
22. My Home's Across the Blue Ridge Mountains :23
23. My Little Georgia Rose :38
24. New River Train – Nine Pound Hammer medley 1:01
25. Nobody's Business :23
26. Oh Death :39
27. Oh Didn't He Ramble – Old Dan Tucker medley 1:06
28. Old Home Place :38
29. Old Joe Clark :21
30. Old Man at the Mill :17
31. Old Paint :37
32. Old Rugged Cross 1:10
33. Old Time Religion :24
34. On and On :43
35. Over the Hills to the Poorhouse :39
36. Pass Me Not 1:03
37. Paul and Silas :21
38. Pig in a Pen :21
39. Poor Ellen Smith :24
40. Precious Memories 1:04
41. Pretty Polly :37
42. Put My Little Shoes Away :44
43. Railroad Bill :23
44. Rain and Snow :37
45. Rank Strangers to Me 1:21
46. Red Rocking Chair :29
47. Red Wing :42
48. Reuben's Train :21
49. Rocky Top :41
50. Roll in My Sweet Baby's Arms :38
51. Roll on Buddy :32
52. Roving Gambler :19
53. Sailor on the Deep Blue Sea :26
54. Sally Goodin :27
55. Shady Grove, bluegrass :21
56. Shady Grove, old time :28
57. Shall We Gather at the River :41
58. Short Life of Trouble, A :22
59. Shortening Bread :26
60. Silver Threads Among the Gold :47
61. Sitting on Top of the World :24
62. Softly & Tenderly :58
63. Somebody Touched Me :35
64. Standing in the Need of Prayer :26
65. Sugar Hill :29
66. Sweet By and By :41
67. Sweet Sunny South :25
68. Swing Low, Sweet Chariot :35
69. Take This Hammer :30
70. Talk about Sufferin' :38
71. There's More Pretty Girls Than One :27
72. They Gotta Quit Kicking My Dawg Around :34
73. This Little Light of Mine :25
74. This Train :22
75. This World is Not My Home :44
76. Train, Train, Train 1:01
77. Train That Carried My Girl From Town, The :32
78. Unclouded Day, The :41
79. Wabash Cannonball :25
80. Walk in Jerusalem Just Like John :29
81. Walking in My Sleep :21
82. Wayfaring Stranger, The 1:06
83. Were You There When They Crucified My Lord?
    What a Friend We Have in Jesus medley 1:32
84. When I Die :31
85. When I Lay My Burden Down :28
86. When My Race is Run 1:09
87. When the Roll is Called Up Yonder
    When the Saints Go Marching In medley 1:02
88. When the Work's all Done This Fall :28
89. When You and I Were Young, Maggie :52
90. Where the Soul Never Dies :39
91. Whitehouse Blues – Who Broke the Lock? medley :57
92. Who Will Sing for Me? :52
93. Wild Bill Jones :22
94. Wildwood Flower :31
95. Will the Circle Be Unbroken
    Will There Be Any Stars in My Crown? medley 1:21
96. Willie My Darling :51
97. Worried Man Blues – Wreck of the Old 97 medley :59
98. You're a Flower Blooming in the Wildwood :41